Lecture Notes in Computer Science 1469

Edited by G. Goos, J. Hartmanis and J. van Leeuwen

Springer-Verlag Berlin Heidelberg GmbH

Ramon Puigjaner   Nunzio N. Savino
Bartomeu Serra (Eds.)

Computer Performance Evaluation

Modelling Techniques and Tools

10th International Conference, Tools'98
Palma de Mallorca, Spain
September 14-18, 1998
Proceedings

 Springer

Series Editors

Gerhard Goos, Karlsruhe University, Germany
Juris Hartmanis, Cornell University, NY, USA
Jan van Leeuwen, Utrecht University, The Netherlands

Volume Editors

Ramon Puigjaner
Nunzio N. Savino
Bartomeu Serra
Universitat de les Illes Balears
Departament de Ciencies Matematiques i Informàtica
Careterra de Valldemossa km 7.6, E-07071 Palma (Balears), Spain
E-mail: {putxi, scidir}@ps.uib.es
        savino@ipc4.uib.es

Cataloging-in-Publication data applied for

Die Deutsche Bibliothek - CIP-Einheitsaufnahme

Computer performance evaluation : modelling techniques and tools
; 10th international conference ; Tools'98, Palma de Mallorca, Spain,
September 14 - 18, 1998 ; proceedings / Ramon Puigjaner ... (ed.). -
Berlin ; Heidelberg ; New York ; Barcelona ; Budapest ; Hong Kong ;
London ; Milan ; Paris ; Singapore ; Tokyo : Springer, 1998
    (Lecture notes in computer science ; Vol. 1469)
    ISBN 978-3-540-64949-6

CR Subject Classification (1991): C.4, D.2.8, D.2.2

ISSN 0302-9743
ISBN 978-3-540-64949-6   ISBN 978-3-540-68061-1 (eBook)
DOI 10.1007/978-3-540-68061-1

Typesetting: Camera-ready by author
SPIN 106838619   06/3142 – 5 4 3 2 1 0   Printed on acid-free paper

Preface

The need to evaluate computer and communication systems performance and dependability is continuously growing as a consequence of both the increasing complexity of systems and the user requirements in terms of timing behaviour. The 10th International Conference on Modelling Techniques and Tools for Computer Performance Evaluation, held in Palma in September 1998, was organised with the aim of creating a forum in which both theoreticians and practitioners could interchange recent techniques, tools, and experiences in these areas. This meeting follows the predecessor conferences of this series:

1984 Paris	1988 Palma	1994 Wien
1985 Sophia Antipolis	1991 Torino	1995 Heidelberg
1987 Paris	1992 Edinburgh	1997 Saint Malo

The tradition of this conference series continued this year where many high quality papers were submitted. The Programme Committee had a difficult task in selecting the best papers. Many fine papers could not be included in the program due to space constraints. All accepted papers are included in this volume. Also, a set of submissions describing performance modelling tools was transformed into tool presentations and demonstrations. A brief description of these tools is included in this volume. The following table gives the overall statistics for the submissions.

Country	Submitted	Accepted	Invited	Tool
Argentina	$\frac{4}{5}$			
Brazil	1			
Canada	$4\frac{2}{3}$	$2\frac{2}{3}$		
France	$9\frac{1}{3}$	$2\frac{2}{3}$		$1\frac{1}{3}$
Germany	$8\frac{2}{3}$	4	1	2
India	1			
Ireland	3			
Israel	1			
Italy	$6\frac{1}{6}$	$1\frac{2}{3}$		
Jordan	$\frac{1}{3}$			
Poland	$\frac{2}{3}$			$\frac{2}{3}$
Singapore	1			
Spain	$12\frac{3}{4}$	$3\frac{3}{4}$		1
South Africa	$\frac{1}{2}$	$\frac{1}{2}$		
Sweden	1			
The Netherlands	1	1		
United Kingdom	$3\frac{1}{2}$	$1\frac{1}{2}$		
USA	$12\frac{1}{2}$	7	1	4
Venezuela	$\frac{1}{4}$	$\frac{1}{4}$		
Total	69	25	9	

The papers address important problems from the application and theoretical viewpoints. The sessions Software Performance Tools, Network Performance, Measurement and Modelling Tools, Case Studies, and Software Performance Evaluation Methods contain papers addressing application problems. The sessions Algorithmic Techniques, Petri Net Techniques and MVA Techniques contain papers addressing theoretical aspects of performance evaluation.

It is impossible to close this text without acknowledging the efforts made by several people to help ensure the success of the conference. I express my thanks to

- The Programme Committee members for the task of reviewing papers and selecting the best of them.
- The external reviewers, without whose help the task of the Programme Committee would become impossible.
- The Organising Committee members, all from Universitat de les Illes Balears, without whose dedicated work the conference could not be set up.
- The scientific societies who have co-organised this conference.
- All public and private organisations that have supported the conference in some way (funding, offering services, or lending material).

Palma, September 1998   Ramon Puigjaner

Programme Committee

Chairman
Ramon Puigjaner

Members

Gianfranco Balbo, Italy
Heinz Beilner, Germany
Maria Calzarossa, Italy
Adrian Conway, USA
Larry Dowdy, USA
Günter Haring, Austria
Peter Harrison, UK
Boudewijn Haverkort, Germany
Peter Hughes, UK
Raj Jain, USA
Pieter Kritzinger, South Africa
Jacques Labetoulle, France
Allen Malony, USA
Raymond Marie, France
Luisa Massari, Italy
Richard Muntz, USA
Ahmed Patel, Ireland
Brigitte Plateau, France
Rob Pooley, UK

Guy Pujolle, France
Daniel Reed, USA
Martin Reiser, Switzerland
Gerardo Rubino, France
William Sanders, USA
Herb Schwetman, USA
Giuseppe Serazzi, Italy
Bartomeu Serra, Spain
Juan-José Serrano, Spain
Kenneth C. Sevcik, Canada
Connie Smith, USA
Arne Solvberg, Norway
Edmundo de Souza e Silva, Brazil
Otto Spaniol, Germany
William Stewart, USA
Hideaki Takagi, Japan
Yutaka Takahashi, Japan
Satish Tripathi, USA
Kishor Trivedi, USA

Secretary
Nunzio Savino

Organising Committee

Chairman
Bartomeu Serra

Members

Bartomeu Adrover
Maribel Barcel
Josep Frau

Roser Lluch
Josep Mañas

Referees

Andreas van Almsick

Juan-Luis Anciano

Gianfranco Balbo

Falko Bause

Heinz Beilner

Guillem Bernat

Madhu Bhabuta

Henrik Bohnenkamp

Peter Buchholz

Maria Carla Calzarossa

Adrian Conway

Paolo Cremonesi

Larry Dowdy

Pedro Gil

Sonia Fahmy

Tony Field

Claudio Gennaro

Mukul Goyal

Rohit Goyal

Gnter Haring

Peter Harrison

Boudewijn Haverkort

Peter Hughes

Raj Jain

Kamyar Kanani

Peter Kemper

Joao-Paulo Kitajima

William Knottenbelt

Pieter Kritzinger

Jacques Labetoulle

Christoph Lindemann

Chunlei Liu

Glenn R. Luecke

Allen Malony

Raymond Marie

Luisa Massari

Richard Muntz

Rafael Ors

Alexander Ost

Ahmed Patel

Brigitte Plateau

Rob Pooley

Ramon Puigjaner

Guy Pujolle

Daniel Reed

Martin Reiser

Gerardo Rubino

William H. Sanders

Vicente Santonja

Nunzio Savino

Herb Schwetman

Giuseppe Serazzi

Bartomeu Serra

Juan-Jos Serrano

Kenneth C. Sevcik

Connie U. Smith

Arne Solvberg

Edmundo A. de Souza e Silva

Otto Spaniol

William Stewart

Hideaki Takagi

Yutaka Takahashi

Satish Tripathi

Kishor Trivedi

Lloyd G. Williams

This conference was organised by

Universitat de les Illes Balears

in co-operation with:

ACM Sigmetrics
IFIP Working Group 6.3 (Performance of Computer Networks)
IFIP Working Group 7.3 (Computer System Modelling)

With the sponsorship of:

Ajuntament de Palma
Conselleria d'Educació, Cultura i Esports del Govern Balear
Direcció General de Tecnologies de la Informació i Comunicacions del Govern Balear

We gratefully acknowledge the support, of various types, of:

Banca March, S.A.
BMC
Caixa d'Estalvis de Balears, Sa Nostra
Digital Equipment Corporation Espaa
Silicon Graphics
Sun Microsystems Ibérica
Telefónica de España, S.A.
TransTOOLs, S.A.

Table of Contents

Invited Paper

Software Performance Tools

Network Performance

Measurement and Modelling Tools

Algorithmic Techniques

Case Studies

Petri Net Techniques

MVA Techniques

Software Performance Evaluation Methods

Tool Presentations

Authors Index

A Modular and Scalable Simulation Tool for Large Wireless Networks

Rajive. Bagrodia, Mario. Gerla

Department of Computer Science
University of California, Los Angeles
Los Angeles, CA 90095

Abstract. This paper describes a modular and scalable simulation environment, called GloMoSim, to evaluate end-to-end performance of integrated wired and wireless networks. GloMoSim has been implemented on sequential and parallel computers and can be used to simulate networks with a large number of nodes. It is designed as a set of library modules, each of which simulates protocols within a specific layer of the communication stack. Common APIs have been specified between neighboring layers on the protocol stacks. The modularity facilitates the study of the interaction between layers as well as the evaluation and comparison of different layers. The parallel structure of the simulator enables the scaling to large network sites without compromising the accuracy. Two sets of experiments (parallel scaling; TCP and MAC layer interaction) illustrate the features of the GloMoSim platform.

1. Introduction

The rapid advancement in portable computing platforms and wireless communication technology has led to significant interest in the design and development of protocols for instantly deployable, wireless networks (often referred to as "Ad Hoc Networks"). Ad hoc networks are required in situations where a fixed communication infrastructure (wired or wireless) does not exist or has been destroyed. The applications span several different sectors of society. In the civilian environment, they can be used to interconnect workgroups moving in an urban or rural area or a Campus and engaged in collaborative operation (e.g., distributed scientific experiments, search and rescue etc). In the law enforcement sector, applications such as crowd control and border patrol come to mind. In the military arena, the modern communications in a battlefield theater require a very sophisticated instant infrastructure, with far more complex requirements and constraints than the civilian applications.

In a nutshell, the key characteristics which make the design and evaluation of ad hoc networks unique and challenging include: (a) mobility, (b) unpredictable wireless channel (fading, interference, obstacles etc), (c) broadcast medium, shared by multiple users, (d) very large number of heterogeneous nodes (e.g., thousands of sensors).

R. Puigjaner et al. (Eds.): Tools'98, LNCS 1469, pp. 1-14, 1998
© Springer-Verlag Berlin Heidelberg 1998

To these challenging physical characteristics of the ad hoc network, we must add the very demanding requirements posed on the network by the typical applications. These include multimedia support, multi-cast and multi-hop communications. Multimedia (including voice, video and image) is a must when several individuals are collaborating in critical applications with real time constraints. Multicasting is a natural extension of the multimedia requirement. Multi-hopping is justified (among other things) by the limited power of the mobile devices, by obstacles and by the desire to reuse frequency and/or code.

Thus, we are confronted with a formidable problem. This problem has been attacked by many researchers leading to several alternative solutions, each offering competitive benefits. It is imperative to have a model and a methodology to compare these various options in a "modular" framework where two protocol modules, say, can be interchanged, all other conditions remaining the same.

In our research, we have addressed this problem by developing a modular, scalable simulation platform, GloMoSim, to evaluate end-to-end performance of integrated wired and wireless networks. The structure of GloMoSim is closely coupled with the actual layering of the protocols in the real ad hoc network. Various options have been proposed in the literature (and some have been implemented and prototyped) for various layers. These options are being incorporated in the platform so as to permit consistent comparison. GloMoSim is designed as a set of library modules (see Figure 1), each of which simulates protocols within a specific layer of the communication stack. Common APIs have been specified between neighboring layers on the protocol stacks. This allows rapid composition of models for the entire stack and facilitates consistent comparison of the performance of protocols at various layers. As detailed simulation models of large networks can become computationally expensive, we have developed GloMoSim using the PARSEC parallel simulation language which has been implemented on diverse sequential and parallel computers [Bagrodia98]. This allows us to use parallel simulation to reduce the simulation time for very large networks.

In this paper we illustrate the salient features of the simulator through various experiments. In the first set of experiments we address scalability. We illustrate two techniques: aggregation and parallelization, which allow us to handle thousands of nodes. In the second experiment we study the interplay of MAC and TCP. Both layers strive to provide efficient transport in a shared environment, with some degree of efficiency and with protection from errors and interference. The MAC layer has only a myopic view of the network, which is a critical limitation in multi-hop networks. In contrast, TCP provides a true end-to-end control on errors and congestion.

The rest of the paper is organized as follows: Section 2 describes the GloMoSim platform, Sections 3 and 4 report the experimental results on scalability and TCP/MAC layer interaction, respectively. Section 5 briefly describes other network simulation platforms and compares them to GloMoSim. Section 6 concludes the paper.

2. GloMoSim: wireless simulation platform

The GloMoSim platform is written using PARSEC, a PARallel Simulation Environment for Complex Systems [Bagrodia98]. PARSEC offers a number of advantages: First, it provides an easy path for the migration of simulation models to operational software prototypes. PARSEC is built around a portable thread-based message-passing programming kernel called MPC, for Message Passing C. The MPC kernel can be used to develop general purpose parallel programs. The only difference between PARSEC and MPC is as follows: a PARSEC model executes in logical time and all messages in the system must be processed in the global order of the timestamps carried in the messages. In contrast, each entity in a MPC program can autonomously process messages in the physical order of their arrival. Because of the common set of message passing primitives used by both environments, it is relatively easy to transform a PARSEC simulation model into operational parallel software in MPC. Such a transformation has already been demonstrated in the domain of network protocols, where simulation models of wireless protocols were directly refined and incorporated into the protocol stack of a network operating system for PCs [Short95]

Second, it is among the few simulation environments that have been implemented on diverse platforms and which support efficient sequential and parallel simulation protocols. In particular, PARSEC has been ported to laptops under Linux, to a distributed memory IBM SP2 running AIX, to a shared memory SPARC1000 running Solaris, and to a 4-processor DELL PC running Windows NT.

Third, PARSEC provides support for visual & hierarchical design of simulation models via an interface called PAVE (for PARSEC Visual Environment). PAVE may be used to visually configure simulation models using pre-defined components for a library in a specific application domain like GloMoSim.

Library Design

The primary goal of the GloMoSim library is to develop a modular simulation environment for wireless networks that is capable of scaling up to networks with thousands of heterogeneous nodes. To provide modularity, the library was developed as a set of models organized into a number of layers as shown in Figure 1. Well-defined APIs are specified to represent the interactions among the layers such that if a protocol model at a given layer obeyed the APIs defined at that layer, it would be easy to swap models of alternative protocols at that layer (e.g., CSMA rather than FAMA as the MAC protocol) without having to modify the models for the remaining layers in the stack. For each layer, the APIs define the format of the data message that is sent to or received from the layer and also describe the control signals that may be required by the layer. Of course, every protocol will not use all the control signals defined at the layer, but must ensure that it obeys the API for the data messages. For instance, interfaces between Data Link/MAC layer and network layer are defined as message passing with the following formats in the simulation library:

Packet_from_NW_to_DLC(P_type, P_dest, P_source, P_payload, P_size, P_VCID)

Packet_from_DLC_to_NW(P_type, P_dest, P_source, P_payload, P_size, P_VCID)

P_type refers to the type of packet (data packets, control packets, etc.), *P_dest* and *P_source* refer respectively to source and destination node, and the other parameters are required for packet processing or quality of service support. Each protocol module at a given layer is required to comply with the APIs defined for that layer

A number of protocols have already been implemented in the GloMoSim library and many more are being added. Available models at each of the layers include:

- Channel propagation models: free space model, analytical models using the log normal distribution, and SIRCIM fading models with shadowing and multipath fading effects[Rappaport90]
- Radio models: Digital spread Spectrum radios with and without capture capability
- MAC layer: CSMA, MACA[Karn90] and FAMA[Fullmer95]
- Network layer: Bellman-Ford routing, flooding, and DSDV
- Transport layer: Free BSD 2.2.4 implementation of TCP; DVMRP, PIM, RSVP
- Applications: replicated file systems, file transfers protocol, web caching

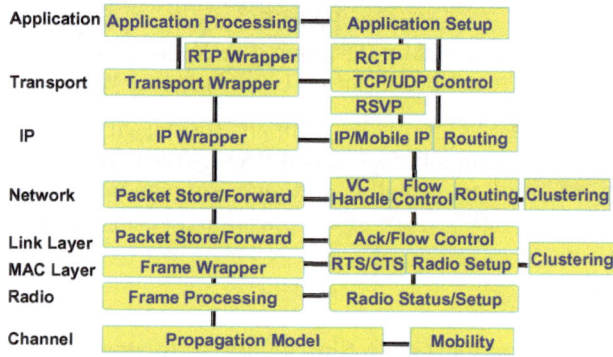

Fig.1. GloMoSim Architecture

GloMoSim provides models at different levels of granularity at each layer. Thus it is possible to simulate TCP either with a detailed model of the lower layers or by using an abstract model where the behavior of the lower layers is represented simply by stochastic delays and bit error rates. Similarly, the channel can be simulated either by using a free space model that typically overstates throughput and other metrics but is computationally fast, or by using the SIRCIM statistical impulse response model, which is considerably more accurate, but is computationally expensive. Many of the preceding models have already been parallelized in the library such that potential users may directly set up their experiments using the appropriate protocol models from each layer of the stack and execute the model on a parallel architecture.

3. Scalability

GloMoSim was designed to be scalable to very large networks. In this section, we describe and illustrate with examples two features of its design that permit this scalability without the use of abstraction: aggregation of multiple physical objects within a single simulation object and the use of parallel execution.

When simulating networks, a common approach is to map each network node to a single simulation object (i.e. a PARSEC entity) or to even map each network node to a set of PARSEC entities, each of which models a single layer in the protocol stack. However, previous experience has indicated that if either of these two approaches is used, a large number of simulation objects (i.e. PARSEC entity instances) have to be created. Such a model can increase the simulation overheads sufficiently to make this approach untenable for simulating large networks. Instead, GloMoSim employs an aggregation approach: it assumes that the network is decomposed into a number of partitions and a single entity is defined to simulate a single layer of the complete protocol stack for all the network nodes that belong to a given partition. This approach reduces the number of simulation objects dramatically (the number of objects can be kept nearly constant rather than be linear as in the earlier case) which in turn reduces the simulation overheads associated with event-list management, event scheduling, and context switching among multiple objects.

Aggregation

To demonstrate the performance improvements that can be derived from entity aggregations, we simulate the MAC layer of a wireless network with only 50 nodes using both the aggregated and non-aggregated approaches. All the network configurations are the same except that in the aggregation method, we create one DLC/MAC entity to simulate 50 network nodes, while in non-aggregation method, we create 50 entity instances, each of which simulates the DLC/MAC layer for a single entity. Table 1 compares the performance of the simulator using the aggregated and non-aggregated implementations of the given model with respect to their execution time, total messages processed, number of entity context switching as well as memory requirement.

Table 1. Performance Comparison of Aggregated Approach vs. Non-aggregated Approach

Approach	Exec. Time(s.)	# of Messages	# of Context Switches	Memory (in pages)
Aggregation	91	7862183	577437	214
Non-	100	7859474	3037297	1029

It is apparent that even for such a small network, the aggregated approach is more efficient. The 10% improvement in execution time is primarily due to the fewer context switches (which are reduced by a factor of 5 for the aggregated model). Note also that the memory requirements are reduced to only 25% and this is likely to be a significant performance issue as the network is scaled to larger sizes. Note that the total number of messages to be processed by both implementations are very close indicating that the improvement in efficiency is primarily a consequence of the reduction in number of simulation objects.

By using the entity aggregation method, we have been able to simulate the protocol stack shown in figure 1 up to the DLC/MAC layer with 10,000 mobile radios, and up to the TCP layer with 1000 nodes.   For this experiment, our purpose was primarily to demonstrate the ability of our simulator to simulate very large networks. The experiment assumed that the nodes are distributed randomly in an area of 1440 X 1440 units, where each radio has a transmission range of 50 units, such that on average a radio has 23 immediate neighbors. The traffic rate at each node was assumed to be exponential with a mean arrival rate of 1 packet/sec, where the average packet length was 100 bytes with a transmission time of 500 microseconds.   The network was simulated for duration of 10 seconds.   Table 2 presents the execution time of the simulator to simulate the MACA, CSMA, and FAMA protocols for the preceding network configuration as the network is scaled up in size form 2000 to 10,000 radios. Note that the absence of a network layer in this configuration implies that all communications are assumed to be single hop. For a given network configuration, even though the number of data packets generated for each of the three MAC protocols is identical, note that the total time to execute the models and the number of internal events (messages) generated for each model are different.   This is primarily due to the additional control messages used in each protocol.

Table 2. Execution Time Increment with Network Size

Node Number	Execution Time (s)			Number of Messages		
	CSMA	MACA	FAMA	CSMA	MACA	FAMA
2000	28	126	172	1056264	4888093	5251246
4000	137	733	1140	4250635	19987812	22449758
6000	385	2280	3756	9640406	45691950	51929666
8000	691	4263	7168	15268500	72608112	82754960
10000	1197	7709	10123	22897268	109097400	13207936

Parallelization

Efficient parallel simulators must address three sets of concerns: efficient synchronization to reduce simulation overheads; model decomposition or partitioning to achieve load balance; efficient process to processor mappings to reduce communications and other overheads in parallel execution.   In general, the parallel performance of simulation models differs among the different protocols because, when other things remaining the same, the model of one protocol may have less inherent concurrency than the other.   Many of the protocols in the GloMoSim library have already been parallelized such that a user need only specify the experimental configuration and provide appropriate parameters to execute the model on a parallel platform [Zeng98].

To demonstrate the capability of GloMoSim with a parallel implementation we present the results from the parallel execution of the experimental configuration whose sequential performance was reported in the previous section. The experiments were executed on an IBM 9076 SP, a distributed memory multi-computer. It consists of a set of RS/6000 workstation processors, each with 128MB RAM connected by a high-speed switch. The graph in Figure 2 shows the time to execute a model of the MACA protocol as a function of both the number of processors available to execute the model and the size of the network. As can be seen from the graph, given a fixed duration of time, the use of multiple processors allows a much larger network to be simulated than would be feasible using only sequential execution. For instance, for this experiment, the use of parallelism allows an analyst to simulate a network with 10,000 nodes in less time than that required for the sequential simulation of a network with 2000 nodes, without any loss of accuracy!

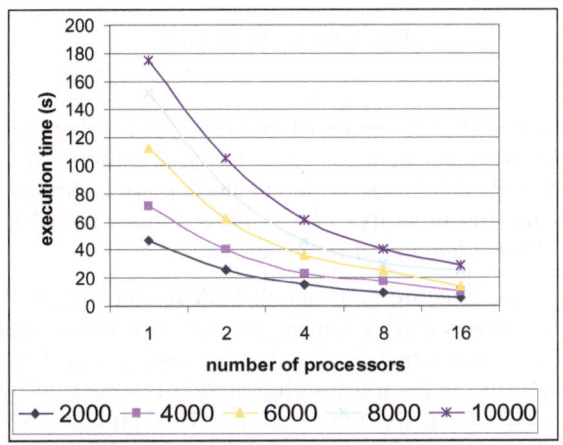

Fig. 2 Parallel Execution Time of Different Size of Networks

4. TCP and MAC layer interaction

Next, we evaluate the performance of TCP in a wireless multi-hop environment and its interaction with two MAC layer protocols (CSMA and FAMA).

The TCP protocol provides reliable delivery (via loss detection and retransmission) as well as congestion control (via dynamic window adjustment). Congestion is inferred from packet loss, which in wired networks is typically caused by buffer congestion and overflow. In a wireless environment, however, there is an additional complication - packet loss is caused not only by buffer overflow, but most often by channel fading, external interference and terminal mobility. These causes are totally unrelated to buffer congestion. The inefficiency of traditional TCP over wireless was recently addressed in [Balakrishnan95]. A "Snoop" agent located in the wired/wireless gateway was proposed to correct the problem. The Snoop solution was developed and evaluated in a wired/wireless interconnection scenario, in which only a single TCP connection is present and the wireless segment is single hop (e.g., cellular system). In our experiment we broaden the scope by considering "multiple" connections in a "multi-hop" environment and by exposing the interference between different hops along the path (hidden terminal problem). We focus on two main issues: the impact of TCP window size on performance, and the fair sharing among multiple connections.

Experimental Configuration

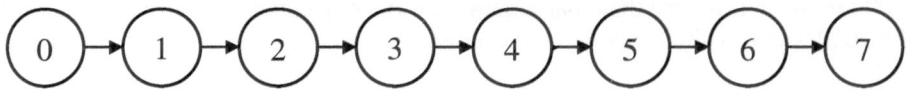

Fig. 3. String Topology

We consider a network with eight nodes (0 through 7) in a string (See Figure 3). The distance between two neighbor nodes is equal to the radio transmission range. TCP connections are established between different node pairs to transfer large files (20 MB). Nodes are static (no mobility). Free space channel model is used. Channel data rate is 2Mbps. Packet length is 1460 bytes.

Two MAC protocols are considered: CSMA and FAMA. CSMA (Carrier Sense Multiple Access) uses carrier sensing to prevent a newly transmitting station from colliding with a station which is already transmitting a packet. CSMA cannot, however, prevent collision if the transmitting station is separated by more than one hop (i.e., it is "hidden") from the new station. This problem, known as "hidden terminal" problem, severely reduces throughput in multihop wireless networks. FAMA (Floor Acquisition Multiple Access) uses the RTS (Request To Send) and CTS (Clear To Send) exchange to prepare the "floor" for data transmission (thus avoiding "hidden terminal" collision in most cases) [Fullmer95].

The TCP simulation model is an accurate replica of the TCP code running in the Internet hosts today. In fact, the TCP simulation code was generated from FreeBSD 2.2.4 code. In TCP, window size grows progressively until it reaches the advertised window (i.e., max window allowed by the receiver) or until packet loss is detected (via duplicate ACKs or timeout). In the latter cases, window size is halved (fast retransmission and fast recovery) or abruptly reduced to 1 (slow start). In our simulation, we can "force" the maximum TCP window to be at a certain value by setting the advertised window to such value (e.g., 1460 bytes).

MAC layer performance

First, we evaluate the behavior of the MAC layer without TCP.

Table 3. Throughput (Kbps), Variable Number of Hops, Without TCP

# of hops	1	2	3	4	5	6	7
CSMA	1891.5	704.3	562.1	561.8	561.7	562.2	561.8
FAMA	1161.6	672.8	584.5	581.5	580.3	580.4	579.8

We start by considering a single UDP session (no TCP) and evaluate the throughput achieved for variable path length (in hops). Both CSMA and FAMA results are shown in Table 3. We note that the performance of CSMA and FAMA alike converges to a fixed (lower) value after 3 hops. This is as expected since in this case packets are pipelined on the path, and packets in the 3rd hop and beyond have no impact on the first link transmissions. We note also that one hop FAMA has lower throughput than one hop CSMA because of the RTS/CTS overhead.

In the second set of experiments, there are file transfer requirements between each node and the next. We use the conventional CSMA and FAMA parameter settings [Fullmer95], and obtain the performance reported in Table 4. CSMA throughput ranges from 0.8 Kbps to 1.7 Mbps. Total throughput is 2.1 Mbps, quite lower than the theoretical maximum, in this case = 6 Mbps. The maximum corresponds to 3 connections separated by "silent" nodes and transmitting at full channel speed (i.e., 2 Mbps each). Throughput degradation and uneven performance are due to hidden terminal and to capture. The 6-7 connection captures the channel since it does not suffer from hidden terminal problems. FAMA behavior is worse, and even less fair than CSMA. Again, the connection 6-7 captures the channel. The other connections have nearly zero throughput.

The cause of this inefficient and/or erratic multi-hop behavior can be in part attributed to the fact that transmitters are too "aggressive". That is, after completing a transmission, a node, after a very short timeout, senses the channel free again and transmits a data packet (in CSMA) or a RTS (in FAMA). This will cause repeated undetected collisions between hidden terminals in CSMA and channel capture in FAMA (where the timeout of blocked terminals is much larger than that of active terminals) [Fullmer95]. The result is poor throughput and strong capture.

Table 4. Throughput (Kbps) in String Topology, No TCP

Streams	0-1	1-2	2-3	3-4	4-5	5-6	6-7	Total Throughput
CSMA	86.0	11.3	90.4	57.3	0.8	183.8	1706.8	2136.3
FAMA	0.2	0.0	1.0	0.0	0.0	0.0	1477.4	1478.6

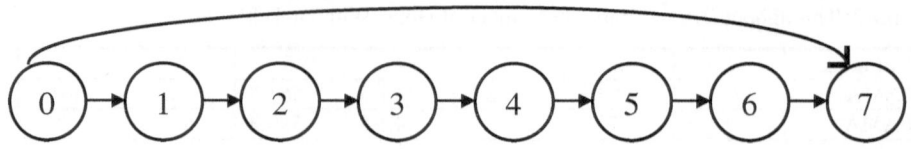

Fig. 5. String Topology with 0 -7 Data Stream

In a third round of experiments, we consider a slightly more complex traffic pattern. There are single hop file transfer requirements like before, plus an end-to-end requirement from 0 to 7 (See Figure 5). We are interested in the impact of this end to end requirement on performance. The results are reported in Table 5. The most important observation is that throughput on connection 0-7 is zero in all runs. This is not unexpected since the packet loss rate on each hop is very high. Therefore, the probability that a packet survives through 7 hops is practically zero. As for the other connections, their performance is similar to that without the end-to-end connection 0-7.

Table 5. Throughput (Kbps) in String Topology with 0-7 Data Stream, No TCP

Streams	0-1	1-2	2-3	3-4	4-5	5-6	6-7	0-7	Total Throughput
CSMA	0.9	13.1	63.6	60.6	0.6	109.9	1780.9	0.0	2029.6
FAMA	0.1	0.0	0.6	0.0	0.0	0.0	1477.5	0.0	1478.2

TCP over the MAC layer

The previous MAC layer experiments have shown that both CSMA and FAMA suffer of capture and of hidden terminal losses. Thus, reliability must be provided by the TCP transport layer protocol. In this section, we examine the interaction of TCP with CSMA and FAMA.

Table 6. Throughput (Kbps), Single TCP Connection, Variable Number of Hops, W = 1460 B

# of Hops	1	2	3	4	5	6	7
CSMA	1838.4	921.3	614.8	461.4	369.2	307.7	263.4
FAMA	1476.5	718.7	475.4	355.3	287.5	239.1	204.7

We start with a single TCP connection that covers a variable number of hops, from 1 to 7. In the first set of experiments, TCP window (W) is 1460 bytes, which is equal to packet size. Thus, the window contains only one packet (i.e., send-and-wait mode). The throughput results for CSMA and FAMA as a function of number of hops H are reported in Table 6. Throughput values match exactly the analytic predictions for a send-and-wait protocol: the throughput is inversely proportional to hop distance. CSMA throughput is slightly higher than FAMA because of RTS/CTS overhead of the latter. It is interesting to compare the TCP results in Table 6 to the non-TCP case reported in Table A. The congestion control mechanism of TCP provides equal or better (in the case of FAMA) performance at low hop distances, while for long hop distances the send-and-wait operation of TCP cannot compete with the pipelining of the UDP case.

Table 7. Throughput (Kbps), Single TCP Connection, Variable Number of Hops, W = 32 KB

# of Hops	1	2	3	4	5	6	7
CSMA	1791.2	439.5	0.5	0.5	0.5	0.5	0.5
FAMA	1458.7	716.2	389.4	71.4	13.5	72.8	66.9

Next, we set W = 32 Kbytes. In this case, the TCP protocol dynamically adjusts the congestion window as required. We would expect that in balance the window increase improves performance since for 7 hops, for example, analysis shows that the optimal throughput is achieved for W = 3 x 1460 bytes. The simulation results shown in Table 7 indicate otherwise. CSMA throughput collapses when H ≥ 3. FAMA does slightly better, but still with throughput much lower than with W = 1460 bytes. Basically, as window is increased, multiple packets and ACKs are outstanding and travel on the path in opposite directions, creating interference and collisions (both in CSMA and FAMA). From these results we conclude that there is no gain in using W larger than single packet size even on connections covering multiple paths. Thus, we will use W = 1460 B in all the following experiments.

Next, we repeat the multiple connection experiment already described in the previous section, this time with TCP on top. Namely, there are 8 nodes (0 through 7) with single hop file transfer connections (0-1, 1-2 etc). In addition, there is a multihop file transfer from 0 to 7. We run both CSMA and FAMA, with and without vacation. The results are reported in Table 8. We only consider W = 1460 B, since we have observed that W > 1460 B typically degrades performance in the multi-hop environment. We start with CSMA, and get zero throughput for the (0-7) connection.

Table 8. Throughput (Kbps) in String Topology, W = 1460 B

TCP Connection	0-1	1-2	2-3	3-4	4-5	5-6	6-7	0-7	Total Throughput
CSMA	358.7	20.6	811.3	960.7	21.8	0.0	1630.1	0.0	3803.3
FAMA	334.2	437.5	336.9	147.0	834.0	248.9	387.7	0.1	2726.3

Similarly, in FAMA, we cannot get any significant throughput from 0 to 7. In comparison with CSMA, we find the behavior of the single hop sources to be more fair. However, the aggregate throughput in FAMA is 2.7 Mbps, less than in CSMA (3.8 Mbps).

In an attempt to favor the 0 to 7 connection, we did increase its window to 32KB. This however had no positive effects, yielding results similar to those of Table 7. In a separate set of experiments, we reduced the length of the multi-hop connection from 7 hops (i.e. 0-7) all the way down to 2 hops (i.e., 2-4). We were able to observe significant traffic (111Kbps) only in the 2-4 case with CSMA. Zero throughput was yielded by FAMA even for the 2-4 connection.

In summary, the following lessons were learned from the TCP experiments in heavy file transfer load: (a) large window has a negative effect especially on CSMA; a window = packet size provides by far the best results; (b) the multi-hop system is very prone to unfairness; (c) unfairness is particularly severe with respect to multi-hop connections - no traffic gets through beyond two hops (when the network is heavily loaded). (d) TCP typically improves fairness especially for FAMA (albeit at the expense of throughput performance). TCP does not improve performance of multihop connections, however.

5. Related Work

Simulation has been a widely used tool for performance evaluation of network protocols and a number of universities and commercial tools have been developed. For instance, a comprehensive survey of commercial products in this domain may be found in the *March 1994 IEEE Communications Magazine*.

A network simulator called NS (http://www-mash.cs.berkeley.edu/ns/) has been developed and is being used to develop a Internet-scale simulator called VINT (http://netweb.usc.edu/vint/). NS is primarily a transport-level simulator that supports several flavors of TCP (include SACK, Tahoe and Reno) and router scheduling algorithms.   Models can be described using a variation of the Tool Command Language, Tcl. Efforts are underway also to include models of wireless protocols in NS [Bakshi97]. To the best of our knowledge, none of the existing commercial or widely used public domain network simulators exploit parallel simulation technology for detailed simulations of very large networks.

Much of the existing research in parallel network simulation has been done in the context of wired networks that include ATM networks, LAN simulators, and interconnection networks for parallel computers [Holvoet97] [Clearly96] [Martini97] or for cellular networks [Carothers94].   Wireless and wired networks differ in fundamental ways: for example, the signal interference and attenuation concerns are inherently more complicated and typically more computationally intensive for wireless mediums than for wired mediums. Also, the broadcast nature of wireless radio transmission makes communication topology in simulation models relatively denser than for an equivalent wired network.

6. Conclusion

The design of ad hoc networks presents unique challenges that involve tradeoffs at multiple levels and there is clear benefit to the evaluation of interactions among the wireless protocol layers. Most of the studies so far have focused on a single layer, using abstracted or approximate models of the remaining layers/protocols.

We have developed a modular and scalable simulation environment, called GloMoSim, to evaluate end-to-end performance of large wireless networks. GloMoSim is designed as a set of library modules, each of which simulates protocols within a specific layer of the communication stack.   Common APIs have been specified between neighboring layers on the protocol stacks. This allows rapid composition of models for the entire stack and facilitates consistent comparison of the performance of a protocol at a given layer as a function of multiple alternatives at another layer.

The paper has presented the results of a study on the interactions between the TCP and MAC layers as a specific example of layer integration in a common simulation model from the radio to the transport layers. In our study, we have shown that some problems can be detected only if the full detail of the various layers is reflected in the simulator.   Thus, we advocate the use of a modular simulation platform which permits the desired degree of accuracy at each layer without a significant deterioration in computation time.   In particular, our study showed the clear impact of the window size in TCP on the throughput and fairness of the wireless connections and the significant impact of the specific MAC protocol that was used at the MAC layer. In the case where multihop connections compete with single hop connections for the same bandwidth, we showed that the multihop connection gets virtually zero throughput. This result suggests that an alternative form of per flow scheduling (e.g., fair queuing) and link level error and loss recovery schemes must be used to improve performance and fairness.

The set of simulation experiments reported in this paper used small networks such that it was possible to both understand the results and identify the primary causes for the observed behavior. We are now in the process of scaling up the simulations models to larger configurations to determine if the effects are replicated in larger networks.

References

1. [Bagrodia98] R. Bagrodia, R. Meyerr, et al., "PARSEC: A Parallel Simulation Environment for Complex System", to appear in Computer Magazine, 1998.

2. [Bakshi97] Bikram Bakshi, Krishna, P., Pradhan, D.K., and Vaidya, N.H., "Performance of TCP over Wireless Networks", 17th Intl. Conf. on Distributed Computing Systems (ICDCS), Baltimore, May, 1997.

3. [Balakrishnan95] Hari Balakrishnan, Srinivasan Seshan, Randy H. Katz, "Improving Reliable Transport and Handoff Performance in Cellular Wireless Networks", ACM Wireless Networks, 1(4), December 1995

4. [Bharghavan94] V. Bharghavan, A. Demers, S. Shenker, and L. Zhang, "MACAW: A Media Access Protocol for Wireless LAN's," ACM SIGCOMM, 1994

5. [Carothers94] C. D. Carothers, Richard M. Fujimoto, Yi-Bing Lin and Paul England, "Distributed Simulation of Large-scale PCS Networks, MASCOTS '94. Proceedings of the

Second International Workshop on Modeling, Analysis, and Simulation of Computer and Telecommunication Systems (Cat. No.94TH0621-3), MASCOTS '94

6. [Clearly96] J.G. Clearly, J. J. Tsai, "Conservative Parallel Simulation of ATM Networks", Proceedings of PADS 1996

7. [Floyd94] S. Floyd, "TCP and Explicit Congestion Notification", ACM Computer Communication Review, V. 24 N. 5, October 1994, p. 10-23.

8. [Fullmer95] C. Fullmer and J.J. Garcia-Luna-Aceves, "Floor Acquisition Multiple Access (FAMA) for packet radio networks", Computer Communication Review, vol.25, (no.4), (ACM SIGCOMM '95, Cambridge, MA, USA, 28 Aug.-1 Sept. 1995.) ACM, Oct. 1995.

9. [Holvoet97] T. Holvoet and P. Verbaeten, "Using Agents for Simulating and Implementing Petri nets", Proceedings of PADS 1997.

10. [Karn90]. P. Karn, "MACA –a New Channel Access Method for Packet Radio", in ARRL/CRRL Amateur radio 9th Computer Networking Conference, ARRL, 1990.

11. [Martini97] P. Martini, M. Rumekasten, J. Tolle, "Tolerant Synchronization for Distributed Simulations of Interconnected Computer Networks", Proceedings of PADS 1997

12. [Morris97] Robert Morris, "TCP Behavior with Many Flows", International Conference on Network Protocols, October 1997

13. [Rappaport90] T. Rappaport and S. Y. Seidel, SIRCIM: Simulation of Indoor Radio Channel Impulse Response Models, VTIP, Inc., 1990

14. [Short95] J. Short, R. Bagrodia, and L. Kleinrock , "Mobile Wireless Network System Simulation,"; Proceedings of ACM Mobile Communication Networking Conference -- Mobicom '95, November 1995

15. [Zeng98] X. Zeng, R. Bagrodia and M. Gerla, "GloMoSim: a Library for the Parallel Simulation of Large-scale Wireless Networks", Proceedings of PADS'1998.

Designing Process Replication and Threading Policies: A Quantitative Approach

M. Litoiu[1], J. Rolia[2], and G. Serazzi[3]

[1]IBM Toronto Lab, Toronto, Canada
marin@ca.ibm.com
[2]Carleton University, Ottawa, Canada
jar@sce.carleton.ca
[3]Politecnico di Milano, Milan, Italy
serazzi@ipmel2.polimi.it

Abstract. When designing and deploying distributed systems it is necessary to determine process activation policy. A process's activation policy determines whether it is persistent or should be created and terminated with each call. For persistent processes the replication or threading levels must be decided. Inappropriate replication/threading levels can lead to unnecessary queuing delays for callers or an unnecessarily high consumption of memory resources. The purpose of this paper is to present quantitative techniques that determine appropriate process replication/threading levels. The results also provide information that can be used to guide the choice of process activation policy. Chosen replication levels are sensitive to the total number of customers using the system and the portion of customers belonging to each class. The algorithms presented consider all workload conditions, are iterative in nature, and are hybrid mathematical programming and analytic performance evaluation methods

1 Introduction

Distributed applications are composed of many classes of objects with instances that interact to accomplish common goals. With the distributed object programming model there are many decisions that must be made with regard to the composition of objects into processes; replication, threading and activation policies for the processes; and the distribution of processes across nodes in a target environment. The results of these decisions affect the performance and hence the Quality of Service (QoS) of the resulting system. Quantitative techniques are needed to support this decision-making process and to determine the policies that capture these decisions.

In many midware platforms, for example CORBA based environments [9], servers can be persistent or created on demand and then terminated. Those servers that are used frequently should be persistent to minimize startup overheads. If the objects within a persistent server are reentrant, their server process can be multithreaded.

R. Puigjaner et al. (Eds.): Tools'98, LNCS 1469, pp. 15-26, 1998
© Springer-Verlag Berlin Heidelberg 1998

Threading level is limited by both operating system and software constraints [4]. For example an operating system configuration may limit the number of file descriptors used by a server process's connections to 64. A threading limit would therefore be 64. When an object's method is a critical section it must not be used by more than one thread at a time and its threading limit is 1. The memory associated with a thread is in use until its current method's demands are satisfied. In systems with layers of server processes, these demands include visits to local processors and disks but also include visits to the methods of other objects that may reside in other processes that are geographically distant. Other objects cannot use the thread and its memory until its method completes. Thus nested software demands and queuing delays affect memory consumption and required threading levels. Furthermore visits to methods in distant locations can take orders of magnitude longer than the sum of local processor and disk demands.

The algorithm presented in this paper gives estimates for the *maximum replication* or *threading levels* required for processes with respect to given software and device utilization limits. Replication beyond this point does not improve user response time. Additional customers simply substitute their delay for access to the process with delays for access to other resources. There is no gain for the accepted customer. On the negative side, the customer may acquire other resources such as memory or database locks that have a negative impact on the already accepted customers. Computing the maximum replication or threading level for a process depends on both the total number of customers in the system and the fraction or mix of customers belonging to each class. The algorithms consider all population mixes for customer classes possible under the design constraints and take into account queuing delays for software entities and devices.

Process replication and threading levels are related to the *maximum utilization level* of the processes. The utilization of a process is the percentage of time it is busy and can be interpreted as the average number of instances of the process or its threads that are active. The aggregate utilization of a process can be greater than one for replicated or multithreaded processes. To compute the maximum process utilization, it is necessary to consider both the workload mix(es) that cause the maximum to occur and the mean object response times for the mix(es). Non-linear programming (NLP) techniques are presented that choose the workload mixes of most interest. Analytic queuing models are used to estimate mean object response times. The combined models are then used to study a system with constraints on device utilization.

The following papers have motivated the proposed algorithms. [1-2] describe an asymptotic bounds analysis technique that determines the workload mixes that cause combinations of devices to saturate. This approach was applied to a Software Performance Engineering case study [4] to estimate maximum object utilization in distributed application systems. However the technique considers only asymptotic conditions under which combinations of devices are saturated and is limited to three classes of requests. We consider an arbitrary number of classes and non-asymptotic conditions, as well. [7] introduces Mean Value Analysis (MVA) for studying the queuing delays of application requests that compete for devices. MVA has been adapted to support Layered Queuing Models (LQMs) that take into account contention for software as well as hardware [8, 10]. These techniques are used to estimate the mean response times of methods and processes in distributed application systems. They take into account the nested demands and queuing delays that affect required threading levels.

The outline of the paper is as follows. Section 2 describes the problem of determining maximum process utilization as a NLP model. In the NLP model, the process utilization is the objective function and the device utilization limits act as constraints. A control algorithm is given in Section 3 that integrates the NLP with LQMs and the Method of Layers [8] to evaluate the process utilization and discover its maximum over all workload conditions. Section 4 shows how the results can be interpreted and used for planning replication and activation policy for distributed application systems. A summary and description of future work are given in Section 5.

2 Process and Object Utilization in a Multi-Class Distributed System

This section develops the notion of object utilization and describes the problem of finding an object's maximum utilization in a system constrained by device utilization limits. The notation describes the model and the subsequent algorithms in terms of classes of objects and their use of devices and other objects. Each process supports one class of objects. As a result, process utilization is described as object utilization. However, the proposed technique is not limited in this way.

2.1 Performance Models for Distributed Applications and Object Utilization

Consider a set of requests that are expected to affect performance most. Each class of request c makes use of a collection of objects with methods that interact with one another. For each class of requests c the response time of an object used by a request includes its own direct demands and queuing delays at its node's devices and its nested demands and queuing delays for access to the methods of the other objects that it visits synchronously. Thus, the average response time R_o^c, of an object o for a request of class c can be expressed as:

$$R_o^c = \sum_{i=1}^{K_o} (D_{io}^c + W_{io}^c) + \sum_{p \varepsilon \mathbf{O}_o} V_{o,p}^c \left(R_p^c + W_p^c \right) \tag{1}$$

where:
- K_o is the number of devices at object o node;
- D_{io}^c is the mean object o demand at device i for a class c request;
- W_{io}^c is the mean waiting time of object o at device i for a class c request;
- $\mathbf{O}_o$ is the set of objects visited synchronously by object o;

- $V^c_{o,p}$ is the number of visits from object o to object p by a class c request;
- R^c_p is the mean response time of object p when servicing a class c request;
- W^c_p is the mean waiting time at object p when servicing class c requests.

Using the utilization law [6], object o utilization U_o is defined as:

$$U_o = \sum_{c=1}^{C} X_c \ R^c_o \qquad (2)$$

where

- C is the number of request classes and X_c is the throughput of class c. We use R^c_o instead of a demand value because it includes both software and device queuing delays. The parameters of (1) and (2) are the input parameters for a system's corresponding Layered Queuing Model (LQM) and the results of performance evaluation.
- K_o, D^c_{io}, O_o, $V^c_{o,p}$, are the input parameters of LQM. Additionally, the system's LQM requires: *application configuration parameters* -- the number of replicates and threading level of each process; *workload conditions* -- per-class think times Z_c and population vector $\underline{N}=(N_1, N_2 \ldots N_c)$, where N_c is class c customer population; and *execution environment policies* -- device scheduling disciplines.
- W^c_{io}, R^c_p, W^c_p, R^c_o and X_c are outputs of a performance evaluation of the LQM. Additional output values include per-class process, object, and device utilizations and mean queue lengths.

[4] estimates maximum object utilization under asymptotic conditions (with at least one device saturated) with the assumptions of no device or software queuing delays. In the presence of one or more saturated devices in the system, throughputs become constant and are determined by the saturated devices. Response times become linear with respect to the number of customers in the system. Since the object utilization components at the bottleneck devices become dominant, the total utilization of an object in the presence of the saturated devices may be considered linear. However, we are interested in studying systems under non-asymptotic conditions and hence non-linear conditions as well. When queuing is taken into account the waiting times at devices and software entities are nonzero. Furthermore they are non-linear with increasing numbers of customers submitting requests. This cause objects utilization to be non-linear with respect to the number of customers as well and motivates the need for NLP techniques.

2.2 An Objective Function for Object Utilization

We assume there are no threading limits for an object o, but there are limits imposed on device utilization. More general constraints are easily introduced and are described in Section 2.4.

The total utilization U_o of an object o is the sum of per-class object utilizations:

$$U_o = U_{o1} + U_{o2} + \ldots + U_{oC} \qquad (3)$$

where U_{oi} is the utilization of object o per class i.

We want to find the maximum utilization of the object o such that device utilizations are less than or equal to their specified bounds. The problem can be expressed for an object o as a non-linear programming problem as follows:

$$\text{Max} \qquad U_o = U_{o1} + U_{o2} + \; .... \; + U_{oC} \tag{4}$$

$$\text{subject to} \quad U_k = \sum_{c=1}^{C} U_{kc} \le b_k$$

$$U_{kc} \ge 0, \quad \forall k \in \mathbf{K}, \; \forall c \in \mathbf{C}$$

where $\mathbf{C}$ and $\mathbf{K}$ are the sets of classes and devices (with cardinalities K and C, respectively), U_k is the total utilization of device k, U_{kc} is the utilization of device k by requests of class c, and b_k is the maximum permitted utilization of device k, referred to as the device k utilization limit. With our notation the use of o as a subscript of U implies a software object o's utilization, and should be distinguished from the U_{kc} terms. Assuming that we know how to solve (4), the solution of this NLP model gives maximum object utilization and request class utilization of devices that cause object o's utilization to reach its maximum within the feasible space imposed by the constraints. The latter is described by $\underline{\mathbf{U}}^+ = (U^+_{11}, \; U^+_{21}, \; U^+_{31}, ..., \; U^+_{12}, \; U^+_{22}, \; U^+_{32}, ...)$.

We now re-express the problem to introduce the object response time R^c_o into the NLP model. For the time being we assume the R^c_o for all the system's objects are known by solving the corresponding LQM, but discuss their relationship to the NLP model in the next section when the queuing models are discussed in more detail.

Using the utilization law, the utilizations of an object o and a device k by a class c request is

$$U_{oc} = X_c R_o^c \quad \text{and} \quad U_{kc} = X_c D_{kc} \; ; \; o \in \mathbf{O}; \; k \in \mathbf{K} \tag{5}$$

where $\mathbf{O}$ denotes the set of all objects in the distributed system.

The total utilization of object o is:

$$U_o = X_1 R_o^1 + X_2 R_o^2 + \; .... \; + X_C R_o^C \tag{6}$$

The total utilization of device i is:

$$U_i = X_1 D_{i1} + X_2 D_{i2} + \; .... \; + X_C D_{iC} \tag{7}$$

Within a customer class, the forced flow law [6] gives the following relations among utilization and demands:

$$U_{ic}/U_{jc} = D_{ic}/D_{jc} \quad \forall i, j \in \mathbf{K}, \; \forall c \in \mathbf{C} \tag{8}$$

$$U_{ic}/U_{jc} = D_{ic}/R_{jc} \quad \forall i \in \mathbf{K}, \; \forall j \in \mathbf{O}, \; \forall c \in \mathbf{C} \tag{9}$$

Assuming that there exists a device r shared by all classes (for example a shared network), and taking this device as reference, we have:

$$U_{jc} = U_{rc} D_{jc}/D_{rc} \; ; \; \forall j \in \mathbf{K}; \; \forall c \in \mathbf{C}; \; \text{and} \tag{10}$$

$$U_{oc} = U_{rc} R_o^c / D_{rc} ; \quad \forall o \in \mathbf{O}; \quad \forall c \in \mathbf{C} \tag{11}$$

Thus, using device r as reference, we can rewrite (4) as:

$$\text{Max} \qquad U_o = U_{r1} R_o^1 / D_{r1} + U_{r2} R_o^2 / D_{r2} + \dots + U_{rC} R_o^C / D_{rC} \tag{12}$$

$$\text{subject to} \quad Uk = \sum_{c=1}^{C} (Dkc / Drc) Urc \leq bk$$

$$U_{r1}, U_{r2}, \dots U_{rC} \geq 0$$

The solution of this problem gives $\underline{U}_r^+ = (U_{r1}^+, U_{r2}^+, \dots, U_{rC}^+)$ from which we can deduce $\underline{U}^+$ using (10). Note that U_0 is a non-linear function since R_o^c depends on $\underline{U}_r = (U_{r1}, \dots, U_{rC})$ in a non-linear manner. Non-linear programming techniques are required to solve (12). The convex simplex method [3] can be used to solve (12), with $U_{r1}, \dots, U_{rC}$ as decision variables. To secure a unique solution to (12) the decision variables should be continuos and object utilization should be convex with regard to decision variables. In section 3 we will show that our NLP model fulfills these conditions.

2.3 Software Constraints

The constraints we introduced so far are linear with respect to per class utilization of a reference device. Sometimes, it is necessary to express software constraints: limits for a method's total utilization to introduce a critical section; a process's total utilization to express a file descriptor limit; or process or device utilization by class for quality of service management. These software constraints are non-linear with respect to the per class device utilizations that we chose as control variables. As long as the utilization limits specified by the software constraints are never met, it is not necessary to include them as NLP constraints. Their non-linear influences are reflected in the analytic queuing model and henceforth captured by the objective function. If these limits can be reached, the software under consideration can become a bottleneck and can affect the entire NLP problem, which becomes a non-linear program with non-linear constraints.

Changing the software to avoid the software bottlenecks is the first choice for the performance engineering process. If it is possible to do this, as mentioned above, the software constraints will have no impact on NLP problem. However, if it is not possible, then we suggest the following strategies:

- Change the problem by reducing the device utilization limits (b_k) so that the software utilization limits are never reached
- Take an optimistic approach and just ignore the software constraints. This strategy will yield overestimated utilization for the object under scrutiny.
- Solve the NLP with non-linear constraints. This requires the use of techniques from the non-linear programming literature [3] to be closely integrated with analytic

models to compute the intermediate values of the objective function. Unfortunately, it comes with a high computational cost.

The following sections do not consider software constraints further. Note that the analytic queuing models always take into account software utilization limits when computing object response times and it is possible to recognize if there are software bottlenecks. Proper treatment of these software constraints in the NLP improves the study of workload mix.

3 Algorithm for Finding Maximum Object Utilization

This section presents an iterative technique that integrates the non-linear programming results with a queuing analysis to estimate R^c_o and a searching technique to find the maximum object utilization and the workload conditions that cause this maximum. The model of Section 2 assumed that the decision variables $\underline{U}_r = (U_{r1}, U_{r2}, ...U_{rd})$, are reachable and continuous. This is achievable by allowing the customer population vector $\underline{N}=(N_1, N_2... N_c)$ to take continuous and real values. This technique assumes the system under study has a corresponding Layered Queuing Model (LQM) and that the model is solved using the Method of Layers [8]. The MOL breaks the LQM into a sequence of two level submodels that can be solved iteratively using MVA techniques. Residence time expressions have been developed that consider the kinds of interactions that arise in distributed applications. For example, synchronous and asynchronous communications, multi-threading, and processes that contain many objects with many methods. Neither MVA nor the MOL introduce discontinuities with regard to the input variables $\underline{N}=(N_1, N_2... N_c)$ within the feasible space.

To secure a unique solution for (12), object utilization must be convex within the feasible space with regard to decision variables. The convex property follows from continuity and monotone-properties of object utilization with regard to per class utilization at a chosen device r. Continuity is secured by the lack of discontinuity points in MVA and MOL with respect to each N_c. The proof of these two properties is out of the scope of this paper.

3.1 The Search Algorithm under Non-Asymptotic Conditions

When solving (12), we assume that the think times associated with each request class are fixed. Also, initial threading levels for processes are set to the sum of the populations of the request classes to ensure they cannot cause queuing delays. The following algorithm is used to determine the find the maximum utilization for an object o. The results provide the population vector $\underline{N}=(N_1, N_2... N_c)$ under which U_o is a maximum when we are on the boundary of the feasible space:

1. Formulate (12), with an initial estimate of R^c_o that does not include waiting times
2. Choose an initial point in the feasible utilization space that gives an initial $\underline{U}_r$
3. Using the simplex algorithm choose a new value $\underline{U}^*_r$ to increase U_o

4. Repeatedly solve the system's LQM using the MOL to get an $\underline{\mathbf{N}}$ that causes $\underline{\mathbf{U}}^*_r$ and provides a new estimate for R^c_o

5. Repeat steps 3 to 4 until $\underline{\mathbf{U}}_r$ can not change without decreasing U_o.

Step 1 follows from Section 2.1 and 2.2 and is not described further. For Step 2, we choose to set the per-class device utilizations to zero. Step 3 is an application of the simplex algorithm. It finds the search direction in utilization space by establishing a new goal for $\underline{\mathbf{U}}_r$, namely $\underline{\mathbf{U}}^*_r$. The search path is based on pivoting using natural and slack utilization variables by computing numeric estimates for the partial derivatives of U_0 from the MOL results. Once a search direction is found, the new value for $\underline{\mathbf{U}}_r$ is computed by a line search method between the current value and the maximum value given by the constraints of (12).

Step 4 iteratively applies the MOL with a hill climbing algorithm; it searches for the customer population $\underline{\mathbf{N}}$ that achieves $\underline{\mathbf{U}}^*_r$. To ensure the reachability of $\underline{\mathbf{U}}^*_r$, the components of $\underline{\mathbf{N}}$ are real values. The algorithm is described as follows.

From an initial population at the 0-th iteration $\underline{\mathbf{N}}^0 = (N^0_1, N^0_2,...,N^0_c)$, for example the zero vector, we search toward the target point $\underline{\mathbf{U}}^*_r$ with the throughput vector $(X^*_1,...,X^*_c) = (U^*_{r1}/D_{r1},.....,U^*_{rc}/D_{rc})$ by varying class population and solving the LQM. With each solution of the LQM we have new estimates for R^c_o and U_o.

3.2 Case Study, an Internet Application

For a concrete example, we introduce the following personnel application. Users interact with the application via a browser. The browser interprets Java applets that interact with a database on the Server Node (Figure 1). The application has two classes of requests that are submitted frequently and are expected to dominate system performance: *query request*: a query returns information about an employee; *update request*: an update modifies some fields of a personnel record.

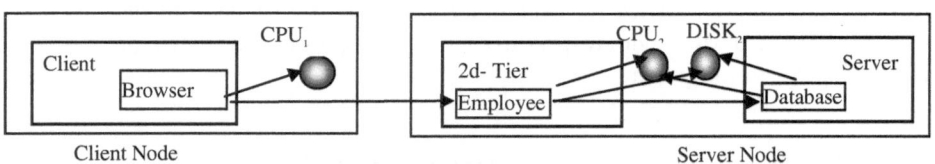

Client Node   Server Node

Figure 1. Personnel application

The example considers three objects: *Browser* on the *Client Node*, and *Employee* and *Database* on the *Server Node*. The *Employee* and *Database* objects reside in the *2d Tier* and *Server* processes respectively. Table 1 gives the total CPU and disk demands of each request and demands per object per request. The *query* and *update* requests are denoted as classes with subscripts *1* and *2*, and the devices with indices *1, 2,* and *3* respectively (as indicated in the first column). In the model per-class think times are 5 seconds.

Table 1. Total request demands and object demands per request (milliseconds)

	Query class 1	Update class 2	Browser/ query	Browser/ update	Employee / query	Employee/ update	Database/ query	Database/ update
CPU$_1$ (Device 1)	D$_{11}$=20	D$_{12}$=10	20	10	0	0	0	0
CPU$_2$ (Device 2)	D$_{21}$=50	D$_{22}$=70	0	0	30	40	20	30
DISK$_2$ (Device 3)	D$_{31}$=64	D$_{32}$=56	0	0	0	56	64	0

Assume that the maximum permitted utilization of the devices *2* and *3* are *0.8* and *0.9*. For an object *o* we want to find the maximum utilization of *o* such that the constraints are satisfied with respect to our chosen reference device *CPU$_2$(device 2)*. Using the demands from Table 1, the equation (12) becomes:

$$ (13) $$

Max $U_{21} R^1_o/50 + U_{22} R^2_o/70$

Subject to

$$ U_{21} + U_{22} = 0.8 $$
$$ (64/50)U_{21} + (56/70) U_{22} = 0.9 $$
$$ U_{21}, U_{22} \geq 0 $$

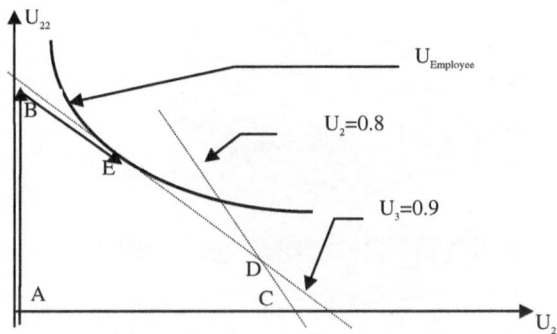

Figure 2. The feasibility region of the Personnel application. ABDC denotes the feasible area and AB and BE are the search directions for maximum utilization of the *Employee* object.

Figure 2 shows a geometrical representation of the feasibility space for the objective function of our example. It is obtained by intersecting the half spaces $U_i \leq b_i$. $U_i = b_i$ are hyper-planes that bound the feasible space. Object *Employee* reaches its maximum utilization at the point E, while the object *Database* reaches its maximum utilization at the point D. The objects' total utilization for the points C, D, E, B and the number of customers in each class that cause these utilizations are presented in Table 2. Points B and C correspond to workload mixes that include only one type of request. The maximum object utilizations for this example are caused by mixes of the requests that are obtained from the solution of the NLP problem.

Table 2. Maximum object utilizations and the request class populations that causes them

	B $\underline{N}$=(78, 0)	D $\underline{N}$= (63,19)	E $\underline{N}$=(33,40)	C $\underline{N}$=(0,63)
Employee	1.34	3.44	3.9	3.7
Database	7.6	9.8	7.0	5.3

4 Using Object Utilization to Define Activation Policy

Replication and activation policies are closely related to the maximum object utilization. A process has utilization that is the sum of its object's utilization. In general, processes with maximum utilization near zero need not be active. Depending on the request arrival distribution, the activation policy should be *shared server* (in which one instance of the object is shared by all requests) or *server per request* (an instance of the object is activated for each request). The latter may be more appropriate if arrivals come in bursts and the startup overheads are low. Terminating a process permits the allocation of system resources to other low frequency processes.

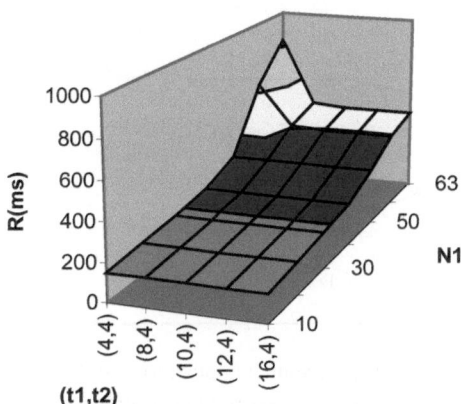

Figure 3. Query response time versus the *Database* threading level and number of customers; (t1,t2) denotes the number of threads of *Database* and *Employee* objects. N_1 denotes the number of customers of class 1 query.

Processes with maximum utilization much greater than zero should be active. For these entities, replication and threading levels must be decided. The maximum utilization gives the appropriate replication levels. If the replication levels are lower than maximum utilization, the customer response times are higher than necessary; if they are beyond the maximum utilization, more memory may be used but there is no improvement in customer response times. Secondary effects from paging overheads may degrade performance. In the following paragraphs we show the impact of threading level for *Database* and *Employee* objects on query response times.

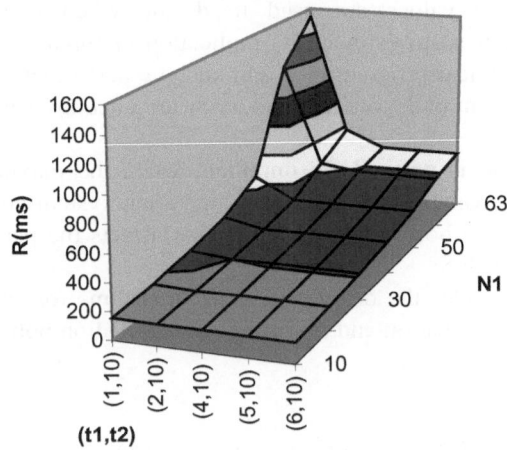

Figure 4. Query response time versus the *Employee* threading level and the number of customers; (t1, t2) denote the number of threads of *Database* and *Employee* objects. N_1 denotes the number of customers of class 1.

Figure 3 and Figure 4 show the *query* response times versus total number of customers in the system and the threading level for the *Database* and *Employee* objects. The total number of customers varies from 10 to 82 by keeping the population of the two classes at a constant ratio 63/19. This corresponds to point D in Figure 2 (see Table 2). In the figures the threading level of one of the objects is kept at its maximum value (4 and 10 respectively) while varying the threading level at the other object.

It is clear from the figures, that too few threads yield high response times since requests suffer queuing delays at the process of the object. Furthermore, more than the maximum number of threads does not improve customer request response times. From Figure 3 and Figure 4, the maximum numbers of threads are 10 and 4. The values predicted using the algorithm of Section 3 were 9.8 and 3.9 respectively (see Table 2). In Figure 3, when we chose the threading levels to be (12,4) the mean response times under high loads are not lowered. Similarly in Figure 4, when we choose threading levels of (5,10) there is no improvement in mean response times under high loads. Corresponding queueing delays are simply incurred at devices or other software servers.

5 Summary and Future Work

A method for deciding process replication and activation policies was presented. The method computes the maximum process utilization under design and implementation constraints.   These values are used to decide whether a process should run continuously, and if so to estimate its replication or threading level. The technique makes use of non-linear programming and analytic performance modeling techniques and takes into account both software and hardware queuing delays under all workload conditions.

This information is particularly important when the maximum utilization of an object exceeds licensing, software design, operating system constraints. Under these conditions a software bottleneck can occur that affects the performance of customer requests and hence QoS.

Future work includes the development of algorithms for automating the study of object placement, replication and threading, and activation policy to achieve scaleable distributed application systems.

Acknowledgments. This work was supported by a grant from IBM Canada, the Telecommunications Research Institute of Ontario (TRIO)/Communications and Information Technology Centre of Ontario (CITO) and the Italian MURST 40% and 60% Projects.

References

1. Balbo G.and Serazzi G.: Asymptotic Analysis of Multiclass Closed Queuing Networks: Common Bottlenecks. Performance Evaluation Journal, Vol. 26 (1996), 51-72
2. Balbo G., Serazzi G.: Asymptotic Analysis of Multiclass Closed Queuing   Networks: Multiple Bottlenecks. Performance Evaluation Journal, Vol. 30, No. 2 (1997) , 115-152
3. Bazaraa M.S., Sherali H.D., Shetty C.M.: Nonlinear Programming, J. Wiley, (1993).
4. Hills G., Rolia J., and Serazzi G.: Performance Engineering of Distributed Software Process Architectures. Lecture Notes in Computer Science, Springer-Verlag, No. 977 (1995) 79-85
5. ISO/IEC JTC1/SC21/WG7 N885: Reference Model for Open Distributed Processing-Part 1: Overview and Guide to Use, (1993)
6. Lazowska et al.: Quantitative System Performance, Computer Systems Analysis Using Queuing Network Models, Prentice-Hall (1984)
7. Reiser M. and Lavenberg S.S.: Mean Value Analysis of Closed Multichain Queuing Networks. Journal of ACM, Vol. 27 (1980), 313-322
8. Rolia J., Sevcik K.: The Method of Layers. IEEE Transactions on Software Engineering, Vol. 21, No. 8 (1995), 689-700
9. Seigel et al.: CORBA Fundamentals and Programming, J. Wiley, (1996)
10.Woodside C.M., Neilson J.E., Petriu D.C., and Majumdar S.: The Stochastic Rendezvous Network Model for the Performance of Synchronous Client-Server-like Distributed Software. IEEE Transactions on Computers, Vol. 44, No. 1 (1995), 20-34

SREPT: Software Reliability Estimation and Prediction Tool *

Srinivasan Ramani, Swapna S. Gokhale, and Kishor S. Trivedi

Center for Advanced Computing and Communication
Department of Electrical and Computer Engineering
Duke University, Durham, NC 27708-0291, USA
{sramani, ssg, kst}@ee.duke.edu

Abstract. Several tools have been developed for the estimation of software reliability. However, they are highly specialized in the approaches they implement and the particular phase of the software life-cycle in which they are applicable. There is an increasing need for a tool that can be used to track the quality of a software product during the software development process, right from the architectural phase all the way up to the operational phase of the software. Also the conventional techniques for software reliability evaluation, which treat the software as a monolithic entity are inadequate to assess the reliability of heterogeneous systems, which consist of a large number of globally distributed components. Architecture-based approaches are essential to predict the reliability and performance of such systems. This paper presents the high-level design of a *Software Reliability Estimation and Prediction Tool* (SREPT), that offers a unified framework containing techniques (including the architecture-based approach) to assist in the evaluation of software reliability at all phases of the software life-cycle.

1 Introduction

Software is an integral part of many critical and non-critical applications, and virtually any industry is dependent on computers for their basic functioning. As computer software permeates our modern society, and will continue to do so in the future, the assurance of its quality becomes an issue of critical concern. Techniques to measure and ensure reliability of hardware have seen rapid advances, leaving software as the bottleneck in achieving overall system reliability.

Various approaches based on the philosophies of *fault prevention, fault removal, fault tolerance* or *fault/failure forecasting* techniques have been proposed to achieve software reliability and many of these techniques have been abstracted into tools. The problem with applying such tools effectively towards improving the quality of software is that these tools are highly specialized in the approaches they implement and the phase of the software life-cycle during which they are

---

* Supported in part by a contract from Charles Stark Draper Laboratory and in part by Bellcore as a core project in the Center for Advanced Computing and Communication and by the National Science Foundation grant number EEC-9714965

R. Puigjaner et al. (Eds.): Tools'98, LNCS 1469, pp. 27–36, 1998.

applicable. There is thus a need for a tool that can track the quality of a software product and provide insights throughout the life-cycle of the software. The high level design of such a tool which provides a unified framework is presented in this paper.

The rest of the paper is organized as follows. In the next section we provide the motivation for a new tool. Section 3 presents the high-level design of SREPT. Section 4 provides an illustration of the use of SREPT in estimating software reliability. Section 5 concludes the paper.

2   Motivation

For state of the art research efforts to become best current practices in the industry, they ought to be made available in a systematic, user-friendly form. This factor has motivated the development of several tools for software reliability estimation. These tools can be broadly categorized as :

- Tools which use static complexity metrics at the end of the development phase as inputs and either classify the modules into fault-prone or non-fault-prone categories, or predict the number faults in a software module. An example of such a tool is the *Emerald* system [5].
- Tools which accept failure data during the functional testing of the software product to calibrate a *software reliability growth model* (SRGM) based on the data, and use the calibrated model to make predictions about the future. SMERFS, AT&T SRE Toolkit, SoRel and CASRE [6] are examples of such tools.

The *Emerald* system [5] uses the Datrix software analyzer to collect about 38 basic software metrics from the source code. Based on the experience in assessing previous software products, these metrics are used to identify *patch-prone* modules. The *Emerald* system can thus be used to determine the quality of a software product after the development phase, or pre-test phase. However it does not offer the capability of obtaining predictions based on the failure data collected during the testing phase. On the other hand, tools [6] like SMERFS, AT&T SRE Toolkit, SoRel, CASRE [11] can be used to estimate software reliability using the failure data to drive one or more of the software reliability growth models (SRGM). However they can only be used very late in the software life-cycle, and early prediction of software quality based on static attributes can have a lot of value. Techniques to obtain the optimal software release times guided by the reliability estimates obtained from the failure data have also been encapsulated in tools like ESTM [14], [15]. But once again, ESTM addresses only a particular problem (though very important) in the software life-cycle. Though some of the conventional techniques are available in the form of tools, these techniques have been shown to be inadequate to predict the reliability of modern heterogeneous software systems. System architecture-based reliability prediction techniques have thus gained prominence in the last few years [7], [16]. Presently there exists no special purpose tool for architecture-based analysis. The above factors highlight the need for a new tool for software reliability estimation and prediction to overcome the limitations of existing tools.

3   Design and Architecture of SREPT

This section presents the high-level design of SREPT. The block diagram in Fig. 1 depicts the architecture of SREPT. As can be seen from the figure, SREPT

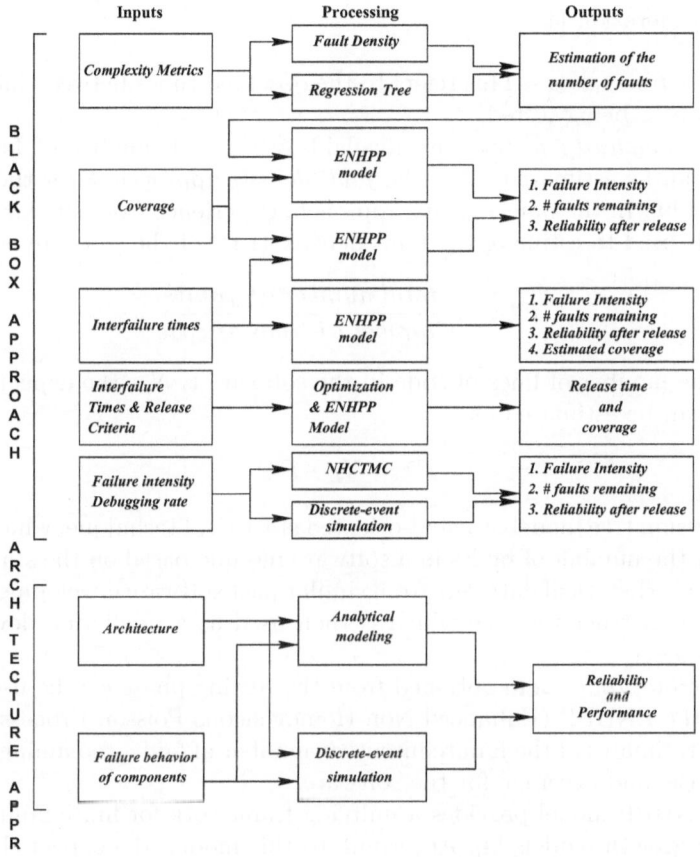

Fig. 1. Architecture of SREPT

supports the *black-box*-based and the *architecture*-based approaches to software reliability prediction.

3.1   Black-Box Based Approaches

Black-box based approaches treat the software as a whole without considering its internal structure. The following measures can be obtained to aid in black-box predictions -

Complexity metrics - These include the number of lines of code, number of decisions, loops, mean length of variable names and other static attributes of the code.

Test coverage - This is defined to be the ratio of potential fault-sites exercised (or executed) by test cases divided by the total number of potential fault-sites under consideration [4].

Interfailure times data - This refers to the observed times between failures when the software is being tested.

When *complexity metrics* are available, the total number of faults in the software can be estimated using the *fault density* approach [8] or the *regression tree* model [9]. In the fault density approach, experience from similar projects in the past is used to estimate the fault density (FD) of the software as,

$$FD = \frac{total\ number\ of\ faults}{number\ of\ lines\ of\ code} . \tag{1}$$

Now, if the number of lines of code in the software is N_L, the expected number of faults can be estimated as,

$$F = N_L * FD . \tag{2}$$

The regression tree model is a goal-oriented statistical technique, which attempts to predict the number of faults in a software module based on the static complexity metrics. Historical data sets from similar past software development projects is used to construct the tree which is then used as a predicting device for the current project.

Interfailure times data obtained from the testing phase can be used to parameterize the ENHPP (Enhanced Non-Homogeneous Poisson Process) model [4] to obtain estimates of the failure intensity, number of faults remaining, reliability after release, and coverage for the software.

The ENHPP model provides a unifying framework for finite failure software reliability growth models [4]. According to this model, the expected number of faults detected by time t, called the *mean value function*, $m(t)$ is of the form,

$$m(t) = a * c(t), \tag{3}$$

where a is the expected number of faults in the software (before testing/debugging begins), and $c(t)$ is the coverage function. Table 1 shows the four coverage functions that the ENHPP model used by SREPT provides by default to reflect four types of failure occurrence rates per fault. Given the sequence of time between failures $(t_1, t_2, \ldots)$ the object is to estimate two or more parameters of the chosen model(s). Commonly, one of these parameters is the expected number faults in the program (before testing/debugging begins), denoted by a, as in Equation (3).

Table 1. Coverage functions and parameters estimated

Coverage Function	Parameters	$m(t)$	Failure Occurrence Rate per fault
Exponential	a, g	$a(1 - e^{-gt})$	Constant
Weibull	a, g, γ	$a(1 - e^{-gt^\gamma})$	Increasing/Decreasing
S-shaped	a, g	$a[1 - (1 + gt)e^{-gt}]$	Increasing
Log-logistic	a, ω, κ	$a\frac{(\omega t)^\kappa}{1+(\omega t)^\kappa}$	Inverse Bath Tub

By explicitly incorporating the time-varying test coverage function in its analytical formulation $(m(t) = a * c(t))$, the ENHPP model is capable of handling any general coverage function and provides a methodology to integrate *test coverage* measurements available from the testing phase into the black-box modeling approach. The user may supply this as coverage measurements at different points in time during the testing phase, or as a time-function. This approach, combining test coverage and interfailure times data is shown in Fig. 1.

The framework of the ENHPP model may also be used to combine the estimate of the total number of faults obtained before the testing phase based on complexity metrics (parameter a), with the coverage information obtained during the testing phase $(c(t))$. This is also shown in Fig. 1.

The ENHPP model can also use interfailure times from the testing phase to obtain *release times* (optimal time to stop testing) for the software on the basis of a specified *release criteria*. Release criteria could be of the following types -

- Number of remaining faults - In this case, the release time is when a fraction ρ of all detectable faults has been removed.
- Failure intensity requirements - The criterion based on failure intensity suggests that the software should be released when the failure intensity measured at the end of the development test phase reaches a specified value λ_f.
- Reliability requirements - This criteria could be used to specify that the required conditional reliability in the operational phase is, say R_r at time t_0 after product release.
- Cost requirements - From a knowledge of the expected cost of removing a fault during testing, the expected cost of removing a fault during operation, and the expected cost of software testing per unit time, the total cost can be estimated. The release time is obtained by determining the time that minimizes this total cost.
- Availability requirements - The release time can be estimated based on an operational availability requirement.

The ENHPP-based techniques described above assume instantaneous debugging of the faults detected during testing. This is obviously unrealistic and leads to optimistic estimates. This drawback can be remedied if the *debugging rate* (repair rate) can be specified along with the *failure intensity*. SREPT offers two approaches to analyze explicit fault removal - *state-space method* [17] and *discrete-event simulation*.

In the state-space approach, SREPT takes the failure occurrence and debugging rates to construct a non-homogeneous continuous time Markov chain (NHCTMC) [3]. The solution of the NHCTMC is obtained using the SHARPE [12] modeling tool that is built into SREPT. The solution of the NHCTMC using SHARPE will enable estimates of *failure intensity, number of faults remaining,* and *reliability after release* to be obtained. The effect of different debugging rates can be studied by specifying the rates accordingly [17]. For example, debugging rates could be constant (say μ), time-dependent (say $\mu(t)$), or dependent on the number of faults pending for removal.

The discrete-event simulation (DES) approach offers distinct advantages over the state-space approach -

- DES accommodates any type of stochastic process. The state-space method is restricted to NHCTMCs with finite number of states, since a numerical solution of the Markov chain is required.
- Simulation approaches are faster for large NHCTMC's that could be very time-consuming to solve using numerical methods.
- The number of states in the Markov chain increases dramatically with an increase in the expected total number of faults in the software. SHARPE imposes restrictions on the number of states in the Markov chain and hence the maximum number of faults possible. DES imposes no such restrictions. But DES requires a large number of runs in order to obtain tight confidence intervals.

3.2   Architecture Based Approach

The second approach to software reliability supported by SREPT (from Fig. 1) is the architecture-based approach. Architecture-based approaches use the internal control structure of the software [7] to predict the reliability of software. This assumes added significance in the evaluation of the reliability of modern software systems which are not monolithic entities, but are likely to be made up of several modules distributed globally. SREPT allows prediction of the reliability of software based on :

Architecture of the Software. This is a specification of the manner in which the different modules in the software interact, and is given by the intermodular transition probabilities, or in a very broad sense, the operational profile of the software [13]. The architecture of the application can be modeled as a DTMC (Discrete Time Markov Chain), CTMC (Continuous Time Markov Chain), SMP (Semi-Markov Process) or a DAG (Directed Acyclic Graph) [3], [18]. The state of the application at any time is given by the module executing at that time, and the state transitions represent the transfer of control among the modules. DTMC, CTMC, and SMP can be further classified into irreducible and absorbing categories, where the former represents an infinitely running application, and the latter a terminating one. The absorbing DTMC, CTMC, SMP and DAG can be analyzed to give performance measures like the expected number of visits to a component during a single execution of the application, the average time spent in a component during a single execution, and the time to completion of the application.

Failure Behavior. This specifies the failure behavior of the modules and that of the interfaces between the modules, in terms of the probability of failure (or reliability), or failure rate (constant/time-dependent). Transitions among the modules could either be instantaneous or there could be an overhead in terms of time. In either case, the interfaces could be perfect or subject to failure, and the failure behavior of the interfaces can also be described by the reliabilities or constant/time-dependent failure rates.

The architecture of the software can be combined with the failure behavior of the modules and that of the interfaces into a *composite model* which can then be analyzed to predict reliability of the software. Various performance measures such as the time to completion of the application, can also be computed from the composite model. Another approach is to solve the architecture model and superimpose the failure behavior of the modules and the interfaces on to the solution to predict reliability. This is referred to as the *hierarchical model.*

SREPT also supports architecture-based software reliability evaluation using *discrete-event simulation* as an alternative to analytical models. Discrete-event simulation can capture detailed system structure, with the advantage that it is not subject to state-space explosion problems like the analytical methods.

4   Illustration

This section gives some examples of the use of SREPT in estimating software reliability. Fig. 2 shows a snapshot of the tool if the ENHPP engine is chosen. Among the details of the tool revealed in this snapshot are - a means of specifying the type of input data (which can be one of *interfailure times data only, interfailure times and coverage data, or estimated # faults and coverage data*). In the snapshot, it has been specified that the input to the ENHPP engine will consist of *interfailure times data only.* The user can then choose one of the coverage functions offered by the ENHPP model to estimate the reliability as well as other metrics of interest. The snapshot shows the *Exponential* coverage function. When asked to "estimate", the tool then brings up a window with suggested initial values of the parameters of the selected model. The convergence of the numerical routines depends largely on the initial guesses, and hence by changing the initial guesses using this window, the user can control it. The results of the estimation including the expected number of faults in the software, the estimated model parameters, and the mean value function are printed in the "Messages" area.

Fig. 3 shows a snapshot of the plot of the mean value function. The figure indicates that initially no faults have been detected, and as time (testing) progresses more and more faults are expected to be detected. Other metrics that can be plotted include the *failure intensity, faults remaining, reliability after release (conditional reliability)* and the *estimated coverage*. Release times can now be obtained based on release criteria.

SREPT also allows the user to let the ENHPP engine determine the best model for the given interfailure times data. This is done on the basis of a *goodness-of-fit, u-plot and y-plot* [10]. Other interfaces will enable the user to access the different techniques supported by SREPT.

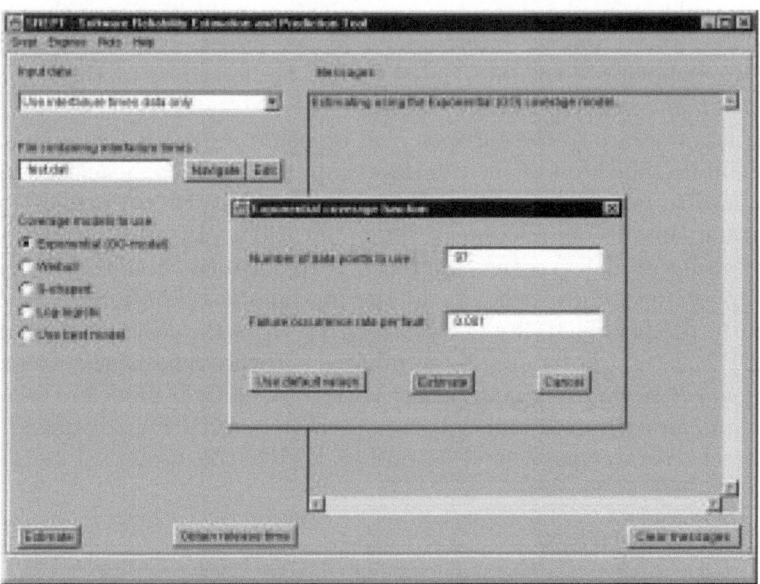

Fig. 2. Choosing the ENHPP engine of SREPT

5   Conclusion

In this paper we presented the high-level design of a tool offering a unified framework for software reliability estimation that can be used to assist in evaluating the quality of the overall software development process right from the architectural phase all the way up to the operational phase. This is because the tool implements several software reliability techniques including complexity metrics-based techniques used in the pre-test phase, interfailure times-based techniques used during the testing phase, and architecture-based techniques that can be used at all stages in the software's life-cycle. Architecture-based techniques are being implemented in a tool in a systematic manner for the first time. SREPT

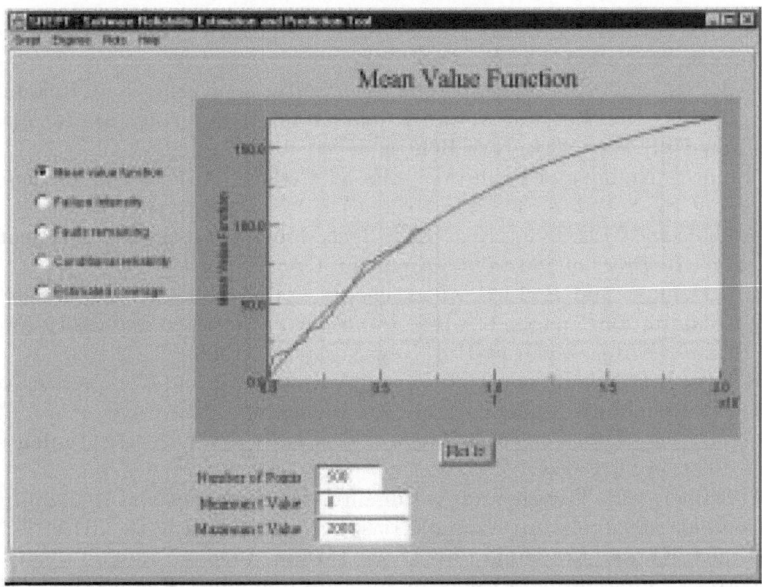

Fig. 3. Plot of the mean value function from the ENHPP engine. The actual number of faults detected is represented by the irregular curve and is derived from the interfailure times data supplied

also has the ability to suggest release times for software based on release criteria, and has techniques that incorporate finite repair times while evaluating software reliability. The tool is expected to have a widespread impact because of its applicability at multiple phases in the software life-cycle, and the incorporation of several techniques in a systematic, user-friendly form in a GUI-based environment.

References

1. S. Gokhale, P.N. Marinos, K.S. Trivedi, "Important Milestones in Software Reliability Modeling", in Proc. of *Software Engineering and Knowledge Engineering*, June 1996.
2. A.L. Goel and K. Okumoto, "Time-Dependent Error-Detection Rate Models for Software Reliability and Other Performance Measures", *IEEE Trans. on Reliability*, Vol.R-28, No.3, pp. 206-211, August 1979.
3. K.S. Trivedi, "Probability and Statistics with Reliability, Queuing and Computer Science Applications", Prentice Hall, Englewood Cliffs, New Jersey, 1982.
4. S. Gokhale, T. Philip, P. N. Marinos, K.S. Trivedi, "Validation and Comparison of Non-Homogeneous Poisson Process Software Reliability Models", *Intl. Symposium of Software Reliability Engineering*, October 1996.
5. J.P. Hudepohl, S.J. Aud, T.M. Khoshgoftaar, E.B. Allen, and J. Mayrand, "Emerald: Software Metrics and Models on the Desktop", *IEEE Software*, September 1996, pp. 56-60.

6. M.R. Lyu (Editor), *Handbook of Software Reliability Engineering*, McGraw-Hill, New York, NY, 1996.
7. J.P. Horgan and A.P. Mathur, chapter "Software Testing and Reliability", pages 531-566, *Handbook of Software Reliability Engineering, M. R. Lyu, Editor*, McGraw-Hill, New York, NY, 1996.
8. M. Lipow, "Number of Faults per Line of Code", *IEEE Trans. on Software Engineering*, SE-8(4):437-439, July 1982.
9. S. Gokhale and M.R. Lyu, "Regression Tree Modeling for the Prediction of Software Quality", In *Proc. of ISSAT'97*, Anaheim, CA, March 1997.
10. S. Brocklehurst and B. Littlewood, chapter "Techniques for Prediction Analysis and Recalibration", pages 119-166, *Handbook of Software Reliability Engineering, M. R. Lyu, Editor*, McGraw-Hill, New York, NY, 1996.
11. M.R. Lyu, A.P. Nikora, and W.H. Farr, "A Systematic and Comprehensive Tool for Software Reliability Modeling and Measurement", *Proceedings of the 23rd International Symposium on Fault-Tolerant Computing (FTCS-23)*, Toulouse, France, June 1993, pp. 648-653.
12. R.A. Sahner, K.S. Trivedi, and A. Puliafito, "Performance and Reliability Analysis of Computer Systems: An Example-Based Approach Using the SHARPE Software Package", Kluwer Academic Publishers, Boston, 1996.
13. J.D. Musa, "Operational Profiles in Software-Reliability Engineering", *IEEE Software*, 10(2):14-32, March 1993.
14. S.R. Dalal and C.L. Mallows, "Some Graphical Aids for Deciding When to Stop Testing Software", *IEEE Journal on Selected Areas in Communications*, Vol.8, No.2, February 1990, pp. 169-175.
15. S. R. Dalal and A. A. McIntosh, "When to Stop Testing for Large Software Systems with Changing Code", *IEEE Trans. on Software Engineering*, Vol.20, No.4, pp. 318-323, April 1994.
16. S. Gokhale and K.S. Trivedi, "Structure-Based Software Reliability Prediction", in *Proc. of Fifth Intl. Conference on Advanced Computing*, Chennai, India, Dec. 1997.
17. S. Gokhale, P.N. Marinos, K.S. Trivedi, M.R. Lyu, "Effect of Repair Policies on Software Reliability", In *Proc. of Computer Assurance'97*, Maryland, June 1997.
18. V.G. Kulkarni, "Modeling and Analysis of Stochastic Systems", Chapman & Hall, London, UK, 1995.

Reusable Software Components for Performability Tools, and Their Utilization for Web-Based Configurable Tools *

Aad P. A. van Moorsel[1] and Yiqing Huang[2]

[1] Distributed Software Research Department
Bell Laboratories Research, Lucent Technologies
600 Mountain Ave., Murray Hill, NJ 07974, USA
aad@bell-labs.com
[2] Center for Reliable and High-Performance Computing
Coordinated Science Laboratory, University of Illinois at Urbana-Champaign
1308 W. Main St., Urbana, IL 61801
yhuang@crhc.uiuc.edu

Abstract. This paper discusses software reusability strategies for performance and reliability modeling tools. Special emphasis is on web-embedded tools, and the potential interaction between such tools. We present the system analysis tools (SAT) application programming interface, which allows for quickly embedding existing tools in the web, and generally simplifies programming analysis tools by structured reuse. We also introduce the FREUD project, which has as primary aim to establish a single point of access to a variety of web-enabled tools. In addition, FREUD facilitates configurable web tools by allowing a user to select from the registered modeling formalisms, solvers and graphics tools, and by providing glue between the tools through scripting. We will argue that this form of reuse is particularly suitable for performability modeling tools because of their predictable usage pattern.

1 Introduction

As witnessed by the contributions to the series of workshops on performance tools [23], the last decade has seen a proliferation of software support for model-based analysis of system reliability, performance and performability. Most software tools, however, support only the modeling formalism or solution methods under investigation, and do not provide a software platform that support future development of similar tools (possibly by other developers). As a consequence, practice shows that similar but incompatible software is being developed at various places, with only limited cross-fertilization through reuse.

The current status of software design and development methodology, and its deployment in the field, seems to create opportunities for some major changes

---

* This work was initiated while Yiqing Huang was with the Distributed Software Research Department, Bell Labs Research, Murray Hill, Summer 1997.

R. Puigjaner et al. (Eds.): Tools'98, LNCS 1469, pp. 37–50, 1998.

in this situation. First of all, readily available software packages like Tcl/Tk or Java's abstract windowing toolkit, already significantly simplify the programming of user interfaces. In addition, methodology underlying software development and reuse becomes more and more widely accepted [28], like that of components [17,31], coordination [11,22], frameworks [8] and patterns [10]. Based on these developments, we discuss in this paper domain-specific opportunities for reuse in the area of performance and reliability modeling tools.

Recently, there have been the first developments in the direction of providing programming interfaces for performability tools. The generic net editor system AGNES, developed at the TU Berlin is the first major effort we know of [20,32]. It provides the necessary C++ classes to create front-ends for tools in the style of TimeNet [12], UltraSAN [30], DyQNtool [15], GISharpe [26], and the like. In the SAT application programming interface (earlier introduced in a hand-out [18]), we provide a subset of the functionality of AGNES, in Java. The SAT API also includes reusable software for creating web-enabled tools, and we will discuss this effort in more detail in this paper. Another recent development is the Mobius Java-based framework developed at the University of Illinois [29]. It takes things one step further than AGNES and SAT in that it also provides reusable software for algorithms, such as state-space generation algorithms.

Certainly other tool developers have considered forms of reuse, but the above are the ones we know off where software is designed with as a primary purpose to assist (other) tool developers with future projects. Of particular interest is the development of generic languages that can be used for specifying a variety of model formalisms, or can be used to interface with a variety of solvers. Examples are the FIGARO workbench [2] developed at Electricité de France, or the SMART language developed at the College of William and Mary [5]. However, languages are only potential (but very important and far reaching) *enablers* for software reuse, they do not deal with the software architecture itself. Similarly, the very successful efforts in the scientific computing community to provide standard implementations and templates for numerical algorithms are reuse enablers, and must be complemented by software solutions [3].

In this paper we discuss two complementary approaches to reuse we followed in providing performability tools over the web. The presented techniques use known reuse methods, tailored specifically to performability modeling tools. First, we introduce the system analysis tools API, which is constructed in the form of a framework [8]. It contains reusable Java classes, and aims at reuse at the source code level. Using the SAT API existing tools can be made web-enabled quickly, and new tools (web-based or not) can be developed very efficiently. Secondly, we introduce the FREUD tool configuration architecture, which allows users to configure a tool from components registered with the FREUD web site (components are for instance graphical modeling interfaces, core mathematical descriptors, solution engines, or display facilities). Each of the components has mature stand-alone functionality, but a combination of components is needed to solve a user's problem. Reuse of components is run-time, using scripting to glue components together [25]. The web-based FREUD implementation assumes that all components are web-embedded, and uses JavaScript as glueing language, but similar approaches can be followed outside the web context.

Before discussing in detail the SAT API and FREUD, we first discuss characteristics common to performability tools. This will help identify what tool modules to consider when configuring tools.

2   Performability Tools Components

We identify typical building blocks for performability tools, and discuss requirements for these tools. We base the search of common structures of performability

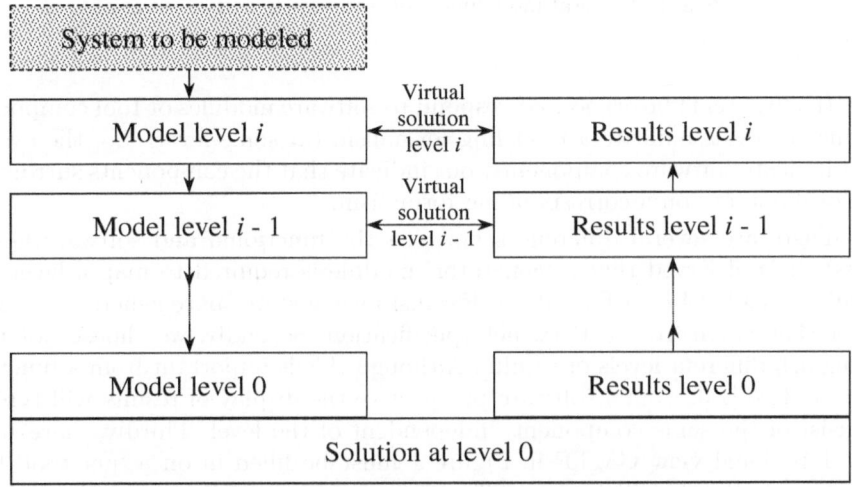

Fig. 1. General modeling tool framework, functional view.

tools on the general modeling tool framework, given in Figure 1. Haverkort [14] formulated the GMTF to classify and compare performability tools with regard to their user-perceived functionality (note that Figure 1 is some what less detailed than the GMTF presented in [14]). In the GMTF a system model is formulated at level i, then transformed into a level $i-1$ formalism, etc. At level 0 the actual solution takes place, after which the results are translated back to the original model level (level i) formalism, so that they can be directly interpreted by the user. As an example, a stochastic Petri-net tool first creates a Petri net description (level 1), then maps it on a Markov chain description (level 0), then solves the Markov chain and gives results in terms of probability distribution of markings in the Petri net.

The above framework is based on a functional view of tools, from a user perspective, but we are interested in discussing tools from an implementation (or software design) perspective. Therefore, we transform Haverkort's 'functional view' GMTF into a 'software view' GMTF, as depicted in Figure 2. In Figure 2

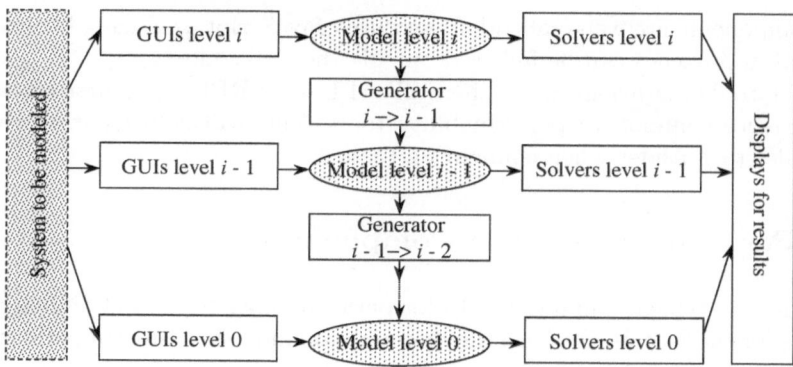

Fig. 2. General modeling tool framework, software view.

the (transparent) boxes now correspond to software modules or tool components, while the ovals indicate a modeling formalism (at some level). So, the ovals do not indicate software components, but indicate that the components surrounding an oval operate on a corresponding formalism.

There are several differences between the functional and software GMTF. First, it is observed that a 'generator' module is required to map a level i formalism to a level $i-1$ formalism. For instance, a state space generator to create a Markov chain from a Petri net specification. Secondly, we choose not to distinguish different levels of results. Although this is important from a functional perspective [14], from a software perspective the display of results will typically consist of the same component, independent of the level. Thirdly, more subtle, the functional view GMTF in Figure 1 must be filled in on a 'per tool' basis, that is, the levels will have a different meaning depending on what tool is fit to the GMTF. In the software-view GMTF, we want to fit different tools into one picture, so that different GUIs, different model formalisms, different solvers can be related to each other. Thus, multiple GUIs are possible in the modified GMTF, as are multiple solvers. Note also that solvers on different levels can be applied (for instance on-the-fly solutions [6] or matrix-geometric solutions [16]).

The software-view GMTF of Figure 2 is not claimed to be the only or preferred way of relating performability tool software components. It is set up so that it motivates the component approach we take in the FREUD configurable tools facility (see Section 4). We have for instance not included libraries, documentation and debugging software components in the GMTF, since it is beyond the scope of this paper to go in too much detail. The point we want to make is that performability modeling tools naturally lend themselves for a component-based software design. All components have clearly defined functionality, and are able to execute largely independently their respective tasks. Moreover, because they operate independently, different implementations of each component may be substituted for each other, without impairing the functioning of any of the other tools. As a consequence, special-purpose GUIs and solvers can be plugged in easily, provided the software is designed to allow for such enhancements.

3   An Application Programming Interface for Web-Embedded Tools

In FREUD, and the configurable tool facility of FREUD, it is assumed that all software components in the GMTF[1] can be accessed and used over the web. We therefore discuss in this section how to make these tool components web-enabled.[2] We introduce the system analysis tools API, which provides reusable Java code for making tools available over the web.

3.1   Web-Enabled Software

Web-embedded applications are being developed in various fields [3,13], and performance modeling tools have been shipped to the web as well [18,26]. The advantages of using tools over the web are plenty, both for the user and tool developer [18]. The major advantages come from the fact that only one version of the tool (put on a web site) is public, and can run in any suitable web browser. In addition, computing facilities on client as well as server side can be used. As a consequence, overhead caused by installation, updating and distributing, and performance degradation caused by inadequate user equipment do no longer play a role. If issues of reliability, security and network performance can be kept in control, and if the process of making tools web-enabled is simple enough, then the web is in many cases the preferred platform. In this paper we make no attempts to tackle quality of service issues, but we do attempt to simplify the development of web-embedded tools.

In its simplest form, a web-based tool is a stand-alone application running fully in the client's web browser; this can be in the form of an applet or plug-in (applets run Java code, plug-ins for instance Tcl/Tk programs, or any other code for which a C++ implemented plug-in is provided). If connection with a server is needed, the HTTP protocol provides the possibility to execute CGI scripts, but this is often not sufficient. Instead, communication will be based on sockets or other higher level protocols, like CORBA's IIOP or Java's RMI.

3.2   SAT API

The system analysis tools application programming interface (SAT API) provides all the necessary code to make tools web-enabled. The SAT API is a framework of Java classes which take care of all aspects of communication, from the applet to the server-side executables. In addition, the SAT API provides performability-tools specific Java classes for user interface creation. The SAT

---

[1] Unless otherwise noted, in what follows GMTF denotes the software-view GMTF of Figure 2.

[2] We interchangeably use 'web-embedded,' 'web-based,' 'web-enabled,' to indicate tools that can be accessed and used over the world-wide web. That is, a front-end is started up in the user's browser, and, if necessary, a back-end server is available (typically for heavy-duty computation).

API is designed such that GUIs, menu options, and communication classes interface through abstract classes, not through their implementations. Hence, implementations of user interface, menu options and communication methods can be changed independently. We introduced an earlier version of the SAT API in a hand-out [18].

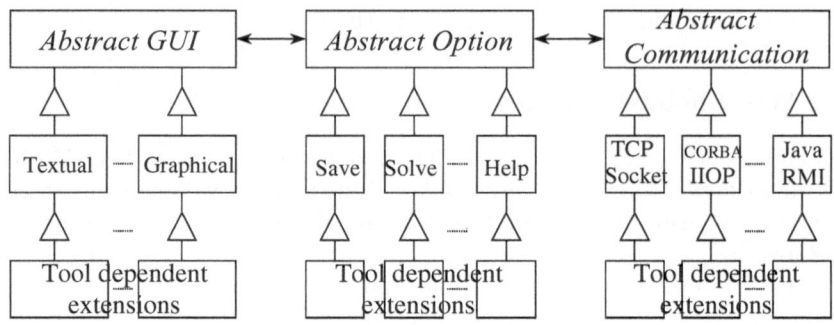

Fig. 3. Client side class hierarchy of System Analysis Tools API.

The SAT API contains classes for the client side and the server side of a web-embedded tool, and we first discuss how the client side is designed, using Figure 3. The main classes are the abstract classes 'GUI', 'Option' and 'Communication,' which interface with each other. Instantiatable subclasses implement (at least) the methods in the abstract classes; if necessary, tool-specific subclasses can be created to override and extend the implemented generic classes. Figure 3 depicts this set-up, using a triangle to indicate a class-subclass relation (as in [10]). So, for instance, there are GUI classes for textual as well as graphical interfaces, and communication classes for socket communication, Java RMI, etc. With this set-up, classes can easily be extended for specific tools, and can easily be replaced by specific implementations or by different technology (the communication can be TCP socket communication, Java RMI, etc., without impacting the GUI and menu options).

The GUI and Option classes are respectively the "view" classes (following the model-view-controller paradigm [7]), corresponding to the visual aspects of the GUI, and the "control" classes, corresponding to the options in the menu bar ('save', 'load', 'help', etc.). There has been made no advanced attempts to create extensive graphical user interfaces (Figure 7 shows a GUI based on the SAT API); the 'textual' classes provide xterm-like functionality to take over the role of the terminal window for textual tools. Of course, there is a need for reusable Java GUI classes for modeling tools, the same as AGNES provides in C++.

On the server side, the SAT API provides a server daemon that continuously listens for users that want to access the back-end, and there is a wrapper provided in which executables are being called. Figure 4 depicts the client and server

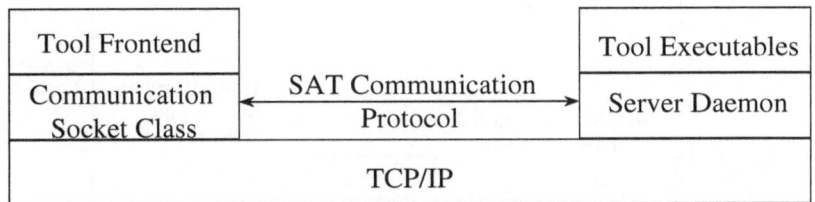

Fig. 4. Client-server functionality in System Analysis Tools API.

modules for the case that a specially developed communication protocol is used. In Figure 4 the 'Tool Frontend' includes the GUI and Option classes from Figure 3, while the 'Communication Socket Class' denotes a particular Communication class. Together they constitute the applet appearing in the user's web browser.

For each individual tool, the server daemon must be configured by setting some parameters, while the wrapper must be adjusted to execute the correct programs depending on the user input. This requires minor effort; we have implementations for SHARPE [27], AMPL [9] and TALISMAN [24], and they only differ through a few lines. The SAT communication protocol mentioned in Figure 4, specifies the message format for communication between front-end and back-end. If this protocol is being used, the construction of messages to be sent, and the parsing of receiving messages can be provided as a reusable class. Note that this communication protocol is based on message passing; if techniques based on remote method invocations (RMI, CORBA) are being used one will not use the SAT communication protocol.

4   FREUD

In this section we discuss the FREUD architecture and implementation. FREUD provides users with a single point of access to web-embedded system analysis tools of the type described in the previous section, and allows users to configure their own software support out of components registered at the FREUD site. We first discuss the basics of FREUD, without the configuration aspects. Then we discuss how FREUD supports configurable tools.

4.1   Registration Service

The provision of a "one-stop-shopping" facility is the original motivation behind FREUD, see Figure 5. Imagine people are interested in analyzing their system for performance or reliability, and want to find the tool that is most suitable. Then it would be attractive if there is a central, well-publicized, site with links to usable tools. This central site, or gateway, does not need to offer much other functionality, since that is left to the individual tools. Effectively, FREUD is thus a regular web site with a database for registered tools (For a more sophisticated view point, we refer to the discussion in [19], where it is argued that authentication, fault tolerance and load balancing may be done centrally. In this

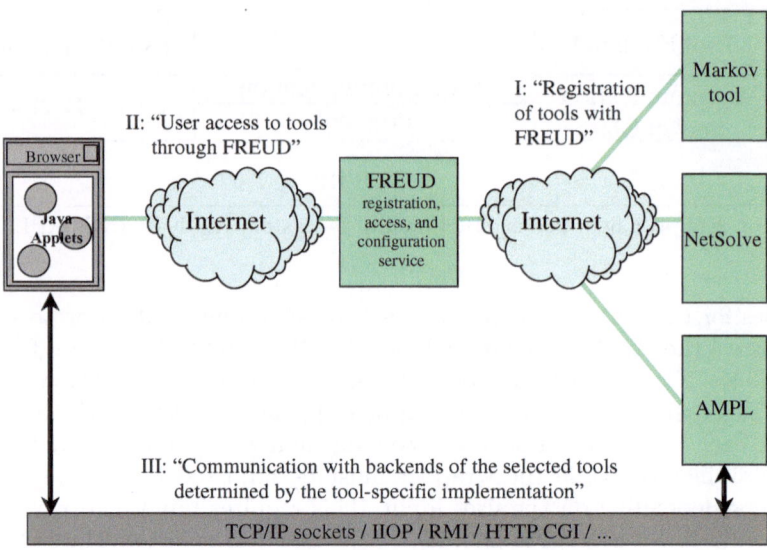

Fig. 5. FREUD.

paper we do not concern ourself with these issues.) In Figure 5, the FREUD site is in the center, and various tools have registered with FREUD (step I); these tools can be accessed by the user from a page with appropriate links dynamically created by FREUD (step II), after which the tool will be downloaded, and future communication is established in any desired way (step III).

Space limitations prohibit us from showing all web pages a user of FREUD may download, but the pages include user authentication displays, tool listings, tool registration forms, etc.

4.2   User View

When the user who accesses FREUD decides to build up a 'new' tool out of registered tool components, the applet in Figure 6 pops up. This configuration applet contains three panels. The left-most panel shows the tool components registered (the shown list contains all tools we have currently available over the web). The user selects desired components in this panel; for instance, a GUI to specify a model, a solution engine to solve the model, and a data display tool to show results. The selected components will then be displayed in the second panel. In Figure 6 Markovtool (a locally developed tool for drawing a hybrid Markov model/Petri net) and NetSolve (a solution engine from the University of Tennessee [3]) are being chosen.

The user then needs to specify how the tool components should interact; that is, which component's output should be forwarded to which component's input. In the example, Markovtool output (a model) will be forwarded as NetSolve input (for solution). Since the formats of Markovtool and NetSolve do

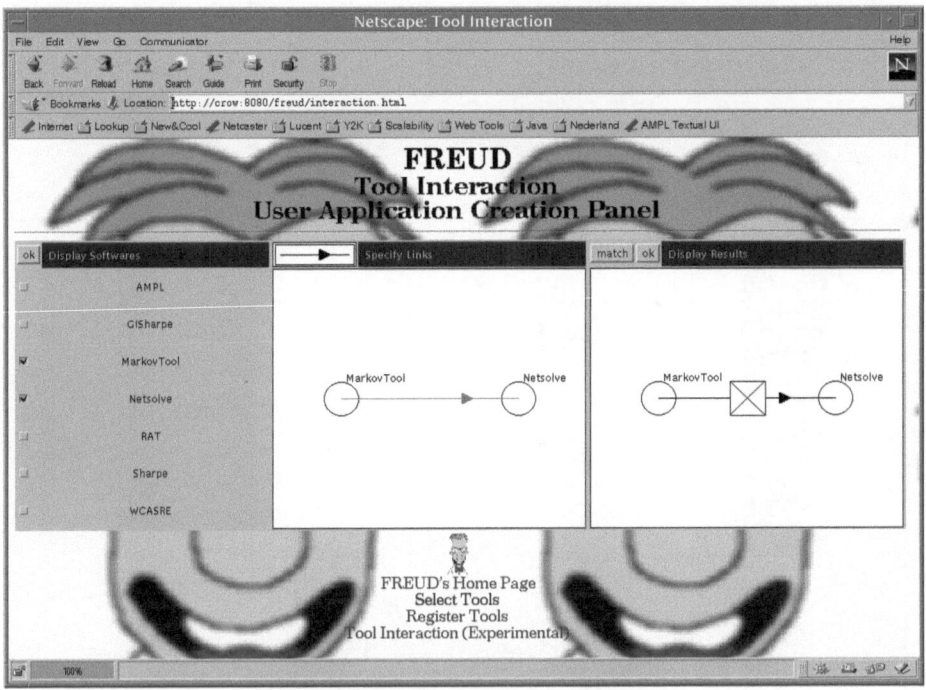

Fig. 6. Configuration facility FREUD.

not match, a translator must exist to convert. The user therefore clicks 'match' to see whether a translator between Markovtool and NetSolve is available. The FREUD gateway will search its database; if the translator exists, it shows up as a marked square between the selected tools. In Figure 6 it can be seen that a translator from Markovtool to NetSolve is available. Finally, the FREUD gateway then dynamically creates an HTML document with the desired collection of tool components and translators (after the user clicks 'OK'). The page in Figure 7 appears (Section 4.3 explains how the page is constructed).

To put this example in context, we illustrate how Markovtool, NetSolve, and the translator fit the GMTF. Markovtool is a level i modeling formalism (for some i; if no further tools are considered one can take $i = 1$), with as output a description of the Markov model, and an initial distribution. The translator then generates a level $i - 1$ model in terms of a system of linear equations, which NetSolve then solves. The translator thus functions as a 'generator' component in this example, while NetSolve is a solver at level $i - 1$.

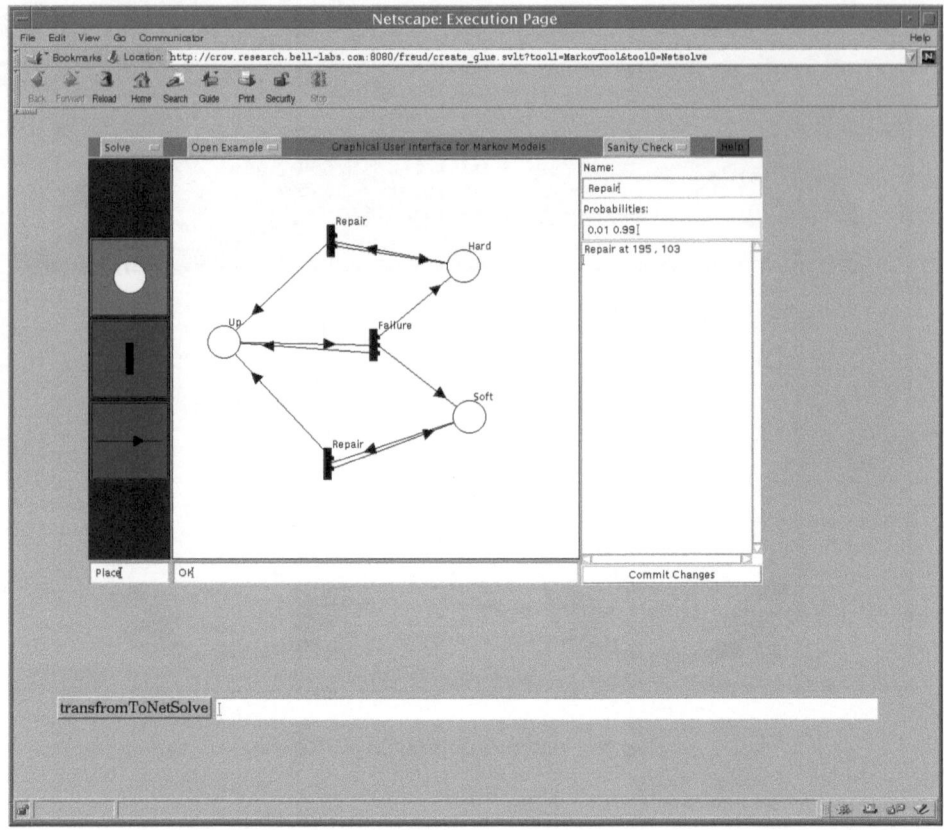

Fig. 7. Configured tool, showing Markovtool and a translator to NetSolve.

4.3 Coordination Mechanisms

In FREUD it is assumed that all registered tools are client-server applications themselves, and there is therefore communication between different components possible on the client side as well as at the server side. We implemented two types of communication, one on the server side based on file I/O, and one on the client side based on scripting using JavaScript. We will concentrate on the client-side coordination through scripting.

The nature of performability tools is such that the pattern of usage of components is typically predictable, as manifested by the GMTF. When we carry out an evaluation, we start with a GUI to create the model, then generate the mathematical model that lends itself for solution, and then display the results. In the GMTF as depicted in Figure 2, this typical user pattern corresponds to a path from left to right. Coordination between components therefore is 'sequential': output of one tool becomes input of the next, possibly after conversion between formalisms and formats. The coordination mechanisms do therefore not need to be very advanced to lead to useful results; in fact, we need a variation of the 'pipe' construct.

JavaScript is a scripting language for controlling browsers, and can be included in HTML documents. Not all browsers know how to interpret JavaScript, but for instance the Netscape browser does. When configuring tools, JavaScript allows for exchanging information between different applets running in the same HTML document. This is even possible if the two applets come from different machines. JavaScript interfaces with Java applets by calling its methods; for instance, to read the model from Markovtool, JavaScript calls Markovtool's public method `model2String()`.

Using JavaScript it is relatively straightforward to construct a translator that functions as a 'pipe' between applets. The remaining task of the translator then is to convert the format. This can be done in JavaScript as well, or one can choose to create a conversion applet, and it depends on the complexity of the operation what method is preferred. In any case, the JavaScript code, including possibly a reference to an applet, is registered with FREUD, and can from then on be used to glue together tool components.

Below we show the JavaScript code used in the Markovtool-NetSolve translator.

```
function transfMtoN() {
        var aPanel = document.Gui.draw_panel;
        var aString = aPanel.model2String();
        document.HighLevel.display.value = aString;
        document.Markov2Netsolve.transform(aString);
}
```

The JavaScript variable `aPanel` takes as 'value' the instantiated object `draw _panel` in the Gui, which is the tag used in the HTML code to identify the Markovtool applet. Then JavaScript calls the method `model2String()` in Markovtool to obtain a string representation of the model. In the last line the string is input to the applet that is part of the translator.

Note that there is no call to a NetSolve method; instead we used the option of file input and output. The reason for this is symptomatic for the current state of Internet software. The NetSolve Java interface (publicly available) uses a later version of the SUN Java development kit than the Netscape browser accepts. The SUN HotJava browser runs the NetSolve interface, but does not yet know how to interpret Netscape's JavaScript. As a consequence, we have to split up the use of the tools (we run NetSolve in HotJava or appletviewer using URL upload of the translator's output). When Netscape is able to use a newer JDK version (hopefully in the near future), or when HotJava starts supporting JavaScript (supposedly in the near future) we may decide that scripting is preferred over file transfer and change the implementation accordingly. It should also be noted that for the in-house developed tools we have combinations of tools that do coordinate through scripting only.

One important element remains to be discussed, namely the posting of interfaces. To create a translator, one must know the methods available to interface with the respective tools. Therefore, at registration with FREUD, a tool posts the public methods available, and gives a description of its semantics. This is done using the same registration page submitted when registering a tool. For the Markovtool, the method `model2String` is posted, as well as the way to access it through `draw_panel`. In the current setting the interfaces are posted in natural language, listing the relevant method calls and their functioning. This could be substituted by a more formal way of describing the interface definition.

4.4   Discussion of the FREUD Implementation

FREUD establishes coordination between software components with minimal requirements on these components. We started from the premise that tools should not have to be adjusted before they can fit in the FREUD configuration service. That is a very important decision with far-reaching consequences, since it limits the level of sophistication one can establish in the coordination between tools (a 'for' loop over a global variable, or interactive display as for the transient solvers in TimeNet [12] are some examples of more complex interaction patterns). We think, however, that performability tools are used in relatively predictable ways, and we therefore establish useful interaction by simple means.

If we are willing to impose further rules on the tool implementations registered with the FREUD configuration service, we can use more advanced coordination mechanisms [1,4,17,21]. These mechanisms have properties like event sharing and state persistence, enabling much more intricate forms of coordination. Then GUIs may interoperate, and front ends and back ends can be registered independently (instead of only full-blown client-server tools as in the FREUD architecture). If developers are willing to code within component architectures more advanced forms of cooperation can be achieved, but it is not beforehand clear whether upgrade to complex existing coordination platforms (Java Beans and the like) is required and advisable for our purposes.

5   Conclusion

In this paper we have presented the FREUD architecture, which offers users a single point of access to web-based performability modeling tools. More importantly, it provides mechanisms to let users configure 'new' tools out of registered components. As a consequence, users are able to leverage of existing tools, like GUIs, numerical solution libraries [3] or linear programming executables [18].

We have embedded the discussion of the FREUD configurable tool facility into the larger issue of programming for reuse, since we expect that performance and reliability modeling tools can benefit from this greatly. We therefore also paid considerable attention to the system analysis tools API we developed. This Java API allows legacy tools as well as new tools to be made web-enabled with minor effort. In addition, we proposed a software-view GMTF (as variation of the functional-view general modeling tool framework in [14]) to help structure software and identify requirements for performability tools.

References

1. R. M. Adler, "Distributed coordination models for client/server computing," *IEEE Computer*, vol. 28, no. 4, pp. 14–22, April 1995.
2. M. Bouissou, "The FIGARO dependability evaluation workbench in use: Case studies for fault-tolerant computer systems," in *23th Annual international Symposium on Fault-Tolerant Computing (FTCS-23)*, pp. 680–685, Toulouse, France, June 1993, IEEE, IEEE Computer Society Press.
3. H. Casanova and J. Dongarra, "NetSolve: A network server for solving computational science problems," *International Journal of Supercomputer Applications and High Performance Computing*, vol. 11, no. 3, pp. 212–223, Fall 1997.
4. P. Ciancarini, A. Knoche, R. Tolksdorf, and F. Vitali, "PageSpace: An architecture to coordinate distributed applications on the web," in *Fifth International World Wide Web Conference*, Paris, France, May 1996.
5. G. Ciardo and A. S. Miner, "SMART: Simulation and Markovian analyzer for reliability and timing," in *Tool Descriptions, Supplement to Proceedings 9th International Conference on Modelling Techniques and Tools for Computer Performance Evaluation*, pp. 41–43, Saint-Malo, France, June 1997.
6. D. D. Deavours and W. H. Sanders, ""On-the-fly" solution techniques for stochastic Petri nets and extensions," in *7th International Workshop on Petri Nets and Performance Models*, pp. 132–141, Saint Malo, France, June 1997, IEEE, IEEE Computer Society Press.
7. A. Eliëns, *Principles of Object-Oriented Software Development*, Addison-Wesley, Reading, MA, USA, 1995.
8. M. E. Fayad and D. C. Schmidt, "Object-oriented application frameworks," *Communications of the ACM*, vol. 40, no. 10, pp. 33–38, October 1997.
9. R. Fourer, D. M. Gay, and B. W. Kernighan, *AMPL: A Modeling Language for Mathematical Programming*, Duxbury Press, Belmont, CA, 1993.
10. E. Gamma, R. Helm, R. Johnson, and J. Vlissides, *Design Patterns: Elements of Reusable Object-Oriented Software*, Addison-Wesley, Reading, MA, USA, 1995.
11. D. Gelernter and N. Carriero, "Coordination languages and their significance," *Communications of the ACM*, vol. 35, no. 2, pp. 97–107, February 1992.
12. R. German, C. Kelling, A. Zimmermann, and G. Hommel, "TimeNET–a toolkit for evaluating non-Markovian stochastic Petri nets," *Performance Evaluation*, vol. 24, pp. 69–87, 1995.
13. O. Günther, R. Müller, P. Schmidt, H. K. Bhargava, and R. Krishnan, "MMM: A web-based system for sharing statistical computing modules," *IEEE Internet Computing*, vol. 1, no. 3, pp. 59–68, May-June 1997.
14. B. R. Haverkort, *Performability Modelling Tools, Evaluation Techniques, and Applications*, PhD thesis, University of Twente, The Netherlands, 1990.
15. B. R. Haverkort, "Performability evaluation of fault-tolerant computer systems using DyQN-tool$^+$," *International Journal of Reliability, Quality and Safety Engineering*, vol. 2, no. 4, pp. 383–404, 1995.
16. B. R. Haverkort and A. Ost, "Steady-state analysis of infinite stochastic Petri nets: Comparing the spectral expansion and the matrix-geometric method," in *Seventh International Workshop on Petri Nets and Performance Models*, Saint Malo, France, June 1997, IEEE Computer Society Press.
17. D. Kiely, "Are components the future of software," *IEEE Computer*, vol. 31, no. 2, pp. 10–11, February 1998.

18. R. Klemm, S. Rangarajan, N. Singh, and A. P. A. van Moorsel, "A suite of internet-accessible analysis tools," in *Tool Descriptions, Supplement to Proceedings 9th International Conference on Modelling Techniques and Tools for Computer Performance Evaluation*, pp. 34–36, Saint-Malo, France, June 1997.
19. R. Klemm and A. P. A. van Moorsel, "Offering computing services on the world wide web," Submitted for publication, February 1998.
20. K. Koischwitz, *Entwurf und Implementierung einer parametrisierbaren Benutzungsoberfläche für hierarchische Netzmodelle (agnes–ein Generische Netz-Editor-System)*, Master's thesis, Technische Universität Berlin, Berlin, Germany, October 1996. In German.
21. D. Krieger and R. M. Adler, "The emergence of distributed component platforms," *IEEE Computer*, vol. 31, no. 3, pp. 43–53, March 1998.
22. T. W. Malone and K. Crowston, "The interdisciplinary study of coordination," *ACM Computing Surveys*, vol. 26, no. 1, pp. 87–119, March 1994.
23. R. Marie, B. Plateau, M. Calzarossa, and G. Rubino, *Computer Performance Evaluation Modelling Techniques and Tools*, volume 1245 of *Lecture Notes in Computer Science*, Springer Verlag, Berlin, Germany, 1997.
24. D. Mitra, J. A. Morrison, and K. G. Ramakrishnan, "ATM network design and optimization: A mutlirate loss network framework," *IEEE/ACM Transactions on Networking*, vol. 4, no. 4, pp. 531–543, August 1996.
25. J. K. Ousterhout, "Scripting: Higher-level programming for the 21st century," *IEEE Computer*, vol. 31, no. 3, pp. 23–30, March 1998.
26. A. Puliafito, O. Tomarchio, and L. Vita, "Porting SHARPE on the web: Design and implementation of a network computing platform using Java," in *Lecture Notes in Computer Science, Vol. 1245, Computer Performance Evaluation Modelling Techniques and Tools*, R. Marie, B. Plateau, M. Calzarossa, and G. Rubino, editors, pp. 32–43, Springer Verlag, Berlin, Germany, 1997.
27. R. A. Sahner, K. S. Trivedi, and A. Puliafito, *Performance and Reliability Analysis of Computer Systems, An Example-Based Approach Using the SHARPE Software Package*, Kluwer, Boston, MA, 1996.
28. J. Sametinger, *Software Engineering with Reusable Components*, Springer Verlag, Berlin, Germany, 1997.
29. W. H. Sanders and D. D. Deavours, "Initial specification of the Modius modeling tool," Internal report, University of Illinois, Urbana-Champaign, IL, Fall 1997.
30. W. H. Sanders, W. D. Obal, M. A. Qureshi, and F. K. Widjanarko, "The *UltraSAN* modeling environment," *Performance Evaluation*, vol. 24, no. 1, pp. 89–115, 1995.
31. O. Sims, *Business Objects: Delivering Cooperative Objects for Client-Server*, IBM McGraw-Hill Series, McGraw-Hill, Berkshire, UK, 1994.
32. A. Zimmermann, *Modellierung und Bewertung von Fertigungssystemen mit speziellen Petri-Netzen*, Dissertation, Technische Universität Berlin, Berlin, Germany, 1997. In German.

Compositional Performance Modelling with the TIPPtool

H. Hermanns, U. Herzog, U. Klehmet, V. Mertsiotakis, M. Siegle

Universität Erlangen-Nürnberg, IMMD 7, Martensstr. 3, 91058 Erlangen, Germany

Abstract. Stochastic Process Algebras have been proposed as compositional specification formalisms for performance models. In this paper, we describe a tool which aims at realising all beneficial aspects of compositional performance modelling, the TIPPtool. It incorporates methods for compositional specification as well as solution, based on state-of-the-art-techniques, and wrapped in a user-friendly graphical front end.

1 Introduction

Process algebras are an advanced concept for the design of distributed systems. Their basic idea is to systematically construct complex systems from smaller building blocks. Standard composition operators allow one to create highly modular and hierarchical specifications. An algebraic framework supports the comparison of different system specifications, process verification and structured analysis. Classical process algebras (e.g. CSP [20], CCS [26] or LOTOS [5]) describe the functional behaviour of systems, but no temporal aspects.

Starting from [17], we developed an integrated design methodology by embedding stochastic features into process algebras, leading to the concept of *Stochastic Process Algebras* (SPA). SPAs allow to specify and investigate both functional and temporal properties, thus enabling early consideration of all major design aspects. Research on SPA has been presented in detail in several publications, e.g. [11, 19, 4, 28, 15, 8] and the series of *Workshops on Process Algebras and Performance Modelling* (PAPM) [1].

This paper is about a modelling tool, the TIPPtool, which reflects the state-of-the-art of SPA research. Development of the tool started as early as 1992, the original aim being a prototype tool for demonstrating the feasibility of our ideas. Over the years, the tool has been extensively used in the TIPP project as a testbed for the semantics of different SPA languages and the corresponding algorithms. Meanwhile, the tool has reached a high degree of maturity, supporting compositional modelling and analysis of complex distributed systems via a user-friendly graphical front end.

The core of this tool is an SPA language where actions either happen immediately or are delayed in time, the delay satisfying a Markovian assumption [15]. Beside support for analysis of functional aspects, the tool offers algorithms for the numerical analysis of the underlying stochastic process. Exact and approximate evaluation techniques are provided for stationary as well as transient analysis. As a very advanced feature, the tool supports semi-automatic compositional reduction of complex models based on equivalence-preserving reduction. This enables the tool to handle large state spaces (the running example given here is small, due to didactical reasons and limited space).

Among related work, the PEPA Workbench [9] is another tool for performance evaluation, where Markov chain models are also specified by means of a process algebra.

The paper is organised as follows: In Sec. 2, we summarise the theoretical background of stochastic process algebras. Sec. 3 gives an overview of the tool's components. All aspects of model specification are discussed in Sec. 4, and analysis algorithms are the subject of Sec. 5. The paper concludes with Sec. 6.

R. Puigjaner et al. (Eds.): Tools'98, LNCS 1469, pp. 51–62, 1998

2   Foundations of Stochastic Process Algebras

2.1   Process algebras

Classical process algebras have been designed as formal description techniques for concurrent systems. They are well suited to describe reactive systems, such as operating systems, automation systems, communication protocols, etc. Basically, a process algebra provides a language for describing systems as a cooperation of smaller components, with some distinguishing features.

Specifications are built from *processes* which may perform *actions*. The description formalism is *compositional*, i.e. it allows to build highly modular and hierarchical system descriptions using composition operators. A parallel composition operator is used to express concurrent execution and possible synchronisation of processes. Another important operator realises *abstraction*: Details of a specification which are internal at a certain level of system description can be internalised by hiding them from the environment. Several notions of *equivalence* make it possible to reason about the behaviour of a system, e.g. to decide whether two systems are equivalent. Apart from a formal means for verification and validation purposes, equivalence-preserving transformation can be profitably employed in order to reduce the complexity of the system. This can also be performed in a compositional way, by replacing system parts through behaviourally equivalent but minimised representations.

Let us exemplify the basic constructs of process algebras on a simple queueing system. It consists of an arrival process $Arrival$, a queue with finite capacity, and a $Server$. First, we model an arrival process as in infinite sequence of incoming arrivals ($arrive$), each followed by an enqueue action (enq), using the *prefix* operator ';'.
$$Arrival := arrive; enq; Arrival$$
The behaviour of a finite queue can be described by a family of processes, one for each value of the current queue population. Depending on the population, the queue may permit to enqueue a job (enq), dequeue a job (deq) or both. The latter possibility is described by a *choice* operator '[]' between two alternatives.
$$Queue_0 := enq; Queue_1$$
$$Queue_i := enq; Queue_{i+1} \ [] \ deq; Queue_{i-1} \qquad 1 \le i < max$$
$$Queue_{max} := deq; Queue_{max-1}$$
Next, we need to define a server process, as follows:
$$Server := deq; serve; Server$$
These separate processes can now be combined by the *parallel composition* operator '|[...]|' in order to describe the whole queueing system. This operator is parametrised with a list '...' of actions on which the partners are required to synchronise:
$$System := Arrival \ |[enq]| \ Queue_0 \ |[deq]| \ Server$$
A formal semantics associates each language expression with an unambiguous interpretation, a *labelled transition system* (LTS). It is obtained by structural operational rules which define for each language expression a specific LTS as the unique semantic model. Fig. 1 (top) shows the semantic model for our example queueing system (assuming that the maximal population of the queue is $max = 3$). There are 16 states, the initial state being indicated by a double circle. A transition between two states is represented by a dashed arrow and labelled with the corresponding action. Since we assume that we are not interested in the inter-

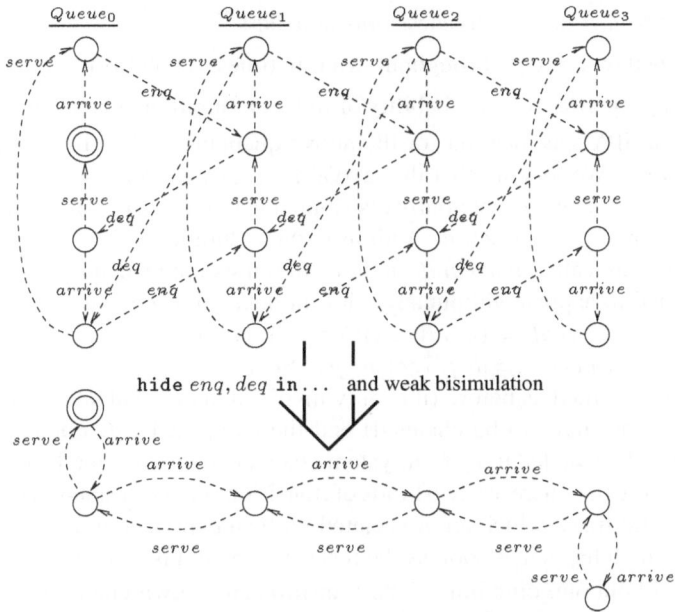

Fig. 1. Semantic model, hiding and reduction

nal details of interaction between *Arrival* and *Queue*, respectively *Queue* and *Server*, we may wish to only observe actions *arrive* and *serve*. This requires *abstraction* from internal details, and is achieved by employing the *hiding* operator:

$$\text{hide } enq, \, deq \text{ in } System$$

As a result, actions *enq* and *deq* are now internal actions, i.e. they are not visible from the environment. Actions hidden from the environment become the distinguished *internal* action τ. In other words, the semantic model of the above expression is obtained by turning all *enq* or *deq* labels appearing in Fig. 1 (top) into τ.

Such τ-actions can be eliminated from the semantic model using an equivalence which is insensitive to internal details of a specification, such as *weak bisimulation*. Weak bisimulation is one of the central notions of equivalence in the general context of process algebras [26]. Fig. 1 (bottom) shows an LTS, which is weakly bisimilar to the one on top (where all *enq*- and *deq*-actions have been replaced by τ). It may be surprising that the resulting LTS has 6 and not 4 states (we assumed $max = 3$). This is due to the fact that the arrival of a customer and its enqueueing into the queue are separate actions, so that one more arrival is possible if the queue is already full. Likewise, dequeueing and serving are modelled as separate actions, such that at the moment the queue becomes empty, the server is still serving the last customer.

2.2 Stochastic Process Algebras

Stochastic Process Algebras (SPA) are aimed at the integration of qualitative-functional and quantitative-temporal aspects in a single specification and modelling approach [11]. In order to achieve this integration, temporal information is attached to actions, in the form of continuous random variables, representing activity durations. The additional time information in the resulting LTS makes it possible to evaluate different system aspects:

- functional behaviour (e.g. liveness or deadlocks)
- temporal behaviour (e.g. throughput, waiting times, reliability)
- combined properties (e.g. probability of timeout, duration of an event sequence)

Let us give a SPA specification for the above queueing system by attaching distributions to actions. We assume that the arrival process is a Poisson process with rate λ and the service time is exponentially distributed with rate μ. We are not forced to associate a duration with every action. Actions without duration happen as soon as possible, therefore they are called *immediate* actions. In our example, enqueueing and dequeueing is assumed to happen without any relevant delay, thus enq and deq are immediate.

$$Arrival := (arrive, \lambda);\ enq;\ Arrival$$
$$Server := deq;\ (serve, \mu);\ Server$$

The queue is specified as before (it is only involved in enq and deq, therefore its specification does not have to be changed) and the composed $System$ is also as above. Fig. 2 depicts the labelled transition system associated with this model (again assuming $max = 3$). Note that there are two kinds of transitions between states: Timed transitions (drawn by solid lines) which are associated with an exponential delay, and immediate transitions which happen as soon as the respective action is enabled.

States without outgoing immediate transition are shown emphasised in the figure. They correspond to states of a Continuous Time Markov Chain (CTMC) (shown at the bottom of the figure) isomorphic to an LTS obtained by applying the notion of weak Markovian bisimulation, after hiding enq and deq. Weak Markovian bisimulation is an adaptation of weak bisimulation to the setting of timed and immediate actions [14]. Abstraction from the two immediate actions enq and deq is an essential prerequisite for unambiguously determining the Markov chain underlying this specification. If, say, enq is hidden, we can be sure that our assumption that enq happens without any delay is justified. Otherwise, it may be the case that $System$ is used as a component in further composition contexts, which require synchronisation on action enq. In this case, the Markov chain depends on additional timing constraints imposed on enq. Therefore it is not possible to remove enq, as long as further synchronisation on enq is still possible (indeed, abstraction rules out any further synchronisation, since τ is not allowed to appear in the list '...' of synchronising actions of a parallel composition operator '$|[...]|$'.)

2.3 Bisimulation and Compositional analysis

As illustrated in the running example, the notion of bisimulation is important. Two states of a process are bisimilar if they have the same possibilities to interact (with a third party) and reach pairwise bisimilar states after any of these interactions [26]. This definition only accounts for immediate actions. On the level of Markov chains, a corresponding definition is provided by the notion of *lumpability*. Two states of a Markov chain are lumpable if they have the same cumulative rate of reaching pairwise lumpable states [23]. *Markovian bisimulation* reflects lumpability and bisimulation on timed transitions, by imposing constraints on actions and rates, see [15, 19] for details. Weak Markovian bisimulation additionally allows abstraction from internal immediate actions, in analogy to ordinary weak bisimulation [16]. Equivalences are defined in terms of states and transitions, i.e. on the level of the LTS. It is possible to characterise their distinguishing power on the level of the language by means of *equational laws* [13].

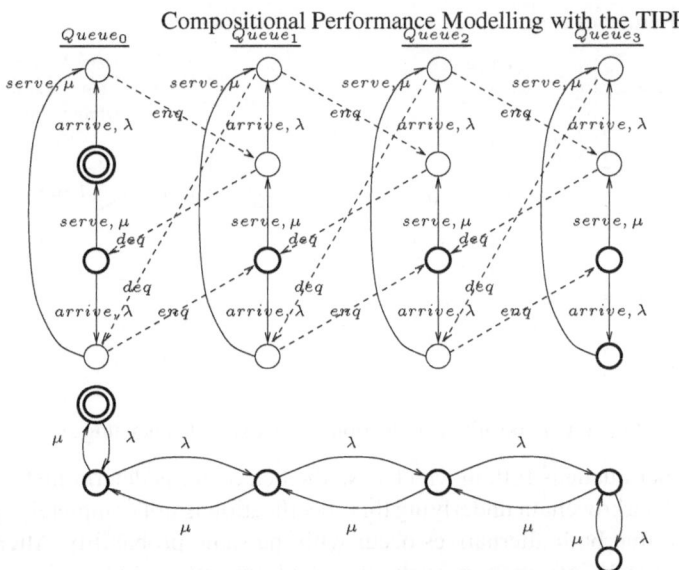

Fig. 2. Top: The LTS for the example queueing system. Bottom: The corresponding CTMC

In the presence of composition operators, such as hiding and parallel composition, it is highly desirable that equivalences are *substitutive*. Intuitively, substitutivity allows to replace components by equivalent ones within a large specification, without changing the overall behaviour. Substitutive equivalences are also called *congruences*. Indeed, Markovian and weak Markovian bisimulation are congruences. Practically important, such equivalences allow *compositional reduction* techniques, where the size of a component's state space may be reduced, without affecting any significant property of the whole model. Compositional reduction has successfully been applied to a variety of systems, see e.g. [7] for an impressive industrial case study.

We return to our queueing example in order to illustrate compositional reduction. We now consider a queueing system with one Poisson arrival process, two queues and two servers. We build this system from the same components, i.e. processes *Arrival*, *Queue* and *Server* are defined as above. The system is now:

$$System := Arrival \ |[enq]| \ ((Queue_0 \ |[deq]| \ Server) \ |||$$
$$(Queue_0 \ |[deq]| \ Server))$$

If the queue sizes are given by $max = 3$, the model has 128 states and 384 transitions. By hiding actions enq and deq and applying weak Markovian bisimulation to the complete system, the state space can be reduced to 22 states and 48 transitions. However, reduction can also be performed in a compositional fashion: The subsystem consisting of one queue server pair has 8 states, which can be reduced down to 5 states. Combining both (reduced) queue-server pairs, we obtain 25 states which can be reduced down to 15 states (this reduction step mainly exploits symmetry of the model). If this reduced system is combined with the arrival process, we get 30 states which can again be reduced to 22 states. This concept of compositional reduction is illustrated in Fig. 3, where the size of the state space and the number of transitions are given for each reduction step.

It is interesting to observe that this system exhibits non-deterministic behaviour: After the completion of a Markovian timed action $arrive$, it is left unspecified which of the two queues synchronises with the arrival process on immediate action enq (provided, of

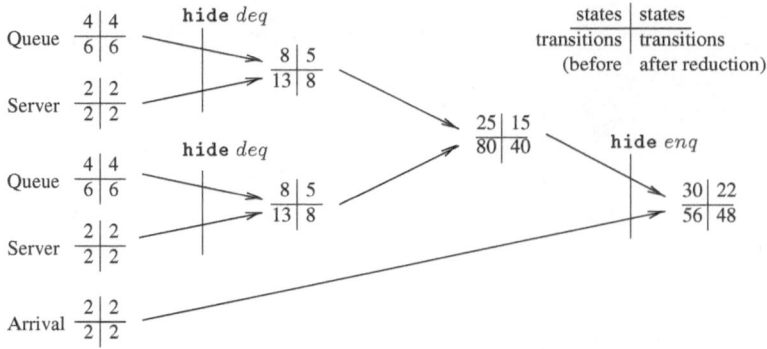

Fig. 3. Compositional reduction of the example queueing system

course, neither queue is full, in which case the behaviour is deterministic). As a consequence, the Markov chain underlying this specification is not completely specified. One
may assume that both alternatives occur with the same probability. Alternatively, one
may explicitly add information (such as a scheduling strategy) in order to resolve non-
determinism. In Sec. 4, we will follow the latter path.

3   Tool overview

The TIPPtool consists of several interacting components. Specifications can be created
with an editor which is part of the tool. A parser checks specifications for syntactic correctness. Another component is responsible for the generation of the LTS and for the
reduction of the LTS according to different bisimulation equivalences (currently, four
bisimulation algorithms are provided). The user can specify performance and reliability
measures to be calculated (such as state probabilities, throughputs and mean values). Experiments can be specified, providing information about activity rates which may vary. A
series of experiments can be carried out automatically in an efficient manner, generating
numerical results for different values of a certain model parameter, while the state space
only needs to be generated once. The tool provides several numerical solution methods
for the steady state analysis as well as for transient analysis of Markov chains. The results of an experiment series are presented graphically with the tool PXGRAPH from
UC Berkeley.

   The export module of the tool provides interfaces to three other tools, PEPP [12],
TOPO [24], and ALDEBARAN [6]. The former interface is based on a special semantics for SPAs which generates stochastic task graphs [18], for which the tool PEPP offers
a wide range of both exact and approximate analysis algorithms, some of which work
even for general distributions. The second interface provides support for the translation
of SPA specifications into a format suitable for the LOTOS tool TOPO. Among other
functionalities, this tool is capable of building C-programs from LOTOS specifications.
The third interface can be used in order to bridge to the powerful bisimulation equivalence algorithms of the tool ALDEBARAN.

4   Model specification

In this section, we explain the details of the specification language supported by the
TIPPtool. It is an extension of basic LOTOS [5], the ISO standardised specification language. To reflect the passing of time in a specification, randomly varying delays may be

attached to actions (at the moment, for reasons of analytical tractability, only exponential distributions are supported).

The available operators are listed in Table 1; Action prefix, choice, hiding and parallel composition (with synchronisation) have already been used in Sec. 2. If no synchronisation between two processes is required, the pure interleaving operator $|\,|\,|$ models independent parallelism. Synchronisation is possible both between immediate or between timed actions. Synchronising a timed with an immediate action is not allowed. When synchronising on timed actions, we define the resulting rate to be the *product* of the two partner rates (this definition preserves compositionality [15]). The intuition of the remaining operators is as follows: stop represents an inactive process, i.e. a process which cannot perform any action. exit behaves like stop after issuing a distinguished signal which is used in combination with the enabling operator >> to model sequential execution of two processes. Disruption with [> is useful to model the interruption of one process by another. Process instantiations $P[a_1, \ldots, a_n]$ resemble the invocation of procedures in procedural programming languages.

Name	Syntax	Name	Syntax
timed action prefix	$(a, r);\ P$	inaction	stop
immediate action prefix	$a;\ P$	successful termination	exit
choice	$P\ [\,]\ Q$	enabling	$P \gg Q$
parallel composition	$P \mid [a_1, \ldots, a_n\,] \mid Q$	disruption	$P\ [> Q$
– pure interleaving	$P \mid\mid\mid Q$	process instantiation	$P[a_1, \ldots, a_n]$
hiding	hide $a_1, \ldots, a_n$ in P		

Table 1. Basic syntax. P, Q are behaviour expressions, a_i are action names.

The concept of process instantiation makes it possible to parameterise processes over action names. In addition, it is often convenient to parameterise a specification with some data values, such as a rate, or the length of a queue (the above specification is a simple example for a data dependent specification, since parameter i governs the synchronisation capabilities of $Queue_i$). We have incorporated the possibility to describe data dependencies in the TIPPtool. In addition, data can also be attached as parameters to actions, and therefore be exchanged between processes, using the concept of inter-process communication [5]. This is highly beneficial, in order to conveniently describe complex dependencies. Data values are declared in the form $!\,value$, attached to an action, where $value$ may be a specific value, a variable or an arithmetic expression. Variable declarations are the counterpart of value declarations. They have the form $?variable:type$ where $variable$ is the name of the variable. These basic ingredients can be combined to form different types of inter-process communication (note that inter-process communication is currently only implemented for immediate actions), among them:

- **value passing:** If value declaration and variable declaration are combined in a synchronisation, the value is transmitted from one process to the other and the variable is instantiated by the transmitted value. An example is:
  $a!2$; stop $|\,[a]\,|$ $a?x$:int ; $b!$(x+1) ; ...
  If several actions are synchronised, each with a variable declaration of the same type, a synchronisation with another process which offers a value of the required type yields a form of multicast communication.
  $a!2$; stop $|\,[a]\,|$ $a?x$:int ; P $|\,[a]\,|$ $a?y$:int ; ...

- **value matching:** If synchronisation on actions is specified where both actions involve value declarations, this synchronisation is only possible if the values turn out to be equal, as in the example given below.

  `a!2 ; stop |[a]| a!(1+1) ; ...`

To illustrate the power of these language elements, we return to our running example of a queueing system. We modify the model in order to represent the join-shortest-queue (JSQ) service strategy. The idea is to insert a new process, `Scheduler`, between arrival and queue, whose task it is to insert an arriving job into the shortest queue. For this purpose, `Scheduler` scans all queues in order to determine the shortest queue, whenever an arrival has occurred. Process `Server` is defined as before. The arrival and queue processes do not communicate directly via action `enq` any more, but via the `Scheduler`. Therefore we simplify the arrival process as follows ('`process`' and '`endproc`' are keywords enclosing a process specification):

```
process Arrival := (arrive, lambda); Arrival endproc
```

i.e. `Arrival` and `Scheduler` now synchronise on the timed action `arrive`. The top-level specification is as follows:

```
( Arrival  |[arrive]|  Scheduler(2,1,1,100,100)  )
   |[ask,repl,enq]|
((Queue(1,0) |[deq]| Server) ||| (Queue(2,0) |[deq]| Server))
```

The `Scheduler` is a parametric process, which can be used for an arbitrary number `noq` of queues. After an arrival (action `arrive` with the "passive" rate 1), the scheduler polls all `noq` queues in order to identify the queue with the smallest population (actions `ask` and `repl`). Each queue sends as a reply its current population. After polling, `Scheduler` has identified the shortest queue. It then enqueues the job into that queue (action `enq`). Parameters `c`, `b`, `nc` and `nb` are needed to store the current queue, the queue with (currently) smallest population, the current population and the (currently) smallest population. In the example, `nc` and `nb` are initialised with the value 100, a value larger than any real queue population (note that the tool provides the possibility to specify choice alternatives which depend on conditions '`[ ...]  ->`').

```
process Scheduler(noq,c,b,nc,nb)  :=
  (arrive, 1); AskQueue(noq,c,b,nc,nb)
where
 process AskQueue(noq,c,b,nc,nb)  :=
  ask!c; repl?x:int; Decide(noq,c,b,x,nb)
 endproc
 process Decide(noq,c,b,nc,nb)  :=
  [c<noq and nc<nb]                -> AskQueue(noq,c+1,c,nc,nc)    []
  [c<noq and (nc>nb or nc=nb)]  -> AskQueue(noq,c+1,b,nc,nb)    []
  [c=noq and nc<nb]      -> (enq!c; Scheduler(noq,1,1,100,100))  []
  [c=noq and (nc>nb or nc=nb)]->(enq!b;Scheduler(noq,1,1,100,100))
 endproc
endproc
```

The `Queue` process has to be modified as well: It now has a parameter `s` which denotes the identity of the queue. In addition, it can now perform actions `ask` and `repl` in order to supply information on the current queue size to the scheduler. Note how value matching is used with actions `ask` and `enq`, and value passing is used with action `repl`.

```
process Queue(s,i)   :=
   ask!s; repl!i; Queue(s,i)
 []
   ([i<3] -> enq!s; Queue(s,i+1)   []
    [i>0] -> deq; Queue(s,i-1)        )
endproc
```

5 Analysing a specification

5.1 Generating and analysing the semantic model

The formal semantics of SPA provides an unambiguous description of how to construct the semantic model in a mechanised way. The structural operational rules can be implemented in a straight-forward fashion. The resulting LTS is either saved directly to files (while a hash-table of all states is maintained in memory) or it is temporarily stored in main memory as an adjacency list, depending on whether equivalence checking algorithms are selected or not.

Once the LTS is generated, it can be used for functional analysis. Our tool provides the capabilities of checking for deadlocks and tracing through the states, i.e. showing a path of actions leading from the initial state to a user-specified target state. Apart from that, equivalence checking algorithms can be used for deciding equivalence of two models. In this way it can be checked, for instance, whether a model meets the requirements of a high-level specification.

5.2 Performance evaluation

Transforming the semantic model into a CTMC and then analysing it by means of numerical solution algorithms for Markov chains, we can obtain performance and reliability measures for a given specification.

Models without immediate actions: For any SPA model with timed actions only and finite state space, the underlying CTMC can be derived directly by associating a Markov chain state with each node of the LTS [10, 19]. The transitions of the CTMC are given by the union of all the arcs joining the LTS nodes, and the transition rate is the sum of the individual rates (see Fig. 4). Transitions leading back to the same node (loops) can be neglected, since they would have no effect on the balance equations of the CTMC. The action names are only taken into account later on, when high-level performance measures are to be computed.

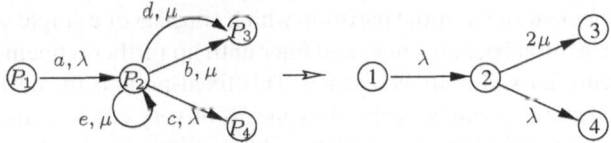

Fig. 4. Deriving a Markov chain

Models with both timed and immediate actions: As discussed in Sec. 2, immediate actions happen as soon as they become enabled. In order to ensure that this enabling cannot be delayed by further composition, abstraction of immediate actions is mandatory. In the stochastic process, these immediate actions correspond to immediate transitions. The presence of immediate transitions leads to two kinds of states in this process: States with outgoing immediate transitions (*vanishing* states) and states without such transitions (*tangible* states). If several immediate transitions emanate from a single state, the decision among these alternatives is non-deterministic, and it may depend on which action is offered by the environment. If we consider the system as a closed system (which is made explicit by hiding all immediate actions) the decision among several immediate transitions still has to be taken. One possible solution is to weight all alternatives with equal probabilities. The standard method used for eliminating immediate transitions is to incorporate transitions into the CTMC which are due to the traversal of some vanishing states between two tangible states. This is done until all vanishing states are bypassed [2]. The rate of these arcs is computed by multiplying the rate of the Markovian transitions leaving the source tangible state with the probability of reaching the target tangible state. However, [29] showed that this technique should be applied with care in the SPA context, essentially because a non-determinstic decision is conceptually different from an equi-probable decision. Therefore, in order to remove immediate transitions, it is more appropriate for SPAs to eliminate them on the basis of bisimulation equivalences, as it has been done in Fig. 2. If non-deterministic alternatives only lead (via some internal, immediate steps) into equivalent states, equivalence-preserving transformations allow to remove this non-determinism, see Sec. 5.3.

In the TIPPtool, standard numerical solution algorithms (Gauß-Seidel, Power method, LU factorisation, refined randomisation) are employed for steady state analysis as well as transient analysis of the CTMC. Apart from these, prototypical implementations of two efficient approximation methods are realised. Both approaches are based on decomposition. *Time Scale Decomposition (TSD)* is a method which can exploit the *Near Complete Decomposability* (NCD) property of many Markov chains. *Response Time Approximation (RTA)* works on the specification level rather than on the CTMC level [25].

5.3   Compositional model reduction

Equivalence relations such as (weak) Markovian bisimulation, introduced in Sec. 2.3, are beneficial both for eliminating immediate transitions, and for reducing models with very large state spaces. Both effects can be achieved by means of the same strategy. For a given specification, say $System$, the key idea is to compute an equivalent specification, $System'$, which is minimal (with respect to the number of states). Performance analysis can then be based on the minimised specification which is obtained by a *partition refinement* strategy: The bisimulation algorithm computes a partition of the state space, such that the subsets correspond to the bisimulation equivalence classes. This is achieved by a successive refinement of an initial partition which consists of a single subset containing all states. The partition becomes finer and finer until no further refinement is needed, or, in algebraic terms, a fixed-point is reached. This fixed-point is the desired result.

This general strategy can be realised by means of very efficient algorithms [21, 27]. For specifications which do not contain timed transitions, we implemented Kanellakis and Smolka's algorithm to compute strong and weak bisimulation. For the converse case (only timed transitions), we implemented an algorithm which is due to Baier [3] for factorising specifications with respect to Markovian bisimulation. These two implementations form the basis of the general case, where timed and immediate transitions coexist: Weak Markovian bisimulation is computed by alternating the algorithms for weak bisimulation (for immediate transitions) and Markovian bisimulation (for timed transitions) until a fixed-point is reached. Since weak Markovian bisimulation abstracts from internal, immediate transitions, this opens a way to eliminate immediate transitions from a specification, as long as they are internal. However, in some cases hiding of immediate transitions is not sufficient, because non-deterministic internal decisions may remain after factorisation. In this case the system is underspecified, and the TIPPtool produces a warning message to the user.

Bisimulation-based minimisation is particularly beneficial if it is applied to components of a larger specification in a stepwise fashion. Since all implemented bisimulations have the algebraic property of *substitutivity*, minimisation can be applied compositionally, as illustrated in Fig. 3. In this way, specifications with very large state spaces become tractable. In the TIPPtool, compositional minimisation is supported in an elegant way. By dragging the mouse inside the editor window, it is possible to highlight a certain component of the specification and to invoke compositional minimisation of this component. When the minimised representation is computed, a new specification is generated automatically, where the selected component has been replaced by the minimised representation.

6 Conclusion

In this paper, we have presented the status quo of the TIPPtool. Although a lot has been achieved, there remain, of course, many open problems for future research. We will briefly present some aspects of ongoing work in the TIPP project.

Several attempts have been made in order to incorporate generally distributed random variables into the model, see e.g. [18, 22]. However, they all suffer from the problem that general distributions lead to intractable stochastic processes. Another problem is that, so far, it is not completely solved how to obtain an algebraic framework (equivalences and equational laws) for a process algebra with general distributions. A promising approach, however, is reported in [8], using *stochastic automata* as a model based on Generalised Semi-Markov processes.

We are currently building a prototype tool for graphical model specification as an easy-to-use front-end for users who are not familiar with the syntax of the TIPPtool's specification language. With the view on models with large state spaces, we are currently investigating techniques for the compact symbolic representation of the semantic model of an SPA description, based on Binary Decision Diagrams [30].

To summarise, the TIPPtool realises state-of-the-art techniques for compositional performance and reliability modelling. As we have indicated, there is a lot of ongoing activity, both in theoretical research, and concerned with the further development and optimisation of the tool.

References

1. *Workshops on Process Algebras and Performance Modelling*, 1993 Edinburgh, 1994 Erlangen, 1995 Edinburgh, 1996 Torino, 1997 Twente, 1998 Nice.
2. M. Ajmone Marsan, G. Balbo, and G. Conte. *Performance Models of Multiprocessor Systems*. MIT Press, 1986.
3. C. Baier. Polynomial time algorithms for testing probabilistic bisimulation and simulation. In *Proc. CAV'96*. LNCS 1102, 1996.
4. M. Bernardo and R. Gorrieri. Extended Markovian Process Algebra. In *CONCUR '96*.

5. T. Bolognesi and E. Brinksma. Introduction to the ISO specification language LOTOS. *Computer Networks and ISDN Systems*, 14:25–59, 1987.

6. M. Bozga, J.-C. Fernandez, A. Kerbrat, and L. Mounier. Protocol verification with the ALDEBARAN toolset. *Int. J. Softw. Tools for Techn. Transf.*, 1(1/2):166–184, 1997.

7. G. Chehaibar, H. Garavel, L. Mounier, N. Tawbi, and F. Zulian. Specification and Verification of the Powerscale Bus Arbitration Protocol: An Industrial Experiment with LOTOS. In *Formal Description Techniques IX*. Chapmann Hall, 1996.

8. P.R. D'Argenio, J-P. Katoen, and E. Brinksma. An algebraic approach to the specification of stochastic systems. In *Programming Concepts and Methods*. Chapman and Hall, 1998.

9. S. Gilmore and J. Hillston. The PEPA Workbench: A Tool to Support a Process Algebra-Based Approach to Performance Modelling. In *7th Int. Conf. on Modelling Techniques and Tools for Computer Performance Evaluation*, Wien, 1994.

10. N. Götz. *Stochastische Prozeßalgebren – Integration von funktionalem Entwurf und Leistungsbewertung Verteilter Systeme*. PhD thesis, Universität Erlangen–Nürnberg, April 1994.

11. N. Götz, U. Herzog, and M. Rettelbach. Multiprocessor and distributed system design: The integration of functional specification and performance analysis using stochastic process algebras. In *Tutorial Proc. of PERFORMANCE '93*. LNCS 729.

12. F. Hartleb and A. Quick. Performance Evaluation of Parallel Programms — Modeling and Monitoring with the Tool PEPP. In Proc. "Messung, Modellierung und Bewertung von Rechen- und Kommunikationssystemen", p. 51–63. Informatik Aktuell, Springer, 1993.

13. H. Hermanns. *Interactive Markov Chains*. PhD thesis, Universität Erlangen-Nürnberg, 1998.

14. H. Hermanns, U. Herzog, and V. Mertsiotakis. Stochastic Process Algebras as a Tool for Performance and Dependability Modelling. In *Proc. of IEEE Int. Computer Performance and Dependability Symposium*, p. 102–111, 1995. IEEE Computer Society Press.

15. H. Hermanns, U. Herzog, and V. Mertsiotakis. Stochastic Process Algebras - Between LOTOS and Markov Chains. *Computer Networks and ISDN Systems*, 30(9-10):901–924, 1998.

16. H. Hermanns, M. Rettelbach, and T. Weiß. Formal characterisation of immediate actions in SPA with nondeterministic branching. In *The Computer Journal* [1], 1995.

17. U. Herzog. Formal Description, Time and Performance Analysis. A Framework. In *Entwurf und Betrieb Verteilter Systeme*. Springer, Berlin, IFB 264, 1990.

18. U. Herzog. A Concept for Graph-Based Stochastic Process Algebras, Generally Distributed Activity Times and Hierarchical Modelling. [1], 1996.

19. J. Hillston. *A Compositional Approach to Performance Modelling*. Cambridge University Press, 1996.

20. C.A.R. Hoare. *Communicating Sequential Processes*. Prentice-Hall, 1985.

21. P. Kanellakis and S. Smolka. CCS Expressions, Finite State Processes, and Three Problems of Equivalence. *Information and Computation*, 86:43–68, 1990.

22. J.P. Katoen, D. Latella, R. Langerak, and E. Brinksma. Partial Order Models for Quantitative Extensions of LOTOS. *Computer Networks and ISDN Systems*, 1998. to appear.

23. J.G. Kemeny and J.L. Snell. *Finite Markov Chains*. Springer, 1976.

24. J.A. Manas, T. de Miguel, and J. Salvachua. Tool Support to Implement LOTOS Specifications. *Computer Networks and ISDN Systems*, 25(7), 1993.

25. V. Mertsiotakis. *Approximate Analysis Methods for Stochastic Process Algebras*. PhD thesis, Universität Erlangen–Nürnberg, 1998. to appear.

26. R. Milner. *Communication and Concurrency*. Prentice Hall, London, 1989.

27. R. Paige and R. Tarjan. Three Partition Refinement Algorithms. *SIAM Journal of Computing*, 16(6):973–989, 1987.

28. C. Priami. Stochastic π-calculus. [1], 1995.

29. M. Rettelbach. *Stochastische Prozeßalgebren mit zeitlosen Aktivitäten und probabilistischen Verzweigungen*. PhD thesis, Universität Erlangen–Nürnberg, 1996.

30. M. Siegle. Technique and tool for symbolic representation and manipulation of stochastic transition systems. TR IMMD 7 2/98, Universität Erlangen-Nürnberg, 1998.

QNA-MC: A Performance Evaluation Tool for Communication Networks with Multicast Data Streams

Gaby Schneider[1], Marko Schuba[1], Boudewijn R. Haverkort[2]

[1] Informatik 4 (Communication and Distributed Systems), RWTH Aachen,
D-52056 Aachen, Germany
marko@i4.informatik.rwth-aachen.de
[2] Laboratory for Distributed Systems, RWTH Aachen,
D-52056 Aachen, Germany
haverkort@informatik.rwth-aachen.de

Abstract. In this paper we present QNA-MC (Queueing Network Analyzer supporting MultiCast), a new performance evaluation tool for the analytical evaluation of multicast protocols. QNA-MC is based on the QNA tool which (approximately) analyses open networks consisting of GI|G|m nodes. We extend this method by allowing a more general input in form of multicast routes. These routes are then converted to serve as input for standard QNA. From the results delivered by QNA our tool derives several performance measures for multicast streams in the network. We validate our approach by comparison to simulation results. Moreover, we give an application example by evaluating different multicast routing algorithms in the European MBONE using QNA-MC.

1 Introduction

Point-to-multipoint (or multicast) communication has become an essential part of today's communication protocols, because a number of applications require the same data to be sent to a group of receivers. Such applications are most efficiently realised via multicast. Moreover, the world-wide deployment and use of the IP multicast protocols (in the MBONE [1, 2]) has driven the development of new applications, which would not have been possible without a multicast infrastructure (e.g. distributed simulation with several thousands of computers involved). Thus, performance investigations of existing and new multicast protocols become more and more important.

Most performance investigations of multicast protocols so far are based on measurement (e.g. [3, 4]), protocol simulation (e.g. [5, 6]) or Monte Carlo simulation on random graphs (e.g [7, 8]). Analytical evaluations are rather seldom because there is still a lack of appropriate analytical models for multicast. Existing analyses make a lot of simplifying assumptions, e.g. they use static delays and do not consider queueing delays in intermediate nodes [9, 10]. Moreover, their results are usually restricted to mean values. Measures like delay variation, which are important for instance in real-time multicast communication, cannot be derived from these models.

Queuing networks (QN), which have proved to be very useful for the performance evaluation of communication systems, have not yet been applied to multicast protocols. The reason for this lies in the fact that existing queueing networks assume communication between different nodes to be point-to-point, i.e. copying of data as

R. Puigjaner et al. (Eds.): Tools'98, LNCS 1469, pp. 63-74, 1998
© Springer-Verlag Berlin Heidelberg 1998

required for multicast data streams is not supported. Moreover, well-known QN approaches such as Jackson networks [11] have a number of limitations, e.g. the restriction to exponentially distributed interarrival or service times, and thus may not model real system behaviour very well. One solution to overcome the disadvantage of exponential distributions is the Queueing Network Analyzer (QNA), which is based on the ideas of Kühn [12] and was extended and tested extensively by Whitt [13, 14]. QNA allows interarrival and service times to be generally distributed (characterized by the first two moments) and yields an approximate analysis of the queueing network. Recently, QNA has been extended in a number of ways, e.g. by Heijenk et al. [15], El Zarki and Shroff [16] and Haverkort [17].

This paper describes QNA-MC, an enhancement of QNA to support the analysis of multicast data streams. An input consisting of one or more multicast routes is converted into the standard input required by Whitt's QNA in order to compute general performance measures. The output of QNA is finally converted back to measures for individual multicast streams, such as the maximum response time and its variation.

The focus of this paper is to present the theoretical background of QNA-MC as well as its practical application. After a brief summary of standard QNA in Section 2 we will describe in Section 3 the conversion from multicast routes to the standard input and from the QNA output to multicast route measures. In Section 4 we will present some implementation aspects of QNA-MC and compare the approximate results delivered by QNA-MC to those of simulations. In Section 5 we will show in a practical application how QNA-MC can be used to compare different multicast routing algorithms. Finally, Section 6 will give some concluding remarks.

2 Standard QNA

Below we very concisely summarize the QNA approach. Details of QNA not directly related to our study are omitted (see [13]). We briefly discuss the QNA model specification, the employed traffic equations and the performance measures computed, focussing only on the single-class case here.

2.1 Model specification

With QNA it is assumed that there are n nodes or queueing stations, with m_i servers at node i, $i \in \{1, ..., n\}$. Service times at node i are characterized by the first moment $E[S_i] = 1/\mu_i$ and the squared coefficient of variation c_{si}^2. From the external environment, denoted as node 0, jobs arrive at node i as a renewal process with rate λ_{0i} and squared coefficient of variation c_{0i}^2. Internally, customers are routed according to Markovian routing probabilities q_{ij}; customers leave the QN from node i with probability q_{i0}. Finally, customers may be combined or created at a node. The number of customers leaving node i for every customer entering node i is denoted by the multiplication factor γ_i. If $\gamma_i < 1$, node i is a combination node; if $\gamma_i > 1$, node i is a creation node. Finally, if $\gamma_i = 1$, node i is a normal node. Created customers are all routed along the same path, or are probabilistically distributed over multiple outgoing routes. Note that this differs fundamentally from multicast routing where also multiple customers are created, but exactly one is routed to each of the successor nodes in the multicast tree (cf. Section 3).

2.2 Traffic equations

Once the model parameters have been set, the analysis of the traffic through the QN proceeds in two main steps:

Elimination of immediate feedback. For nodes with $q_{ii} > 0$ it is advantageous for the approximate procedure that follows to consider the possible successive visits of a single customer to node i as one longer visit. This transformation is taken care of in this step.

Calculation of the internal flow parameters. In this step, the arrival streams to all the nodes are characterized by their first two moments. This proceeds in two steps:

First-order traffic equations. Similarly as in Jackson QNs, traffic stream balance equations are used to calculate the overall arrival rate λ_i for node i. Next the node utilizations $\rho_i = \lambda_i/m_i\mu_i$ can be computed. They all should be smaller than 1, otherwise the QN does not show stable behaviour. If this is the case, the second step can be taken.

Second-order traffic equations. QNA approximately derives the squared coefficients of variation of the customer flows arriving at the nodes (c_{ai}^2). The squared coefficient of the customer stream departing node i (c_{di}^2) is computed with Marschall's formula [18] using the Krämer and Langenbach-Belz approximation for the expected waiting time at GI|G|1 nodes.

2.3 Performance measures

Once the first and second moment of the service and interarrival time distributions have been calculated, the single nodes can be analysed in isolation.

An important measure for the congestion in a node is the average waiting time. To derive this value in general GI|G|1 queues, only approximate results are available, most notably, the Krämer and Langenbach-Belz approximation [19]. It delivers an exact result whenever we deal with M|G|1 and M|M|1 queues.

From the waiting time, other congestion measures such as the mean response time, and (using Little's law) the average queue length and the average node population can be derived. Using a series of approximations, also the squared coefficient of variation for the waiting time at a node is computed (see Whitt [13]: (50)-(53)).

From the per-node performance measures, QNA calculates network-wide (end-to-end) performance measures by appropriately adding the per-node performance measures. Performance measures for multi-server nodes are only computed approximately, using the evaluation of the M|M|m queue, with average interarrival and service time as in the corresponding G|G|1 queue, as a starting point (see Whitt [13]: (70)-(71)).

3 Integration of Multicast Routes

QNA as defined in Section 2 does only support the analysis of point-to-point connections, either given by the routing probabilities, i.e non-deterministic, or by deterministic routes. In order to allow customers or packets to be duplicated at certain nodes QNA-MC generalizes the route input of QNA to support multicast routes. The conversion of multicast routes to the standard input of QNA is quite simple, if the route conversions given in [13] are taken as an example.

3.1 Input Conversion

In QNA-MC the network is described first:

- n : number of nodes in the network,
- m_i : number of servers at node i, $i \in \{1, ..., n\}$, and
- r : number of routes.

Each multicast route $k \in \{1, ..., r\}$ is described in the form of a tree with input:

- N_k : set of nodes in route k,
- $first_k \in N_k$: first node in route k,
- λ_{route_k} : external arrival rate for route k, and
- $c^2_{route_k}$: squared coefficient of variation of external arrival process for route k.

For each node $l \in N_k$ of a multicast route k the following additional information is required (using the typical record notation "$l.$"):

- $l.number$: node number,
- $l.\mu$: node service rate,
- $l.c^2_s$: squared coefficient of variation of the service-time distribution of the node,
- $l.\gamma$: creation/combination factor of the node (default value 1),
- $l.\lambda$: modified external arrival rate of the node, i.e. the creation/combination factors of previous nodes are taken into account (automatically calculated by QNA-MC),
- $l.succ\_no$: number of successors of the node,
- $l.succ_i$: ith successor of the node.

Note that there is a difference between a "route node" $l \in N_k$ and a "network node" $l.number \in \{1, ..., n\}$. The same "network node" may occur several times in a route, i.e. as several different "route nodes" with possibly different values $l.\mu$, $l.\gamma$, etc.

This input is converted by QNA-MC to obtain the standard input for QNA. First, the external arrival rate λ_{0i} per node i is derived as the sum of all route arrival rates:

$$\lambda_{0i} = \sum_{k=1}^{r} \lambda_{route_k} \cdot \mathbf{1}\{first_k.number = i\}, \tag{1}$$

where the function $\mathbf{1}\{condition\}$ denotes the indicator function, i.e. $\mathbf{1}\{A\} = 1$, if A = TRUE, and $\mathbf{1}\{A\} = 0$, if A = FALSE.

The overall flow rate λ_{ij} between two nodes i and j is the sum of the flow rates in each route going from i to j. It can be written as

$$\lambda_{ij} = \sum_{k=1}^{r} \sum_{l \in N_k} l.\lambda \cdot l.\gamma \cdot \mathbf{1}\{l.number = i \text{ and } \exists s \in \{1,...,l.succ\_no\} : l.succ_s.number = j\}. \tag{2}$$

Similarly, the departure rate λ_{i0} from node i, i.e. the flow from the node out of the network, is given by the sum of the departure rates of all route nodes with number i and no successor (leaf nodes):

$$\lambda_{i0} = \sum_{k=1}^{r} \sum_{l \in N_k} l.\lambda \cdot l.\gamma \cdot \mathbf{1}\{l.number = i \text{ and } l.succ\_no = 0\}. \tag{3}$$

Based on these rates the Markovian routing probabilities q_{ij}, i.e. the proportion of the customers that go from i to j to those leaving i, can be calculated by normalizing the flow rate λ_{ij} to the overall flow rate out of node i:

$$q_{ij} = \lambda_{ij} \Big/ \Big(\lambda_{i0} + \sum_{k=1}^{r} \sum_{l \in N_k} l.\lambda \cdot l.\gamma \cdot \mathbf{1}\{l.number = i \text{ and } l.succ\_no \neq 0\} \Big). \tag{4}$$

Next the average creation/combination factor γ_i of node i can be computed. It depends on the arrival rates and creation/combination factors of the individual multicast routes and is given as a weighted average of the individual node factors $l.\gamma$ (marked grey):

$$\gamma_i = \frac{\displaystyle\sum_{k=1}^{r} \sum_{l \in N_k} l.\lambda \cdot l.\gamma \cdot \mathbf{1}\{l.number = i\}}{\displaystyle\sum_{k=1}^{r} \sum_{l \in N_k} l.\lambda \cdot \mathbf{1}\{l.number = i\}}. \tag{5}$$

Similarly, the average service-time μ_i per customer at node i and the corresponding squared coefficient of variation c_{si}^2 can be derived as weighted averages as follows:

$$E[S_i] = \frac{1}{\mu_i} = \frac{\displaystyle\sum_{k=1}^{r} \sum_{l \in N_k} l.\lambda \cdot \frac{1}{l.\mu} \cdot \mathbf{1}\{l.number = i\}}{\displaystyle\sum_{k=1}^{r} \sum_{l \in N_k} l.\lambda \cdot \mathbf{1}\{l.number = i\}}, \tag{6}$$

and

$$E[S_i^2] = \frac{1}{\mu_i^2}\big(c_{si}^2 + 1\big) = \frac{\displaystyle\sum_{k=1}^{r} \sum_{l \in N_k} l.\lambda \cdot \frac{1}{l.\mu^2}\big(l.c_s^2 + 1\big) \cdot \mathbf{1}\{l.number = i\}}{\displaystyle\sum_{k=1}^{r} \sum_{l \in N_k} l.\lambda \cdot \mathbf{1}\{l.number = i\}}. \tag{7}$$

Note that (7) uses the fact that the second moment of a mixture of distributions, i.e. $(c_{si}^2 + 1)/\mu_i^2$, equals the mixture of the second moments of the mixed distributions.

Finally, the squared coefficient of variation c_{0i}^2 for all external arrival processes is determined (see Whitt [13]: (10) - (12)). If the external arrival rate $\lambda_{0i} = 0$, then c_{0i}^2 is set to 1 and thus has no further impact on the QNA calculations. If $\lambda_{0i} \neq 0$ then

$$c_{0i}^2 = (1 - w_i) + w_i \Bigg[\sum_{k=1}^{r} \frac{c_{route_k}^2 \cdot \lambda_{route_k}}{\lambda_{0i}} \cdot \mathbf{1}\{first_k.number = i\} \Bigg], \tag{8}$$

where the value for w_i is defined as

$$w_i = \Big[1 + 4(1-\rho_i)^2(v_i - 1)\Big]^{-1} \text{ with } v_i = \Bigg[\sum_{k=1}^{r} \Big(\frac{\lambda_{route_k}}{\lambda_{0i}}\Big)^2 \cdot \mathbf{1}\{first_k.number = i\} \Bigg]^{-1}. \tag{9}$$

and $\rho_i = \lambda_i/(\mu_i m_i)$.

After calculation of all these values QNA-MC starts the standard QNA method as described in Section 2, which delivers several network and node measures.

3.2 Output Conversion

In addition to the results delivered by standard QNA, QNA-MC computes measures for individual multicast routes and for different paths p within these routes, i.e. measures for individual receivers of the stream. Note that we define a path to be the unambiguous node sequence from the sender to a single receiver in a multicast route.

Let P_k denote the set of paths of multicast route k. From the standard QNA output we know the mean and variance of the waiting time of an arbitrary customer in network node i (denoted $E[W_i]$ and $V[W_i]$, resp.). Thus, the response time $E[R_p]$ of the receiver at the end of path $p \in P_k$ is the sum of the expected service times and expected waiting times of all nodes l in the path p:

$$E[R_p] = \sum_{l \in p} \left(\frac{1}{l.\mu} + E[W_{l.number}] \right) \tag{10}$$

and the variance is calculated in a similar way as

$$V[R_p] = \sum_{l \in p} \left(\frac{1}{l.\mu^2} \cdot l.c_s^2 + V[W_{l.number}] \right). \tag{11}$$

Of particular interest for many analyses (see e.g. the application of QNA-MC in Section 5) are the maximum response times and variances within a multicast route. Hence, these values are computed as well.

Finally, if we define the weight ω_p as the proportion of the customers leaving the network at the end of path p to those departing from the overall route

$$\omega_p = \frac{\sum_{l \in p} l.\lambda \cdot 1\{l.succ\_no = 0\}}{\sum_{p \in P_k} \sum_{l \in p} l.\lambda \cdot 1\{l.succ\_no = 0\}} \tag{12}$$

then (similar to equations (5) - (7)) the mean response time of the overall route k, i.e. for a "general" customer of the multicast stream, can be written as

$$E[R_{P_k}] = \sum_{p \in P_k} \omega_p E[R_p] \tag{13}$$

and the corresponding variance can be calculated from the weighted second moments of the individual paths minus the squared expectation value delivered by (13):

$$V[R_{P_k}] = \sum_{p \in P_k} \omega_p \left(V[R_p] + E[R_p]^2 \right) - E[R_{P_k}]^2. \tag{14}$$

4 Tool Support: QNA-MC

We implemented QNA-MC in C++ on a Solaris platform based on the C code of QNAUT (QNA, University of Twente). After rewriting most of the code in C++ we added the input and output conversions described in the last Section.

We tested QNA-MC for a number of different parameter sets and network scenarios by comparing the QNA-MC results to the results of equivalent simulations. Here, we present only those results relevant for our example application in Section 5. However, results for other parameter combinations had the same quality (see [20]). The simple test scenario is shown in Fig. 1.

The investigated network consists of four nodes. The only "real" multicast route (black) enters the network at node 1, passes on to node 2 and then goes on to node 3 and 4, where the customers leave the network. The other routes (grey) model background traffic and are used to increase the overall load ρ in the nodes. Customers of these routes leave the network directly after having passed their entrance node.

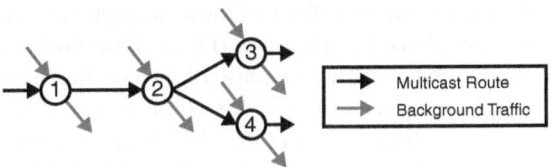

Fig. 1. Test scenario for QNA-MC validation

The following parameter combinations have been selected according to our application example (cf. Section 5), i.e. constant interarrival times for the multicast data stream, constant service times at the nodes and background traffic with high variance. The respective parameter values are given in Table 1.

Table 1. Model parameters

Load	Multicast Route		Background Traffic[a]		Node Service[b]	
ρ	λ_{route_mc}	c_{route_mc}	λ_{route_bg}	c_{route_bg}	μ	c_s
0.25	1	0	4	{2, 3}	20	0
0.5	2	0	8	{2, 3}	20	0
0.7	3	0	11	{2, 3}	20	0
0.9	4	0	14	{2, 3}	20	0

a. The same values are used for all background traffic routes in the network.
b. The node parameters are the same for all nodes in all routes.

Fig. 2 compares the results of QNA-MC to those of simulation. Since the 95% confidence intervals of the simulations were too small to be distinguishable from the mean values (less than 0.02) they are not explicitly shown. Because of the symmetric multicast tree the performance measures for individual receiver response times (see (10) and (11)) and overall multicast route response time (see (13) and (14)) are the same.

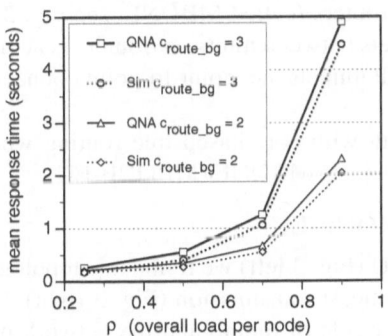
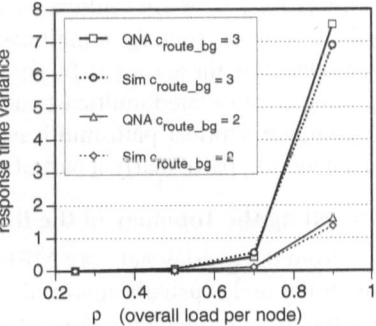

Fig. 2. QNA-MC and simulation results for the test scenario

The left diagram of Fig. 2 shows the load dependent mean response times for both multicast receivers. For small load the results of QNA-MC are very close to the simulation results. When the load is increased the absolute difference becomes slightly larger but is still within an (from our point of view) acceptable range. Looking at the response time variance calculated by QNA-MC (Fig. 2 right) the values are even better.

It should be mentioned that a further increase of the coefficient of variation leads to a more significant overestimation of the response time by QNA-MC. If a high coefficient of variation is used then the results of QNA-MC have to be interpreted more carefully because of the pessimistic approximations delivered by QNA-MC.

Overall (also if all other validation results are taken into account, see [20]) QNA-MC has shown to be an appropriate tool for the calculation of approximate measures in general QNs with multicast data streams. Because of its short run time QNA-MC can be applied to multicast QN models for which simulation times are no longer acceptable (see e.g. the example in Section 5). The run times of QNA on a Sun Ultra for all examples in this paper were less than a second. In contrast to this even the simple model shown in Fig. 1 required a simulation time between 15 and 30 minutes (30.000 seconds simulated time, simulation tool OPNET, Sun Ultra), i.e. QNA-MC yields a speed up factor of 1000 to 2000 even for simple networks.

5 Example Application: Multicast Routing Algorithms

We will now show in an example how QNA-MC can be applied to analyse multicast protocols. Particularly, we describe the application of QNA-MC to evaluate multicast routing algorithms in the European Internet.

5.1 Introduction

The most popular multicast protocol used in wide area networks is IP multicast. Its routing algorithm calculates multicast routes based on *shortest path trees* between the source and all members of the multicast group or as *core-based trees* (e.g. in the Protocol Independent Multicast Architecture [21]), where all senders share a delivery tree rooted at a special node called core. To realize such a point-to-multipoint routing algorithm in the Internet, where most routers do not support multicast routing, an overlay network topology between multicast-capable routers (called MBONE, see Fig. 3 left) is required. "Direct" routing of multicast packets between multicast routers is achieved by interconnecting these routers by so-called IP tunnels, i.e. point-to-point connections transporting encapsulated multicast packets.

To compare shortest path multicast routing with core-based tree routing we first model a network, particularly a part of the European MBONE (MBONE-EU).

5.2 Modelling the Topology of the Basic MBONE-EU

Starting from the overlay network MBONE-EU (Fig. 3 left) we refine this topology by adding all the nodes usually involved in a multicast transmission (Fig. 3 right). Note, that the topology refinements are just made by rule of thumb and the network might look different in reality. We add non-multicast routers (white nodes) for tunnels in the backbone and local area, local area multicast routers (small black nodes), members of the multicast group (white squares) and two different cores (black squares) used only for core-based tree routing. The distinction between all the different router types is meaningful, because backbone routers usually have a higher performance than local routers and handling of a multicast packet usually takes more time than handling of a unicast packet. Finally, we have to consider the constant propagation delay between the backbone multicast routers. We make the simplifying assumption that it is proportional to the distance as the crow flies and model this by GI/D/100 nodes (grey). Our investigations showed that the queuing delay in nodes with 100 servers is negligible. The propagation delay in the local area, i.e. between a receiver, sender, or core and its nearest backbone router is neglected.

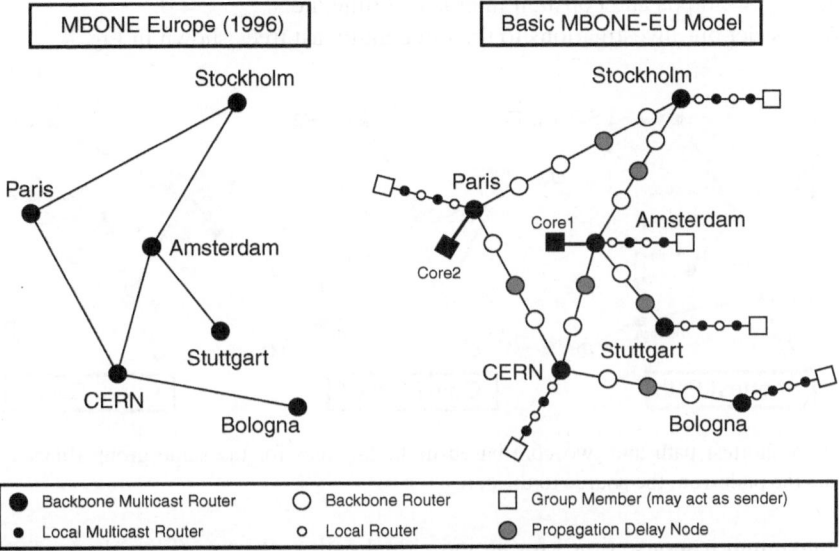

Fig. 3. European MBONE: overlay network topology (left) and basic model (right)

5.3 Parameterization of the Basic MBONE-EU

In the next step we define the node service rates. Both, for background and multicast packets, the service rates μ of all routers (pps = packets per second) are assumed to be constant (i.e. $c_s = 0$) as given in Table 2.

Table 2. Node service rates

Node Type	Background Service Rate	Multicast Service Rate
Backbone Multicast Router	200,000 pps	100,000 pps
Local Multicast Router	10,000 pps	2000 pps
Backbone Router	200,000 pps	190,000[a] pps
Local Router	10,000 pps	9000[a] pps
Source / Receiver	- (not required)	500 pps
Core	- (not required)	10,000 pps

a. Encapsulated packets have a larger packet length and thus a longer service time.

Similar to Fig. 1 we model background traffic in routers as independent cross data streams. According to arguments given in [22] the coefficients of variance of the background streams are chosen to be larger than 1 (namely $c_{bg} = \{3, 5, 7\}$), i.e. they represent traffic with high burstiness. The overall network load ρ is modified by proportionally increasing or decreasing the background traffic arrival rate at all nodes.

5.4 Definition of Multicast Routes

Finally, we have to define the external arrival process for the multicast data stream under investigation. We assume the sender to be the source of an audio stream (e.g. a PCM encoded stream of the MBONE tool "vat" [23]), which produces packets with rate $\lambda_{route\_mc} = 50$ pps and constant interarrival time, i.e. $c_{route\_mc} = 0$.

We restrict our investigations to the three multicast trees shown in Fig. 4.

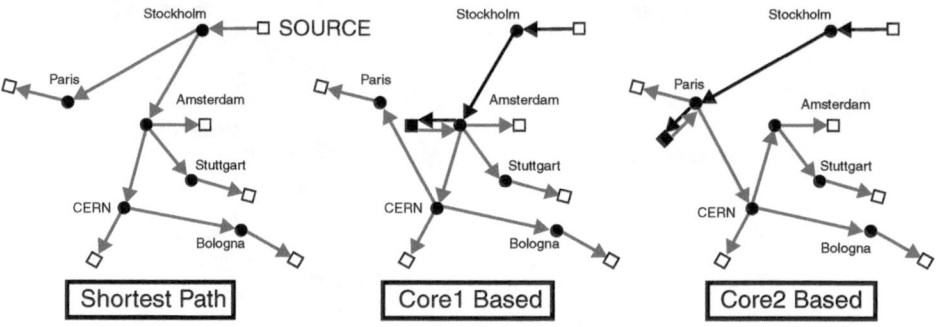

Fig. 4. A shortest path and two core-based multicast trees for the same group (black arrows indicate the path from the source to the core)

The maximum response times for an individual path in the tree (here always from the source near Stockholm to a receiver near Bologna at the right bottom) and the mean response times for the overall tree (calculated according to (10) and (13) resp.) are shown in Fig. 5 for $c_{bg} = 3$.

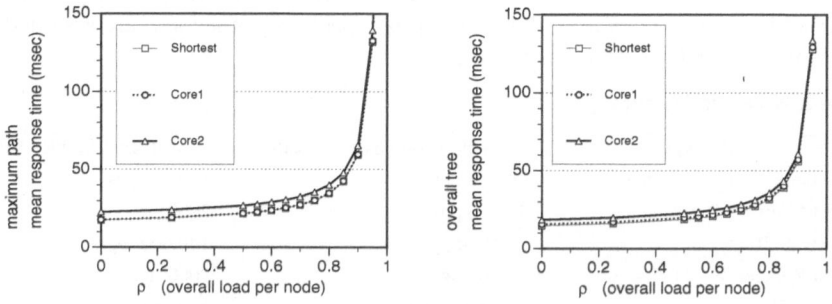

Fig. 5. Response times for the maximum path (left) and overall tree (right) for $c_{bg} = 3$.

In both diagrams the values are very similar independent of the routing tree used. Even the "longer" paths via core number 2 do not influence the overall delay very strongly. Furthermore, if we take 150 ms as the maximum acceptable delay for audio transmissions (see e.g. [24]) then this delay bound is reached by the mean response time only if the load is higher than 95%.

Let us now take a closer look at the influence of the background traffic burstiness on the response time measures (shown for the shortest path tree only) in Fig. 6. In order to obtain traffic with higher burstiness we set the coefficients of variation c_{bg} to 3, 5 and 7. Although the absolute response time and variance values are overestimated by QNA-MC for coefficients of variation larger than 3 (cf. Section 4) we think that the results shown in Fig. 6 accurately represent the general tendency of response time and variance for increasing burstiness.

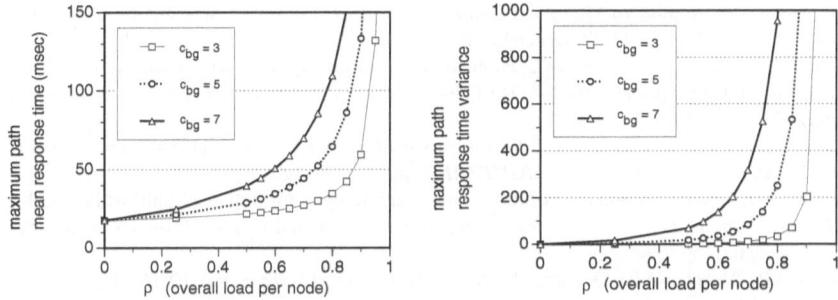

Fig. 6. Maximum path response time and variance for bursty traffic

The influence of the background traffic burstiness on both mean response time and response time variance is rather strong. The higher the burstiness the earlier the critical delay bound of 150 ms for audio samples is reached. Because the variance values increase rather fast with the overall load the response time of individual packets will often be larger than 150 ms even for less load. For an audio data stream this leads to the dropping of audio samples and thus to quality loss.

6 Conclusions

In this paper we have presented QNA-MC, which can be used for the performance evaluation of large communication networks with multicast data streams. We have described the theoretical background and have shown by comparison to simulations that QNA-MC delivers accurate results at low cost. Moreover, we have shown in an example based on the European MBONE, how QNA-MC can be used to compare different multicast routing algorithms. Whereas similar simulations cannot be performed in reasonable time, QNA-MC calculates the performance measures of interest immediately. Moreover, these measures include response time variances. Thus it is possible to use e.g. Chebyshev's inequality to determine the probability that packets arrive within a certain delay bound, what is very important all sorts of real time multicast applications. Overall QNA-MC shows itself to be a promising alternative to existing analysis and simulation methods of multicast protocols.

References

1. Deering S. E., "Multicast Routing in Internetworks and Extended LANs", *Proc. of ACM SIGCOMM*, pp. 55-64, 1988
2. Eriksson H., "MBONE: The Multicast Backbone", *Communications of the ACM*, Vol. 37, No. 8, pp. 54-61, August 1994
3. Yavatkar R., Griffioen J., Sudan M., "A Reliable Dissemination Protocol for Interactive Collaborative Applications", *Proc. of ACM Multimedia*, pp. 333-44, 1995
4. Paul S., Sabnani K.K., Lin J.C.-H., Bhattacharyya S., "Reliable Multicast Transport Protocol (RMTP)", *IEEE Journal on Selected Areas in Communications*, Vol. 15, No. 3, pp. 407-21, April 1997
5. Hermanns, O., Schuba, M., "Performance Investigations of the IP Multicast Protocols", *Computer Networks and ISDN Systems*, Vol. 28, pp. 429-39, 1996
6. Billhartz T., Cain J.B., Farrey-Goudreau E., Fieg D., Batsell S.G., "Performance and Resource Cost Comparison for the CBT and PIM Multicast Routing Protocols", *IEEE Journal on Selected Areas in Communications*, Vol. 15, No. 3, pp. 304-15, April 1997
7. Waxman B. M., "Routing of Multipoint Connections", *IEEE Journal on Selected Areas in Communications*, Vol. 6, No. 9, pp. 1617-22, December 1988
8. Salama H.F., Reeves D.S., Viniotis Y., "Evaluation of Multicast Routing Algorithms for Real-Time Communication on High-Speed Networks", *IEEE Journal on Selected Areas in Communications*, Vol. 15, No. 3, pp. 332-45, April 1997
9. Pingali S., Towsley D., Kurose J. F., "A Comparison of Sender-Initiated and Receiver-Initiated Reliable Multicast Protocols", *Proc. of ACM SIGMETRICS*, pp. 221-30, 1994
10. Schuba M., Reichl P., "An Analysis of Retransmission Strategies for Reliable Multicast Protocols", *Proc. of The International Conference "Performance of Information and Communication Systems" PICS '98*, Lund, Sweden, May 1998
11. Jackson J.R., "Jobshop-Like Queueing Systems", *Management Science*, Vol. 10, No. 1, pp. 131-42, 1963
12. Kühn P. J., "Approximate Analysis of General Queueing Networks by Decomposition", *IEEE Transactions on Communications*, Vol. 27, No. 1, pp. 113-26, January 1979
13. Whitt W., "The Queueing Network Analyzer", *The Bell System Technical Journal*, Vol. 62, No. 9, pp. 2779-815, November 1983
14. Whitt W., "Performance of the Queueing Network Analyzer", *The Bell System Technical Journal*, Vol. 62, No. 9, pp. 2817-43, November 1983
15. Heijenk G., El Zarki M., Niemegeers I.G., "Modelling Segmentation and Reassembly Processes in Communication Networks", *Proc. of ITC-14*, North-Holland, pp. 513-24, 1994
16. El Zarki M., Shroff N., "Performance Analysis of Packet-Loss Recovery Schemes in Interconnected LAN-WAN-LAN Networks", *Proc. of the Third Conference on High-Speed Networking*, Danthine A., Spaniol O., (Eds.), North-Holland, pp. 2817-43, 1991
17. Haverkort B.R., "Approximate Analysis of Networks of PH/PH/1/K Queues: Theory & Tool Support", *Lecture Notes in Computer Science 977*, "Quantitative Evaluation of Computing and Communication Systems", Beilner H., Bause F. (Eds.), Springer, pp. 239-53, September 1995
18. Marshall K.T., "Some Inequalities in Queueing", *Operations Research*, Vol. 16, No.3, pp. 651-65, 1968
19. Krämer W., Langenbach-Belz M., "Approximate Formulae for the Delay in the Queueing System GI|G|1", *Proc. of ICT-8*, pp. 235-1/8, 1976
20. Schneider G., "Enhancement of QNA for Approximate Analysis of Networks with Multicast Data Traffic" (in german), *Diploma Thesis, Aachen University of Technology*, Germany, April 1998
21. Deering S., Estrin D. L., Farinacci D., Jacobson V., Liu C.-G., Wei L., "The PIM Architecture for Wide-Area Multicast Routing", *IEEE/ACM Transactions on Networking*, Vol. 4, No.2, pp. 153- 62, April 1996
22. Paxson V., Floyd S., "Wide Area Traffic: The Failure of Poisson Modeling", *IEEE/ACM Transactions on Networking*, Vol. 3, No. 3, pp. 226-44, June 1995
23. Jacobson V., McCanne S., "vat - LBNL Audio Conferencing Tool,", on-line available at http://www-nrg.ee.lbl.gov/vat/
24. ITU-T Recommendation G.114, "Transmission systems and media - general recommendations on the transmission quality for an entire international telephone connection - one-way transmission time", 1993

Response Times in Client-Server Systems

A.J. Field[*], P.G. Harrison[*], J. Parry[†]

Abstract. Response time is the key performance measure in on-line transaction processing systems and other client-server architectures. Not only is it important to achieve a low average value and correspondingly high throughput, but response time should also be fairly consistent in order to provide a good quality of service. We develop a new algorithm for computing the probability density function of response times in Markovian models of client-server systems. We model the clients and servers by central server queueing networks and obtain response time densities as simple functions of time under independence assumptions that are shown to hold asymptotically as network size increases. The communication network is modelled as a single server queue with mean service time determined by its operational characteristics. We consider an Ethernet and construct a new model, of interest in its own right, that captures details not modelled hitherto. This model is validated against simulation and shows good agreement up to moderate utilisations, the normal operating environment for Ethernets. The whole client-server model is implemented in the Metron Athene Client-Server capacity planning tool and sample runs are examined.

1. Introduction

The proliferation of client-server systems in business continues unabated, as applications are split into local tasks run on "client" workstations and resource-intensive computations run on a "server" mainframe. The architecture is diverse, typically supplied by several vendors using several operating systems. It is also complex with new levels of systems software such as the Distributed Computing Environment (DCE) superimposed on the traditional layers of operating system, database and application. Many of these systems are provided for non-IT staff, so inadequate performance is directly exposed.

Quality of service in client-server systems is typically measured by *response time*. This is the time elapsed between a client issuing a request to the server and the arrival at the client of the response (e.g. data); alternately, it is sometimes considered as the elapsed time between successive requests, i.e. including processing time and thinking time at the client. Not only is it important to achieve a low average response time and correspondingly high throughput, but response time should also be fairly consistent in order to provide a good quality of service. In other words, it is important to be able to estimate the probability distribution of response time and, indeed, 95th quantiles are specified in the TPC benchmarks.

[*] Department of Computing, Imperial College, London

[†] Metron Technology Limited, Taunton

R. Puigjaner et al. (Eds.): Tools'98, LNCS 1469, pp. 75-92, 1998
© Springer-Verlag Berlin Heidelberg 1998

We derive an approximate algorithm for computing response time probability density functions for client-server systems and demonstrate it through the capacity planning tool Athene Client-Server developed by Metron Technology Ltd, [5]. The clients and servers are represented by standard central server queueing networks and the communication network by a novel, customised model of the Ethernet [4]. This model captures details not modelled hitherto and is of interest in its own right, but we use it here to determine the service rate of a single server queue that we use to approximate the behaviour of the network in the wider model. A similar approach can be used for other types of network such as token rings. Under appropriate independence assumptions, which are shown to hold asymptotically as network size increases, response time is a convolution which can be simplified and then inverted analytically to give the probability density directly as a function of time. Implementation is thereby easy compared with conventional methods that rely on numerical inversion of Laplace transforms.

The paper is set out as follows. In section 2, the model structure for client server systems is described and in the next two sections the sub-models corresponding to clients and servers (viz. central server queueing networks) and the Ethernet are presented in detail. Section 5 presents some numerical results as computed by Athene Client-Server and the paper concludes in section 6.

2. Client-server models

In the simplest of client-server systems, there are logically three sources of delay: the client (a sum of sub-delays comprising user "think time" at a terminal and further ones in the host computer system), the network (in two directions corresponding to a request and a reply) and the server. More generally, a client-server system consists of a more complex network of nodes linked by communication networks of various kinds. These nodes comprise the clients and various levels of server. If a client's request can be satisfied at a 'local' server, then only that one server and the network connecting to it are involved in the transaction. Otherwise the request must be forwarded, over another network, to a 'second level' server and possibly to higher level servers until the request can be satisfied. The topology of such systems can therefore be quite complex with the sharing of applications and databases, for example. Response time now becomes dependent on the level of server to which a transaction has to be sent and response time distribution or average response time is a weighted sum of the corresponding quantity conditioned on the transaction path required.

In order to calculate average response time for a given transaction path, we merely need to sum the average delays in each component in that path. In the simplest case this is just $m_c + m_{n1} + m_s + m_{n2}$ where m_c, m_{n1}, m_s, m_{n2} are the mean delays at the client, network (from client to server), server and network (from server to client) respectively. More generally, the sum will be

$$m_c + \sum_{servers,i} m_{s_i} + \sum_{networks,j} (m_{n_j1} + m_{n_j2})$$

For response time distribution, we make the approximating assumption that each node and network yields an independent contribution to a transaction delay, with corresponding probability distribution functions $F_c(t), F_{s_i}(t), F_{n_j1}(t), F_{n_j2}(t)$. We denote the density (which will always exist) and Laplace-Stieltjes transform (LST) of a probability distribution function $F(t)$ by $f(t)$ and $F^*(s)$ respectively. Then the LST of response time distribution is approximated by

$$R*(s) = F_c*(s) \prod_{servers, i} F_{s_i}*(s) \prod_{networks, j} F_{n_j 1}*(s)F_{n_j 2}*(s)$$

It therefore remains to compute the LSTs for each component and invert where possible to find the required probability density function of response time. To this end, in the next section we represent both client and server nodes by central-server queueing network models of the type shown in Figure 1. More generally, specific models should be tailored to the type of node in question, for example a parallel database server. However, the resulting LST would then be exceedingly complex, perhaps only available numerically and almost certainly requiring numerical inversion. We do not pursue this further in this paper.

Regarding network delays, we develop a detailed model of the ubiquitous Ethernet in section 4 and obtain a good approximation for its mean. At reasonably low utilisations, the ethernet can be adequately modelled as a single server queue and, using the value calculated for the mean delay to calibrate it, a highly efficient approximate algorithm has been implemented for transaction response time density. Greater accuracy can be obtained, particularly at higher loading, at increased computational cost by using the LST directly and inverting numerically. However, the normal operating load on an Ethernet must usually be kept at a low level to achieve adequate performance.

3. Central Server Models

We use a central server model of the type shown in Figure 1 to represent both client and server nodes; see [2] for example. This is a single class queueing network consisting of a CPU (the central server) and M devices parameterized as follows:

   1) The average total CPU time of a task, T;

   2) The average number of visits a task makes to each device i, v_i $(1 \le i \le M)$

   3) The average service time (per visit) at each device i, $1/\mu_i$ $(1 \le i \le M)$

   4) The external arrival rate to the CPU, λ

The CPU is labelled 0, and the M devices are labelled 1 to M. We therefore define the visit count and service rate of the CPU to be

$$v_0 = 1 + \sum_{i=1}^{M} v_i \quad \text{and} \quad \mu_0 = \frac{v_0}{T}$$

In addition, the routing probabilities shown in Figure 1 are defined to be $p_i = v_i/v_0$ and the probability of departing the network after visiting the CPU is $d = 1/v_0$.

Now, the response time of a task in a queueing network is the sum of its busy times at each of the nodes it visits. Hence, average response time is the sum of the average busy times, an easy calculation. We consider central server networks with several devices in which tasks make a large number of cycles before departing. We then make the approximating assumption that a task's busy times at each node are independent random variables. This appears a strong assumption which is clearly not

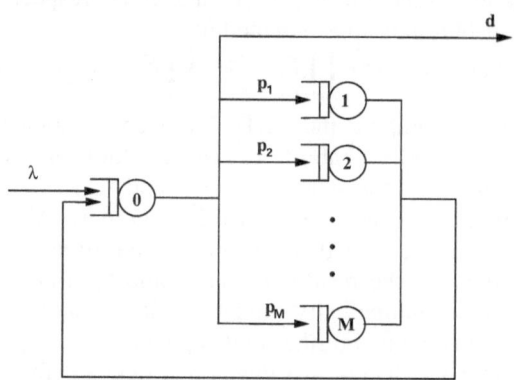

Figure 1. A central server queueing network

valid in networks with only one device, for example. This is because the number of visits to the CPU must be the same as the number of visits to the device; hence the respective visit times are strongly correlated. However, as the number of devices M increases, the assumption holds asymptotically provided no small set of devices dominates, i.e. only a few of the visit counts are significant. This is formalised in the following:

Proposition 1

Let V_i denote the random variable for the number of visits a task makes to device i $(1 \leq i \leq M)$ and $V = V_1 + \ldots + V_M$ denote the number of cycles made by a task. Then

$$P(V_1 = n_1, \ldots, V_M = n_M \mid V = n) \approx \prod_{i=1}^{M} P(V_i = n_i \mid V = n)$$

as $n \to \infty$ provided no device i dominates.

Proof

The left hand side of the equation is

$$L = \frac{n!}{\prod_{i=1}^{M} n_i!} \prod_{i=1}^{M} p_i^{n_i}$$

and the right hand side can be written $R = L \times U$ where

$$U = (n!)^{M-1} \prod_{i=1}^{M} \frac{(1 - p_i)^{n - n_i}}{(n - n_i)!}$$

We therefore need to show that $U \to 1$ as $n \to \infty$. Now write $p_i = k_i / n$ where $\sum_{i=1}^{M} k_i = n$ and each k_i is small compared to n under the hypothesis that no device i dominates. Applying Stirling's formula to the factorial terms, as $n \to \infty$,

$$U \approx \left(\frac{n}{e}\right)^{(M-1)n} \prod_{i=1}^{M} \frac{(1-k_i/n)^{n-n_i}}{(n/e)^{n-n_i}(1-n_i/n)^{n-n_i}}$$

Thus, as $n \to \infty$, for n_i small in comparison to n,

$$U \approx \prod_{i=1}^{M} \frac{e^{-k_i}}{e^{-n_i}} = \frac{e^{-n}}{e^{-n}} = 1$$

However, if any n_i is large enough to be comparable with n, both the probabilities L and R are neglibible. QED

We now need to compute the busy time distribution at each node, $B_i(t)$ at node i say. Let the jth waiting time of a given task at node i be denoted by W_j and let the task make V visits to node i. Then the LST of the busy time distribution is

$$B*(s) = E[e^{-s(W_1+...+W_V)}] = E[E[e^{-s(W_1+...+W_V)} \,|\, V]] = E[(E[e^{-sW_1}])^V] = G_V(W*(s))$$

where G_V is the probability generating function of the random variable V and $W*(s)$ is the LST of the waiting time distribution at node i. In an open Markovian network, the waiting time density at node i is $W_i*(s) = (\mu_i - \lambda_i)/(s + \mu_i - \lambda_i)$ where $\lambda_i = \lambda v_i$ for $(0 \le i \le M)$.

For the CPU, the number of visits made by a task is geometric so that

$$G_{V0}(z) = \sum_{n=0}^{\infty} d(1-d)^n z^{n+1} = \frac{zd}{1-z(1-d)}$$

and hence, after simple algebra,

$$B_0*(s) = (\mu_0 - \lambda_0)/(v_0 s + \mu_0 - \lambda_0)$$

For the devices, to find the probability that a task makes v visits, we condition on the number of cycles n, i.e. visits made to the CPU. Hence we find for device i $(1 \le i \le M)$

$$G_{Vi}(z) = \sum_{v=0}^{\infty} \sum_{n=v}^{\infty} d(1-d)^n \binom{n}{v} q_i^v z^v (1-q_i)^{n-v}$$

where $q_i = p_i/(1-d)$. Changing the order of summation (with $n \ge v$) and rearranging, we obtain

$$G_{Vi}(z) = \sum_{n=0}^{\infty} d(1-d)^n (1-q_i^n) \sum_{v=0}^{n} \binom{n}{v} \left(\frac{q_i z}{1-q_i}\right)^v = \frac{d}{d + p_i(1-z)}$$

Substituting $W*(s)$ for z then yields

$$B_i*(s) = \frac{s + \mu_i - \lambda_i}{(v_i+1)s + \mu_i - \lambda_i} = \frac{1}{v_i+1} + \frac{(\mu_i - \lambda_i)v_i/(v_i+1)}{(v_i+1)s + \mu_i - \lambda_i}$$

Under our independence of busy times assumption, the LST of the response time distribution for the central server queuing network is now

$$R*(s) = \prod_{i=0}^{M} B_i*(s)$$

This can be inverted analytically, using the method described below, to give the density $r(t)$ of response time. However, to illustrate the method, we make the further simplifying assumption that $d \ll p_i$ for all i. This is frequently reasonable; for example if $d = 1/M^2$ and all the p_i are equal, then each p_i is of the order $1/M$. When the assumption does not hold, the problem of LST inversion becomes a collection of inversions of the type we now consider when it does hold.

For $d \ll p_i$ for all $i>0$, i.e. $v_i \gg 0$, we find that $B_i *(s) \approx \dfrac{\mu_i - \lambda_i}{(v_i + 1)s + \mu_i - \lambda_i}$

and hence that

$$R^*(s) = K \prod_{i=0}^{M}\left(\frac{1}{s + a_i}\right) \tag{1}$$

where $a_i = (\mu_i - \lambda_i)/(v_i + 1)$ for $i > 0$, $a_0 = (\mu_0 - \lambda_0)/v_0$ and $K = \prod_{i=0}^{M} a_i$.

The problem has now been reduced to finding an expression for $R^*(s)$ which can be straightforwardly inverted, for example by using the method of partial fractions. If all the a_i's are distinct, we obtain:

$$R^*(s) = K \sum_{i=0}^{M} \frac{r_i}{(s + a_i)}$$

where the factors r_i are given by

$$r_i = \frac{(-1)^M}{\prod_{j=0, j \neq i}^{M} (a_i - a_j)}$$

This can be proved either by standard linear algebra, or (more straightforwardly) by induction on M. Using the facts that $R*(0) = 1$ and $R*'(0) = -\sum_{i=0}^{M} 1/a_i$ (from equation (1)), we find that

$$\sum_{i=0}^{M} \frac{r_i}{a_i} = \frac{1}{K} \quad \text{and} \quad \sum_{i=0}^{M} \frac{r_i}{a_i^2} = \frac{1}{K}\sum_{i=0}^{M} \frac{1}{a_i}$$

We have now decomposed $R^*(s)$ into a linear combination of Laplace transforms of exponential densities, and thus, since the Laplace transformation is a linear operator, we can invert it to give the density function r(t) as

$$\boxed{r(t) = K \sum_{i=0}^{n} r_i e^{-a_i t}}$$

Finally in this section we note that a transaction path consists of a client node, a number of server nodes and corresponding network nodes which we shall represent as M/M/1 queues. We assume that all of these components are independent and hence that the LST of system response time distribution is a product of products of the form of $R*(s)$ in equation (1). This is just another expression of the same form and hence is invertible in the same way to give response time density as a function of time.

4.   The Ethernet and its Modelling

The methodology described in section 2 applies to all types of client-server network; it is necessary to determine only the mean latency of the network so that the appropriate service rate can be chosen for the M/M/1 queue used to represent it. If the basis of the contention for the network is queueing, then the service rate must be chosen so that the resulting waiting time matches the mean latency. If the basis of contention is sharing, a delay ('infinite') server can be used instead whereupon service time will be the same as latency.

We choose the Ethernet for our network because of its predominance as a local area network (LAN). From its origins at Xerox in the mid-seventies, Ethernet [4] has become the most successful LAN technology. Recent developments such as Fast Ethernet and GigaBit Ethernet offer a relatively easy way to improve the bandwidth of an existing Ethernet to cope with the ever increasing demand.

Boggs, Mogul and Kent [1] give a detailed account of the many attempts which have been made to model Ethernets. As they point out, many models which have been developed do not model the correct Medium Access Control layer. There are many models which aim to find the throughput for various values of the 'offered load', but yield no information on the average packet delay. Many models make unrealistic assumptions such as constant message lengths. The model presented here is based on simple probability theory, gives the average packet delay and any assumptions made are explicitly stated.

4.1 Modus Operandi

Upper layer protocols are not considered here: this discussion centres primarily on the Medium Access Control layer. In the case of an Ethernet, the process by which a message gets access to the wire is called Carrier Sense Multiple Access with Collision Detection (CSMA/CD). The classic analogy of this process is a dinner party conversation. Everybody around the dinner table must listen for a period of quiet before speaking. Once a space occurs, each person has an equal chance to say something. If two people start talking at once, they both realise and both try to speak again a short time later.

The following algorithm is followed each time a message requires access to the medium:

1) If the medium is idle, **transmit**. Otherwise go to step 2.
2) If the medium is busy, continue to listen until the channel is idle, then **transmit**.
3) If a collision is detected during transmission, transmit a brief **jamming signal** to ensure that all stations know there has been a collision. After transmitting this signal, wait (back off) a random amount of time, then attempt to transmit again – step 1.

The collision time is determined by the truncated binary exponential backoff algorithm (not to be confused with the exponential distribution) before attempting to retransmit. This is described below. The 'slot time' referred to is the time taken to transmit the smallest possible message (64 octets) = 51.2 microseconds for a 10Mbit Ethernet.

1. After the **first** collision, a station waits either 0 or 1 slot times. The probability of each is ½.
2. After the **second**, the station waits one of (0,1,2,3) slot times with probability ¼.
3. .
4. .

5. .
6. After the **tenth**, the station waits one of $(0, ..., 2^{10}-1)$ slot times, with probability $1/2^{10}$
7. ... 15) Subsequently, the backoff time is chosen as if it were the tenth collision.

Thus the maximum back-off time picked subsequent to a collision is 2^{10} slot times = 51.2 milliseconds. After fifteen collisions (sixteen transmission attempts) the message is 'dropped' and this situation is handled by the higher level protocol. The time to process the exception is typically up to 100 - 1000 times longer than the transmission time.

4.2 An Ethernet Model
The following assumptions are made in the model described here.
1. The offered arrivals have an exponentially distributed inter-arrival time (Poisson arrival process).
2. The combined arrivals (offered arrivals plus retries) also have an exponentially distributed inter-arrival time.
3. All stations are separated by a constant distance (star formation).
4. Backoff times are truncated binary exponential.
5. A message fails if the 16th attempt to acquire the network fails.

We use the following notation and parameter values in the numerical results of section 4.3.

Ethernet speed = v = 10 MegaBits/Second
Propagation time (maximum possible) = Δ =25.6 μS
Preamble time (8 Bytes) = T_{PRE} = 2.6 μS
Jamming time (4 Bytes) = T_{JAM} =1.3 μS
Interframe gap = T_{IFG} =9.6 μS
Slot time (64 Bytes) = T_{SLOT} =51.2 μS
Minimum message time (64 Bytes) = T_{MIN} =51.2 μS
Maximum message time (1518 Bytes) = T_{MAX} = 1214 μS

4.2.1 A Model with Constant Message Lengths
To simplify the presentation, we first consider an Ethernet that carries messages of constant length, before generalising to arbitrary message lengths in the next subsection. Message transmission time, which excludes time due to collisions and backoffs, is denoted by T. The offered arrival rate, which excludes arrivals due to retries, is denoted λ. The utilisation – the probability of observing the Ethernet transmitting a successful message – is therefore given by $\rho = \lambda T$. The total arrival rate, which includes retries, is denoted by Λ, which we calculate below.

The probability of a message colliding is dependent both on the current backoff state of the message and the backoff state of any message it has previously collided with. For example, take two messages which collide together on their first attempt. Each choose a backoff time of either 0 or 1 slot times. If they choose the same time they will collide again, so the probability of another collision is at least a half.

We make the following three simplifying assumptions:
1) All collisions involve only two messages.
2) If two messages choose the same backoff time after a collision, they will collide again.
3) If two messages choose different backoff times after a collision, the probability of a collision is the same as that of the first attempt, with a modified network utilisation term (described below).

The first assumption is expected to give good results for low utilisations (the usual operating domain of an Ethernet) but may under-estimate the collision rate when the network is busier. Note as any message's backoff state becomes large, the probability of it colliding at the next attempt should tend to the probability of a collision at its first attempt, simply because it will have waited a long time before attempting to transmit again.

In this model, each incoming message has a *state number*, with state number 1 meaning the message is making its first attempt, etc. Denote the probability of failure at the nth attempt as p_n. Then the total arrival rate is given by

$$\Lambda = \lambda(1 + p_1 + p_1 p_2 + ... + \prod_{j=1}^{15} p_j).$$

The upper limit, 15, of the product reflects that each message tries up to sixteen times before giving up. The probability q_j of an arbitrary incoming message being in state j is given by

$$q_j = \frac{\lambda}{\Lambda} \prod_{k=1}^{j-1} p_k, \qquad 1 \le j \le 16$$

where the empty product is defined to be 1.

We first consider a message which is making its first attempt at transmission. The message suffers a collision if either
1) the network is busy and there is at least one other arrival during the transmission of that message or during the original message's initialisation phase (one propagation time, Δ) immediately preceding it; or
2) the network is idle and at least one other message arrives within two propagation times (one before and one after the arrival instant).

In the steady state, the probability that the network is busy on arrival is given by ρ by the random observer property of Poisson processes. Since the total arrival process is assumed to be Poisson, p_1, the probability of a collision at the first attempt, is

$$p_1 = (1 - \rho)(1 - e^{-2\Lambda\Delta}) + \rho(1 - e^{-\Lambda(T+\Delta)})$$

Here, Δ is the propagation time (assumed constant) between stations – the time taken for a signal to traverse the Ethernet from one station to another. This equation should be compared to Kleinrock's collision probability for CSMA [3], where message transmission times are not taken into account.

If a message suffers a collision, it must have collided with at least one other message; by the first assumption above, *exactly* one other message. If both messages choose the same backoff time, they will collide again (assumption two). If they choose different backoff times, the probability of successful transmission is assumed to be the same as at the first attempt (assumption three). Thus the probability of failure at the ith attempt is

$$p_i = \sum_{j=1}^{16} q_j (P_{i-1,j} + (1 - P_{i-1,)j}) p_{1i}), \quad 2 \le i \le 16$$

where P_{ij} is the probability of a direct clash between a message that was previously in state i and one which was previously in state j,

$$P_{ij} = (0.5)^{\max(\min(i,10),\min(j,10))}$$

i.e., the probability that the messages choose the same backoff time. Recalling assumption (3),

$$p_{1i} = (1 - \rho_i)(1 - e^{-2\Lambda\Delta}) + \rho_i (1 - e^{-\Lambda(T+\Delta)})$$

where ρ_i is the probability that a message sees the network busy on its ith attempt ($2 \le i \le 16$). Now, if the preceding backoff time was large in comparison with message transmission time, ρ_i is well approximated by ρ. However, if the backoff time, B say, was small, the network would only be busy if another message arrived during that backoff time. Hence a better approximation would be $\rho_i = \lambda B$. We combine these approximations by defining

$$\rho_i = \sum_{j=0}^{2^i-1} 2^{-i} \mathrm{Min}[\lambda j T_{SLOT}, \rho]$$

The above equations for $\{p_i\}$ are solved iteratively with the starting values $p_i = \rho$ for all i. The iteration was always found to be convergent for $0 < \rho < 1$ in a wide range of tests.

The dropping probability – the probability that a message fails at the 16th attempt – is given by

$$P_{DROP} = \prod_{i=1}^{16} p_i$$

An additional definition is now needed: that of the *average residual wait time*, R_i, which is the average time between a message in backoff state i arriving at the network and the discovery of a collision, given that the message actually has a collision. This is given by

$$R_i = \Delta + \frac{T}{2} w_i$$

where w_i is the *waiting probability* for backoff state i, i.e. the probability that a message, on suffering a collision, had seen the network busy on its arrival. This is given by

$$w_1 = \frac{\rho\left(1 - e^{-\Lambda(T+\Delta)}\right)}{p_1}$$

$$w_i = \frac{\sum_{j=1}^{16} q_j \rho_i \left[P_{i-1,j} + (1 - P_{i-1,j})\left(1 - e^{-\Lambda(T+\Delta)}\right)\right]}{p_i} \quad 2 \le i \le 16$$

The average time for a message to successfully transmit is then given by:

$$T_{TOTAL} =$$

$$T + T_{IFG} + \rho T/2$$

$$+ \sum_{i=1}^{16} \left(\frac{\left(\prod_{j=1}^{i-1} p_j \right)(1-p_i)}{1-p_{DROP}} \left((i-1)(T_{IFG} + T_{JAM}) + \sum_{j=1}^{i-1} \left(R_j + \left(\frac{2^{\min(j,10)}-1}{2} \right) T_{SLOT} \right) \right) \right) \quad (2)$$

The term $\rho T/2$ arises because the successful transmission attempt may have to wait for the network to become idle before transmitting.

4.2.2 General Message Length Distribution

It is well documented that the shape of the message length distribution has a significant effect on the throughput of an Ethernet; see [1, 6] for example. Let the message propagation time random variable (not including any back offs, jams, etc.) be denoted by X. This quantity is directly related to the message length L via $X=L/v$, where v is the Ethernet's speed. Let the message propagation time probability density function be $p(t)$. Now, when observing the network, there is a greater chance of seeing longer messages because they spend a longer amount of time on the network. This means the probability density of *observed* message propagation times, $b(t)$ say, has to be weighted by the message propagation time itself; this is just the familiar argument used to find (non-rigorously) the observed renewal period probability density in renewal theory. Thus we find:

$$b(t) = \frac{p(t)t\,dt}{\int_{y=0}^{\infty} p(t)t\,dt} = \frac{1}{T} p(t)t$$

where $T = E[X]$ is the average propagation time. The probability of failure at the first attempt is now

$$p_1 = (1-\rho)(1-e^{-2\Lambda\Delta}) + \rho \int_0^{\infty} b(t)(1-e^{-\Lambda(t+\Delta)})\,dt$$

and similarly p_i is given by the same formula with ρ replaced by ρ_i which is now defined by

$$\rho_i = \sum_{j=0}^{2^i-1} 2^{-i} \text{Min}[\lambda \int_0^{\infty} \text{Min}[jT_{SLOT}, t]p(t)\,dt, \rho]$$

$$= \sum_{j=0}^{2^i-1} 2^{-i} \text{Min}\left[\lambda \left[\int_0^{jT_{SLOT}} tp(t)\,dt + jT_{SLOT} \int_{jT_{SLOT}}^{\infty} p(t)\,dt \right], \rho \right]$$

In practice, the integrals above will be bounded due to the minimum and maximum message lengths as defined in the Ethernet specification. The waiting probabilities w_i are now given by:

$$w_1 = \frac{\rho \int\limits_0^\infty b(t)\left(1 - e^{-\Lambda(t+\Delta)}\right)dt}{P_1}$$

$$w_i = \frac{\sum\limits_{j=1}^{16} q_j \rho_i \left[P_{i-1,j} + (1 - P_{i-1,j}) \int\limits_0^\infty b(t)\left(1 - e^{-\Lambda(t+\Delta)}\right)dt \right]}{P_i} \qquad \text{for } 1 < i < 16$$

Now let T_{WAIT} denote the average time a message spends waiting before attempting to transmit, if on arrival it finds the network busy. Then

$$T_{WAIT} = \frac{1}{2}\int\limits_0^\infty t b(t)dt = \int\limits_0^\infty \frac{t^2}{2T} p(t)dt$$

(This is just the mean residual life in renewal theory.) The average residual wait time is now $R_i = \Delta + w_i T_{WAIT}$. These expressions can now be substituted into equation (2) for the average total transmission time in the previous section. As expected, if we take $p(t) = \delta(t-T)$, the equation is exactly the same.

Measurements of real Ethernets have shown that the most common message lengths are either minimum size or maximum size – typically the small messages are acknowledgements or requests, while the large messages are chunks of data. Thus a *bimodal* probability distribution is an appropriate model. Let α be the fraction of messages which are short; this quantity may be measured by any network 'sniffer'. Then the propagation time probability density function is equal to a weighted sum of two delta functions:

$$p(t) = \alpha\delta(t - T_{short}) + (1 - \alpha)\delta(t - T_{long})$$

All the expressions above can be computed very simply using this. For example, the quantity T_{WAIT} is:

$$T_{WAIT} = \frac{1}{2T}\left(\alpha T_{short}^2 + (1 - \alpha)T_{long}^2\right)$$

5.   Numerical Results

The graphs below show the total message transmission time as a function of Ethernet utilisation as predicted by the analytical model, in comparison with simulation results. Over 10000 message transmissions were simulated for each point on the graphs giving narrow confidence bands at the 95% confidence level. The simulation models the Ethernet's modus operandi exactly as described in section 4.1 and so its output results from an entirely different basis compared to that of the analytical predictions. Consequently, good agreement instils confidence in the models.

For constant message lengths, we obtained the following graphs.

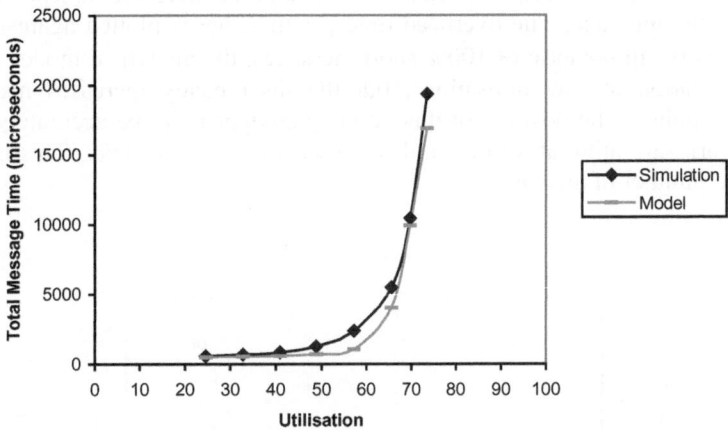

Figure 2. Transmission time versus utilisation

Generally, the analytical results compare favourably to the simulation results. In particular, the point at which performance starts to degrade seriously is clearly identified, at a utilisation of about 60%, which agrees closely with the simulation. This is the measure of most importance to capacity planners when designing their client-server system.

The next graph shows the dropping probabilities plotted against utilisation; recall that a message is dropped when it suffers 16 consecutive collisions. Again, it is clear that the network becomes saturated at utilisations of just over 60%. This is confirmed by simulation and is entirely consistent with the folk-lore surrounding the Ethernet.

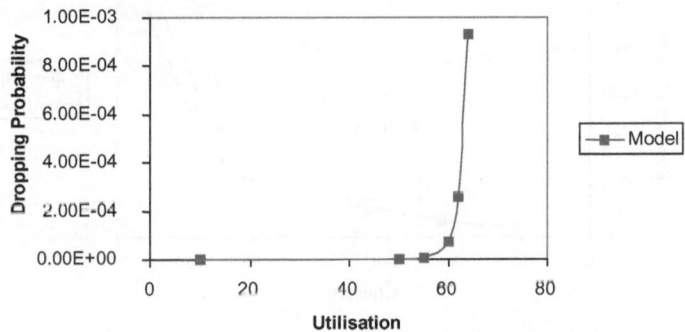

Figure 3. Dropping Probability vs Utilisation

The behaviour of the bimodal model parameterisation for T_{short} corresponding to 64 bytes and T_{long} corresponding to 1518 bytes and for various values of α is now examined. We define the response overhead as the average time for a message transmission minus that message's propagation time. This is the overhead time due to collisions before successful transmission, and is therefore independent of the length of the message. The overhead time per message is plotted against utilisation for various α. In the case of 100% short messages, the analytical model agrees well with simulation at low utilisations, but the discrepancy increases nearer to the saturation point. The position of this point again appears to be accurately predicted, the network saturating at a lower utilisation between 25 and30%. This is due to an increased number of arrivals.

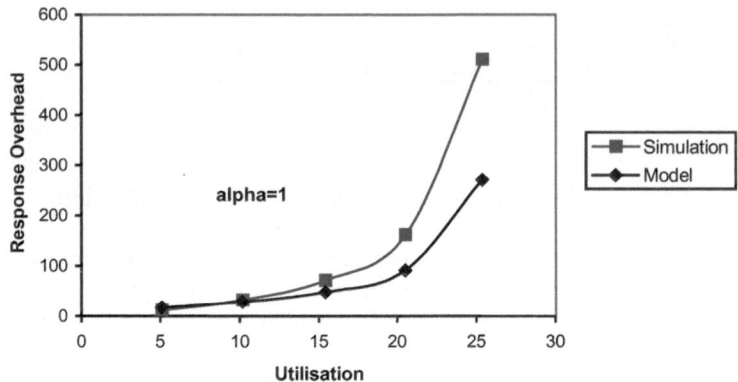

Figure 4. Response overhead with all short messages

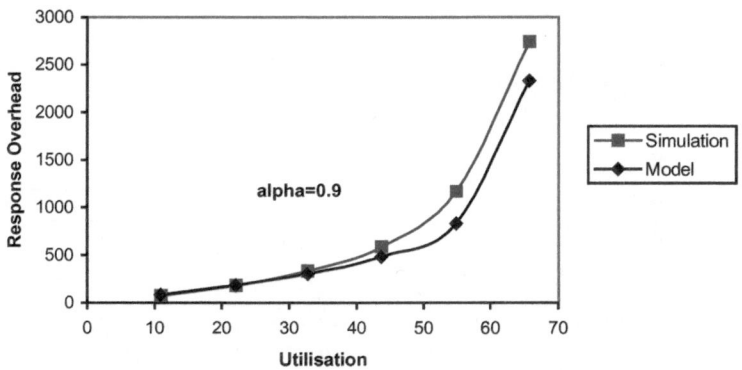

Figure 5. Response overhead with 90% short messages

With only a small proportion of long messages, the agreement between the analytical model and simulation is greatly improved and both models show that the Ethernet saturates at utilisation between 50 and 60%.

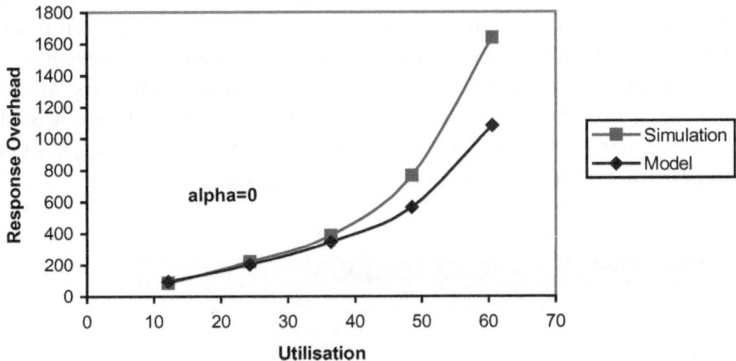

Figure 6. Response overhead with all long messages

The saturation point does not change very much as the proportion of long messages increases and with 100% long messages it is still between 50 and 60%. Note the larger scale in Figure 6. These graphs are similar to those of Tobagi and Hunt [6].

5.1 Efficiency of the Analytical Model

The number of iterations needed by the model is a crucial parameter of the algorithm's performance. As expected the number of iterations necessary increases as the utilisation increases. However, to achieve results with a relative error of one part in a thousand, at most twelve iterations of the 16+1 equations for p_i must be performed. On a fast machine, this takes milliseconds. This should be compared with the simulation, which takes up to half an hour for highly utilised Ethernets. Simulation, whilst being slightly more accurate, is machine intensive: for typical capacity planning questions, the analytical model can provide very similar answers in a fraction of the time.

5.2 Parameterisation of an M/M/1 Queue

We now wish to model the Ethernet as an M/M/1 queue in order to incorporate it into our response time model of section 3. Given the mean waiting time (total transmission time) at the Ethernet we have two choices:

- To consider the Ethernet as a queueing system where messages have to spend some time waiting before they transmit;
- To consider it as a shared resource where each message receives service continuously from the instant of its arrival, at a reducing rate as the number of messages there increases.

The operation of the Ethernet is closer to the first alternative, which is the one we choose.

If the service rate of the queue is μ, the mean waiting time is $1/(\mu-\lambda)$ where λ is as given in the Ethernet model. Hence we solve the Ethernet model for T_{TOTAL} and then match this with $1/(\mu-\lambda)$ to give $\mu = \lambda + 1/T_{TOTAL}$. This is the service rate we use in the response time model, which is now complete.

6.   The Athene Client-Server tool

Athene Client-Server is a capacity planning tool from Metron Technology Ltd, which contains the models outlined in this paper.   It contains a flexible topology editor to link clients, networks and servers. An example three-tier topology is shown in Figure 7.   This model has ten NT clients communicating with an application server over an Ethernet. The application server calls a large back-end database. Data for modelling the clients and servers can be taken from NT and UNIX.   Workloads are linked across machines over networks. Evaluation of the underlying queueing network is done near-instantaneously, on-line, as and when the parameters of the model are changed.

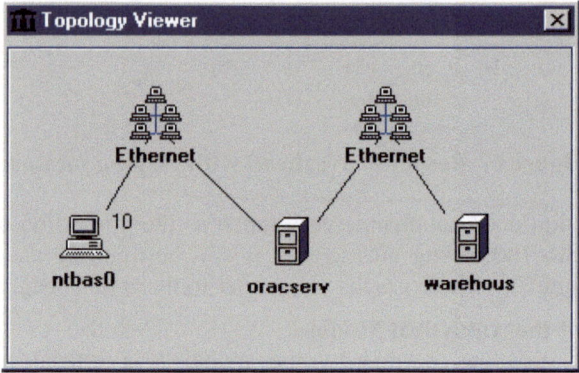

Figure 7. Network specification window

Response times of distributed workloads can be broken down into constituent parts, and even by device. This information is displayed as a bar chart in a new window, as shown in Figure 8 for example.

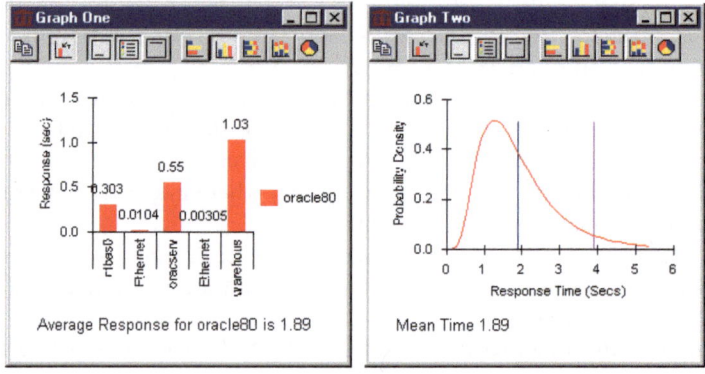

Figure 8. Constituents of response time and its probability density

The response time density calculation is implemented as described in section 3. The Ethernet contribution to response time is often negligible, as in this instance, whereupon its representation as an M/M/1 queue does not introduce a significant error. What is important is to be able to predict when the network will saturate, and we have seen that our model finds the corresponding level of utilisation accurately. The charts in Figure 8 change in real time as the user varies the parameters of the model, for example the number of clients, the rate at which transactions are generated by each client, Ethernet speed and the mean service time at the database.

'What-if' questions the model caters for include how the performance will change at increasing transaction rates, both on individual machines and across the enterprise, with greater numbers of clients, higher utilisation of Ethernets, etc. Long term forecasting, which can facilitate the maintenance of service levels, is also possible; a typical display is shown in Figure 9.

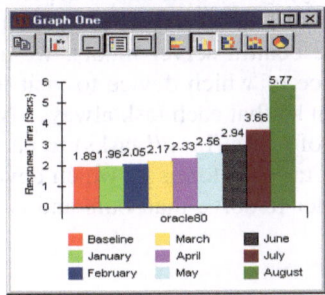

Figure 9. Long term forecasting

Here the growth in the usage of Oracle 80 over a period of eight months has been anticipated by installation management. It is required to find out whether system performance will remain adequate in terms of response time, which is characterised by its mean value. In this case we see after about six months (June) there is some cause for concern and an upgrade may be needed.

7. Summary and Future Work

We have developed a simple but effective and efficient model for predicting mean response times and response time densities in client-server systems. We have also demonstrated its use by incorporating it into a capacity planning tool for client-server installation management. This software is in production and can provide a significant, live tool demonstration.

In terms of the mathematics involved, we have found a new approximate result for response time density in central server networks that holds under appropriate independence assumptions. Although these assumptions do not hold in practice, we have shown that they do asymptotically as network size increases and should not lead to undue inaccuracy for moderately sized networks. In addition, we have derived a new model of the Ethernet, which is of interest in its own right and produces accurate results at low utilisations and predicts well the maximum utilisation possible before performance degrades sharply. We used this model to parameterise the Ethernet as a single server Markovian queue in order to incorporate it into the above response time model. Again, at low utilisation, this does not introduce a significant error. Future work will consider the increasingly prevalent *switched* Ethernets which offer significant increase in bandwidth as well as reduced contention. This will require a radically different network model but will not affect the client-server modelling tool.

A major limitation of the current models is their reliance on exponential service times. We believe that the Ethernet sub-model will generalise straightforwardly to approximate response time densities for arbitrary message length distributions. The same cannot be said for the response times in central server systems. However, we do have the property that the numbers of visits made to each node in these queueing networks are (asymptotically) geometric and independent. Hence an exponential form for the time spent by a task at each node is not an unreasonable approximation. Finally, we note that in the central server model, we assumed that any given task makes an independent choice of which device to visit next every time it leaves the CPU. In reality, it will often be that each task always visits the *same* device on every cycle, the average number of visits (by *all* tasks) to each device being the same by virtue of the distribution of tasks in terms of which device they do choose. In fact, this problem is rather simpler to solve than ours and is an obvious extension of the model.

8. Acknowledgements

The authors would like to thank Mike Garth and Adam Grummitt for helpful comments on the manuscript. The work was supported by the Department of Trade and Industry's SPUR initiative.

9. References

[1] Boggs, Mogul & Kent, 'Measured Capacity of an Ethernet: Myths and Reality', WRL Research Report 88/4, (1988)

[2] Harrison P G, Patel N M; "Performance Modelling of Communication Networks and Computer Architectures", Addison-Wesley, 1993.

[3] Kleinrock, 'Queueing Systems, Volume Two: Computer Applications', Wiley, (1976)

[4] Metcalfe & Boggs, 'Ethernet: Distributed Packet Switching for Local Computer Networks', Communications of the CSM, 19, 5, 395, (1976)

[5] Metron; "Athene / Client-Server User Guide", Metron Technology Limited, Taunton, UK, 1995.

[6] Tobagi & Hunt, 'Performance Analysis of Carrier Sense Multiple Access with Collision Detection', Computer Networks, 4, 245, (1980)

A Queueing Model with Varying Service Rate
for ABR

Rudesindo Núñez-Queija

CWI, P.O. Box 94079, 1090 GB Amsterdam, The Netherlands
sindo@cwi.nl

Abstract. In this paper we study a queueing model with a server that
changes its service rate according to a finite birth and death process.
The object of interest is the simultaneous distribution of the number
of customers in the system and the state of the server in steady-state.
Both infinite and finite storage capacity for customers is considered. The
influence of the operating time-scale is investigated by letting the underlying birth-death process move infinitely fast as well as infinitely slow.
The model can be applied to the performance analysis of (low priority)
Available Bit Rate (ABR) traffic at an ATM switch in the presence of
traffic with a higher priority such as Variable Bit Rate (VBR) traffic and
Constant Bit Rate (CBR) traffic. For a specific example we illustrate
by numerical experiments the influence of the latter traffic types on the
ABR service.

1 Introduction

This work was motivated by the introduction of the *Available Bit Rate* (ABR)
service class in *Asynchronous Transfer Mode* (ATM) networks. The ABR service is a low-priority service that was designed for carrying data connections in
ATM networks. The amount of transmission capacity that is reserved for ABR
traffic is typically a very small portion of the total network capacity and, in general, not sufficient to handle all ABR traffic. Apart from this low-level reserved
capacity, ABR connections can profit from (temporarily) unused capacity from
other service classes, such as the more traditional *Constant Bit Rate* (CBR) and
Variable Bit Rate (VBR) services. Thus, ABR connections will receive a varying
service capacity. Other specific characteristics of the ABR service class are (i)
the ability to react dynamically to network congestion by means of feedback
information from the network's links to the ABR sources, and (ii) fair sharing
of the available capacity among ABR connections. For ABR connections, the
cell loss fraction should be very small. This can be achieved by incorporating
large storage buffers at the switches, that can be controlled with the already
mentioned feedback mechanisms: As soon as traffic congestion is detected at a
switch, for instance because the contents of the switch's storage buffer exceed
some threshold level, the switch sends a feedback signal to the ABR sources,
that forces them to lower their input rates. When the congestion is released, the

R. Puigjaner et al. (Eds.): Tools'98, LNCS 1469, pp. 93–104, 1998.

sources are notified in a similar way. For more detailed specifications of ABR we refer to the ATM Forum [2].

In this paper we focus on the ABR service *at the connection level*. We assume that all transient effects of the feedback mechanism, that operates at the cell-level, can be ignored. This seems to be a reasonable assumption, since the durations of ABR connections are typically large, compared to oscillations at the cell level. An active ABR source continuously sends cells to the network at the permitted rate. When a source has no more cells to send, the connection is terminated.

We propose a queueing model for the analysis of the ABR service at the connection level. We model a single ATM switch by a server that can be in different states. The state of the server determines the service capacity. We assume that the state of the server changes according to some general finite birth and death process. For ABR, the service capacity is determined by the load of higher priority traffic. In the queueing model, an ABR connection is represented by a customer (the service requirement of the customer corresponds to the amount of cells to be transmitted). All customers present at the service station – i.e. all active ABR sources – are served according to the (egalitarian) *processor sharing* service discipline, which is the mathematical translation of the 'fair sharing' requirement for ABR connections.

Our model is a two-dimensional Markov process, and we study it through its steady-state distribution. The two components of the process are (i) the number of customers at the service station and (ii) the state of the server. We assume that customers (ABR calls) arrive according to a Poisson process. This is a reasonable assumption for ABR calls at the connection level: There are many sources and each of them can become active (with small probability) at any point in time. We further assume that the service requirement of a customer (i.e. the amount of data that an ABR source transmits) is drawn from an exponential distribution.

Although the assumption of exponentially distributed service requirements is quite restrictive, the presented model may be used to gain useful qualitative insights into the performance of low priority traffic (ABR) that is offered a varying service capacity. For our model we determine the steady-state distribution of the number of active ABR sources, and compare it to the case with a fixed available link capacity. Note that, because of the exponentially distributed service requirements, the queue length process is identical to that of the same model with *First Come First Served* (FCFS) service discipline, instead of processor sharing. However, in future studies we will investigate the *sojourn time* (delay) of customers in this model, for which the processor sharing discipline complicates the analysis considerably, even under the above mentioned assumptions. For a review on processor sharing queues, see Yashkov [22].

In our model we consider both an infinite and a finite storage capacity for customers. The latter corresponds to the situation where the individual customers are assigned a guaranteed minimum capacity, see Sect. 6.

The presented model is a generalisation of the priority model analysed by Núñez Queija and Boxma [18]. In that report, the state of the server is explicitly given by the number of higher priority customers in the system (e.g. VBR and CBR connections), which form an $M/M/n/k$ queue. In Núñez Queija [19] the results were generalised and extended for the present model with infinite capacity.

Variants of the priority model were studied by several authors. The case where both types of customers have an infinite waiting space and within each customer type the service discipline is FCFS, was solved first by Mitrani and King [15] and later by Gail et al. [7]. Falin et al. [6] analysed the case with processor sharing among the low priority customers. An extensive treatment of the spectral analysis of $M/G/1$-type Markov chains is given in Gail et al. [8]. Daigle and Lucantoni [5] analysed a model that contains our model with infinite storage capacity. However, we use somewhat different arguments and we are able to carry the analysis somewhat further (see Sect. 4). In addition, we also discuss the case with finite storage capacity.

Recently, several other studies were concerned with the application of similar models to the performance analysis of ABR. Blaabjerg et al. [3] consider a model similar to the one in [18] and give various performance measures in terms of the steady-state distribution, rather than analysing this distribution in greater detail. Independent from our studies, Altman et al. [1] obtained different results for a model that is contained in [19]. Kulkarni and Li [11] analysed a similar model with finite storage capacity by means of Laplace-Stieltjes Transforms.

The remainder of the paper is organised as follows. We present the model in Sect. 2. In Sect. 3, a starting point for the analysis is provided using the matrix-geometric theory of Neuts [17]. A detailed spectral analysis is presented in Sect. 4. The steady-state distribution for the infinite storage model is given in Sect. 5. For the model with finite storage capacity the results are mentioned in Sect. 6. In Sect. 7 the influence of fast- and slowly-changing service modes is discussed, and illustrated by a numerical example. Finally, in Sect. 8, conclusions are drawn and current research is mentioned.

2   The Model

We consider a service station where customers arrive according to a Poisson process with rate λ. The probability distribution of the service requirement of each customer is assumed to be exponential with mean 1 (this is no restriction) and independent of everything else. All customers present at the station are served according to the *processor sharing* discipline. I.e., if the station would work at constant rate μ then the model would become the standard $M/M/1$ processor sharing queue, and each customer would be served at rate μ/j, whenever there are $j > 0$ customers present.

The service capacity of the service station changes according to a birth and death process. More precisely: Let $[Y(t)]_{t \geq 0}$ be a birth and death process on $\{0, 1, \ldots, N\}$, N being a positive integer, with birth rate $q_i^{(+)} > 0$

$(i = 0, 1, \ldots, N - 1)$, and death rate $q_i^{(-)} > 0$ $(i = 1, 2, \ldots, N)$, whenever $Y(t) = i$ (for notational convenience we set $q_0^{(-)} = q_N^{(+)} = 0$). We further define $q_i := q_i^{(-)} + q_i^{(+)}$. We assume $Y(t)$ to be independent of the arrival times and service requirements of the customers. The station works at rate $\mu_i > 0$ when $Y(t) = i \in \{0, 1, \ldots, N\}$. The restriction $\mu_i > 0$, $\forall i$, is purely for compactness of presentation. The case where some of the μ_i are equal to 0 can be treated in the same manner, see Remark 1.

We already mentioned in Sect. 1 that, because of the exponentiality assumption on the service requirements, the fact that the service discipline is processor sharing has no effect on the queue length process: It is equivalent to the queue length process of the same model with FCFS service discipline.

We will consider both the case where there is an infinite storage buffer for customers at the station, and the case with a finite storage buffer for L customers, $L \in \{1, 2, 3, \ldots\}$. In the latter model, if a customer arrives at the service station and finds L other customers present, the new customer is rejected and is lost.

In this paper we will use the superscript $^{(\infty)}$ for the model with infinite buffer, and the superscript $^{(L)}$ for the finite buffer model. When it concerns both models, no superscripts are given.

Let $X(t)$ be the number of customers present in the system at time t. Then the process $(X(t), Y(t))$ is an irreducible and aperiodic Markovian process. Moreover, by definition, $Y(t)$ is not influenced by $X(t)$, i.e. if we define $p_i := \mathbf{P}\{Y = i\} := \lim_{t \to \infty} \mathbf{P}\{Y(t) = i\}$:

$$
p_0 = \left(1 + \sum_{i=1}^{N} \prod_{k=1}^{i} \frac{q_{k-1}^{(+)}}{q_k^{(-)}} \right)^{-1},
$$

$$
p_i = p_0 \prod_{k=1}^{i} \frac{q_{k-1}^{(+)}}{q_k^{(-)}}, \qquad\qquad i = 1, \ldots, N, \qquad (1)
$$

see for instance Sect. I.4.1 of Cohen [4]. The vector of these steady-state probabilities is denoted by $\bar{p} = (p_0, p_1, \ldots, p_N)$.

We define the simultaneous equilibrium probabilities

$$
\pi_{j,i} := \mathbf{P}\{X = j, Y = i\} := \lim_{t \to \infty} \mathbf{P}\{X(t) = j, Y(t) = i\}, \qquad (2)
$$

and partition them into vectors $\bar{\pi}_j := (\pi_{j,0}, \pi_{j,1}, \ldots, \pi_{j,N})$ of length $N + 1$. Note that $\bar{\pi}_j$ is associated with the states in which j customers are present. This partition enables us to write the equilibrium vector as a block vector $\bar{\pi}^{(\infty)} = (\bar{\pi}_0^{(\infty)}, \bar{\pi}_1^{(\infty)}, \bar{\pi}_2^{(\infty)}, \ldots)$ for the model with infinite storage buffer, and $\bar{\pi}^{(L)} = (\bar{\pi}_0^{(L)}, \bar{\pi}_1^{(L)}, \ldots, \bar{\pi}_L^{(L)})$ for the model with a storage buffer for L customers. The corresponding infinitesimal generators of the processes $(X^{(\infty)}(t), Y(t))$ and $(X^{(L)}(t), Y(t))$ are given by:

$$
\mathcal{Q}^{(\infty)} := \begin{bmatrix} Q_d^{(0)} & \lambda I & 0 & \cdots & & \\ M & Q_d & \lambda I & 0 & \cdots & \\ 0 & M & Q_d & \lambda I & 0 & \cdots \\ \vdots & & \ddots & \ddots & \ddots & \ddots & \ddots \end{bmatrix},
\tag{3}
$$

$$
\mathcal{Q}^{(L)} := \begin{bmatrix} Q_d^{(0)} & \lambda I & 0 & \cdots & \cdots & 0 \\ M & Q_d & \lambda I & 0 & \cdots & \\ 0 & \ddots & \ddots & \ddots & \ddots & \vdots \\ \vdots & \ddots & & M & Q_d & \lambda I \\ 0 & \cdots & & 0 & M & Q_d^{(L)} \end{bmatrix}.
\tag{4}
$$

Here, $Q_d^{(0)} = Q_Y - \lambda I$, $Q_d = Q_Y - \lambda I - M$, and $Q_d^{(L)} = Q_Y - M$.

$\mathcal{Q}^{(L)}$ consists of $L + 1$ block rows and block columns. The matrices Q_Y, I, and M are of dimension $(N + 1) \times (N + 1)$. I is the identity matrix, M is the diagonal matrix $\mathrm{diag}[\mu_0, \mu_1, \ldots, \mu_N]$ and Q_Y is the (tri-diagonal) infinitesimal generator of the process $Y(t)$:

$$
Q_Y := \begin{bmatrix} -q_0 & q_0^{(+)} & 0 & \cdots & \cdots & \cdots & 0 \\ q_1^{(-)} & -q_1 & q_1^{(+)} & 0 & \cdots & \cdots & 0 \\ 0 & q_2^{(-)} & -q_2 & q_2^{(+)} & 0 & \cdots & 0 \\ \vdots & \ddots & \ddots & \ddots & \ddots & \ddots & \vdots \\ 0 & \cdots & \cdots & \cdots & \cdots & q_N^{(-)} & -q_N \end{bmatrix}.
\tag{5}
$$

By Theorem 3.1.1 of Neuts [17], we have that the process $(X^{(\infty)}(t), Y(t))$ is ergodic if and only if

$$
\lambda < \bar{p} M \bar{e} = \sum_{i=0}^{N} p_i \mu_i.
\tag{6}
$$

Here $\bar{e}$ is the $N + 1$ dimensional column vector with all entries equal to 1.

In the sequel, when addressing the infinite buffer model, we assume that (6) holds. For the finite buffer model the steady-state distribution also exists when (6) is not satisfied. The case $\lambda = \bar{p} M \bar{e}$ can be analysed by the same techniques, but requires some extra work and does not add significantly to the results. Therefore we restrict ourselves to the case when $\lambda \neq \bar{p} M \bar{e}$.

3   Infinite Buffer Model

This section is concerned with providing a starting point for the analysis of the model with infinite capacity. For this, we use arguments from the matrix-geometric theory developed by Neuts [17] and the highly related spectral expansion technique (see for instance Mitrani and Mitra [16] and Mitrani and Chakka

[14]). In Sect. 6 we discuss the implications for the finite capacity model.

When the ergodic condition (6) holds, the unique probability vector $\overline{\pi}^{(\infty)} = (\pi_0^{(\infty)}, \pi_1^{(\infty)}, \pi_2^{(\infty)}, \ldots)$ satisfying $\overline{\pi}^{(\infty)} \mathcal{Q}^{(\infty)} = 0$ has the matrix-geometric form,

$$\pi_{j+1}^{(\infty)} = \pi_j^{(\infty)} R, \tag{7}$$

where the matrix R has all its eigenvalues *inside* the unit disc, and is the minimal nonnegative solution to the quadratic matrix equation,

$$\lambda I + R Q_d + R^2 M = 0, \tag{8}$$

(see Theorem 3.1.1 of Neuts [17]). For an interpretation of the elements of the matrix R, see Sect. 1.7 of [17].

In Sect. 4 we show that the matrix R has a full set of eigenvectors. When this is the case, we can rewrite (7) to the 'spectral expansion' form

$$\overline{\pi}_j^{(\infty)} = \sum_{k=0}^{N} \alpha_k \, (r_k)^j \, \overline{v}_k. \tag{9}$$

Here, $r_0, \ldots, r_N$ are the eigenvalues of the matrix R and $\overline{v}_0, \ldots, \overline{v}_N$ the corresponding left eigenvectors, i.e. $\overline{v}_k R = r_k \overline{v}_k$, $k = 0, 1, \ldots, N$. In Sect. 5 we show how the coefficients α_k can be found, once all the r_k and $\overline{v}_k$ are determined.

We now define the quadratic matrix polynomial $T(z)$ by,

$$T(z) := \lambda I + z Q_d + z^2 M. \tag{10}$$

Note that if $\overline{v}$ is an eigenvector of the matrix R corresponding to the eigenvalue r, then $\overline{v}$ is in the left nullspace of the matrix $T(r)$ (this can be seen by premultiplying (8) with $\overline{v}$), and so $\det[T(r)]=0$. It follows immediately that R is nonsingular, since $T(0) = \lambda I$ is nonsingular. Therefore, using (8), we may write

$$T(z) = (R - zI) \, R^{-1} \lambda I \, (I - zG), \tag{11}$$

where $G = \frac{1}{\lambda} RM$. To the author's knowledge, the factorisation (11) of the matrix $T(z)$ has not been reported before in the literature.

The matrix G is stochastic, and satisfies

$$\lambda G^2 + Q_d \, G + M = 0.$$

For more on the matrix G see Sect. 3.3 of Neuts [17].

The factorisation (11) is very useful, since $\det[R - zI]$ is precisely the characteristic polynomial of R, and for $z \neq 0$: $\det[I - zG] = z^{N+1} \det[\frac{1}{z} I - G]$. The polynomial $\det[T(z)]$ is of degree $2(N+1)$. In the ergodic case, the zeros of $\det[T(z)]$ *inside* the complex unit disk coincide with the eigenvalues of R, and the remaining zeros coincide with the eigenvalues of G^{-1}. In Sect. 4 we show that the zeros of $\det[T(z)]$ are all different, positive reals, and hence, so are all eigenvalues of R and G^{-1} (and also G).

Note that if some of the μ_i are zero, then G is singular, and the degree of the polynomial $\det[I - zG]$ becomes smaller than $N + 1$, see Remark 1.

4 Spectral Analysis

In this section we investigate the roots of the polynomial $\det[T(z)]$. We show that, unless $\lambda = \bar{p}M\bar{e}$, all these roots are different, real and positive. Some of the results in this section, concerned with the case where (6) holds, were already obtained by Daigle and Lucantoni [5]. In particular they found the number of zeros of $\det[T(z)]$ in $(0,1)$ and in $(1,\infty)$. However, they did not prove that these zeros are different but *assumed* they were, so that the spectral expansion (9) holds. Also, our methods are different from theirs: We use continuity arguments to prove our results, whereas they use the fact that the matrices λI, Q_Y and M are semidefinite.

Because of space limitations, most proofs in this section had to be omitted. Partial proofs concerning the case $\lambda < \bar{p}M\bar{e}$ can be found in [19][1]. Full proofs are given in the extended version of this paper, see [20].

Lemma 1. *For real $z \neq 0$ the matrix $T(z)$ has $N+1$ different real eigenvalues.*

The fact that the eigenvalues of $T(z)$ are real for real z, simplifies the analysis considerably. In the sequel we only consider the eigenvalues as real functions of the real variable z. Therefore, using Lemma 1, for real $z \neq 0$, we may denote the eigenvalues of $T(z)$ by

$$\tau_0(z) < \tau_1(z) < \ldots < \tau_N(z). \tag{12}$$

Obviously, $\tau_0(0) = \tau_1(0) = \ldots = \tau_N(0) = \lambda$.

Lemma 2. *All eigenvalues $\tau_k(z)$, $k = 0,1,\ldots,N$, are continuous functions of $z \in \mathbb{R}$.*

Lemma 3. *$\tau_N(1) = 0$, and for $k = 0,1,\ldots,N-1$ the equation $\tau_k(z) = 0$ has (at least) one solution for $z \in (0,1)$ and (at least) one solution for $z \in (1,\infty)$.*

Lemma 4. *If $\lambda < \bar{p}M\bar{e}$, then $\tau_N(z) = 0$ for some $z \in (0,1)$. If $\lambda > \bar{p}M\bar{e}$, then $\tau_N(z) = 0$ for some $z \in (1,\infty)$. If $\lambda = \bar{p}M\bar{e}$, then the zero of $\tau_N(z)$ at $z = 1$ is of multiplicity 2.*

Theorem 1. *If $\lambda \neq \bar{p}M\bar{e}$ then all roots of $\det[T(z)]$ are different. If $\lambda < \bar{p}M\bar{e}$ then $N+1$ of them lie in (0,1), one at $z = 1$ and N in $(1,\infty)$. If $\lambda > \bar{p}M\bar{e}$ then N of them lie in (0,1), one at $z = 1$ and $N+1$ in $(1,\infty)$.*

Proof. By Lemmas 3 and 4 we have found all $2(N+1)$ roots of $\det[T(z)]$ with the required positions. ⊓

Remark 1. Let n_0 be the number of states i, of the process $Y(t)$, for which $\mu_i = 0$. The degree of $\det[T(z)]$ is $2(N+1) - n_0$. If $n_0 > 0$, then the number of zeros of $\det[T(z)]$ in the interval $(1,\infty)$ becomes $N - n_0$ when $\lambda < \bar{p}M\bar{e}$, and $N+1-n_0$ when $\lambda > \bar{p}M\bar{e}$. This can be proved using the same arguments as in the analysis with strictly positive service rates.

---

[1] see ~http://www.cwi.nl/static/publications/reports/PNA-1997.html.

5   Steady State Distribution for the Infinite Buffer Model

In Sect. 4, we have shown that, under the ergodicity condition (6), R has $N+1$ *different* eigenvalues in the interval (0,1); therefore the equilibrium distribution can be written as in (9). We order the eigenvalues of R as $0 < r_0 < r_1 < \ldots < r_N < 1$, and construct the diagonal matrix $\Lambda = \mathrm{diag}[r_0, r_1, \ldots, r_N]$. The corresponding (normalised) eigenvectors $\overline{v}_0, \overline{v}_1, \ldots, \overline{v}_N$ compose the matrix V, $\overline{v}_k$ being the $k + 1^{\mathrm{st}}$ row of V. We have the (obvious) Jordan decomposition $R = V^{-1}\Lambda V$.

Having determined the r_k and $\overline{v}_k$, it remains to find the coefficients α_k in (9). Writing $\overline{\alpha} = (\alpha_0, \alpha_1, \ldots, \alpha_N)$, and using the obvious relation $\sum_{j=0}^{\infty} \overline{\pi}_j^{(\infty)} = \overline{p}$, we have,

$$\overline{\alpha}\,(I - \Lambda)^{-1}\,V = \overline{p}. \tag{13}$$

The probability vector $\overline{p}$ is given by (1). Equation (13) uniquely determines $\overline{\alpha}$.

Now, the steady state probability vectors $\overline{\pi}_j^{(\infty)}$, $j \geq 0$, are determined through (9). In particular, the marginal queue length distribution is given by

$$\mathbf{P}\{X^{(\infty)} = j\} = \overline{\alpha}\Lambda^j V\overline{\mathbf{e}} = \sum_{k=0}^{N} \alpha_k\,(r_k)^j\,\overline{v}_k\overline{\mathbf{e}}. \tag{14}$$

Remark 2. From (14) the moments of the number of customers in the system are easily determined, in particular the mean $\mathbb{E}\left[X^{(\infty)}\right]$ and the variance $\mathrm{var}\left[X^{(\infty)}\right]$. Using Little's formula we immediately obtain the mean processing time (or sojourn time) from $\mathbb{E}\left[X^{(\infty)}\right]$.

6   Finite Buffer Model

In this section we discuss the finite buffer model using the results obtained in Sect. 4. In the finite buffer model, if a customer arrives at the service station and finds L other customers present, the new customer is rejected and leaves the station. Therefore, the minimum rate at which an individual customer is served, is $\min_{i \in \{0,1,\ldots,N\}} \frac{\mu_i}{L}$. For the application of the model to ABR this is an important matter: Individual ABR connections are assigned a guaranteed Minimum Cell Rate (MCR). In our model the service rates μ_i, $i = 0, 1, \ldots, N$ and the buffer size L can be designed such that the chosen MCR is guaranteed. The parameter L determines the Call Acceptance Control policy for ABR. The rates μ_i are determined by the link capacity and the traffic characteristics of higher priority traffic.

Unlike the infinite buffer model, the steady-state probability vector for the finite buffer model does not satisfy a matrix geometric relation like (7). However, since the model is an irreducible finite Markov process, we know that the (unique) steady-state distribution exists, see Theorem 3.4 of Cohen [4]. Then, from the standard theory of difference equations (for instance by using Theorem S1.8 of

Gohberg et al. [9]), it follows that if the matrix $T(z)$ has a complete set of null-values and corresponding null-vectors, then the steady-state probabilities must be of the form,

$$\overline{\pi}_j^{(L)} = \sum_{k=0}^{2N+1} \alpha_k \left(r_k\right)^j \overline{v}_k, \qquad j = 0, 1, \ldots, L, \tag{15}$$

where $r_0, \ldots, r_{2N+1}$ are the zeros of $\det[T(z)]$ and $\overline{v}_0, \ldots, \overline{v}_{2N+1}$ are the corresponding left null-vectors. In Theorem 1 we showed that, unless $\lambda = \overline{p}M\overline{e}$, all the r_k are different (and positive real numbers), and therefore (15) holds.

It can be shown that the coefficients α_k are uniquely determined by combining (15) with the boundary equations,

$$\overline{\pi}_0^{(L)}\left[Q_Y - \lambda I\right] + \overline{\pi}_1^{(L)}M = \overline{0},$$
$$\overline{\pi}_{L-1}^{(L)}\lambda I + \overline{\pi}_L^{(L)}\left[Q_Y - M\right] = \overline{0},$$

and the normalisation $\sum_{j=0}^L \overline{\pi}_j^{(L)}\overline{e} = 1$.

7   Numerical Experiment

In this section, we illustrate how the results can be used in numerical experiments. We investigate how the queue length distribution is influenced by fast and slowly changing service modes. More precisely, we replace Q_Y, the generator of the process $Y(t)$, by sQ_Y, with $s \in (0, \infty)$. The factor s is a *time-scale* parameter.

If $s \to \infty$, the queue length distribution converges to that of the $M/M/1/L$ model (including $L = \infty$) with service capacity fixed at the average $\sum_{i=0}^N p_i\mu_i$. Also, if $s \downarrow 0$, in the limit, with probability p_i, customers arrive at an $M/M/1/L$ queue with fixed service capacity μ_i. If at least one μ_i is smaller than or equal to λ, the infinite model becomes unstable. In [20] these statements are proved formally, by first showing that the null-values of the (new) matrix $T(z)$, with Q_Y replaced by sQ_Y, are continuous functions of s.

We now illustrate these effects numerically. For this we use the model specified in [18]. In that model, $Y(t)$ is the number of higher priority connections on the link, for instance VBR (or CBR) connections. It is assumed that VBR connections are requested according to a Poisson process (with rate ν). Holding times of VBR connections are assumed to be drawn from an exponential distribution (with mean h). A maximum number N of VBR connections can be carried simultaneously on the link, and new requests for VBR connections when this maximum number is reached, are rejected and lost. Thus, $Y(t)$ is the queue length process of the $M/M/N/N$ loss model, and its generator Q_Y is given by

$$q_i^{(+)} = \nu, \ i = 0, 1, \ldots, N - 1,$$
$$q_i^{(-)} = \tfrac{i}{h}, \ i = 1, 2, \ldots, N.$$

All other off-diagonal entries are zero.

In particular the steady-state distribution of $Y(t)$ is:

$$p_i = \frac{(\rho_Y)^i/i!}{\sum_{m=0}^{N}(\rho_Y)^m/m!}, \qquad i = 0, 1, \ldots, N,$$

where $\rho_Y := \nu h$ is the *offered* load by VBR traffic. The mean number of VBR connections will be denoted by $\mathbb{E}[Y]$.

During the complete holding time, a VBR connection uses a fixed capacity 1 (this is no restriction). The capacity that is not required by VBR connections is assigned to ABR traffic. It is assumed that the link capacity is equal to N, i.e. when there are N VBR connections, no capacity is left over for ABR traffic. The matrix M is therefore determined by,

$$\mu_i = N - i, \qquad i = 0, 1, \ldots, N.$$

For more details on this model we refer to [18].

In our experiments, $N = 17$ (in accordance with data supplied by KPN Research for The Netherlands). Further, we also fix $\rho_Y = 10$. This value for ρ_Y is not of any particular interest, the resulting graphs are of the same form for other values of ρ_Y. Note however, that for fixed ρ_Y the steady-state probabilities p_i of the process $Y(t)$, and in particular the average number of service units available to the low-priority traffic ($N - \mathbb{E}[Y]$), are also fixed.

We set $\nu = 10s$ (and consequently $h = 1/s$), where, as before, $s \in (0, \infty)$ is a time-scale parameter.

For $s = \frac{1}{5}, 1$ and ∞, we have plotted, in Fig. 1, the mean number of ABR connections for increasing λ. The lowest curve, denoted by 'limit' ($s = \infty$), corresponds to the regular $M/M/1$ queue with fixed service capacity $N - \mathbb{E}[Y]$. We already indicated above that the curves converge to this lowest curve as $s \to \infty$. In Fig. 2 we have done the same for the variance of the number of ABR connections. Again we observe the indicated convergence as s increases.

Space limitations do not allow for an extensive numerical study at this point. However, we do spend a few words on the efficiency of our computations. In general, use of spectral methods instead of matrix-geometric routines to find the matrix R, improve computational efficiency. Using matrix-geometric techniques, the computation time increases with L (for the finite buffer model), and with λ (for the infinite buffer model). The computational effort using spectral methods is insensitive to these parameters. For a comparison of the spectral method with traditional matrix-geometric methods, see Mitrani and Chakka [14]. However, it must be noted that the matrix-geometric techniques used in that comparison are not the most efficient. For an improvement of these techniques, see Latouche and Ramaswami [12]. Still, these procedures are sensitive to L and λ.

In our case, numerical evaluation is further facilitated by the fact that the nullvalues of $T(z)$ are positive real numbers. They can essentially be found using bisection.

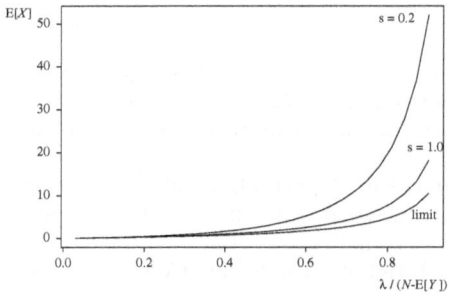

Fig. 1.

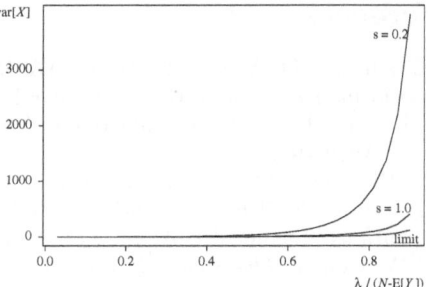

Fig. 2.

8 Concluding Remarks

In this paper we have studied a queueing model with a server that changes its service rate according to a finite birth and death process. Both the cases of an infinite and a finite buffer were considered. This model captures many features of ABR traffic at the connection level on an ATM link, in the presence of other traffic types with higher priority (CBR, VBR). Under exponentiality assumptions, regarding the distributions of the service requirements and the process regulating the available service capacity (finite birth-death process), we were able to give a detailed analysis of the distribution of the number of ABR connections. Although the assumption on the exponential distribution of the service requirements is restrictive, we believe that the model is useful to gain qualitative insights into the performance of ABR traffic, because of the detailed analysis. Currently, these models are used in joint experiments with KPN Research for performance studies of ABR traffic. In this paper, only a small numerical experiment was presented to illustrate the effect of the varying service rate on the queue length distribution. We observed that, depending on time-scale differences, ignoring the service variability and fixing the capacity at the mean, can be a very bad approximation.

Through Little's formula we also obtained the mean processing time. Of course, in practice one would also like to know the variance of the processing time and possibly higher moments. Also the (mean) processing time conditioned on the amount of work is a valuable performance measure. These issues are the subject of our current research.

Acknowledgement
The author is indebted to dr. J.L. van den Berg (KPN Research) and dr. I. Norros (VTT) for interesting discussions about the modelling aspects of ABR, and to Professor J.W. Cohen for several discussions and comments. The author wants to thank in particular Professor O.J. Boxma for reading previous versions of this paper and providing many helpful comments on them.

References

1. E. Altman, D. Artiges, K. Traore. *On the integration of best-effort and guaranteed performance services.* INRIA Research Report 3222 (1997).
2. The ATM Forum Technical Committee. *Traffic Management Specification.* Version 4.0, April 1996.
3. S. Blaabjerg, G. Fodor, M. Telek, A.T. Andersen. *A partially blocking-queueing system with CBR/VBR and ABR/UBR arrival streams.* Institute of Telecommunications, Technical University of Denmark (internal report, 1997).
4. J.W. Cohen. *The Single Server Queue.* North-Holland Publishing Company, Amsterdam, 2nd edition, 1982.
5. J.N. Daigle, D.M. Lucantoni. *Queueing systems having phase-dependent arrival and service rates.* Numerical Solution of Markov Chains (1991), W.J. Stewart (ed.), 161–202.
6. G. Falin, Z. Khalil, D.A. Stanford. *Performance analysis of a hybrid switching system where voice messages can be queued.* Queueing Systems 16 (1994), 51-65.
7. H.R. Gail, S.L. Hantler, B.A. Taylor. *On a preemptive Markovian queue with multiple servers and two priority classes.* Mathematics of Operations Research 17 (1992), 365-391.
8. H.R. Gail, S.L. Hantler, B.A. Taylor. *Spectral analysis of $M/G/1$ and $G/M/1$ type Markov chains.* Advances in Applied Probability 28 (1996), 114-165.
9. I. Gohberg, P. Lancaster, L. Rodman. *Matrix Polynomials.* Academic Press, New York, 1982.
10. R.A. Horn and C.R. Johnson. *Matrix Analysis.* Cambridge University Press (1987).
11. L.A. Kulkarni, S.-Q. Li. *Performance analysis of rate based feedback control for ATM networks.* Proceedings of IEEE INFOCOM '97, Kobe, Japan (1997), 795–804.
12. G. Latouche, V. Ramaswami. *A logarithmic reduction algorithm for quasi-birth-death processes.* J. Appl. Probab. 30 (1993), no. 3, 650–674.
13. M. Marcus, H. Minc. *A Survey of Matrix Theory and Matrix Inequalities.* Allyn and Bacon, Inc., Boston, 1964.
14. I. Mitrani, R. Chakka. *Spectral expansion solution for a class of Markov models: Application and comparison with the matrix-geometric method.* Performance Evaluation 23 (1995), 241-260.
15. I. Mitrani, P.J.B. King. *Multiprocessor systems with preemptive priorities.* Performance Evaluation 1 (1981), 118-125.
16. I. Mitrani, D. Mitra. *A spectral expansion method for random walks on semi-infinite strips.* In: Iterative Methods in Linear Algebra, ed. by R. Beauwens and P. de Groen, Proceedings of the IMACS international symposium, Brussels, Belgium (1991).
17. M.F. Neuts. *Matrix-geometric Solutions in Stochastic Models - An Algorithmic Approach.* The Johns Hopkins University Press, Baltimore, 1981.
18. R. Núñez Queija, O.J. Boxma. *Analysis of a multi-server queueing model of ABR.* To appear in J. Applied Mathematics and Stochastic Analysis.
19. R. Núñez Queija. *Steady-state analysis of a queue with varying service rate.* CWI Report PNA-R9712 (1997).
20. R. Núñez Queija. *A queue with varying service rate for ABR.* Internal report (1998).
21. B.N. Parlett. *The Symmetric Eigenvalue Problem.* Prentice-Hall, Englewood Cliffs, 1980.
22. S.F. Yashkov. *Mathematical problems in the theory of shared-processor queueing systems.* J. Soviet Mathematics 58 (1992), no. 2, 101–147.

Simulative Performance Evaluation of the Temporary Pseudonym Method for Protecting Location Information in GSM Networks

Peter Reichl, Dogan Kesdogan[*], Klaus Junghärtchen, Marko Schuba

Department of Computer Science • Informatik IV (Communication Systems)
Aachen University of Technology • D-52056 Aachen • Germany
{peter, dogan, klausj, marko}@i4.informatik.rwth-aachen.de

Abstract. The information about the location of a mobile user belongs to the most sensitive data within mobile communication networks. One possibility to protect it especially against curious insiders with access to the network consists of storing the actual information in so-called "home trusted devices" and using temporary pseudonyms for user registration in the network databases. This paper presents a detailed OPNET simulation and evaluation of the signalling cost of this approach compared to standard GSM.

1 Introduction

In contrast to previous mobile communication networks, GSM offers a much higher level of security to its users and the network operator, e.g. by authentication and speech encryption procedures as well as the use of temporary identities protecting the user's privacy. Despite these features, there are some security weaknesses in the GSM standard, e.g. the issue of protecting location information about the user (as it is contained within the GSM signalling information). The temporary pseudonym method [11, 7] is one recent approach for protecting this rather sensitive information against attacks coming from inside the network (especially against corrupt network providers). This paper presents a thorough simulative investigation and performance evaluation of this method.

GSM networks have roughly the following structure [13]: The total supply area of the network consists of several MSC areas (managed by a Mobile Switching Center MSC each) which are subdivided into several Location Areas LA (each of them managed by a Base Station Controler BSC), each being constituted of several cells, where a respective Base Transceiver Station BTS emits and receives radio waves in a certain frequency spectrum. The distributed location management consists of a central database, the Home Location Register HLR, containing the respective current MSC area of each user, whereas for each MSC area a local database, the Visitor Location Register VLR, contains the current LA in the respective MSC area.

Each user moves within the supply area, and her mobility is managed by procedures for mobile originated (MO) calls setup, mobile terminated (MT) calls setup, Handover and Location Update (LU). The latter one is initiated by the Mobile Station (MS) while leaving one LA and entering a new one and performs the update of the user location information in the network databases (HLR and VLRs). The

[*] The work of Dogan Kesdogan was supported by the Gottlieb Daimler- and Karl Benz-Foundation

R. Puigjaner et al. (Eds.): Tools'98, LNCS 1469, pp. 105-116, 1998
© Springer-Verlag Berlin Heidelberg 1998

procedure is handled locally as soon as both LAs belong to the same MSC, otherwise the MSC of the new LA forwards the LU request to the HLR which thereupon cancels the record in the VLR of the old MSC and confirms the insertion of the new record in the VLR of the new MSC which in turn acknowledges the MS request.

The so-called Gateway MSC (GMSC) allows to establish MT calls from the Public Switched Telephone Network PSTN to a GSM subscriber. In order to route the call to the MSC in whose area the MS of the respective user currently is roaming, the GMSC requests routing information from the HLR and the respective VLR. The MSC then manages the establishment of a radio connection between the MS and the BTS of the cell where the user currently is registred.

There are already several different approaches for protecting the location of a mobile user (see [7] for a comprehensive overview). This paper focusses on the concept of "temporary pseudonyms", which has been developed in order to comply with the following demands:

- the user location information should be protected as long as the user moves with the mobile switched on and no MT call arriving;
- the implementation should avoid major changes of the GSM standard and should allow real-time communication;
- the responsibility for sensitive data should be moved to the user as far as possible.

Having introduced the idea of temporary pseudonyms in section 2, the following section 3 presents the results of a detailed OPNET simulation of the TP method compared to standard GSM signalling, before some concluding remarks finish the paper. Note that the companion paper [11] is much more focussed towards investigating this method analytically and discussing a generalization of it in depth.

2 The Method of Temporary Pseudonyms

"Temporary Pseudonyms" (TP) have been proposed first in [9, 10]. The basic idea relies heavily on the concept of trusted parties: In the simplest case, this means that a Home Trusted Device (HTD) is used for storing sensitive data (authentication keys, location information etc.) or even handles the complete location management (thus replacing the VLR) confidentially. It is important to note that the HTD is completely under the control of the user.

In the TP method, the trusted region is no longer used for saving the actual LAI of the user. Instead, the basic idea consists of protecting a mobile user's location information (within a mobile network) by protecting her identity. Hence, the user is assigned a pseudonym (Pseudo Mobile Subscriber Identity PMSI). As long as the user is registered under a pseudonym, the network provider may know that a user under a certain pseudonym currently is at a certain place, but he cannot connect the real identity of the user with her actual location.

The pseudonym is generated time-synchronously in the MS and the HTD, i.e. both stations generate at the same time a random number by using identically parameterized random generators PRG (the seed for initializing the PRG must have previously been exchanged between MS and HTD). This random number works as an *implicit address*, i.e. as "identity" of the user, under which she may register in the data bases (HLR and VLR) of the mobile network. Within the procedures in the GSM network, the implicit address plays the role of the standard IMSI (International Mobile

Subscriber Identification Number). [5, 8] present a much more detailed discussion of implicit addressing.

As soon as a call is arriving at the network, the HTD of the user (which is reachable e.g. through a fixed network like ISDN) is asked for the currently used pseudonym. This information allows the network provider to find out the necessary location information and to set up the call as usual. Note that the user remains anonymous as long as no call arrives for him from outside. If moreover the user uses prepaid phone cards, even MO calls may take place anonymously. Note that the user must not be assigned an unambiguous secret key in order to prevent the possibility of linking her often changing pseudonyms. Encryption of the data sent via the air interface during an MO call is guaranteed by the MS itself informing the network provider about the key that is used for communication.

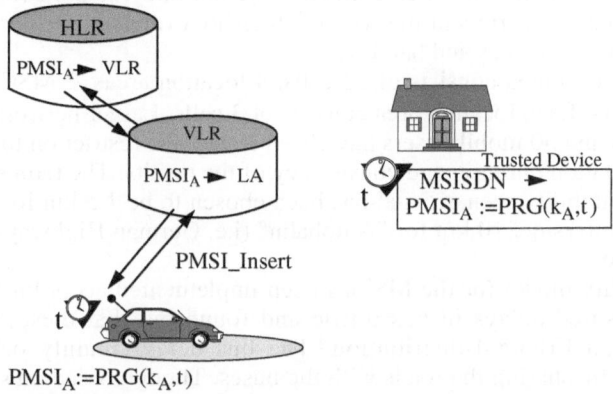

Fig. 1. Generation and insertion of a new pseudonym

Fig. 1 demonstrates how pseudonym changes between MS and HTD are performed in time-synchronous manner. Changing them exactly while changing the location area, i.e. by registering in the new location area under a different pseudonym (without cancelling the old one, because otherwise the two pseudonyms could be linked) might be the most efficient way, because then any information about a direction of the pseudonym is hidden. On the other hand, the user anonymity is lost (as e.g. a constant driving velocity yields constant pseudonym changes which can be linked). Note that it is not possible to directly inform the HTD about the pseudonym update as every message between the user and her HTD allows the user's identity to be combined with her location area. This may be solved by drawing the time between two changes from an exponential (memoryless) distribution. This approach moreover prevents situations in which the channel capacity of the mobile network might be exceeded as all users have to update their pseudonyms at the same time.

3 Simulation Results

The TP method has been integrated into an existing GSM model for the simulation platform OPNET [3]. The model consists of the OPNET network layer for building the network topology, the OPNET node layer for modelling the data flow within network components, and the OPNET process layer, in which the behaviour of the components is characterized by finite automatas. In this model, the main GSM hardware and signalling procedures are simulated (see fig. 2). Included are mobile stations (MS), base transceiver stations (BTS), base station controlers (BSC), mobile switching centers (MSC), visited location registers (VLR), home location registers (HLR), gateway mobile switching centers (GMSC) and the public switched telephone network (PSTN).

Signalling has been modelled close to the GSM standard down to layer 3 of the protocol model. In addition to [3], packets sent over the SS7 network are piggybacked by appropriate packets of the lower layers TCAP, SCCP and MTP3.

The simulation comprises the procedures Mobile Originated Call, Mobile Terminated Call, (Inter-BSC, Inter-MSC) Location Update, (Inter-BSC, Inter-MSC) Handover and Paging. Service handling and authentication are not integrated, in contrast to System Information and Measurement messages, which are evaluated for deciding on the initiation of location updates and handovers.

The simulation area consists of 12 cells, 4 location areas, 2 MSC/VLRs and $N = 21$ mobile users. Each location area consists of 3 cells. Larger networks with up to 40 cells, 4 MSCs and 50 mobile users have been tested, the restriction to the smaller one is due to simulation duration and consistency of the results. The radius of the cells depends on the mobility scenario and has been chosen to be 1.5 km for a city scenario, 15 km for countryside, 10 km for "Autobahn" (i.e. German Highway) and 9 km for a mixed scenario.

The mobility model for the MS has been implemented according to results from [2] who measured delays in bus traffic and found out that these delays could be modeled by an Erlang-4-distribution. The bus delays mainly occur due to the individual traffic sharing the roads with the buses. Though based on slightly different driving conditions (e.g. time schedule at every bus stop), the results can be transfered to individual traffic. Hence, the mean delay may be calculated as "perturbation" of the usual mean driving time according to

$$t_{mean} = t_{min} + X_{Erl} \cdot t_{min} = (1 + X_{Erl}) \cdot t_{min} \qquad (3.1)$$

where X_{Erl} is drawn from an Erlang-4 distribution. This yields a mean simulated speed of

$$v_{mean} = \frac{v_{max}}{1 + X_{Erl}}. \qquad (3.2)$$

This leads to the following mobility algorithm that is executed for every mobile node during the simulation:
1. Mobile users are distributed randomly across the simulation area.
2. Each mobile user draws a random destination from a uniform distribution.
3. Each mobile node has parameters indicating the real mean speed and the maximum speed. Thus the delay for part of the way and the simulated speed may be calculated.
4. At certain times each mobile node decides whether it performs a 90° turn towards the destination or not. The distance between these points and the turn probability are given as parameters and depend on the simulation scenario; they have been calculated based on typical respective scenarios in the region of Aachen.
5. The mobile node moves according to its calculated speed and direction.
6. If the destination is reached, a new destination as chosen according to step 2, and the algorithm continues from step 3 onwards.

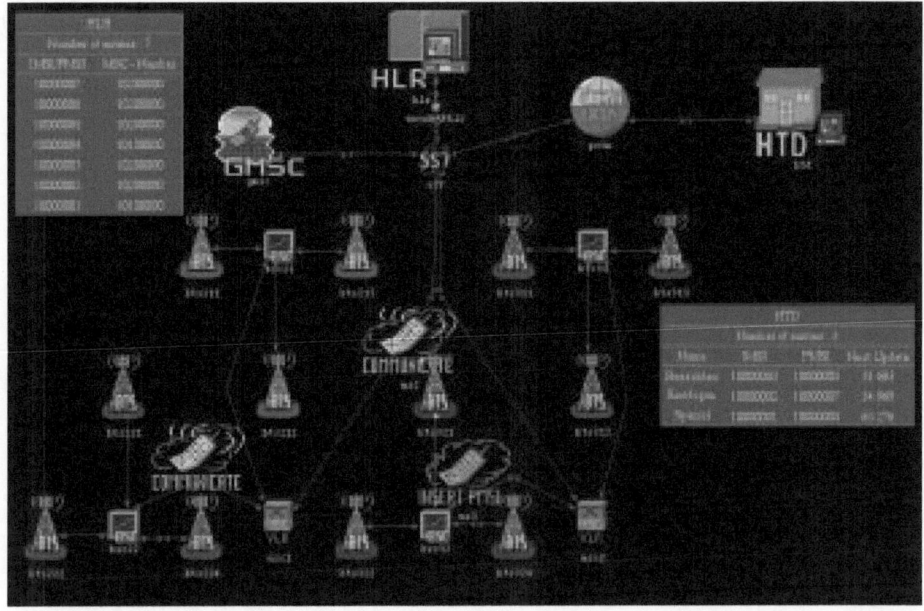

Fig. 2. The OPNET model for the simulated GSM network

Note that the mean speed of mobile nodes has been assumed to be 10 *km/h* in the city, 65 *km/h* in the countryside, 100 *km/h* in the "Autobahn" and 58 *km/h* in the mixed scenario (cf. [12]).

Measurements in real mobile networks [1] state that during the busy hour approximately 2/3 of the calls are mobile originated whereas 1/3 are mobile terminated calls. Measured mean call setup rates are around 0.45 calls/hour for mobile originated calls and 0.225 calls/hour for mobile terminated ones, yielding a global call interarrival time of about 5333 seconds. Furthermore, the mean duration of mobile terminated calls has been measured to be 115 seconds in contrast to 105 seconds for outgoing calls. According to [4, 6], call holding times as well as interarrival times may be drawn from exponential distributions.

Finally, the length of the pseudonyms has been set to 100 bits, which is perfect for avoiding collisions between pseudonyms (as derived in [11]).

3.1 Variation of the Mobility Behaviour

In this section it is demonstrated how changes in the mobility behaviour effect the load of the mobile network. To this end, the three scenarios "city", "countryside" and "Autobahn" are explored. The simulation parameters are given in table 1.

Fig. 3 shows the total signalling load generated by one user in the mobile network. On the one hand, the network load depends strongly on the mobility environment of the user. A user in the countryside scenario with large location areas and medium speed causes less load than a user who is fast or moves in areas with small cell sizes. This demonstrates the influence of the rate of location area updates. On the other hand, the difference between the signaling in the GSM network and with the TP method appears to increase proportionally to the mobility behaviour as well, being 75% in the countryside, 80% in the city and 96% in the Autobahn scenario.

	city	countryside	Autobahn
cell radius [km]	1.5	15	10
speed [km/h]	10	65	100
turning probability	0.7	0.4	0.2
distance between two turns	0.5	3.0	9.0
PMSI updates/h	2.4	1.88	3.9
time between two PMSI updates [min]	25	32	15
PMSI length [bit]	100		
call setup rate MO [attempts/h]	0.45		
time between two MO calls [min]	133		
call setup rate MT [attempts/h]	0.225		
time between two MT calls [min]	266		

Table 1. Simulation parameters for variation of mobility behaviour

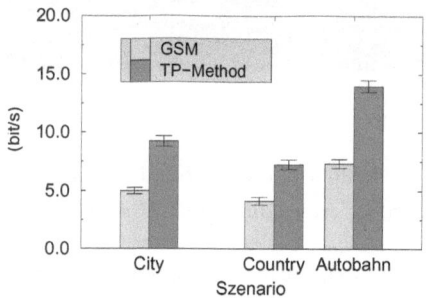

Fig. 3. Total network load in the three scenarios

Fig. 4. Mean duration of the procedures for location update and pseudonym change

The mean duration of the procedures for location update and pseudonym change is demonstrated in fig. 4. On the air interface the location update procedure uses the TMSI for either method. Thus the length of the PMSI here is of no influence at all. Within the SS7 network PCM30-connections are used. The 64 kbit/s speed of their signalling channel is high enough to prevent the location update delay from rising heavily. The PMSI Insertion procedure has to send one pseudonym across the air interface. Due to its length and the low rate of the dedicated signalling channel the duration of the procedure increases by 67%. Nevertheless it is not as time-critical as a handover procedure.

Where does the high signalling load come from? The responsible factor turns out to be the share of the location update procedure, which is extended for the PMSI insertion procedure, in the global load. Fig. 5 left shows that in the chosen simulation environment the location updates (inter-MSC and inter-BSC) cause nearly 60% of the global load, whereas the low impact of the call procedures results from the call rates being adjusted to the values given in [1]. With the TP method being implemented, location updates and pseudonym insertions amount to 74% of the global load. The load increase under the TP method is caused by the concept of adapting the pseudonym change rate to the location update rate in order to reveal as little as possible over the connection of a movement path and the corresponding pseudonym. Hence, increasing the location update rate yields a load increase under the TP method by the location update expense plus the pseudonym change expense. As we use a modified Inter-MSC-location-update procedure for changing pseudonyms, this corresponds approximately to double the expense.

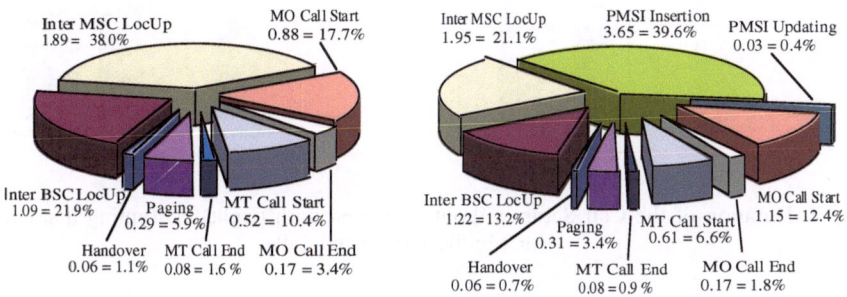

Fig. 5. Distribution of the global load w.r.t. the different GSM procedures (in bit/s) for the case of the city scenario

Fig. 6 shows the share of system information and measurement messages with respect to the total load. Note that system information messages are between 22 and 23 bytes long and cause – sent continuously every 0.235 seconds – more than 90% of the total load, whereas measurement messages are sent every 0.48 seconds and cause about 4% of the total load.

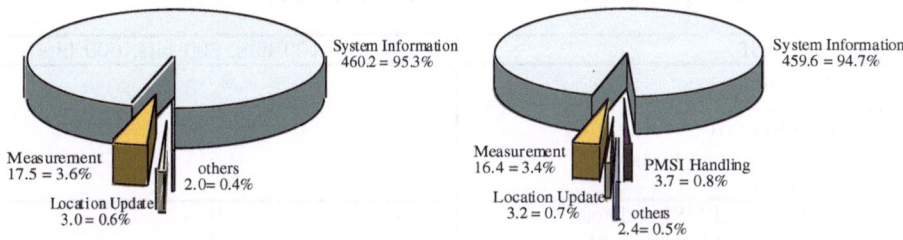

Fig. 6. Load distribution to the different procedures for the GSM network (left) and the TP method (right) with system information and measurement messages

Fig. 7 finally presents the call setup time for incoming and outgoing calls. The call setup times for both kinds of calls coincide as long as no (public key encrypted) session key is sent from the mobile to the network. Conveying a session key causes a delay of 0.66 seconds per direction if sent over a dedicated signalling channel with netto bit rate of 782 bit/s. The pseudonym has to be sent twice with an initial message in order to prevent two users from accessing the same traffic channel: First a random number is sent from the user to the network which afterwards is contained in the answer of the network to indicate that the user is now owner of the channel which is assigned by the network. Then the initial message is sent "piggybacked" to a layer 2 LAPDm SABM-message which is answered by an exact copy of it within an LAPDm UA-message (see [13]). If the mobile does not receive an exact copy of its initial message, it has to clear the connection.

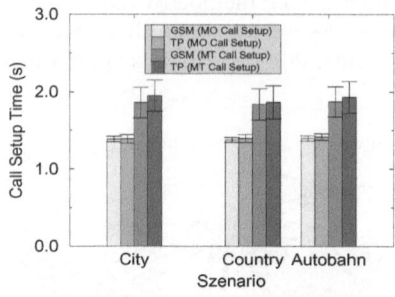 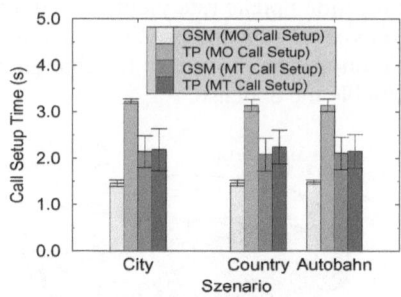

Fig. 7. Duration of the Call Setup without (left) and with (right) encrypting a session key for Mobile Originated calls

3.2 Variation of the Pseudonym Length

This section deals with the influence of the pseudonym length to the signalling load in the mobile network. The signalling under the TP method is compared to standard GSM signalling. Moreover it is investigated how the load behaves if instead of the TMSI (Temporary Mobile Subscriber Identity as used in standard GSM) in all relevant signalling messages the IMSI or the PMSI, resp., are used. The mobility behaviour and pseudonym change rates are modelled as averages over the values shown in the last section. The important parameters are listed in table 2.

Lenght of PMSI	50 bits, 100 bits, 200 bits, 600 bits
cell radius [km]	9
speed [km/h]	58
turning probability	0.43
distance between two turns	0.5
PMSI updates/h	6
time between two PMSI updates [min]	10
call setup rate MO [attempts/h]	1.2
time between two MO calls [min]	50
call setup rate MT [attempts/h]	0.6
time between two MT calls [min]	100

Table 2. Simulation parameters for variation of pseudonym length

As in the previous section, the TP method shows again a significant load increase in the different scenarios compared to the signalling expense of standard GSM. Fig. 8 left shows for example that the total network load is doubled. Moreover, the load varies linearly with the pseudonym length. Note that a pseudonym length of 600 bits has only be simulated to demonstrate the trend of the load development. It may be shown [7, 11] that in fact a pseudonym length of 70 bits is sufficient for preventing two users from choosing the same pseudonym.

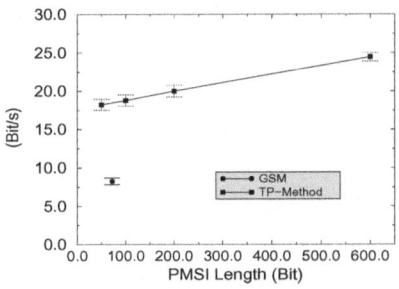 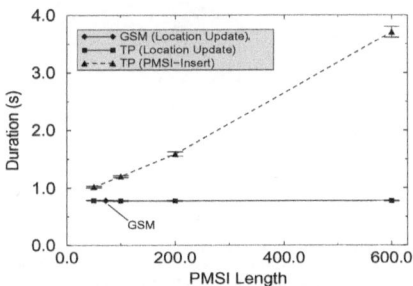

Fig. 8. Global load (left) and duration for location update and PMSI insertion (right), depending on the length of the pseudonym

The duration of location update and call setup procedures does not depend on the length of the pseudonym as shown in fig. 8 right, the reason being that the location update and call setup procedures use the TMSI while sending messages on the air interface; only in the fixed network with its much higher transmission capacity GSM uses IMSI, whereas TP uses PMSI. In contrast, the duration of the PMSI insertion procedure is heavily depending on the PMSI length, as the new PMSI has to be transmitted on the air interface, where e.g. 100 bits long pseudonyms delay the insertion by 128 ms.

3.3 Variation of Pseudonym Change Rate

This section explores the influence of the pseudonym change rate on the load of the GSM network. We have investigated pseudonym change intervals from two minutes up to one hour. The mobility and call model is the same as in the previous section. The parameters correspond to those of table 2 for a PMSI length of 100 bits except for those listed in table 3.

PMSI updates/hour	30	6	2	1
time between two PMSI updates [min]	2	10	30	60

Table 3. Simulation parameters for variation of pseudonym change rates

Fig. 9 left shows that the shorter the interval between two pseudonym changes, the larger the increase in the global load and vice versa. Note that the load may be influenced to a much larger extent than e.g. by the call rate (or PMSI length, as further experiments have shown). Fig. 9 right demonstrates how the PMSI insertion procedure becomes more and more responsible for the total network load: For the time between two PMSI changes being 600 sec (corresponding to 6 changes/hour) the insertion causes 47% whereas for a time of 120 sec between two changes (i.e. 30 changes/hour) this share is already approximately 81%. The reason for this lies in the "length" of the PMSI insertion procedure (i.e. the sum of lengths of all respective messages) which is a couple of times the length of the PMSI. Hence it can be concluded that increasing the PMSI exchange rate has much more effect than prolonging the PMSI.

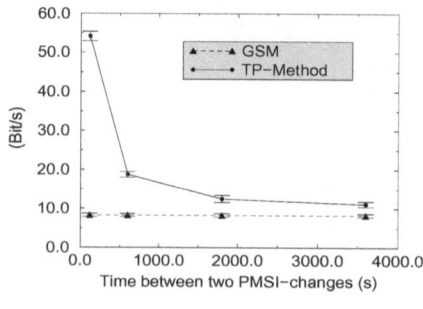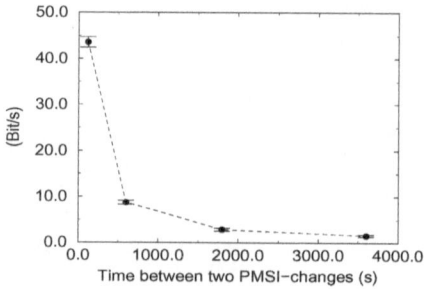

Fig. 9. Global load for different PMSI change rates (left)
and load caused by the PMSI insertion procedure (right)

Fig. 10 shows the distribution of the total load at the different GSM interfaces. Obviously, the air interface U_m is affected most by the signalling of a user. As the dedicated signalling channels at the air interface are assigned exclusively to the users, whereas the signalling messages of all users use the ressources of the same SS7 network, the load in the SS7 network must be viewed in relation to the user number. A load increase of 0.1 bit/s (as caused by increasing the pseudonym change rate from 2 to 6 changes/hour) increases the total load in the SS7 network for a user number of 1 million by approximately 98 Kbit/s.

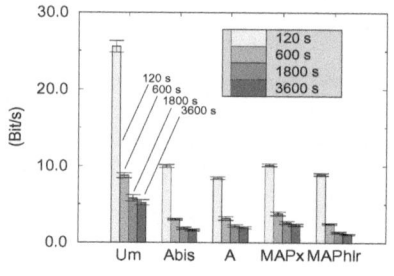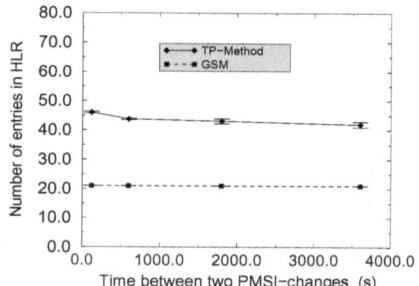

Fig. 10. Load at different air interfaces
for different pseudonym change rates

Fig. 11. Average number of entries in the
HLR database

Finally, the average number A of entries in the HLR has been simulated. In [11], we have derived analytically that for the case of our TP scenario, $A = 2 \cdot N$ (N being the number of active users, 21 in our case), i.e. double the value as in standard GSM. Fig. 11 shows the close matching between theoretical prediction and measurement. The slight increase for the case of very high pseudonym change rates is caused by an artifact: Drawing the TTL from an exponential distribution one may get values of under some seconds, which in turn may cause the deletion of a pseudonym during an on-going signalling procedure due to normal transmission delay and possible high signalling traffic in the network. To avoid simulation errors, the minimum TTL has been set to values between 2 and 10 seconds, thus guaranteeing that the use of a pseudonym is finished before it is deleted. Therefore, increasing pseudonym update rates may yield new pseudonyms arriving faster than they can be served (i.e. deleted), thus causing an increasing number of entries in the database.

3.4 Variation of the Call Rate

In this section the effect of varying the call attempt rate is investigated. The ratio between outgoing and incoming calls is assumed to be 2:1. The parameter values of table 3 remain unchanged except for the ones listed in table 4. Note that the sending of a transmission key is neglected here.

call setup rate MO [attempts/h]	4	2.4	1.6	1.2
time between two MO calls [min]	15	25	38	50
call setup rate MT [attempts/h]	2	1.2	0.8	0.6
time between two MT calls [min]	30	50	75	100
average time between call attempts [sec]	600	1000	1500	2000
PMSI updates/hour	6			

Table 4. Simulation parameters for variation of call attempt rates

Fig. 12 shows two characteristic results. It may be concluded that the total network load as well as the load on the HLR interfaces increases with the rate of arriving calls. The increase is equal for the GSM network and the TP method, hence the request at the user's HTD does not matter because of the high transmission rates.

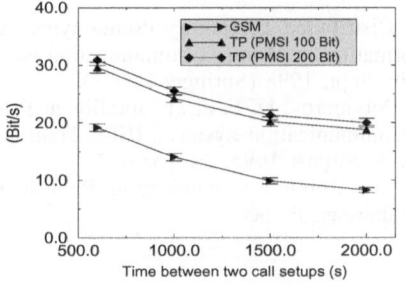 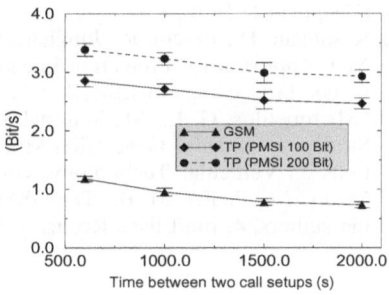

Fig. 12. Global load for varying call attempt rates (left)
and load on the HLR interface (right)

4 Concluding Remarks

This paper has dealt with the question of how to protect information about user location against insider attackers in a GSM network. It has been demonstrated that the TP method yields feasible solutions to this problem by hiding the relation between user identity and location with pseudonyms whose unavoidable changes can be protected from being linked together by an attacker. The performance aspects of this approach have been thoroughly investigated by a detailed OPNET simulation and evaluation that has dealt with the influence of mobility behaviour, pseudonym length, their change rate and the call setup rate on the performance of the method.

References

1. Brass, V.; Fuhrmann, W. F.: Traffic Engineering Experience from Operating Cellular Networks. IEEE Communication Magazine, August 1997, 66–71.
2. Dauber, F.-J.: QoS Parameters of Bus Traffic with respect to Time-Tables and Subsequent Variability. Ph.D. Thesis (in German). Aachen University of Technology, July 1986.
3. Institute Eurecom, Delta Partners: A GSM OPNET Model (incl. documentation). © 1994–95.
4. Fuhrmann, W.; Brass, V.: Performance Aspects of the GSM Radio Subsystem. Proceedings of the IEEE, vol. 82 no. 9, 1994, 1449–1466.
5. Farber, D. J.; Larson, K. C.: Network Security via Dynamic Process Renaming. Proceedings of the 4th Data Communications Symposion, Quebec (Canada), Oct. 1975, 8/13–8/18.
6. Guérin, Roch A.: Channel Occupancy Time Distribution in a Cellular Radio System. IEEE Transactions on Vehicular Technology, vol. VT-35 no. 3, 1987, 89–99.
7. Junghärtchen, K.: Simulative Investigation of Methods for Protecting Location Information in Mobile Networks. Diploma Thesis. Aachen University of Technology, November 1997 (in German).
8. Karger, P. A.: Non-Discretionary Access Control for Decentralized Computing Systems. M.Sc. Thesis, Techn. Report MIT/LCS/TR-179, MIT 1975.
9. Kesdogan, D.; Fouletier, X.: Secure Location Information Management in Cellular Radio Systems. Proceedings of the IEEE Wireless Communication Systems Symposion WCSS'95, Long Island, 1995, 35–46.
10. Kesdogan, D.; Federrath, H.; Jerichow, A.; Pfitzmann, A.: Location Management Strategies increasing Privacy in Mobile Communication Systems. Proceedings of the 12th IFIP International Information Security Conference SEC'96, May 1996 (Chapman & Hall).
11. Kesdogan, D.; Reichl, P.; Junghärtchen, K.: Distributed Temporary Pseudonyms: A New Approach for Protecting Location Information in Mobile Communication Networks. Proceedings of ESORICS'98. Louvain, Sept. 1998 (Springer LNCS).
12. Lyberopoulos, G. L.; Markoulidakis, J. G.; Polymeros, D. F. et al.: Intelligent Paging Strategies for Third Generation Mobile Telecommunication Systems. IEEE Transactions on Vehicular Technology, vol. 44 no. 3, August 1995, 543–553.
13. Mouly, M.; Pautet, M. B.: The GSM System for Mobile Communication. Published by the authors, 4, rue Elisée Reclus, F-91120 Palaiseau, France.

A Model Driven Monitoring Approach to Support the Multi-view Performance Analysis of Parallel Responsive Applications

Javier García; Joaquín Entrialgo; Francisco Suárez; Daniel F. García

Universidad de Oviedo
Area de Arquitectura y Tecnología de Computadores
Campus de Viesques s/n, 33204 Gijón, Spain
E-mail: javier@atc01.etsiig.uniovi.es

Abstract. This paper describes an approach to carry out performance analysis of parallel responsive applications. The approach is mainly based on measurement, but in addition, the idea of driving the measurement process (application instrumentation and monitoring) by a behavioral model is introduced. Using this model, highly comprehensible performance information can be collected. The combined use of both modeling and measurement techniques is referred to as Model Driven Monitoring. The whole approach relies on this behavioral model, one instrumentation method and two tools, one for monitoring and the other for visualization and analysis. Each of these is briefly described, and the steps to carry out performance analysis based on them are clearly defined. They are explained by means of a case study. Finally, one method to evaluate the intrusiveness of the monitoring approach is proposed, and the intrusiveness results for the case study are presented.

1 Introduction

Monitoring tools for parallel computers have been a very active field of research for the last decade, as they have always been considered indispensable for parallel application development. Most of them are oriented to measuring the computational behavior of large scientific applications [5,11] (normally related to numerical simulation of very complex systems), providing two typical views of application behavior: 1) how the application programming structures (processes, threads, procedures, etc.) are executed — *program execution view* —; and 2) how the resources are utilized — *resource utilization view* —. Starting from the measurements obtained according to these views, the metrics which explain the performance of these applications, e.g. the *execution time*, the *speedup* and so forth, can be easily calculated.

However, other types of applications, such as the so called *responsive applications* [7], cannot be fully understood using these two views exclusively. *Responsive applications* are constantly interchanging information with the environment in which they work. They receive external requests, elaborate responses and issue them to the environment. Thus, their behavior could well be understood in terms of *external events* (external request arrivals) and the sequences of partially ordered activities (*activity execution paths*) carried out in response to these events; and their performance should be expressed by

R. Puigjaner et al. (Eds.): Tools'98, LNCS 1469, pp. 117–128, 1998.
© Springer-Verlag Berlin Heidelberg 1998

means of two metrics: *response time* and *processing throughput* for each external event. All of this represents an additional behavioral view — *activity execution path view* — complementary to those offered by standard monitoring tools.

Therefore, monitoring tools for parallel systems (those oriented to executing responsive applications) should ideally provide performance information for this *activity execution path view*, in order that analysts can asses application performance (*response times* and *throughputs*) precisely and easily. The use of such monitoring tools must inevitably be driven by a modeling process. Thus, applications must first be modeled (defining for each external event the sequence of activities which make up the response), and later, measured in accordance with their models. This special monitoring procedure provides a full method to carry out application performance analysis (in contrast to simulation or analytical modeling), which takes advantage of the full integrated use of modeling and measurement techniques. We refer to it as *Model Driven Monitoring* (MDM) [3].

In this paper, we present the *MDM approach* to support the performance analysis of responsive applications developed on parallel architectures. In Section 2, an overview of the approach is shown. Section 3 outlines the main characteristics of the behavioral model used as the basis of the approach. Section 4 briefly describes the instrumentation system and the monitoring tool developed to support the approach on two different parallel architectures. Section 5 summarizes the use of the approach by means of a case study. Finally, in Section 6, the problem of monitor intrusiveness is posed, and a simple method to calculate the instrumentation impact on application response time is presented.

2   The MDM Approach For Performance Analysis: Overview

The aim of the MDM approach is to provide a complete method to support the performance analysis of responsive applications developed on multiprocessors. The approach is based on the following elements:

1. *A behavioral model* which allows the definition of application behavior in terms of external events and the sequences of activities which must be carried out as responses. We refer to these sequences as *activity graphs*, which will be defined in Section 3.
2. *An instrumentation method* — called *model driven instrumentation* — which translates the behavioral information held in the model into instrumentation probes into the application source code.
3. *A monitoring tool* to measure instrumented applications.
4. *A visualization and analysis tool* to show the measured behavior of an application in accordance with its behavioral model (activity graphs), and to provide the automatic calculation of the application performance metrics (response times and processing throughputs for each external event).

Before applying these elements in the performance analysis of an application, the functional specification and one implementation of this application must be available, given that the MDM approach is based on measurement. This does not mean that the application must be completely finished, only a prototype, developed to a greater or lesser extent, is needed. Prototypes can be easily obtained using fast prototyping tools [8], thus, the MDM approach can be used with little effort from the early stages of the application design. Once a preliminary implementation of the application is available (referred to in Figure 1 as *preliminary development stages*), the four steps of the MDM approach can begin (these are also summarized in Figure 1).

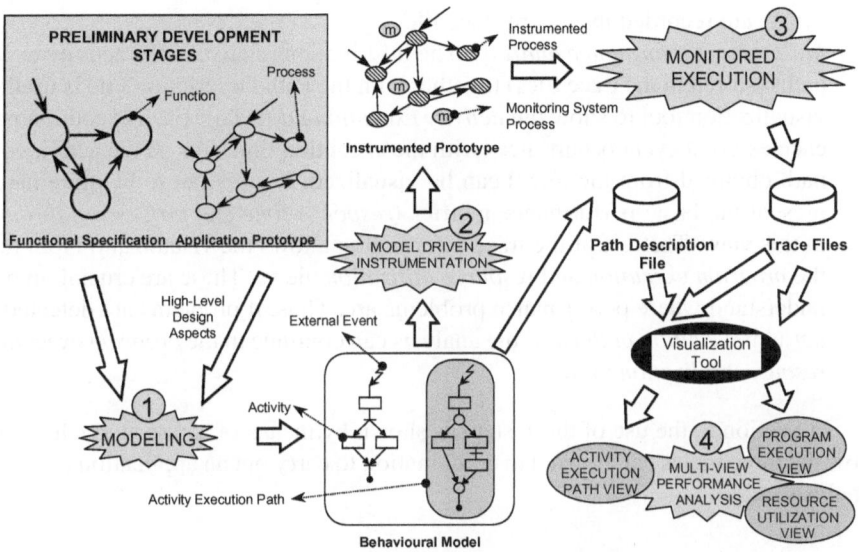

Fig. 1. *Model Driven Monitoring (MDM) approach*

1. *Modeling.* This is the process by which a behavioral model of the application is obtained. Starting from the functional specification, all the external events (requests) to which the application must respond are determined. Then, an *activity graph* describing the activities which must be carried out as response, is defined for each one of them, generating one *activity graph* for each external event. In the prototype, each activity must be implemented by a piece of software, however, some of them may be refined by parallelization (to reduce their execution times), or by replication (to improve the throughput). These high-level design details can also be added to the *activity graphs* in order to improve the expressiveness of the model. When the modeling process is finished, all the information relative to the model is stored in the *Path Description File*.
2. *Model Driven Instrumentation.* As each activity of the behavioral model must be associated to a determined piece of code of the application software, they can be easily instrumented on the source code with a "beginning" and "end" of execution.

In addition, the points of the source code where external events are recognized must also be instrumented.

3. *Monitored Execution*. The instrumented application is executed together with the monitoring system. During the execution, the events relative to the behavioral model ("external event occurrences" and "beginnings" and "ends" of activity executions) are captured by the instrumentation probes and stored in the monitoring system buffers. These events are the basis for the *activity execution path view*. In addition, other types of events (e.g. "communications", "synchronization primitives", "I/O services", etc.) are also captured, providing the information for the *program execution* and *resource utilization* views. When the application execution finishes, all the events are recorded in a set of trace files.

4. *Multi-view performance analysis*. The information relative to the activity execution paths (stored in the trace files) together with the Path Description File is used by the visualization tool to show the *activity execution path view*. Each execution path for each external event occurrence (with the execution times for all the activities of the path obtained from the trace) can be visualized. It turns out to be quite natural to present the basic performance metrics (*response time* and *processing throughput*) in this view. The rest of the trace information allows the visualization tool to show the *program execution* and *resource utilization* views. These are crucial, in order to understand where performance problems are. Thus, if problems are detected in the *activity execution path view*, the analysis can continue in the *program execution* and *resource utilization* views.

In Section 5, the use of these steps is shown by means of a case study, highlighting how the three views can be used in combination to carry out an application performance analysis.

3   Behavioral Model Description

One behavioral model must be defined to represent applications in terms of *activity execution paths*. In the MDM approach, we have chosen the model proposed in [10]. This is a graph based model called *activity graph*. These graphs are made up of two main elements:

1. *Activities*. These represent the functions which must be carried out by applications, and how they are executed, explained in temporal terms. Thus, activity executions can be represented by means of a sequence of three events, which are added to the model. They are the following:
   - "Ready": when the activity is ready to begin executing, i.e., when all its predecessors in the graph have already completed their executions.
   - "Begin": when it actually begins to execute.
   - "End": when it finishes its execution.
   Starting from these events, the model describes activity executions using three times:
   - Waiting time: the difference between the times of "ready" and "begin" events. Normally, it is related to synchronization problems.

- Service time: the difference between the times of "begin" and "end" events. It is related to the resources demanded by the activity.
- Response time: the sum of waiting and service times.

2. *Precedence and synchronization relationships.* These are used to describe the partial ordering of the activities making up a path. They are: "direct sequence", "and-fork", "and-join", "or-fork" and "or-join".

In Section 5, the two uses of these *activity graphs* can be observed during the application of the MDM approach in a case study. The former deals with the behavioral modeling of the application, in order to drive the instrumentation process; this is represented in Figure 5. The latter is related to the visualization tool, which employs the activity graphs, as can be seen in the left window of Figure 6, to display the application behavior, using the event trace obtained after the application execution. In this display, activity executions are represented by two colored boxes; the light part depicts the activity *waiting time*, and the dark part the *service time*.

In the context of this visualization tool, the activity graphs are called *macroactivities*, so, throughout this paper, the terms: *activity graph*, *activity execution path* and *macroactivity* will be considered as synonymous.

4   The Monitoring System

The MDM approach can be considered a general methodology which can be applied to any multiprocessor: the behavioral model and the instrumentation method relies on general concepts, independent of target architectures, and the visualization tool can interpret traces coming from different multiprocessors (by simply using some configuration options). However, monitoring systems are inevitably dependent on target architectures, and hence, must be specifically developed for each kind of multiprocessor.

In the context of this research work, two full software monitoring tools have been developed: one for a SN9500 computer based on T9000 transputers [4], and the other for an embedded multiprocessor based on C40 DSPs [9]. Although both monitors are quite similar, some differences exist between them. Their main characteristics will now be described.

4.1   Monitor Functionality

The function of the monitoring system is to trace the occurrence of the most relevant events during application execution, and store information related to them in a set of trace files. Therefore, in order to specify the functionality of the monitoring system, the set of relevant software events has been defined.

1. *Run-Time system events.* These represent calls to the run-time system. The main ones are: communications, synchronization primitives and I/O operations. The information provided by these events is the basis for the *program execution* and *resource utilization* views.

2. *Activity execution events.* These determine: the moment an activity is executed; in response to what external event; and its execution state (waiting or executing). They provide the information for the *activity execution path view.*
3. *Monitoring system state events.* These express important states reached by the monitoring system, such as, the start and end of monitoring, or the filling of the monitoring buffer. They are very important in order to interpret the trace correctly.

4.2 Monitor Structure

The monitoring system is structured in two main components, a *distributed monitor* and a collection of *instrumentation probes* spread over the application processes.

The *distributed monitor*, as shown in Figure 2, is made up of a set of *monitoring processes* (one per CPU of the multiprocessor), and a *central monitor.* The *monitoring processes* hold the buffers in which events are stored. The *central monitor* is devoted to synchronizing the main activities that must be carried out by the monitoring system during a measurement session.

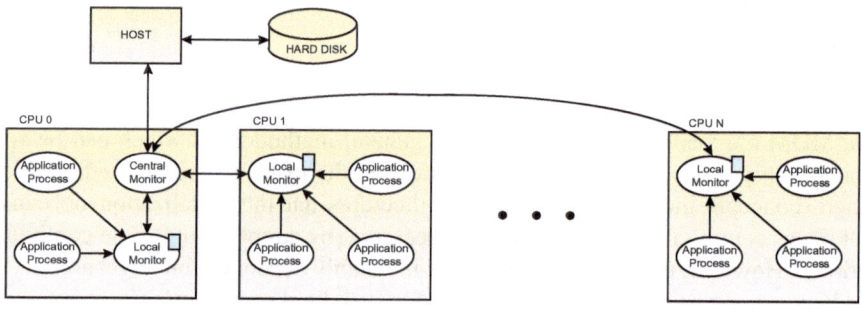

Fig. 2. *Distributed monitor structure*

The *instrumentation probes* are the elements that capture event occurrence. They are inserted in the source code of the application in two ways: either by using instrumented runtime functions (provided by an instrumented runtime library, following the same approach as in [2,6]); or by using special instrumentation functions, supplied by a special purpose instrumentation library. The latter allows the introduction of probes in the code, in order to capture activity execution events.

4.3 Monitor Operation

The operation of the monitor is divided into three stages:

1. *Initial monitoring tasks.* At this stage, the monitoring system is initiated. First, it loads configuration information in a set of internal data structures. Secondly, the

clocks of the CPUs are synchronized. The synchronization is performed by a master-slave algorithm, and using, if necessary, several repetitions to guarantee minimum error [1]. Finally, the *central monitor* sends a signal to all *monitoring processes* to begin the execution and measurement of the application.

2. *Execution and measurement of the application.* During this phase, the monitoring processes behave as passive entities (buffers). The instrumentation probes carry out the work. All the probes share the monitoring buffers placed in the CPU where they are located.

3. *Final monitoring tasks.* When the application finishes, the central monitor collects all the information stored in the monitoring buffers in order to store it in the filesystem. At this point the measurement session is finished.

5   Case Study Analysis

5.1   Case Study Description

Now, a brief description of a case study to illustrate the MDM approach is presented using a simple graph. It consists of a high performance router with encryption capabilities. This case is a variation of an example presented in [6]. Figure 3 shows the functionality required for this system.

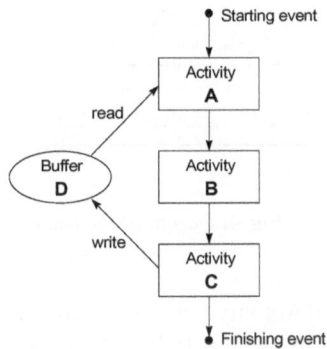

Fig. 3. *Sequence of activities in the router*

When a packet arrives at the system, the network interface places the packet in Buffer D. The first task is devoted to checking the integrity of data and calculating its checksum. This task is called Activity A in Figure 3. Next, using the checksum, a hardware key is consulted to obtain a code. Using this code and the header and tail of the original packet, an algorithm is executed to obtain an encryption sequence. All these functions are grouped in Figure 3 as Activity B. The next task involves the calculation of the new header, including the target destination of the packet. Following this, the encryption sequence is combined with the original packet and the resulting values are the new encrypted data. The new header, tail and encrypted data overwrite the old packet stored in Buffer D. This task is called Activity C in Figure 3. Finally, the packet is retransmitted to the network.

The design used to implement this functionality is shown in Figure 4. This design uses four CPUs (represented by rhombs) and eight processes (represented by ellipses). Each activity is implemented using a block of sequential code (represented by rectangles). Figure 4 also shows the association of these code blocks (and therefore of activities) to processes and the mapping of processes on CPUs. The arrows represent the calling sequence of activities.

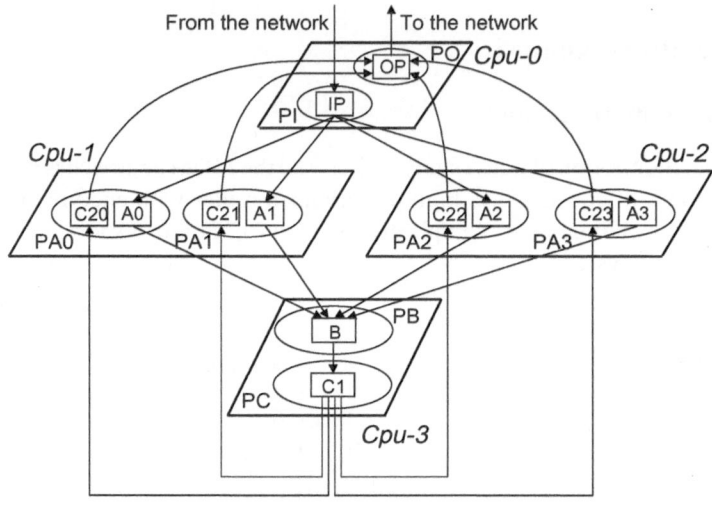

Fig. 4. *Design of the router*

In this design, the original Activity A has been replicated four times (A0, A1, A2, A3). Activity C has been divided in two, C1 (which finds the new destination of the packet) associated to Process PC, and C2 (which rebuilds the packet) associated to Processes PA. Activity C2 is also replicated four times (C20, C21, C22, C23).

5.2   Behavioral Modeling and Model Driven Instrumentation

In the left part of Figure 5, the behavioral model of the router, representing the sequence of activities carried out to process a packet, is shown. This model was obtained from the functional specification and the preliminary design, and it is used to guide the instrumentation of the application source code. In the following paragraphs this process is described.

The behavioral model of the router, composed of only one macroactivity (activity execution path), determines all the events which must be instrumented. These are the "begin" of the macroactivity (represented by the thick black segment, in which the chain of activities starts), and one "begin" and "end" for each activity (IP, A(0), A(1), ...) of the model.

The instrumentation library of the monitoring system provides three functions to instrument these three types of events, called m_BeginMacroAct(), m_BeginAct() and m_EndAct(). So, in order to carry out the instrumentation, the analyst need only determine at which point of the application source code he must insert the corresponding instrumentation functions. Figure 5 shows the instrumentation of the "beginning" of the *macroactivity* in Process PI. Additionally, it also shows the instrumentation of Activities IP, in Process PI, and A(3) and C2(3), in Process PA.

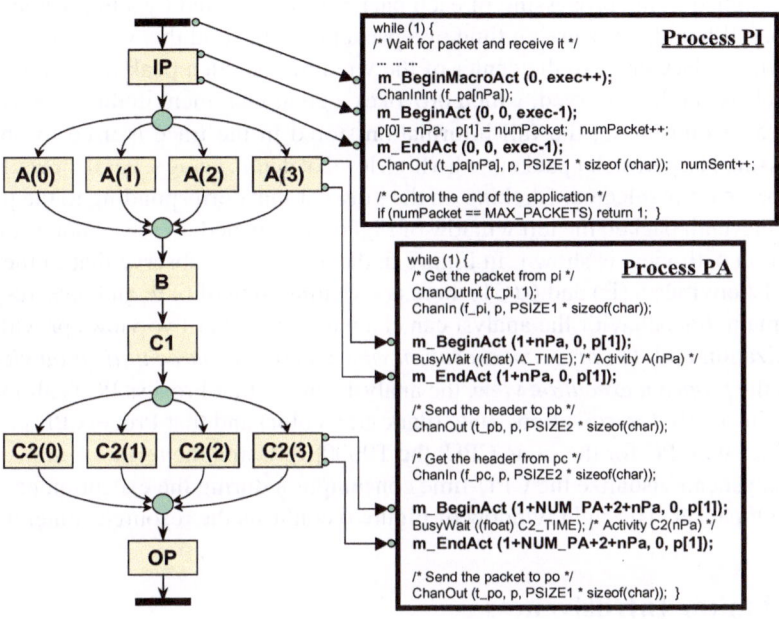

Fig. 5. *The model driven instrumentation process*

This manual instrumentation process is only used to observe the sequence of activities carried out in the router in response to the arrival of each packet. To track the evolution of the state of the software entities (processes), and the utilization of resources (CPUs), additional instrumentation is used. This instrumentation is automatically attached to the application by the monitoring tool.

5.3 Monitored Execution

The instrumented source code of the application is compiled and linked with the object monitoring libraries to obtain an instrumented executable application. The monitor and the application are executed together in the target multiprocessor. After the execution the programmer obtains an event trace which allows the analysis of the router.

5.4 Multi-View Performance Analysis

The information captured by this monitoring system allows the performance analysis of parallel responsive applications in a two-phase manner.

In the first phase, the analyst observes the temporal behavior of the system from an external point of view. The time used by the router to process each packet is visualized considering only two events, the arrival and the departure of the packet. In the top window of Figure 6, each gray bar represents the processing of a packet. The maximum response time assigned to the processing of each packet is represented by a black line above the gray bar. When the processing time of a packet goes beyond this value, the color of the bar turns to dark gray. In the center of the window a sudden peak in the arrival-rate of the packets can be observed, which provokes a great increment in the response time.

In a second phase, the full information stored in the trace is used to observe the processing of a particular packet with a high level of detail, using several views. Logically, the worst case is selected. Clicking on the gray bar that corresponding to the processing of the eleventh packet, the left window of Figure 6 is opened. In this window, the activity execution path view is shown. In Figure 6, the analyst can observe that in the response time of Activities 5 (B) and 6 (C1) there is a waiting time of 68% and 35% respectively. To explain this behavior the analyst can change to the other two views provided by the visualization tool, the *program execution view* and the *resource utilization view*.

In the *program execution view*, the analyst can see that Process PC is almost permanently in "ready for execution" state (dark gray color) and that Process PB periodically competes with PC for the same CPU, the T9000[3]. Using the *resource utilization view* the analyst can visualize the CPU-time consumption during the execution period of the eleventh packet. The right window of Figure 6 confirms the resource contention.

6   Monitor Intrusiveness

Minimizing the intrusiveness and predicting the perturbation introduced by any monitoring approach is always of primary importance. The software monitoring approach presented in this work is intrusive, that is, it introduces perturbation and overhead in the target application. In this section, the technique used to evaluate and control intrusiveness is explained. It consists of a two step procedure:

1. A monitored execution of the application, using only the probes for capturing the *macroactivity* related events, is performed. Thus, a trace of the application with only the *macroactivity* "begin" and "end" events is obtained. In this way, the perturbation introduced is negligible, as the number of events captured is very small. For each execution i of each macro-activity m, a start time $s_i(m)$ and a final time $f_i(m)$ are obtained. The total execution time for the execution i of the macro-activity m will be $t_i(m) = f_i(m) - s_i(m)$.

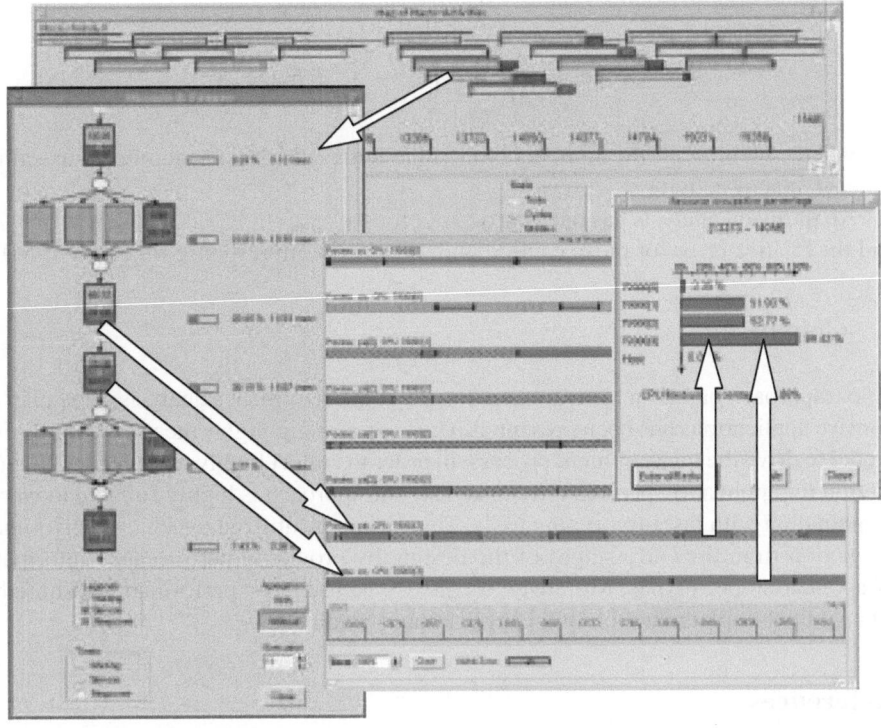

Fig. 6. *Performance views obtained from the measured trace*

2. Reproducing the conditions of the measurement session, a second trace of the application is obtained. However, at this point, all the probes to capture "run-time system" and "activity execution" related events are added to the "begin" and "end" *macroactivity* probes used in the first execution. This means adding all the monitoring overhead and maximizing the perturbation. New $s_i'(m)$ and $f_i'(m)$ are obtained and a new $t_i'(m)$ can be computed for each macro-activity m and each execution i.

With the measurements obtained in these steps, the absolute error for each macroactivity execution, $AE_i(m)=t_i'(m)-t_i(m)$, gives the expansion of the execution time due to the monitoring overhead. The relative error, $RE_i(m)=(t_i'(m)-t_i(m))/t_i(m)$, gives the perturbation introduced by the monitoring system in a particular macroactivity execution. Thus, it is possible to establish how accurately the measurements represent the application behavior, when the application is suffering the whole monitoring overhead. A detailed performance analysis of an application requires the monitoring of all events, but the results of such analysis must only be accepted if the error due to the intrusiveness is reasonably small. The Mean Relative Error (MRE) can be used as a global metric of the intrusiveness of the monitor:

$$MRE = \frac{1}{M} \sum_{m=1}^{M} \left(\frac{1}{N_m} \sum_{i=1}^{N_m} RE_i(m) \right)$$

where M represents the number of macro-activities and N_m the number of executions for each macro-activity m.

An intrusion analysis has been carried out for the case study. The MRE was of 7.78% and the relative error for the execution with the maximum response time was of 5.07%.

7   Conclusions

A new approach based on measurement to carry out performance analysis of parallel responsive applications has been presented. The approach highlights the use of a behavioral model to drive the measurement process, in order to collect highly understandable information for application performance analysis. The approach is highly suitable to work in combination with fast prototyping tools. Thus, it can be utilized to achieve performance prediction from the early stages of the design, by providing performance information of application prototypes. Moreover, it can also be used as a performance test method, when a final implementation of an application is available.

References

1. F. Cristian. Probabilistic clock synchronization. *Distributed Computing*, March 1989.
2. G. A. Geist, M. T. Heath, B. W. Peyton, and P. H. Worley. A user's guide to picl, a portable instrumented communication library. Technical Report TM-11616, ORNL, 1990.
3. R. Hofmann, R. Klar, B. Mohr, A. Quich, and M. Siegle. Distributed performance monitoring: Methods, tools, and applications. *IEEE Trans. on Parallel and Distributed Systems*, 5(6), June 1994.
4. Parsys Ltd. *SN 9500 Technical Overview*, 1994.
5. D. A. Reed, R. A. Aydt, R. J. Noe, P. C. Roth, K. A. Shields, W. Schwartz, and L. F. Tavera. Scalable performance analysis: The pablo performance analysis environment. In *Scalable Parallel Libraries*, 1993.
6. L. Schäfers and C. Scheidler. Monitoring the t9000: the trapper approach. In *Transputer Applications and Systems*, 1994.
7. C. U. Smith. *Performance Engineering of Software Systems*. Addison-Wesley, 1990.
8. Francisco J. Suárez, Javier García, Joaqu acutein Entrialgo, Daniel F. García, Santiago Grana, and Pedro de Miguel. A toolset for visualization and analysis of parallel real-time embedded systems based on fast prototyping techniques. In *Euromicro Workshop on Parallel and Distributed Processing*, pages 186–194, Madrid, Spain, January 1998.
9. Texas Instrument. *C40 Reference Manual*, 1993.
10. C. M. Woodside. A three-view model for performance engineering of concurrent software. *IEEE Transactions on Software Engineering*, 21(9):754–767, September 1995.
11. B. J. N. Wylie and E. Endo. Annai/pma multi-level hierarchical parallel program performance engineering. In *1st International Workshop on Highlevel Programming Models and Supportive Environments*, April 1996.

Instrumentation of Synchronous Reactive Systems for Performance Analysis: A Case Study *

Alberto Valderruten, Javier Mosquera, Víctor M. Gulías

LFCIA, Departamento de Computación, Universidad de La Coruña
Campus de Elviña, 15071 La Coruña, Spain
{valderruten,mosky,gulias}@dc.fi.udc.es

Abstract. A performance evaluation methodology, which integrates performance modeling techniques into the Synchronous Reactive Modeling method supported by ESTEREL, is presented. It is based on timing and probabilistic quantitative constructs which complete the functional models. A monitoring mechanism provides performance results during the simulation. This methodology is applied to study a multithreaded runtime system for a distributed functional programming language. Performance metrics are computed and validated with experimental results.

Keywords: Performance Engineering, Synchronous Reactive Models, Multithreaded Runtime Systems, Model Development, Instrumentation, Simulation and Monitoring, Functional Programming.

1 Introduction

Declarative languages are characterized as having no implicit state and thus the emphasis is placed entirely on programming with *expressions*. In order to improve the execution time of declarative programs, a great deal of effort has to be done to implement languages that exploit automatically (in part, at least) the implicit parallelism in the side-effect-free expressions of declarative languages, in our case, functional languages [8]. There are plenty of problems in implementing an actual distributed system using a functional language. In our previous work [14,15], the necessity of introducing hints or annotations which guide the compiler and runtime system to exploit properly the system resources is presented. This set of *performance annotations* [13] supply quantitative information needed to complete the functional design to carry out the performance modeling tasks.

This paper leads with the performance modeling approach that will support and guide the strategy used by the scheduler to balance the workload. The use of a formal modeling method allows an unambiguous and precise description of the system and leads to easier formal verification and validation. Thus, a

---

* Work partially funded by XUGA10504B96 and XUGA10505B96, *Xunta de Galicia*.

R. Puigjaner et al. (Eds.): Tools'98, LNCS 1469, pp. 129–141, 1998.
© Springer-Verlag Berlin Heidelberg 1998

Synchronous Reactive Model, well suited to describe computer-based systems which must react *instantaneously* to external events, is used to represent the behaviour of a task scheduler in a cluster of computers.

However, this modeling method was not intended to support quantitative analysis and the prediction of the system behaviour with respect to non-functional requirements. In order to fill this gap, the idea is to consider the performance requirements of a design as dedicated constructs for checking performance constraints by simulation. The semantics of these constructs must differ from those of the Synchronous Reactive System, and then ambiguities must be avoided.

Hence, we focus on the integration of performance evaluation and Synchronous Reactive Models. That will allow specification, implementation and analysis of our systems taking into account both functional and non-functional requirements [12]. When formal models include inputs with regard to performance evaluation, we can obtain performance models addressing the service quality (speed, reliability...), very early in the system development life-cycle. The main goal of this approach is to define and validate rules allowing an easier definition of performance models and then to compute performance metrics. In our case study, performance evaluation techniques may advise the programmer about the estimated performance of a given scheduling strategy.

By obtaining a performance model from a Synchronous Reactive Model, and solving it by simulation, we would have to get a similar behaviour as the observed by the actual system, an earlier prototype described in [6]. In order to support the modeling methodology, ESTEREL [3,1,2], a language for Synchronous Reactive Modeling, is used.

2   The Multithreaded Runtime System for DFL

DFL (*Distributed Functional Language*) [6] is a distributed implementation of the functional language O'CAML [9] designed to speed up the computation by spawning tasks to different nodes in a cluster of computers. At a first glance, O'CAML is extended with primitives to perform higher-order explicit communication among distributed threads in a distributed memory framework, typically a cluster of computers. With this primitives, the core of DFL may be proved to be equivalent to Milner's π-calculus [10] with asynchronous channels.

On top of this explicit framework, Multilisp's futures [7] have been implemented in order to perform side-effect free lenient evaluation [11] (evaluation of function body and its arguments simultaneously). A future is a *suggestion* for the runtime system to spawn a new task. In this approach, the programmer uses sequential O'CAML enriched with future annotations for identifying potential tasks. Some of these expressions will be evaluated as remote tasks, while some will be carried out locally depending on system workload.

The key problem is to distribute efficiently the workload among all the sites. We have adopted a work-stealing scheduler, similar to CILK's multithreaded runtime system [4]. With this approach, each site owns a pool of pending tasks (futures) to be executed by an *evaluator thread*. The pool of local tasks is ma-

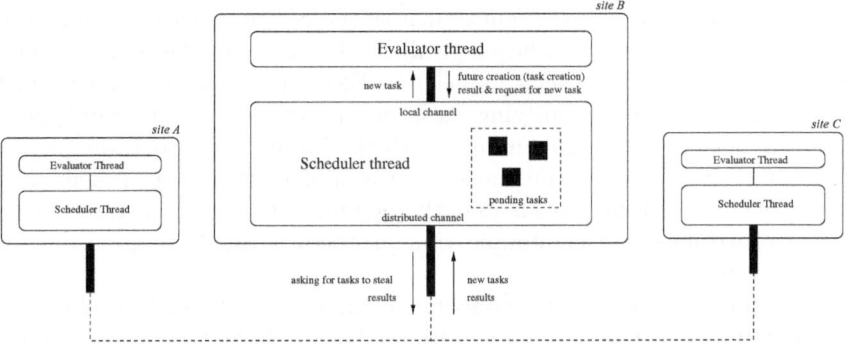

Fig. 1. Distributed threads to implement concurrent future evaluation

naged by an *scheduler thread*, which is asked for work by the evaluator when it becomes idle and delivers results to their destination. When the workload at a given site falls under a threshold (for instance, no pending tasks are available), a work-stealing cycle begins: the scheduler thread (the *thief*) polls other locations for new tasks and, if a site with enough workload is found (the *victim*), some tasks are *stolen* from it, being migrated to the idle site. This strategy seems to behave quite well in dynamic and highly asynchronous concurrent programs.

3   The Modeling Process

In order to obtain performance estimations of the system described in section 2, and hence to analyze different design options, a Synchronous Reactive Model has been built using ESTEREL and its **C** interface. The modeling process involves two main steps:

1. A Synchronous Reactive Model corresponding to the functional point of view is implemented using the deterministic mechanisms provided by ESTEREL; this first model is called the *Functional* [1] *Model*.
2. The Functional Model is completed using performance constructs and instrumented with a suitable monitoring mechanism to obtain performance measures during the simulation; the result is a *Performance Model*.

3.1   The Functional Model

Synchronous Reactive Modeling provides an optimal framework for the modular decomposition of programs that engage in complex patterns of deterministic interaction, such as many real-time and communication entities. Synchronous Reactive Models are used to describe computer-based systems which must react

---

[1] Note that, starting from now, *functional* should be understood as a description of *what* a system does instead of the *functional programming* meaning of section 2.

instantaneously to external events, such as the commands sent to an embedded system in a satellite or the alarms produced by sensors. The ESTEREL language was designed to develop such models. In ESTEREL, a module reacts instantly to each input event by modifying its internal state and creating output events. Thus, the reactions are *synchronous* with the inputs: the processing of an event must not be interrupted, and the system is sufficiently fast to process its input events. Such a system has an underlying finite state machine. Real-time embedded controllers and communication protocol entities are good examples of reactive systems.

ESTEREL is an imperative concurrent language, with high level control and event handling constructs. Modules are the basic entities which can be interfaced with the environment or with other modules. Each module has an event interface used to communicate with its environment. Events are the main objects handled by the modules: they may be composed of several signals, which can be either present or absent during the reaction to an input. The `present` construct (figure 2, left) is used to test the presence of a signal in the current event.

In order to be present in a reaction, an output signal can be emitted by a module using the `emit <signal>` instruction. This signal is *broadcast* to all modules having the signal defined as input. Hence, signals are used for synchronization and communication description.

There are two kinds of ESTEREL instructions:

- *Instantaneous instructions*, in the basis of the perfect synchrony hypothesis, which are completed in the same reaction they were activated: signal emission (`emit`), signal presence test (`present`) and sequencing (`<instruction-1> ; <instruction-2>`) are examples of such instructions.
- *Waiting instructions*, the simplest of which is the `await <signal>` statement. The execution of a waiting instruction will block until an specified event occurs.

```
present <signal>                    [weak] abort <instruction-1>
    [then <instruction-1>]          when <signal>
    [else <instruction-2>]          [ do <instruction-2> ]
end present                         end abort
```

Fig. 2. The `present` and `abort` constructs

A parallel operator || allows the control flow to be transmitted to several instructions simultaneously. It terminates when its two branches terminate, and again, it takes no time by itself.

The `abort` statement deals with preemption, one of the most important features of ESTEREL. The `abort` construct is shown in figure 2 (right). Here, `instruction-1` will be interrupted and `instruction-2` executed if an occurrence of `signal` happens before `instruction-1` ends. This instruction terminates when `instruction-1` does, or when `instruction-2` does if a timeout occurs.

In general, more user-friendly statements are derived from a set of primitive or kernel statements. A detailed description of its semantics is presented in [1].

3.2   Considering Performance

Taking into account performance issues during the system life-cycle is done by means of a performance modeling process, involving a set of system designers and modeling expert activities [5]. The aims of modeling include performance requirements, which may consider throughput, timing and utilization rate constraints. The proposed approach completes the functional specification with all performance (non functional) information, allowing the computation of performance results by simulation. In order to add this kind of information to the ESTEREL functional specification, the necessary quantitative information below must be introduced:

1. The estimated processing time relevant to each *timed action*. A timed action is an action which consumes time, e.g. the time for processing a frame, the transmission time... They are relevant to performance modeling, but have no sense in a Synchronous Reactive Model. Our modeling choices must avoid any semantical incongruence with the perfect synchrony hypothesis.
2. The probability associated with each possible *alternative behaviour*. When a probability defines the system behaviour, a degree of non-determinism must be introduced in the Synchronous Reactive Model, which is deterministic by nature. Once again, the modeling choices must treat this point carefully.

Thus, the *performance constructs*, which introduce this quantitative information, must not violate the synchronous reactive model hypothesis of both determinism and instantaneous reaction. The timed actions can be viewed as requests to external modules that must reply after a certain amount of time. Both requests and replies are signals emitted from and received to the reactive module, respectively. The model allows to manage this type of behaviour. The determinism is maintained too, because this principle is only referred to the way of the synchronous reactive module is going to react whenever an input event occurs. As timed actions are considered external for the synchronous reactive module, they can have variable or even random duration, without violating the determinism principle of the synchronous reactive model.

The constructs that allow alternative behaviours maintain the instantaneous reaction principle. Nevertheless, the determinism seems to be violated, as long as different behaviours are wanted with same inputs. Again, the problem can be solved moving the source of the alternative behaviours out of the synchronous reactive model. As for timed actions, the alternative behaviours can be viewed as replies from external sources that determine the behaviour in the reactive module. This module is deterministic because always reacts in the same way when the reply of the external decision is the same. The non-deterministic behaviour is delegated by the reactive kernel and managed separately, so the determinism is maintained inside it.

Timed actions can be implemented as a two-fold procedure: (i) request for a finalization signal to an external module and (ii) wait for the finalization signal. In ESTEREL, they can be implemented as shown in figure 3 (left). However, by doing this, the time management is left entirely to the external module, and the time control feature supported by the synchronous reactive model is not used. In order to unify the time management, the construct can be implemented as in figure 3 (right), where the signal TIME_SIGNAL is the one that counts the time passing across the entire synchronous reactive model (for example, the predefined ESTEREL signal tick). The external module only must respond to a GET_TIMED_ACTION_DURATION request by sending the amount of time of the timed action, which is carried within the TIMED_ACTION_DURATION signal.

```
emit TIMED_ACTION_STARTS;          emit GET_TIMED_ACTION_DURATION;
await TIMED_ACTION_FINISHES;       await immediate TIMED_ACTION_DURATION;
                                   await (?TIMED_ACTION_DURATION) TIME_SIGNAL;
```

Fig. 3. Implementing timed actions

A way to implement the alternative behaviours is shown in figure 4. The external module that receives the signal GET_ALTERNATIVE_BEHAVIOUR takes a decision based on some rules, which are external to the synchronous reactive model.

```
emit GET_ALTERNATIVE_BEHAVIOUR;
await
   case ALTERNATIVE_BEHAVIOUR_1 do <behaviour_1_statement>
   ...
   case ALTERNATIVE_BEHAVIOUR_n do <behaviour_n_statement>
end await;
```

Fig. 4. Implementing alternative behaviours

In addition, in order to obtain performance measures from these models, a suitable monitoring mechanism must be implemented. A trace file must be generated with the results of the observation of a set of signals defined by the designer based on the desired performance metrics. The result of this *model instrumentation* step is an operative performance model.

4   The Case Study

In this section, we present the Synchronous Reactive Model and the derived Performance Evaluation Model for a multithreaded runtime system as the one exposed in section 2.

4.1   The Functional Model

The ESTEREL Functional Model, whose architecture is shown in figure 5, describes the sequencing and synchronization operations involved in the multithreaded runtime system. The implementation of data structures as tasks queues, the probabilistic behaviour mechanism and the trace generation are supported by the C interface of ESTEREL.

The number of nodes involved in the distribution is a parameter of the model. The module **Processor** implements the functionalities at each node, while the main module, `WrkStl`, handles the parallelisation of all the processor instances, the communication medium among nodes and the time signal sender. In figure 5, an n-processor system is represented.

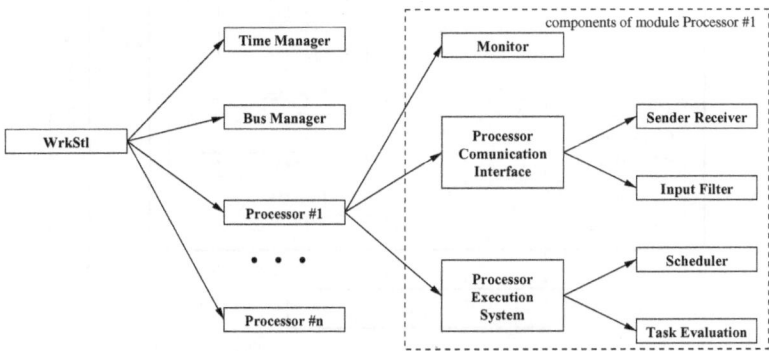

Fig. 5. Instances diagram of `WrkStl` model

The `Time Manager` module sends to the rest of the modules a signal that represents the logical time of the simulation. On the other hand, the `Bus Manager` models a typical bus medium which properly routes messages among sites and solves the collisions.

Figure 6 presents a processor module and its interaction with the rest of modules in the system. Communication with other processors, via the `Bus Manager`, is performed by the `Processor Communication Interface` inside each processor. Two modules cooperate inside this one: The `Input Filter` and the `Sender Receiver`. The former extracts the messages from the bus and then sends them to the `Sender Receiver` module. The latter can send messages directly to the `Bus Manager`.

All messages are modeled as a valued signal that contains sender and receiver identifications as well as data transmitted between them. This signal is sent by the `Processor Evaluation System` to the `Processor Communication Interface`, which converts the valued signal into a multi-valued one in order to be handled by the `Bus Manager`. Here, this signal may be combined with other signals of the same type eventually sent by other processors. The `Bus Manager` takes these signals, splits them into individual messages and sends them to the destination processor, whose `Processor Communication Interface` extracts the information and sends it to its `Processor Evaluation System`.

From the site point of view, messages can arrive at any time during its normal processing cycle. The communication system assumes an asynchronous basis, using a local queue to store the incoming messages. The additional processing of the message (like marshalling and unmarshalling of data) starts when the normal processor operation is interrupted.

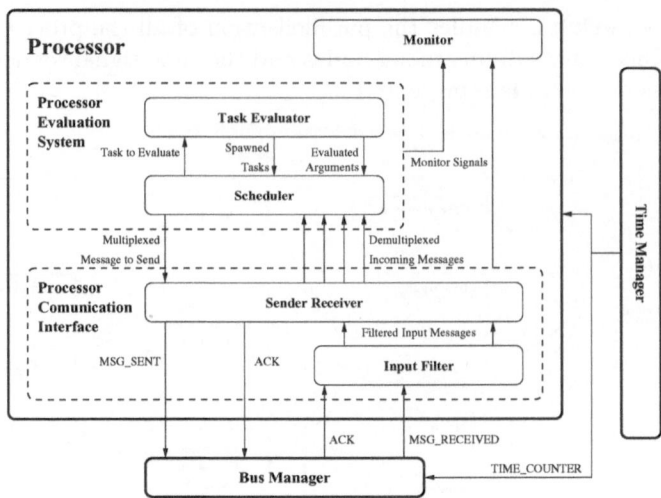

Fig. 6. A processor module

Task scheduling and processing are mainly supported by the `Scheduler` and `Task Evaluator` modules. The `spawn` (creation of a new task) and `spawn_next` (successor of a task waiting for results) operations are considered into the task processing. The model supposes the following restrictions for the programs:

- If a task does not spawn any child, then it does not create a successor task.
- When a task spawns a set of children, a `spawn_next` statement has already been executed, and then the task terminates.
- Every child task sends arguments to the successor of its parent, so a successor cannot become ready until all the children terminate.
- A successor cannot spawn any child.

The evaluation modules are considered as two threads running in the same processor. The `Scheduler` only can be interrupted by an incoming message when it is not busy. On the other hand, the `Task Evaluator` can be interrupted at any time.

The scheduler decides that the work-stealing procedure must be started, playing the *thief* role, when its local ready queue becomes empty. The *victim* is randomly chosen and it receives a work-stealing attempt. The normal activities of the victim processor are interrupted in order to handle this attempt. If the victim has ready tasks, it sends one to the thief, who finishes then the work-stealing procedure. If the victim has no ready tasks, then notifies this condition to the thief. In this case, the thief must wait for an exponentially growing random period of time before a new attempt.

The proposed model is quite detailed because we are interested on low-level performance results to tune the system scheduler under some workload configurations. Then, this functional model is an appropriate starting point to support the performance analysis.

4.2   Considering Performance

As discussed in section 3.2, the ESTEREL functional model must be extended to include timed actions and alternative behaviours, as well as the instrumentation needed to obtain the performance model that fulfills the requirements.

Timed actions implement variable durations using external functions to quantify the amount of time consumed by actions such as transmissions, argument marshalling and unmarshalling, etc. Figure 7 shows the ESTEREL code corresponding to a message reception which uses the `Time_Tx` function.

```
await MSG_RECEIVED_FILTERED;      % message reception
var Time:integer in              % temporized event starts
  Time:=Time_Tx();
  await Time tick;
end var;                         % temporized event finishes
emit MSG_RECEIVED_ACK;           % message acknowledgement
```

Fig. 7. Message reception

Alternative behaviours are based on probabilistic functions which return different values following a given distribution. These values can be used to establish some model parameters, such as the number of spawns for a task or the timed action durations. Figure 8 shows how to determine the victim processor, randomly chosen as previously stated.

```
Victim:= DecideVictim(ID_P);         % choosing victim processor
Msg:=MakeReqSteal(ID_P,Victim);      % building request message
...
weak abort
    ...
    sustain MSG_TO_SEND(Msg)         % sending request message
    ...
when immediate MSG_TO_SEND_ACK;
```

Fig. 8. Choosing a victim

The model instrumentation for performance analysis is supported by the `Monitor` modules, which check the presence of a set of specific signals during the simulation process and produce a trace file. Each trace register includes a time reference (the current time), a locality reference (the processor) and the identification of the signal. Some additional parameters can be included if needed.

An observation point in the model corresponds to the emission of a monitoring signal, as shown in figure 9. In this case, the start of the task evaluation is monitorized with the `MON_STARTS_EVALUATE_TASK` signal, which carries information about the task that will be run. The `Monitor` modules wait for these monitoring signals and write a trace entry with each one received. Figure 10 shows the control loop for a the aforementioned monitoring signal.

```
emit MON_STARTS_EVALUATE_TASK(Task); % monitor signal emitted
var Time:integer in                  % temporized event inits
  Time=Time_Evaluation(Task,ID_P);
  await Time tick;
end var;                             % temporized event finishes
```

Fig. 9. An observation point

The proposed monitoring mechanism only offers the basic observation functionality that is needed for performance measuring. A complete statistical tool must include at least the computation of the confidence intervals that are needed to control the simulation time.

```
loop
  await MON_STARTS_EVALUATE_TASK;
  call Mon_STARTS_EVALUATE_TASK () (ID_P,?TIME_COUNTER,?MON_STARTS_EVALUATE_TASK);
end loop
```

Fig. 10. A monitoring control loop

5   Performance Analysis of the Case Study

The verification and validation of the performance model has been carried out with the study of a set of workload scenarios. We study the behaviour of a (quite ideal) divide-and-conquer algorithm, which is the typical skeleton used in the applications for which the actual system is designed for. In particular, the workload has been modeled with the following settings:

- Non-trivial input is always divided into two balanced partitions.
- The partition and fusion stages take a time that follows an exponential distribution, whose mean value is function of the input size.
- Granularity for the trivial input also follows an exponential distribution whose mean is fixed as a parameter of the simulation.

Three performance metrics were considered: the system speedup, the number of steal requests and the number of ready tasks (every task but the successors that have not received their results yet) on the whole system. Figure 11 shows some results obtained from simulations with different input sizes (100 and 800 times the size of the trivial input) on a different number of identical processors (1, 2, 4, 8, and 16). As expected, the system gets better speedup when we increase the input size, as shown in figures 11(a) and 11(b), as long as the number of tasks in the system also increases. The speedup is the relation between the execution time of the whole process on a single processor (without scheduling overheads) and the corresponding execution time on an n-processor configuration. Hence, the analysis program must determine the value of the accumulated speedup at every time.

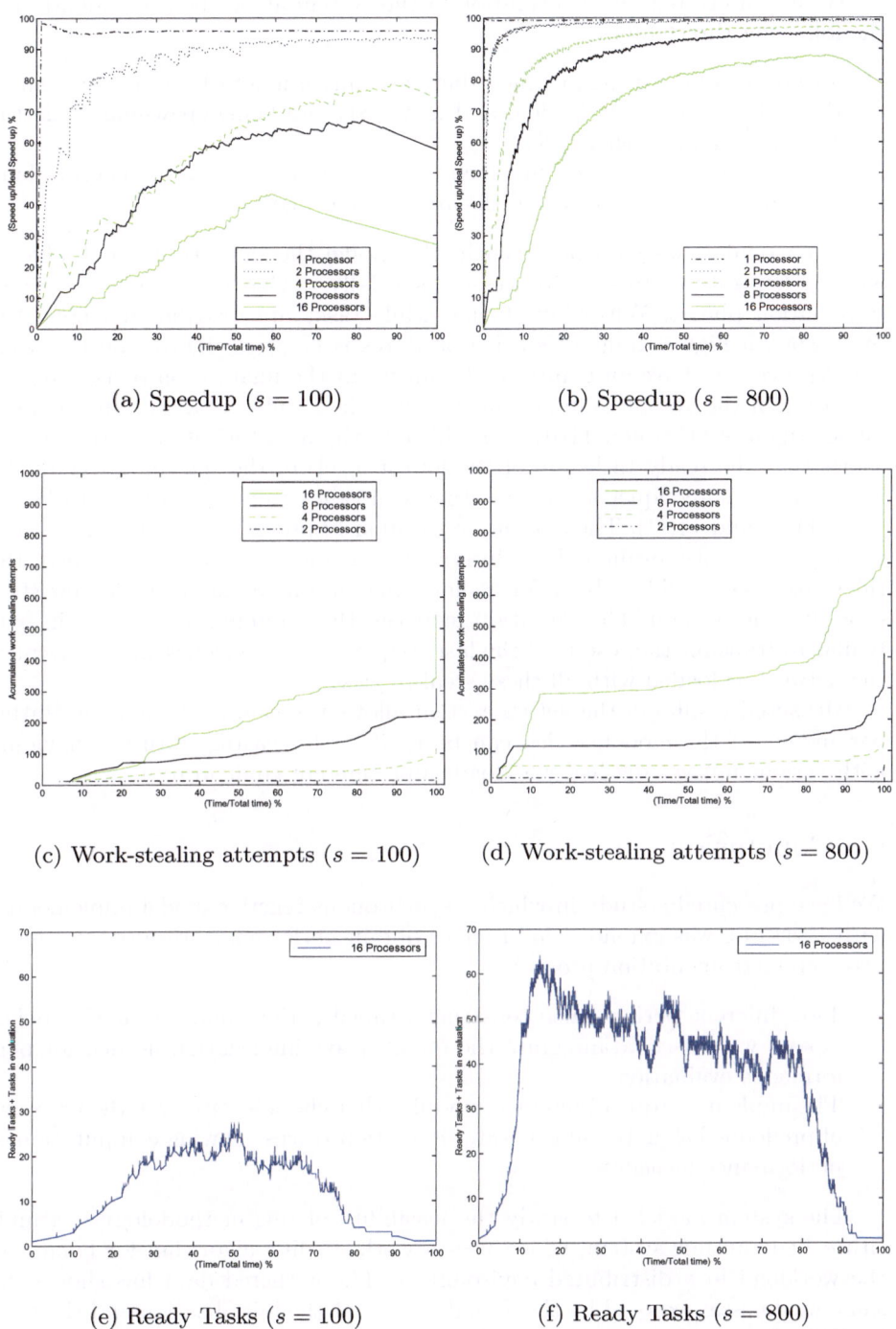

(a) Speedup ($s = 100$)

(b) Speedup ($s = 800$)

(c) Work-stealing attempts ($s = 100$)

(d) Work-stealing attempts ($s = 800$)

(e) Ready Tasks ($s = 100$)

(f) Ready Tasks ($s = 800$)

Fig. 11. Simulation results with different number of processors and input sizes (s)

We are interested on the evolution of the system along the time, identifying the following three stages:

1. an *initialization stage*, in which there are only a few tasks on the system;
2. then, the system gets loaded, and new tasks are being spawning while the system evaluates other tasks;
3. and the *finalization stage*, in which the system becomes empty again as long as tasks terminate and new tasks are not spawned.

In particular, we have observed in the model the same transient problems when a low rate of tasks is processed, specially during the initialization and termination phases. When initializing, while tasks are distributed among the processors, a high volume of steal procedures is engaged due to the fact that many processors have an empty ready queue. In the finalization phase, the degradation of the system is important because the number of disturbing steals is higher (figures 11(c) and 11(d)). In addition, the monitorization of the queues shows that the ready tasks are of the lowest levels of the spawning tree of the ideal divide-and-conquer layout, i.e. they will generate less additional tasks (figures 11(e) and 11(f)). The sites are continuously processing steal requests and the tasks currently evaluated are interrupted. If any request were satisfied, the thief processor would be busy for a short time and it would engage a new steal procedure quite soon. This situation increases the communication time, in particular to transmit the results of the lasts requests of the given scenario, because the network is loaded with all these steal requests.

Measured results in the actual system allows the tuning of the quantitative parameters of the model, which can be used for forecasting future behaviours with various not yet reached workloads and different configurations.

6   Conclusion

We have presented a study in which a synchronous reactive model implemented with ESTEREL was extended in order to obtain performance results by using a two-step instrumentation procedure:

- Two different performance constructs, timed actions and alternative behaviours, were used to integrate the quantitative information needed for performance evaluation.
- The implementation of monitor modules that check at any time the presence of predefined signals and generate simulation traces allowing computation of performance measures.

The system modeled to study the feasibility of this methodology is a multithreaded runtime system, which uses a work-stealing algorithm for balancing the workload in a distributed environment. The gathered data has shown the same weaknesses exposed by the actual system at the initialization and the finalization phases, when the number of tasks is low and most of the work-stealing attempts fail.

There are some open issues that should be considered as future work:

1. Further measuring in the actual system must be performed in order to tune different workload models.
2. Determine the proper mechanism to adjust the parameters of the actual scheduler using the model results to improve the efficiency of the distributed functional programs.
3. Compare the simulation process with other simulation tools, paying attention to features related with the simulation time control, modeling capabilities, scalability...

References

1. G. Berry. The semantics of pure esterel. In M. Broy, editor, *Program Design Calculi*, Computer and System Sciences 118, NATO ASI Series, pages 361–409. 1993.
2. G. Berry. *The Esterel v5 Language Primer. Version 5.10, release 1.0.*, 1997.
3. G. Berry and G. Gonthier. The ESTEREL synchronous programming language: design, semantics, implementation. *Science of Computer Programming*, 19(2):87–152, November 1992.
4. R.D. Blumofe, C.F. Joerg, B.C. Kuszmaul, C.E. Leiserson, K.H. Randall, and Y. Zhou. Cilk: An efficient multithreaded runtime system. *Journal of Parallel and Distributed Computing*, 37(1):55–69, August 1996.
5. E. Conquet, A. Valderruten, R. Trémoulet, Y. Raynaud, and S. Ayache. Un modèle du processus de l'activité d'évaluation des performances. *Génie Logiciel et Systèmes Experts*, (27):27–31, 1992.
6. V. Gulias. *DFL: Distributed Functional Computing*. PhD thesis, University of La Coruña, SPAIN, 1998 (to appear).
7. R.H. Halstead. Multilisp: A language for concurrent symbolic computation. *ACM Transactions on Programming Languages and Systems*, 7(4):501–538, Oct. 1985.
8. P. Hudak. Conception, evolution, and application of functional programming languages. *ACM Computing Surveys*, 21(3):359–411, September 1989.
9. X. Leroy. *The Objective Caml System, release 1.05*. INRIA, 1997.
10. R. Milner, J. Parrow, and D. Walker. A calculus of mobile processes. *Information and Computation*, 100(1):1–77, September 1992.
11. K. Schauser and S. Goldstein. How much non-strictness do lenient programs Require? In *ACM FPCA '95*, San Diego, June 1995.
12. A. Valderruten. *Modélisation des Performances et Développement de Systèmes Informatiques: une étude d'intégration*. PhD thesis, Université Paul Sabatier, 1993.
13. A. Valderruten and V. Gulias. An information model for performance engineering. In *Proceedings of the International Conference on Information Systems Analysis, ISAS'96*, Orlando, 1996.
14. A. Valderruten, V. Gulias, and J.L. Freire. Instrumentation strategies in distributed functional computing. In *Proceedings of the International Conference on Information Systems Analysis, ISAS'97*, Caracas, 1997.
15. A. Valderruten, M. Vilares, and J. Graña. Instrumentation of synchronous reactive models for performance engineering. *LNCS*, 989:76–89, 1995.

A Perturbation and Reduction Based Algorithm

J.-M. Fourneau[1]   &   L. Mokdad[1,2]

(1) PR*i*SM
Université de Versailles Saint-Quentin
45 av. des Etats Unis
78 035 Versailles Cedex, FRANCE
(2) LERI,
Université de Reims Champagne-Ardenne
Reims, FRANCE

Abstract. We present a new algorithm for solving discrete-time Markov chains where transition probabilities have several orders of magnitude. Our method combines the decomposition by perturbation and the reduction approaches. In the decomposition phase, we remove from the chain some transitions with very small probabilities. But we assume that the reduced graph is still strongly connected after the deletion. A transversal (a cut set of the directed cycles) is then obtained and the reduction method is used to compute the first approximation of the steady-state distribution. Further approximations may be computed iteratively to obtain the desirable accuracy. We prove the algorithm and present some examples.

1   Introduction

The analysis of a lot of queueing models requires the computation of the steady-state distribution of a Markov chain. Thus, this problem receives a considerable attention (see Stewart's book [15] for an exhaustive presentation of the various algorithms proposed). Among these algorithms, direct methods, decomposition methods and iterative methods are clearly related to our work because of some of their drawbacks.

Direct methods, in general related to Gaussion elimination, require an important memory space because the matrix is filled during the elimination process. Iterative methods consist of successive approximations until the solution is obtained with a fixed accuracy. The number of operations used in such methods is a priori unknown. The problem with these methods is that they can require a long time to converge if the subdominant eigenvalue is close to one. Decomposition techniques perform some graph operation on the chain to obtain smaller problems which are usually simpler to solve. An example in which decomposition approach gives good results is a class of problems in which the state space can be partitioned into disjoint subsets with strong probabilities among the states of a subset but with small probabilities among the subsets ([2], [3]). This kind of problems, known as Nearly Completely Decomposable (NCD) problems, have

R. Puigjaner et al. (Eds.): Tools'98, LNCS 1469, pp. 142–153, 1998.
© Springer-Verlag Berlin Heidelberg 1998

typically very bad convergence rate for iterative algorithms because of the eigenvalues but ad-hoc algorithms ([10] or [15]) give very good results. However, these algorithms only work for the class of NCD matrices.

In this paper, we present a new algorithm based on perturbation and reduction which is devoted to the analysis of matrices which are not NCD, even if they contain probabilities of several orders of magnitude. These matrices are often considered in the analysis of ATM networks. For instance, a discrete-time queue with Markov Modulated Batch arrival Process and finite capacity (i.e. a *MMBP/D/1/K* queue) exhibits such a structure if the tail probabilities of the batch distribution are very small. These matrices may be difficult to solve using other techniques because of their size, their structure and their eigenvalues.

For these matrices, we propose an approximate method based on the following four steps:

1. deletion of arcs of small probabilities to obtain an irreducible chain on the same space but with a better structure,
2. computation of a cut set of the directed cycles of the modified chain,
3. reduction to a smaller problem to obtain the first approximation of the steady-state distribution,
4. iteration on the perturbation formula to obtain better approximates.

The deletion step is closely related to the technique described by Mahlis and Sanders in [12]. Briefly, they decompose the matrix into two matrices on the same space. This decomposition is based on the transition probabilities. The matrix which contains high probabilities is kept into memory while the other matrix is sent on disk. Iterative techniques are used on the matrix in memory and when a given accuracy is reached, the other matrix is used to further improve the approximates. Such an approach is mostly useful to optimize the number of disk accesses when we solve a chain whose matrix is too large for the memory. Our paper is more theoretical in nature. We prove that the perturbation due to the deletion has an effect on the steady-state distribution which has the same order than the threshold used for the deletion. We also proved the iteration to obtain further approximates of the distribution. Our results also establish the convergence and the accuracy of Sanders's method.

In section 2, we describe our method. We present the assumptions and the computation of the different approximations of the steady-state distribution and we prove the algorithm. In section 3, we give a description of the different steps of the algorithm. Finally, the last section is devoted to numerical experiments that show the effectiveness of our method.

2 Perturbation and Reduction

We consider a discrete-time finite aperiodic and irreducible Markov chain and our objective is to compute its steady-state distribution π :

$$\begin{cases} \pi P = \pi \\ \pi e = 1 \end{cases} \tag{1}$$

where P is the matrix of the Markov chain and e, a column vector of 1. Let N be the size of the Markov chain, so the size of matrix P is $N \times N$.

2.1   Assumptions

First let us define the assumptions we use. Remember that our objective is to compute the approximation of π, solution of system 1 for some matrices whose structure is now introduced. The key idea is that the decomposition process which is described in the following will lead to two non zero matrices.

We decompose matrix P into two matrices P_1 and E on the same space, using threshold ε :

- All transitions in matrix E carry a probability smaller than ε
- Matrix P_1 is irreducible. All transitions of P with probability greater than ε are in P_1. This matrix may also contain some transitions with a probability smaller than ε.

$$P = P_1 + \varepsilon E \tag{2}$$

It is not necessary to be more precise on the decomposition at this step because the perturbation analysis only takes advantage of the ergodicity of P_1 and the small values of the transitions in matrix E. The decomposition we used in the context of cut set of the directed cycle is further illustrated in section 3 and 4 and in the paragraph on the computation of a_i. Finally, remark that if we completely remove transitions with small probabilities from an NCD matrix, we will obtain a reducible matrix P_1.

Then, we normalize the two matrices to make matrix P_1 stochastic. We put on the diagonal elements of P_1 the sum of probabilities which have been carried by arcs transferred into matrix E.

$$P_1(i, i) = P_1(i, i) + \varepsilon \Sigma_{j=1, j \neq i}^{N} E(i, j)]$$

This sum of probabilities is also subtracted from the diagonal elements of E. Thus, we have:

$$\Sigma_{j=1}^{N} E(i, j) = 0 \quad and \quad \Sigma_{j=1}^{N} P_1(i, j) = 1 \ \forall \ 1 \leq i \leq N$$

Note that after the normalization phase, relation 2 still holds. The main assumption is that such a decomposition leads to matrices which are both non zero.

2.2   Using P_1 Rather Than P

Now, the two questions we may consider are related to the computation of π_1 the steady-state distribution of P_1: is π_1 a good approximation of π the steady-state distribution of P and is it easier to compute π_1 rather than π ? The answer to the first question comes from the analysis of the perturbation while several answers may be given to the second question. In this paper, we focus on the use of the reduction technique applied on P_1. As this technique is based on the computation and the use of a cut set of the directed cycles of the graph, it is clear that this cut set is easier to obtain and smaller, in general, when we consider matrix P_1 instead of matrix P. Other possible answers to the second question are introduced in the conclusion. The theoretical foundations of our method comes from [4] where it is proved that there is continuity of steady-state distribution of discrete-time Markov chain when we continuously change the transition rates, assuming that the chain remains ergodic.

Before proceeding with the perturbation analysis, remark that P_1 is aperiodic because it is irreducible (as stated in the assumptions) and it contains at least one loop since matrix E is non zero. Therefore, the chain associated to P_1 has a steady-state distribution π_1.

Perturbation Let δ be the difference between vectors π and π_1.

$$\delta = \pi - \pi_1 \Leftrightarrow \pi = \delta + \pi_1 \tag{3}$$

After substitution of equations (3) and (1) into (2), we obtain:

$$(\delta + \pi_1)(P_1 + \varepsilon E) = \delta + \pi_1$$

We develop and after cancellation of terms (as we have $\pi_1 P_1 = \pi_1$), we get:

$$\delta = \delta(P_1 + \varepsilon E) + \varepsilon \pi_1 E \tag{4}$$

Following [7] (for the first part of the description of Courtois's method), assume that the solution of system (4) is a classical solution for a perturbation and can be expressed as follows: $\delta = \Sigma_{i=1}^{\infty} a_i \varepsilon^i$ with $\sum_j a_i(j) = 0$ for all i. We substitute δ in equation (4) and, after identification of terms, we find that the a_i vectors must follows relations (5). In theorem 1, we state that these relations are consistent and allow the computation of vectors a_i. We also proved that, for an arbitrary k, the effect at order ε^k (i.e. the vector a_k) is upper bounded.

$$\begin{cases} a_1 = a_1 P_1 + \pi_1 E \quad and \quad a_1 e = 0 \\ a_{i+1} = a_{i+1} P_1 + a_i E \quad and \quad a_i e = 0 \end{cases} \tag{5}$$

Theorem 1 *The a_i vectors exist and are upper bounded.*

Proof : Remember that P_1 is an irreducible aperiodic stochastic matrix of size N. Therefore the linear operator Q defined by $(N - 1)$ columns of P_1 and one column full of 1 is not singular. But system (5) is also defined as a linear problem using operator Q. Therefore a_1 exists and a_i exist by induction on i.

Now consider the equation $a_1 = a_1 P_1 + \pi_1 E$ and substitute a_1 in the r.h.s. We obtain:

$$a_1 = \pi_1 E + \pi_1 E P_1 + a_1 P_1^2$$

Performing n times the substitution, we get:

$$a_1 = \pi_1 E(\sum_{j=0}^{n} P_1^j) + a_1 P_1^{n+1}$$

But as P_1 is ergodic, $P_1^{+\infty}$ exists and it rows are constant. As the sum of the elements of a_1 is zero, $\lim_n a_i P_1^i = 0$. Thus:

$$a_1 = \pi_1(\sum_{j=0}^{+\infty} E P_1^j)$$

Using the same argument on the rows of $P_1^{+\infty}$, and as the sums of the elements in each row of E is 0, $E P_1^{+\infty}$ is the zero matrix. Therefore,

$$a_1 = \pi_1(\sum_{j=0}^{+\infty} E(P_1^j - P_1^{+\infty}))$$

As P_1 is finite, irreducible and aperiodic, we have a geometric convergence of P_1^j to $P_1^{+\infty}$. More precisely, it exists a $\alpha > 0$ and $\beta < 1$ such that $\| P_i^n - P_1^{+\infty} \|_\infty \leq \alpha \beta^n$, for all n (see Hunter, theorem 7.1.3 [8]). Therefore,

$$\| a_i \|_\infty \leq \frac{\| \pi_1 E \|_\infty}{1 - \beta} \qquad (6)$$

The proof for an arbitrary a_i is quite the same.

As a corollary, we obtain a formula for an approximation of π with a given accuracy. Let us now define δ by $\frac{\varepsilon}{1-\beta}$.

Corollary 1 *Assume that $\delta < 1$, π may be approximated by $\pi_1 + \Sigma_{i=1}^{k-1} a_i \varepsilon^i$ with an error smaller than $\| \pi_1 E \|_\infty \delta^i/(1 - \delta)$.*

Let us remark that this applies for all decomposition based on the partition of transitions according to a threshold ϵ as soon as $\delta < 1$. Note that this condition is not very restrictive because, in general, ε is much smaller than $(1 - \beta)$. Thus, we also state the accuracy of the first part of Sanders's method. Finally note that the proof is not exactly the same in Courtois's approach since matrix P is not NCD.

In the following, we show how to compute π_1, the first approximation of π. We also present the computation of further approximates of π using more terms from the perturbation formula to obtain a desirable accuracy.

First Approximation of π Using P_1 rather than P may be useful in a numerical computation of the steady-state distribution. The first idea is the gain of memory space and the speedup in the product of vectors by the matrix. Therefore, iterative algorithms use less space and are quicker to perform the elementary product $x_n P$. This is roughly Sanders and Malhis's approach. However, it is not clear that the subdominant eigenvalue of P_1 is smaller that the one of P. So, computation of π_1 may be a more difficult problem for some badly defined matrix P.

In this paper we advocate a different approach based on a generalisation of recursive algorithms and a direct resolution of a subproblem. We follow some graph arguments to partition the state space. These arguments are known as the reduction technique (see [11] for the theory and [5] for an application to Stochastic Automata Networks). The easiest solution to perform the reduction is the computation of a cut set of the directed cycles of the graph without loops associated to the chain. This cut set is usually denoted as a transversal.

Definition 1 (transversal) *[1] Let $G = (V, E)$ be a directed graph with a set of vertices denoted as V and a set of directed edges denoted as E. $T_G \subset V$ is a transversal of G if each directed cycle of G has at least one vertex in T_G.*

Remember that when we have built matrix P_1, we have removed some transitions from P and we may have also add some loops. But as we consider the graphs without loops associated to the chain we have the following relation between the sets of vertices.

Proposition 1 *The vertices of the graph without loops associated to P_1 are element of the set of vertices of the graph without loops associated to P (i.e. $E(P_1) \subset E(P)$)*

But, the cut set of the directed cycles is a monotone parameter.

Proposition 2 *Let $G = (V, E)$ and $G_1 = (V, E_1)$ two graphs with the same set of nodes V, if $E_1 \subset E$ then an arbitrary transversal of G is a transversal of G_1.*

Computing a minimal transversal is an NP complete problem [6] but we only need an arbitrary transversal for the reduction. So, very efficient heuristics may be used to obtain such sets. In general, we use several of them and consider the smallest set. The general framework for the heuristics is presented in the next section. As the set of edges V_1 is smaller, the algorithms usually perform better on G_1. So, the transversal computed on the graph associated to P_1 will, in general, be smaller than the transversal computed on the graph associated to P. This is important because the complexity of the whole method depends on the size of the transversal. Let N_1 be the size of the transversal and $N_2 = N - N_1$.

When the transversal is computed, we reorder the states of P such that the states in the transversal receive a number between 1 and N_1. Assuming that matrix P_1 may be represented as blocks: $\begin{pmatrix} A & B \\ C & D \end{pmatrix}$. The following property is proved in [5].

Proposition 3 *There exists an ordering of the vertices such that D is upper triangular. And $I - D$ is not singular.*

Therefore, computing $(I - D)^{-1}$ is quite simple. Let us now present the last part of algorithm. We decompose π_1 and e into 2 subvectors (π_1^1, π_1^2) and (e_1, e_2) to botain:

$$\begin{cases} \pi_1^1(I - A) = \pi_1^2 C \\ \pi_1^2(I - D) = \pi_1^1 B \\ \pi_1^1 e_1 + \pi_1^2 e_2 = 1 \end{cases} \tag{7}$$

As $(I - D)$ is not singular, matrix $H = B(I - D)^{-1}$ is well defined. After substitution, we get:

$$\begin{cases} \begin{cases} \pi_1^1(I - A - HC) = 0 \\ \pi_1^1(e_1 + He_2) = 1 \end{cases} \\ \pi_1^2 = \pi_1^1 H \end{cases} \tag{8}$$

The first two equations consist of a reduced system in π_1^1. The size of the system is now N_1 instead of N. We solve it with an usual Gaussian elimination algorithm. π_1^2 is then obtained using the third equation: a simple product of a vector by a sparse matrix which represents the propagation of the values of π_1^1. This method is related to the stochastic complementation theory [13] and is a generalization of the ad-hoc algorithm proposed by Robertazzi to solve Markov models of some protocols [14].

Thus, using this method, we have obtained a first approximation of π. And this computation is in general much more quicker than for the exact result.

Computation of the a_i We begin by the computation of a_1 which is solution of a slightly different equation. Then we show how to solve the general a_i using some information already computed for a_1. Remember that we have to solve:

$$a_1 = a_1 P_1 + \pi_1 E \quad and \quad a_1 e = 0 \tag{9}$$

where π_1 is the steady-state distribution of P_1, i.e. the first approximation of the solution.

Now, we define more precisely the partition of the arcs we used to build P_1. We assume that the arcs of P with a probability smaller than ϵ which are incident to a node of the transversal of P_1 we consider are kept in matrix P_1. Even if such a definition seams to be recursive (we use P_1 to build P_1), the decomposition is feasible in two steps because of the property of the transversal.

- First we remove from P all the arcs with a probability smaller than ε to obtain an irreducible P_1. We compute a transversal of P_1.
- We add into P_1 the arcs of P with a probability smaller than ε which are incident to the nodes of the transversal. The transversal computed on the first version of P_1 is still a cut set of directed cycles of this new version of P_1. Indeed, the arcs added in the second step may add cycles. But these new

cycles always use a vertex in the transversal as the new arcs are incidents to vertices of this cut set.

Therefore using the decomposition into blocks we already used for P_1, we show that the non zero elements of matrix E are associated to block D of P_1, (i.e $E = \begin{pmatrix} 0 & 0 \\ \hline 0 & E_\varepsilon \end{pmatrix}$).

We decompose a_1 into (a_1^1, a_1^2) and π_1 in (π_1^1, π_1^2).

$$(a_1^1, a_1^2) = (a_1^1, a_1^2) \left(\frac{A | B}{C | D} \right) + (\pi_1^1, \pi_1^2) \begin{pmatrix} 0 & 0 \\ \hline 0 & E_\varepsilon \end{pmatrix}$$

¿From the previous expression, we obtain the following system:

$$\begin{cases} a_1^1(I - A) = a_1^2 C \\ a_1^2(I - D) = a_1^1 B + \pi_1^2 E_\varepsilon \\ a_1^1 e_1 + a_1^2 e_2 = 0 \end{cases} \tag{10}$$

Again let H be $(I - D)^{-1}$:

$$\begin{cases} a_1^1(I - A - HC) = \pi_1^2 E_\varepsilon (I - D)^{-1} C \\ a_1^1(e_1 + He_2) = -\pi_1^2 E_\varepsilon (I - D)^{-1} e_2 \\ a_1^2 = a_1^1 H + \pi_1^2 E_\varepsilon (I - D)^{-1} \end{cases} \tag{11}$$

Given $G = E_\varepsilon (I - D)^{-1}$, system (11) becomes:

$$\begin{cases} a_1^1(I - A - HC) = \pi_1^2 GC \\ a_1^1(e_1 + He_2) = -\pi_1^2 Ge_2 \\ a_1^2 = a_1^1 H + \pi_1^2 G \end{cases} \tag{12}$$

So, we solve the reduced system of a_1^1 and then we obtain a_1^2 by a simple product by a sparse matrix. To solve system (12), we build the linear operator M from the $N_1 + 1$ linear equations. And using a Gaussian elimination, we compute M^{-1} which is kept in memory because it is also used in the next steps of the algorithm. The computation of a_1 has roughly the same complexity as the computation of π_1. Furthermore, the resolution of the linear system for a_1 only differ by one equation from the linear system for π_1. Similarly, the computation of matrix $(I - A - HC)$ and G will be done only once. This may lead to important savings in time. Remember that a_{i+1} is defined as :

$$\begin{cases} a_{i+1} = a_{i+1} P_1 + a_i E \\ a_{i+1} e = 0 \end{cases} \tag{13}$$

Using the block structure of matrices P_1 and E we obtain, using the same algebraic manipulation we used to get a_1:

$$\begin{cases} a_{i+1}^1(I - A - HC) = a_i^2 GC \\ a_{i+1}^1(e_1 + He_2) = -a_i^2 Ge_2 \\ a_{i+1}^2 = a_{i+1}^1 H + a_i^2 G \end{cases} \tag{14}$$

Most of the computation was already done : M, M^{-1}, H and G. It only remains to perform the matrix vector multiplications. So the computation of a_i for $i > 1$ does not take a lot of time, if a_1 is already computed.

3   Description of the Whole Algorithm

Let us now give the complete description of the algorithm including the heuristics
to compute the transversal.

1. Let $\varepsilon \in [0, 1]$. We decompose matrix P into P_1 and E such that P_1 is irreducible and the transitions with probability smaller than ε which are not
   needed for the irreducibility of P_1 are in E.
2. We compute the transversal T associated to P_1 using the following heuristics.
   We usually consider the function f to be the input and output degree or their
   sum or their product. The complexity of these heuristics is linear.
   a) T is empty,
   b) remove from G the vertex x which maximize function f, put it into T,
      remove the edges incident to x,
   c) remove from G all the nodes y with input degree or output degree equal
      to 0. Remove the edges incident to y. Loop until it is no more possible
   d) if G is not empty, go to 2.c,
   e) perform the heuristic for all f in the set of functions. Take the transversal
      with the smallest size.
3. We add into P_1 the transitions of E incident to nodes of the transversal.
4. We compute the steady-state distribution π_1 using reduction method.
5. We compute a_1 using reduction (equation (12)), matrix M defined by $N_1 - 1$
   colums of $(I - A - HC)$ and $(e_1 + He_2)$ is computed as well as M^{-1}. Matrices
   M^{-1}, H, G are kept in memory.
6. for all i between 2 and k, we compute a_{i+1} using the reduced system (equation (14)), and the matrices already obtained in the former phases.
7. the approximation of π is $\pi_1 + \sum_{i=1}^{k} a_i \varepsilon^i$.

4   Numerical Experiments

We now present some numerical results for our algorithm. In the first part, we
compare it with a direct algorithm (i.e. GTH) on random matrices. Then we
present a model of a voice and data multiplexer which may be easily solved
using our approach.

4.1   Comparison on Random Matrices

Our method needs a preprocessing (the partition and the reduction) before proceeding to a direct analysis of a subsystem. For some matrices, this preprocessing
does not allow a significant reduction of the state space. Therefore, our algorithm
will be, in this case, a little bit worst than the direct algorithm (i.e. the preprocessing is linear in the number of transitions). So we compare the algorithms on
a sufficiently large set of random structures and we perform statistical tests on
the results.

We have generated random matrices using the following algorithm. The irreducibility is insured by a Hamiltonian directed loop which is deterministic. Then random edges have been added according to an i.i.d Bernoulli process. Let p_{edge} be the probability to add an edge and let p_{edge_ε} be the probability that this transition has a probability smaller than ε. We have considered different values of p_{edge} and p_{edge_ε} and for each case, we have generated 20 matrices and we have computed the average execution time for our method and the GTH method. Typical results are depicted in figure 1. The important fact is that the efficiency of our method increases with the size of the matrix.

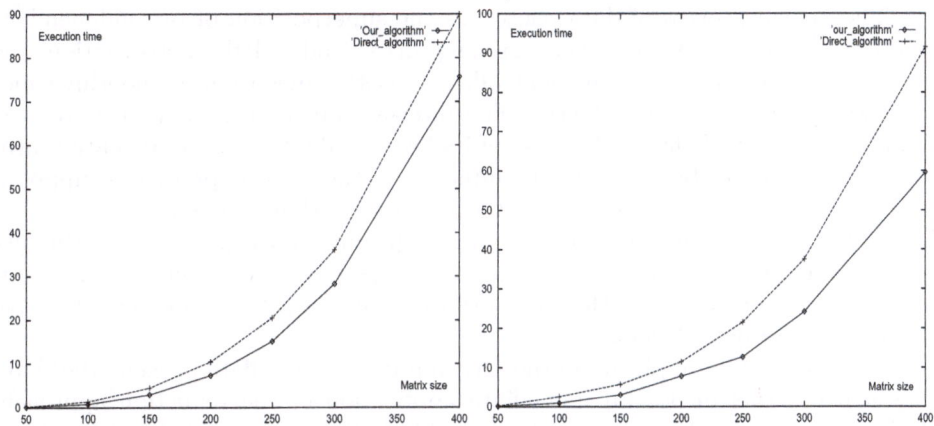

Fig. 1. Computation time for $p_{edge} = 0.1$ and $p_{edge_\varepsilon} = 0.005$.

For each case, we have computed the mean μ and the standard deviation σ of the difference of time between the two methods. The time for our method is the total time (i.e. the computation of the partition, the tranversal and the reduction). We have also computed the 95% confidence interval IC and performed the test of significance for these variables [9]. For all confidence intervals obtained, we established that zero is not include in the interval, so both algorithms are significantly different. Our algorithm takes significanlty less time even if for some matrices the direct algorithm is better. This is typically the case when the transversal is large.

	$p_{edge} = 0.1$ and $p_{edge_\varepsilon} = 0.005$			$p_{edge} = 0.01$ and $p_{edge_\varepsilon} = 0.05$		
Size	μ	σ	IC	μ	σ	IC
50	4.8E-02	9E-03	[4.49E-02, 5.19E-02]	3.2E-02	1E-02	[2.84E-02, 3.62E-02]
100	4.8E-01	3E-02	[4.68E-01, 4.93E-01]	1.6E+00	2E-01	[1.55E+00, 1.75E+00]
150	1.4E+00	6E-02	[1.41E+00, 1.45E+00]	1.6E+00	4E-01	[1.44E+00, 1.79E+00]
200	2.6E+00	2E-01	[2.51E+00, 2.73E+00]	3.4E+00	4E-01	[3.33E+00, 3.64E+00]
300	6.6E+00	6E-01	[6.37E+00, 6.86E+00]	7.7E+00	2E-01	[7.64E+00, 7.89E+00]
400	1.1E+01	2E+00	[1.02E+01, 1.19E+01]	2.5E+01	6E+00	[2.22E+01, 2.96E+01]

4.2 A Small Example

We consider a voice and data multiplexer for one channel. There is a buffer to store data packets. When the voice is active, it keeps the channel until the communication finishes. The distribution of the communication time for voice is assumed to follow an exponential distribution. When data packets are present in the buffer, the voice packets is not allowed to begin a connection. The channel is used by data and the connection demand for voice is lost (it is not buffered). The inter-arrivals of voice connection follow a Poisson process. The service distribution of the data packets are assumed to be i.i.d exponential. The buffer is of size B.

The arrival process of data packets is the superposition of two independent sources of arrivals: a controlled arrival process and a light perturbation due to more variable process. The controlled process comes from a smoothing mechanism such as a Leaky Bucket. The inter-arrival for this flow of arrivals is represented by an Erlang k because of its low variability. The perturbation process is supposed to be Poisson. The intensity of the Poisson process is supposed to be very small compared to the intensity of the Erlang process.

The first step of the numerical analysis is the uniformization of the continuous-time chain. The chain has $2 \times K \times (B+1)$ states and his very sparse : the maximum degree of a node is 6. However, for some values of the parameters, iterative techniques are not efficient.

Because of the complexity of the arrival process of the data packets, the chain has a bad structure for an immediate application of the reduction approach. Indeed, the minimal transversal has roughly half the nodes of the chain. Note that in this case, we are able to prove that the cut set is minimal.

However after removing the arcs with small probabilities (which are associated to Poisson arrivals), the chain becomes much more simple for the structural analysis. The minimal cut set has now a cardinality of $K + B$. Then, we have to solve two linear systems of size $K + B$ rather than a linear system of size $2K(B+1)$. Our algorithm is in this case much more efficient than the iterative techniques, due to the parameters, and than the direct algorithm, due to the structural properties we are able to take into account.

5   Conclusion

Finally, we want to stress that the perturbation argument is much more general that the algorithm we have designed. We suggest now some new approaches based on the perturbation argument we present in section 2. The first idea is to combine perturbation and product form solutions. For instance, a network of $M/M/1$ with exponential services, Markov routing, and external arrivals following a superposition of Poisson processes and some Markovian perturbation may be approximated by a Jackson's network. However we have to characterize the relations which define a_1 when π_1 has a product form. Remember that the sets of linear equations which define both quantities are almost the same. So it may be expected some kind of analytical results for networks of queues.

Another approach, more numerical, consists of an analysis of terms $\pi_1 E P_1^i$ used in the explicit construction of a_i. In some cases, a very fast approximation of a_i may be found after only some iterations on the summation. This may lead to a new class of algorithms to obtain the steady-state distribution of Markov chains.

References

1. C. Berge. *Graphes et Hypergraphes*. Dunod, 1970.
2. P.-J. Courtois. Error analysis in nearly-completely decomposable stochastic systems. *Econometrica*, 43(4):691–709, 1975.
3. P.-J. Courtois. *Decomposability: queuing and computer system applications*. Academic Press, 1977.
4. G. Fayolle, V.A. Malyshev, and Menshikov M.V. *Topics in the constructive theory of countable Markov chain*. 1993.
5. J.-M. Fourneau and Quessette F. Graphs and stochastic automata networks. In *Computations with Markov Chains, Kluwer, Edited by W.J. Stewart*, 1995.
6. M.R. Garey and D.S. Johnson. *Computers and Intractability, a Guide to the theory of NP- Completeness*. W.H. Freeman and Company, 1979.
7. E. Gelenbe and I. Mitrani. *Analysis and synthesis of computer systems*. Academic press, 1980.
8. J.J. Hunter. *Mathematical Techniques of Applied Probability*. Academic Press, 1933.
9. R. Jain. *The art of computer systems performance analysis*. Wiley, 1992.
10. R. Koury, D.F. McAllister, and W.J. Stewart. Methods for computing stationary distribution of a large markov chain. *SIAM J. Algebraic and Discrete Mathematics*, 5:164–186, 1984.
11. R. Lal and U.N. Bhat. Reduced systems in markov chains and their applications in queueing theory. *Queueing Systems*, 2, 1987.
12. L.M. Malhis and W.H. Sanders. An efficient two-stage iterative method for the steady-state analysis of markov regenerative stochastic petri net models. In *Performance Evaluation*, pages 583–601, 1996.
13. C.D. Meyer. Stochastic complementation, uncoupling markov chains, and the theory of nearly reducible systems. *SIAM review*, 31(2):240–272, June 1989.
14. R. Robertazzi. Recursive solution of a class of non-product form protocol models. In *INFOCOM*, 1989.
15. W.J. Stewart. *An Introduction to the Numerical Solution of Markov Chains*. Princeton, 1993.

A Comparison of Numerical Splitting-based Methods for Markovian Dependability and Performability Models [*]

Víctor Suñé and Juan A. Carrasco

Departament d'Enginyeria Electrònica,
Universitat Politècnica de Catalunya,
Diagonal 647, plta. 9, 08028 Barcelona, Spain

Abstract. Iterative numerical methods are an important ingredient for the solution of continuous time Markov dependability models of fault-tolerant systems. In this paper we make a numerical comparison of several splitting-based iterative methods. We consider the computation of steady-state reward rate on rewarded models. This measure requires the solution of a singular linear system. We consider two classes of models. The first class includes failure/repair models. The second class is more general and includes the modeling of periodic preventive test of spare components to reduce the probability of latent failures in inactive components. The periodic preventive test is approximated by an Erlang distribution with enough number of stages. We show that for each class of model there is a splitting-based method which is significantly more efficient than the other methods.

1 Introduction

Continuous time Markov chains (CTMCs) are widely used for dependability modeling. For these models, several measures of interest can be computed from the solution vector of a linear system of equations. Typically, such a system is sparse and may have hundreds of thousands of unknowns, so it must, in general, be solved numerically using an iterative method.

Several currently available tools allow us to solve dependability models. These are, among others, SAVE [7], SPNP [3], UltraSAN [5] and SURF-2 [2]. SPNP uses Successive Overrelaxation (SOR) with dynamic adjustment of the relaxation parameter ω [4]. SAVE uses SOR for the computation of the steady-state probability vector and SOR combined with an acceleration technique [10] for computation of mean time to failure ($MTTF$) like measures. UltraSAN offers a direct method with techniques to reduce the degree of fill-in and SOR, being ω selected by the user. Finally, SURF-2 uses the gradient-conjugate method (see, for instance, [14]).

---

[*] This work has been supported by the Comisión Interministerial de Ciencia y Tecnología (CICYT) under the research grant TIC95–0707–C02–02.

R. Puigjaner et al. (Eds.): Tools'98, LNCS 1469, pp. 154–164, 1998.

Several papers have compared numerical methods for solving the linear systems of equations which arise when solving CTMC models. In an early paper [8], performance models are considered and several iterative methods are compared for the computation of the stationary probability vector of an ergodic Markov chain. These methods include Gauss-Seidel (GS), SOR, block SOR and Chebyshev acceleration with GS preconditioning. For SOR, an algorithm based on the theory of p-cyclic matrices [17] is used to select a value for ω. In [14], failure/repair models are considered and SOR with dynamic adjustment of ω also based on the theory of p-cyclic matrices is compared with GS and the power methods, showing that SOR is considerably more efficient specially for the linear systems arising in $MTTF$ computations. In [11] a number of direct and iterative methods are reviewed in the context of performance models. Among others, three spliting-base methods are considered: GS, SOR and symmetric SOR. In [6] the generalized minimal residual method and two variants of the quasi-minimal residual algorithm are compared. In [9], direct and splitting-based iterative methods are considered for solving CTMC models arising in communication systems and the authors suggest to use SOR with suitable values for ω in combination with some aggregation/disaggregation steps.

In this paper we compare splitting-based iterative methods for the solution of linear systems which arise in the computation of the steady-state reward rate ($SSRR$) defined over rewarded CTMC models. We start by defining formally the measure and establishing the linear system which has to be solved. Let $X = \{X(t); t \geq 0\}$ be a finite irreducible CTMC. X has state space Ω and infinitesimal generator $\boldsymbol{Q} = (q_{ij})_{i,j \in \Omega}$. Let r_i, $i \in \Omega$ be a reward rate structure defined over X. The steady-state reward rate is defined as:

$$SSRR = \lim_{t \to \infty} E[r_{X(t)}]$$

and can be computed as

$$SSRR = \sum_{i \in \Omega} r_i \pi_i \ ,$$

where $\boldsymbol{\pi} = (\pi_i)_{i \in \Omega}$ is the steady-state probability distribution vector of X, which is the only normalized ($\|\boldsymbol{\pi}\|_1 = 1$) solution of:

$$\boldsymbol{Q}^T \boldsymbol{\pi} = \boldsymbol{0} \ , \tag{1}$$

where matrix $\boldsymbol{Q}^T$ is singular and the superscript T indicates transpose. The steady-state unavailability is a particular case of $SSRR$ obtained by defining a reward rate structure $r_i = 0$, $i \in U$, $r_i = 1$, $i \in D$, where U is the subset of Ω including the up (operational) states and D is the subset of Ω including the down states.

In this paper we are concerned with numerical iterative methods to solve the linear system (1). Two classes of models will be considered. The first class include failure/repair models like those which can be specified by the SAVE modeling language [7]. Basically, these models correspond to fault-tolerant systems

made up of components which fail and are repaired with exponential distributions. There is an state in which all components are unfailed having only outgoing
failure transitions. The remaining states have at least an outgoing repair transition. Note that in this class of models the detection of the failure of a component
is assumed to be instantaneous, i.e. all failed components are immediately scheduled for repair. In the second class of models which we will consider, failures of
"spare" (inactive) components will be detected only when they are tested. Test
of spare components will be assumed to be performed periodically with deterministic intertests times. To be able to use CTMCs to represent such systems the
deterministic intertests time will be approximated by a K-Erlang distribution
with K large enough to obtain convergence in $SSRR$ as K is incremented.

We will analyze and compare GS, SOR and block Gauss-Seidel (BGS). A
more complete comparison including an efficient implementation of GMRES
(see, for instance, [13]) and $MTTF$ like measures can be found in [16]. We will
show that GS is guaranteed to converge for (1) when the chain X is generated
breadth-first and the first generated state is exchanged with the last generated
state. Also, an algorithm to select dynamically ω in SOR will be briefly reviewed.
The rest of the paper is organized as follows. Section 2 reviews the iterative
methods. Section 3 analyzes convergence issues. Section 4 presents examples
and numerical results and Sect. 5 presents the conclusions.

2   Numerical Methods

We are interested in solving a linear system of the form

$$Ax = b \ , \tag{2}$$

where $A = Q^T$ and $b = 0$. In the following we will let n be the dimension of A.
We next review splitting-based iterative numerical methods which can be used
to solve (2).

2.1   Gauss-Seidel, SOR and Block Gauss-Seidel

Splitting-based methods are based on the decomposition of matrix A in the form
$A = M - N$, where M is nonsingular. The iterative method is then:

$$x^{(k+1)} = M^{-1}Nx^{(k)} + M^{-1}b \ ,$$

where $x^{(k)}$ is the k-th iterate for x.

Both GS and SOR are easily derived by considering the decomposition $A =
D - E - F$, where D is the diagonal of A and $-E$ and $-F$ are, respectively,
the strict lower and upper part of A. GS is obtained by taking $M = D - E$ and
$N = F$. The iterative step of GS can then be described as:

$$x^{(k+1)} = (D - E)^{-1}Fx^{(k)} + (D - E)^{-1}b \ ,$$

or in terms of the components of A as:

$$x_i^{(k+1)} = \frac{1}{a_{i,i}}\left(-\sum_{j=1}^{i-1} a_{i,j}x_j^{(k+1)} - \sum_{j=i+1}^{n} a_{i,j}x_j^{(k)} + b_i\right), \ i = 1,\dots,n \ . \quad (3)$$

SOR is obtained by taking $M = (D - \omega E)/\omega$ and $N = ((1 - \omega)D + \omega F)/\omega$. The iterative step of SOR can then be described as:

$$x^{(k+1)} = (D - \omega E)^{-1}\big((1 - \omega)D + \omega F\big)x^{(k)} + (D - \omega E)^{-1}\omega b \ ,$$

or in terms of the components of A as:

$$x_i^{(k+1)} = \omega\, x_i^{GS} + (1 - \omega)x_i^{(k)}, \ i = 1,\dots,n \ ,$$

where x_i^{GS} is the right-hand side of (3).

BGS is the straightforward generalization of GS when the coefficient matrix, the right-hand side and the solution vector of (2) are partitioned in p blocks as follows:

$$A = \begin{pmatrix} A_{1,1} & \cdots & A_{1,p} \\ \vdots & \ddots & \vdots \\ A_{p,1} & \cdots & A_{p,p} \end{pmatrix}, x = \begin{pmatrix} x_1 \\ \vdots \\ x_p \end{pmatrix}, b = \begin{pmatrix} b_1 \\ \vdots \\ b_p \end{pmatrix}.$$

The iterative step of BGS is:

$$x_i^{(k+1)} = A_{i,i}^{-1}\left(-\sum_{j=1}^{i-1} A_{i,j}x_j^{(k+1)} - \sum_{j=i+1}^{p} A_{i,j}x_j^{(k)} + b_i\right), \ i = 1,\dots,p \ . \quad (4)$$

Hence, each iteration of BGS requires to solve p systems of linear equations of the form $A_{i,i}x_i = z_i$. Depending on the sizes of the matrices $A_{i,i}$, such systems may be solved using direct or iterative methods.

2.2   An Algorithm for the Optimization of ω in SOR

In this section we briefly describe an algorithm for the optimization of the relaxation parameter ω of SOR. The algorithm does not assume any special property on the matrix of the linear system and searches the optimum ω in the interval $[0, 2]$.

The algorithm is based on estimations of the convergence factor (modulus of the sub-dominant eigenvalue of the iteration matrix). After each iteration k such that the last two iterations have been performed with the same value of ω, the convergence factor η is estimated as:

$$\tilde{\eta} = \frac{\|x^{(k)} - x^{(k-1)}\|_\infty}{\|x^{(k-1)} - x^{(k-2)}\|_\infty} \ .$$

Stabilization of $\tilde{\eta}$ is monitored and it is assumed that a good estimate has been achieved when the relative difference in $\tilde{\eta}/(1 - \tilde{\eta})$ is smaller than or equal to a given threshold parameter $TOLNI$ three consecutive times. For a given ω, except $\omega = 1$, for which no limit is imposed, a maximum of $M = \max\{MAXITEST, est/RATIOETAST\}$ iterations are allocated for the stabilization of $\tilde{\eta}/(1 - \tilde{\eta})$, where est is the number of iterations required for the stabilization of $\tilde{\eta}/(1 - \tilde{\eta})$ for $\omega = 1$. If after M iterations $\tilde{\eta}/(1 - \tilde{\eta})$ has not been stabilized, SOR is assumed not to converge for the current ω. Selection of appropriate values for $TOLNI$ is a delicate matter. If $TOLNI$ is chosen too large an erroneous estimate of the convergence factor may result and the optimization method may become confused. If $TOLNI$ is chosen too small non-convergence may be assumed when the method converges but $\tilde{\eta}/(1-\tilde{\eta})$ takes a large number of iterations to stabilize. Selection of values for $MAXITEST$ and $RATIOETAST$ also involves a tradeoff. If the resulting M is too small, non-convergence may be assumed erroneously. If the resulting M is too large, iterations may be wasted for a bad ω. After some experimentation we found $TOLNI = 0.0001$, $MAXITEST = 150$, and $RATIOETAST = 5$ to be appropriate choices.

The algorithm starts with $\omega = 1$ and, while the estimate for η decreases, makes a scanning in the interval $[1, 2]$ taking increments for ω of 0.1. If a minimum for η is bracketed, a golden search (see, for instance, [12]) is initiated. If for an ω it is found that the method does not converge, the increment for ω is divided by 10 and the search continues to the right starting from the last ω for which the method converged. This process is repeated till the increment for ω is 0.001 (the minimum allowed). If the estimate for η for $\omega > 1$ is found to increase a similar scanning is made to the left in the interval $[0, 1]$. At any point of the algorithm, the best ω is recorded and used till convergence or the maximum number of allowed iterations is reached when the algorithm becomes "lost". The complete algorithm is implemented using an automaton with 13 different states corresponding to different states of the search. Due to lack of space we cannot give a precise description of the automaton, but only highlight the main ideas on which it is based.

3   Convergence

$-\boldsymbol{Q}^T$ is a singular M-matrix and it is well known that SOR converges for $-\boldsymbol{Q}^T\boldsymbol{\pi} = \boldsymbol{0}$ (and, therefore, for (1)) if $0 < \omega < 1$ [15, Theorem 3.17]. We prove next that if X is generated breadth-first and the first state and the last one are exchanged, convergence of GS when solving (1) is also guaranteed.

First we briefly describe breadth-first generation. The initial state is put in an empty FIFO queue. From that point, the generation process continues by taking a state from the queue, generating all its successors and putting in the queue the successors not previously generated. The generation process finishes when the queue becomes empty.

Given the $n \times n$ matrix $\boldsymbol{A}$, its associated directed graph $\Gamma(\boldsymbol{A}) = (V, E)$ is defined by a set of vertices $V = \{1, \ldots, n\}$ and a set of edges $E = \{(i, j) \in$

$V \mid a_{i,j} \neq 0\}$. A sequence of vertices $\alpha = (i_0, i_1, \ldots, i_l, i_0)$ is called a cycle of $\Gamma(A)$ if $i_j \neq i_k$, $j \neq k$, $0 \leq j, k \leq l$ and, $(i_k, i_{(k+1)} \mod (l+1)) \in E$, $0 \leq k \leq l$. The cycle is said to be monotone increasing if $i_0 < i_1 < \ldots < i_l$ and it is said to be monotone decreasing if $i_0 > i_1 > \ldots > i_l$ [1].

Theorem 1. *Let Q be the infinitesimal generator of a finite and irreducible CTMC obtained by generating the CTMC breadth-first and exchanging the first and last states. Forward[1] Gauss-Seidel converges for the linear system $Q^T \pi = 0$ for each initial guess $\pi^{(0)}$.*

Proof. Let $\Gamma(Q) = (V, E)$ be the directed graph associated to Q, infinitesimal generator of X, and let $i_n = n$ be the index of the last state of X. Also, let i_{n-1} be any state with $(i_{n-1}, i_n) \in E$. Because of irreducibility of Q, some state i_{n-1} exists. More generally, since X is generated breadth-first, each state i_l has a predecessor which was generated before it. Such a precedessor may be i_n (the state from which X is generated) or $i_{l-1} < i_l$. Then, it is clear that a cycle $(i_n, i_k, \ldots, i_{n-2}, i_{n-1}, i_n)$ with $i_{l-1} < i_l$, $1 \leq k < l \leq n$ can be formed in $\Gamma(Q)$. Such a cycle becomes $(i_n, i_{n-1}, i_{n-2}, \ldots, i_k, i_n)$ in $\Gamma(Q^T)$, which is monotone decreasing. Then [1, Corollary 1], forward Gauss-Seidel converges for solving $Q^T \pi = 0$ for each $\pi^{(0)}$.   □

Of course, with $\pi^{(0)} = 0$ the method will converge to 0, a trivial solution of the linear system which is not of interest. Thus, we should start with any $\pi^{(0)} > 0$.

Regarding BGS when applied to solve (1), it is known that there always exists a convergent block splitting for Q^T provided that an appropriate ordering of the states is used [8].

As convergence test we require the relative variation on $SSRR$ to be smaller than or equal to a specified tolerance ϵ three consecutive times. The rationale for this test is that it takes into account only "important" components of the solution vector.

4   Numerical Results

In this section we compare the performance of the numerical methods to solve (1) using two examples. The first example is a model with failure and repair transitions and immediate detection of component failures; the second example is a model with failure and repair transitions and K-Erlang intertests time of spare components.

For all methods, the relative tolerance for convergence is taken $\epsilon = 1 \times 10^{-8}$ and a maximum of 100,000 iterations is allowed. In all cases, the CTMC is generated breadth-first and, when the GS and SOR methods (SOR reverts to GS when it cannot find an appropriate $\omega \neq 1$) are used for the solution of (1),

---

[1] The method we have called Gauss-Seidel should be more properly called forward Gauss-Seidel.

the first state (state with all components unfailed) is exchanged with the last generated state so that convergence of GS is guaranteed (Theorem 1). CPU times have been all measured on a Ultra 1 SPARC workstation.

The first example is the distributed fault-tolerant database system depicted in Fig. 1. The system includes two processors, two controllers and three disk clusters, each with four disks. When both processors are unfailed, one of them is in the active state and the other in the spare state. Similarly, when both controllers are unfailed, one of them is active and the other spare. The system is operational if at least one processor, one controller and three disks of each cluster are unfailed. Processors, controllers and disks fail with constant rates 2×10^{-5}, 2×10^{-4} and 3×10^{-5}, respectively. Spare components fail with rate 0.2λ, where λ is the failure rate of the active component. There are two failure modes for processors: "soft" mode, which occurs with probability 0.8, and "hard" mode, which occurs with probability 0.2. Soft failures are recovered by an operator restart, while hard failures require hardware repair. Coverage is assumed perfect for all failures except those of the controllers, for which the coverage probability is C. Uncovered controller failures are propagated to two failure free disks of a randomly chosen cluster. Processor restarts are performed by an unlimited number of repairmen. There is only one repairman who gives preemptive priority first to disks, next to controllers, and last to processors in hard failure mode. Failed components with the same priority are taken at random for repair. Repair rates for processors in soft and hard failure mode are, respectively, 0.5 and 0.2. Controllers and disks are repaired with rates 0.5 and 1, respectively. Components continue to fail when the system is down. The measure of interest is the steady-state unavailability (UA), a particular case of the $SSRR$ generic measure. The generated CTMC has 2,250 states and 19,290 transitions. Four values for the coverage probability are considered: $C = 0.9, 0.99, 0.999,$ and 0.9999. For this example we only experimented with GS and SOR. The CPU time required for the generation of the model was 0.263 s.

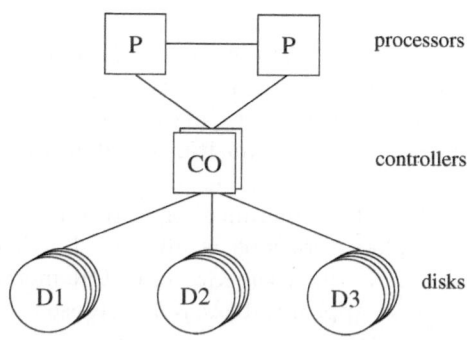

Fig. 1. Distributed fault-tolerant database system

In Table 1 we show the number of iterations and CPU times in seconds for the first example. The GS method is the faster. SOR requires the same number of iterations to achieve convergence as GS because the convergence is so fast that it is achieved before any adjustment on ω can be done. The time per iteration for SOR is slightly greater than for GS.

Table 1. Number of iterations under, respectively, GS and SOR, it_{GS}, it_{SOR}, CPU time in seconds under, respectively, GS and SOR, t_{GS}, t_{SOR}, and UA for the first example

C	it_{GS}	t_{GS}	it_{SOR}	t_{SOR}	UA
0.9	20	0.097	20	0.12	4.054×10^{-5}
0.99	19	0.094	19	0.12	4.461×10^{-6}
0.999	19	0.094	19	0.12	8.537×10^{-7}
0.9999	19	0.094	19	0.12	4.929×10^{-7}

The system considered in the second example is exactly the same as the system of the first example, with the only difference that spare processors and controllers are tested with deterministic intertests times T approximated by a K-Erlang distribution with expected value T with K large enough to make the approximation error small. The measure of interest is again the steady-state unavailability UA. It is clear that the greater T the greater UA. Intuitively, the fact that faulty spare units are not immediately scheduled for repair "increases" the repair times of such units and so increases UA. Then, only values for the intertests time not much greater than the average repair times of the components are reasonable choices. Since the minimum repair rate is 0.2, we consider the following five values for T: 100, 10, 1, 0.1, and 0.01. For the sake of brevity, we will give only results for a coverage probability C equal to 0.99. The value of K is chosen as the minimum value which makes the relative difference between UA for two consecutive K's smaller than or equal to 5×10^{-4}. In Table 2 we show, for each value of T, the number of Erlang stages K, the number of states and transitions of the CTMC X and its generation time.

Table 2. Number of Erlang stages K, number of states, number of transitions and generation time t_g in seconds for the second example and $C = 0.99$

T	K	states	transitions	t_g
0.01	3	12,000	125,766	1.98
0.1	3	12,000	125,766	1.98
1	6	24,000	251,532	4.14
10	9	36,000	377,298	6.36
100	25	100,000	1,048,050	18.7

The state descriptions of the second example have a component ϕ, $1 \leq \phi \leq K$ used to indicate the phase of the K-Erlang distribution. For BGS, the blocks are chosen to include all states which only differ in the value of the state variable ϕ. In addition, states within each block are sorted following increasing values of ϕ (from 1 to K). With that ordering, the diagonal matrices $\boldsymbol{A}_{ii}$ of BGS have the form:

$$
\begin{pmatrix}
q_{m,m} & 0 & \cdots & & 0 & q_{n,m} \\
q_{m,m+1} & q_{m+1,m+1} & 0 & & \cdots & 0 \\
& q_{m+1,m+2} & q_{m+2,m+2} & & \cdots & 0 \\
& & & \cdots & & \\
0 & \cdots & & q_{n-2,n-1} & q_{n-1,n-1} & 0 \\
0 & \cdots & & 0 & q_{n-1,n} & q_{n,n}
\end{pmatrix}.
$$

Taking advantage of this form, we solve efficiently the linear systems (4) of BGS using Gaussian elimination with fill-in only in the last column.

The iterative methods considered for the second example are GS, SOR and BGS. Table 3 shows the results obtained. Notice first that although UA tends fast to the value corresponding to instantaneous detection of failed spare components (4.461×10^{-6}), its dependence on T is significant, at least for moderate values of the intertests time. The performance of the numerical methods is also affected by T. For large values of T, the GS method performs very well, but its performance degrades quickly as T decreases. The same type of comments can be made for the SOR algorithm. Note, however, that as the number of iterations required by GS increases, the relative reduction in the number of iterations achieved by SOR is greater. This means that the algorithm used for selecting the relaxation parameter ω is efficient. BGS is the method which requires less iterations. For $T = 100$ it requires more CPU time than GS and SOR. This is due to the time required to sort the states as explained before. For $T = 10$ BGS is as fast as GS and SOR, and for smaller values of T it should be clearly considered as the method of choice. Overall, BGS seems to be the method of choice for the second example.

Table 3. Number of iterations under, respectively, GS, SOR and BGS, it_{GS}, it_{SOR}, it_{BGS}, CPU time in seconds under, respectively, GS, SOR and BGS, t_{GS}, t_{SOR}, t_{BGS}, and UA for the second example, $C = 0.99$ and several values of T

T	it_{GS}	t_{GS}	it_{SOR}	t_{SOR}	it_{BGS}	t_{BGS}	UA
100	21	10.5	21	11.9	10	15.6	6.129×10^{-6}
10	31	5.01	31	5.74	11	4.92	4.641×10^{-6}
1	162	14.8	162	17.5	12	3.15	4.480×10^{-6}
0.1	1,391	58.4	1,045	51.4	12	1.43	4.463×10^{-6}
0.01	12,632	527	5,953	284	12	1.45	4.461×10^{-6}

5 Conclusions

In this paper three splitting-based iterative numerical methods for solving linear systems have been analyzed in the context of two classes of dependability models and the measure *SSRR*. A new and robust algorithm to dynamically tune the relaxation parameter ω of SOR has been briefly described. It has been proved that Gauss-Seidel converges for the solution of the linear system which results when the steady-state probability vector of an irreducible CTMC has to be computed if the CTMC is generated breadth-first and the first and last state are exchanged. Experimental results have shown that the method of choice for each class of model is different (GS for the first class and BGS for the second class).

References

1. G. P. Barker and R. J. Plemmons, "Convergent Iterations for Computing Stationary Distributions of Markov Chains", SIAM J. Alg. Disc. Math., vol. 7, no. 3, July 1986, pp. 390–398.
2. C. Béounes, M. Aguéra, J. Arlat, S. Bachman, C. Bourdeau, J. E. Doucet, K. Kanoun, J. C. Laprie, S. Metge. J. Moreira de Souza, D. Powell and P. Spiesser, "SURF-2: A Program for Dependability Evaluation of Complex Hardware and Software Systems," *Proc. 23rd IEEE Int. Symp. on Fault-Tolerant Computing (FTCS-23)*, Toulouse, 1993, pp. 668–673.
3. G. Ciardo, J. K. Muppala and K. S. Trivedi, "SPNP: Stochastic Petri Net Package", *Proc. 3rd IEEE Int. Workshop on Petri Nets and Performance Models (PNPM89)*, Kyoto, December 1989, pp. 142–150.
4. G. Ciardo, A. Blakemore, P. F. Chimento, J. K. Muppala, and K. S. Trivedi, "Automated Generation and Analysis of Markov Reward Models Using Stochastic Reward Nets", in C. Meyer and R. Plemmons, editors, *Linear Algebra, Markov Chains and Queuing Models*, IMA Volumes in Mathematics and its Applications, Springer-Verlag 1983, pp. 145–191.
5. J. Couvillon, R. Freire, R. Johnson, W. O. II, A. Qureshi, M. Rai, W. Sanders, and J. Tvedt, "Performability modeling with UltraSAN", *IEEE Software*, September 1981, pp. 69–80.
6. R. W. Freund and M. Hochbruck, "On the Use of Two QMR Algorithms for Solving Singular Systems and Applications in Markov Chain Modeling", Numerical Linear Algebra with Applications, vol. 1, no. 4, 1994, pp. 403–420.
7. A. Goyal, W. C. Carter, E. de Souza e Silva, S. S. Lavenberg, and K. S. Trivedi, "The System Availability Estimator", *Proc. of the 16th Int. Symp. on Fault-Tolerant Computing (FTCS-16)*, 1986, pp. 84–89.
8. L. Kaufmann, B. Gopinath and nE. F. Wunderlich, "Analysis of Packet Network Congestion Control using Sparse Matrix Algortihms", IEEE Trans. on Communications, vol COM-29, no. 4, April 1981, pp. 453–465.
9. U. R. Krieger, B. Müller-Clostermann, M. Sczittnick, "Modeling and Analysis of Communication Systems Based on Computational Methods for Markov Chains", IEEE J. on Selected Areas in Comm., vol. 8, no. 9, December 1990, pp. 1630–1648.
10. P. Heidelberger, J. K. Muppala and K. Trivedi, "Accelerating Mean Time to Failure Computations", IBM Research Report RC–0415, 1996 (to appear in Performance Evaluation).

11. B. Philippe, Y. Saad and W. J. Stewart, "Numerical Methods in Markov Chain Modeling", Operations Research, vol. 40, no. 6, Nov.–Dec. 1992, pp. 1156–1179.
12. W. H. Press, B. P. Flannery, S. A. Teukolsky and W. T. Vetterling, *Numerical Recipes. The Art of Scientific Computing*, Cambridge University Press, Cambridge, 1986.
13. Y. Saad and M. H. Schultz, "GMRES: A Generalized Minimal Residual Algorithm for Solving Nonsymmetric Linear Systems", SIAM J. Sci. Stat. Comput., vol. 7, no. 3, July 1986, pp. 856–869.
14. W. J. Stewart and A. Goyal, "Matrix Methods in Large Dependability Models", IBM Thomas J. Watson Research Center, Technical Report RC-11485, November 1985.
15. W. J. Stewart, *Introduction to the Numerical Solution of Markov Chains*, Princeton University Press, Princeton, 1994.
16. V. S. Suñé and J. A. Carrasco, "A Comparison of Numerical Iterative Methods for Markovian Dependability and Performability Models", Technical Report, Universitat Politècnica de Catalunya, June 1998.
17. R. S. Varga, *Matrix Iterative Analysis*, Prentice-Hall, Englewood Cliffs, NJ, 1962.

Probability, Parallelism and the State Space Exploration Problem

William Knottenbelt[1], Mark Mestern[2], Peter Harrison[1], and Pieter Kritzinger[2]

[1] Department of Computing, Imperial College, 180 Queens Gate, London SW7 2BZ, United Kingdom, email: {wjk,pgh}@doc.ic.ac.uk
[2] Computer Science Department, University of Cape Town, Rondebosch 7701, South Africa, email: {mmestern,psk}@cs.uct.ac.za

Abstract. We present a new dynamic probabilistic state exploration algorithm based on hash compaction. Our method has a low state omission probability and low memory usage that is independent of the length of the state vector. In addition, the algorithm can be easily parallelised. This combination of probability and parallelism enables us to rapidly explore state spaces that are an order of magnitude larger than those obtainable using conventional exhaustive techniques. We implement our technique on a distributed-memory parallel computer and we present results showing good speedups and scalability. Finally, we discuss suitable choices for the three hash functions upon which our algorithm is based.

1 Introduction

Complex systems can be modelled using high-level formalisms such as stochastic Petri nets and process algebras. Often the first phase in the logical and numerical analysis of these systems is the explicit generation and storage of the model's underlying state space and state transition graph. In special cases, where the state space has sufficient structure, an efficient analytical solution can be obtained without the explicit enumeration of the entire state space. Several ingenious techniques, predominantly based on the theory of queueing networks, can be applied in such cases [3]. Further, certain restricted hierarchical structures allow states to be aggregated and the state space to be decomposed [5, 16]. In this paper, however, we consider the general problem where no symmetry or other structure is assumed.

Conventional state space exploration techniques have high memory requirements and are very computationally intensive; they are thus unsuitable for generating the very large state spaces of real-world systems. Various authors have proposed ways of solving this problem by either using shared-memory multiprocessors [2] or by distributing the memory requirements over several computers in a network [7, 6].

Allmaier *et al.* [2] present a parallel shared memory algorithm for the analysis of Generalised Stochastic Petri Nets (GSPNs) [1]. The shared memory approach means that there is no need to partition the state space as must be done in the case of distributed memory. This also brings the advantage of simplifying the

R. Puigjaner et al. (Eds.): Tools'98, LNCS 1469, pp. 165-179, 1998

load balancing problem. However, it does introduce synchronisation problems between the processors. Their technique is tested on a Convex SPP 1600 shared memory multiprocessor with 4GB of main memory. The authors observe good speedups for a range of numbers of processors employed and the system can handle 4 000 000 states with 2 GB of memory.

Caselli *et al.* [6] offer two ways to parallelise the state space generation for massively parallel machines. In the data-parallel method, a marking of a GSPN with t transitions is assigned to t processors. Each processor handles the firing one transition only and is responsible for determining the resulting state. This method was tested on a Connection Machine CM-5 and showed computation times linear in relation to the number of states. In the message-passing method the state space is partitioned between processors by a hash function and newly discovered states are passed to their respective processors. This method achieved good speedups on the CM-5, but was found to be subject to load imbalance.

Ciardo *et al.* [7] present an algorithm for state space exploration on a network of workstations. Their approach is not limited to GSPNs but has a general interface for describing state transition systems. Their method partitions the state space in a way similar to [6] but no details on the storage techniques used are given. The importance of a hashing function which evenly distributes the states across the processors is emphasised, but the method also attempts to reduce the number of states sent between processors. It was tested on a network of SPARC workstations interconnected by an Ethernet network and an IBM SP-2 multiprocessor. In both cases a good reduction in processing time was reported although with larger numbers of processors, diminishing returns occurred. The largest state space successfully explored had 4 500 000 states; this required four hours of processing on a 32-node IBM SP-2.

All the techniques proposed so far do not take advantage of the considerable gains achieved by using dynamic storage techniques based on hash compaction. The dynamic storage method we present here has several important advantages: memory consumption is low, space is not wasted by a static allocation and access to states is simple and rapid. We also present a parallel version of our technique which results in further performance gains.

After introducing the problem of state space exploration in Section 2, we give the details of the storage allocation algorithm in Section 3 and of the parallel state space generation algorithm in Section 4. Numerical results on the performance of the algorithm are in Section 5 and Section 6 discusses suitable hashing and partition functions. Section 7 concludes and considers future work.

2   State Space Exploration

Fig. 1 shows an outline of a simple sequential state space exploration algorithm. The core of the algorithm performs a breadth-first search (BFS) traversal of a model's underlying state graph, starting from some initial state s_0. This requires two data structures: a FIFO queue F which is used to store unexplored states and a table of explored states E used to prevent redundant state exploration.

```
begin
    E = {s₀}
    F.push(s₀)
    A = ∅
    while (F not empty) do begin
        F.pop(s)
        for each s' ∈ succ(s) do begin
            if s' ∉ E do begin
                F.push(s')
                E = E ∪ {s'}
            end
            A = A ∪ {id(s) → id(s')}
        end
    end
end
```

Fig. 1. Sequential state space generation algorithm

The function $succ(s)$ returns the set of successor states of s. Some formalisms (such as GSPNs) include support for "instantaneous events" which occur in zero time. A state which enables an "instananeous event" is known as a *vanishing state*. We will assume that our successor function implements one of several known on-the-fly techniques available for eliminating vanishing states [8] [17]. In addition, we will not consider the case where s_0 is vanishing.

As the algorithm proceeds, it constructs A, the state graph. To save space, the states are identified by a unique state sequence number given by the function $id(s)$. If we require the equilibrium state space probability distribution, we must construct a Markov chain by storing in A the transition rate between state s and s' for every arc $s \to s'$. The graph A is written out to disk as the algorithm proceeds, so there is no need to store it in main memory.

3   Dynamic Probabilistic Hash Table Compaction

The memory consumed by the state exploration process depends on the layout and management of the two main data structures of Fig. 1. The FIFO queue can grow to a considerable size in complex models. However, since it is accessed sequentially at either end, it is possible to manage the queue efficiently by storing the head and tail sections in main memory, with the central body of the queue stored on disk. The table of explored states, on the other hand, enjoys no such locality of access, and it has to be able to rapidly store and retrieve information about every reachable state. A good design for this structure is therefore crucial to the space and time efficiency of a state generator.

One way to manage the explored state table is to store the full state descriptor of every state in the state table. Such *exhaustive* techniques guarantee complete state coverage by uniquely identifying each state. However, the high memory requirements of this approach severely limit the number of states that can be stored. *Probabilistic* techniques, on the other hand, use hashing techniques to drastically reduce the memory required to store states. This reduction comes at a cost, however, and it is possible that the hash table will represent two distinct states in the same way. If this should happen, the state hash table will incorrectly report a state as previously explored. This will result in incorrect transitions in the state graph and the omission of some states from the hash table. This risk may be acceptable if the probability of inadvertently omitting even one state can be quantified and kept very small.

Probabilistic methods first gained widespread popularity with the development of Holzmann's bit-state hashing technique [13, 14]. This technique aims at maximizing state coverage in the face of limited memory by using a hash function to map each state onto a single bit position in a large bit vector. Holzmann's method was subsequently improved upon by Wolper and Leroy's hash compaction technique [19], and Stern and Dill's enhanced hash compaction method [18]. These techniques hash states onto compressed values which are inserted into a large pre-allocated hash table with a fixed number of slots.

All of these probabilistic methods rely on *static* memory allocation, since they pre-allocate large blocks of memory for the explored-state table. Since the number of states in the system is in general not known beforehand, the preallocated memory may not be sufficient, or may be a gross overestimation. We now introduce a new probabilistic technique which uses *dynamic* storage allocation and which yields a good collision avoidance probability.

The system is illustrated in Fig. 2. The explored state table takes the form of a hash table with several rows. Attached to each row is a linked list which stores compressed state descriptors. Two independent hash functions are used. The *primary* hash function $h_1(s)$ is used to determine which hash table row should be used to store a compressed state and the *secondary* hash function $h_2(s)$ is used to compute the compressed state descriptor values (also known as secondary keys). If a state's secondary key $h_2(s)$ is present in the hash table row given by its primary key $h_1(s)$, then the state is deemed to have been explored. Otherwise the secondary key is added to the hash table row and it's successors are pushed onto the FIFO queue. Note that two states s_1 and s_2 are classified as being equal if and only if $h_1(s_1) = h_1(s_2)$ and $h_2(s_1) = h_2(s_2)$; this may happen even when the two state descriptors are different, so collisions may occur (as in all other probabilistic methods).

3.1   Reliability of the probabilistic dynamic state hash table

We consider a hash table with r rows and $t = 2^b$ possible secondary key values, where b is the number of bits used to store the secondary key. In such a hash table, there are rt possible ways of representing a state. Assuming that $h_1(s)$ and $h_2(s)$ distribute states randomly and independently, each of these representations are equally likely. Thus, if there are n distinct states to be inserted into the hash

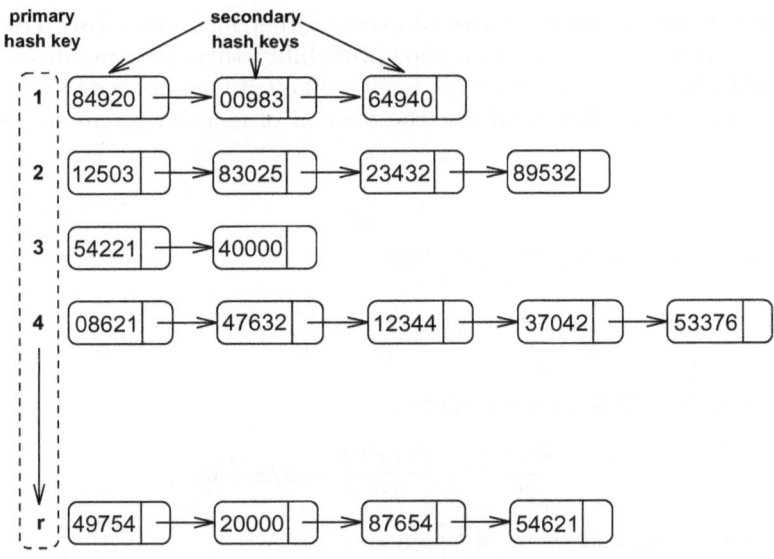

Fig. 2. Hash table with compressed state information

table, the probability p that all states are uniquely represented is given by:

$$p = \frac{(rt)!}{(rt - n)!(rt)^n} \tag{1}$$

Using Stirling's approximation for $n!$ in Eq. (1) yields:

$$p \approx e^{-\frac{n^2}{rt}}$$

If $n^2 << rt$ (as will be the case in practical schemes with p close to 1), we can use the fact that $e^x \approx (1 + x)$ for $|x| << 1$ to approximate p by:

$$p \approx 1 - \frac{n^2}{rt}$$

The probability q that all states are not uniquely represented, resulting in the omission of one or more states from the state space, is of course simply:

$$q = 1 - p \approx \frac{n^2}{rt} = \frac{n^2}{r2^b} \tag{2}$$

Thus the probability of state omission q is proportional to n^2 and is inversely proportional to the hash table size r. Increasing the size of the compressed state descriptors b by one bit halves the omission probability.

3.2   Space complexity

If we assume that the hash table rows are implemented as dynamic arrays, the number of bytes of memory required by the scheme is:

$$M = hr + nb/8. \tag{3}$$

Here h is the number of bytes of overhead per hash table row. For a given number of states and a desired omission probability, there are a number of choices for r and b which all lead to schemes having different memory requirements. How can we choose r and b to minimize the amount of memory required? Rewriting Eq. (2):

$$r \approx \frac{n^2}{q2^b} \tag{4}$$

and substituting this into Eq. (3) yields

$$M \approx \frac{hn^2}{q2^b} + \frac{nb}{8}$$

Minimizing M with respect to b gives:

$$\frac{\partial M}{\partial b} \approx -\frac{n^2(\ln 2)h}{q2^b} + n/8 = 0$$

Solving for the optimal value of b yields:

$$b \approx \log_2\left(\frac{hn\ln 2}{q}\right) + 3$$

The corresponding optimal value of r can then be obtained by substituting b into Eq. (4).

q	number of states											
	10^5			10^6			10^7			10^8		
	Mb	b	r	Mb	b	r	Mb	b	r	Mb	b	r
0.001	0.4186	32	2328	4.608	35	29104	50.21	39	181899	543.2	42	2273737
0.01	0.3774	29	1863	4.186	32	23283	46.08	35	291038	502.1	39	1818989
0.1	0.3363	25	2980	3.774	29	18626	41.86	32	232831	460.8	35	2910383

Table 1. Optimal values for memory usage and the values for b and r used to obtain them for various system state sizes and omission probabilities q

Table 1 shows the the optimal memory requirements in megabytes (Mb) and corresponding values of b and r for state space sizes ranging from 10^5 to 10^8. We have assumed a hash table row overhead of $h = 8$ bytes per row. In practice, it is difficult to implement schemes where b does not correspond to a whole number of bytes. Consequently, 4-byte or 5-byte compression is recommended.

4   Parallel State Space Exploration

We now investigate how our technique can be further enhanced to take advantage of the memory and processing power provided by a network of workstations or a distributed-memory parallel computer. We will assume that there are N nodes available. Each node has its own processor and local memory and can communicate with other nodes via a network.

In the parallel algorithm, the state space is partitioned between the nodes so that each node is responsible for exploring a portion of the state space and for constructing a section of the state graph. A partitioning hash function $h_0(s) \to (0, \ldots, N - 1)$ is used to assign states to nodes, such that node i is responsible for exploring the set of states E_i and for constructing the portion of the state graph A_i where:

$$E_i = \{s : h_0(s) = i\}$$
$$A_i = \{(s_1 \to s_2) : h_0(s_1) = i\}$$

It is important that $h_0(s)$ achieves a good spread of states across nodes in order to achieve good load balance. Naturally, the values produced by $h_0(s)$ should also be independent of those produced by $h_1(s)$ and $h_2(s)$ to enhance the reliability of the algorithm.

The operation of node i in the parallel algorithm is shown in Fig. 3. Each node i has a local FIFO queue F_i used to hold unexplored local states and a hash table used to store the set E_i representing the states that have been explored locally. State s is assigned to processor $h_0(s)$, which stores the state's compressed state descriptor $h_2(s)$ in the local hash table row given by $h_1(s)$.

As in the sequential case, node i proceeds by popping a state off the local FIFO queue and determining the set of successor states. Successor states for which $h_0(s) = i$ are dealt with locally, while other successor states are sent to the relevant remote processors via calls to send-state(k, g, s). Here k is the remote node, g is the identity of the parent state and s is the state descriptor of the child state. The remote processors must receive incoming states via matching calls to receive-state(k, g, s) where k is the sender node. If they are not already present, the remote processor adds the incoming states to both the remote state hash table and FIFO queue.

For the purpose of constructing the state graph, states are identified by a pair of integers (i, j) where $i = h_0(s)$ is the node number of the host processor and j is the local state sequence number. As in the sequential case, the index j can be stored in the state hash table of node i. However, a node will not be aware of the state identity numbers of non-local successor states. When a node receives a state it returns its identity to the sender by calling send-id(k, g, h) where k is the sender, g is the identity of the parent state and h is the identity of the received state. The identity is received by the original sender via a call to receive-id(g, h).

In practice, it is inefficient to implement the communication as detailed in Fig. 3, since the network rapidly becomes overloaded with too many short messages. Consequently state and identity messages are buffered and sent in large blocks. In order to avoid starvation and deadlock, nodes that have very few states left in their FIFO queue or are idle broadcast a message to other nodes requesting them to flush their outgoing message buffers.

```
begin
    if h₀(s₀) = i do begin
        Eᵢ = {s₀}
        Fᵢ.push(s₀)
    end else
        Eᵢ = {}
    Aᵢ = ∅
    while (shutdown signal not received) do begin
        if (Fᵢ not empty) do begin
            Fᵢ.pop(s)
            for each s' ∈ succ(s) do begin
                if h₀(s') = i do begin
                    if s' ∉ Eᵢ do begin
                        Fᵢ.push(s')
                        Eᵢ = Eᵢ ∪ {s'}
                    end
                    Aᵢ = Aᵢ ∪ {id(s) → id(s')}
                end else
                    send-state(h₀(s'), id(s), s')
            end
        end
        while (receive-id(g, h)) do
            Aᵢ = Aᵢ ∪ {g→h}
        while (receive-state(k, g, s')) do begin
            if s' ∉ Eᵢ do begin
                Fᵢ.push(s')
                Eᵢ = Eᵢ ∪ {s'}
            end
            send-id(k, g, id(s'))
        end
    end
end
```

Fig. 3. Parallel state space generation algorithm for node i

The algorithm terminates when all the F_i's are empty and there are no outstanding state or identity messages. We use Dijkstra's circulating probe algorithm [10] to determine when this occurs.

In terms of reliability of the parallel technique, two distinct states s_1 and s_2 will mistakenly be classified as identical states if and only if $h_0(s_1) = h_0(s_2)$ and $h_1(s_1) = h_1(s_2)$ and $h_2(s_1) = h_2(s_2)$. Since h_0, h_1 and h_2 are independent functions, the reliability of the parallel algorithm is essentially the same as that of the sequential algorithm with a large hash table of Nr rows, giving a state omission probability of

$$q = \frac{n^2}{Nr2^b} \tag{5}$$

5   Results

To illustrate the potential of our technique, we consider a 22-place GSPN model of a flexible manufacturing system. This model, which we will refer to as the FMS model, was originally presented in detail in [9], and was subsequently used in [7] to demonstrate distributed exhaustive state space generation. A detailed understanding of the model is not required. It suffices to note that the model has a parameter k (corresponding to the number of initial tokens in places $P1, P2$ and $P3$), and that as k increases, so does the number of states n and the number of arcs a in the state graph (see Fig. 4).

k	n	a
1	54	155
2	810	3 699
3	6 520	37 394
4	35 910	237 120
5	152 712	1 111 482
6	537 768	4 205 670
7	1 639 440	13 552 968
8	4 459 455	38 533 968
9	11 058 190	99 075 405
10	25 397 658	234 523 289
11	54 682 992	518 030 370
12	111 414 940	1 078 917 632

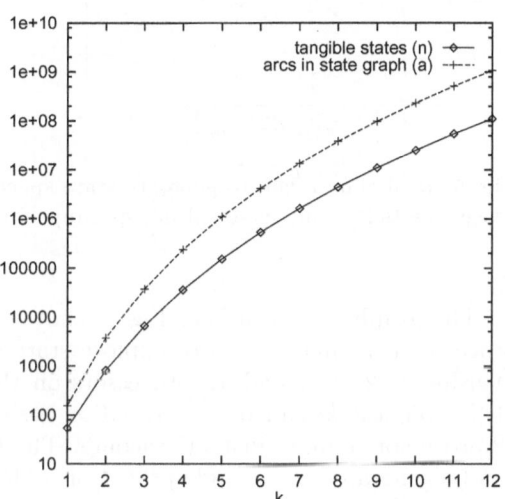

Fig. 4. The number of tangible states (n) and the number of arcs in the state graph (a) for various values of k

We implemented the state generator algorithm of Fig. 3 using hash tables with $r = 350\,003$ rows per processor and $b = 40$ bit secondary keys. The generator was written in C++, with support for two popular parallel programming interfaces, viz. the Message Passing Interface (MPI) [12] and the Parallel Virtual Machine (PVM) interface [11]. Models are specified using the DNAmaca interface language [17] which allows the high-level specification of generalised timed transition systems including GSPNs, queueing networks and Queueing Petri nets [4]. The high-level specification is then translated into a C++ class which is compiled and linked to a library implementing the core state generator. The state space and state graph are written to disk in compressed format as the algorithm proceeds.

We obtained our results on a Fujitsu AP3000 distributed-memory parallel computer with 12 processing nodes [15]. Each node has a 200 MHz UltraSparc processor, 256Mb RAM and 4GB local disk space. The nodes run the Solaris operating system and support MPI. They are connected by a high-speed wormhole-routed network with a peak throughput of 200Mb/s (the AP-net).

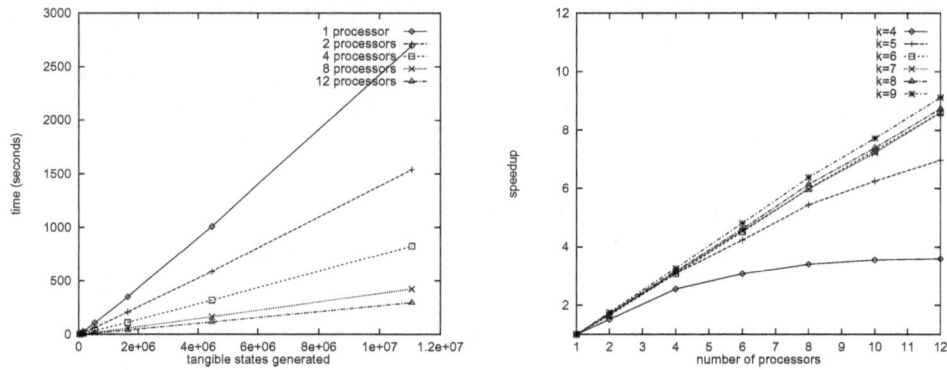

Fig. 5. Real time taken to generate state spaces up to $k = 9$ using 1, 2, 4, 8 and 12 processors (left), and the resulting speedups for $k = 4, 5, 6, 7, 8$ and 9 (right)

The graph on the left in Fig. 5 shows the time (defined as the maximum processor run time) taken to explore state spaces of different sizes (up to $k = 9$) using 1, 2, 4, 8 and 12 processors on the AP3000. The $k = 8$ state space (4 459 455 states) can be generated on a single processor in under 17 minutes; 12 processors require just 115 seconds. The $k = 9$ state space (11 058 190 states) can be generated on a single processor in 45 minutes; 12 processors require just 296 seconds.

The graph on the right in Fig. 5 shows the speedups for the cases $k = 4, 5, 6, 7, 8, 9$. The speedup for N processors is given by the run time of the sequential generation ($N = 1$) divided by the run time of the distributed generation with N processors. For $k = 9$ using 12 processors we observe a speedup of 9.12, giving an efficiency of 76%. Most of the lost efficiency can be accounted for by communication overhead and buffer management, which is not present in the sequential case. Since speedup increases linearly in the number of processors for $k > 6$, there is evidence to suggest that our algorithm scales well.

The memory utilization of our technique is low: a single processor generating the $k = 8$ state space uses a total of 74Mb RAM (16.6 bytes per state), while the $k = 9$ state space requires 160Mb RAM (14.5 bytes per state). 9 bytes of the memory used per state can be accounted for by the 40-bit secondary key and the 32-bit unique state identifier; the remainder can be attributed to factors such as hash table overhead and storage for the front and back of the unexplored state queue. By comparison, a minimum of 48 bytes would be required to store a state descriptor in a straightforward exhaustive implementation (22 16-bit integers plus a 32-bit unique state identifier). The difference will be even more marked with more complex models that have longer state descriptors, since the memory consumption of our technique is independent of the number of elements in the state descriptor.

Moving beyond the maximum state space size that can be generated on a single processor, the graph on the left in Fig. 6 shows the real time required to generate larger state spaces using 12 processors. For the largest case ($k = 12$) 55 minutes are required to generate a state space with 111 414 940 tangible states and a state graph with 1 078 917 632 arcs. The graph on the right in Fig. 6 shows the distribution of the states generated by each processor for the case $k = 12$.

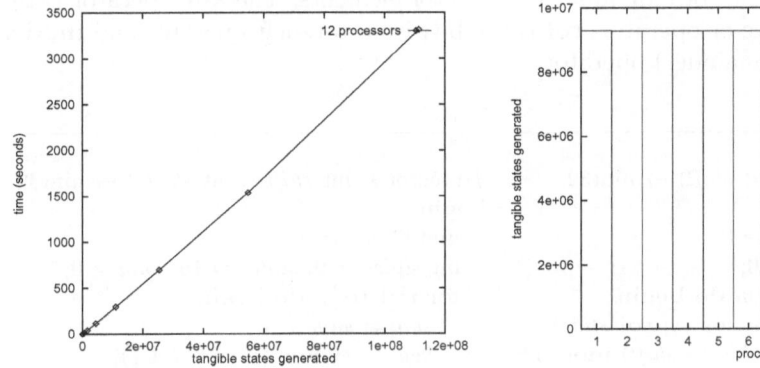

Fig. 6. Real time taken to generate state spaces up to $k = 12$ using 12 processors (left) and distribution of states across processors for $k = 12$ (right)

In comparison to the results reported above (see Table 4), Ciardo *et al* used conventional exhaustive distributed generation techniques to generate the same sample model for the case $k = 8$ in 4 hours using 32 processors on an IBM SP-2 parallel computer [7]. They were unable to explore state spaces for larger values of k.

To enhance our confidence in our results for the case $k = 12$, we use Eq. (5) to compute the probability of having omitted at least one state. For a state space of size $n = 10^8$ states, the omission probability q is given by:

$$q \approx \frac{n^2}{Nr2^b} = \frac{10^{16}}{12 * 350\,003 * 2^{40}} = 0.00217$$

i.e. the omission probability is approximately 0.2%. This is a small price to pay for the ability to explore such large state spaces, and is probably less than the chance of a serious (man-made) error in specifying the model.

To further increase our confidence in the results, we changed all three hash functions and regenerated the state space. This resulted in exactly the same number of tangible states and arcs. This process could be repeated several times to establish an even higher level of confidence in the results.

6   Choosing good hash functions

The reliability of our technique depends on the behaviour of the hash functions h_0, h_1 and h_2 in three important ways. Firstly, h_0 and h_1 should randomly partition states across the processors and hash table rows. Secondly, h_2 should result in a random distribution of compressed values. Finally, h_0, h_1 and h_2 should distribute states independently of one other.

Before we consider each of these functions individually, consider the two general hash functions f_1 and f_2 shown in Fig. 7. Both map an m-element state vector $s = (s_1, s_2, \ldots, s_m)$ onto a 32-bit unsigned integer by manipulating the bit representations of individual state vector elements. The **xor** operator is the bitwise exclusive or operator, **rol** is the bitwise rotate-left operator and **mod** is the modulo (remainder) operator.

```
f₁(vector s, int shift) → uint32        f₂(vector s, int shift₁ , int shift₂) → uint32
begin                                   begin
   uint32 key = 0;                         uint32 key = 0;
   int slide = 0;                          int slide₁ = 0, slide₂ = 16, sum = 0;
   for i=1 to m do begin                   for i=1 to m do begin
      key = key xor (sᵢ rol slide);           sum = sum + sᵢ
      slide = (slide + shift) mod 32;         key = key xor (sᵢ rol slide₁);
   end                                        key = key xor (sum rol slide₂);
   return key;                               slide₁ = (slide₁ + shift₁) mod 32;
end                                          slide₂ = (slide₂ + shift₂) mod 32;
                                          end
                                          return key;
                                       end
```

Fig. 7. Two general hash functions for mapping states onto 32 bit unsigned integers.

Hash function $f_1(s, shift)$ uses exclusive or to combine rotated bit representations of the state vector elements. State vector element s_i is rotated left by an offset of $(i \times shift)$ mod 32 bits. Hash function $f_2(s, shift_1, shift_2)$ is based on encoding not only element s_i rotated left by an offset of $i \times shift_1$ mod 32, but also the sum $\sum_{j<i} s_i$ rotated left by an offset of $i \times shift_2$ mod 32. This technique makes the hash function resistant to any symmetries and invariants that may be present in the model.

We make use of functions f_1 and f_2 to derive suitable choices for $h_0(s)$, $h_1(s)$ and $h_2(s)$ as follows:

- For the **partitioning hash function**, we use either

$$h_0(s) = f_1(s, shift) \bmod prime \bmod N$$

or

$$h_0(s) = f_2(s, shift_1, shift_2) \bmod prime \bmod N$$

where $shift$, $shift_1$ and $shift_2$ are arbitrary shifting factors relatively prime to 32 and $prime$ is some prime number $>> N$.

- For the **primary hash function**, we use either

$$h_1(s) = f_1(s, shift) \bmod r$$

or

$$h_1(s) = f_2(s, shift_1, shift_2) \bmod r$$

where $shift$, $shift_1$ and $shift_2$ are arbitrary shifting factors relatively prime to 32 and r, the number of rows in the hash table, is a prime number.

- For the **secondary hash function**, we consider 32-bit (4-byte compression) based on either f_1 or f_2:

$$h_2(s) = f_1(s, shift)$$

or

$$h_2(s) = f_2(s, shift_1, shift_2)$$

where $shift$, $shift_1$ and $shift_2$ are relatively prime to 32. Function f_2 has the desirable property that it is resistant to symmetries and invariants in the model; this prevents similar (but distinct) states from having the same secondary hash values. Consequently, f_2 gives a better spread of secondary values then f_1. For 40-bit secondary hash keys (i.e. five-byte state compression), f_2 can easily be modified to produce a 40-bit hash key instead of a 32-bit hash key.

It is important to ensure the independence of the values produced by $h_0(s)$, $h_1(s)$ and $h_2(s)$. The following guidelines assist this:

- Some hash functions should be based on f_1 while others are based on f_2; hash functions which use the same base function should use different shifting factors.
- The hash functions should consider state vector elements in a different order.
- the value of r used by $h_1(s)$ should not be the same as the value of $prime$ used by $h_0(s)$.

The results presented in Section 5 made use of partitioning and primary functions based on f_1 and a 40-bit secondary hash function based on f_2.

7   Conclusion and future work

We have presented a new dynamic probabilistic state exploration technique and developed an efficient, scalable parallel implementation. In contrast to conventional state exploration algorithms, the memory usage of our technique is very low and is independent of the length of the state vector. Since the method is probabilistic, there is a chance of state omission, but the reliability of our technique is excellent and the probability of omitting even one state is extremely small. Moreover, by performing multiple runs with independent sets of hash functions, we can reduce the omission probability almost arbitrarily at linear computational cost.

Our results to date show good speedups and scalability. It is the combination of probability and parallelism that dramatically reduces both the space and time requirements of large-scale state space exploration. We note here that the same algorithm could also be effectively implemented on a shared-memory multiprocessor architecture, using a single shared hash table and a shared breadth first search queue. There would be no need for a partitioning function and contention for rows in the shared hash table would be very small. Consequently, it should again be possible to achieve good speedups and scalability.

Our technique is based on the use of hashing functions to assign states to processors, hash table rows, and compressed state values. The reliability analysis requires that the hash functions distribute states randomly and independently and we have shown how to generate hashing functions which meet these requirements. To illustrate its potential, we have explored a state space with more than 10^8 tangible states and 10^9 arcs in under an hour using 12 processors on an AP3000 parallel computer. The probability of state omission is just 0.2%.

Previously, the memory and time bottleneck in the performance analysis pipeline has been state space exploration. We believe that our technique shifts this bottleneck away from state space generation and onto stages later in the analysis pipeline. Future work will focus on completing the performance analysis pipeline with a parallel functional analyser and a parallel steady-state solver. The functional analyser will ensure that the generated state graph maps onto an irreducible Markov chain by eliminating transient states and by verifying that the remaining states are strongly connected. The steady-state solver will then solve the state graph's underlying Markov chain for its steady-state probability distribution using standard techniques for linear simultaneous equations.

8   Acknowledgements

The authors would like to thank the Imperial College Parallel Computing Centre for the use of the AP3000 distributed-memory parallel computer. The authors would also like to thank the anonymous referees for their helpful comments. William Knottenbelt gratefully acknowledges the support and funding provided by the Beit Fellowship for Scientific Research.

References

1. M. Ajmone-Marsan, G. Conte, and G. Balbo. A class of Generalised Stochastic Petri Nets for the performance evaluation of multiprocessor systems. *ACM Transactions on Computer Systems*, 2:93–122, 1984.
2. S.C. Allmaier and G. Horton. Parallel shared-memory state-space exploration in stochastic modeling. *Lecture Notes in Computer Science*, 1253, 1997.
3. F. Basket, K.M. Chandy, R.R. Muntz, and F.G. Palacios. Open, closed and mixed networks of queues with different classes of customers. *Journal of the ACM*, 22:248 – 260, 1975.
4. F. Bause. Queueing Petri nets: A formalism for the combined qualitative and quantitative analysis of systems. In *Proceedings of the 5th International Workshop on Petri nets and Performance Models*. IEEE, October 1993.
5. P. Buchholz. Hierarchical Markovian models: Symmetries and aggregation. *Performance Evaluation*, 22:93–110, 1995.
6. S. Caselli, G. Conte, and P. Marenzoni. Parallel state exploration for GSPN models. In *Lecture Notes in Computer Science 935: Proceedings of the 16th International Conference on the Application and Theory and Petri Nets*. Springer Verlag, Turin, Italy, June 1995.
7. G. Ciardo, J. Gluckman, and D. Nicol. Distributed state-space generation of discrete-state stochastic models. *INFORMS J. Comp.* To appear.
8. G. Ciardo, J.K. Muppula, and K.S. Trivedi. On the solution of GSPN reward models. *Performance Evaluation*, 12(4):237–253, 1991.
9. G. Ciardo and K.S. Trivedi. A decomposition approach for stochastic reward net models. *Performance Evaluation*, 18(1):37–59, 1993.
10. E.W. Dijkstra, W.H.J. Feijen, and A.J.M. van Gasteren. Derivation of a termination detection algorithm for distributed computations. *Information Processing letters*, 16:217–219, June 1983.
11. A. Geist, A. Beguelin, J. Dongarra, W. Jiang, R. Manchek, and V. Sunderam. *PVM Parallel Virtual Machine: A Users' Guide and Tutorial for Networked Parallel Computing*. MIT Press, Cambridge, Massachussetts, 1994.
12. W. Gropp, E. Lusk, and A. Skjellum. *Using MPI: Portable Parallel Programming with the Message Passing Interface*. MIT Press, Cambridge, Massachussetts, 1994.
13. G.J. Holzmann. *Design and Validation of Computer Protocols*. Prentice-Hall, 1991.
14. G.J. Holzmann. An analysis of bitstate hashing. In *Proceedings of IFIP/PSTV95: Conference on Protocol Specification, Testing and Verification*. Chapman & Hall, Warsaw, Poland, June 1995.
15. H. Ishihata, M. Takahashi, and H. Sato. Hardware of AP3000 scalar parallel server. *Fujitsu Scientific and Technical Journal*, 33(1):24–30, June 1997.
16. P. Kemper. Numerical analysis of superposed GSPNs. In *Proc. of the Sixth International Workshop on Petri Nets and Perfromance Models*, pages 52–62. IEEE Computer Society Press, 1995.
17. W.J. Knottenbelt. Generalised Markovian analysis of timed transition systems. Master's thesis, University of Cape Town, 1996.
18. U. Stern and D.L. Dill. Improved probabilistic verification by hash compaction. In *IFIP WG 10.5 Advanced Research Working Conference on Correct Hardware Design and Verification Methods*, 1995.
19. P. Wolper and D. Leroy. Reliable hashing without collision detection. In *Lecture Notes in Computer Science 697*, pages 59–70. Springer-Verlag, 1993.

An Improved Multiple Variable Inversion Algorithm for Reliability Calculation

Tong Luo[1] and K. S. Trivedi[2]

[1] GTE Laboratories, 40 Sylvan Rd, Waltham, MA 02254, USA
tluo@gte.com
[2] Electrical Engineering Department, Duke University, Durham, NC 27708, USA
kst@ee.duke.edu

Abstract. An improved algorithm based on the one proposed by Veeraraghavan and Trivedi(VT) to calculate system reliability using sum of disjoint products (SDP) and multiple variable inversion (MVI) techniques is presented. We compare the improved algorithm with several well known algorithms. The run time comparison shows that the computational saving achieved by our algorithm is quite significant.

1   Introduction

Fault trees and reliability graphs (also known as s-t connected networks) are frequently used for reliability modeling of complex systems. The advantage that they possess over Markov chains (and stochastic Petri nets) is a concise representation and efficient solution algorithms. The class of algorithms known as sum-of-disjoint-products (SDP) is the most often used for such reliability calculations. Early versions of SDP algorithms used single variable inversion (SVI) techniques while the newer versions employ multiple variable inversion (MVI). Three well known MVI algorithms are VT [12], KDH88 [6] and CAREL [10]. We propose a new algorithm based on the VT [12] algorithm and show that the new algorithm is faster than all the three algorithms cited above.

All SDP methods start by generating minpaths for reliability graphs or the mincuts for fault trees. The system reliability is then the probability of the union of the minpaths or the mincuts. This is a union of product problem (UPP). The idea of SDP method is to convert the sum of products into the sum of disjoint products so that the probability of the sum of products can be expressed as the sum of the probability of each disjoint product. Single variable inversion(SVI) methods [5,2,8,1,7,3] generally produce very large number of products in the intermediate and the final results while MVI methods such as VT [12], KDH88 [6], and CAREL [10] achieve shorter computation time and appreciably fewer disjoint products. Obtaining fewer disjoint products is important because it reduces the computation time, the storage space, and the rounding error. However, all these MVI algorithms are quite complex. A comparison of the operators used in these algorithms is given in [9].

By carefully studying all possible combinations of two products (we call each possible combination of two products a *state*), we divide the state space into four

R. Puigjaner et al. (Eds.): Tools'98, LNCS 1469, pp. 180–192, 1998.
© Springer-Verlag Berlin Heidelberg 1998

disjoint subsets each satisfying a given condition, namely, "subset condition", "x1 condition", "disjoint condition" and "split recursive condition". Following this idea, we have developed an improved algorithm (we call it I_VT algorithm) over VT [12]. The improved algorithm has a simple formulation, and is more efficient over the original VT [12] algorithm. The proof is also quite short so we include it in this paper. A run time comparison of I_VT with VT [12], KDH88 [6] and CAREL [10] algorithms over nine examples of different complexity shows that the time saving of I_VT is very significant.

2   Terminology

path A set of events such that if all of them are true the system is functional.

minpath A subset of a path with minimal number of events that still make the system functional.

minpath set The set of all the minpaths of a network. It can be generated by Tarjan's algorithm [11].

cut A set of events such that if all the events in the set are true then the system is failed.

mincut A subset of a cut with minimal number of events that still make the system fail.

mincut set The set of all the mincuts of a fault tree. It can be generated by Bennetts' algorithm [4].

cube A representation of the Boolean product of all variables in a system. For a system consists of n variables $e_1, e_2, ..., e_n$, cube $A = a_1 a_2 ... a_n$, where

$$a_i = \begin{cases} 1 & \text{if variable } e_i \text{ is true,} \\ x & \text{if variable } e_i \text{ does not matter,} \\ 0_\mu & \text{if the event that all the variables} \\ & \quad e_j \text{ for which } a_j = 0_\mu \text{ are true is false.} \end{cases}$$

Symbol 0_μ is used to represent inverted products. For example, the cube representation of Boolean product $\overline{w_1 w_2} w_3 \overline{w_4} w_5 \overline{w_6 w_7}$ is $0_1 0_1 1 0_2 1 0_3 0_3$.

coordinate The ith element of a cube is called the ith coordinate.

coordinate pair The coordinates of two cubes at the same index.

minproduct The cube representation of either a minpath or a mincut according to the context.

disjoint products A set of minproducts disjoint from each other.

3   Problem to Solve

The reliability of a network (or a fault tree) G, $R(G)$, can be expressed as:

$$R(G) = \begin{cases} P(\bigcup_{i=1}^{p} MP_i) & \text{if } MP_i \text{ is a minpath,} \\ 1 - P(\bigcup_{i=1}^{p} MP_i) & \text{if } MP_i \text{ is a mincut.} \end{cases}$$

where $MP_i, i = 1, 2, ..., p$, are all the minproducts of the network(or fault tree). The minproducts are generally not disjoint from each other. So we are dealing with the problem of computing the probability of a union of non-disjoint products. One way to solve this problem is to use the sum of disjoint product(SDP) equation:

$$P(\bigcup_{i=1}^{p} MP_i) = P(MP_1) + P(MP_2 \cdot \overline{MP_1}) + ...$$

$$+P(...((MP_p \cdot \overline{MP_1}) \cdot \overline{MP_2}) \cdot ... \cdot \overline{MP_{p-1}}) \tag{1}$$

To use Equation 1, we must know how to calculate Boolean product $A \cdot \overline{B}$. In SVI algorithms, $A \cdot \overline{B}$ is decomposed into the form that does not have group inverted variables. The problem becomes more complicated when we try to use MVI techniques. Following lemma suggests an alternative way to calculate the Boolean product $A \cdot \overline{B}$. Its proof is given in the Appendix.

Lemma 1. *Let A, B and R be Boolean variables. $A \cdot \overline{B} = R$ iff R satisfy the following two Properties:*

Property 1: *R is disjoint from B, i.e., $R \cdot B = 0$*
Property 2: *$R + B = A + B$*

This lemma forms the basis of our LVT and the VT [12] algorithm. The operator "♮"(pronounced "little") introduced in this paper satisfies the above two Properties.

4   State Space Division

Applying "♮" operator, we can write Equation 1 as:

$$P(\bigcup_{i=1}^{p} MP_i) = P(MP_1) + P(MP_2 ♮ MP_1) + ...$$

$$+P(...((MP_p ♮ MP_1) ♮ MP_2)...♮ MP_{p-1})$$

For operation $A♮B$, the coordinates in cube A can have $1, x, 0_\mu$ as their values (0_μ may be generated by previous operations), while the coordinates in cube B can only have $1, x$ as their values because B is an original minproduct. If we consider the tuple (A, B) of the two cubes in the operation $A♮B$ as a *state*, then the state space is $S = \{(A, B)|a_i = 1, x, 0_\mu, \ b_i = 1, x\}$. As shown in Figure 1, each state in S can have all possible combinations of the coordinate pairs. S can be divided into two disjoint subspaces S_1 and S_2 by requiring that each state in S_1 must have the coordinate pair $(a_i = 0_\mu, b_i = 1)$ for some index i, and by requiring that each state in S_2 can not have such coordinate pair. To illustrate this condition in Figure 1, coordinate pair $(a_i = 0_\mu, b_i = 1)$ is highlighted by a small surrounding frame in S_1, and is taken out from S_2. S_1 can be further divided into disjoint subspaces S_{11} and S_{12} by requiring S_{12} satisfy the condition that for each zero group 0_μ in cube A, we can find a coordinate pair $(a_j = 0_\mu,$

$b_j = x$) for index $j \neq i$, and by requiring that S_{11} not satisfy such a condition. To illustrate this condition in Figure 1, this special requirement on coordinate pair $(a_j = 0_\mu, b_j = x)$ is marked with an asterisk and highlighted by a surrounding frame in S_{12}, and is crossed out in S_{11}. We denote this coordinate pair with an asterisk in S_{12} in order to indicate this requirement does not simply mean it must appear in each state of this subspace. We do not drop this coordinate pair from S_{11} because this requirement does not mean it can not appear in any state of S_{11}. Considering the requirement S_{11} inherited from S_1, this actually means that for each state of S_{11} there exists a zero group 0_μ in cube A such that for all $a_i = 0_\mu$ their corresponding coordinates in B has $b_i = 1$. We will illustrate in the next section that A is disjoint from B for every state of S_{11}. S_2 also can be further divided into two disjoint subspaces S_{21} and S_{22} by requiring that each state in S_{21} must have the coordinate pair $(a_i = x, b_i = 1)$ for some index i, and by requiring that each state in S_{22} can not have such a coordinate pair. As shown in Figure 1, coordinate pair $(a_i = x, b_i = 1)$ is highlighted by a small surrounding frame in S_{21}, and is dropped from S_{22}. The two cubes of each state in subspaces S_{11}, S_{12}, S_{21}, and S_{22} satisfy the interesting conditions illustrated in the following section.

5 Basic Cube Relationships

The following two propositions were illustrated in VT[12]:

Proposition 2 (Disjoint Condition). *Given two cubes A and B with $A = a_1 a_2 ... a_n$ where $a_i \in \{1, x, 0_\nu\}$, and $B = b_1 b_2 ... b_n$ where $b_i \in \{1, x\}$, the two cubes are disjoint, i.e., $A \cdot B = 0$, if $\exists \mu$ such that for all $a_i = 0_\mu$ we have $b_i = 1$.*

Proposition 3 (Subset Condition). *Given two cubes A and B with $A = a_1 a_2 ... a_n$ where $a_i \in \{1, x, 0_\nu\}$, and $B = b_1 b_2 ... b_n$ where $b_i \in \{1, x\}$, A is a subset of B, i.e., $A + B = B$ if $\forall i \in [1, n]$ either $a_i = b_i$ or (if $a_i \neq b_i$) $b_i = x$.*

It is easy to check that the two cubes of each state in subspace S_{11} satisfy the disjoint condition($A \cdot B = 0$) and the two cubes of each state in subspace S_{22} satisfy the subset condition($A + B = B$). We say that the two cubes of each state in subspace S_{21} satisfy "x1 condition" because they must have a $(a_i = x, b_i = 1)$ coordinate pair. We say that the two cubes of each state in subspace S_{12} satisfy "split recursive condition" because this is the case we need to take special care of, and we will use split and recursive method to process it. The definitions of the "x1 condition" and the "split recursive condition" are given as:

Definition 4 (x1 Condition). *Given two cubes A and B with $A = a_1 a_2 ... a_n$ where $a_i \in \{1, x, 0_\nu\}$, and $B = b_1 b_2 ... b_n$ where $b_i \in \{1, x\}$, A and B satisfy the "x1 condition" if we can find a coordinate pair $(a_i = x, b_i = 1)$ at some index i, and all the other coordinate pairs at index $j \neq i$, can only have one of the following combinations: $(a_j = x, b_j = 1)$, $(a_j = b_j)$, or (if $a_j \neq b_j$) $b_j = x$.*

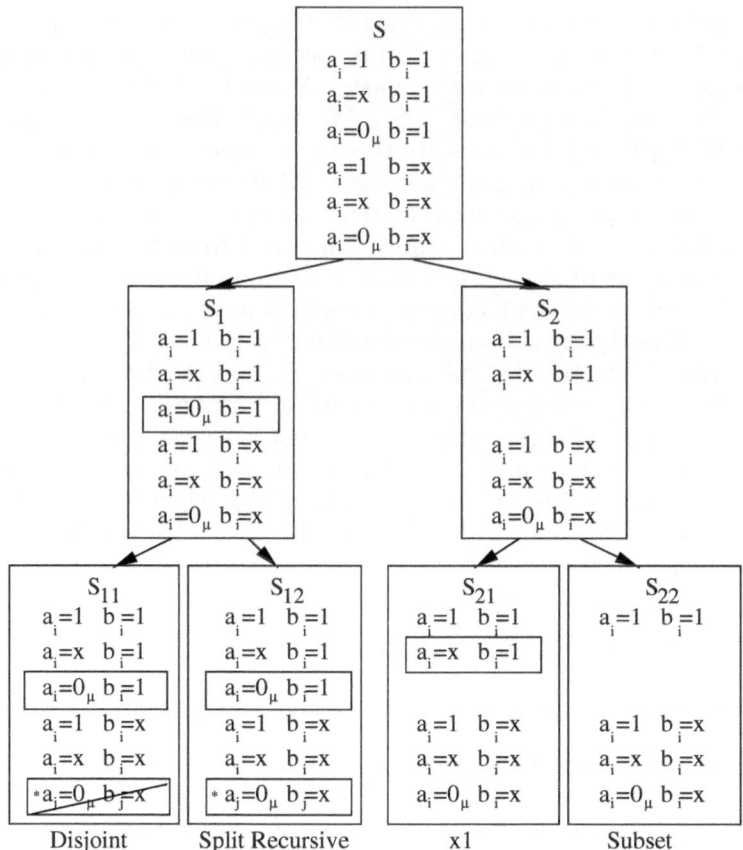

Fig. 1. State Space Division.

Definition 5 (Split Recursive Condition). *Given two cubes A and B with* $A = a_1a_2...a_n$ *where* $a_i \in \{1, x, 0_\mu\}$, *and* $B = b_1b_2...b_n$ *where* $b_i \in \{1, x\}$, *A and B satisfy the "split recursive condition" if we can find a coordinate pair* $(a_i = 0_\nu, b_i = 1)$ *at index i for some zero group* 0_ν, *and for every zero group* 0_μ *in cube A we can find a coordinate pair* $(a_j = 0_\mu, b_j = x)$ *at index* $j \neq i$.

6 The "little" Operator "♮"

With the four exhaustive and mutually exclusive conditions defined above, we are ready to introduce the operator "♮".

Definition 6 (Operator "♮"). *Given two cubes A and B with* $A = a_1a_2...a_n$ *where* $a_i \in \{1, x, 0_\mu\}$ *with the largest index of grouped zeros being* γ ($\gamma = 0$ *if cube A has no grouped zeros*), $B = b_1b_2...b_n$ *where* $b_i \in \{1, x\}$, *the operator "♮"*

is defined as:

$$A \natural B = \begin{cases} 0 & \text{if ``subset condition'' holds,} \\ C & \text{if ``x1 condition'' holds,} \\ A & \text{if ``disjoint condition'' holds,} \\ (A_1 \natural B) + A_x & \text{if ``split recursive condition'' holds.} \end{cases}$$

A_1 and A_x are cubes obtained from A by splitting over a zero group 0_μ that has both $(a_i = 0_\mu, b_i = 1)$ and $(a_j = 0_\mu, b_j = x)$ coordinate pairs. A_1 is obtained from A by setting all those a_i's that have $(a_i = 0_\mu, b_i = 1)$ pairs to 1. A_x is obtained from A by setting all those a_j's that have $(a_j = 0_\mu, b_j = x)$ pairs to x. For example, let $A = 0_1 0_1$ and $B = 1x$. So we have $A = A_1 + A_x = 10_1 + 0_1 x$. Its corresponding boolean expression is probably more clear: $A = \overline{ab} = a\overline{b} + \overline{a}$. $C = c_1 c_2 ... c_n$ where

$$c_i = \begin{cases} 0_{(\gamma+1)} & \text{if } a_i = x \text{ and } b_i = 1 \\ a_i & \text{otherwise} \end{cases}$$

Having defined the operator "$\natural$", we introduce the following theorem that establishes the I_VT algorithm. Its proof is given in the Appendix.

Theorem 7 $(A \cdot \overline{B} = A \natural B)$. *Given two cubes A and B where $A = a_1 a_2 ... a_n$ with $a_i \in \{1, x, 0_\mu\}$ and $B = b_1 b_2 ... b_n$ where $b_i \in \{1, x\}$, and the operator "$\natural$" defined as above, we have $A \cdot \overline{B} = A \natural B$.*

7   Examples

In this section we give nine examples as shown in Figure 2. A link without direction arrow is bidirectional. We present the operation steps of Example 1 in detail in Table 1 to illustrate our algorithm. The condition column labels the condition of the two cubes under the "$\natural$" operation. "x1" means the "x1 condition" and "sr" means the "split recursive condition". The γ column labels the largest zero group index in the corresponding cube. In order to compare the execution time (in second) of I_VT with VT [12], KDH88 [6], and CAREL [10] algorithms, we implement the four algorithms on the same platform Solaris and run the nine examples on a Sun Sparc 10 work station. The result is shown in Table 2, where the "Ex" column gives the example index, the "mp#" column gives the number of minpaths.

8   Compare I_VT with VT

In this section we give a step by step comparison of the I_VT and VT [12] algorithms. Comparison of VT [12], KDH88 [6], and CAREL [10] is given in [9]. In VT [12] algorithm, the exclusive sharpe operator "$\$$" is introduced to make two cubes A and B disjoint. The "$\$$" operator is defined as follows:

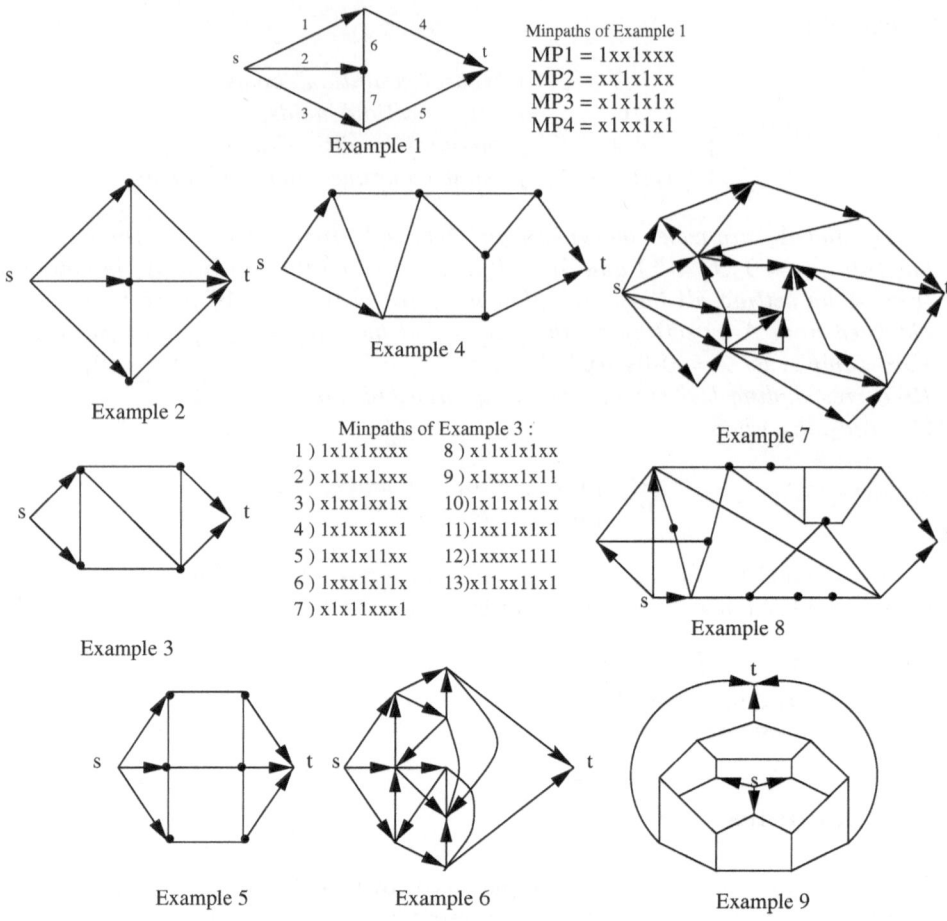

Minpaths of Example 1
MP1 = 1xx1xxx
MP2 = xx1x1xx
MP3 = x1x1x1x
MP4 = x1xx1x1

Example 1

Example 2

Example 4

Example 7

Minpaths of Example 3 :
1) 1x1x1xxxx   8) x11x1x1xx
2) x1x1x1xxx   9) x1xxx1x11
3) x1xx1xx1x   10)1x11x1x1x
4) 1x1xx1xx1   11)1xx11x1x1
5) 1xx1x11xx   12)1xxxx1111
6) 1xxx1x11x   13)x11xx11x1
7) x1x11xxx1

Example 3

Example 8

Example 5

Example 6

Example 9

Fig. 2. Exmaple 1-9

Definition of Operator "$": For two cubes A and B, $A = a_1a_2...a_n$ where $a_i \in \{1, x, 0_\mu\}$, and $B = b_1b_2...b_n$ where $b_i \in \{1, x\}$, the sharpe operator "$" is defined as:

$$A\$B = \begin{cases} \emptyset & \text{if } A + B = B & (1) \\ D_k & \text{if } \exists i \text{ such that } ((a_i = 0_\nu) \land (b_i = 1)) & (2) \\ C & \text{otherwise} & (3) \end{cases}$$

where k is the largest zero group index in cube A. $D_j = D_{j-1}@_jB$, for $j = 2, 3, ..., k$ and $D_1 = A@_1B$.
$C = c_1c_2...c_n$ with

$$c_i = \begin{cases} 0_{\gamma_1} & \text{if } a_i = x \text{ and } b_i = 1 \\ a_i & \text{otherwise} \end{cases}$$

where γ_1 is the index of cube B.

Table 1. LVT operations on Example 1

mp	♮ operations	cond	γ	dp
MP_1	1 x x 1 x x x		0	1xx1xxx
MP_2	x x1 x 1 x x		0	
	♮MP_1 1 x x 1 x x x	x1		
	0_1 x 1 0_1 1 x x		1	$0_1 x 1 0_1 1 x x$
MP_3	x 1 x 1 x 1 x		0	
	♮MP_1 1 x x 1 x x x	x1		
	0_1 1 x 1 x 1 x		1	
	♮MP_2 x x1 x 1 x x	x1		
	0_1 1 0_2 1 0_2 1 x		2	$0_1 1 0_2 1 0_2 1 x$
MP_4	x 1 x x 1 x 1		0	
	♮MP_1 1 x x 1 x x x	x1		
	0_1 1 x 0_1 1 x 1		1	
	♮MP_2 x x1 x 1 x x	x1		
	0_1 1 0_2 0_1 1 x 1		2	
	♮MP_3 x 1 x 1 x 1 x	sr		
	(A_1) 0_1 1 0_2 1 1 x 1		2	(A_x) $x 1 0_2 0_1 1 x 1$
	♮MP_3 x 1 x 1 x 1 x	x1		
	0_1 1 0_2 1 1 0_3 1		3	$0_1 1 0_2 1 1 0_3 1$

Table 2. Execution time of LVT, VT, KDH88, and CAREL

Ex	mp#	LVT	VT	KDH	CAREL
1	4	0.0	0.0	0.0	0.0
2	9	0.0	0.0	0.0	0.0
3	13	0.0	0.0	0.0	0.0
4	24	0.0	1.0	1.0	1.0
5	29	1.0	2.0	2.0	3.0
6	64	4.0	45.0	5.0	53.0
7	36	5.0	51.0	8.0	17.0
8	106	6.0	241.0	12.0	401.0
9	780	1025.0	37411.0	2356.0	12862.0

Definition of Operator "$@_j$": For two cubes A and B defined as above, the operator "$@_j$" is defined as:

$$
A@_jB = \begin{cases}
A & \text{if } A \cdot B = 0 & (4) \\
A & \text{if } \forall(a_i = 0_j), b_i \neq 1 & (5) \\
A & \text{if } \forall i, a_i \neq 0_j, \text{ i.e., zero group } 0_j \text{ doesn't exist} & (6) \\
(A_1 \% B) + A_x & \text{otherwise} & (7)
\end{cases}
$$

Where A_1 is a cube obtained from A by setting to 1 all $a_i = 0_k$, for which $b_i = 1$. A_x is a cube obtained from A by setting to x all $a_i = 0_k$, for which $b_i = x$.

Definition of Operator "%": For two cubes A and B defined as above, the operator "%" is defined as:

Table 3. Steps of VT on Example 3 (Part I)

path#	op	VT steps	cond	k
11		$1\ x\ x\ 1\ 1\ x\ 1\ x\ 1$		
1	$	$1\ x\ 1\ x\ 1\ x\ x\ x\ x$		
		$1\ x\ 0_1\ 1\ 1\ x\ 1\ x\ 1$	3	1
2	$	$x\ 1\ x\ 1\ x\ 1\ x\ x\ x$		
		$1\ 0_2\ 0_1\ 1\ 1\ 0_2\ 1\ x\ 1$	3	2
3	$,@_1	$x\ 1\ x\ x\ 1\ x\ x\ 1\ x$	2	
		$1\ 0_2\ 0_1\ 1\ 1\ 0_2\ 1\ x\ 1$	5	
	$@_2$	$x\ 1\ x\ x\ 1\ x\ x\ 1\ x$		
	A_1	$1\ 1\ 0_1\ 1\ 1\ 0_2\ 1\ x\ 1$	7	
	%	$x\ 1\ x\ x\ 1\ x\ x\ 1\ x$		
		$1\ 1\ 0_1\ 1\ 1\ 0_2\ 1\ 0_3\ 1$	3	3
4	$,@_1	$1\ x\ 1\ x\ x\ 1\ x\ x\ 1$	2	
		$1\ 1\ 0_1\ 1\ 1\ 0_2\ 1\ 0_3\ 1$	4	
	$@_2$	$1\ x\ 1\ x\ x\ 1\ x\ x\ 1$		
		$1\ 1\ 0_1\ 1\ 1\ 0_2\ 1\ 0_3\ 1$	4	
	$@_3$	$1\ x\ 1\ x\ x\ 1\ x\ x\ 1$		
		$1\ 1\ 0_1\ 1\ 1\ 0_2\ 1\ 0_3\ 1$	4/5	3

path#	op	VT steps	cond	k
5	$,@_1	$1\ x\ x\ 1\ x\ 1\ 1\ x\ x$	2	
		$1\ 1\ 0_1\ 1\ 1\ 0_2\ 1\ 0_3\ 1$	4/5	
	$@_2$	$1\ x\ x\ 1\ x\ 1\ 1\ x\ x$		
		$1\ 1\ 0_1\ 1\ 1\ 0_2\ 1\ 0_3\ 1$	4	
	$@_3$	$1\ x\ x\ 1\ x\ 1\ 1\ x\ x$		
		$1\ 1\ 0_1\ 1\ 1\ 0_2\ 1\ 0_3\ 1$	4/5	3
6	$,@_1	$1\ x\ x\ x\ 1\ x\ 1\ 1\ x$	2	
		$1\ 1\ 0_1\ 1\ 1\ 0_2\ 1\ 0_3\ 1$	4/5	
	$@_2$	$1\ x\ x\ x\ 1\ x\ 1\ 1\ x$		
		$1\ 1\ 0_1\ 1\ 1\ 0_2\ 1\ 0_3\ 1$	4/5	
	$@_3$	$1\ x\ x\ x\ 1\ x\ 1\ 1\ x$		
		$1\ 1\ 0_1\ 1\ 1\ 0_2\ 1\ 0_3\ 1$	4/5	3
7	$	$x\ 1\ x\ 1\ 1\ x\ x\ x\ 1$		
		$\emptyset$	1	

$$A\%B = \begin{cases} \emptyset & \text{if } A + B = B & (1) \\ A & \text{if } \exists i \text{ such that } ((a_i = 0_\nu) \wedge (b_i = 1)) & (2) \\ C & \text{otherwise} & (3) \end{cases}$$

where C is the same as defined in "$" operator.

We use Example 3 shown in Figure 2 and give the detailed steps on how the two algorithms make MP_{11} disjoint from minpaths $MP_1, MP_2, ..., MP_{10}$. The operating steps of VT [12] algorithm are shown in Table 3 and Table 4, and the steps of I_VT are shown in Table 5. The A_x in Table 4 and Table 5 is generate at the same time when A_1 is generated in Table 3 and Table 5 respectively. It is made disjoint from the consequent $MP_4, MP_5, ..., MP_{10}$ in parallel with A_1. We put the process of A_x in a separate table only due to the limitation of the page size. We assign a number to each condition of the "$", "$@_j$" and the "%" operators of the VT algorithm [12] so as to refer to them more easily in the "cond" column of Table 3 and Table 4. Condition 1 is the same as our "subset condition" and Condition 4 is the same as our "disjoint condition". The "4/5" in the "cond" column of Table 3 means that either Condition 4 or 5 is taken. Same notation applies to "4/6". The "$,$@_1$" in the "op" column of Table 3 means that the "$" is first used on the cube in the same row, then because Condition 2 is taken, "$@_1$" is used to do the real work. The conditions of the "$" and the "%" operator are assigned the same number because they are the same. Readers can tell which condition is taken by checking the context of the operator we are discussing. In the "cond" column of Table 5, the "s", "d", "x1", and "sr" stand for the "subset condition", the "disjoint condition", the "x1 condition", and the "split and recursive condition" in the "♮" operator definition.

Table 4. Steps of VT on Example 3 (Part II)

path#	op	VT steps	cond	k
	A_x	1 0_2 0_1 1 1 x 1 x 1	7	2
4	\$, @$_1$	1 x 1 x x 1 x x 1	2	
		1 0_2 0_1 1 1 x 1 x 1	4	
	@$_2$	1 x 1 x x 1 x x 1		
		1 0_2 0_1 1 1 x 1 x 1	4/5	
5	\$	1 x x 1 x 1 1 x x		
		1 0_2 0_1 1 1 0_5 1 x 1	3	5
6	\$	1 x x x 1 x 1 1 x		
		1 0_2 0_1 1 1 0_5 1 x 0_6	3	6
7	\$, @$_1$	x 1 x 1 1 x x x 1	2	
		1 0_2 0_1 1 1 0_5 1 x 0_6	4/5	
	@$_2$	x 1 x 1 1 x x x 1		
		1 0_2 0_1 1 1 0_5 1 x 0_6	4	
	@$_3$	x 1 x 1 1 x x x 1		
		1 0_2 0_1 1 1 0_5 1 x 0_6	4/6	
	@$_4$	x 1 x 1 1 x x x 1		
		1 0_2 0_1 1 1 0_5 1 x 0_6	4/6	
	@$_5$	x 1 x 1 1 x x x 1		
		1 0_2 0_1 1 1 0_5 1 x 0_6	4/5	
	@$_6$	x 1 x 1 1 x x x 1		
		1 0_2 0_1 1 1 0_5 1 x 0_6	4	6
8	\$, @$_1$	x 1 1 x 1 x 1 x x	2	
		1 0_2 0_1 1 1 0_5 1 x 0_6	4	
	@$_2$	x 1 1 x 1 x 1 x x		
		1 0_2 0_1 1 1 0_5 1 x 0_6	4	
	@$_3$	x 1 1 x 1 x 1 x x		
		1 0_2 0_1 1 1 0_5 1 x 0_6	4/6	
	@$_4$	x 1 1 x 1 x 1 x x		
		1 0_2 0_1 1 1 0_5 1 x 0_6	4/6	
	@$_5$	x 1 1 x 1 x 1 x x		
		1 0_2 0_1 1 1 0_5 1 x 0_6	4/5	
	@$_6$	x 1 1 x 1 x 1 x x		
		1 0_2 0_1 1 1 0_5 1 x 0_6	4/5	6
9	\$, @$_1$	x 1 x x x 1 x 1 1	2	
		1 0_2 0_1 1 1 0_5 1 x 0_6	4/5	
	@$_2$	x 1 x x x 1 x 1 1		
		1 0_2 0_1 1 1 0_5 1 x 0_6	4	
	@$_3$	x 1 x x x 1 x 1 1		
		1 0_2 0_1 1 1 0_5 1 x 0_6	4/6	
	@$_4$	x 1 x x x 1 x 1 1		
		1 0_2 0_1 1 1 0_5 1 x 0_6	4/6	
	@$_5$	x 1 x x x 1 x 1 1		
		1 0_2 0_1 1 1 0_5 1 x 0_6	4	
	@$_6$	x 1 x x x 1 x 1 1		
		1 0_2 0_1 1 1 0_5 1 x 0_6	4	6
10	\$, @$_1$	1 x 1 1 x 1 x 1 x	2	
		1 0_2 0_1 1 1 0_5 1 x 0_6	4	
	@$_2$	1 x 1 1 x 1 x 1 x		
		1 0_2 0_1 1 1 0_5 1 x 0_6	4/5	
	@$_3$	1 x 1 1 x 1 x 1 x		
		1 0_2 0_1 1 1 0_5 1 x 0_6	4/6	
	@$_4$	1 x 1 1 x 1 x 1 x		
		1 0_2 0_1 1 1 0_5 1 x 0_6	4/6	
	@$_5$	1 x 1 1 x 1 x 1 x		
		1 0_2 0_1 1 1 0_5 1 x 0_6	4	
	@$_6$	1 x 1 1 x 1 x 1 x		
		1 0_2 0_1 1 1 0_5 1 x 0_6	4/6	

VT algorithm [12] takes 52 steps while I_VT algorithm takes only 15 steps. The work load of each step is almost the same ($O(n)$, where n is the number of coordinates in the cubes) for both algorithms because it is basically a coordinate-wise operation of the two cubes under operation. And, we believe that I_VT algorithm also saves in the condition calculations because the conditions in our "♮" operator are mutually exclusive while some conditions, such as Conditions 4, 5, and 6, in VT [12] algorithm are not. Also, in VT algorithm [12], Conditions 1 and 2 must be checked in order to take Conditions 3, and Condition 4, 5, 6, must be checked in order to take Condition 7. Thus, I_VT algorithm is more efficient.

The redundant operations, which are time consuming, of VT algorithm [12] also result from the operator "@$_j$", which is a simple iteration over zero groups from index 1 to the maximum index number as long as there is a (0,1) coordinate pair in the two cubes. As the zero groups on which the "@$_j$" is operating

Table 5. Steps of I_VT on Example 3

path#	op	♮ steps	cond	γ
11		1 x x 1 1 x 1 x 1		
1	♮	1 x 1 x 1 x x x x		
		1 x 0_1 1 1 x 1 x 1	x1	1
2	♮	x 1 x 1 x 1 x x x		
		1 0_2 0_1 1 1 0_2 1 x 1	x1	2
3	♮	x 1 x x 1 x x 1 x		
	A_1	1 1 0_1 1 1 0_2 1 x 1	sr	2
	♮	x 1 x x 1 x x 1 x		
		1 1 0_1 1 1 0_2 1 0_3 1	x1	3
4	♮	1 x 1 x x 1 x x 1		
		1 1 0_1 1 1 0_2 1 0_3 1	d	
5	♮	1 x x 1 x 1 1 x x		
		1 1 0_1 1 1 0_2 1 0_3 1	d	
6	♮	1 x x x 1 x 1 1 x		
		1 1 0_1 1 1 0_2 1 0_3 1	d	
7	♮	x 1 x 1 1 x x x 1		
		∅	s	

path#	op	♮ steps	cond	γ
	A_x	1 0_2 0_1 1 1 x 1 x 1	sr	2
4	♮	1 x 1 x x 1 x x 1		
		1 0_2 0_1 1 1 x 1 x 1	d	
5	♮	1 x x 1 x 1 1 x x		
		1 0_2 0_1 1 1 0_3 1 x 1	x1	5
6	♮	1 x x x 1 x 1 1 x		
		1 0_2 0_1 1 1 0_3 1 x 0_4	x1	6
7	♮	x 1 x 1 1 x x x 1		
		1 0_2 0_1 1 1 0_3 1 x 0_4	d	
8	♮	x 1 1 x 1 x 1 x x		
		1 0_2 0_1 1 1 0_3 1 x 0_4	d	
9	♮	x 1 x x x 1 x 1 1		
		1 0_2 0_1 1 1 0_3 1 x 0_4	d	
10	♮	1 x 1 1 x 1 x 1 x		
		1 0_2 0_1 1 1 0_3 1 x 0_4	d	

may not need to be processed (as Condition 5) or may not even exist at all (as Condition 6), and each unnecessary "$@_j$" needs $O(n)$ operations to check the conditions. Furthermore, we can see the larger the discontiguous interval, the more unnecessary "$@_j$" loops will be incurred. Consider the disjoint product MP_{24} of Example 3, the maximum zero group number is 20 and the discontiguous intervals are large. If there is a $(0,1)$ coordinate pair in the process, it may incur 20 "$@_j$" loops and most of them are unnecessary. Other redundant operations of VT [12] come from the A_x generated in Condition 7 of the operator "$@_j$". It will be carried on to the next step $@_{j+1}$ to make it disjoint from B, which is unnecessary because A_x is disjoint from B by definition.

I_VT algorithm removes all these unnecessary operations, so it is faster.

9   Conclusion

In this paper, we propose an improved algorithm (I_VT) over VT [12]. The I_VT is simpler and more efficient. We introduce and prove a lemma (Lemma 1) which forms the foundation of I_VT algorithm, and is used implicitly by VT [12]. A state space division idea is presented, which makes the I_VT algorithm easy to understand and prove. We implement the I_VT and the well known MVI algorithms on the same platform. The run time comparison shows I_VT is the fastest. Finally, we give a step by step comparison of I_VT vs VT [12], and explain why I_VT is faster than VT [12].

Appendix

Proof of Lemma 1: We need to show both the sufficient and necessary condition.

Sufficient: If $A = 0$ and $B = 0$, from Property 2 we have $R = 0$, thus $A \cdot \overline{B} = R$. If $A = 0$ and $B = 1$, from Property 1 we have $R = 0$, thus $A \cdot \overline{B} = R$. If $A = 1$ and $B = 0$, from Property 2 we have $R = 1$, thus $A \cdot \overline{B} = R$. If $A = 1$ and $B = 1$, from Property 1 we have $R = 0$, thus $A \cdot \overline{B} = R$.

Necessary: It is easy to verify that for each value of $R = A \cdot \overline{B}$ in the truth table of A and B, R satisfies the two Properties.

Proof of Theorem 7: We only need to show the result of $A \natural B$ satisfies the two Properties of Lemma 1. Because the "$\natural$" operator is recursive, we discuss the "subset condition", "disjoint condition" and "x1 condition" as boundary conditions before the "split recursive condition".

Case 1: If A and B satisfy the subset condition, then $A + B = B$. So we have $0 + B = A + B$. Also we have $0 \cdot B = 0$, So 0 satisfies the two Properties. hence $A \natural B = 0 = A \cdot \overline{B}$.

Case 2: If A and B satisfy the disjoint condition, then $A \cdot B = 0$. It is also trivial to see that $A + B = A + B$, so A satisfies the two Properties, hence $A \natural B = A = A \cdot \overline{B}$.

Case 3: If A and B satisfy the "$x1$ condition", we notice this condition is different from the subset condition only in that we can find a coordinate a_i in A such that $a_i = x$ and $b_i = 1$. Let γ be the largest zero group number in cube A, we can construct a cube C by setting all the coordinates in A such that $a_i = x, b_i = 1$ to zero group $0_{\gamma+1}$. Also we can construct a cube C_1 by setting all the coordinates in A such that $a_i = x, b_i = 1$ to 1. So we have $A = C + C_1$. By checking with the "subset condition" and the "disjoint condition" we have $C \cdot C_1 = 0$, $C \cdot B = 0$ (i.e. C satisfies Property 1) and $C_1 + B = B$. Thus $A \natural B = (C \natural B) + (C_1 \natural B) = C$. (using the results of the "subset condition" and "disjoint condition" proved above). Also it trivial to see $A + B = C + C_1 + B = C + B$, so C satisfies Property 2. Hence $A \natural B = C = A \cdot \overline{B}$.

Case 4: If A and B satisfy the "split-recursive condition", then we can find a zero group μ that has $(a_i = 0_\mu, b_i = 1)$ and $(a_j = 0_\mu, b_j = x, i \neq j)$. We can split A into $A = A_1 + A_x$, where A_1 is a cube obtained from A by setting to 1 all $a_i = 0_\mu$ for which $b_i = 1$, and A_x is a cube obtained from A by setting to x all $a_i = 0_\mu$ for which $b_i = x$. It is easy to verify (as illustrated in VT[12]) that $A_1 \cdot A_x = 0$ and $A_x \cdot B = 0$. So we have:

$$A \natural B = (A_1 + A_x) \natural B$$
$$= (A_1 \natural B) + (A_x \natural B)$$
$$= (A_1 \natural B) + A_x$$

Here the "♮" operator is used recursively. Because these four conditions are exhaustive and mutually exclusive and the number of such zero groups are limited, after all zero groups are taken care of, the algorithm will hit one of the boundary conditions. As we proved above, all "♮" operations of the boundary conditions satisfy the two Properties, so the final result also satisfies the two Properties. Hence $A♮B = (A_1♮B) + A_x = A \cdot \overline{B}$

References

1. J. A. Abraham. An improved algorithm for network reliability. *IEEE Transactions on Reliability*, R-28:58–61, April 1979.
2. K. K. Aggarwal, K. B. Misra, and J. S. Gupta. A fast algorithm far reliability evaluation. *IEEE Transactions on Reliability*, R-24:83–85, 1975.
3. F. Beichelt and L. Spross. An improved abraham-method for generating disjoint sums. *IEEE Transactions on Reliability*, R-36:70–74, April 1987.
4. R. G. Bennetts. On the analysis of fault trees. *IEEE Transactions on Reliability*, R-24:175–185, August 1975.
5. L. Fratta and U. G. Montanari. A boolean algebra method for computing the terminal reliability in a communication network. *IEEE Transactions on Circuit Theory*, CT-20:203–211, May 1973.
6. Klaus D. Heidtmann. Smaller sum of disjoint products by subproduct inversion. *IEEE Transactions on Reliability*, 38:305–311, August 1989.
7. M. O. Locks. A minimizing algorithm for sum of disjoint products. *IEEE Transactions on Reliability*, R-36(4):445–453, October 1987.
8. S. Rai and K. K. Aggarwal. An efficient method for reliability evaluation of a general network. *IEEE Transactions on Reliability*, R-27:206–211, August 1978.
9. S. Rai, M. Veeraraghavan, and K. S. Trivedi. A suvey of efficient reliability computation using disjoint products approach. *Networks*, 25:147–163, 1995.
10. S. Soh and Rai. Carel: Computer aided reliability evaluator for distributed computing networks. *IEEE Transactions on Parallel and Distributed Systems*, pages 199–213, April 1991.
11. R. E. Tarjan. A unified approach to path problems. *Journal ACM*, 28:577–593, 1981.
12. M. Veeraraghavan and K. S. Trivedi. An improved algorithm for symbolic reliability analysis. *IEEE Transactions on Reliability*, 40:347–358, August 1991.

Performance Evaluation of
Web Proxy Cache Replacement Policies

Martin Arlitt, Rich Friedrich, and Tai Jin

Hewlett-Packard Laboratories, 1501 Page Mill Road, Palo Alto, CA 94304

`{arlitt, richf, tai}@hpl.hp.com`

Abstract. The continued growth of the World-Wide Web and the emergence of new end-user technologies such as cable modems necessitate the use of proxy caches to reduce latency, network traffic and Web server loads. In this paper we analyze the importance of different Web proxy workload characteristics in making good cache replacement decisions. Trace-driven simulation is used to evaluate the effectiveness of various replacement policies for Web proxy caches. The extended duration of the trace (117 million requests collected over five months) allows long term side effects of replacement policies to be identified and quantified.

Our results indicate that size-based replacement policies maximize request hit rates while frequency-based policies maximize byte hit rates. With either approach it is important that inactive objects be removed from the cache to prevent pollution.

1 INTRODUCTION

The World-Wide Web ("The Web") has grown tremendously in the past few years to become the most prevalent source of traffic on the Internet today. This growth has led to congested backbone links, overloaded Web servers and frustrated users. These problems will become more severe as new end-user technologies such as cable modems are deployed. One solution that could help relieve these problems is object caching[18].

In this paper we present a trace-driven simulation study of a Web proxy cache. Our goal in this study is to evaluate the effects of different workload characteristics on the replacement decisions made by the cache. The workload characteristics that we consider include object size, recency of reference, frequency of reference and turnover in the active set of objects. These characteristics were identified in our Web proxy workload characterization study[1].

Our research on Web proxies has utilized measurements of an actual Web proxy workload. We collected data from a proxy cache that is located in an Internet Service Provider (ISP) environment. Subscribers to this ISP access the Web using high-speed cable modems. Measurements of this proxy were collected over a five month period (January 3rd - May 31st, 1997). In total more than 117 million requests were recorded.

A Web proxy[12] can be used to resolve client requests for Web objects. When the proxy receives a request from a client the proxy attempts to fulfill the request from among the objects stored in the proxy's cache. If the requested object is found (a *cache*

R. Puigjaner et al. (Eds.): Tools'98, LNCS 1469, pp. 193-206, 1998

hit) the proxy can immediately respond to the client's request. If the requested object is not found (a *cache miss*) the proxy then attempts to retrieve the object from another location such as a peer or parent proxy cache or the origin server. Once a copy of the object has been retrieved the proxy can complete its response to the client. If the requested object is *cacheable* (based on information provided by the origin server or determined from the URL) the proxy may decide to add a copy of the object to its cache. If the object is *uncacheable* (again determined from the URL or information from the origin server) the proxy should not store a copy in its cache.

An important first step in proxy research is understanding Web proxy workloads. A quantitative way to understand these workloads is through workload characterization. A number of recent efforts[6][8], including our own[1], have identified numerous characteristics of proxy workloads. We use this knowledge to help identify the strengths and weaknesses of different replacement policies for proxy caches.

Currently there are two approaches to cache management. One approach is to provide the cache with abundant resources so that few (if any) replacement decisions need to be made[9][13]. The alternative approach is to use as few resources as possible by making good replacement decisions when the cache is full[4][11][16][17]. While some organizations may be willing to continuously add resources to their proxy cache we feel that the majority of enterprises will be more interested in achieving the best possible performance for the lowest possible cost. Thus, throughout the remainder of this paper, we focus on maximizing either the hit rate or byte hit rate of a proxy cache that has limited cache space. Although other researchers have performed caching simulations of Web proxies these previous studies have been limited to either short-term traces of busy proxies[4][6][8] or long-term traces of relatively inactive proxies[11][16][17]. Our study is the first to examine a busy proxy over an extended period of time. Caching is more important in a busy environment as it reduces the demand on the shared external network link. Long-term traces are important in order to identify potential side effects of replacement policies. Furthermore, our study identifies which workload characteristics merit consideration in cache replacement decisions and discusses why these characteristics are important. We then use these characteristics to evaluate the achieved hit rates and byte hit rates of several existing replacement policies and to identify their strengths and weaknesses.

The remainder of this paper is organized as follows. Section 2 describes the collection and reduction of the workload data set. Section 3 summarizes the results of our workload characterization study focusing on the characteristics that merit consideration when making cache replacement decisions. Section 4 provides the design of our trace-driven simulation study while Section 5 presents the simulation results. The paper concludes in Section 6 with a summary of our findings and a discussion of future work.

2 DATA COLLECTION AND REDUCTION

2.1 Data Collection

In order to characterize the workload of a Web proxy and to conduct a trace-driven simulation of a Web proxy cache, measurements of an actual Web proxy workload were collected. The site under study provides interactive data services to residential and business subscribers using cable modems. The services available to the subscribers include email, network news and the World-Wide Web. Figure 1 shows a simplified view of the system under study. To access the available services a subscriber uses a cable modem to connect to the server complex through the Signal Conversion System (SCS). The SCS routes all requests for Web objects (i.e., HTTP, FTP, and Gopher requests) to the Web proxy. This proxy includes an object cache so some of the client requests can be satisfied within the server complex. On a cache miss the proxy retrieves the object from an origin server on the Internet. The access logs of this proxy were collected. Customer requests for other services such as Email and News are forwarded to a separate server; the workload of the Email and News server was not measured and is not used in this study.

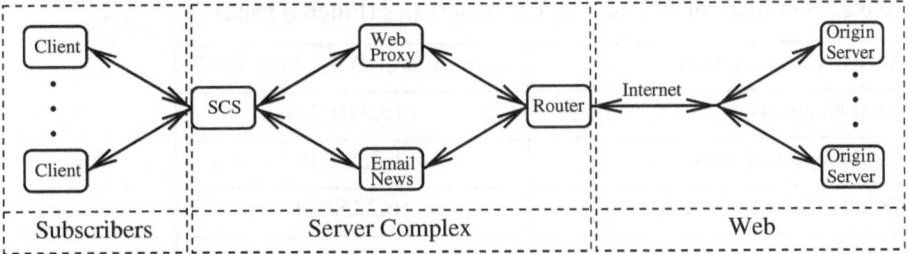

Figure 1. Diagram of the System Under Study

The collected access logs contain information on all client requests for Web objects from January 3rd, 1997 until May 31st, 1997[1]. Each entry in an access log contains information on a single request received by the Web proxy from a client. Each entry includes the client IP address (dynamically assigned), the time of the request, the requested URL, the status codes for both the proxy and origin server responses, the size of the response (in bytes) and the time required to complete the response. A summary of the amount of raw data collected is given in Table 1.

Table 1. Summary of Access Log Characteristics (Raw Data)

Access Log Duration	January 3rd - May 31st, 1997
Total Requests	117,652,652
Total Content Data Transferred	1,340 GB

[1.] The access logs were collected on a daily basis. The access logs were not available on 13 days and were incomplete on 4 other days.

2.2   Data Reduction

Due to the extremely large access logs created by the proxy (nearly 30 GB of data) we found it necessary to create a smaller, more compact log due to storage constraints and to ensure that the workload analyses and caching simulations could be completed in a reasonable amount of time. We performed these reductions in several ways while still maintaining as much of the original information as possible. One very effective method of reduction is to represent the access log information in a more efficient manner (e.g., map the unique URLs to distinct integer identifiers). We also removed information that we felt would be of little or no value in either the workload analysis or the simulation study (e.g., we kept only GET requests which accounted for 98% of all requests and 99.2% of all content data). After reducing the access logs the overall statistics were recalculated. The results are shown in Table 2. The reduced data set is 4.5 GB (1.5GB compressed). This represents not only a tremendous space savings but also a time savings as the log is in a format that dramatically improves the efficiency of our analysis tools and cache simulator.

Table 2. Summary of Access Log Characteristics (Filtered Data)

Access Log Duration	January 3rd - May 31st, 1997
Total Requests	115,310,904
Total Content Bytes	1,328 GB
Unique Cacheable Requests	16,225,621
Total Uncacheable Requests	9,020,632
Unique Cacheable Content Bytes	389 GB
Total Uncacheable Content Bytes	56 GB

Unfortunately, not all information of interest is available in the access logs. One problem that we faced was trying to correctly identify object modifications and user aborted connections. To address this problem we assumed that modifications and aborts could be identified by a change in the size of the object. If the size changed by less than 5% we hypothesized that the object had been modified[2]; otherwise, we speculated that a user abort had occurred (either during the current request or on a previous one). If no change in size occurred, we assumed that the object had not been modified.

---

[2] We chose 5% as a threshold after an in-depth analysis of object size changes seen in the log[1].

3 WORKLOAD CHARACTERIZATION

In this section we present a summary of our workload characterization study[1]. In particular we focus on the characteristics that we feel could impact proxy performance and cache replacement decisions.

Cacheable Objects. In order for Web caching to improve performance it is vital that most objects be cacheable. Our analysis of the data set under study revealed that 92% of all requested objects (96% of the data transferred) were cacheable.

Object Set Size. In Table 2 we reported that there were over 16 million unique cacheable objects requested during the measurement period. This is several orders of magnitude larger than the number of unique objects seen in Web server workloads[2]. Due to the extremely large object set size the proxy cache must be able to quickly determine whether a requested object is cached to reduce response latency. The proxy must also efficiently update its state on a cache hit, miss or replacement.

Object Sizes. One of the obstacles for Web caching is working effectively with variable-sized objects. While most of the requested objects are small (the median object size in this data set was 4 KB) there are some extremely large objects available. The largest object requested during the measurement period was a 148 MB video. We speculate that the higher access speeds available to the clients are increasing the number of large transfers as well as the maximum size of transfers. The issue for the proxy cache is to decide whether to cache a large number of small objects (which could potentially increase the hit rate) or to cache a few large objects (possibly increasing the byte hit rate).

Recency of Reference. Most Web proxy caches in use today utilize the Least Recently Used (LRU) replacement policy (or some derivative of LRU). This policy works best when the access stream exhibits strong temporal locality or recency of reference (i.e., objects which have recently been referenced are likely to be re-referenced in the near future). In our workload characterization study[1] we found that one-third of all re-references to an object occurred within one hour of the previous reference to the same object. Approximately two-thirds (66%) of re-references occurred within 24 hours of the previous request. These results suggest that recency is a characteristic of Web proxy workloads.

Frequency of Reference. Several recent studies[2][5] have found that some Web objects are more popular than others (i.e., Web referencing patterns are non-uniform). Our characterization study of the Web proxy workload revealed similar results[1]. These findings suggest that popularity, or frequency of reference, is a characteristic that could be considered in a cache replacement decision. We also found that many objects are extremely unpopular. In fact, over 60% of the distinct objects (i.e., unique requests)[3] seen in the proxy log were requested only a single time (we refer to these

---

[3.] The number of distinct objects represents an upper bound on the number of objects that could be cached; the size of these objects (i.e., the unique bytes transferred) indicates the maximum useful cache size.

objects as "one-timers"[2]). Obviously there is no benefit in caching one-timers. Thus, a replacement policy that could discriminate against one-timers should outperform a policy that does not.

Turnover. One final characteristic that could impact proxy cache replacement decisions is turnover in the active set of objects (i.e., the set of objects that users are currently interested in). Over time the active set changes; objects that were once popular are no longer requested. These inactive objects should be removed from the cache to make space available for new objects that are now in the active set.

4   EXPERIMENTAL DESIGN

This section describes the design of the Web proxy cache simulation study. Section 4.1 introduces the factors and levels that are examined. Section 4.2 presents the metrics used to evaluate the performance of each replacement policy. Section 4.3 discusses other issues regarding the simulation study.

4.1   Factors and Levels

Cache Sizes. The cache size indicates the amount of space available for storing Web objects. We examine seven different levels for this factor: 256 MB, 1 GB, 4 GB, 16 GB, 64 GB, 256 GB and 1 TB. Each level is a factor of four larger than the previous size; this allows us to easily compare the performance improvement relative to the increase in cache size. The smaller cache sizes (e.g., 256 MB to 16 GB) indicate likely cache sizes for Web proxies. The larger values (64 GB to 1 TB) indicate the performance of the cache when a significant fraction of the total requested object set is cached. The largest cache size (1 TB) can store the entire object set and thus indicates the maximum achievable performance of the cache. The other cache sizes can hold approximately 0.06% (256 MB), 0.25% (1 GB), 1% (4 GB), 4% (16 GB), 16% (64 GB) and 64% (256 GB) of the entire object set.

Cache Replacement Policies. The second factor that we investigate in this simulation study is the replacement policy used by the cache. The replacement policy determines which object(s) should be evicted from the cache in order to create sufficient room to add a new object. There are many proposed cache replacement policies, too many to focus on in this study. We examine six different, previously proposed replacement policies in this study: two "traditional" policies (Least Recently Used and Least Frequently Used), two replacement policies recommended for Web proxy caches (Size[16] and GreedyDual-Size[4]) and two policies designed for other computer systems (Segmented LRU[10] and LRU-K[14]). We chose these six policies because each one considers at least one of the proxy workload characteristics when making a replacement decision.

The Least Recently Used (LRU) policy removes the object which has not been accessed for the longest period of time. This policy works well in workloads which exhibit strong temporal locality (i.e., recency of reference). LRU is a very simple policy requiring no parameterization.

The Least Frequently Used (LFU) policy maintains a reference count for every object in the cache. The object with the lowest reference count is selected for replacement. If more than one object has the same reference count a secondary policy can be used to break the tie (our implementation uses LRU as the secondary policy). One potential drawback of LFU is that some objects may accumulate large reference counts and never become candidates for replacement, even if these objects are no longer in the active set (i.e., the cache could become polluted with inactive objects). To alleviate this problem an aging policy can be implemented[15]. This aging policy requires two parameters.

The Size policy, designed by Williams *et. al.*[16] specifically for Web proxy caches, removes the largest object(s) from the cache when space is needed for a new object. This policy requires no parameterization.

The GreedyDual-Size policy proposed by Cao and Irani[4] considers both the size of the object and its recency of reference when making a replacement decision. Cao and Irani have proposed several variations of this policy[4]. We examine two of these policies: GreedyDual-Size (Hits), which attempts to maximize the hit rate of the proxy cache, and GreedyDual-Size (Bytes) which attempts to maximize the byte hit rate. Neither GreedyDual-Size policy requires parameterization.

The Segmented LRU (SLRU) policy was originally designed for use in a disk cache[10]. We include it in this study because it considers both frequency and recency of reference when making a replacement decision. The SLRU policy partitions the cache into two segments: an unprotected segment and a protected segment (reserved for popular objects). This policy requires one parameter.

The LRU-K replacement policy proposed by O'Neil et. al. [14] also considers both frequency and recency of reference when selecting an object for replacement. In an attempt to improve performance this policy retains historical information (the last K reference times) on objects even if they have been removed from the cache. This policy requires two parameters.

4.2   Performance Metrics

In this study two metrics are used to evaluate the performance of the proxy cache: *hit rate* and *byte hit rate*. The hit rate is the percentage of all requests that can be satisfied by searching the cache for a copy of the requested object. The byte hit rate represents the percentage of all data that is transferred directly from the cache rather than from the origin server.

A third metric of interest is response time or latency. We do not use this metric in this study for several reasons. High variability in transfer times for the same object make replacement decisions more difficult. Inaccuracies in our recorded response times also factored in our decision to not use this metric. Furthermore, Cao and Irani found that maximizing the hit rate reduced latency more effectively than policies designed to reduce response times[4].

4.3   Other Design Issues

Simulator Description. Due to the extremely large data set that we use in our simulation study it was necessary to implement the simulator as efficiently as possible. Our focus was on reducing the complexity of the actions performed by the simulator. We began with the simulator used by Arlitt and Williamson[3] and modified it to handle the large number of unique objects seen in Web proxy workloads and to perform additional replacement policies. The updated simulator requires $O(1)$ time to determine if a cache hit or miss has occurred, $O(1)$ time to determine which object to replace when space is required, and $O(1)$ to $O(\log n)$ time (depending on the replacement policy being evaluated) to update the cache state information. As a result our simulator requires only 30 to 45 minutes to simulate all 115 million requests.

An important aspect of any simulation study is validation of the simulator. While we cannot guarantee that our results are accurate when all 115 million requests are considered we did take precautions to ensure correctness. For example, the simulator was initially tested using short traces (e.g., 100 requests) which could be verified by hand. The results obtained from our simulator are repeatable. Furthermore, the performance of various policies using our simulator is similar to the results reported in other studies[4][11].

Simulation Warm-up. When monitoring a system only the steady-state behaviour is of interest. During the initial or transient state of a cache simulation, many of the cache misses occur simply because the cache is empty (i.e., cold misses). To identify the transient state we monitored all cache misses on a day-by-day basis. Initially most of the misses were indeed cold misses. After several weeks other types of misses (e.g., capacity misses) had more effect on cache performance. We used the first three weeks of trace data (8% of all requests) to warm the cache. During this period the simulated cache operates in its usual manner but no statistics are collected. Statistics are only collected once the warm-up period has finished. We use the same warm-up period in all experiments.

Assumptions. In our study all requests except for aborted (i.e., incomplete) transfers are used to drive the simulation. All status 200, 203, 300, 301 and 410 responses (except for dynamic requests) are considered to be cacheable[7]. We also consider status 304 responses to be cacheable even though no data is transferred. We use status 304 responses to update the state information maintained by the proxy cache on the object being validated. We believe that this information helps the replacement policy in determining the active set of objects. This does not imply that the cache would not forward Get-If-Modified requests to the origin server should such actions be necessary. All remaining responses are considered to be uncacheable.

Our simulator does not perform cache consistency functions such as asynchronous validations. We do update the state information on objects that we know have changed. Since our data set does not include Time-to-Live information we do not collect statistics on the number of validation messages that would occur. Also, we do not consider issues like security or authentication. These issues, along with consistency, require more in-depth coverage than we can provide in this study. Since our simulator does not provide all of the functionality of a real proxy cache we expect our results (i.e., hit rates and byte hit rates) to be somewhat optimistic.

5 SIMULATION RESULTS

This section provides the simulation results of the proxy cache replacement policy study. Section 5.1 examines the effects of parameterization on the performance of the replacement policies. Section 5.2 compares the performance of the different cache replacement policies. All of our results are shown in graphical format (Figure 2 - Figure 5). Each figure consists of two graphs, with the graph on the left indicating the achieved hit rate for a cache of a particular size while the graph on the right shows the achieved byte hit rate for a similarly configured cache.

5.1 Parameterization

Three of the replacement policies under study (LFU, SLRU and LRU-K) require parameterization in order to function properly. We examine each policy individually in an attempt to determine the effects of each parameter on the performance of the replacement policy.

The LFU replacement policy requires two parameters in order to age objects in the cache. We experimented with different settings for these parameters[4]. Figure 2 compares the performance of LFU without aging (LFU) to LFU with aging (LFU-Aging). LFU-Aging clearly outperforms LFU. These results indicate that it is important for the replacement policy to be able to make changes to the active set of objects. The performance of LFU is similar to that of LFU-Aging in two situations. When cache sizes are large (e.g., 256 GB and up) few replacement decisions are needed and cache pollution is not a factor so the policies have similar performance. When cache sizes are very small (e.g., 256 MB), adding a single large object can result in the removal of a large number of smaller objects reducing the effects of cache pollution.

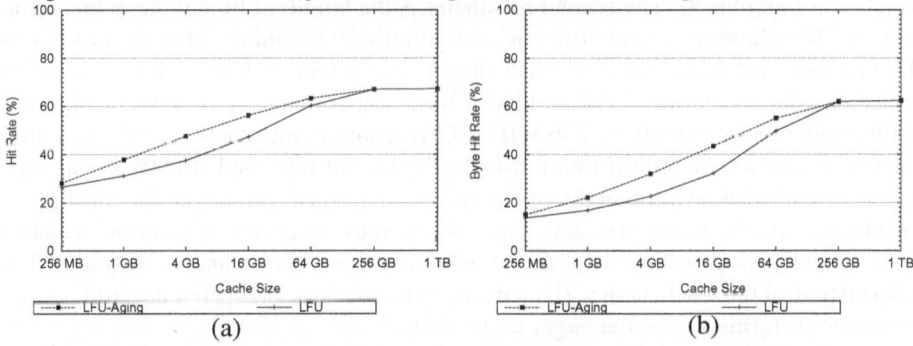

Figure 2. Analysis of LFU performance: (a) Hit Rate; (b) Byte Hit Rate

---

4. We found that as long as the aging policy was periodically invoked the choice of values for these parameters did not have a significant impact on performance.

The SLRU replacement policy uses a single parameter to set the size of the protected cache segment. We examined a wide range of values for this parameter. Figure 3 shows the results when either 10, 60 or 90 per cent of the available cache space is reserved for the protected segment. There is one curve on the graph for each parameter setting. For example, the SLRU-90 curves indicate the hit and byte hit rate achieved when the SLRU policy reserves 90% of the cache space for the protected segment. The general trend seen in Figure 3 is that performance improves as the size of the protected segment gets larger. The exception to this observation occurs for large cache sizes (e.g., 16, 64 and 256 GB). At these sizes the performance of the SLRU-90 policy degrades compared to smaller partition sizes. This degradation occurs due to the partitioning of resources (i.e., capacity misses are occurring in the unprotected segment even though space is available in the protected segment). The best overall results occur for a protected segment size of 60 per cent. Since similar results were obtained in the original study using disk caches[10] we believe that this parameter setting is not specific to our data set.

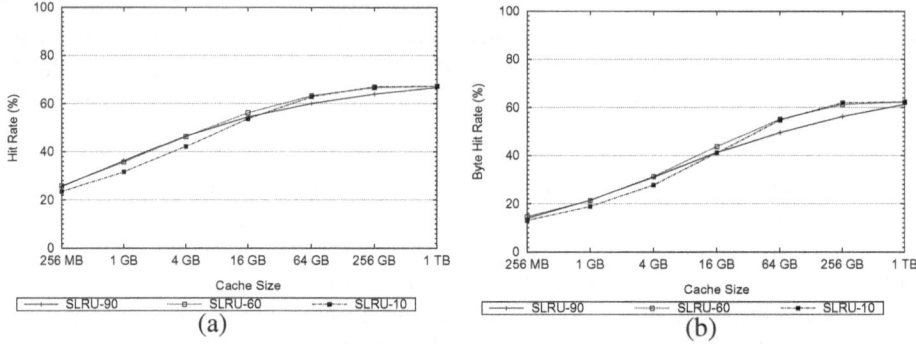

Figure 3. Analysis of SLRU performance: (a) Hit Rate; (b) Byte Hit Rate

The final replacement policy under study that requires parameterization is LRU-K. LRU-K requires two parameters. The first parameter is the number of reference times to retain for an object. The second parameter is the length of time to keep this information. We examine several different configurations: retaining either the last two or the last three reference times to each object, and retaining history information for either one day or forever. The results of these experiments are shown in Figure 4. With smaller cache sizes (e.g., 256 MB - 1 GB) retaining information on the last three references (for any length of time) provides higher hit rates and slightly higher byte hit rates. This can be attributed to the policy giving higher priority to the most popular objects. As the cache size gets larger it becomes necessary to retain information for a longer period of time in order to achieve better performance. Requiring less information about each object (i.e., using only the last two reference times) also improves performance for the larger cache sizes.

5.2   Comparison of Replacement Policies

In this section we compare the performance of all of the replacement policies. To make the comparison easier we include only the "best" curve for each of the policies

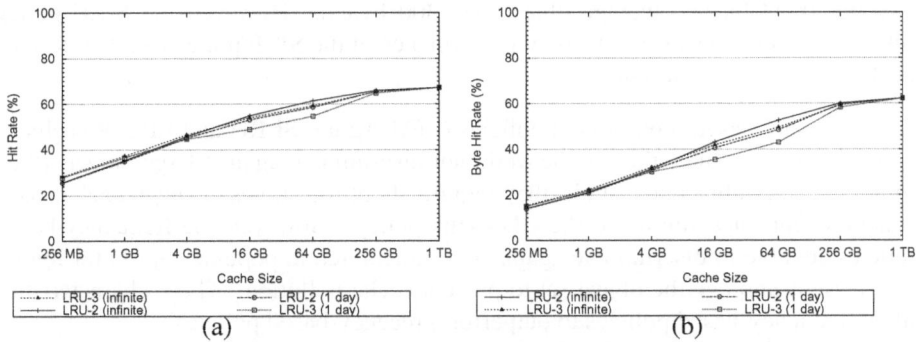

Figure 4. Analysis of LRU-K performance: (a) Hit Rate; (b) Byte Hit Rate

that required parameterization (i.e., we use LFU-Aging for the LFU policy, SLRU-60 for the SLRU policy and LRU-2 with infinite history for the LRU-K policy). We have also sorted the legend in each graph by the performance of the policies. For example, in Figure 5(a), the first policy listed in the legend is GDS-Hits. The GDS-Hits policy achieved the highest hit rate. The last policy in the legend is LRU. LRU obtained the lowest hit rate of the policies that we examined.

Figure 5(a) compares the hit rates achieved by each policy. The results indicate that the maximum achievable hit rate is 67% (obtained by all policies with a cache size of 1 TB). The remaining 33% of requests are for the initial requests for objects, for uncacheable objects (e.g., output from dynamic or cgi objects) or for the updates of objects which have been modified and cannot be served from the cache. Figure 5(a) shows that even small caches can perform quite well if the correct replacement policy is used. For example, a 256 MB cache using the GreedyDual-Size (Hits) policy achieved a hit rate of 35% which is 52% of the maximum achievable rate. This rate was achieved while allowing for only 0.06% of the entire object set size to be cached.

Figure 5(a) shows that the GreedyDual-Size (Hits) policy is vastly superior to other policies when hit rate is used as the metric. For small cache sizes (256 MB to 16 GB) GDS-Hits outperforms all other policies by at least 6 percentage points. The success of the GDS-Hits policy can be attributed to two characteristics of the policy: it discriminates against large objects, allowing for more small objects to be cached; and it ages the object set to prevent cache pollution from occurring. During our experiments we monitored the number of objects kept in the cache under the various replacement policies. With a 256 MB cache the GDS-Hits policy held 170,000 objects (average object size 1.5 KB) at the end of the simulation. The LFU-Aging policy, by comparison, held only 20,000 objects (an average object size of 13 KB). By inflating the number of objects kept in the cache GDS-Hits increases the probability that an object will be in the cache when it is requested. The other size-based policies (GDS-Bytes and SIZE) have much lower hit rates. GDS-Bytes attempts to improve the byte hit rate by favoring larger objects (it kept 26,000 objects in the 256 MB cache). Thus, the lower hit rate of GDS-Bytes is not unexpected. The SIZE policy discriminates even more harshly against large objects. In the 256 MB cache the SIZE policy collected over 900,000 objects (average object size 300 bytes). However, the SIZE policy failed to age the object set. The poor performance of the SIZE policy can therefore be attributed to cache pollution.

The frequency-based replacement policies (LFU-Aging, SLRU and LRU-K) achieve similar hit rates. Since these policies do not discriminate against large objects (they do not consider object size at all) they require about four times as much cache space to achieve hit rates similar to the GDS-Hits policy. However, the frequency-based policies are able to discriminate against one-timers, retain popular objects for longer time periods and age the object set to prevent cache pollution. These characteristics allow frequency-based policies to outperform recency-based policies.

The only recency-based policy that we examine is LRU. LRU achieves the lowest hit rate since it does not consider enough information when making replacement decisions and therefore tends to make poorer choices. Because of this the LRU policy requires almost eight times as much cache space as the GDS-Hits policy to achieve similar hit rates. One positive feature of LRU is that it ages the object set which prevents cache pollution.

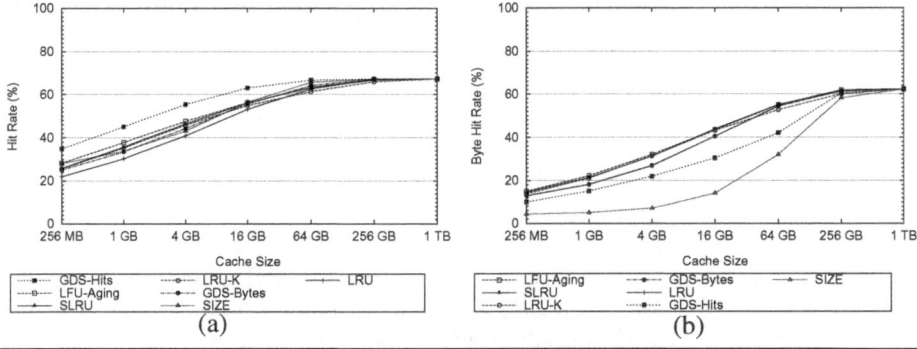

Figure 5. Comparison of all Replacement Policies: (a) Hit Rate; (b) Byte Hit Rate

Figure 5(b) shows the achieved byte hit rates for the replacement policies under study. Figure 5(b) reveals a maximum byte hit rate of 62% for the data set under study. The remaining 38% of the data needed to be transferred across the external network link. The results also indicate that it is more difficult to achieve high byte hit rates than high hit rates. For example, a 256 MB cache can achieve a byte hit rate of 15% which is only one quarter of the maximum achievable byte hit rate.

According to the results in Figure 5(b) the frequency-based policies (LFU-Aging, SLRU and LRU-K) are the best choice for reducing network traffic. The three frequency-based policies achieve similar byte hit rates, approximately 2-4 percentage points higher than LRU. The frequency-based policies work well because they do not discriminate against the large objects which are responsible for a significant amount of the data traffic. Frequency-based policies also retain popular objects (both small and large) longer than recency-based policies, another reason that frequency-based policies achieve higher byte hit rates.

The LRU and GDS-Bytes policies have almost identical performance in terms of byte hit rates. LRU does not discriminate against large objects which allows it to outperform size-based policies which do. Although GDS-Bytes is a size-based policy it has been designed to treat large objects more favorably in an attempt to improve the byte hit rate. Both LRU and GDS-Bytes require about twice the cache space to achieve byte hit rates comparable to the frequency-based policies.

Since size-based policies (generally) discriminate against large objects it is not surprising that these policies have the worst byte hit rate performance. The GDS-Hits policy requires four times more cache space to achieve the same byte hit rate as a frequency-based policy. The byte hit rate of the SIZE policy is even worse than GDS-Hits because of more unfavorable treatment of large objects and cache pollution.

6 SUMMARY AND CONCLUSIONS

This paper has presented our performance study of a Web proxy cache. This study is the first to include the effects of high-speed cable modems by clients and also has the largest data set of any proxy workload. Trace-driven simulations were used to evaluate the performance of different cache replacement policies. Our results indicate that size-based policies achieve higher hit rates than other policies while frequency-based policies are more effective at reducing external network traffic. The results show that a properly chosen replacement policy can reduce the purchase cost of Web proxy caches by making better use of available resources. The results also indicate that it is important to examine the performance of replacement policies over extended time durations to test for side effects such as cache pollution.

The intent of this paper was not to promote the use of a single replacement policy for Web proxies. Instead, our goal was to explain the performance of different policies by examining the workload characteristics that each policy used or did not use when making replacement decisions. This information can be applied in the design of a new replacement policy that achieves both high hit rates and byte hit rates.

Acknowledgments

The authors would like to thank Mike Rodriquez of HP Labs and all the people in the Telecommunication Platforms Division (TPD) who supplied us with access logs; John Dilley, Gita Gopal and Jim Salehi of HP Labs and the anonymous reviewers for their constructive comments on the paper; and Greg Oster of the University of Saskatchewan for his assistance with the development of the simulator.

REFERENCES

[1] M. Arlitt, R. Friedrich, and T. Jin, "Using Workload Characterization to Improve Proxy Cache Management", Technical Report HPL-98-07, Hewlett-Packard Laboratories, January 1998.

[2] M. Arlitt and C. Williamson, "Internet Web Servers: Workload Characterization and Performance Implications", *IEEE/ACM Transactions on Networking,* Vol. 5, No. 5, pp. 631-645, October 1997.

[3] M. Arlitt and C. Williamson, "Trace-Driven Simulation of Document Caching Strategies for Internet Web Servers", *The Society for Computer Simulation SIMULATION Journal,* Vol. 68, No. 1, pp. 23-33, January 1997.

[4] P. Cao and S. Irani, "Cost-Aware WWW Proxy Caching Algorithms", *Proceedings of USENIX Symposium on Internet Technologies and Systems (USITS),* Monterey, CA, pp. 193-206, December 1997.

[5] C. Cunha, A. Bestavros, and M. Crovella, "Characteristics of WWW Client-based Traces", Technical Report TR-95-010, Boston University Department of Computer Science, April 1995.

[6] B. Duska, D. Marwood, and M. Feeley, "The Measured Access Characteristics of World-Wide Web Client Proxy Caches", *Proceedings of USENIX Symposium of Internet Technologies and Systems (USITS),* Monterey, CA, pp. 23-35, December 1997.

[7] R. Fielding, J. Gettys, J. Mogul, H. Frystyk, and T. Berners-Lee, "RFC 2068 - Hypertext Transfer Protocol - - HTTP/1.1", January 1997.

[8] S. Gribble and E. Brewer, "System Design Issues for Internet Middleware Services: Deductions from a Large Client Trace", *Proceedings of USENIX Symposium on Internet Technologies and Systems (USITS),* Monterey, CA, pp. 207-218, December 1997.

[9] Inktomi homepage. Available at http://www.inktomi.com

[10] R. Karedla, J. Love and B. Wherry, "Caching Strategies to Improve Disk System Performance", IEEE Computer, Vol. 27, No. 3, pp. 38-46, March 1994.

[11] P. Lorenzetti and L. Rizzo, "Replacement Policies for a Proxy Cache", Technical Report, Universita di Pisa, December 1996.

[12] A. Luotonen, *Web Proxy Servers*, Prentice Hall, Upper Saddle River, NJ, 1998.

[13] Mirror Image homepage. Available at http://www.mirror-image.com

[14] E. O'Neil, P. O'Neil and G. Weikum, "The LRU-K Page Replacement Algorithm for Database Disk Buffering", *Proceedings of SIGMOD '93*, Washington, DC, May 1993.

[15] J. Robinson and M. Devarakonda, "Data Cache Management Using Frequency-Based Replacement", *Proceedings of the 1990 ACM SIGMETRICS Conference on the Measurement and Modeling of Computer Systems*, Boulder, CO, pp. 134-142, May 1990.

[16] S. Williams, M. Abrams, C. Standridge, G. Abdulla, and E. Fox, "Removal Policies in Network Caches for World-Wide Web Documents", *Proceedings on ACM SIGCOMM '96*, Stanford, CA, pp. 293-305, August 1996.

[17] R. Wooster and M. Abrams, "Proxy Caching that Estimates Page Load Delays", Proceedings of the 6th International World-Wide Web Conference, Santa Clara, CA, April 1997.

[18] World-Wide Web Consortium, "Replication and Caching Position Statement", August 1997. Available at: http://www.w3.org/Propogation/activity.html

Performance Analysis of a WDM Bus Network Based on GSPN Models *

Giuliana Franceschinis[1], Andrea Fumagalli[2], and Roberto Grasso[2]

[1] Università degli Studi di Torino, Dipartimento di Informatica
Corso Svizzera 185, 10149 Torino, Italy
Tel: +39-11-7429111 – Fax: +39-11-751603
giuliana@di.unito.it
[2] The University of Texas at Dallas
P.O. Box 830688 – MS EC33 – Richardson, TX 75083-0688
Tel: (972) 883-6853 – Fax: (972) 883-2710
{andreaf,grasso}@utdallas.edu

Abstract. Recent progress in optical technology makes it possible to design innovative high speed network architectures. One possible architecture consists of a folded bus fiber in which parallel transmission channels are obtained using Wavelength Division Multiplexing (WDM). Nodes connected to the bus exchange data using the channels in parallel. Signals are transmitted from the source to the destination node in an all-optical fashion, thus avoiding the bottleneck of electronic processing at the intermediate nodes.

The aim of the paper is to study the performance of the WDM bus network controlled by a novel access protocol proposed by the authors. The analysis is based on two GSPN models that allow to determine the access delay of the proposed protocol and its fairness throughout the nodes. As a result, it is possible to quantitatively determine the effect that some design choices have on system fairness. The paper discusses the strength and limits of GreatSPN, the tool used to perform the analysis.

1 Introduction

The available 30 THz of fiber bandwidth makes optical technology the most adequate to realize future high speed data networks necessary to support the exponentially increasing traffic of today Internet. Although first experimental results of high speed transmission in fiber show that rates in the range of 100 Gbps and above are possible on a single channel [17], Wavelength Division Multiplexing (WDM) [5] seems to be a more practical approach with today technology [19]. By means of WDM, the fiber bandwidth can be subdivided to obtain parallel and independent channels in the same fiber, each operating at a transmission rate compatible with extant electronic technology, e.g., 2.5 Gbps.

* This research is sponsored by NSF under contracts # NCR-9628189 and # NCR-9596242, by CSELT, by the EEC HCM Project MATCH (CHRX-CT94-0452) and the Italian MURST. A. Fumagalli is currently on leave from the Politecnico di Torino.

R. Puigjaner et al. (Eds.): Tools'98, LNCS 1469, pp. 207–218, 1998.

Beside the "multiplication factor" on the transmission bandwidth, WDM offers a more fundamental innovation in modern data networking. According to the concept of all-optical transmission, transmitted data on a given wavelength can be optically propagated towards the intended destination without requiring electronic conversion at the intermediate nodes along the path from the source to the destination [13]. By so doing, the available optical bandwidth can be exploited without encountering the problem of "electronic bottleneck", generating from the about 3 orders of magnitude of rate difference between optics and electronics.

A number of networking solutions (called *single hop* solutions) have been proposed that are based on this principle (see [13] for a complete survey). Single hop topologies include passive coupler star [6], ring [9] and folded bus [4]. The remaining part of the paper focuses on the WDM folded bus topology proposed in [4], consisting of a transmission bus and a reception bus.

The advantages of using folded bus network are: (1) re-circulation of the optical signal is not possible, thus preventing undesired effects caused by residual transmission due to non-ideal optical filtering [16], (2) if time is divided into fixed slots, each containing one packet per wavelength, random transmission of (fixed length) packets is possible without generating collision by simply sensing the transmission bus at the beginning of each slot prior to the packet transmission, (3) the folding point of the bus, i.e., where the transmission bus joins the reception bus, is the natural place for connecting a gateway that provides system scalability [8].

However, as well know from the Distributed Queue Dual Bus (DQDB) standard [18], if not properly controlled, random transmission of packets at the nodes of a bus topology may generate unfair network response throughout the nodes, i.e., upstream nodes can freely use all the available bandwidth making downstream nodes starve for bandwidth. In addition, to minimize individual channel congestion multi-channel bus requires that channels be evenly loaded. A solution to these two problems was proposed in FairNet [4]. Under the assumption that the transmission queue is limited to one (fixed length) packet, and packets are generated according to a geometric arrival process, a close form for the average access delay is derived in [4] as a function of p_i, $i = 1, \ldots, N$, where p_i is the probability that node i decides to attempt transmission during the current time slot, and N is the number of nodes in the system. The set of values for p_i's that generate even access delay throughout the nodes can be derived from the close form under any given traffic distribution that does not generate instability in the system.

In the attempt to address a more realistic scenario than the single buffer case, the authors have recently developed a modified version of the FairNet protocol that takes into account a multi packet transmission queue [11]. The proposed access protocol determines when and *which* packet to transmit according to the packets currently stored in the transmission queue. The packet for transmission is selected to balance the packets stored at the node with respect to their transmission channel. The proposed protocol is expected to balance the load throughout the channels, and consequently decrease the individual channel congestion and the average access delay of the system.

This paper presents two models devised to take into account the multi-packet nature of the transmitter queue and characterize the performance of the proposed access protocol. The models, based on the Generalized Stochastic Petri Net (GSPN) formalism [2], allow to compute the average access delay of a transmitted packet as a function of both the position of the source node along the bus and the channel used for transmission.

As shown in the paper, the proposed modeling technique allows to determine with good accuracy 1) what level of unfairness arises when multi packet transmission queue is used, 2) how system fairness is affected by the way reception channels are assigned to destination nodes, and 3) what reduction of average access delay is achieved by the proposed protocol with respect to the FairNet protocol.

2 System Description

The network under consideration is an optical folded bus based structure in which a number (W) of parallel unidirectional channels (wavelength), are shared among a number (N) of nodes. A 4 node-2 channel network is depicted in Fig.1. Nodes transmit packets using the *transmitter bus* and receive packets

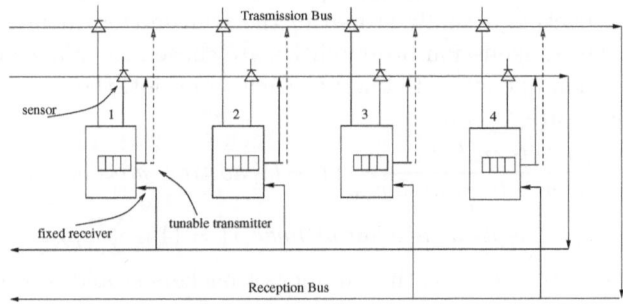

Fig. 1. A two channel bus with four nodes.

from the *reception bus*. Once transmitted, the optical signal circulates in the folded bus and it is broadcast to all nodes as it propagates within the reception bus. Destination node receives only packets intended to it. Time is slotted on each channel, and the slot length is equal to the packet transmission time plus the guard band necessary to take into account the finite tuning speed of optical transmitters. Slots are aligned across the channels and aligned slots arrive at node simultaneously. Each node is equipped with three basic components: a tunable transmitter that can be tuned on any of the W channels, a fixed receiver which receives from a preassigned channel, (e.g., node i is tuned on wavelength λ_j, $j = \left\lceil \frac{i \times W}{N} \right\rceil$) and a sensor that detects whether or not wavelengths in the transmission bus are occupied with packets transmitted by the upstream nodes. Notice that a wavelength can be shared by several destinations. Each node has W FIFO transmission queues, one for each channel. The packet's channel is automatically determined by the channel assigned to the packet's destination node. Source nodes willing to transmit to a destination must tune their transmitter on the corresponding destination's channel prior to transmitting the packet.

Access protocols As previously explained, an appropriate access protocol is necessary to assure that, independently from their location in the bus, nodes can evenly share the bus bandwidth. This is achieved using a probabilistic scheduling strategy according to which, at any time slot, node i either chooses channel c for transmission with probability p_{ic} or does not attempt transmission at all with probability $(1 - \sum_c p_{ic})$. When channel c is selected for transmission, the node transmits the first packet in the transmitter queue corresponding to that channel if the queue is not empty and channel c in the arriving slot is sensed empty.

In a simplified scenario where each node has only one transmission queue shared by the channels the values for p_{ic}'s that guarantee a given fairness criterion (in our case an even average packet delay throughout the nodes) can be analytically derived [4] assuming that the network traffic matrix is known, and the offered load is stable. Once determined, the values for p_{ic}'s are fixed.

However, in a more practical scenario where node has multi packet transmission queues, the use of constant p_{ic}'s limits network performance. A better approach makes use of transmission probabilities, p_{icp}, that are dynamic and depend on the packets actually stored in the transmitter queues. In particular, at each node the transmission probabilities are chosen to balance the occupancy of the transmission queues as follows: at each time slot, the transmission probabilities for node i are

$$p_{icp} = \frac{\#packets\ in\ buffer\ c}{\sum_k \#packets\ in\ buffer\ k}(1 - P\{no\ transmission\ at\ node\ i\}) \qquad (1)$$

$$P\{no\ transmission\ at\ node\ i\} = (1 - \sum_c p_{ic}) \qquad (2)$$

where $\#$ *packets in buffer* c is the number of packets stored in the transmission queue associated with channel c at node i, and $P\{no\ transmission\ at\ node\ i\}$ is the probability that node i decides not to transmit as derived in [4].

3   GSPN Models

A complete and exact model of the proposed system requires a state definition that takes into account the joint distributions of the packets at every node and the packets propagating in the bus on the parallel channels. The complexity for such a model becomes prohibitive already with few nodes and few channels.

A practical approach, consists of deriving approximated performance indices by separately analyzing as many (relatively small) models as the number of nodes in the system. The method consists of sequentially analyzing the model of each node, starting from the most upstream one and gradually moving towards the most downstream one with respect to the transmission bus. A similar serial solution technique has been presented in [12]. The model used to analyze the node is Markovian [15], and automatically obtained by means of a graphical formalism called Generalized Stochastic Petri Net (GSPN) [2]. GSPN is a stochastic-timed Petri Net formalism [2] in which the firing time of a transition is either exponentially distributed (timed transition) or deterministically equal to zero (immediate transition) [1,2]. Timed transitions are associated with events that take time to occur. Immediate transitions are used to model logical operations. Timed transitions can fire only when none of the immediate transitions is enabled. For a complete description of the GSPN formalism, the interested reader may refer to [2].

In this paper GSPN is adopted to model a (slotted) synchronous system using the following technique [14,10,3]: a timed transition is used to model the slotted time, i.e., its firing represents the beginning of a new time slot. Immediate transitions are then used to model the events that occur at the node during that time slot, i.e., packet generation and packet transmission. The embedded Discrete Time Markov Chain obtained sampling the system when the timed transition becomes enabled represents the slotted system at the end of the time slot. It can be shown that independently from the firing time of the timed transition, the steady state solution of the GSPN model equals the solution of the embedded chain and consequently of the slotted system.

The tool used to construct and analyze the models is GreatSPN [7]. While building the models we took advantage of the structural property analysis modules of the tool to check the models consistency: for example invariant computation was used to quickly find erroneous or missing arcs in the more complex model. The tool uses the results of structural analysis (e.g., place bounds) for a more efficient encoding of the *marking* (state) during state space generation.

To model the bus system, marking dependent immediate transition weights are necessary. Unfortunately, GreatSPN allows only marking dependent timed transition rates, while it imposes constant immediate transition weights (see [2] for a thorough discussion on this choice motivations). The equivalent functionality of marking dependent immediate transitions is thus achieved in the proposed models using a set of timed transitions that are marking dependent. In particular a timed transition followed by an immediate transitions free choice subnet is replaced by a set of timed transitions (one for each immediate transition in the subnet). The firing of any of these timed transitions represents the start of a new time slot and determines the choice of a subset of possible state evolution during that slot.

Two GSPN models of the node are described next. The first model is simpler as it does not take into account the joint distribution of packets in consecutive slots. This model is accurate when the offered load is low. The second model is more complicated as it attempts to capture the increasing fluctuation of traffic in the bus as network load increases and as slots propagate along the transmission bus. The models assume that both traffic matrix and network load are known. The packets arrival process at source nodes is geometric.

Node model without traffic memory Fig. 2 shows the GSPN model of node i in a 2 channel bus network. Places *Buffer_1* and *Buffer_2* represent the two transmission queues at the node, each storing the packets awaiting transmission on one of the channels. Each token in place *Buffer_i* represents one packet in the corresponding queue.

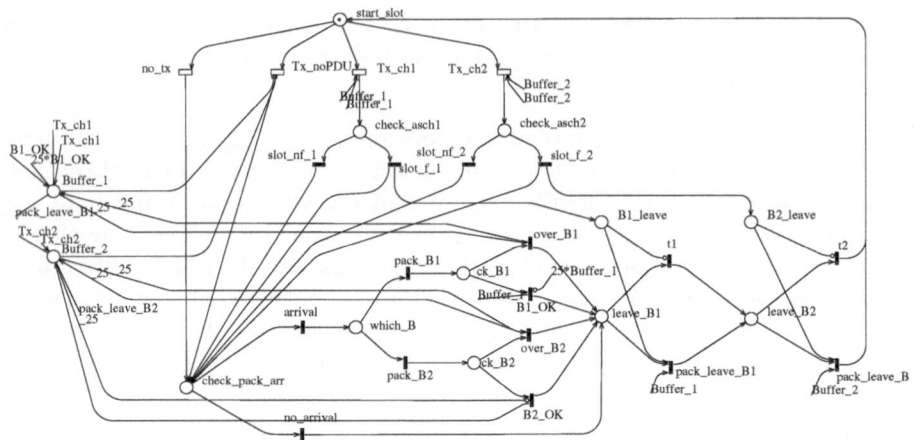

Fig. 2. Node model without traffic memory. $W = 2$.

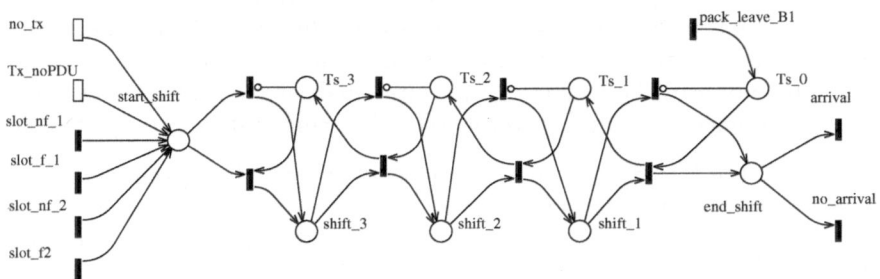

Fig. 3. GSPN model with traffic memory: most upstream node. $W = 2$.

Place *start_slot* contains one token that concurrently enables four timed transitions. The firing on any of these transitions represents the beginning of a new time slot. The transition that actually fires is stochastically determined. The firing probability of each transition t is proportional to the corresponding firing rate λ_t, which is determined according to the behavior of the access protocol, as follows: *no_tx* represents the beginning of a slot in which the node chooses not to transmit, and its rate is computed using Eq. (2); *Tx_no_PDU* is enabled when both *Buffer_1* and *Buffer_2* are empty and its firing rate is $\lambda_{Tx\_no\_PDU} = 1 - \lambda_{no\_tx}$; transition *Tx_ch1* (*Tx_ch2*) represents the beginning of a slot in which the node wants to attempt transmission of a packet in queue 1 (queue 2), it has a marking dependent rate computed using Eq. 1. The last two transitions are never enabled simultaneously with Tx_no_PDU, and $\lambda_{Tx\_ch1} + \lambda_{Tx\_ch2} = 1 - \lambda_{no\_tx}$.

Following the firing of any of the timed transitions (that removes the token from $start\_slot$), a sequence of immediate transitions fire until a token is placed back into $start\_slot$. The firing of the immediate transitions perform the change of the marking of places $Buffer\_1$ and $Buffer\_2$, according to the access protocol and the packet arrival process. If the node attempts transmission on channel i (firing of transition Tx_ch_i), the status of the corresponding channel is sensed. The firing probability associated with transition $slot\_nf\_i$ ($slot\_f\_i$) is set to the probability to find the slot busy (free). If the slot is busy transmission does not occur (firing of $slot\_nf\_i$, $t1$, $t2$). Conversely, if the slot is free, one packet is transmitted, removing one token from place $Buffer\_i$ (firing of transitions $slot\_f\_i$, $pack\_leave\_B\_i$ and $t\_(3-i)$). The firing probabilities of transitions $slot\_nf\_i$ and $slot\_f\_i$ are functions of traffic distribution, network load, position of the nodes in the bus and assignment policy of reception channels.

Packet generation at the node is modeled by two conflicting transitions, namely, $arrival$ and $no\_arrival$, whose weight is a function of the load offered by the node. When a packet is generated, a token is placed in one of the two places $Buffer\_1$ or $Buffer\_2$, according to the destination chosen for the packet (firing of $pack\_B\_i$). If the corresponding buffer is full, the generated packet is discarded (firing of $over\_B\_i$), otherwise transition B_i_OK fires.

The maximum number of packets $bmax$ buffered in a queue is a model parameter. This parameter is encoded in the weight of some arcs connected with places $Buffer\_i$. In Fig. 2 the capacity for each buffer, $bmax$, is 25 packets. It must be observed that the number of states of the model is equal to $bmax^W$, thus the maximum size for the transmission queue is quite limited as the number of wavelengths grows. However, as shown in [10], under the assumption of uniform offered load on the wavelengths, it is possible to take advantage of special state space reduction techniques by using an high level Petri net formalism capable of automatically exploiting system symmetries.

Node model with traffic memory The simple model in Fig. 2 does not take into account the fluctuations of the busy slots in the transmission bus caused by the concurrent transmissions of source nodes. In fact, only the average probability of sensing a busy slot on each channel is modeled by the weight of transitions $slot\_nf\_i$. Since the level of traffic fluctuation tends to increase in the transmission bus as the network load grows and as slots move towards the most downstream node, a more complex model is necessary to determine the effect of this phenomenon that may intuitively lead to increased access delay.

To capture the fluctuation of busy slots in the transmission bus the model in Fig. 2 is modified to compute the joint distribution of busy slots in WL consecutive time slots. The modification consists of refining place $check\_pack\_arr$ as shown in Fig. 3. The place in the original model must be substituted by the subnet so that all the input arcs of $check\_pack\_arr$ enter place $start\_shift$ while all the output arcs of *check_pack_arr* exit from place *end_shift*. Moreover an arc is added going from transition *pack_leave_B1* to place *Ts_0*.

Places *Ts_3*, *Ts_2*, *Ts_1*, *Ts_0*, in the subnet represent the states of the current slot (*Ts_0*) and of the past three slots. If the node transmits a packet on channel 1, a token is placed in *Ts_0*. That token is then shifted one place to the left at each time slot, until it is discarded 4 time slots later.

The conditional probability of the state of a slot, given the states of the previous three slots, is calculated as

$$P\{\#Ts\_0 = i_0 \mid \#Ts\_1 = i_1, \#Ts\_2 = i_2, \#Ts\_3 = i_3\}, i_j = 0, 1 \qquad (3)$$

where $P\{\#Ts\_0 = i_0\}$ is the probability that i_0 tokens are in place *Ts_0*.

This joint distribution computed with the modified model is fed into the model of the next downstream node to characterize the distribution of the arriving busy slots at that node. This feed-forward approach maintains partial memory of the distribution of the packets transmitted by upstream nodes. Clearly, as WL tends to infinity, the model becomes asymptotically exact. However since both the model and state space size grows with the length of the window memory, only small values of WL can be used.

For the sake of space we do not show the model of node j (with $j > 1$). This complex model includes an additional subnet used to generate the next busy slot on the basis of the joint distribution computed through the previous node model. The additional subnet is composed of 10 places and 25 immediate transitions (16 of which would reduce to 1 if GreatSPN allowed marking dependent weights).

Solution of the models using GreatSPN The models were solved using the solution modules of GreatSPN [7] for the generation of the reachability graph (RG), the derivation of the corresponding Markov chain and its steady state solution. The RG generation module computes and stores both tangible and vanishing markings, and it passes on only the tangible ones to the next modules (these are the markings in which the model spends non zero time). GreatSPN can build state spaces of up to a few million states, depending on the model complexity and on the characteristics of the computer platform. However, the maximum size of RG that the tool can generate drops to a few hundred thousand states if most of the states are vanishing (as in the two proposed models).

The table at the end of this section shows the number of tangible and vanishing states of the two models, the time required to generate the RG (we do not report the time required to generate and solve the MC since it is negligible), and the memory requirement for different queue sizes. The computer platform consists of a Pentium II, 300Mhz, and 64Mb RAM. The limiting resource is the memory: the most demanding models that we could solve used up to 122Mb. The first model with buffer size of 30, stopped for exhausted memory at 14.680 tangible states. The second model with buffer size of 9 stopped at 4.960 tangible states having used 130Mb of memory.

Although the number of tangible states in our models is quite small, the much higher number of vanishing states limits the size of the analyzable models. Probably, techniques that eliminate vanishing marking on the fly would allow to solve larger models, although increasing considerably the time. Moreover, it might be the case that the implementation of immediate firing sequences exploration in GreatSPN is not optimized, especially for lengthy sequences. Although handling immediate transition firings is heavy due to the considerable amount of information needed to compute the correct firing probabilities in the MC generation step, it is surprising how much inefficient it is in comparison with timed transitions handling: for comparison purposes, we solved the second model changing all immediate transitions into timed ones (which of course does not lead to correct results, but generates a RG of comparable size), affording to generate a state space of 821.442 states, with buffer capacity of 20, using approximately 90Mb of memory and short time.

Another possible solution to increase the size of solvable models, is to allow more complex state changes in a single firing: for example shifting left the tokens in places Tsp_i, $i = 0, \ldots, 3$ requires a sequence of four immediate transition firings in our model. If the same operation was done in a single step, the number of vanishing states would greatly reduce. This solution requires a change in the formalism.

Model type	buffers size	# Tangible states	# Vanishing states	user+system time	Memory (Mb)
simple	10	1.848	32.208	<3s	14
simple	25	10.608	191.508	14+3s	91
simple	29	14.160	256.484	19+4s	122
simple	30	>14.680	n.c.	n.c.	>127
complex	5	1.836	63.612	7+1s	48
complex	8	4.212	150.714	19+4s	114
complex	9	>4.960	n.c.	n.c.	>130

4   Performance

This section discusses some results obtained resolving the GSPN models. The analysis is carried out assuming a uniform traffic distribution, i.e., nodes generate the same load, defined as number of generated packets per slot, and packets are evenly destined to any node except for the source node itself. Access delay is defined as the time spent by a packet as the head-of-the-line in the queue until transmission takes place. Access delay is measured in time slots.

Fig. 4 shows average access delay versus network load obtained in a 10 node-2 wavelength using the FairNet protocol (dashed curve) and the proposed protocol (solid curve). The average access delay is calculated at the most upstream node and considering both transmission queues. The simple GSPN model was used to derive the results for the proposed protocol that reduces the average access delay by a factor of two when compared to the FairNet performance. This reduction increases as load grows. Simulation results obtained using a custom object oriented simulator [11] are also shown (+ symbol) in the graph and reveal the good accuracy of the simple GSPN model.

We have computed the average access delay at the most upstream node for three different bus networks, assuming a network load that is 50% the network capacity; The first bus has 2 wavelengths and 10 nodes. The second bus has 4 wavelengths and 20 nodes. The third bus has 6 wavelengths and 30 nodes. The ratio $\frac{N}{W}$ is constant and equal to 5. The reduction factor of the average access delay achieved by the proposed protocol with respect to FairNet grows with the number of wavelengths. With 2 wavelengths the proposed protocol had a delay of 2 slots against the 4.22 slots of Fairnet. With 4 wavelengths, the access delay is reduced to 25% (2.45 against 9.176). With 6 wavelengths, the access delay is reduced to 15% (2.25 against 14.15).

Fig. 5 shows the average access delay at each node and on each channel, separately, in a 10 node-2 wavelength network. Two bus configurations are considered. The first one (dotted curves) uses the reception channel assignment proposed for FairNet, in which the 5 most upstream nodes receive from channel 1 and the remaining 5 nodes receive from channel 2. With this channel assignment, although the global average access delay remains constant throughout the nodes, the per channel access delay reveals a substantial unfairness. The cause of this unfairness is the fact that nodes do not transmit to themselves. Thus, under uniform traffic distribution a node tends to transmit less often on its own reception channel than on the other. This unfairness can be significantly reduced by changing the way channels are assigned for reception. By alternating the channels for reception as we move from the most upstream node to the most downstream node, a better result is obtained (solid curves).

Figs. 6 and 7 show the per channel average access delay throughout the nodes of a 10 node-2 wavelength bus for two network loads, 20% and 70% of the network capacity, respectively. These results are obtained using the complex GSPN model that takes into account the fluctuation of the busy slots in the transmission bus. With 20% load the model already captures the effect of traffic fluctuation, together with the effect determined by the alternating pattern of the receiver channels. Practically speaking, the system is fair. At higher load, 70%, the unfairness due to traffic fluctuation becomes more pronounced and may require the use of some additional control mechanism.

In Fig. 7 results (symbol +) obtained via simulation are shown for comparison. The comparison shows that the GSPN model is only partially able to capture the effect of traffic fluctuation. This is due to the finite memory that the model has of the busy slots in the transmission bus, i.e., $WL = 4$ slots. However the complex model reveals the presence of the delay drift: if we used the simple model in this load situation we would obtain a flat curve.

5   Discussion

The paper proposed two GSPN models to analyze average access delay and fairness in a WDM multi-channel folded bus in which nodes have transmitter queues larger than one packet. In the bus, channel access is regulated by a novel protocol proposed by the authors that sorts the packets for transmission at the node according to the occupancy of the transmission queues, with the goal of balancing the packets awaiting transmission on their transmission channel and consequently minimize traffic congestion on each individual channel.

The GSPN models were numerically resolved using GreatSPN tool [7]. The tool is capable of handling Markovian models with a few million states. However, due to the specific technique adopted in this paper to model *slotted system*, long sequences of immediate transitions must be fired in order to determine the underlying Markov chain. Since the current implementation of the tool is not optimized for handling lengthy sequences of immediate transition firings, the number of states that could be managed in our case was lower. In spite of the above limitation of the tool, numerical results obtained by solving the GSPN models showed that (1) reduction of access delay with respect to previous work [4] is possible, with improvements proportional to the number of channels (wavelengths), (2) the multi-packet transmission queue may lead to unfair network behavior, (3) network unfairness can be mitigated by alternating the channels for reception at the nodes. Practically speaking, the measured unfairness is acceptable when load conditions are not heavy (load below 50% originates delay differences that are within few percentages).

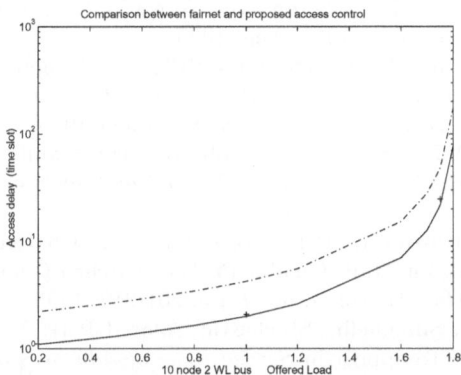

Fig. 4. Comparison between FairNet (dashed) and proposed protocol (solid). Simulation is indicated with +.

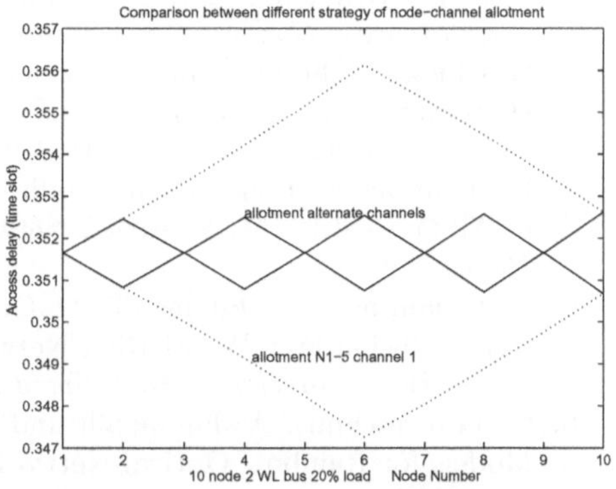

Fig. 5. Two strategies to assign reception channels to nodes: FairNet (dotted), alternating technique (solid).

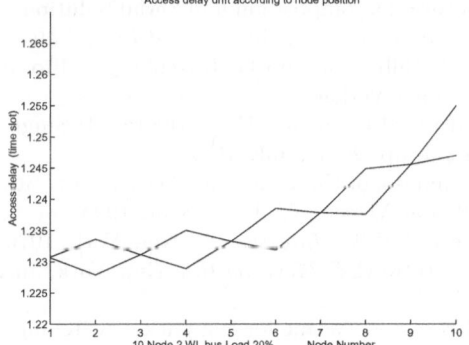

Fig. 6. Access delay drift at low load on the two channels.

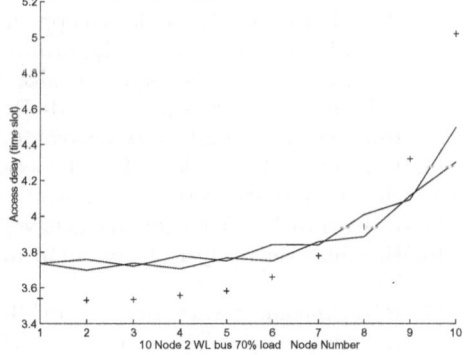

Fig. 7. Results of simulation (+) vs. GSPN model with traffic memory.

References

1. M. Ajmone Marsan, G. Balbo, G. Conte, "A Class of Generalized Stochastic Petri Nets for the Performance Analysis of Multiprocessor Systems," *ACM Transactions on Computer Systems*, vol. 2, no. 1, May 84.
2. M. Ajmone Marsan, G. Balbo, G. Conte, S. Donatelli, G. Franceschinis "Modelling with generalized stochastic Petri Nets," *John Wiley & Sons*, 1996.
3. M Ajmone Marsan and R. Gaeta. GSPN models for ATM networks. In *Proc. 7th Int. Workshop on Petri Nets and Performance Models*, St. Malo', France, June 1997. IEEE-CS Press.
4. S. Banerjee, B. Mukherjee, "Fairnet: A WDM-based Multiple Channel Lightwave Network with Adaptive and Fair Scheduling Policy," *Journal of Lightwave Technology*, vol. 11, no. 5-6, pp. 1104-1111, May/June 1993.
5. C.A.Brackett, "Dense Wavelength Division Multiplexing Networks: Principles and Applications," *IEEE Journal on Selected Areas in Communications*, vol. 8, pp. 948-964, Aug. 1990.
6. M.-S. Chen, N.R. Dono, R. Ramaswami, "A Media-Access Protocol for Packet-Switched Wavelength Division Multiaccess Metropolitan Area Networks," *IEEE I. Selected Areas Commun.*, vol. 8, no. 6, pp. 1048-1057, Aug. 1990.
7. G. Chiola, G. Franceschinis, R. Gaeta, and M. Ribaudo. GreatSPN 1.7: Graphical Editor and Analyzer for Timed and Stochastic Petri Nets. *Performance Evaluation, special issue on Performance Modeling Tools*, 24(1&2):47–68, November 1995.
8. I. Chlamtac, V. Elek, A. Fumagalli, "A Fair Slot Routing Solution for Scalability in All-Optical Packet Switched Networks," *accepted in the Journal of High Speed Networks*.
9. I. Chlamtac, A. Fumagalli, L.G. Kazovsky, P.T. Poggiolini, "A Contention/Collision Free WDM Ring Network for Multi Gigabit Packet Switched Communication," *Journal of High Speed Networks*, vol. 4, no. 2, pp. 201-219, 1995.
10. G. Franceschinis, A. Fumagalli and A. Silinguelli. Stochastic Colored Petri Net Models for Rainbow Optical Networks. To appear in *Special issue of Advances of Petri Nets on Communication Network Applications*, J. Billington and G. Rozenberg (editors), *Lecture Notes in Computer Science*, Springer Verlag
11. R. Grasso, "Equità nell'accesso alle reti ottiche a bus a trama fissa," *Electrical Degree Thesis*, Politecnico of Turin, Oct. 1997.
12. B.R. Haverkort and H.P. Idzenga, Structural Decomposition and Serial Solution of the ATM GAUSS Switch, To appear in *Special issue of Advances of Petri Nets on Communication Network Applications*, J. Billington and G. Rozenberg (editors), *Lecture Notes in Computer Science*, Springer Verlag
13. J. P. Jue, B. Mukherjee, "WDM- Based Local Lightwave Networks Part1: Single-Hop System," *IEEE Network*, vol. 6, no. 4, pp. 20-32, July 1992.
14. L. Kant, W,H, Sanders "Loss Process Analysis of the Knockout Switch using Stochastic Activity Networks," *ICCCN '95*, Las Vegas, NV, USA, Sept. 1995.
15. L. Kleinrock, "Queueing systems vol I e II," *Wiley Interscience*, New York, 1976.
16. B. Mukherjee, "Optical Communication Networks" *McGraw-Hill*, New York, July 1997.
17. P.R. Prucnal, P.A. Perrier, "Optically-Processed routing for fast packet switching," *Lightwave Comm. Mag.*, 1, No. 1, 54-67.
18. "Distributed Queue Dual Bus," *IEEE 802.6*.
19. *IEEE Communications Magazine*, vol. 36, no. 2, February 1998.

Scheduling Write Backs for Weakly-Connected Mobile Clients

Kevin W. Froese and Richard B. Bunt

Department of Computer Science,
University of Saskatchewan,
Saskatoon, SK, Canada, S7N 5A9
{froese, bunt}@cs.usask.ca

Abstract. The emerging demand for mobile computing has created a need for improved file system support for mobile clients. Current file systems with support for mobility provide availability through file replicas cached at the client. However, the wide range in the quality of network connections a mobile client may experience makes cache management a complex task.

One important cache management decision is how (and when) modifications that have been made to cached files at a weakly-connected client can and should be propagated back to the file server. This paper presents the results of a trace-driven simulation study of two write-back scheduling policies: a simple statistical policy and a more explicit "reader preference" policy. Emphasis is placed on the interaction between the workload created by loading files demanded by a user and background writes performed to maintain file consistency.

1 Introduction

The ability to work from any location has rapidly become a requirement for many users, and systems and network designers must respond to the challenge of supporting mobile computing. Our interest is in providing file system support to mobile users where only a low-bandwidth[1] (or *weak*) network connection to a file server (and other resources provided by a local-area network) is available. The high latency and/or unreliability of a weak network connection means that the mobile client cannot rely exclusively on the network for file system services. File caching at the client appears to offer the best solution for maintaining file system performance in a weakly-connected mobile environment.

The use of client file caching to support mobility originally arose in the context of disconnected operation, where the mobile client has no network connection at all. While operating in disconnected mode the client relies on cached copies of optimistically replicated files, all cache misses are fatal (there is no way to retrieve a requested file which is not present at the client), and reintegration

---

[1] "Low bandwidth" may arise from a low-technology connection, from network congestion, from distance from the home network, or from a combination of all three.

R. Puigjaner et al. (Eds.): Tools'98, LNCS 1469, pp. 219-230, 1998

with the home file system cannot occur until reconnection takes place (increasing the likelihood of conflicts when both the cached and permanent copies of a file are updated independently). These issues become less problematic when the mobile client has even a weak network connection. Cache misses can be serviced, albeit slowly, and file updates can be sent back to the file server much more quickly, reducing the chance of update conflicts occurring.

File systems with support for weakly-connected operation have been described by Mummert (Coda) [8] and Huston (AFS) [6]. These systems are based on the same caching techniques which are used to support disconnected operation – whole-file caching of optimistically replicated files. Prior to "going mobile" the client's cache gathers files for use while weakly-connected. (This process is called *hoarding* in the Coda file system [10].) While mobile, any updates made to cached files are stored in a *log file*. The weak network connection is used to retrieve any requested files which are not present in the client's cache, and can also be used to send log file entries back to the file server. (This is called *trickle reintegration* in Coda and *background replay* in AFS.) Regardless of the specific file system in use, client caching is the central component of these systems.

As with much of the current work in mobility, the client caching techniques currently used in systems which support weakly-connected operation have been developed with *functionality* as their primary goal. However, the cache is also the key to achieving acceptable file system *performance*. We feel that users will be willing to sacrifice some performance for the advantages of mobility, but that a large degradation will be unacceptable. If acceptable file system performance is to be achieved while mobile, appropriate caching decisions must be made.

One important cache management decision is how (and when) modifications that have been stored in the client's log file can and should be propagated back to the file server. Two conflicting goals complicate this problem. First, it is desirable to write back the contents of the log file as soon as possible in order to reduce the likelihood of update conflicts occurring due to sharing of files under an optimistic replication scheme [6, 8]. As well, performing write backs promptly helps reduce the size of the log file, which is desirable for freeing local client resources (disk space), as well as for reducing reintegration time once the client regains a strong connection [2]. Write backs also help protect file modifications from loss due to failure, damage or theft of the mobile client [8].

Conflicting with the benefits of eagerly performing write backs is the need for reads to have priority for network usage. Any time a file must be transfered from a server (in response to a read miss), it is likely that both the application which requested the file and the user will be stalled until the read has been completed. Therefore it is desirable that reads start (and complete) as soon as possible, and performing write backs could easily interfere with this goal, particularly if "whole-file" caching is being used. An advantage of delaying (and thus a disadvantage of eagerly performing) write backs is the fact that it is common for several modifications to be made to a file over a short period of time, and the number of actual I/O operations which need to be performed can be reduced by delaying the write back. Huston and Honeyman found that 70% of operations stored in a log file could be eliminated by delaying write backs [6].

We use trace-driven simulation to investigate the performance of two write-back scheduling policies: a simple statistical policy and a more explicit "reader preference" policy. Our results indicate that even at low bandwidths, even a simple write-back policy, can reintegrate changes to cached files with the home file system in an acceptable period of time, and can do so with very little interference with read traffic. This performance can be achieved with quite reasonably sized caches at the mobile client.

2   Experimental Setup

The approach taken in this study was to gather detailed traces of real file system activity from users performing "everyday" work, and to use these traces to drive simulations of a mobile client's file cache. We begin with a description of the type of mobile environment envisioned by this work. The techniques used to collect the traces are described next, followed by a discussion of the simulation model. Some notes on the simulation methodology conclude the section.

2.1   The Mobile Environment

We envision a style of location-independent computing that is based on current LAN-based client-server distributed systems. Each mobile user is assumed to originate from such a LAN, which is called his/her "home" location. This is where the home file server resides. Apart from his/her home location (say, the workplace), a user may work from several other locations from time to time, such as his/her place of residence, a hotel room, or another laboratory.

The type of work being performed is assumed to be that found in a typical academic/research environment: such things as text editing, compiling programs from source code, document preparation and viewing, and information browsing (such as using a World Wide Web client). We focus on this type of workload despite the arguments that this is *not* the type of work which users will likely do in a mobile environment [7]. Since it is impossible to predict accurately what future workloads from mobile environments will look like, we feel that stronger results can be obtained by using a workload model based on current data rather than some speculative model of future user behaviour.

Figure 1 shows the system model used in this work. The client file cache manager prepares for going mobile by hoarding (whole) files while the client is strongly connected. Optimistic replication [1] and whole-file caching are assumed. Whenever the client attempts to read from a file, the cache is searched for the file. If the file is present in the cache no network access is needed. If not, then the read request is placed in the read queue where it waits for access to the network. When the network becomes available, the request is sent to the file server over the weak connection, and the file is then transfered to the client. When a client issues a write, the operation is saved in the log file, and is placed in the write

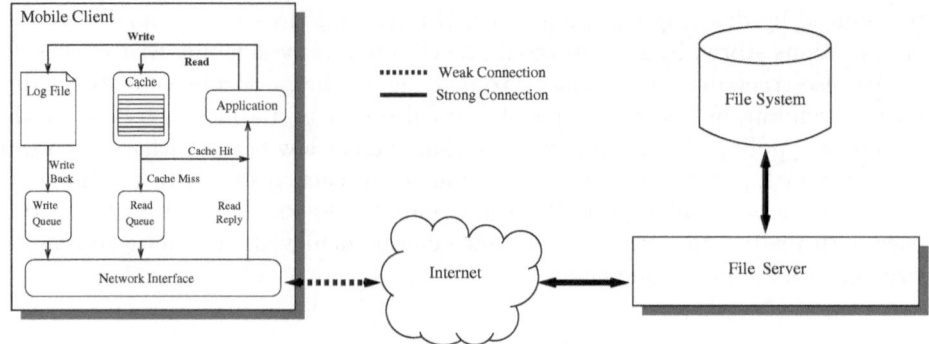

Fig. 1. System Model

queue. The write may later be sent to the file server over the weak connection for file system reintegration.

2.2   Collection of Workload Traces

In order to obtain the traces of file system activity, modifications were made to the HP-UX 9.05 operating system kernel to record all `read()` and `write()` system calls. Information such as the device and inode numbers of files, user ID's, and file sizes was recorded. A complete list of the parameters recorded is given in Table 1.

A series of traces was collected from a set of four HP Series 700 workstations by capturing all file system activity over a seven-day period. This data was broken into seven day-long segments, and were combined into a set of four week-long, continuous traces, each from a single workstation. From these four traces, the activity of single users was isolated and stored in separate trace files. These individual-user traces from each workstation were then combined (maintaining the time stamps on each event), resulting in traces which recorded the file activity of a single user (on all four workstations) over a period of one week. In the interests of space we limit this analysis to two of these week-long single-user traces, the characteristics of which are summarised in Table 2. "Active Time" is the duration of the trace (24 hours times seven days) minus any periods of inactivity greater than 15 minutes in length. "Total Requests" is the sum of the

Table 1. System Calls and Parameters Recorded

System Calls Recorded	Parameters Recorded
`read()` `write()`	time, process ID, user ID, error status, vnode pointer, file type, device, inode, file size, file offset, transfer size, file name

Table 2. Trace Characteristics

Trace	Active Time (Hours)	Total Requests	Unique Files	Unique Bytes (MB)	Read Transfers (MB)	Write Transfers (MB)	Write Requests (% of total)
Trace 1	12.9	21013	383	17	4596	4	37.8
Trace 2	7.0	53860	1000	18	4718	35	67.9

number of read and write requests in the trace. "Unique Files" is the number of files which are either read from or written to in the trace, counting each distinct file only once. "Unique Bytes" is the total size of all unique files seen in the trace. "Read Transfers" and "Write Transfers" are the total amount of data read and written, and "Write Requests" indicates the fraction of requests which are writes. Trace 1 was chosen because it is typical of the traces collected, and has characteristics similar to those of traces used in other studies (such as [1]). Trace 2 was chosen because it has an unusually high level of write activity – roughly two-thirds of all events are writes. This trace is included as a "stress test" of the write-back scheduling policies considered.

2.3 Simulation Model

The simulator reads and processes each read/write event in the input trace file sequentially. The client is considered to be strongly connected (with a 10 Mb/sec network link) at first, and prepares for weak connection by operating in a "hoarding" mode for some specified period of simulation time. The client cache (which is of a fixed size) begins empty, but stores copies of all files referenced while in hoarding mode. If there is insufficient space in the cache to store a file, files are removed (according to the replacement policy currently in use) until there is enough space in the cache for the new file. After some period of time the client becomes weakly connected, at which time hoarding activity is halted. The client remains weakly connected for the remainder of the simulation.

When a read event occurs, the client cache is searched for the requested file. If the file is present in the cache (a hit), no action is required. Otherwise, a read miss has occurred and the file is transfered from a file server to the client over the weak connection, and the file is placed in the cache (potentially replacing other files if the cache is full). Since reads are assumed to be blocking events, no other activity occurs at the client.

When a write event occurs, the log file is updated. For the purposes of simulation the log file stores only the content of write operations and a time stamp. After each write the log file is searched for an entry that overlaps the current write. An entry is said to *overlap* if it is from the same file and any portion of the data in the entry is from the same segment of the file as the new entry. All overlapping log file entries are deleted, and the new entry is added to the log file. No simulation time is consumed processing a write. All writes are assumed to be non-blocking.

A write back can be performed at any time, as determined by the write-back policy in use (LRU). Regardless of policy, the oldest entry in the log file is always written back first.

The simulation runs until all trace events have been processed. It is possible (and common) for there to be entries remaining in the log file when the simulation completes.

A series of initial experiments was performed to determine reasonable values for various simulation parameters, which were then fixed for the remainder of the study. The client is considered to be strongly connected for an initial period of 24 hours (the hoarding phase), during which the cache is "heated" in preparation for subsequent mobile activity (as is done in [5]). While mobile, LRU replacement is used regardless of the type of connection and size of cache.

2.4   Performance Metrics

As noted in [9], there is a need to develop metrics for effectively evaluating caching strategies for mobile environments, since the constraints imposed by the mobile environment make the resource/performance trade-offs pertaining to caching significantly different from those in a LAN environment. The metrics used in this study aim to characterise important relationships between resource consumption and performance when managing a mobile client's file cache.

One important measure of performance is the amount of time required to service all I/O requests in a reference trace. This quantity consists of two components: *read service time*, the amount of time spent transferring files requested by applications that resulted in cache misses, and *write interference time*, the amount of time spent waiting for write backs to complete when the read queue is not empty. For this study, the total (simulation) time required to process all events is reported as a "time expansion" value. This is computed by dividing the total time simulation time by the time required to process the same trace while strongly connected. The resulting ratio provides an indication of the "slowdown" resulting from the weakly connected environment. Write interference time is also of interest since it directly measures the amount by which the decisions of a given write-back policy extend the total time required to service all requests in a trace.

The size of the mobile client's log file is also measured. The maximum size of the log file indicates a minimum level of available disk capacity needed at the client (in addition to that required for the file cache and other local files) to operate in weakly-connected mode for the duration of the trace.

The period of time from when a file is modified until it is written back is of interest since it is during this period that update conflicts can occur or changes can be lost due to some sort of failure. The less time an update spends in the log file, the less chance there is of such problems occurring.

Finally, since the reason for delaying write backs is to reduce the number which need to be performed, the fraction of log file entries which are overwritten by subsequent overlapping write activity is examined. If the frequency of log file overwrites is low, the disadvantages of delaying writes outweigh the advantages.

3   The Experiments

3.1   Policies

Our study focuses on the problem of accommodating both reads and writes over a low bandwidth connection. Since the demand placed on a mobile client's network connection will often exceed the bandwidth available, it is necessary to implement policies which control access to the network. In this study, there are two sources of network traffic – the read queue and the write queue (see Section 2.1). Requests in the read queue are given access to the network immediately upon the network becoming idle. While weakly connected, requests in the write queue (i.e. write backs) are given access according to one of the following write-back scheduling policies[2]:

- No Write Back (No WB) – perform no write backs while weakly connected
- Lotto – hold a lottery (with the write queue receiving W tickets and the read queue receiving R tickets[3]) after each transfer (read or write) has completed, or if the network has been idle for some fixed period I (set to 0.1 seconds for this study[4]); write back the oldest log file entry in its entirety whenever the write queue wins a lottery
- Delayed Write Back with Preemption (DWB-P) – begin writing back the oldest log file entry if it has been in the log file for at least some fixed aging period A (set to 15 minutes for this study) and if the network is idle; if a read request occurs before the write back has completed, halt the write back and resume from the same point when the network becomes idle

Each of these policies attempts to perform writes whenever possible while giving priority to read traffic. No Write Back is included simply to provide a basis for comparison. (At the other extreme is the Write Through policy, in which writes are performed immediately with the application blocking until the write has been completed. We do not examine Write Through, since its appropriateness is doubtful even in a strongly connected environment, and it is even more poorly suited for a mobile client.) Delayed Write Back with Preemption gives priority to reads by performing writes only when the network is otherwise idle. A write back in progress will be halted if a read request is received, and will be resumed from the same point at a later time. Lotto is based on the policy described in [11] (and used in AFS [6]), with modifications to work on a whole-file (rather than packet) basis. Lotto attempts to detect idleness using fixed timer-based prediction [4].

---

[2] Additional polices are considered in [3]

[3] The number of read tickets (R) is set to 11, and the number of write tickets (W) is set to 1. These values were used to maintain the same ratio of tickets for write backs to other traffic used in [6].

[4] Based on preliminary experiments to determine reasonable values.

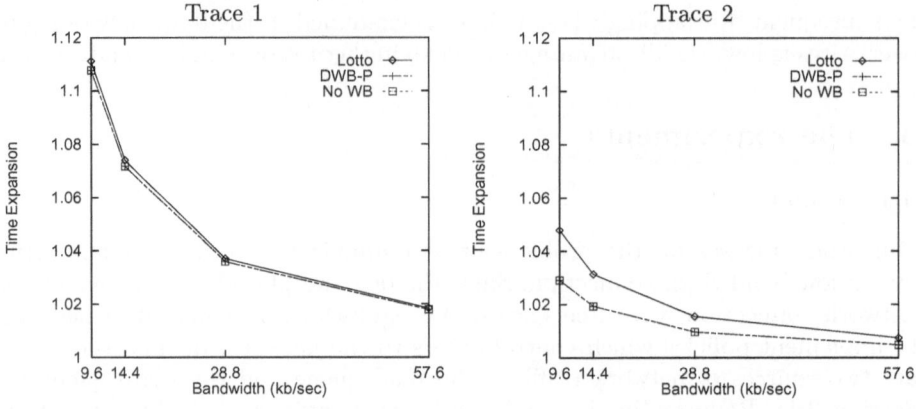

Fig. 2. Time Expansion with a 10 MB Cache

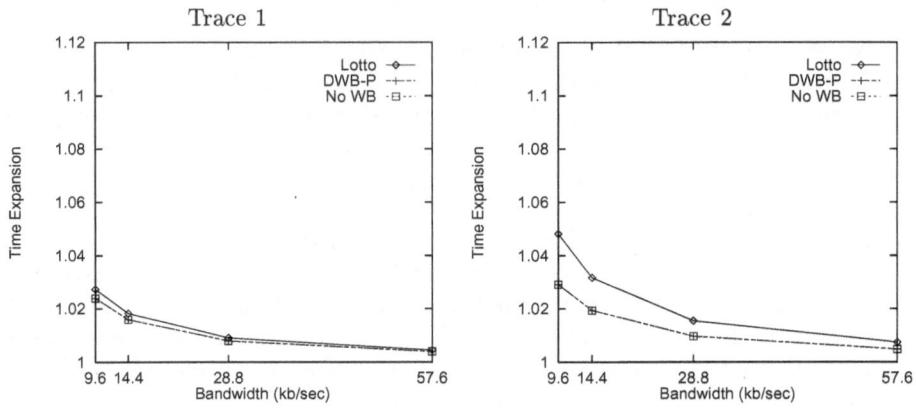

Fig. 3. Time Expansion with a 20 MB Cache

3.2 Results

Figures 2 and 3 show the time expansion experienced for each write-back policy for client cache sizes of 10 MB and 20 MB respectively. Very little difference in performance is seen between the various policies. With Trace 1 there is essentially no difference in performance, and there is only a very small difference with Trace 2. Regardless of write-back policy, with a relatively small client cache of 10 MB, the time expansion values are all small enough (less than 15%) that a user should be able to work effectively even with a very low-bandwidth connection of 9.6 kb/sec[5]. Increasing the cache size to 20 MB reduces the upper bound on time expansion to 5%.

---

[5] This represents a "net" (i.e. effective) bandwidth value, ignoring any bandwidth lost to congestion, routing delays, retransmissions, etc.

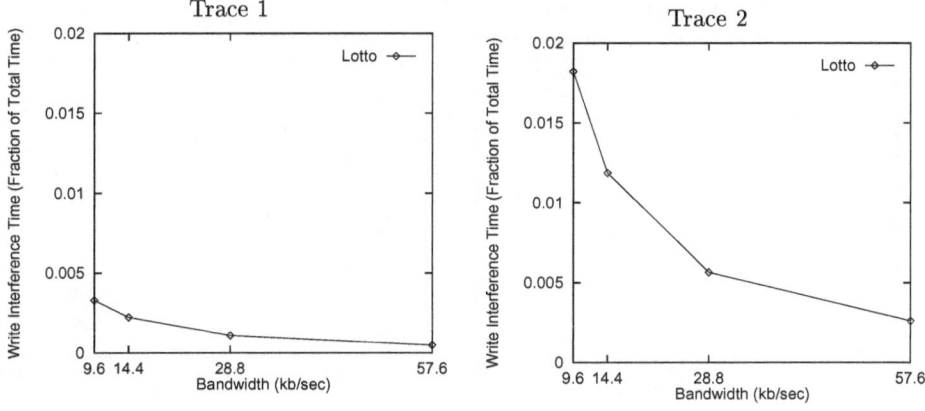

Fig. 4. Write Interference Time with the Lotto Policy (20 MB cache)

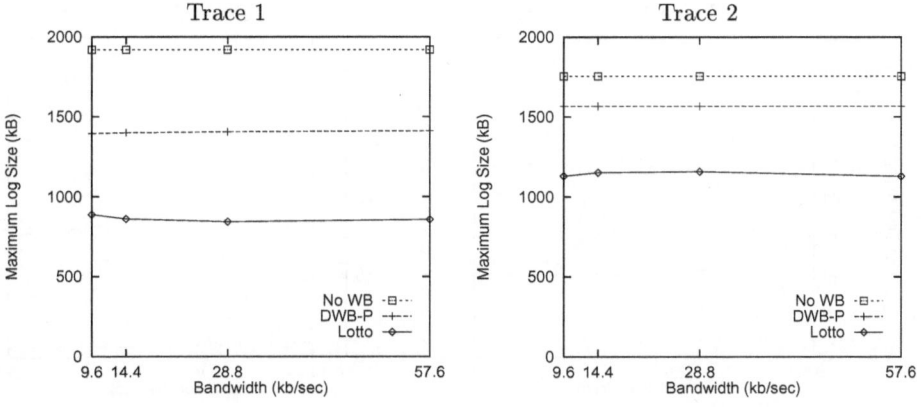

Fig. 5. Maximum Log File Size (20 MB cache)

Results for all remaining experiments are presented only for a client cache size of 20 MB, a size that is not unreasonable by today's standards.

The fraction of total run time attributable to write interference for the Lotto policy can be seen in Figure 4. As expected, interference time is reduced by increasing bandwidth, but even at low bandwidths very little write interference is observed. By design the Delayed Write Back with Preemption policy does not experience write interference.

Figure 5 demonstrates the cost of write-back policies, as reflected by the maximum size of the log file at the client. Bandwidth has almost no effect on the size of the log file for any of the write-back policies. The log file size of the No Write Back policy is provided to show the extent to which each policy reduces the size of the log file. For both traces, the maximum size of the log file is under

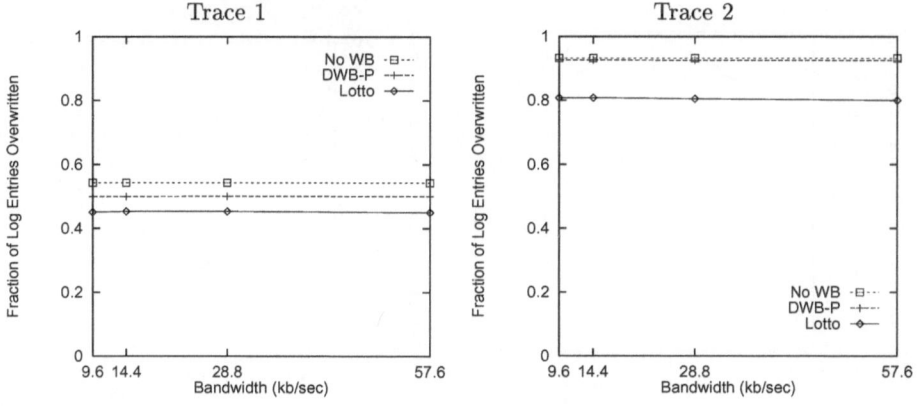

Fig. 6. Fraction of Log Entries Overwritten (20 MB cache)

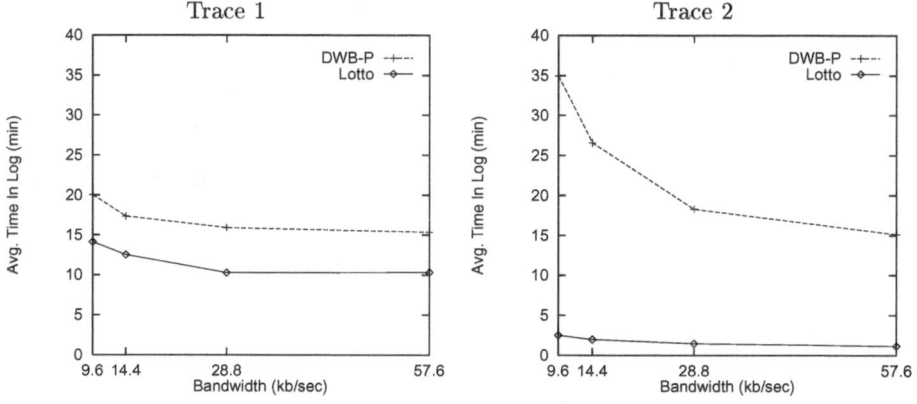

Fig. 7. Average Time Entries Remain in Log File (20 MB cache)

2 MB. This is particularly surprising for Trace 2, since 35 MB of write activity is present in that trace.

The small log file sizes observed for all policies are due in part to the large number of log file entries which are overwritten while in the log file, as seen in Figure 6. Although the values shown for Trace 2 are in line with those reported in [3], they are much larger than was observed for Trace 1, where approximately 45%-55% of log file entries were overwritten. This is likely due to the higher percentage of write requests present in Trace 2 (see Table 2). Again, the difference in performance between the various write-back policies is small.

Finally, Figure 7 shows the average period of time log file entries remain in the log file. The time in log file is reduced as bandwidth increases, since it is possible to perform more write backs. This reduction is relatively small in most cases. As is expected, use of a more "aggressive" write back-policy (such as Lotto) results in log file entries being reintegrated more quickly than with a more "conservative" write-back policy (such as Delayed Write Back), with the amount of difference depending on the number of writes which are performed. For Trace 1, the difference between the two policies is small, but in Trace 2, where many more writes are performed, the difference is significant. In all cases, the average time a log file entry remains in the log file is quite short, ranging from 15 to 35 minutes (depending on network bandwidth), even with a conservative write-back policy. We deem this to be an acceptable period of time since it is likely within the length of a user's working session, which means that the majority of changes made to files will likely be propagated to the server before he/she is finished working.

4   Conclusions

Our simulation results show that it is possible to provide quite good file system support in a weakly-connected environment, servicing read requests in a timely manner while at the same time providing acceptable write service. Even when bandwidth is low, there is enough unused network capacity that even a conservative write-back policy, such as Delayed Write Back, results in writes being reintegrated with the home file system in an acceptable period of time – less than 30 minutes in most cases. This is accomplished with very little interference with read traffic, increasing the total time required to perform all read operations by less than 5% in most cases. This level of performance can be achieved even at a resource-poor client. For the traces examined in this study, a 20 MB file cache was found to be large enough to support this type of activity. While there are definitely performance benefits to be gained from higher-bandwidth connections, even a 9.6 kb/sec network link proved to be enough to provide acceptable levels of performance.

The performance benefits of delaying write backs were found to be quite substantial. By ensuring that log file entries remain in the log file for even 15 minutes, the number of entries in the log file can be dramatically reduced by overlapping writes, in turn significantly reducing the number of write backs which need to be performed.

Interestingly, the Delayed Write Back with Preemption policy did not perform significantly better than Lotto. This is encouraging since it shows that it is not necessary for write-back policies to be complex in order to achieve acceptable levels of performance.

File access is an important requirement of a mobile computing environment. The presence of a weak network connection provides a mobile client with an opportunity to have the same file access functionality as a strongly connected client. Although such functionality comes with an attendant cost (in both resource needs and performance), our study suggests that these costs should be acceptable, even when simple write-back scheduling policies are used.

Acknowledgements

This research was funded, in part, by the Natural Sciences and Engineering Research Council of Canada (NSERC), through a Postgraduate Scholarship and Research Grant OGP0003707. We are also grateful for support from Telecommunications Research Laboratories (TR*Labs*), IBM Canada's Centre for Advanced Studies (CAS), and from Hewlett Packard.

References

1. M. Baker, J. Hartman, M. Kupfer, K. Shirriff, and J. Ousterhout. Measurements of a distributed file system. In *Proc. Thirteenth ACM Symposium on Operating System Principles*, pages 198–212, Pacific Grove, CA, Oct. 1991.
2. M. Ebling, L. Mummert, and D. Steere. Overcoming the network bottleneck in mobile computing. In *Proc. Workshop on Mobile Computing Systems and Applications*, Santa Cruz, CA, Dec. 1994.
3. K. Froese. File cache management for mobile computing. Master's thesis, Dept. of Computer Science, University of Saskatchewan, Saskatoon, SK, 1997.
4. R. Golding, P. Bosch, C. Staelin, T. Sullivan, and J. Wilkes. Idleness is not sloth. In *Proc. USENIX Conf.*, pages 201–212, New Orleans, LA, Jan. 1995.
5. L. Huston and P. Honeyman. Disconnected operation for AFS. In *Proc. First USENIX Symposium on Mobile and Location-Independent Computing*, pages 1–10, Cambridge, MA, April 1993.
6. L. Huston and P. Honeyman. Partially connected operation. In *Proc. Second USENIX Symposium on Mobile and Location-Independent Computing*, pages 91–97, Ann Arbor, MI, April 1995.
7. J. Landay and T. Kaufmann. User interface issues in mobile computing. In *Proc. Fourth Workshop on Workstation Operating Systems*, Napa, CA, Oct. 1993.
8. L. Mummert, M. Ebling, and M. Satyanarayanan. Exploiting weak connectivity for mobile file access. In *Proc. Fifteenth ACM Symposium on Operating Sytems Principles*, pages 143–155, Copper Mountain Resort, CO, Dec. 1995.
9. M. Satyanarayanan. Fundamental challenges of mobile computing. Technical report, School of Computer Science, Carnegie Mellon University, Pittsburgh, PA, 1996.
10. M. Satyanarayanan, J.J. Kistler, L.B. Mummert, M.R. Ebling, P. Kumar, and Q. Lu. Experience with disconnected operation in a mobile computing environment. In *Proc. First USENIX Symposium on Mobile and Location-Independent Computing*, pages 11–28, Cambridge, MA, April 1993.
11. C. Waldspurger and W. Weihl. Lottery scheduling: Flexible proportional-share resource management. In *Proc. First Symposium on Operating System Design and Implementation*, pages 1–11, Monterey, CA, November 1994.

On Choosing a Task Assignment Policy for a Distributed Server System

Mor Harchol-Balter[*,1], Mark E. Crovella[**,2], and Cristina D. Murta[***,2]

[1] Laboratory for Computer Science, MIT
harchol@theory.lcs.mit.edu
[2] Department of Computer Science, Boston University
{crovella,murta}@bu.edu

Abstract. We consider a distributed server system model and ask which policy should be used for assigning tasks to hosts. In our model each host processes tasks in First-Come-First-Serve order and the task's service demand is known in advance. We consider four task assignment policies commonly proposed for such distributed server systems: Round-Robin, Random, Size-Based, in which all tasks within a give size range are assigned to a particular host, and Dynamic-Least-Work-Remaining, in which a task is assigned to the host with the least outstanding work. Our goal is to understand the influence of task size variability on the decision of which task assignment policy is best. We find that no *one* of the above task assignment policies is best and that the answer depends critically on the variability in the task size distribution. In particular we find that when the task sizes are not highly variable, the Dynamic policy is preferable. However when task sizes show the degree of variability more characteristic of empirically measured computer workloads, the Size-Based policy is the best choice. We use the resulting observations to argue in favor of a specific size-based policy, SITA-E, that can outperform the Dynamic policy by almost 2 orders of magnitude and can outperform other task assignment policies by many orders of magnitude, under a realistic task size distribution.

1 Introduction

To build high-capacity server systems, developers are increasingly turning to distributed designs because of their scalability and cost-effectiveness. Examples of this trend include distributed Web servers, distributed database servers, and high performance computing clusters. In such a system, requests for service arrive and must be assigned to one of the host machines for processing. The rule for assigning tasks to host machines is known as the *task assignment policy*.

* Supported by the NSF Postdoctoral Fellowship in the Mathematical Sciences.
** Supported in part by NSF Grants CCR-9501822 and CCR-9706685.
*** Supported by a grant from CAPES, Brazil. Permanent address: Depto. de Informática, Universidade Federal do Paraná, Curitiba, PR 81531, Brazil.

R. Puigjaner et al. (Eds.): Tools'98, LNCS 1469, pp. 231-242, 1998
© Springer-Verlag Berlin Heidelberg 1998

In this paper we concentrate on the particular model of a distributed server system in which each incoming task is immediately assigned to a host machine, and each host machine processes its assigned tasks in first-come-first-served (FCFS) order. We also assume that the task's service demand is known in advance. Our motivation for considering this model is that it is an abstraction of some existing distributed servers, described in Section 3.

We consider four task assignment policies commonly proposed for such distributed server systems: Round-Robin, in which tasks are assigned to hosts in a cyclical fashion; Random, in which each task is assigned to each host with equal probability; Size-Based, in which all tasks within a certain size range are sent to an individual host; and Dynamic (also known as Least-Work-Remaining) in which an incoming task is assigned to the host with the least amount of outstanding work left to do (based on the sum of the sizes of those tasks in the queue).

Our goal is to study the influence of task size variability on the decision of which task assignment policy is best. We are motivated in this respect by the increasing evidence for high variability in task size distributions, witnessed in many measurements of computer workloads. In particular, measurements of many computer workloads have been shown to fit a heavy-tailed distributions with very high variance, as described in Section 2.2.

In comparing task assignment policies, we make use of simulations and also analysis or analytic approximations. We show that the variability of the task size distribution makes a crucial difference in choosing a task assignment policy, and we use the resulting observations to argue for a specific task assignment policy that works well under conditions of high task size variance.

2   Background and Previous Work

2.1   Fundamental Results in Task Assignment

The problem of task assignment in a model like ours has been extensively studied, but many basic questions remain open. In the case where task sizes are unknown, the following results exist: Under an exponential task size distribution, the optimality of Shortest-Line task assignment policy (send the task to the host with the shortest queue) was proven by Winston [14] and extended by Weber [12] to include task size distributions with nondecreasing failure rate. The actual performance of the Shortest-Line policy is not known exactly, but is approximated by Nelson and Phillips [9]. In fact as the variability of the task size distribution grows, the Shortest-Line policy is no longer optimal, Whitt [13].

In the case where the individual task sizes are known, as in our model, equivalent optimality and performance results have not been developed for the task assignment problem, to the best of our knowledge. For the scenario in which the ages of the tasks currently serving are known, Weber [12] has shown that the Shortest-Expected-Delay rule is optimal for task size distributions with increasing failure rate, and Whitt [13] has shown that there exist task size distributions for which the Shortest-Expected-Delay rule is not optimal.

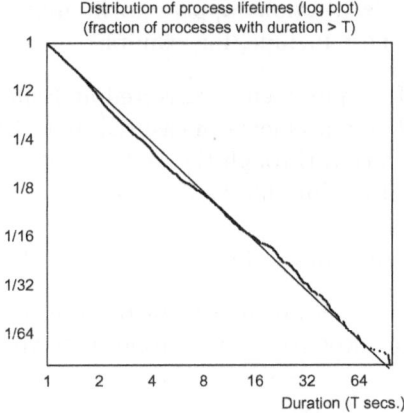

Fig. 1. Measured distribution of UNIX process CPU lifetimes, from [5]. Data indicates fraction of jobs whose CPU sevice demands exceed T seconds, as a function of T.

2.2 Measurements of task size distributions in computer applications

Many application environments show a mixture of task sizes spanning many orders of magnitude. In such environments there are typically many small tasks, and fewer large tasks. Much previous work has used the exponential distribution to capture this variability, as described in Section 2.1. However, recent measurements indicate that for many applications the exponential distribution is a poor model and that a heavy-tailed distribution is more accurate. In general a heavy-tailed distribution is one for which $\Pr\{X > x\} \sim x^{-\alpha}$, where $0 < \alpha < 2$.

Task sizes following a heavy-tailed distribution show the following properties:

1. Decreasing failure rate: In particular, the longer a task has run, the longer it is expected to continue running.
2. Infinite variance (and if $\alpha \leq 1$, infinite mean).
3. The property that a very small fraction ($< 1\%$) of the very largest tasks make up a large fraction (half) of the load. We will refer to this important property throughout the paper as the *heavy-tailed property*.

The lower the parameter α, the more variable the distribution, and the more pronounced is the heavy-tailed property, *i.e.* the smaller the faction of large tasks that comprise half the load.

As a concrete example, Figure 1 depicts graphically on a log-log plot the measured distribution of CPU requirements of over a million UNIX processes, taken from paper [5]. This distribution closely fits the curve

$$\Pr\{\text{Process Lifetime} > T\} = 1/T.$$

In [5] it is shown that this distribution is present in a variety of computing environments, including instructional, reasearch, and administrative environments.

In fact, heavy-tailed distributions appear to fit many recent measurements of computing systems. These include, for example:

- Unix process CPU requirements measured at Bellcore: $1 \leq \alpha \leq 1.25$ [8].
- Unix process CPU requirements, measured at UC Berkeley: $\alpha \approx 1$ [5].
- Sizes of files transferred through the Web: $1.1 \leq \alpha \leq 1.3$ [1,3].
- Sizes of files stored in Unix filesystems: [7].
- I/O times: [11].
- Sizes of FTP transfers in the Internet: $.9 \leq \alpha \leq 1.1$ [10].

In most of these cases where estimates of α were made, $1 \leq \alpha \leq 2$. In fact, typically α tends to be close to 1, which represents very high variability in task service requirements.

3   Model and Problem Formulation

We are concerned with the following model of a distributed server. The server is composed of h hosts, each with equal processing power. Tasks arrive to the system according to a Poisson process with rate λ. When a task arrives to the system, it is inspected by a dispatcher facility which assigns it to one of the hosts for service. We assume the dispatcher facility knows the size of the task. The tasks assigned to each host are served in FCFS order, and tasks are not preemptible. We assume that processing power is the only resource used by tasks.

The above model for a distributed server was initially inspired by the xolas batch distributed computing facility at MIT's Laboratory for Computer Science. Xolas consists of 4 identical multiprocessor hosts. Users specify an upper bound on their job's processing demand. If the job exceeds that demand, it is killed. The xolas facility has a dispatcher front end which assigns each job to one of the hosts for service. The user is given an upper bound on the time their job will have to wait in the queue, based on the sum of the sizes of the jobs in that queue. The jobs queued at each host are each run to completion in FCFS order.

We assume that task sizes show some maximum (but large) value. As a result, we model task sizes using a distribution that follows a power law, but has an upper bound. We refer to this distribution as a *Bounded Pareto*. It is characterized by three parameters: α, the exponent of the power law; k, the smallest possible observation; and p, the largest possible observation. The probability mass function for the Bounded Pareto $B(k, p, \alpha)$ is defined as:

$$f(x) = \frac{\alpha k^{\alpha}}{1 - (k/p)^{\alpha}} \, x^{-\alpha-1} \quad k \leq x \leq p. \tag{1}$$

Throughout this paper we model task sizes using a $B(k, p, \alpha)$ distribution, and vary α over the range 0 to 2 in order to observe the effect of changing variability of the distribution. To focus on the effect of changing variance, we keep the distributional mean fixed (at 3000) and the maximum value fixed (at

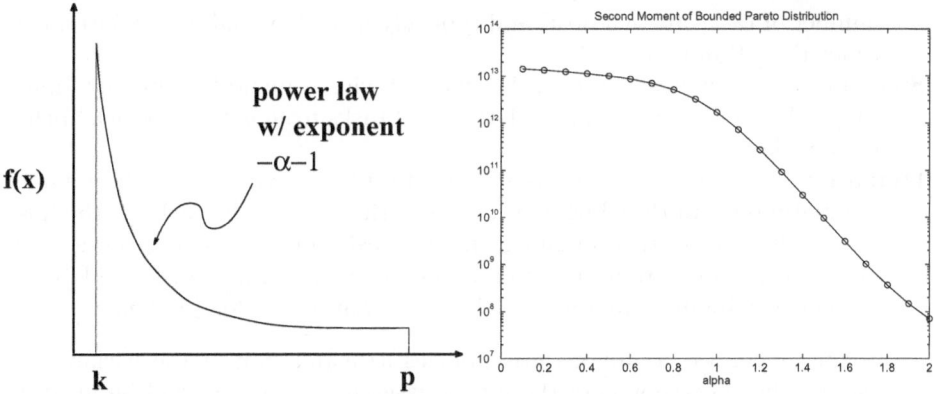

Fig. 2. Parameters of the Bounded Pareto Distribution (left); Second Moment of $B(k, 10^{10}, \alpha)$ as a function of α, when $\mathbf{E}\{X\} = 3000$ (right).

Number of hosts	$h = 8$.
System load	$\rho = .8$.
Mean service time	$\mathbf{E}\{X\} = 3000$ time units
Task arrival process	Poisson with rate $\lambda = \rho \cdot 1/\mathbf{E}\{X\} \cdot h = .0021$ tasks/unit time
Maximum task service time	$p = 10^{10}$ time units
α parameter	$0 < \alpha \leq 2$
Minimum task service time	chosen so that mean task service time stays constant as α varies ($0 < k \leq 1500$)

Table 1. Parameters used in evaluating task assignment policies

$p = 10^{10}$). In order to keep the mean constant, we adjust k slightly as α changes ($0 < k \leq 1500$). The above parameters are summarized in Table 1.

Note that the Bounded Pareto distribution has all its moments finite. Thus, it is not a heavy-tailed distribution in the sense we have defined above. However, this distribution will still show very high variability if $k \ll p$. For example, Figure 2 (right) shows the second moment $\mathbf{E}\{X^2\}$ of this distribution as a function of α for $p = 10^{10}$, where k is chosen to keep $\mathbf{E}\{X\}$ constant at 3000, ($0 < k \leq 1500$). The figure shows that the second moment explodes exponentially as α declines. Furthermore, the Bounded Pareto distribution also still exhibits the heavy-tailed property and (to some extent) the decreasing failure rate property of the unbounded Pareto distribution.

Given the above model of a distributed server system, we ask how to select the best task assignment policy. The following four are common choices:

Random : an incoming task is sent to host i with probability $1/h$. This policy equalizes the expected number of tasks at each host.
Round-Robin : tasks are assigned to hosts in cyclical fashion with the ith task being assigned to host $i \bmod h$. This policy also equalizes the expected

number of tasks at each host, and typically has less variability in interarrival times than Random.

Size-Based : Each host serves tasks whose service demand falls in a designated range. This policy attempts to keep small tasks from getting "stuck" behind large tasks.

Dynamic : Each incoming task is assigned to the host with the smallest amount of outstanding work, which is the sum of the sizes of the tasks in the host's queue plus the work remaining on that task currently being served. This policy is optimal from the standpoint of an individual task, and from a system standpoint attempts to achieve instantaneous load balance.

In this paper we compare these policies as a function of the variability of task sizes. The effectiveness of these task assignment schemes will be measured in terms of mean waiting time and mean slowdown, where a task's slowdown is its waiting time divided by its service demand. All means are per-task averages.

3.1   A New Size-Based Task Assignment Policy: SITA-E

Before delving into simulation and analytic results, we need to specify a few more parameters of the size-based policy.

In size-based task assignment, a size range is associated with each host and a task is sent to the appropriate host based on its size. In practice the size ranges associated with the hosts are often chosen somewhat arbitrarily. There might be a 15-minute queue for tasks of size between 0 and 15 minutes, a 3-hour queue for tasks of size between 15 minutes and 3 hours, a 6-hour queue, a 12-hour queue and an 18-hour queue, for example. (This example is used in practice at the Cornell Theory Center IBM SP2 job scheduler [6].)

In this paper we choose a more formal algorithm for size-based task assignment, which we refer to as SITA-E — Size Interval Task Assignment with Equal Load. The idea is simple: define the size range associated with each host such that the total work (load) directed to each host is the same. The motivation for doing this is that balancing the load minimizes mean waiting time.

The mechanism for achieving balanced expected load at the hosts is to use the *task size distribution* to define the cutoff points (defining the ranges) so that the expected work directed to each host is the same. The task size distribution is easy to obtain by maintaining a histogram (in the dispatcher unit) of all task sizes witnessed over a period of time.

More precisely, let $F(x) = \Pr\{X \leq x\}$ denote the cumulative distribution function of task sizes with finite mean M. Let k denote the smallest task size, p (possibly equal to infinity) denote the largest task size, and h be the number of hosts. Then we determine "cutoff points" x_i, $i = 0 \ldots h$ where $k = x_0 < x_1 < x_2 < \ldots < x_{h-1} < x_h = p$, such that

$$\int_{x_0=k}^{x_1} x \cdot dF(x) = \int_{x_1}^{x_2} x \cdot dF(x) = \cdots = \int_{x_{h-1}}^{x_h=p} x \cdot dF(x) = \frac{M}{h} = \frac{\int_k^p x \cdot dF(x)}{h}$$

and assign to the ith host all tasks ranging in size from x_{i-1} to x_i.

SITA-E as defined can be applied to *any* task size distribution with finite mean. In the remainder of the paper we will always assume the task size distribution is the Bounded Pareto distribution, $B(k, p, \alpha)$.

4   Simulation Results

In this section we compare the Random, Round-Robin, SITA-E, and Dynamic policies via simulation. Simulation parameters are as shown in Table 1.

Simulating a server system with heavy-tailed, highly variable service times is difficult because the system approaches steady state very slowly and usually from below [2]. This occurs because the running average of task sizes is typically at the outset well below the true mean; the true mean isn't achieved until enough large tasks arrive. The consequence for a system like our own is that simulation outputs appear more optimistic than they would in steady-state. To make our simulation measurements less sensitive to the startup transient, we run our simulation for 4×10^5 arrivals and then capture data from the next single arrival to the system only. Each data point shown in our plots is the average of 400 independent runs, each of which started from an empty system.

We consider α values in the range 1.1 (high variability) to 1.9 (lower variability). As described in Section 2.2, α values in the range 1.0 to 1.3 tend to be common in empirical measurements of computing systems.

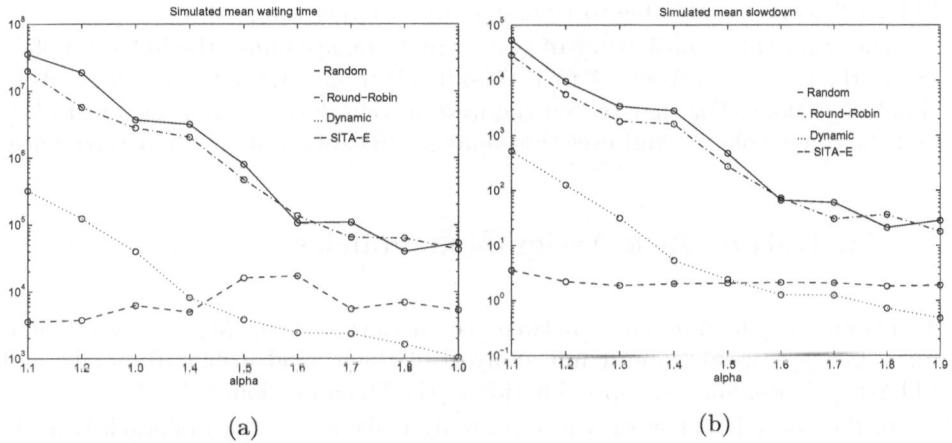

(a)   (b)

Fig. 3. Mean Waiting Time (a) and Mean Slowdown (b) under Simulation of Four Task Assignment Policies as a Function of α.

Figure 3 shows the performance of the system for all four policies, as a function of α (note the logarithmic scale on the y axis). Figure 3(a) shows mean waiting time and 3(b) shows mean slowdown. Below we simply summarize these results; in the next section, we will use analysis to explain these results.

First of all, observe that the performance of the system under the Random and Round Robin policies is similar, and that both cases perform much more poorly than the other two (SITA-E and Dynamic). As α declines, both of the performance metrics under the Random and Round-Robin policies explode approximately exponentially. This gives an indication of the severe impacts that heavy-tailed workloads can have in systems with naive task assignment policies.

The Dynamic policy shows the benefits of instantaneous load balancing. Dynamic is on the order of 100 times better for both metrics when compared to Random and Round Robin. For large α, this means that Dynamic performs quite well—with mean slowdown less than 1. However as the variability in task size increases (as $\alpha \to 1$), Dynamic is unable to maintain good performance. It too suffers from roughly exponential explosion in performance metrics as α declines.

In contrast, the behavior of SITA-E is quite different from that of the other three. Over the entire range of α values studied, the performance of the system under SITA-E is relatively unchanged, with mean slowdown always between 2 and 3. This is the most striking aspect of our data: in a range of α in which performance metrics for Random, Round Robin, and Dynamic all explode, SITA-E's performance remains remarkably insensitive to increase in task size variability.

As a result we find that when task size is less variable, Dynamic task assignment exhibits better performance; but when task sizes show the variability that is more characteristic of empirical measurements ($\alpha \approx 1.1$), SITA-E's performance can be on the order of 100 times better than that of Dynamic.

In [4] we simulate a range of loads (ρ) and show that as load increases, SITA-E becomes preferable to Dynamic over a larger range of α.

The remarkable consistency of system performance under the SITA-E policy across the range of α from 1.1 to 1.9 is difficult to understand using the tools of simulation alone. For that reason the next section develops analysis of SITA-E and the other policies, and uses that analysis to explain SITA-E's performance.

5   Analysis of Task Assignment Policies

To understand the differences between the performance of the four task assignment policies, we provide a full analysis of the Round-Robin, Random, and SITA-E policies, and an approximation of the Dynamic policy.

In the analysis below we will repeatedly make use of the Pollaczek-Kinchin formula below which analyzes the M/G/1 FCFS queue:

$$\mathbf{E}\{\text{Waiting Time}\} = \lambda \mathbf{E}\{X^2\}/2(1-\rho) \qquad \text{[Pollaczek-Kinchin formula]}$$
$$\mathbf{E}\{\text{Slowdown}\} = \mathbf{E}\{W/X\} = \mathbf{E}\{W\} \cdot \mathbf{E}\{X^{-1}\}$$

where λ denotes the rate of the arrival process, X denotes the service time distribution, and ρ denotes the utilization ($\rho = \lambda \mathbf{E}\{X\}$). The slowdown formulas follow from the fact that W and X are independent for a FCFS queue.

Observe that every metric for the simple FCFS queue is dependent on $\mathbf{E}\left\{X^2\right\}$, the second moment of the service time. Recall that if the workload is heavy-tailed, the second moment of the service time explodes, as shown in Figure 2.

Random Task Assignment. The Random policy simply performs Bernoulli splitting on the input stream, with the result that each host becomes an independent $M/B(k,p,\alpha)/1$ queue. The load at the ith host, is equal to the system load, that is, $\rho_i = \rho$. So the Pollaczek-Kinchin formula applies directly, and all performance metrics are proportional to the second moment of $B(k,p,\alpha)$. Performance is generally poor because the second moment of the $B(k,p,\alpha)$ is high.

Round Robin. The Round Robin policy splits the incoming stream so each host sees an $E_h/B(k,p,\alpha)/1$ queue, with utilization $\rho_i = \rho$. This system has performance close to the Random case since it still sees high variability in service times, which dominates performance.

SITA-E. The SITA-E policy also performs Bernoulli splitting on the arrival stream (which follows from our assumption that task sizes are independent). By the definition of SITA-E, $\rho_i = \rho$. However the task sizes at each queue are determined by the particular values of the interval cutoffs, $\{x_i\}, i = 0, ..., h$. In fact, host i sees a $M/B(x_{i-1}, x_i, \alpha)/1$ queue. The reason for this is that partitioning the Bounded Pareto distribution into contiguous regions and renormalizing each of the resulting regions to unit probability yields a new set of Bounded Pareto distributions. In [4] we show how to calculate the set of x_is for the $B(k,p,\alpha)$ distribution, and we present the resulting formulas that provide full analysis of the system under the SITA-E policy for all the performance metrics.

Dynamic. The Dynamic policy is not analytically tractable, which is why we performed the simulation study. However, in [4] we prove that a distributed system of the type in this paper with h hosts which performs Dynamic task assignment is actually equivalent to an M/G/h queue. Fortunately, there exist known approximations for the performance metrics of the M/G/h queue [15]:

$$\mathbf{E}\left\{Q_{M/G/h}\right\} = \mathbf{E}\left\{Q_{M/M/h}\right\} \cdot \mathbf{E}\left\{X^2\right\}/\mathbf{E}\left\{X\right\}^2,$$

where X denotes the service time distribution and Q denotes the number in queue. What's important to observe here is that the mean queue length, and therefore the mean waiting time and mean slowdown, are all proportional to the second moment of the service time distribution, as was the case for the Random and Round-Robin task assignment policies.

Using the above analysis we can compute the performance of the above task assignment policies over a range of α values. Figure 4 shows the analytically-derived mean waiting time and mean slowdown of the system under each pol icy over the whole range of α. Figure 5 again shows these analytically-derived metrics, but only over the range of $1 \le \alpha \le 2$, which is the range of α corresponding to most empirical measurements of process lifetimes and file sizes (see Section 2.2). (Note that, because of slow simulation convergence as described at the beginning of Section 4, simulation values are generally lower than analytic predictions; however all simulation trends agree with analysis).

First observe that the performance of the Random and Dynamic policies in both these figures grows worse as α decreases, where the performance curves follow the same shape as the second moment of the Bounded Pareto distribution, shown in Figure 2. This is expected since the performance of Random and Dynamic is directly proportional to the second moment of the service time distribution. By contast, looking at Figure 5 we see that in the range $1 < \alpha < 2$, the mean waiting time and especially mean slowdown under the SITA-E policy is remarkably constant, with mean slowdowns around 3, whereas Random and Dynamic explode in this range. The insensitivity of SITA-E's performance to α in this range is the most striking property of our simulations and analysis.

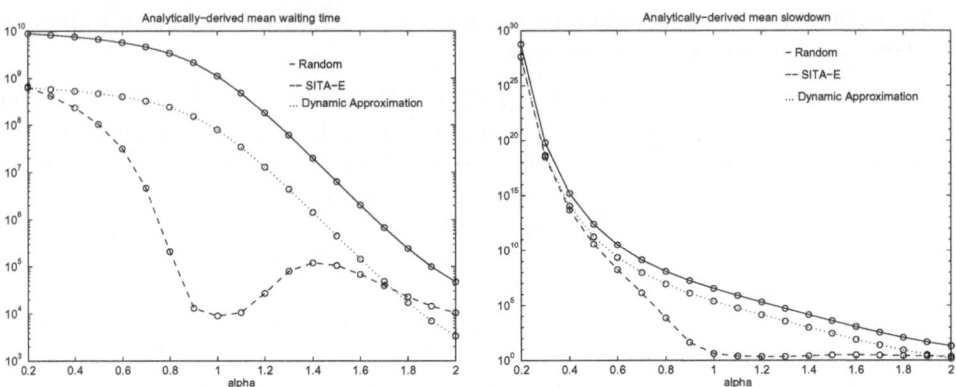

Fig. 4. Analysis of mean waiting time and mean slowdown over whole range of α, $0 < \alpha \le 2$.

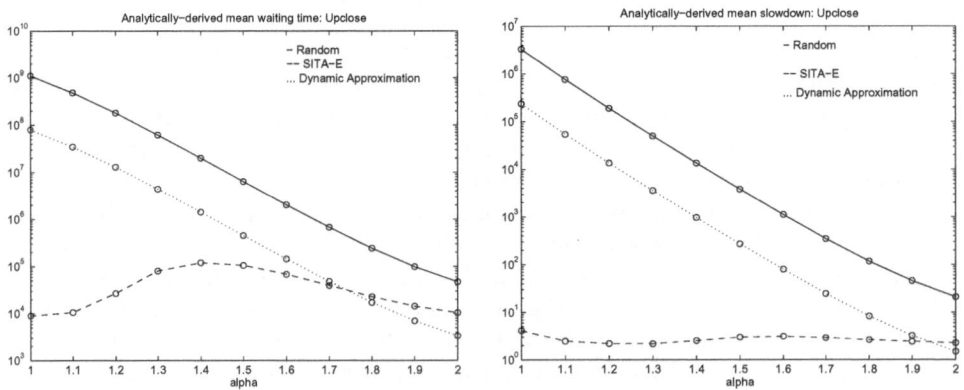

Fig. 5. Analysis of mean waiting time and mean slowdown over empirically relevant range of α, $1 \le \alpha \le 2$.

Why does SITA-E perform so well in a region of task size variability wherein a Dynamic policy explodes? A careful analysis of the performance of SITA-E at each queue of the system (see [4]) leads us to the following answers:

1. By limiting the range of task sizes at each host, SITA-E greatly reduces the variance of the task size distribution witnessed by the lowered-numbered hosts, thereby improving performance at these hosts. In fact the performance at most hosts is superior to that of an M/M/1 queue with utilization ρ.
2. When load is balanced, the majority of tasks are assigned to the low-numbered hosts, which are the hosts with the best performance. This is intensified by the heavy-tailed property which implies that *very* few tasks are assigned to high numbered hosts.
3. Furthermore, mean slowdown is improved because small tasks observe proportionately lower waiting times.

For the case of $\alpha \leq 1$, shown in Figure 4, even under the SITA-E policy, system performance eventually deteriorates badly. The reason is that as overall variability in task sizes increases, eventually even host 1 will witness high variability. Further analysis [4] indicates that adding hosts can extend the range over which SITA-E shows good performance. For example, when the number of hosts is 32, SITA-E's performance does not deteriorate until $\alpha \leq .8$.

6   Conclusion

In this paper we have studied how the variability of the task size distribution influences which task assignment policy is best in a distributed system. We consider four policies: Random, Round-Robin, SITA-E (a size-based policy), and Dynamic (sending the task to the host with the least remaining work).

We find that the best choice of task assignment policy depends critically on the variability of task size distribution. When the task sizes are not highly variable, the Dynamic policy is preferable. However, when task sizes show the degree of variability more characteristic of empirical measurements ($\alpha \approx 1$), SITA-E is best.

The magnitude of the difference in performance of these policies can be quite large: Random and Round-Robin are inferior to both SITA-E and Dynamic by several orders of magnitude. And in the range of task size variability characteristic of empirical measurements, SITA-E outperforms Dynamic by close to 2 orders of magnitude.

More important than the above results, though, is the insights about these four policies gleaned from our analysis:

Our analysis of the Random, Round-Robin and Dynamic policies shows that their performance is directly proportional to the second moment of the task size distribution, which explains why their performance deteriorates as the task size variability increases. Thus, even the Dynamic policy, which comes closes to achieving instantaneous load balance and directs each task to the host where it waits the least, is not capable of compensating for the effect of increasing variance in the task size distribution.

To understand why size-based policies are so powerful, we introduce the SITA-E policy which is a simple formalization of size-based policies, defined to equalize the expected load at each host. This formalization allows us to obtain a full analysis of the SITA-E policy, leading to a 3-fold characterization of its power: (i) By limiting the range of task sizes at each host, SITA-E greatly reduces the variability of the task size distribution witnessed by each host – thereby improving the performance at the host. (ii) When load is balanced, most tasks are sent to the subset the hosts having the best performance. (iii) Mean slowdown is improved because small tasks observe proportionately lower waiting times. These 3 properties allow SITA-E to perform very well in a region of task size variability in which the Dynamic policy breaks down.

References

1. M. E. Crovella and A. Bestavros. Self-similarity in World Wide Web traffic: Evidence and possible causes. *IEEE/ACM Transactions on Networking*, 5(6):835–846, December 1997.
2. M. E. Crovella and L. Lipsky. Long-lasting transient conditions in simulations with heavy-tailed workloads. In *1997 Winter Simulation Conference*, 1997.
3. M. E. Crovella, M. S. Taqqu, and A. Bestavros. Heavy-tailed probability distributions in the world wide web. In *A Practical Guide To Heavy Tails*, pages 1–23. Chapman & Hall, New York, 1998.
4. M. Harchol-Balter, M. E. Crovella, and C. D. Murta. On choosing a task assignment policy for a distributed server system. Technical Report MIT-LCS-TR-757, MIT Laboratory for Computer Science, 1998.
5. M. Harchol-Balter and A. Downey. Exploiting process lifetime distributions for dynamic load balancing. *ACM Transactions on Computer Systems*, 15(3), 1997.
6. S. Hotovy, D. Schneider, and T. O'Donnell. Analysis of the early workload on the Cornell Theory Center IBM SP2. Technical Report 96TR234, CTC, Jan. 1996.
7. G. Irlam. Unix file size survey. http://www.base.com/gordoni/ufs93.html, 1994.
8. W. E. Leland and T. J. Ott. Load-balancing heuristics and process behavior. In *Proceedings of Performance and ACM Sigmetrics*, pages 54–69, 1986.
9. R. D. Nelson and T. K. Philips. An approximation for the mean response time for shortest queue routing with general interarrival and service times. *Performance Evaluation*, 17:123–139, 1998.
10. V. Paxson and S. Floyd. Wide-area traffic: The failure of Poisson modeling. *IEEE/ACM Transactions on Networking*, pages 226–244, June 1995.
11. D. L. Peterson and D. B. Adams. Fractal patterns in DASD I/O traffic. In *CMG Proceedings*, December 1996.
12. R. W. Weber. On the optimal assignment of customers to parallel servers. *Journal of Applied Probability*, 15:406–413, 1978.
13. Ward Whitt. Deciding which queue to join: Some counterexamples. *Operations Research*, 34(1):226–244, January 1986.
14. W. Winston. Optimality of the shortest line discipline. *Journal of Applied Probability*, 14:181–189, 1977.
15. R. W. Wolff. *Stochastic Modeling and the Theory of Queues*. Prentice Hall, 1989.

Structured Characterization of the Markov Chain of Phase-Type SPN

Susanna Donatelli[1][*], Serge Haddad[2], and Patrice Moreaux[2,3]

[1] Università di Torino, Dipartimento di Informatica susi@di.unito.it
[2] LAMSADE {haddad, moreaux}@lamsade.dauphine.fr
[3] Université de Reims Champagne-Ardenne

Abstract. This paper presents a characterization of the Markovian state space of a Stochastic Petri Nets with phase-type distribution transitions as a union of Cartesian products of a set of "components" of the net. The method uses an abstract view of the net based on the vectors of enabling degrees of phase-type transitions, as well as on the sets of "interrupted clients". Following the decomposition used for the state space characterization, a tensor algebra expression for the infinitesimal generator (actually for its rate matrix) is given, that allows the steady state probability to be computed directly from a set of matrices of the size of the components, without the need of storing the whole infinitesimal generator.

1 Introduction

Since the introduction of Stochastic Petri Nets (SPN) [17]), the need for more general distributions of firing time have been recognized as necessary to adequately model many real life phenomena. Two general directions have been taken in this area: the first one [1,10,2] introduces general distributions of firing time with specific conditions which allows one to extract "subordinated" Markov chains and compute steady state and transient probabilities of the states. The second approach [17,11,9] introduces phase-type (PH) distribution firing time without further restrictions, and computes the resulting embedded Continuous Time Markov Chain (CTMC). Two problems then arise: to precisely define the stochastic semantics of phase-type (PH-)transitions and to cope with the state space problem since we are faced with a "bi-dimensional" complexity: exponential with respect to the size of the net, and that can be exponential under specific hypotheses with respect to the number of stages of the PH distributions.

Previous works on SPN with PH-transitions (PH-SPN for short) have taken into account the stochastic semantics problem either at the net level [9], or at the underlying CTMC level directly [11].

For what concerns the net level approach, the works reported in [17,9] alter the initial SPN with PH-transitions: each phase type (including special cases like

---

[*] This work has been developed within the project HCM CT94-0452 (MATCH) of the European Union. At time of writing S. Donatelli was visiting professor at Lamsade, at the University of Paris-Dauphine.

R. Puigjaner et al. (Eds.): Tools'98, LNCS 1469, pp. 243–254, 1998.

Erlang, Coxian) transition is replaced in the net with a sub-net which translates its stochastic semantics. This expansion may be automated and integrated in a tool. However only the single server policy is studied and, moreover, each PH-transition must have only one input and one output place in [9].

The second approach [11] expands the embedded Markov chain, and the net is not modified. The PH distributions are taken into account during the reachability graph (RG) computation. This method allows the management of any combination of the three elements of the execution policy (that we shall define later), and may be also integrated in a tool.

It is now well-known [19,4,12,14] that tensor expressions applied to queuing networks and SPN solution can provide substantial memory savings which enable management of Markov chains with large state space. In fact, it was recognized (for example in [16]) that the main memory bottleneck with tensor methods is the size of the steady state probabilities vector, and not of the infinitesimal generator.

In a first attempt to reduce the complexity of the *resolution* of the Markov chain derived from an SPN with PH-distributions, the work in [15] presents a method based on structural decomposition of the net, leading to a tensor expression of the generator of the chain. Such a decomposition builds a superset of the state space of the chain as a *Cartesian product* of smaller state spaces and classify state transitions as local, that is to say changing only one component of the state, or global, changing simultaneously several components of the state.

A serious drawback of the work in [15] is in the number of elements of the Cartesian product that are not legal states of the system. This may lower the efficacy of the method since a lot of space and time can be lost in those states that are part of the Cartesian product. This problem is common also to other approaches using tensor algebra.

In this paper we show instead how tensor algebra can be used to *exactly* characterize the state space of a PH-SPN, in a way that does not depend on the structure of the net, by following the approach based on high level state information, introduced in the context of marked graphs [6], and used for hierarchical GSPN [3], and, recently, to the asynchronous composition of components[8,7].

Using this characterization, we derive a tensor expression of the rate matrix of the Markov chain of the net which allows the computation of the steady state probabilities coping with the growth of the Markovian state space induced by the PH-transitions.

The method is presented in the context of exponentially distributed, transition timed, Petri nets, without immediate transitions and inhibitor arcs and assumes that the net is small enough for the tangible reachability set TRS, and for the tangible reachability graph TRG, to be built and stored in memory.

The paper is organized as follows: Section 2 introduces the definition of PH distributions, the semantics of PH-transitions, the definition of PH-SPN, and discusses the definition of Markovian state of an SPN which is at the root of the construction of the Markovian state space presented in Section 3 for single server transitions. Section 4 introduces the tensor expressions for the corresponding rate matrix. Section 5 outlines the results in the more complicated case of PH-transitions with multiple servers semantics. The method presented is summarized and evaluated in Section 6 that concludes the paper. The reader will find in [13] an extended version of the paper with detailed examples and proofs.

2   Phase-Type SPN

PH distributions have been defined [18] as the time until absorption of a CTMC with $s + 1$ states and a single absorbing state. A PH distribution can also be seen as a network of exponential servers, the initial distribution of the chain being $(c_{O,j})_{1 \leq j \leq s}$ and the absorbing state being the state 0. Leaving a stage i, a client may enter stage j with probability $C_{i,j}$ or enter the absorbing state with probability $C_{i,0}$ ($\sum_{j=0}^{j=s} C_{i,j} = 1$).

We firstly study stochastic semantics of PH-transitions and we give the definition of PH-SPN; then we discuss how to define a state of the system that is consistent with the given specifications.

2.1   Stochastic Semantics of PH-Transitions

In order to provide a full definition of PH-SPN, a number of additional specifications should be added to each non-exponential transitions.

• *Memory Policy:* the memory policy specifies what happens to the time associated to transition when a change of state occurs.

With the *Enabling Memory* policy, the elapsed time is lost only if t is not enabled in the new marking. Transitions with enabling memory therefore do not loose the past work, as long as they are enabled. Time-out transition usually have this memory policy.

With *Age Memory* policy the elapsed time is always kept (of course unless it is transition t itself that causes the change of state) whatever the evolution of the system: the next time the transition will be enabled, the remaining firing time will be the *residual time* from the last disabling and not a new sampling. Time-sharing service may be modelled by age memory policies.

In this paper we do not consider *resampling policy* which realizes a conflict at the temporal specification level, that may not have a counterpart at the structure level.

The memory policy of transition t is denoted by $mp(t)$, and the possible values are E, for enabling, or A, for age.

The enabling memory policy of PH-transitions needs a precise definition, giving how its internal state is modified when another transition fires. Since a firing is considered as an "atomic" action, in this paper we use the following interpretation of enabling memory: the memory of a transition t_h, enabling memory, is reset when either in the new state the transition is disabled, or in the new state the transition has kept its enabling, but it is the transition t_h itself that has caused the change of state.

• *Service Semantics:* the service semantics specifies how many clients can be served in parallel by a transition. The use of the term "client" is imported from queuing networks, and we use it in the paper as a synonymous of active server.

The service semantics is defined around the concept of *enabling firing degree* edf(t, **m**) of t in **m** which gives the number of time the transition t may be fired consecutively from **m**:

$$\text{edf(t, \textbf{m})} = k \quad \text{iff} \quad \begin{cases} \forall p \in {}^\bullet t, \ \mathbf{m}(p) \geq k \cdot \mathbf{Pre}(p, t) \\ \exists p \in {}^\bullet t, \ \mathbf{m}(p) < (k+1) \cdot \mathbf{Pre}(p, t) \end{cases}$$

The service policy of transition t is denoted by $sp(t)$. We have the three classical policies: single server (S), multiple (K) and infinite (I) server.

We shall denote by ed(t, **m**) the enabling degree of transitions, *according with the service policy*, that is to say: ed(t, **m**) = min$(K, \text{edf(t, \textbf{m})})$, where $K = 1$ for single server, $K = K$ for K-multiple server, and $K = +\infty$ for infinite server.

As usual, the firing rate of an exponential transition t in **m** is ed(t, **m**)) · w(t, **m**). For single server PH-transition, the firing rate is $\mu_s \cdot C(t)[s, 0]$ if a client in stage s ends its service and no new client enters in service, and $\mu_s \cdot C(t)[s, 0] \cdot C(t)[0, s']$ if another client enters immediately in service in stage s'. The multiple and infinite server cases introduce several complex problems so that we have chosen to present the method first for the single server case, then to generalize the results to the multiple and infinite server cases in Section 5.

• *Clients and Interrupt/Resume Policies:* two other parameters have to be defined for multiple and infinite server policies: the Clients policy (cp) and the interrupt/resume policy (ip). For the single server case, we suppose the interrupt/resume semantics which resumes the interrupted client (if any), when a transition firing increases the enabling degree (from 0 to 1). The study of cp and ip for multiple and infinite server PH-transitions is outlined in Section 5.

The specification of the stochastic semantics of a PH-transition is then $\theta = (s, \mu, C, mp, sp, cp, ip)$, with $s(t)$ the number of stages of t and $\forall 1 \leq i \leq s(t)$:

– $\mu_i(t)$ the rate of the ith stage of t;
– $C(t)[i, j]$ the probabilities of routing a client from the ith stage to the jth stage $(0 \leq j \leq s(t))$ stage after the end of service of the ith stage. $C[i, 0] = 1 - \sum_{j=1}^{j=s(t)} C(t)[i, j]$ is the probability to leave the service of the transition. $C[0, j]$, the probabilities for an incoming client to enter the system in stage j, with $\sum_{j=1}^{j=s(t)} C(t)[0, j] = 1$ (it is not possible to leave the transition in zero time);
– $mp(t)$ the memory policy of t $(E$ or $A)$, $sp(t)$ the service policy of t $(S, K$ or $I)$, $cp(t)$ the clients policy of t, if needed $(O$ or $U)$, and $ip(t)$ the interrupt policy of t, if needed.

Let us now introduce the definition of PH-SPN.

Definition 1. *A PH-SPN is a tuple* $\mathcal{N} = (P, TX, TH, \mathbf{Pre}, \mathbf{Post}, \mathbf{w}, \theta)$:
– *P is the set of places;*
– *TX is the set of exponential transitions;*

- TH is the set of phase-type (PH-)transitions; $\mathrm{TX} \cap \mathrm{TH} = \emptyset$ and $\mathrm{TX} \cup \mathrm{TH} = T$ is generically called the set of transitions.
- **Pre** and **Post** : $P \times T \to \mathbb{N}$ are the incidence functions: **Pre** is the input function, and **Post** the output function
- $\mathbf{w} : T \times \mathrm{Bag}(P) \to \mathbb{R}^+$: $\mathbf{w}(t, \mathbf{m})$ is the firing rate of the exponential distribution associated to transition t in marking[1] $\mathbf{m}$, if t is exponential, and it is instead equal to 1 for PH-transitions.
- θ is a function that associates to each transition $t_h \in \mathrm{TH}$ its specification θ_h.

The choice of an initial marking $\mathbf{m_0}$, defines a marked PH-SPN also called a PH-SPN system $\mathcal{S} = (\mathcal{N}, \mathbf{m_0})$. We denote with TRS and TRG the reachability set and graph.

The definition of a Markovian state of a PH-SPN is therefore an $(H+1)$-tuple,

$$(\mathbf{m}, \mathrm{d}(t_1, \mathbf{m}), \ldots, \mathrm{d}(t_H, \mathbf{m}))$$

where $\mathbf{m}$ is the marking, and $\mathrm{d}(t_h, \mathbf{m})$ is the "descriptor" of phase-type transition t_h in marking $\mathbf{m}$. In the next section we shall define the descriptors in such a way for the state to be Markovian, and we shall see that, for the age memory case, the descriptors depend on information that can be computed only from the reachability graph, so that it may be more precise to write $(\mathbf{m}, \mathrm{d}(t_1, \mathbf{m}, \mathrm{TRG}),$ $\ldots, \mathrm{d}(t_H, \mathbf{m}, \mathrm{TRG}))$. We call MS the set of Markovian states of a PH-SPN.

2.2   Descriptors for Single Server Ph-Transitions

When there are PH-transitions the marking process of the net is not Markovian any longer, but it is still possible to build a Markovian state by considering more detailed information [18,11]. We shall consider the enabling memory and the age memory case separately.

• *Descriptors for Enabling Memory:* for an enabling memory transition the only relevant information is the stage of the current client. Let $d(t, \mathbf{m})$ (d for short, if t and $\mathbf{m}$ are implicit from the context) denote the descriptor of a PH- transition t. We have

$$d = i \in \{0, 1, \ldots, s(t)\}$$

where i is the index of the stage in which the client is receiving service. $i = 0$ means no client is currently in service.

• *Descriptors for Age Memory:* for the case of age memory we need the additional information on the interrupted client giving in which stage it has been interrupted. This information can be stored explicitly or implicitly. We can add to the descriptor a number indicating the stage at which the client has been interrupted (explicit info), or we can encode this information into the descriptor already defined (implicit info): since a single server transition has either a client interrupted, or a client in service, but never the two together, then $d(t, \mathbf{m}) = i$

---

[1] $\mathrm{Bag}(P)$ is the set of multi-sets on P.

means: client in service in stage i if $\mathrm{ed}(\mathrm{t}, \mathbf{m}) > 0$ and client interrupted in stage i if $\mathrm{ed}(\mathrm{t}, \mathbf{m}) = 0$.

In this paper we choose the implicit encoding. Note however, that we need to explicitly encode the descriptor for no client at all (either in service or interrupted) with the value $d(t, \mathbf{m}) = 0$.

3   Characterization of the Markovian State Space of a PH-SPN in the Single Server Case

In this section we show the first main result of the paper which gives an exact structured description of the MS of a PH-SPN. The method, presented and used in [6] for marked graphs, in [8] for DSSP systems, and, more recently, in [7] exploits two ideas: the first one is a description of the MS as Cartesian product of K subspaces following the classical tensor based approach [3,12,15]. The second one is the introduction of a high level (abstract) description of the MS, used in the asynchronous context in [4,6,7,8], "compatible" with the previous subspaces product. This leads to an expression of MS as a disjoint union of Cartesian products with the same high level description. In a formal way, if $\mathcal{A}$ is the set of abstract views $av(s)$ of the Markovian states s, we have:

$$MS = \biguplus_{a \in \mathcal{A}} S_1(a) \times \ldots \times S_K(a)$$

where $S_k(a)$ denotes the subset of states of the kth component such that

$$(\forall\, 1 \leq k \leq K, s_k \in S_k(a)) \Leftrightarrow \begin{cases} s = (s_1, \ldots, s_K) \in MS \\ av(s) = a \end{cases}$$

The existence of an high level description of the system allows to appropriately pre-select the subsets of the states that should enter in the Cartesian product: only states of the different components that share the same high level view of the system are multiplied in the Cartesian product. Without such a high level description, Cartesian products provide only Potential Markovian state Spaces (PMS) with $MS \subset PMS$ and, in the general case, $|PMS| \gg |MS|$.

Since a Markovian state of a PH-SPN is a $H+1$ tuple $(\mathbf{m}, \mathrm{d}(t_1, \mathbf{m}), \ldots \mathrm{d}(t_H, \mathbf{m}))$, we consider MS as a set of $H+1$ components, one component defines the marking of the net and the other H the state of the H phase-type-transitions.

For what concerns the high level view, although we might use the marking $\mathbf{m}$ of a state (any other "high level" information computable from the TRS in linear time and space, may also be a choice), it is not the most efficient choice. Indeed, as we have seen in the previous section, the descriptor of a PH-transition only depends on its enabling degree for enabling memory, and on the enabling degree and on the number of interrupted clients for age memory. It is then suitable to define a coarser high level view exploiting these weaker dependencies. We shall consider the two cases enabling and age separately.

- *Enabling Memory Case:* from the definition of the descriptors, the set $D_h(\mathbf{m})$ of legal descriptors of a transition t_h for a marking $\mathbf{m}$ only depends on the enabling degree $\mathrm{ed}(t_h, \mathbf{m}) = e_h$ of t_h in $\mathbf{m}$: $D_h(\mathbf{m}) = D_h(e_h) = \{i : 1 \le i \le s(t_h)\}$ if $e_h = 1$ and $D_h(e_h) = \{0\}$ if $e_h = 0$. This key observation leads us to define the equivalence relation ρ over the set of markings in TRS:

$$\mathbf{m} \; \rho \; \mathbf{m}' \quad \text{iff} \quad \forall t_h \in \text{TH} \;\; \mathrm{ed}(t_h, \mathbf{m}) = \mathrm{ed}(t_h, \mathbf{m}')$$

and to take the vector $\mathbf{ed} = (e_1, \ldots, e_H)$ of enabling degrees of transitions in TH as the high level description of Markovian states. We use as representative of a class the vector $\mathbf{ed}$ and indicate the set of markings of equivalence class $\mathbf{ed}$ with $[\mathbf{ed}]$ and the set of distinct vectors of enabling degrees of a given TRS with $\mathcal{ED}$. The following proposition gives the structure of MS.

Proposition 1. *If all phase-type transitions of a PH-SPN $\mathcal{S}$ are enabling memory then*

$$\mathrm{MS}(\mathcal{S}) = \biguplus_{\mathbf{ed} \in \mathcal{ED}} [\mathbf{ed}] \times D_1(e_1) \times \cdots \times D_H(e_H) \tag{1}$$

Proof. The proof is based on the property of the sets $D_h(\mathbf{m})$. By definition,

$$\mathrm{MS}(\mathcal{S}) = \biguplus_{\mathbf{ed} \in \mathcal{ED}} \{(\mathbf{m}, \mathrm{d}(t_1, \mathbf{m}), \ldots \mathrm{d}(t_H, \mathbf{m})) \in \mathrm{MS}(\mathcal{S}); \mathbf{m} \in [\mathbf{ed}]; \forall h, \; \mathrm{d}(t_h, \mathbf{m}) = e_h\}$$

Since, $\forall m \in [\mathbf{ed}] : \; \mathrm{d}(t_h, \mathbf{m}) = e_h$ for all h, and $\forall \mathbf{m}, \mathbf{m}' \in \mathrm{TRS}(\mathcal{S})$ such that $\mathbf{m} \; \rho \; \mathbf{m}'$:

$$(\mathbf{m}, \mathrm{d}^1, \ldots \mathrm{d}^H) \in \mathrm{MS}(\mathcal{S}) \;\; \text{iff} \;\; (\mathbf{m}', \mathrm{d}^1 \ldots \mathrm{d}^H) \in \mathrm{MS}(\mathcal{S})$$

we can decompose the $(H + 1)$ tuple to obtain the result.

- *The Age Memory Case:* in this case, the set of legal descriptors of a transition t_h in the marking $\mathbf{m}$ is $\{s_1, \ldots, s_{t_h}\}$ if the enabling degree of t_h in $\mathbf{m}$ is 1 and is fully determined by the number of interrupted clients, which may be 0 or 1, if the enabling degree of t_h in $\mathbf{m}$ is 0.

   In fact, for a given marking, the number of interrupted clients in t_h may depend on the different possible ways to get to that marking, and for makings with the same enabling degree for t_h, the number of interrupted clients of t_h may differ (see [13] for an example). We now partition the MS accordingly to the enabling degree and to the set of the possible numbers of interrupted clients in each phase type transition.

   Let $\mathcal{IC}(t_h, \mathbf{m})$ indicate the set of possible numbers of interrupted client in transition t_h for marking $\mathbf{m}$ ($\mathcal{IC}(t_h, \mathbf{m}) = \{0\}$ or $\{1\}$ or $\{0, 1\}$). We have developed an algorithm which may be applied for both single and multiple server cases, providing the $\mathcal{IC}(t_h, \mathbf{m})$ sets in polynomial time with respect to the size of the reachability graph (see [13] for details).

   Since the set $D_h(\mathbf{m})$ of legal descriptors of a transition t_h for a marking $\mathbf{m}$ only depends on the enabling degree $\mathrm{ed}(t_h, \mathbf{m}) = e_h$ of t_h in $\mathbf{m}$ and the number of interrupted clients in $\mathbf{m}$, we can write $D_h(\mathbf{m}) = D_h(e_h, i_h)$ with i_h the set of possible numbers of interrupted clients in $\mathbf{m}$. Consequently, the equivalence relation ρ over the set of markings in TRS is now defined by:

$$\mathbf{m} \; \rho \; \mathbf{m'} \; \text{iff} \; \forall t_h \in \text{TH} \;\; \text{ed}(t_h, \mathbf{m}) = \text{ed}(t_h, \mathbf{m'}) \; \text{and} \; \mathcal{IC}(t_h, \mathbf{m}) = \mathcal{IC}(t_h, \mathbf{m'})$$

and the high level description of Markovian states is the pair of vectors $(\mathbf{ed}, \mathbf{ic})$ where $\mathbf{ic} = (i_1, \ldots, i_H)$ is the vector of possible numbers of interrupted clients in phase-type transitions (remember that each element i_h is a set), and $\mathbf{ed}$ is the vector of their enabling degrees, as before. We shall use as representative of a class the pair of vectors $(\mathbf{ed}, \mathbf{ic})$, and we shall indicate the set of markings of equivalence class $(\mathbf{ed}, \mathbf{ic})$ with $[\mathbf{ed}, \mathbf{ic}]$.

Let $\mathcal{EI}$ be the set of pairs $(\mathbf{ed}, \mathbf{ic})$; if all phase-type transitions of a PH-SPN $\mathcal{S}$ are age memory then

$$\text{MS}(\mathcal{S}) = \biguplus_{(\mathbf{ed}, \mathbf{ic}) \in \mathcal{EI}} [\mathbf{ed}, \mathbf{ic}] \times D_1(e_1, i_1) \times \cdots \times D_H(e_H, i_H) \tag{2}$$

where $D_h(e_h, i_h)$ is the set of descriptors of transition t_h compatible with (e_h, i_h).

• *General Expression for the Markovian State Space of PH-SPN:* obviously there is no problem in mixing age memory transitions with enabling memory ones in the same PH-SPN $\mathcal{S}$. Indeed we can rewrite MS in more general form in the following theorem that summarize the two previous results:

Theorem 1. *Given a PH-SPN $\mathcal{S}$, we have*

$$\text{MS}(\mathcal{S}) = \biguplus_{\mathbf{ei} \in \mathcal{EI}} [\mathbf{ei}] \times D_1(ei_1) \times \cdots \times D_H(ei_H) \tag{3}$$

where $\mathbf{ei} = (ei_1, \ldots, ei_H)$, and $ei_h = e_h$ if t_h is enabling memory, and $ei_h = (e_h, i_h)$ if t_h is age memory.

4   Expression of the Infinitesimal Generator and Rate Matrix

This section shows the second main result of the paper, namely how the rate matrix of a PH-SPN with H phase-type transitions can be characterized through a tensor algebra expression of matrices of the size of the $(H + 1)$ components that have been used to characterize the state space in the previous section. The rate matrix $\mathbf{R}$ is defined as:

$$\mathbf{Q} = \mathbf{R} - \boldsymbol{\Delta} \tag{4}$$

where $\mathbf{Q}$ is the infinitesimal generator, $\boldsymbol{\Delta}$ is a diagonal matrix and $\boldsymbol{\Delta}[i, i] = \sum_{k \neq i} \mathbf{Q}[i, k]$; $\mathbf{R}$ can therefore be obtained from $\mathbf{Q}$ by putting to null all diagonal elements. The use of the rate matrix $\mathbf{R}$ instead of the infinitesimal generator $\mathbf{Q}$, allows for a simpler tensorial expression, as pointed out in numerous papers [16,3], at the cost of either computing the diagonal elements on the fly, or of explicitly storing the diagonal.

Following the approach presented in [3,8,6], a characterization of the set of reachable states as the disjoint union of Cartesian products naturally leads to an organization of $\mathbf{R}$ in block form (disjoint union) and to a tensor expression for each block (Cartesian product). Since we have considered the vector of enabling degrees and, for the age memory case, the vector of sets of numbers of interrupted clients, as high level states, the blocks are determined by the equivalence classes built on these vectors denoted by $\mathbf{ei}$ in a generic form. The structure of $\mathbf{R}$ is given by the next theorem.

Theorem 2. *The block matrices of* $\mathbf{R}$ *are:*

$$\mathbf{R}(\mathbf{ei}, \mathbf{ei}') = \mathbf{K}_0(\mathrm{TX})(\mathbf{ei}, \mathbf{ei}') \bigotimes_{h=1}^{H} \mathbf{Dc}_h(\mathrm{ei}_h, \mathrm{ei}'_h)$$
$$+ \sum_{t_h \in T(\mathbf{ei}, \mathbf{ei}') \cap \mathrm{TH}} \mathbf{K}_0(t_h)(\mathbf{ei}, \mathbf{ei}')$$
$$\bigotimes_{l=1}^{h-1} \mathbf{Dc}_l(\mathrm{ei}_l, \mathrm{ei}'_l) \bigotimes \mathbf{Dr}_h(\mathrm{ei}_h, \mathrm{ei}'_h) \bigotimes_{l=h+1}^{H} \mathbf{Dc}_l(\mathrm{ei}_l, \mathrm{ei}'_l)$$
$$(5)$$

$$\mathbf{R}(\mathbf{ei}, \mathbf{ei}) = \bigoplus_{h=1}^{H} \mathbf{R}_h(\mathrm{ei}_h, \mathrm{ei}_h)$$
$$+ \sum_{t_h \in T(\mathbf{ei}, \mathbf{ei}) \cap \mathrm{TH}} \mathbf{K}_0(t_h)(\mathbf{ei}, \mathbf{ei}) \bigotimes_{l=1}^{h-1} \mathbf{I}_{\mathrm{ei}_l} \bigotimes \mathbf{Dr}_h(\mathrm{ei}_h, \mathrm{ei}_h) \bigotimes_{l=h+1}^{H} \mathbf{I}_{\mathrm{ei}_l}$$
$$(6)$$

Due to lack of space, we omit in the present paper, technical details and proofs (which may be found in [13]) about the expression of $\mathbf{R}$ and we give only an intuitive explanation of the theorem.

We have two types of blocks in the matrix, the $(\mathbf{ei}, \mathbf{ei})$ diagonal blocks and the off-diagonal $(\mathbf{ei}, \mathbf{ei}')$.

The off-diagonal block matrices correspond to a change of marking either due to the firing of an exponential transition (gathered in $\mathbf{K}_0(\mathrm{TX})(\mathbf{ei}, \mathbf{ei}')$) which simultaneously (hence the $\bigotimes$ operator) produces modifications of the descriptors of the PH-transitions ($\mathbf{Dc}_h(\mathrm{ei}_h, \mathrm{ei}'_h)$); or due to the external firing (α-firings in [15], the firing of the stage is followed by the choice to leave the transition) of a phase-type transition ($\mathbf{K}_0(t_h)(\mathbf{ei}, \mathbf{ei}')$ and $\mathbf{Dr}_h(\mathrm{ei}_h, \mathrm{ei}'_h)$) which also produces simultaneous modifications of other descriptors ($\mathbf{Dc}_l(\mathrm{ei}_l, \mathrm{ei}'_l)$).

The diagonal block matrices come either from internal (or "local", hence the $\bigoplus$ operator) state changes (β-firings in [15], the firing of the stage is followed by the choice of moving to another stage of the same transition) of PH-transitions ($\mathbf{R}_h(\mathrm{ei}_h, \mathrm{ei}_h)$) or from an external firing of a PH-transition which must leave the descriptors of other PH-transitions unchanged ($\mathbf{K}_0(t_h)(\mathbf{ei}, \mathbf{ei})$, $\mathbf{Dr}_h(\mathrm{ei}_h, \mathrm{ei}_h)$ and $\mathbf{I}_{\mathrm{ei}_l}$).

The reader will find examples of matrices involved in the theorem in [13].

5   Extension to the Multiple Server Case

In this section, we only briefly review the consequences of the introduction of multiple server PH-transitions; a detailed presentation is given in [13].

The first problem is to precisely define the stochastic semantics of these transitions. In particular, the clients policy (*cp*) together with the interrupt/resume policy (ip) must be refined so that the following property holds: starting from a Markovian state, the decrease of k in the enabling degree of the correspon- ding marking **m** of the net, leading to interrupt k clients, immediately followed by the increase of k in the enabling degree, leading to activate k clients, resto- res the initial Markovian state. We propose two types of clients ("ordered" and "unordered" with respect to time) and three adapted interrupt/resume policies ("FIFO", "LIFO" and "Static") covering many encountered modelling needs.

From the definition of these policies we derive new descriptors for multiple server PH-transitions in the enabling as well as in the age memory case.

With these new descriptors, we are able to extend the results of sections 3 and 4. The Markovian state space may still be exactly described as an union of Cartesian products and we present an algorithm providing the sets $\mathcal{IC}(t_h, \mathbf{m})$ (these sets are more complex to compute than for the single server case). The rate matrix **R** has the same structure as in Theorem 2 (obviously the $\mathbf{R}_h, \mathbf{Dr}_h$ and $\mathbf{Dc}_h$ matrices are modified accordingly).

6   Evaluation of the Method and Conclusions

In this paper we have presented a characterization of the state space of SPN with H PH-transitions as a disjoint union of Cartesian products of $H + 1$ terms, and an associated tensor expression for the rate matrix of the underlying Markovian process. The memory policies considered are enabling and age memory, with single server as well as multiple/infinite server semantics.

The approach followed is inspired to the tensor algebra method for hierar- chical Petri nets [3], and for DSSP [8], but we were able to find a definition of abstract view of the system that leads to a precise characterization of the state space (all and only the reachable states are generated), which was not possible for the mentioned papers. The abstract view is the vector of enabling degree of PH-transitions for enabling memory, enriched by the information on the set of possible numbers of interrupted clients for each age memory transition. Both in- formation can be computed from the reachability graph of the net, the enabling degree computation is straightforward, and we have given an algorithm for the computation of the set of possible interrupted clients.

Tensor algebra has already been applied to PH-SPN in [15], following an SGSPN-like approach [12]: unfortunately the number of non reachable states generated could be very high, a problem that we have completely solved with the method here presented, at the price of a slightly more complicated tensorial expression.

Following the characterization of the state space a tensor formula for the rate matrix has been derived. This formula allows the computation of the state space probability vector without the need to explicitly compute and store the infinitesimal generator of the CTMC underlying the PH-SPN, resulting in a saving in storage, and thus in the possibility of solving more complex models. The probability vector need still to be stored in full, and *this is the real limitation of the approach proposed*. At present state of hardware, the tensor based approach can solve systems with up to some millions states on a workstation, depending on the memory available on the machine [16]; in [5] it is also shown that the amount of memory required for storing the component matrices is negligible with respect to that required for the probability vector.

The contribution of the method proposed is, we hope, twofold. Practical: once implemented and integrated in an SPN tool, it shall enlarge the set of solvable PH-SPN models, thus providing a greater applicability of the model. Theoretical: the characterization of the state space given shows the dependencies between markings, different types of transitions and different types of firing of the same transition, descriptors and memory policies, thus providing, we hope, a step forwards a deeper understanding of PH-SPN.

Acknowledgements We would like to thank Andrea Bobbio for fruitful discussions and explanations on PH-SPN.

References

1. M. Ajmone Marsan and G. Chiola. On Petri nets with deterministic and exponentially distributed firing times. In G. Rozenberg, editor, *Advances in Petri Nets 1987*, number 266 in LNCS, pages 132–145. Springer–Verlag, 1987.

2. A. Bobbio and M. Telek. Markov regenerative SPN with non overlapping activity cycles. In *International Computer Performance and Dependability Symposium - IPDS95*, pages 124–133. IEEE CS Press, 1995.

3. P. Buchholz. A hierarchical view of GCSPN's and its impact on qualitative and quantitative analysis. *Journal of Parallel and Distributed Computing*, 15(3):207–224, July 1992.

4. P. Buchholz. Aggregation and reduction techniques for hierarchical GCSPN. In *Proc. of the 5th International Workshop on Petri Nets and Performance Models*, pages 216–225, Toulouse, France, October 19–22 1993. IEEE Computer Society Press.

5. P. Buchholz, G. Ciardo, S Donatelli, and P. Kemper. Complexity of Kronecker operations on sparse matrices with applications to the solution of Markov models, 1997. submitted for publication.

6. P. Buchholz and P. Kemper. Numerical analyisis of stochastic marked graphs. In *Proc. 6th Intern. Workshop on Petri Nets and Performance Models*, pages 32–41, Durham, NC, USA, October 1995. IEEE-CS Press.

7. J. Campos, S. Donatelli, and M. Silva. Structured solution of asynchronously communicating stochastic modules: from DSSP to general P/T systems, 1997. submitted for publication.

8. J. Campos, S. Donatelli, and M. Silva. Structured solution of stochastic DSSP systems. In *Proc. of the 7th International Workshop on Petri Nets and Performance Models*, pages 91–100, Saint-Malo, France, June 3–6 1997. IEEE Computer Society Press.

9. P. Chen, S. C. Bruell, and G. Balbo. Alternative methods for incorporating nonexponential distributions into stochastic timed Petri nets. In *Proc. of the third International Workshop on Petri Nets and Performance Models*, pages 187–197, Kyoto, Japan, December 11–13 1989. IEEE Computer Society Press.

10. G. Ciardo, R. German, and C. Lindemann. A characterization of the stochastic process underlying a stochastic Petri net. In *Proc. of the 5th International Workshop on Petri Nets and Performance Models*, pages 170–179, Toulouse, France, October 19–22 1993. IEEE Computer Society Press.

11. A. Cumani. ESP - a package for the evaluation of stochastic Petri nets with phase-type distributed transition times. In *Proc. of the International Workshop on Timed Petri Nets*, pages 144–151, Torino, Italy, July 1-3 1985. IEEE Computer Society Press.

12. S. Donatelli. Superposed generalized stochastic Petri nets: definition and efficient solution. In Robert Valette, editor, *Proc. of the 15th International Conference on Application and Theory of Petri Nets*, number 815 in LNCS, pages 258–277, Zaragoza, Spain, June 20–24 1994. Springer–Verlag.

13. S. Donatelli, S. Haddad, and P. Moreaux. Srtuctured characterization of the markov chains of phase-type SPN. http://www.lamsade.fr/m̃oreaux/tools98/extended.ps, June 1998.

14. S. Haddad and P. Moreaux. Asynchronous composition of high level Petri nets: a quantitative approach. In *Proc. of the 17th International Conference on Application and Theory of Petri Nets*, number 1091 in LNCS, pages 193–211, Osaka, Japan, June 24–28 1996. Springer–Verlag.

15. S. Haddad, P. Moreaux, and G. Chiola. Efficient handling of phase-type distributions in generalized stochastic Petri nets. In *Proc. of the 18th International Conference on Application and Theory of Petri Nets*, number 1248 in LNCS, pages 175–194, Toulouse, France, June 23–27 1997. Springer–Verlag.

16. P. Kemper. Numerical analysis of superposed GSPNs. In *Proc. of the 6th International Workshop on Petri Nets and Performance Models*, pages 52–61, Durham, NC, USA, October 3–6 1995. IEEE Computer Society Press.

17. M. K. Molloy. *On the integration of delay and throughput in distributed processing models*. PhD dissertation, University of California, Los Angeles, CA, USA, September 1981.

18. M. F. Neuts. *Matrix-geometric solutions in stochastic models - an algorithmic approach*. The John Hopkins University Press, London, 1981.

19. B. Plateau. On the stochastic structure of parallelism and synchronization models for distributed algorithms. In *Proc. of the 1985 ACM SIGMETRICS Conference on Measurement and Modeling of Computer Systems*, pages 147–154, Austin, Texas, USA, August 1985. ACM.

Markov Regenerative Stochastic Petri Nets with General Execution Policies: Supplementary Variable Analysis and a Prototype Tool

Reinhard German

Technische Universität Berlin, Prozeßdatenverarbeitung und Robotik,
Franklinstr. 28/29, 10587 Berlin, Germany, rge@cs.tu-berlin.de

Abstract. Stochastic Petri nets (SPNs) with general firing time distributions are considered. The generally timed transitions can have general execution policies: the preemption policy may be preemptive repeat different (prd) or preemptive resume (prs) and the firing time distribution can be marking-independent or marking-dependent through constant scaling factors. A stationary analysis method covering all possible combinations is presented by means of supplementary variables. The method is implemented in a prototype tool based on Mathematica. An example illustrates the analysis method and the use of the tool.

1 Introduction

In order to increase the modeling power of *stochastic Petri nets* (SPNs), various methods for the numerical analysis in case of transitions with general firing time distributions (*general transitions*) have been investigated. For a proper specification of the execution semantics of the SPN, it is necessary to exactly specify the execution policy of the general transitions [1]. Since the general distributions do not enjoy the memoryless property, the behavior in case of preemptions and the meaning of marking-dependent firing time distributions has to be defined. In [1], two *preemption policies* were defined: *race enabling* (memory is lost when the transition is preempted) and *race age* (memory is preserved when the transition is preempted). Furthermore, *marking dependence through constant scaling factors* was defined, in which the transition can change its speed from marking to marking and keeps a relative age variable. In a later paper [18] it was suggested to use the terms *preemptive repeat different* (prd), corresponding to race enabling and *preemptive resume* (prs), corresponding to race age.

Besides phase-type approximation [8] many authors use the results of Markov renewal theory for the analysis of SPNs with general transitions. In this approach, the analysis is based on an embedded discrete time Markov chain (DTMC). A first algorithm was developed for *deterministic and stochastic Petri nets* (DSPNs), in which in each marking besides transitions with exponentially distributed firing times (*exponential transitions*) at most one transition with deterministic firing time (*determistic transitions*) with prd-policy may be enabled.

R. Puigjaner et al. (Eds.): Tools'98, LNCS 1469, pp. 255–266, 1998.

The method is based on an embedded DTMC. As an extension it was proposed in [15] to deal with marking-dependent deterministic firing times, which is a special case of marking-dependence through constant scaling factors. In [5,6] it was shown how to generalize the analysis algorithm for DSPNs to *Markov regenerative SPNs*, in which at most one general transition with prd-policy can be enabled in each marking. The stationary analysis algorithm is automated in the software tool TimeNET [11]. [5] also suggested a transient analysis method for this class of SPNs. The approach has been generalized in several papers to the case of prs-policy [16,4,17], preemptive repeat identical policy (pri) [3], as well as the case of all policies mixed [18], always under the assumption of marking-independent firing time distributions.

Alternatively, the method of supplementary variables [7] can be employed for the analysis. This was suggested in [12] for the stationary analysis of Markov regenerative SPNs with prd-policy and marking-independent firing time distributions and extended to the transient analysis in [9,13]. The transient analysis algorithm is automated in TimeNET for DSPNs.

In this paper Markov regenerative SPNs are considered in which the execution policy of general transitions can be either prd or prs and the distribution can also be marking-dependent through constant scaling factors. The method of supplementary variables is extended in order to analyze all possible cases. As a result a condensed algorithm can be given in which each combination leads to a different computation of submatrices. The overall method is to solve an *embedded continuous time Markov chain* (CTMC) and to convert the solution to the solution of the actual process. The algorithm has been implemented in a prototype tool *SPNica* based on Mathematica [19]. The prototype is not optimized for efficiency (however, models with up to a few hundred states can be solved) but allows a good flexibility in model specification, evaluation, and result presentation. An example is used to illustrate both the analysis algorithm and the tool usage.

2   Considered Model Class and Notation

SPNs are considered which consist of places, immediate and timed transitions, arcs, guards, and undistinguishable tokens, as described in, e.g., [1]. Transitions with an exponential and general firing time distribution are referred to as exponential and general transitions, respectively. The execution policy of each general transition can be specified by three attributes in arbitrary combinations: 1) the firing time distribution, 2) the *preemption policy*: prd or prs, and 3) the *marking dependence type*: marking-independent (constant) or marking-dependent through constant scaling factors (scaling). The meaning of scaling is explained in Sec. 3.2. As an analysis restriction, in each marking at most one general transition may be *active*. A prd-transition is active if it is enabled and a prs-transition is active if it is enabled or preempted.

Let G denote the set of general transitions and let $g \in G$ denote a general transition. In the marking-dependent case, denote by $F_n(x)$ the firing time distribution of a general transition enabled in marking n. We assume that $F_n(x)$ has no mass at zero, i.e., $F_n(0) = 0$. The maximum support of $F_n(x)$ is denoted by $x_{n_{\max}} \in \mathbb{R}^+ \cup \{\infty\}$. In related notation we write: the density $f_n(x) = \frac{d}{dx} F_n(x)$, the complementary distribution function $\bar{F}_n(x) = 1 - F_n(x)$, and the instantaneous firing rate $\mu_n(x) = f_n(x)/\bar{F}_n(x)$ for $x < x_{n_{\max}}$. In the marking-independent case the subscript is omitted and instead the superscript $g \in G$ is used in order to denote the affiliation to the transition: $F^g(x)$, $f^g(x)$, $x^g_{\max}$, etc.

Let $\mathcal{S}$ denote the set of tangible markings which is required to be finite. Define subsets of $\mathcal{S}$ as:

- $\mathcal{S}^E = \{n \in \mathcal{S} \mid$ no general transition active in $n\}$,
- $\mathcal{S}^g = \{n \in \mathcal{S} \mid$ general transition g enabled in $n\}$,
- $\mathcal{S}^{g^*} = \{n \in \mathcal{S} \mid$ prs-transition g can be preempted in $n\}$,
- $\mathcal{S}^G = \bigcup_{g \in G} \mathcal{S}^g$, and $\mathcal{S}^{G^*} = \bigcup_{g \in G} \mathcal{S}^{g^*}$.

The sets $\mathcal{S}^E$, $\mathcal{S}^g$, and $\mathcal{S}^{g^*}$, $g \in G$, from a partition of $\mathcal{S}$. For a prd-transition g, the set $\mathcal{S}^{g^*}$ is empty. A prs-transition g is active both in $\mathcal{S}^g$ and $\mathcal{S}^{g^*}$. Note that it may be possible that the states of $\mathcal{S}^{g^*}$ are reached without preemption of g, e.g., from $\mathcal{S}^E$.

An SPN describes a *marking process* $\{N(t), t \geq 0\}$. The aim of the analysis are the *state probabilities* $\pi_n = \lim_{t \to \infty} Pr\{N(t) = n\}$ and *general firing frequencies* φ_n (the mean firing rate of a general transition in state n). If the limits are not existing, time-averaged limits are taken. $\boldsymbol{\pi}$ and $\boldsymbol{\varphi}$ denote the corresponding vectors. We refer to a state transition caused by the firing of an exponential or general transition as exponential or general state transition, respectively. The marking process is uniquely described by the matrices $\mathbf{Q}$, $\bar{\mathbf{Q}}$, and $\boldsymbol{\Delta}$:

- the q_{ij}, $i \neq j$, are the rates of all exponential state transitions from i to j except for those which preempt a prd-transition, q_{ii} is the negative sum of all rates of exponential state transitions out of state i, including those which preempt a prd-transition,
- $\bar{q}_{ij}$ is the rate of the exponential state transitions from i to j which preempt a prd-transition, (the case of $\bar{q}_{ij} \neq 0$, for $i, j \in \mathcal{S}^g$ is included),
- δ_{ij} is the *branching probability* that the firing of a general transition g in state i leads to state j, given that g fires in i.

In order to filter out values of the vectors and matrices corresponding to certain subsets of $\mathcal{S}$, *filter matrices* are defined: $\mathbf{I}^F$ is a diagonal matrix whose ith diagonal element is equal to one if $i \in \mathcal{S}^E$ and equal to zero otherwise, $\mathbf{I}^g$, $\mathbf{I}^{g^*}$, $\mathbf{I}^G$, and $\mathbf{I}^{G^*}$ are defined analogously. The vector which contains the state probabilities of $\mathcal{S}^E$ and zeroes at other positions is written as $\boldsymbol{\pi}^E = \boldsymbol{\pi}\mathbf{I}^E$. The matrix in which all rows not corresponding to states of $\mathcal{S}^E$ are set to zero is denoted by $\mathbf{Q}^E = \mathbf{I}^E\mathbf{Q}$, the matrix in which additionally all columns not corresponding to states of $\mathcal{S}^g$ are set to zero is given by $\mathbf{Q}^{E,g} = \mathbf{I}^E\mathbf{Q}\mathbf{I}^g$. Similarly, $\mathbf{Q}^{E,E+G^*} = \mathbf{I}^E\mathbf{Q}(\mathbf{I}^E + \mathbf{I}^{G^*})$. Other filtered vectors and matrices can be defined analogously.

3   Supplementary Variable Analysis

The method of supplementary variables [7] is extended in order to analyze Markov regenerative SPNs with mixed preemption policies and marking-dependent firing time distributions. The analysis is performed in three steps. In Sec. 3.1 the case of mixed preemption policies is investigated under the assumption of marking-independent firing time distributions and in Sec. 3.2 marking dependence is investigated under the assumption of preemption policy prd. In Sec. 3.3 a summary of the algorithm is given which includes also the case in which preemption policy prs is combined with marking dependence.

3.1   Preemption Policies prd and prs

SPNs with mixed preemption policies prd and prs and with marking-independent firing time distributions are considered in this section. The discrete marking process is supplemented by a continuous component: $\{(N(t), X(t)), t \geq 0\}$, $X(t) \in \mathbb{R}_0^+ \cup \{\infty\}$. $X(t)$ is the supplementary variable if $N(t) \in \mathcal{S}^G \cup \mathcal{S}^{G^*}$ and equal to infinity if $N(t) \in \mathcal{S}^E$. In case of a prd-transition the interpretation of $X(t)$ is the time since the enabling of the transition, in case of a prs-transition the interpretation of $X(t)$ is the performed work since the enabling. Note that in states of $\mathcal{S}^{G^*}$ the value of $X(t)$ does not change. Furthermore, if a state of $\mathcal{S}^{G^*}$ has been reached by the preemption of a prs-transition, $X(t) > 0$, and $X(t) = 0$ otherwise.

In order to express state equations the following quantities are defined. *Age densities* are defined as $\pi_n(x) = \lim_{t \to \infty} \frac{d}{dx} Pr\{N(t) = n, X(t) \leq x\}$ (alternatively defined as time-averages, if not existing) and *age intensities* as $p_n(x) = \pi_n(x)/\bar{F}^g(x)$ for $n \in \mathcal{S}^g \cup \mathcal{S}^{g^*}$, $x \leq x_{\max}^g$, and $p_n(x) = 0$ for $n \in \mathcal{S}^E$. $\boldsymbol{\pi}(x)$ and $\mathbf{p}(x)$ are the corresponding vectors.

State equations are now derived for the stationary case. For the states of $\mathcal{S}^E$ and $\mathcal{S}^{G^*}$ a first balance equation is given by

$$0 = \boldsymbol{\pi}^E \mathbf{Q}^{E,E+G^*} + \boldsymbol{\varphi} \boldsymbol{\Delta}^{G,E+G^*} + \boldsymbol{\pi}^G \bar{\mathbf{Q}}^{G,E+G^*} + \mathbf{p}^{G^*}(0) \mathbf{Q}^{G^*,E+G^*}. \quad (1)$$

The equation expresses the balance of "flow-in" and "flow-out" due to exp. state transitions when no general transition is active; the first term corresponds to exp. state transitions out of $\mathcal{S}^E$, the second to the firings of general transitions, the third to preemptions of prd-transitions, and the fourth to exp. state transition out of $\mathcal{S}^{G^*}$ when no prs-transition is active. For each $g \in G$, the dynamics in the states of $\mathcal{S}^g$ is described by the following ordinary differential equation (ODE) for $x > 0$:

$$\frac{d}{dx} \mathbf{p}^g(x) = \mathbf{p}^g(x) \mathbf{Q}^{g,g} + \mathbf{p}^{g^*}(x) \mathbf{Q}^{g^*,g}. \quad (2)$$

The first term corresponds to exp. state transitions when a general transition g is enabled and the second to exp. state transitions which enable the preempted prs-transition g again. For the states of $\mathcal{S}^{g^*}$ and for $x > 0$ a second balance equation is valid:

$$0 = \mathbf{p}^g(x) \mathbf{Q}^{g,g^*} + \mathbf{p}^{g^*}(x) \mathbf{Q}^{g^*,g^*}. \quad (3)$$

The equation expresses the balance of "flow-in" and "flow-out" due to exp. state transitions when a prs-transition g is preempted. A boundary condition is given by

$$\mathbf{p}^G(0) = \boldsymbol{\pi}^E \mathbf{Q}^{E,G} + \varphi \boldsymbol{\Delta}^{G,G} + \boldsymbol{\pi}^G \bar{\mathbf{Q}}^{G,G} + \mathbf{p}^{G^*}(0) \mathbf{Q}^{G^*,G}. \tag{4}$$

It expresses the enabling of a general transition and consists of the same terms as the first balance equation except for the different destination as indicated by the superscript G. The general firing frequencies and the state probabilities can be given by three integrals in terms of the age densities:

$$\varphi = \sum_{g \in G} \int_0^\infty \mathbf{p}^g(x) f^g(x)\, dx, \tag{5}$$

$$\boldsymbol{\pi}^G = \sum_{g \in G} \int_0^\infty \mathbf{p}^g(x) \bar{F}^g(x)\, dx, \quad \boldsymbol{\pi}^{G^*} = \boldsymbol{\pi}^{G^*}(0) + \sum_{g \in G} \int_{0+}^\infty \mathbf{p}^{g^*}(x) \bar{F}^g(x)\, dx. \tag{6}$$

Finally, the normalization condition $\boldsymbol{\pi}\mathbf{e} = 1$ has to be satisfied ($\mathbf{e}$ is a vector of ones).

For the analysis of the equations, define

$$\mathbf{A}^g = -\mathbf{Q}^{g,g^*}\left(\mathbf{Q}^{g^*,g^*}\right)^{-1}, \quad \mathbf{B}^g = \mathbf{Q}^{g,g} - \mathbf{Q}^{g,g^*}\left(\mathbf{Q}^{g^*,g^*}\right)^{-1}\mathbf{Q}^{g^*,g}, \tag{7}$$

where $\left(\mathbf{Q}^{g^*,g^*}\right)^{-1}$ denotes the inversion restricted to the rows and columns which correspond to $\mathcal{S}^{g^*}$. Let $\mathbf{A} = \sum_{g \in G} \mathbf{A}^g$. The inversion represents a key step in the analysis of SPNs with prs-transitions and has also been used in [17]. $\mathbf{B}^g$ is the generator matrix of the *subordinated CTMC* of g. The subordinated CTMC represents exponential state transitions when g is enabled and also takes into account the exponential state transitions when g is preempted. Based on $\mathbf{B}^g$, the matrices $\boldsymbol{\Omega}^g$ and $\boldsymbol{\Psi}^g$ can be defined representing the conditional state probabilities and conditional sojourn times in the subordinated CTMC when g fires, respectively:

$$\boldsymbol{\Omega}^g = \mathbf{I}^g \int_0^\infty e^{\mathbf{B}^g x} f^g(x)\, dx, \quad \boldsymbol{\Psi}^g = \mathbf{I}^g \int_0^\infty e^{\mathbf{B}^g x} \bar{F}^g(x)\, dx. \tag{8}$$

Let the sums of the matrices be $\boldsymbol{\Omega} = \sum_{g \in G} \boldsymbol{\Omega}^g$ and $\boldsymbol{\Psi} = \sum_{g \in G} \boldsymbol{\Psi}^g$. Finally, a matrix $\mathbf{S}$ and a conversion matrix $\mathbf{D}$ can be defined:

$$\mathbf{S} = \mathbf{Q}^{E+G^*} + \boldsymbol{\Omega}\boldsymbol{\Delta} + \boldsymbol{\Psi}\bar{\mathbf{Q}} - \mathbf{I}^G, \quad \mathbf{D} = \mathbf{I}^{E+G^*} + \boldsymbol{\Psi}(\mathbf{I} + \mathbf{A}), \tag{9}$$

Using similar arguments as in [10] it can be shown that $\mathbf{S}$ is the generator matrix of a CTMC, referred to as the *embedded CTMC*. Defining the solution vector $\mathbf{w} = \boldsymbol{\pi}^E + \mathbf{p}^G(0) + \mathbf{p}^{G^*}(0)$, the solution of the marking process can be obtained by first solving the embedded CTMC

$$\mathbf{w}\mathbf{S} = \mathbf{0}, \text{ subject to } \mathbf{w}\mathbf{D}\mathbf{e} = 1, \tag{10}$$

and by backsubstitution:

$$\boldsymbol{\pi} = \mathbf{w}\mathbf{D}, \quad \varphi = \mathbf{w}\boldsymbol{\Omega}. \tag{11}$$

Proof (of Eqns. (10) and (11)). It follows from the second balance equation that

$$\mathbf{p}^{g^*}(x) = -\mathbf{p}^g(x)\mathbf{Q}^{g,g^*}\left(\mathbf{Q}^{g^*,g^*}\right)^{-1} = \mathbf{p}^g(x)\mathbf{A}^g, \tag{12}$$

insertion into the ODE yields

$$\frac{d}{dx}\mathbf{p}^g(x) = \mathbf{p}^g(x)\left[\mathbf{Q}^{g,g} - \mathbf{Q}^{g,g^*}\left(\mathbf{Q}^{g^*,g^*}\right)^{-1}\mathbf{Q}^{g^*,g}\right] = \mathbf{p}^g(x)\mathbf{B}^g, \tag{13}$$

hence $\mathbf{p}^g(x) = \mathbf{p}^g(0)e^{\mathbf{B}^g x}$. Insertion into the integrals leads to

$$\varphi = \sum_{g \in G}\mathbf{p}^g(0)\mathbf{\Omega}^g = \mathbf{p}^G(0)\mathbf{\Omega}, \ \ \pi^G = \sum_{g \in G}\mathbf{p}^g(0)\mathbf{\Psi}^g = \mathbf{p}^G(0)\mathbf{\Psi}, \tag{14}$$

and

$$\pi^{G^*} = \mathbf{p}^{G^*}(0) + \sum_{g \in G}\mathbf{p}^g(0)\mathbf{\Psi}^g\mathbf{A}^g = \mathbf{p}^{G^*}(0) + \mathbf{p}^G(0)\mathbf{\Psi}\mathbf{A}. \tag{15}$$

Insertion of these results into the sum of the first balance equation and of the boundary conditions leads to $\mathbf{wS} = \mathbf{0}$ and insertion into the normalization condition leads to $\mathbf{wDe} = 1$. These two equations allow to compute $\mathbf{w}$. Backsubstitution into the integrals leads to $\pi = \mathbf{wD}$ and $\varphi = \mathbf{w\Omega}$. □

3.2   Marking Dependence through Constant Scaling Factors

SPNs with preemption policy prd and with marking-dependent firing time distributions through constant scaling factors are considered in this section. First a discussion of this type of marking-dependence is given.

The *absolute age variables* in state n are denoted by X_n and x_n (the random variable and its value, respectively). $F_n(x_n) = Pr\{X_n \le x_n\}$ is the firing time distribution of the absolute age variable in state n. The $F_n(x_n)$ are marking-dependent through constant scaling factors if 1) a marking-independent *relative firing time distribution* $\hat{F}(\hat{x})$ exists, 2) a *constant scaling factor* $c_n \in \mathbb{R}^+$ exists for each state n such that $F_n(x_n) = \hat{F}\left(\frac{x_n}{c_n}\right)$. An example is a uniform distribution for which the interval boundaries are scaled by the same factor. The *relative age variables* are then defined by $\hat{X} = \frac{X_n}{c_n}$ and $\hat{x} = \frac{x_n}{c_n}$. The execution semantics of a transition with a firing time distribution which is marking-dependent through constant scaling factors is: when a marking change takes place, the absolute age variable is scaled appropriately such that the relative age variable remains unchanged, i.e., $X_i = c_i\hat{X} = \frac{c_i}{c_j}X_j$. For the density and moments of the relative age variables one can derive:

$$f_n(x_n) = \frac{1}{c_n}\hat{f}(\hat{x}), \ \ E[X_n^k] = c_n^k E[\hat{X}^k]. \tag{16}$$

Choosing $c_n = E[X_n]$ leads to $E[\hat{X}] = 1$ and $\hat{F}(\hat{x})$ represents a *normalized firing time distribution*.

For the derivation of state equations, the age intensities are required in absolute and normalized versions. *Absolute age densities* are defined as $\pi_n(x_n) = \lim_{t \to \infty} \frac{d}{dx_n} Pr\{N(t) = n, X_n(t) \le x_n\}$, *absolute age intensities* as $p_n(x_n) = \pi_n(x_n)/\bar{F}_n(x_n)$ for $n \in \mathcal{S}^G$, $x_n \le x_{n_{\max}}$ and $p_n(x_n) = 0$ for $n \in \mathcal{S}^E$. *Normalized age intensities* are then $\hat{p}_n(\hat{x}) = p_n(c_n\hat{x})$ for $n \in \mathcal{S}^g$, $\hat{x} \le \hat{x}^g_{\max}$. $\boldsymbol{\pi}(x)$, $\mathbf{p}(x)$, and $\hat{\mathbf{p}}(\hat{x})$ are the corresponding vectors, $\mathbf{c}$ denotes the vector of scaling factors and the matrix $\hat{\mathbf{Q}} = \text{diag}(\mathbf{c})\,\mathbf{Q}$ is defined by scaling the rows of $\mathbf{Q}$ with the corresponding scaling factors ($\text{diag}(\cdot)$ converts a vector to a diagonal matrix).

The balance equations and boundary conditions are a special case of the previous case since the set $\mathcal{S}^{G^*}$ is empty (no prs-transitions):

$$0 = \boldsymbol{\pi}^E \mathbf{Q}^{E,E} + \boldsymbol{\varphi} \boldsymbol{\Delta}^{G,E} + \boldsymbol{\pi}^G \bar{\mathbf{Q}}^{G,E}, \quad \mathbf{p}^G(0) = \boldsymbol{\pi}^E \mathbf{Q}^{E,G} + \boldsymbol{\varphi} \boldsymbol{\Delta}^{G,G} + \boldsymbol{\pi}^G \bar{\mathbf{Q}}^{G,G}, \quad (17)$$

and the normalization condition is still $\boldsymbol{\pi}\mathbf{e} = 1$.

A difference equation for a state $j \in \mathcal{S}^g$, $g \in G$, is

$$\pi_j(c_j\hat{x} + c_j \Delta t) = \pi_j(c_j\hat{x}) + \sum_{i \in \mathcal{S}^g} \pi_i(c_i\hat{x}) q_{ij} c_i \Delta t - \pi_j(c_j\hat{x}) \mu_j(c_j\hat{x}) c_j \Delta t + o(\Delta t) \quad (18)$$

and the integral equations for $j \in \mathcal{S}^G$ are

$$\varphi_j = \int_0^{x_{n_{\max}}} \pi_j(x_j) \mu_j(x_j)\, dx_j, \quad \pi_j = \int_0^\infty \pi_j(x_j)\, dx_j, \quad (19)$$

Forming an ODE for $x > 0$ from the difference equation yields:

$$\frac{d}{d(c_j\hat{x})} \pi_j(c_j\hat{x}) = \sum_{i \in \mathcal{S}^g} \pi_i(c_i\hat{x}) \frac{c_i}{c_j} q_{ij} - \pi_j(c_j\hat{x}) \mu_j(c_j\hat{x}), \quad (20)$$

replacing the absolute age densities by the normalized age intensities leads to

$$\frac{d}{d\hat{x}} \hat{p}_j(\hat{x}) = \sum_{i \in \mathcal{S}^g} \hat{p}_i(\hat{x}) \hat{q}_{ij}. \quad (21)$$

Insertion of the normalized age intensities into the integral equations and integration by substitution leads to:

$$\boldsymbol{\varphi} = \int_0^\infty \hat{\mathbf{p}}^g(\hat{x}) \hat{f}^g(\hat{x})\, d\hat{x}, \quad \boldsymbol{\pi}^G = \int_0^\infty \hat{\mathbf{p}}^g(\hat{x})(1 - \hat{F}^g(\hat{x}))\, d\hat{x}\, \text{diag}(\mathbf{c}^g). \quad (22)$$

From the ODE it follows that $\hat{\mathbf{p}}^g(\hat{x}) = \hat{\mathbf{p}}^g(0) e^{\hat{\mathbf{Q}}^g \hat{x}}$. Matrices $\boldsymbol{\Omega}^g$ and $\boldsymbol{\Psi}^g$ are therefore defined as

$$\boldsymbol{\Omega}^g = \mathbf{I}^g \int_0^\infty e^{\hat{\mathbf{Q}}^g \hat{x}} \hat{f}^g(\hat{x})\, d\hat{x}, \quad \boldsymbol{\Psi}^g = \mathbf{I}^g \int_0^\infty e^{\hat{\mathbf{Q}}^g \hat{x}} (1 - \hat{F}^g(\hat{x}))\, d\hat{x}\, \text{diag}(\mathbf{c}^g), \quad (23)$$

the multiplication with the diagonal matrix from the right leads to a columnwise scaling of the matrix. The rest of the analysis can be performed as in the previous case.

3.3 Summary of the Algorithm

All results can be condensed in a single framework. The generator matrix $\mathbf{S}$ of the embedded CTMC and the conversion matrix $\mathbf{D}$ are defined as:

$$\mathbf{S} = \mathbf{Q}^{E+G^*} + \mathbf{\Omega}\mathbf{\Delta} + \mathbf{\Psi}\bar{\mathbf{Q}} - \mathbf{I}^G, \ \ \mathbf{D} = \mathbf{I}^{E+G^*} + \mathbf{\Psi}(\mathbf{I} + \mathbf{A}). \tag{24}$$

The required submatrices are given as sums of the corresponding matrices for each general transition g: $\mathbf{\Omega} = \sum_{g \in G} \mathbf{\Omega}^g$, $\mathbf{\Psi} = \sum_{g \in G} \mathbf{\Psi}^g$, and $\mathbf{A} = \sum_{g \in G} \mathbf{A}^g$. The definition of $\mathbf{\Omega}^g$, $\mathbf{\Psi}^g$, and $\mathbf{A}^g$ depends on the combination of preemption policy and marking dependence of g. The following four cases have to be distinguished (cases a)-c) have been derived explicitly in the last two sections, case d) can be obtained with similar arguments):

a) prd, constant:

$$\mathbf{\Omega}^g = \mathbf{I}^g \int_0^\infty e^{\mathbf{Q}^g x} f^g(x)\,dx, \ \ \mathbf{\Psi}^g = \mathbf{I}^g \int_0^\infty e^{\mathbf{Q}^g x} \bar{F}^g(x)\,dx, \tag{25}$$

b) prd, scaling:

$$\mathbf{\Omega}^g = \mathbf{I}^g \int_0^\infty e^{\hat{\mathbf{Q}}^g \hat{x}} \hat{f}^g(\hat{x})\,d\hat{x}, \ \ \mathbf{\Psi}^g = \mathbf{I}^g \int_0^\infty e^{\hat{\mathbf{Q}}^g \hat{x}}(1 - \hat{F}^g(\hat{x}))\,d\hat{x}\,\mathrm{diag}\,(\mathbf{c^g}), \tag{26}$$

c) prs, constant:

$$\mathbf{\Omega}^g = \mathbf{I}^g \int_0^\infty e^{\mathbf{B}^g x} f^g(x)\,dx, \ \ \mathbf{\Psi}^g = \mathbf{I}^g \int_0^\infty e^{\mathbf{B}^g x} \bar{F}^g(x)\,dx, \tag{27}$$

d) prs, scaling:

$$\mathbf{\Omega}^g = \mathbf{I}^g \int_0^\infty e^{\mathbf{B}^g \hat{x}} \hat{f}^g(\hat{x})\,d\hat{x}, \ \ \mathbf{\Psi}^g = \mathbf{I}^g \int_0^\infty e^{\mathbf{B}^g \hat{x}}(1 - \hat{F}^g(\hat{x}))\,d\hat{x}\,\mathrm{diag}\,(\mathbf{c}^g). \tag{28}$$

The matrix $\mathbf{A}^g$ is equal to zero in cases a) and b), in case c), the matrices $\mathbf{A}^g$ and $\mathbf{B}^g$ are as defined in Sec. 3.1, and in case d), $\mathbf{A}^g = -\mathrm{diag}\,(\mathbf{c}^g)^{-1}\hat{\mathbf{Q}}^{g,g^*}(\mathbf{Q}^{g^*,g^*})^{-1}$ and $\mathbf{B}^g = \hat{\mathbf{Q}}^{g,g} - \hat{\mathbf{Q}}^{g,g^*}(\mathbf{Q}^{g^*,g^*})^{-1}\mathbf{Q}^{g^*,g}$ (the inverse of the diagonal matrix is restricted to the states of $\mathcal{S}^g$). The scaling of $\mathbf{Q}$ has to be taken into account in case d).

The stationary solution of the marking process can then be obtained by the following algorithm: 1) compute the matrices $\mathbf{\Omega}$, $\mathbf{\Psi}$, and $\mathbf{A}$, 2) solve the embedded CTMC: $\mathbf{wS} = \mathbf{0}$, subject to $\mathbf{wDe} = 1$, and 3) convert to the actual marking process: $\boldsymbol{\pi} = \mathbf{wD}$, $\boldsymbol{\varphi} = \mathbf{w\Omega}$.

It often happens that the embedded CTMC consists of one recurrent and one transient class. In step 2 it is sufficient to restrict $\mathbf{w}$, $\mathbf{S}$, and the rows of $\mathbf{D}$ to the recurrent class (and also to restrict the rows of $\mathbf{\Omega}$ and $\mathbf{\Psi}$ to these states). [10] shows that a formal relationship is existing to the solution approach based on Markov renewal theory in which an embedded DTMC is constructed. It is also possible to extend the analysis to the case of more than one recurrent classes.

4   SPNica: A Prototype Analysis Tool

A prototype tool *SPNica* for the analysis of SPNs has been implemented based on Mathematica 3.0 [19]. The main goal is to test the presented analysis algorithms. Mathematica was chosen since it provides a large number of functions for linear algebra and numerical mathematics. Furthermore, the list processing, symbolic manipulation, functional programming, pattern matching, and graphics facilities can be used for a flexible model specification, evaluation, and result presentation. The code is of medium size (several hundred lines). Although it is not optimized for efficiency, it is possible to solve models with up to a few hundred states in some minutes on a PC (233 MHz Pentium processor, 32 MB RAM).

4.1   Tool Architecture

Different layers can be identified in the evaluation of an SPN: the SPN itself, the reduced reachability graph (RRG), the marking process, the result vectors (π and φ), and the results of the measures. In SPNica, all information corresponding to one layer is collected in a structured list: SPN, RRG, Q (the generator matrix of a CTMC), SV1P (a process in which each state is supplemented with at most one age variable), {pi,phi}, and measures. Several functions are existing which perform the mapping between the layers.

4.2   SPN Specification

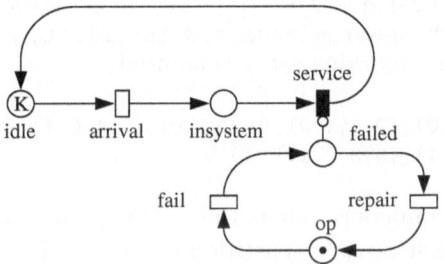

Fig. 1. SPN of an M/G/1/K system with failure and repair

An SPN is specified as a list SPN={P,T,IA,OA,HA,MO,measures}, where P is the list of places, T is the list of transitions, IA, OA, and HA are the lists of input, output, and inhibitor arcs, MO is the initial marking, and measures is the list of requested measures. The behavior of a transition is specified by a list of attributes (such as the distribution, policy, etc.), an attribute is given as a Mathematica transformation rule. The distribution can either be exponential or *expolynomial* (defined by polynomial and exponential pieces, [14,12,6]). The definition of measures is based on the concept of expected rate and impulse rewards [13]. In order to minimize the notational effort, default values are assumed (e.g., for the policy, arc multiplicity, marking, etc.), just values which differ from the default ones have to be given by a transformation rule. As an example, consider the SPN shown in Fig. 1 representing an M/G/1/K queuing system with failures and repairs The service unit has a prs-policy. Assume that the guard `#insystem>0` is attached to transition `fail`, meaning that failures are only possible if the system is busy. An SPNica representation is:

```
K=3;l=0.5;r=0.25;s=1;t=1;
P={idle,insystem,op,failed};
T={{arrival,{dist->exp[l]}},
   {service,{dist->I[t],policy->"prs"}},
   {fail,{dist->exp[r],guard->rr[insystem]>0}},
   {repair,{dist->exp[s]}}};
IA={{idle,arrival}, {insystem,service},{op,fail},{failed,repair}};
OA={{arrival,insystem},{service,idle},{fail,failed},{repair,op}};
HA={{failed,service}};
MO={idle->K,op->1};
measures={N->mean[rr[insystem]],S1->mean[ir[service]],
          S2->mean[ir[arrival]],W->N/S1};
SPN={P,T,IA,OA,HA,MO,measures};
```

4.3 Analysis

From the SPN first the RRG is generated by the function `ReducedReachabilityGraph`. The resulting data structure is of the form `RRG={netclass,markingset,edgesset,Slist,flist,measures,pi0}`. In the example, the following marking set is generated:

```
markingset={{3,0,1,0},{2,1,1,0},{1,2,1,0},{2,1,0,1},{0,3,1,0},
            {1,2,0,1},{0,3,0,1}}
```

(the order of token numbers is as in P, the marking number is according its occurrence). The following state space partition is generated: `Slist={{1},{{2,3,5},{4,6,7}}}`, representing $\mathcal{S}^E = \{1\}$, $\mathcal{S}^{\text{service}} = \{2,3,5\}$, $\mathcal{S}^{\text{service}^*} = \{4,6,7\}$.

`SV1Process` generates the list `SV1P={Slist,flist,Q,Qbar,Delta}` as a representation of the underlying stochastic process in terms of the state partition, the list of transition attributes and the three matrices $\mathbf{Q}$, $\bar{\mathbf{Q}}$, and $\boldsymbol{\Delta}$:

$$\mathbf{Q} = \begin{bmatrix} -0.5 & 0.5 & 0 & 0 & 0 & 0 & 0 \\ 0 & -0.75 & 0.5 & 0.25 & 0 & 0 & 0 \\ 0 & 0 & -0.75 & 0 & 0.5 & 0.25 & 0 \\ 0 & 1 & 0 & -1.5 & 0 & 0.5 & 0 \\ 0 & 0 & 0 & 0 & -0.25 & 0 & 0.25 \\ 0 & 0 & 1 & 0 & 0 & -1.5 & 0.5 \\ 0 & 0 & 0 & 0 & 1 & 0 & -1 \end{bmatrix}, \quad \bar{\mathbf{Q}} = \mathbf{0}, \quad (29)$$

$$\mathbf{\Delta} = \begin{bmatrix} 0 & 0 & 0 & 0 & 0 & 0 & 0 \\ 1 & 0 & 0 & 0 & 0 & 0 & 0 \\ 0 & 1 & 0 & 0 & 0 & 0 & 0 \\ 0 & 0 & 0 & 0 & 0 & 0 & 0 \\ 0 & 0 & 1 & 0 & 0 & 0 & 0 \\ 0 & 0 & 0 & 0 & 0 & 0 & 0 \\ 0 & 0 & 0 & 0 & 0 & 0 & 0 \end{bmatrix} \tag{30}$$

The function SV1Pstationary computes the stationary solution according to the algorithm given in Sec. 3.3. The numerical computation of the integrals of the matrix exponentials required for the matrices $\mathbf{\Omega}^g$ and $\mathbf{\Psi}^g$ is performed by an extended version of Jensen's method [14,12,6]. The result is the pair of lists {pi,phi} representing the vectors π and φ, in the example:

{{0.419,0.285,0.139,0.047,0.041,0.039,0.030},{0,0.210,0.17,0,0.089,0,0}}

GetMeasures takes measures and {pi,phi} in order to compute a new transformation rule list in which all right hand sides are the final results, in the example: {N->0.900,S1->0.464,S2->0.464,W->1.938}. (N is the mean number of customers, S1 the effective arrival rate, S2 the effective service rate, and W the mean waiting time). It is also easily possible to plot curves in case of experiments and in case of transient evaluations.

5 Conclusions

The analysis of Markov regenerative SPNs with mixed preemption policies and marking-dependent firing time distributions has been presented. The analysis is based on the method of supplementary variables. All possible combinations of execution policies fit well in a single framework. An algorithm has been formulated which is close to implementation. The tool provides good support in the testing of the developed formulas. Due to space limitations the transient case was not considered although state equations can be derived with similar arguments.

References

1. M. Ajmone Marsan, G. Balbo, A. Bobbio, G. Chiola, G. Conte, A. Cumani. The Effect of Execution Policies on the Semantics of Stochastic Petri Nets. *IEEE Trans. Softw. Engin.* **15** (1989) 832-846.
2. M. Ajmone Marsan, G. Chiola. On Petri Nets with Deterministic and Exponentially Distributed Firing Times. *Advances in Petri Nets 1986*, Springer-Verlag, LNCS 266, pp. 132–145, 1987.
3. A. Bobbio, V.G. Kulkarni, A. Puliafito, M. Telek, K. Trivedi. Preemptive Repeat Identical Transitions in Markov Regenerative Stochastic Petri Nets. *Proc. 6th Int. Conf. on Petri Nets and Performance Models*, Durham, North Carolina, USA, pp. 113–122, 1995.
4. A. Bobbio, M. Telek. Markov Regenerative SPN with Non-Overlapping Activity Cycles. *Proc. Int. Performance and Dependability Symp.*, 124–133, Erlangen, Germany, 1995.

5. H. Choi, V. G. Kulkarni, K. S. Trivedi. Markov Regenerative Stochastic Petri Nets. *Perf. Eval.* **20** (1994) 337–357.
6. G. Ciardo, R. German, C. Lindemann. A Characterization of the Stochastic Process Underlying a Stochastic Petri Net. *IEEE Trans. Softw. Engin.* **20** (1994) 506–515.
7. D. R. Cox. The Analysis of Non-Markov Stochastic Processes by the Inclusion of Supplementary Variables. *Proc. Camb. Phil. Soc. (Math. and Phys. Sciences)* **51** (1955) 433–441.
8. A. Cumani. ESP - A Package for the Evaluation of Stochastic Petri Nets with Phase-Type Distributed Transition Times. *Proc. Int. Workshop Timed Petri Nets*, Torino, Italy, pp. 278–184, 1985.
9. R. German. New Results for the Analysis of Deterministic and Stochastic Petri Nets. *Proc. IEEE Int. Performance and Dependability Symp.*, Erlangen, Germany, pp. 114–123, 1995.
10. R. German. About the Relationship of Embedding and Supplementary Variables in the Analysis of Markov Regenerative Models. Technical Report, TU Berlin, 1998.
11. R. German, C. Kelling, A. Zimmermann, G. Hommel. TimeNET: A Toolkit for Evaluating Non-Markovian Stochastic Petri Nets. *Perf. Eval.* **24** (1995) 69–87.
12. R. German, C. Lindemann. Analysis of Stochastic Petri Nets by the Method of Supplementary Variables. *Perf. Eval.* **20** (1994) 317–335.
13. R. German, A. P. van Moorsel, M. A. Qureshi, W. H. Sanders. Solution of Stochastic Petri Nets with General Distributions, Rate and Impulse Rewards. *Application and Theory of Petri Nets 1996*, Proc. 17th Int. Conf. Osaka, Japan, Springer-Verlag, LNCS 1091, pp. 172-191, 1996.
14. W. K. Grassmann. The GI/PH/1 Queue: A Method to Find the Transition Matrix, *INFOR* **20** (1982) 144–156.
15. C. Lindemann, R. German. Modeling discrete event systems with state-dependent deterministic service times. *Discrete Event Dynamic Systems: Theory and Applications* **3** (1993) 249–270.
16. M. Telek, A. Bobbio. Markov Regenerative Stochastic Petri Nets with Age Type General Transitions. *Application and Theory of Petri Nets*, Proc. 16th Int. Conf., Springer-Verlag, LNCS 935, pp. 471–489, 1995.
17. M. Telek, A. Bobbio, L. Jereb, A. Puliafito, K.S. Trivedi. Steady State Analysis of Markov Regenerative SPN with Age Memory Policy. *Quantitative Evaluation of Computing and Communication Systems*, pp. 165–179, Springer-Verlag, LNCS 977, 1995.
18. M. Telek, A. Bobbio, A. Puliafito. Steady State Solution of MRSPNs with Mixed Preemption Policies. *Proc. IEEE Int. Performance and Dependability Symp.*, Urbana-Champaign, Illinois, USA, pp 106–115, 1996.
19. S. Wolfram. *The Mathematica Book.* 3rd ed. Wofram Media/Cambridge Unversity Press 1996.

A Queue-Shift Approximation Technique for Product-Form Queueing Networks

Paul J. Schweitzer[1]*, Giuseppe Serazzi[2]**, and Marco Broglia[3]

[1] W. E. Simon Graduate School of Business Administration,
University of Rochester, Rochester, NY 14627, USA
[2] Politecnico di Milano, Dip. Elettronica e Informazione,
P.za L. da Vinci 32, 20133 Milano, Italy, serazzi@elet.polimi.it
[3] NSA srl, Via F. Baracca 9, 20035 Lissone (MI), broglia@nsa.it

Abstract. Increasing complexity of actual computer systems has made exact modelling techniques prohibitively expensive, and the need for approximation techniques for performance evaluation is well-recognized. A new approximation technique is given for product-form queueing networks with constant-rate servers. It estimates the shift in mean queue lengths rather than the fractional deviations used in the Chandy-Neuse linearizer. Experimental results are reported which show that the new approximation 92% of the times has superior accuracy to linearizer. As population grows, the superior accuracy over linearizer increases. In 58% of the test cases, the new approximation technique gave errors of zero (at least 6 digits) while linearizer achieves such accuracy in less than 2.5% of cases. In some of the stress cases described, the new approximation technique has roughly five orders of magnitude less error than linearizer.

1 Introduction

Queueing network models are a fundamental tool for performance evaluation engineering. Originally these models had relatively small number of servers and of customer classes. However, in recent years computer-communication systems have become increasingly complex. Client-server, intranet and extranet architectures involve interconnection of a large number of components via LANs and WANs. In addition, there has been a vast proliferation of workloads with widely varying resource demands, both between different load types and also within each type. A representative workload model must allow the description of a large number of distinct classes of customers.

For these reasons, single-workload models have limited use, and will be replaced by models allowing large numbers of load classes, customers, and stations. Exact solution techniques (when applicable) become prohibitively expensive, and

---

* This work was partially supported by the Center for Manufacturing and Operations Management of the W. E. Simon Graduate School of Business Administration at the University of Rochester
** This work was partially supported by MURST 40% Project and CESTIA-CNR Italy

R. Puigjaner et al. (Eds.): Tools'98, LNCS 1469, pp. 267–279, 1998.

approximation techniques are becoming fundamental for the future of systems modelling.

Several approximation techniques able to provide estimates of the most important indices have been proposed (see e.g., [1], [8], [3], [5], [11]).

In this paper we restrict our attention to the *linearizer* approximation [3], the most accurate among the proposed techniques. In Sect. 2 we introduce the notation that will be used through the paper. The linearizer algorithm together with some of its variants in the literature [11], [9] are also discussed in this section. In Sects. 3 and 4 the new approximation technique and the solution algorithms are presented. Computational results obtained from this approximation and comparisons with the results of the linearizer and Schweitzer-Bard [1], [8] are discussed in Sect. 5. Accuracy and complexity of the method are also presented.

2   The Model and Notation

Consider a closed product-form queueing network [2], [7] with M constant-rate servers and R customer classes. The population vector is denoted by $\underline{K} = (K_1, K_2, \ldots, K_R)$ and the total population by $K_{\text{sum}} = K_1 + K_2 + \cdots + K_R$. Customers do not change class. The other data for the model are:

- S_{ri} = mean service time of a class-r customer for each visit to server i (if i is FCFS, this must be independent of r);
- V_{ri} = mean number of visits by a class-r customer to server i;
- $L_{ri} = V_{ri}S_{ri}$ = mean load placed on server i by one customer of class-r.

The servers are numbered $1, 2, \ldots, M$ and the customer classes are numbered $1, 2, \ldots, R$. We let DC denote the set of Delay Centers and QC denote the set of Queueing Centers (first-come-first-served, or processor share, or last-come-first-served pre-emptive resume, or service in random order [10]). Note $\{1, 2, \ldots, M\} \equiv DC + QC$.

The desired performance measures of the queueing network are:

- $Q_{ri}(\underline{K})$ = mean number of class-r customers at server i (either in service or in queue);
- $Q_i(\underline{K})$ = mean number of customers at server i (any class, either in service or in queue);
- $X_{ri}(\underline{K})$ = throughput of class-r customers at server i;
- $X_r(\underline{K})$ = throughput of class-r customers;
- $W_{ri}(\underline{K})$ = mean sojourn time (service plus queueing) of a class-r customer during one visit to server i.

Exact Mean Value Analysis (MVA) permits these to be computed recursively from [7]:

$$W_{ri}(\underline{K}) = S_{ri}\left[1 + Q_i(\underline{K} - \underline{e}^r)\right] \qquad K_r \geq 1, \quad 1 \leq r \leq R, \quad i \in QC \qquad (1a)$$
$$W_{ri}(\underline{K}) = S_{ri} \qquad\qquad\qquad 1 \leq r \leq R, \quad i \in DC \qquad\qquad (1b)$$

$$X_r(\underline{K}) = \frac{K_r}{\displaystyle\sum_{i=1}^{M} V_{ri}\, W_{ri}(\underline{K})} \qquad\qquad 1 \le r \le R \qquad\qquad (2)$$

$$X_{ri}(\underline{K}) = X_r(\underline{K})\, V_{ri} \qquad\qquad 1 \le r \le R, \quad 1 \le i \le M \qquad (3)$$

$$Q_{ri}(\underline{K}) = X_{ri}(\underline{K})\, W_{ri}(\underline{K}) \qquad\qquad 1 \le r \le R, \quad 1 \le i \le M \qquad (4)$$

$$Q_i(\underline{K}) = \sum_{r=1}^{R} Q_{ri}(\underline{K}) \qquad\qquad 1 \le i \le M \qquad\qquad (5)$$

with initial conditions $Q_i(\underline{0}) = 0$ for $1 \le i \le M$. Here $\underline{e}^r$ denotes a unit vector along the r-th axis: $(\underline{e}^r)_i = \delta_{ri}$. In order to avoid having to attach the condition $K_r \ge 1$ to every equation, we employ the convention that any class-r unknown $X_r(\underline{K})$, $X_{ri}(\underline{K})$, $Q_{ri}(\underline{K})$, $W_{ri}(\underline{K})$, etc. is zero if $K_r \le 0$. Note that the conservation law

$$\sum_{i=1}^{M} Q_{ri}(\underline{K}) = K_r \qquad\qquad 1 \le r \le R \qquad\qquad (6)$$

is automatically satisfied by the recursion. Note also that the X's and W's can be eliminated, leaving only a recursion for the M Q's (actually only for $\{Q_i,\ i \in QC\}$):

$$Q_i(\underline{K}) = \sum_{r=1}^{R} Q_{ri}(\underline{K}) = \sum_{\substack{r=1 \\ K_r \ge 1}}^{R} \frac{K_r\, L_{ri}\,[1 + \chi(i \in QC)\, Q_i(\underline{K} - \underline{e}^r)]}{\displaystyle\sum_{j=1}^{M} L_{rj}\,[1 + \chi(j \in QC)\, Q_j(\underline{K} - \underline{e}^r)]}$$

$$1 \le i \le M \quad (7)$$

where the indicator function is

$$\chi(i \in QC) \equiv \begin{cases} 1 & i \in QC \\ 0 & i \in DC \end{cases}.$$

Server utilizations can be subsequently computed from

$$U_i(\underline{K}) = \sum_{r=1}^{R} U_{ri}(\underline{K}) = \sum_{\substack{r=1 \\ K_r \ge 1}}^{R} \frac{K_r\, L_{ri}}{\displaystyle\sum_{j=1}^{M} L_{rj}[1 + \chi(j \in QC)\, Q_j(\underline{K} - \underline{e}^r)]} \qquad i \in QC.$$

Unfortunately the exact recursion (1) to (5), or (7), has time computational complexity of $\mathrm{O}(MR\prod_{r=1}^{R}(1+K_r))$ and is usually impractical if $R \ge 5$. The same computational complexity and conclusion holds [7] when the convolution algorithm [6] is used to solve constant-rate product-form networks. This has motivated the investigation of approximation methods, in particular Schweitzer-Bard [1], [8] and linearizer [3]. The original linearizer uses the fractional deviations

$$D_{rit}(\underline{K}) \equiv \frac{Q_{ri}(\underline{K} - \underline{e}^t)}{K_r - \delta_{rt}} - \frac{Q_{ri}(\underline{K})}{K_r}$$

$$K_r \geq 1 + \delta_{rt}, K_t \geq 1, \quad 1 \leq r, t \leq R, \quad i \in QC \quad (8)$$

and rewrites (7) as

$$Q_{ri}(\underline{K}) = \frac{K_r L_{ri} \left\{ 1 + \chi(i \in QC) \sum_{\substack{t=1 \\ K_t \geq 1}}^{R} (K_t - \delta_{tr}) \left[D_{tir}(\underline{K}) + \frac{Q_{ti}(\underline{K})}{K_t} \right] \right\}}{\sum_{j=1}^{M} L_{rj} \left[1 + \chi(j \in QC) \left\{ \sum_{\substack{t=1 \\ K_t \geq 1}}^{R} (K_t - \delta_{tr}) \left[D_{tjr}(\underline{K}) + \frac{Q_{tj}(\underline{K})}{K_t} \right] \right\} \right]}$$

$$1 \leq r \leq R, \quad 1 \leq i \leq M . \quad (9)$$

The fixed point system (9) is called the *core problem* (for population $\underline{K}$) and its solution for the Q_{ri}'s, with $\underline{K}$ and D_{tir} fixed, is called the *core algorithm* (successive approximations appears to always work, if initialized with a uniform customer distribution $Q_{ri}(\underline{K}) \simeq K_r/M$). Actually it suffices to just solve (9) for $\{Q_{ri}, 1 \leq r \leq R, i \in QC\}$ and only afterwards to compute Q_{ri} for $i \in DC$.

With the replacement of $\underline{K}$ by $\underline{K} - \underline{e}^s$ and the approximation

$$D_{rit}(\underline{K} - \underline{e}^s) \simeq D_{rit}(\underline{K}) \quad 1 \leq r, s, t \leq R, \quad i \in QC \quad (10)$$

(9) becomes

$$Q_{ri}(\underline{K} - \underline{e}^s) =$$

$$\frac{(K_r - \delta_{rs}) L_{ri} \left\{ 1 + \chi(i \in QC) \sum_{\substack{t=1 \\ K_t \geq 1 + \delta_{ts}}}^{R} (K_t - \delta_{tr} - \delta_{ts}) \left[D_{tir}(\underline{K}) + \frac{Q_{ti}(\underline{K} - \underline{e}^s)}{K_t - \delta_{ts}} \right] \right\}}{\sum_{j=1}^{M} L_{rj} \left[1 + \chi(j \in QC) \left\{ \sum_{\substack{t=1 \\ K_t \geq 1 + \delta_{ts}}}^{R} (K_t - \delta_{tr} - \delta_{ts}) \left[D_{tjr}(\underline{K}) + \frac{Q_{tj}(\underline{K} - \underline{e}^s)}{K_t - \delta_{ts}} \right] \right\} \right]}$$

$$K_s \geq 1, \quad 1 \leq r, s \leq R, \quad 1 \leq i \leq K . \quad (11)$$

The original linearizer algorithm treats (8), (9), (11) together as a *fixed point problem* for the triple of unknowns $\{Q_{ri}(\underline{K}), Q_{ri}(\underline{K} - \underline{e}^s), D_{ris}(\underline{K}), 1 \leq r, s \leq R, i \in QC\}$. They may be solved by a specialized form of successive approximations (fix D's; solve (9), (11) separately for $\{Q_{ri}(\underline{K})\}$ and $\{Q_{ri}(\underline{K} - \underline{e}^s)\}$ by $R+1$

invocations of core algorithm; update D's via (8), and repeat). Generally less than 10 iterations are needed ([3] uses 3 iterations). Once the Q's are available, all other performance measures can be computed.

Several variants have been proposed to simplify the core problem. One, in [9], notes that the D's enter (9) only in the combination

$$E_{ri}(\underline{K}) \equiv \sum_{\substack{t=1 \\ K_t \geq 1}}^{R} (K_t - \delta_{tr})\, D_{tir}(\underline{K}) \ .$$

This reduces the number of unknowns (D's or E's) by a factor of R, but does not alter the numerical value of the variables.

Another variant [8] rewrites (9) as

$$Q_{ri}(\underline{K}) = \frac{K_r\, L_{ri}\left(1 + E_{ri}(\underline{K}) + Q_i(\underline{K}) - Q_{ri}(\underline{K})/K_r\right)}{C_r} \qquad 1 \leq r \leq R, \quad i \in QC$$

where C_r, the denominator in (9), is the mean cycle time for class-r customers. This permits elimination of Q_{ri} in favor of Q_i and C_r, thereby reducing the number of unknowns from $R|QC|$ to $R + |QC|$. The original core problem (9) (for fixed $\underline{K}$ and E_{ri}) is replaced by a joint fixed point problem in $\{Q_i\}$ and $\{C_r\}$. The numerical values are not altered by this change of variables.

Another variant, the AQL approximation in [11], uses

$$D_{it}^*(\underline{K}) \equiv \frac{Q_i(\underline{K} - \underline{e}^t)}{K_{\text{sum}} - 1} - \frac{Q_i(\underline{K})}{K_{\text{sum}}}$$

rather then $D_{rit}(\underline{K})$, and replaces (10) by the analogous approximation for D^*. This changes the numerical values. It has been found to produce comparable accuracy to the original linearizer, while reducing time and space complexity by a factor of R.

For the sake of consistency, all comparisons are done with original linearizer.

3   The New Approximation Technique

3.1   Approximation of the Absolute Deviations

The new approximation (referred to as QSA for Queue-Shift Approximation) is based upon *absolute* deviations, i. e., the shift in mean queue lengths, rather than upon the *fractional* deviations in (8). Specifically, we define

$$Y_{ri}(\underline{K}) \equiv Q_i(\underline{K} - \underline{e}^r) - [Q_i(\underline{K}) - 1] \qquad K_r \geq 1, \quad 1 \leq r \leq R, \quad i \in QC \quad (12)$$

(this replaces (8)) and rewrite (7) as

$$Q_i(\underline{K}) = \sum_{\substack{r=1 \\ K_r \geq 1}}^{R} \frac{K_r\, L_{ri}\,[Q_i(\underline{K}) + Y_{ri}(\underline{K})]}{\sum_{j \in QC} L_{rj}\,[Q_j(\underline{K}) + Y_{rj}(\underline{K})] + \sum_{j \in DC} L_{rj}} \qquad i \in QC \qquad (13a)$$

$$Q_i(\underline{K}) = \sum_{\substack{r=1 \\ K_r \geq 1}}^{R} \frac{K_r\, L_{ri}}{\sum_{j \in QC} L_{rj}\,[Q_j(\underline{K}) + Y_{rj}(\underline{K})] + \sum_{j \in DC} L_{rj}} \qquad i \in DC\ . \qquad (13b)$$

This replaces (9). Similarly, with $\underline{K}$ in (13) replaced by $\underline{K} - \underline{e}^s$, a replacement for (11) is obtained. The *new core algorithm* now denotes solving (13a) for $\{Q_i,\ i \in QC\}$, for fixed $\underline{K}$ and Y's. Then compute $\{Q_i,\ i \in DC\}$ via (13b). Note again that (6) and

$$\sum_{i=1}^{M} Q_i(\underline{K}) = K_{\text{sum}}$$

are satisfied automatically.

The remaining task is to specify an approximation for all $\{Y_{ri}(\underline{K})\}$ and for all $\{Y_{ri}(\underline{K} - \underline{e}^s)\}$. The simplest approach (cf. (10)) is to approximate

$$Y_{ri}(\underline{K} - \underline{e}^s) \simeq Y_{ri}(\underline{K}) \qquad 1 \leq r, s \leq R \quad i \in QC$$

which has an error of $O(1/K_{\text{sum}})$. It leads to a *two-level* QSA, and involves the fixed point triple of equations

$$\begin{aligned}
&\text{for } Q_i(\underline{K}) : \text{(13a) as written} &&(14a)\\
&\text{for } Q_i(\underline{K} - \underline{e}^s) : \text{(13a) with } \underline{K} \text{ replaced by } \underline{K} - \underline{e}^s, &&(14b)\\
&\qquad Q_i(\underline{K}) \text{ by } Q_i(\underline{K} - \underline{e}^s) \text{ and } Y_{ri}(\underline{K}) \text{ unchanged}\\
&\text{for } Y_{ri}(\underline{K}) : \text{(12) as written} &&(14c)
\end{aligned}$$

for the triple of unknowns $\{Q_i(\underline{K}),\ Q_i(\underline{K} - \underline{e}^s),\ Y_{ri}(\underline{K}),\ i \in QC, 1 \leq r, s \leq R\}$.

A more accurate approach is a *three-level* QSA with the approximation

$$Y_{ri}(\underline{K} - \underline{e}^s - \underline{e}^t) \simeq Y_{ri}(\underline{K} - \underline{e}^s) + Y_{ri}(\underline{K} - \underline{e}^t) - Y_{ri}(\underline{K})$$
$$1 \leq r, s, t \leq R \quad i \in QC \quad (15)$$

with an error of $O(1/K_{\text{sum}}^2)$. Note that (15) preserves the symmetry in s and t, which halves the effort in computing $Y_{ri}(\underline{K} - \underline{e}^s - \underline{e}^t)$ and $Q_i(\underline{K} - \underline{e}^s - \underline{e}^t)$. Equation (15) would be exact if $Y_{ri}(\underline{K})$ were an affine linear function of $\underline{K}$.

One now has a *fixed-point problem* for the quintuple of variables $\{Q_i(\underline{K}),\ Q_i(\underline{K} - \underline{e}^s),\ Q_i(\underline{K} - \underline{e}^s - \underline{e}^r),\ Y_{ri}(\underline{K}),\ Y_{ri}(\underline{K} - \underline{e}^s),\ i \in QC, 1 \leq r, s \leq R\}$. The five sets of equations are:

$$\text{for } Q_i(\underline{K}) \ : \ (13a) \text{ as written} \tag{16a}$$

$$\text{for } Q_i(\underline{K} - \underline{e}^s) \ : \ (13a) \text{ with } \underline{K} \text{ replaced by } \underline{K} - \underline{e}^s, \tag{16b}$$
$$Q_i(\underline{K}) \text{ by } Q_i(\underline{K} - \underline{e}^s)$$
$$\text{and } Y_{ri}(\underline{K}) \text{ by } Y_{ri}(\underline{K} - \underline{e}^s)$$

$$\text{for } Q_i(\underline{K} - \underline{e}^s - \underline{e}^t) \ : \ (13a) \text{ with } \underline{K} \text{ replaced by } \underline{K} - \underline{e}^s - \underline{e}^t, \tag{16c}$$
$$Q_i(\underline{K}) \text{ by } Q_i(\underline{K} - \underline{e}^s - \underline{e}^t) \text{ and}$$
$$Y_{ri}(\underline{K}) \text{ by } Y_{ri}(\underline{K} - \underline{e}^s) + Y_{ri}(\underline{K} - \underline{e}^t) - Y_{ri}(\underline{K})$$
$$[\text{cf. } (15)]$$

$$Y_{ri}(\underline{K}) \equiv 1 + Q_i(\underline{K} - \underline{e}^r) - Q_i(\underline{K}) \tag{16d}$$
$$K_r \geq 1, \quad 1 \leq r \leq R, \quad i \in QC$$

$$Y_{ri}(\underline{K} - \underline{e}^s) \equiv 1 + Q_i(\underline{K} - \underline{e}^r - \underline{e}^s) - Q_i(\underline{K} - \underline{e}^s) \tag{16e}$$
$$K_r, K_s \geq 1 + \delta_{rs}, \quad 1 \leq r, s \leq R, \quad i \in QC \ .$$

The storage requirements are comparable to the linearizer.

3.2   Remarks

1. The exact properties

$$\sum_{i=1}^{M} Q_i(\underline{K}) = K_{\text{sum}}$$

$$\sum_{i=1}^{M} Q_i(\underline{K} - \underline{e}^s) = K_{\text{sum}} - 1 \qquad K_s \geq 1$$

$$\sum_{i=1}^{M} Q_i(\underline{K} - \underline{e}^s - \underline{e}^t) = K_{\text{sum}} - 2 \qquad K_s, K_t \geq 1 + \delta_{st}$$

are maintained by the approximation. If there are no delay centers

$$\sum_{i=1}^{M} Y_{ri}(\underline{K}) = M - 1 \qquad 1 \leq r \leq R$$

$$\sum_{i=1}^{M} Y_{ri}(\underline{K} - \underline{e}^s) = M - 1 \qquad 1 \leq r, s \leq R$$

are also maintained.

2. Just as for linearizer, the fixed point problems (14) and (16) lacks a proof that a solution with non-negative Q's (and utilizations below unity) exists and is unique (empirically both properties hold).

4   Solution Algorithms for the Fixed-Point Problem

The user can choose any standard algorithm to solve the fixed point problem (16). We used our own implementation of a sophisticated Newton's method with global convergence [4], and we also implemented a version of successive substitutions, as in [3], exploiting the decomposition into $\frac{(R+1)\,(R+2)}{2}$ core problems. For solving the core problem, Newton worked well for us, but is known to fail occasionally. In a few percent of the cases, Newton terminated at unphysical solutions with some negative components. Successive approximations also usually worked well for solving the core problem, but in the few percent of the cases where it diverged, convergence was achieved by under-relaxation. However, applying successive approximations to the *whole* set (16) is not recommended, because [11] found similar examples where this "simultaneous iteration" diverged in 20% of the cases.

Our conclusion is that no single algorithm is guaranteed to always work well, but in practice one can always somehow solve the equations by taking suitable precautions.

The fixed point problems for linearizer (8), (9), (11) and QSA (14), (16) have similar structure and can be solved by similar iterative algorithms, e.g. successive substitutions or Newton's method. Of course, the solution should be independent of the computational algorithm chosen.

Iterative algorithms are sensitive to starting points, so similar starting points were used when solving the linearizer and QSA fixed point problems by either successive substitutions or Newton's method. The general observation is that the algorithms are robust for "reasonable" starting points, e. g. customers of each class equidistributed among the resources, but behave poorly if poor starting points are used: Newton can converge to unphysical solutions while the outer loop in successive substitutions can require dozens of iterations rather than the 3 iterations recommended in [3]. In addition, we found that the individual core problems for both linearizer and QSA were frequently very time consuming when solved by successive substitutions, requiring many hundreds of iterations. This justifies the additional attention given to starting points as well as the use of acceleration (extrapolation) techniques, to be reported separately, when solving the core problems.

Iterative algorithms are also sensitive to the termination criterion, so similar criteria were employed when comparing algorithms. In particular, there is the danger of premature termination without the desired accuracy. [11] describe ways of preventing premature termination. An appropriate termination criterion should involve both the change in the variables and the residual error between the left and right sides of (16). The suggestion in [3] to terminate after three iterations is not robust [11].

Just as for the linearizer algorithm, we lack formal proof that the algorithms will converge. Empirically the algorithms with precautions *always* converged and always led to the *same* solution despite varying the starting point: the fixed point with side conditions of non-negativity (and of utilizations at most one) appears to always exist and be unique.

5   Accuracy of the Approximation

We have implemented the four algorithms:

Acronym	Name	Main reference
MVA	Mean Value Analysis	[7]
SB	Schweitzer-Bard Algorithm	[1], [8]
LIN	Linearizer Algorithm	[3]
QSA	QSA Algorithm	This paper (16)

To evaluate the accuracy of the algorithms an extensive experimentation has been performed. The experiments consisted of randomly generated test cases (Sect. 5.1) and stress cases (Sect. 5.2).

5.1   Randomly Generated Test Cases

A large set of test cases were generated similar to those in [3], as follows: $M = 5$ stations, $R = 1$ to 4 classes. K_{sum} ranges from 50 to 500 in steps of 50. In all, there are 40 choices of the triple (M, R, K_{sum}), with 100 samples run for each, leading to 4000 test cases.

The 100 samples for each triple were generated as follows:

- All stations were either QC (with probability 0.95) or DC (with probability 0.05);
- The elements of the $R \times M$ matrix $[V_{ri}]$ were generated independently from the same continuous uniform distribution on $[0, 10]$;
- The elements of the $R \times M$ matrix $[S_{ri}]$ were generated as follows: if server i is DC, each S_{ri} was chosen independently from the same continuous uniform distribution on $[0, 10]$; if server i is QC, $S_{ri} = S_i$ for all r, where S_i is chosen from the same continuous uniform distribution on $[0, 10]$;
- The $R \times M$ matrix $[L_{ri}]$ was then generated as $[V_{ri}S_{ri}]$ and then 10% of the L_{ri} values were set to 0;
- The population vector $\underline{K} = (K_1, K_2, \dots, K_R)$ was chosen equally-likely from the set of integers vectors satisfying the conditions

$$\sum_{r=1}^{R} K_r = K_{sum}, \qquad K_r \geq 1 \text{ for } 1 \leq r \leq R .$$

The four algorithms were run on the 4000 samples. For each of the 100 samples of each triple (M, R, K_{sum}), we compute the errors (relative to MVA):

$$error\ on\ Q = \max_{ri}\left\{\frac{|Q_{ri}^{appr} - Q_{ri}^{MVA}|}{K_r}\right\}, \qquad error\ on\ U = \max_{ri}\{|U_{ri}^{appr} - U_{ri}^{MVA}|\}$$

$$(17)$$

where Q_{ri}^{appr} and U_{ri}^{appr} are obtained from the approximation considered and Q_{ri}^{MVA} and U_{ri}^{MVA} are given by the exact MVA. Table 1 entries are average error.

Table 1. Average errors for the approximations

number of classes	number of samples	approximation algorithm	average error	
			Q	U
$R = 1$	1000	SB	0.000144	0.000109
		LIN	0.000043	0.000024
		QSA	0.000000	0.000000
$R = 2$	1000	SB	0.002540	0.001892
		LIN	0.000290	0.000124
		QSA	0.000056	0.000028
$R = 3$	1000	SB	0.007468	0.005491
		LIN	0.000752	0.000492
		QSA	0.000245	0.000105
$R = 4$	1000	SB	0.022579	0.013798
		LIN	0.002485	0.001152
		QSA	0.001604	0.000625

Figure 1 shows the average errors for LIN and QSA as a function of the number of classes.

These results show that QSA has average errors at most half as big as those of LIN and in some cases was accurate to six or eight significant figures. As usual for all the approximation techniques, for a given population the average error increases with R (empirically by a factor of 2-10 as R increases by 1) due to the decrease in the number of jobs per class. As expected all methods had decreased errors as the population increased.

Let us remark that in 58% of the test cases, QSA gave errors of zero (at least 6 digits) while LIN achieves such accuracy in less than 2.5% of cases.

5.2   Stress Cases

For the stress cases we choose among the 4000 randomly generated test cases the ones in which LIN exhibited large errors and we compared them with the ones given by QSA. In most of the cases QSA significantly outperforms LIN.

As an example in Table 2 are reported the loadings (rounded) of the case exhibiting the largest errors in LIN. The network parameters are: $K = 5$ queueing stations, $R = 2$ classes, $\underline{K} = (21, 29)$.

The corresponding errors (17) on Q are 0.004459 for LIN and 0.001812 for QSA while the errors on U are 0.001900 for LIN and 0.000639 for QSA. QSA has roughly 1/2 the errors of LIN.

As another stress case we present the network, whose loadings are reported in Table 3, for which the ratio between the corresponding errors given by LIN and QSA is maximized. The network parameters are: $K = 5$ queueing stations, $R = 2$ classes, $\underline{K} = (111, 89)$.

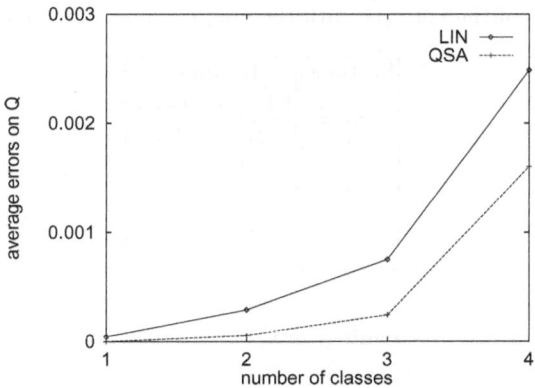

Fig. 1. Average errors on Q for LIN and QSA

Table 2. Loadings of the network with the largest error on LIN

Stations	Loadings	
	Class 1	Class 2
1	16	50
2	19	28
3	0	42
4	12	25
5	39	29

The errors on Q are $4.04\,10^{-5}$ for LIN and $4.18\,10^{-10}$ for QSA while the errors on U are $6.73\,10^{-5}$ for LIN and $5.54\,10^{-10}$ for QSA. QSA has roughly five orders of magnitude less error than LIN.

For a three-class stress case, we tested our algorithm on the example presented in [3]. The network parameters are: $K = 3$ queueing stations, $R = 3$ classes, $\underline{K} = (2,2,2)$ and the corresponding loadings are reported in Table 4. Let us remark that, in spite of the small number of jobs in this example the error of QSA with respect to that of LIN is very small.

The errors on Q are 0.000318 for LIN and 0.000185 for QSA while the errors on U are 0.000716 for LIN and 0.000415 for QSA. QSA has roughly 1/2 the errors of LIN.

6   Conclusions

A new approximation method is presented for closed product-form queueing networks with constant-rate servers. While this approximation has memory and computational requirements comparable to linearizer methods, its accuracy is generally better than linearizer for populations as small as 10-20, and its superiority increases as populations grow. Several stress cases are given where QSA

Table 3. Loadings of the network with the max ratio between errors of LIN and QSA

Stations	Loadings	
	Class 1	Class 2
1	16	73
2	59	15
3	6	26
4	2	36
5	10	0

Table 4. Loadings of the three-class stress case

Stations	Loadings		
	Class 1	Class 2	Class 3
1	10	1	1
2	1	10	1
3	1	1	10

outperforms linearizer. The accuracy achieved, on the order of 4-6 digits, appears sufficient to justify abandoning exact solution methods in favor of the approximation method, especially since the model input data is almost never this accurate. In 58% of the test cases, QSA gave errors of zero (at least 6 digits) while LIN achieves such accuracy in less than 2.5% of cases.

References

1. Y. Bard. Some extensions to multiclass queueing network analysis. In A. Butrimenko M. Arato and E. Gelenbe, editors, *Proceedings of the 4th International Symposium on Modelling and Performance Evaluation of Computer Systems*, Performance of Computer Systems, pages 51–62, Amsterdam, Netherlands, 1979. North-Holland Publishing Company.
2. F. Baskett, K. M. Chandy, R. R. Muntz, and F. G. Palacios. Open, closed, and mixed networks of queues with different classes of customers. *Journal of the ACM*, 22(2):248–260, April 1975.
3. K. M. Chandy and D. Neuse. Linearizer: A heuristic algorithm for queueing network models of computing systems. *Communications of the ACM*, 25(2):126–134, February 1982.
4. J. E. Dennis, Jr and R. B. Schnabel. *Numerical Methods for Unconstrained Optimization and Nonlinear Equations*. Prentice-Hall Series in Computational Mathematics. Prentice-Hall, Englewood Cliffs, New Jersey, 1983.
5. D. L. Eager and K. C. Sevcik. Bound hierarchies for multiple-class queueing networks. *Journal of the ACM*, 33(1):179–206, January 1986.
6. M. Reiser and H. Kobayashi. Queueing networks with multiple closed chains: Theory and computational algorithms. *IBM Journal of Research and Development*, 19:283–294, 1975.

7. M. Reiser and S. S. Lavenberg. Mean-value analysis of closed multichain queueing networks. *Journal of the ACM*, 27(2):313–322, April 1980.
8. P. J. Schweitzer. Approximate analysis of multiclass closed networks of queues. In *Proceedings of International Conference on Stochastic Control and Optimization*, Free University, Amsterdam, Netherlands, April 1979.
9. E. de Souza e Silva and R. R. Muntz. A note on the computational cost of the linearizer algorithm for queueing networks. *IEEE Transactions on Computers*, 39:840–842, 1990.
10. J. R. Spirn. Queueing networks with random selection for service. *IEEE Transactions on Software Engineering*, 3:287–289, 1979.
11. J. Zahorjan, D. L. Eager, and H. M. Sweillam. Accuracy, speed and convergence of approximate mean value analysis. *Performance Evaluation*, 8(4):255–270, 1988.

Experiments with Improved
Approximate Mean Value Analysis Algorithms [*]

Hai Wang and Kenneth C. Sevcik

Department of Computer Science
University of Toronto
Toronto, Ontario, Canada M5S 3G4
{hai,kcs}@cs.toronto.edu

Abstract. Approximate Mean Value Analysis (MVA) is a popular technique for analyzing queueing networks because of the efficiency and accuracy that it affords. In this paper, we present a new software package, called the *Improved Approximate Mean Value Analysis Library (IAMVAL)*, which can be easily integrated into existing commercial and research queueing network analysis packages. The IAMVAL packages includes two new approximate MVA algorithms, the Queue Line (QL) algorithm and the Fraction Line (FL) algorithm, for analyzing multiple class separable queueing networks. The QL algorithm is always more accurate than, and yet has approximately the same computational efficiency as, the Bard-Schweitzer Proportional Estimation (PE) algorithm, which is currently the most widely used approximate MVA algorithm. The FL algorithm has the same computational cost and, in noncongested separable queueing networks where queue lengths are quite small, yields more accurate solutions than both the QL and PE algorithms.

1 Introduction

Queueing network models have been widely adopted for the performance evaluation of computer systems and communication networks. While it is infeasible to compute the exact solution for the general class of queueing network models, solutions can be computed for an important subset, called *separable* (or *product-form*) queueing networks [2]. The solution for separable queueing networks can be obtained with modest computational effort using any of several comparably efficient exact algorithms. *Mean Value Analysis (MVA)* [9] is the most widely used of these algorithms. However, even for separable queueing networks, the computational cost of an exact solution becomes prohibitively expensive as the number of classes, customers, and centers grows. Numerous approximate MVA algorithms have been devised for separable queueing networks [1,10,4,3,6,14,17,15,11]. Among them, the Bard-Schweitzer Proportional Estimation (PE) algorithm [10] is a popular algorithm that has gained wide acceptance

---

[*] This research was supported by the Natural Science and Engineering Research Council of Canada (NSERC), and by Communications and Information Technology Ontario (CITO).

R. Puigjaner et al. (Eds.): Tools'98, LNCS 1469, pp. 280–291, 1998.

among performance analysts [5,8], and is used in most commercial and research queueing network solution packages.

In this paper, we present a new software package, called the *Improved Approximate Mean Value Analysis Library (IAMVAL)*, which includes two new approximate MVA algorithms for analyzing multiple class separable queueing networks. Both algorithms have approximately the same computational cost as the PE algorithm. The Queue Line (QL) algorithm always yields more accurate solutions, and hence it dominates the PE algorithm in the spectrum of different algorithms that trade off accuracy and efficiency. The Fraction Line (FL) algorithm yields more accurate solutions than both the QL and PE algorithms, but only for noncongested separable queueing networks where queue lengths are quite small. These two new algorithms have the accuracy, speed, limited memory requirements, and simplicity to be appropriate for inclusion in existing commercial and research queueing network analysis packages, and the IAMVAL library can be integrated into these software packages to replace the PE algorithm library.

The remainder of the paper is organized as follows. Section 2 reviews material relating to approximate MVA algorithms. Section 3 presents the QL and FL algorithms and their computational costs. Section 4 contains a comparison of the accuracy of the solutions of the PE, QL, and FL algorithms and discusses their relative merits. Finally, a summary and conclusions are provided in Section 5.

2   Background

Consider a closed separable queueing network [2,9] with C customer classes, and K load independent service centers. The customer classes are indexed as classes 1 through C, and the centers are indexed as centers 1 through K. The customer population of the queueing network is denoted by the vector $\overrightarrow{\mathbf{N}} = (N_1, N_2, ..., N_C)$ where N_c denotes the number of customers belonging to class c for $c = 1, 2, ..., C$. Also, the total number of customers in the network is denoted by $N = N_1 + N_2 + \cdots + N_C$. The mean service demand of a class c customer at center k is denoted by $D_{c,k}$ for $c = 1, 2, ..., C$, and $k = 1, 2, ..., K$. The think time of class c, Z_c, is the sum of the delay center service demands of class c.

For network population $\overrightarrow{\mathbf{N}}$, we consider the following performance measures of interest:

$R_{c,k}(\overrightarrow{\mathbf{N}})$ = the average residence time of a class c customer at center k.
$R_c(\overrightarrow{\mathbf{N}})$ = the average response time of a class c customer in the network.
$X_c(\overrightarrow{\mathbf{N}})$ = the throughput of class c.
$Q_{c,k}(\overrightarrow{\mathbf{N}})$ = the mean queue length of class c at center k.
$Q_k(\overrightarrow{\mathbf{N}})$ = the mean total queue length at center k.

Based on the *Arrival Instant Distribution* theorem [7,12], the exact MVA algorithm [9] involves the repeated applications of the following six equations, in which $\overrightarrow{\mathbf{n}} = (n_1, n_2, ..., n_C)$ is a population vector ranging from $\overrightarrow{\mathbf{0}}$ to $\overrightarrow{\mathbf{N}}$; $A_k^{(c)}(\overrightarrow{\mathbf{n}})$ is the average number of customers a class c customers finds already at center k

when it arrives there, given the network population $\vec{n}$; $\vec{1}_c$ is a C-dimensional vector whose c^{th} element is one and whose other elements are zeros; and $(\vec{n} - \vec{1}_c)$ denotes the population vector $\vec{n}$ with one class c customer removed:

$$A_k^{(c)}(\vec{n}) = Q_k(\vec{n} - \vec{1}_c), \tag{1}$$

$$R_{c,k}(\vec{n}) = D_{c,k} \cdot \left(1 + A_k^{(c)}(\vec{n})\right), \tag{2}$$

$$R_c(\vec{n}) = \sum_{k=1}^{K} R_{c,k}(\vec{n}), \tag{3}$$

$$X_c(\vec{n}) = \frac{n_c}{Z_c + R_c(\vec{n})}, \tag{4}$$

$$Q_{c,k}(\vec{n}) = R_{c,k}(\vec{n}) \cdot X_c(\vec{n}), \tag{5}$$

$$Q_k(\vec{n}) = \sum_{c=1}^{C} Q_{c,k}(\vec{n}), \tag{6}$$

with initial conditions $Q_k(\vec{0}) = 0$ for $k = 1, 2, ..., K$.

The key to the exact MVA algorithm is recursive expression in equation (1) which relates performance with population vector $\vec{n}$ to that with population vector $(\vec{n} - \vec{1}_c)$. This recursive dependence of the performance measures for one population on lower population levels causes both space and time complexities of the exact MVA algorithm to be $\Theta(KC \prod_{c=1}^{C}(N_c + 1))$. Thus, for large numbers of classes (more than ten) or large populations per class, it is not practical to solve networks with the exact MVA algorithm.

The approximate MVA algorithms for separable queueing networks improve the time and space complexities by substituting approximations for $A_k^{(c)}(\vec{N})$ that are not recursive. Among all approximate MVA algorithms, the Bard-Schweitzer Proportional Estimation (PE) algorithm [10] is a popular algorithm that is currently in wide use. The PE algorithm is based on the approximation

$$Q_{j,k}(\vec{N} - \vec{1}_c) \approx \begin{cases} \frac{N_c - 1}{N_c} Q_{c,k}(\vec{N}) & \text{for } c = j, \\ Q_{j,k}(\vec{N}) & \text{for } c \neq j. \end{cases}$$

Hence, the approximation equation that replaces equation (1) in the PE algorithm is

$$A_k^{(c)}(\vec{N}) = Q_k(\vec{N} - \vec{1}_c) = \sum_{j=1}^{C} Q_{j,k}(\vec{N} - \vec{1}_c) \approx Q_k(\vec{N}) - \frac{1}{N_c} Q_{c,k}(\vec{N}). \tag{7}$$

The system of nonlinear equations (2) through (7) of the PE algorithm can be solved iteratively by any general purpose numerical techniques, such as the successive substitution method or Newton's method [10,3,17,8]. Zahorjan et al. [17] found that no single implementation of the PE algorithm is guaranteed to always work well. When the PE algorithm is solved by Newton-like methods, the algorithm involves solving a nonlinear system of at least C equations [3,8], and the algorithm may fail to converge, or may converge to infeasible solutions [17]. When the PE algorithm is solved by the successive substitution method, the algorithm may converge very slowly in some cases, although it always yields feasible solutions [5] and converges very quickly for most networks [17]. When the PE algorithm is solved by the successive substitution method, the space complexity of the algorithm is $O(KC)$, and the time complexity is $O(KC)$ per iteration [10]. Thus, application of the PE algorithm is practical even for networks of up to about 100 classes and about 1000 service centers. The number of customers per class does not directly affect the amount of computation (although it may influence the speed of convergence).

3   The Queue Line and Fraction Line Approximate MVA Algorithms

In this section, two new iterative approximate MVA algorithms, the Queue Line (QL) algorithm and the Fraction Line (FL) algorithm, for multiple class separable queueing networks are presented. Both algorithms improve on the accuracy of the PE algorithm while maintaining approximately the same computational efficiency as the PE algorithm. The improvement with the FL algorithm occurs only in lightly loaded separable queueing networks, but the QL algorithm is more accurate than the PE algorithm in all cases.

3.1   The Queue Line Algorithm

The QL approximation is motivated by observing the graph of $Q_{c,k}(\vec{n})$ versus $\vec{n}$ (as shown in Figure 1). The PE approximation is equivalent to interpolating the value between the values of $Q_{c,k}(\vec{n})$ for 0 and n_c. The QL approximation interpolates instead between the values at 1 and n_c. As can be seen in Figure 1, the QL approximation is more accurate than the PE approximation for both bottleneck and non-bottleneck centers. The QL algorithm is based on the following approximations:

Approximation 1 (Approximations of the QL Algorithm).

(1) when $N_c = 1$ and $c = j$,
$$Q_{j,k}(\vec{N} - \vec{1}_c) = 0,$$
(2) when $N_c > 1$ and $c = j$,
$$\frac{Q_{j,k}(\vec{N}) - Q_{j,k}(\vec{N} - \vec{1}_c)}{1} = \frac{Q_{j,k}(\vec{N})\; Q_{j,k}(\vec{N} - (N_c - 1)\vec{1}_c)}{N_c - 1},$$
(3) when $N_c \geq 1$ and $c \neq j$,
$$Q_{j,k}(\vec{N} - \vec{1}_c) = Q_{j,k}(\vec{N}),$$

where $\vec{N} - \vec{1}_c$ denotes the population $\vec{N}$ with one class c customer removed, and $\vec{N} - (N_c - 1)\vec{1}_c$ denotes the population $\vec{N}$ with $N_c - 1$ class c customers removed.

Like the PE algorithm, the QL algorithm assumes that removing a class c customer does not affect the proportion of time spent by customers of any other classes at each service center. However, as shown in Figure 1, while the PE algorithm assumes the linear relationship between $Q_{c,k}(\overrightarrow{\mathbf{N}})$ and N_c, the QL algorithm estimates $Q_{c,k}(\overrightarrow{\mathbf{N}} - \overrightarrow{\mathbf{1}}_c)$ by linear interpolation between the points $(1, Q_{c,k}(\overrightarrow{\mathbf{N}} - (N_c - 1)\overrightarrow{\mathbf{1}}_c))$ and $(N_c, Q_{c,k}(\overrightarrow{\mathbf{N}}))$.

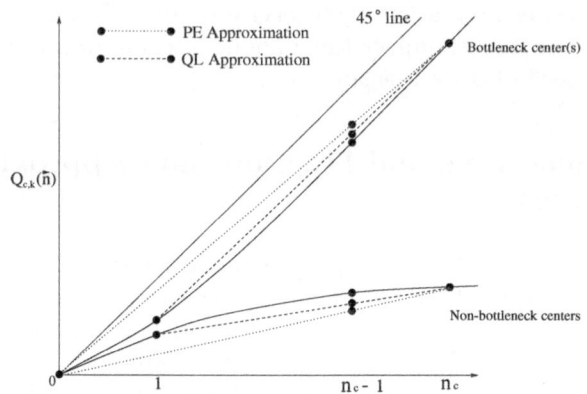

Fig. 1. Approximations of the PE and QL algorithms

Approximation 1 leads to the following approximation equation that replaces equation (1) in the QL algorithm [13,16].

QL Approximation Equation: *Under Approximation 1, the approximation equation of the QL algorithm is*

$$
\begin{cases}
\textbf{(1) when } N_c = 1, \quad A_k^{(c)}(\overrightarrow{\mathbf{N}}) = Q_k(\overrightarrow{\mathbf{N}}) - Q_{c,k}(\overrightarrow{\mathbf{N}}), \\
\textbf{(2) when } N_c > 1, \\
\quad A_k^{(c)}(\overrightarrow{\mathbf{N}}) = Q_k(\overrightarrow{\mathbf{N}}) - \frac{1}{N_c - 1}\left[Q_{c,k}(\overrightarrow{\mathbf{N}}) - Q_{c,k}(\overrightarrow{\mathbf{N}} - (N_c - 1)\overrightarrow{\mathbf{1}}_c)\right] \\
\qquad = Q_k(\overrightarrow{\mathbf{N}}) - \frac{1}{N_c - 1}\left\{Q_{c,k}(\overrightarrow{\mathbf{N}}) - \dfrac{D_{c,k}\left[1 + Q_k(\overrightarrow{\mathbf{N}}) - Q_{c,k}(\overrightarrow{\mathbf{N}})\right]}{Z_c + \sum_{l=1}^{K}\left\{D_{c,l}\left[1 + Q_l(\overrightarrow{\mathbf{N}}) - Q_{c,l}(\overrightarrow{\mathbf{N}})\right]\right\}}\right\}
\end{cases}
$$
$$\tag{8}$$

Note that when there is a single customer in class c, its residence time at a center k is given by

$$
R_{c,k}(\overrightarrow{\mathbf{N}} - (N_c - 1)\overrightarrow{\mathbf{1}}_c) = D_{c,k}\left[1 + Q_k(\overrightarrow{\mathbf{N}}) - Q_{c,k}(\overrightarrow{\mathbf{N}})\right],
$$

because it is expected that the arrival instant queue length is simply the equilibrium mean queue length of all other classes, excluding class c. This fact is used in the final substitution in equation (8) (and also equation (9)).

3.2   The Fraction Line Algorithm

The FL approximation is motivated by observing the graph of $\frac{Q_{c,k}(\vec{\mathbf{n}})}{n_c}$ versus n_c (as shown in Figure 2). In this case, the PE approximation takes the value of this ratio to be the same at $(n_c - 1)$ as at n_c. The FL approximation estimates the value at $(n_c - 1)$ by interpolating between the values at 1 and n_c. As can be seen in Figure 2, when n_c is sufficiently small, the FL approximation becomes more accurate than that of PE approximation for both bottleneck and non-bottleneck centers. The FL algorithm is based on the following approximations:

Approximation 2 (Approximations of the FL Algorithm).

(1) when $N_c = 1$ and $c = j$,
$$Q_{j,k}(\vec{\mathbf{N}} - \vec{\mathbf{1}}_c) = 0,$$
(2) when $N_c > 1$ and $c = j$,
$$\frac{Q_{j,k}(\vec{\mathbf{N}})}{N_c} - \frac{Q_{j,k}(\vec{\mathbf{N}} - \vec{\mathbf{1}}_c)}{N_c - 1} = \frac{1}{N_c - 1}\left[\frac{Q_{j,k}(\vec{\mathbf{N}})}{N_c} - \frac{Q_{j,k}(\vec{\mathbf{N}} - (N_c - 1)\vec{\mathbf{1}}_c)}{1}\right],$$
(3) when $N_c \geq 1$ and $c \neq j$,
$$Q_{j,k}(\vec{\mathbf{N}} - \vec{\mathbf{1}}_c) = Q_{j,k}(\vec{\mathbf{N}}),$$

where $\vec{\mathbf{N}} - \vec{\mathbf{1}}_c$ denotes the population $\vec{\mathbf{N}}$ with one class c customer removed, and $\vec{\mathbf{N}} - (N_c - 1)\vec{\mathbf{1}}_c$ denotes the population $\vec{\mathbf{N}}$ with $N_c - 1$ class c customers removed.

Like the PE and QL algorithms, the FL algorithm assumes that removing a class c customer does not affect the proportion of time spent by customers of any other classes at each service center. Furthermore, as shown in Figure 2, the FL algorithm estimates $Q_{c,k}(\vec{\mathbf{N}} - \vec{\mathbf{1}}_c)$ by linear interpolation between the points $(1, Q_{c,k}(\vec{\mathbf{N}} - (N_c - 1)\vec{\mathbf{1}}_c))$ and $(N_c, \frac{Q_{c,k}(\vec{\mathbf{N}})}{N_c})$.

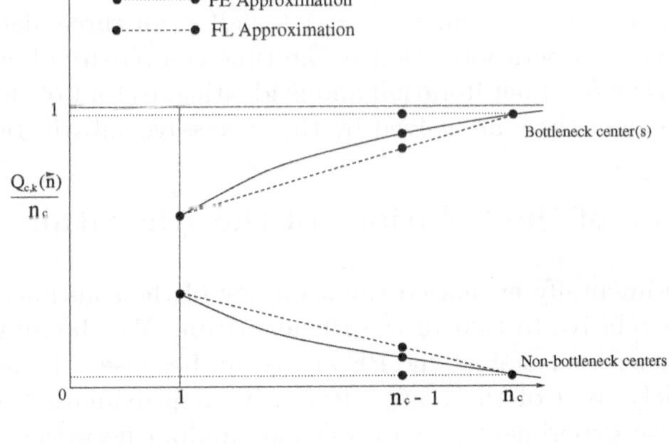

Fig. 2. Approximations of the PE and FL algorithms

Approximation 2 leads to the following approximation equation that replaces equation (1) in the FL algorithm [13,16].

FL Approximation Equation: *Under Approximation 2, the approximation equation of the FL algorithm is*

$$
\begin{cases}
\textbf{(1)} \text{ when } N_c = 1, \quad A_k^{(c)}(\vec{\mathbf{N}}) = Q_k(\vec{\mathbf{N}}) - Q_{c,k}(\vec{\mathbf{N}}), \\
\textbf{(2)} \text{ when } N_c > 1, \\
\quad A_k^{(c)}(\vec{\mathbf{N}}) = Q_k(\vec{\mathbf{N}}) - \frac{2}{N_c} Q_{c,k}(\vec{\mathbf{N}}) + Q_{c,k}(\vec{\mathbf{N}} - (N_c - 1)\vec{\mathbf{1}}_c) \\
\quad\quad = Q_k(\vec{\mathbf{N}}) - \frac{2}{N_c} Q_{c,k}(\vec{\mathbf{N}}) + \dfrac{D_{c,k}\left[1 + Q_k(\vec{\mathbf{N}}) - Q_{c,k}(\vec{\mathbf{N}})\right]}{Z_c + \sum_{l=1}^{K}\left\{D_{c,l}\left[1 + Q_l(\vec{\mathbf{N}}) - Q_{c,l}(\vec{\mathbf{N}})\right]\right\}}.
\end{cases}
$$

$$(9)$$

The system of nonlinear equations of the FL algorithm consists of (9) and (2) through (6), while that of the QL algorithm consists of (8) and (2) through (6). As with the PE algorithm, the system of nonlinear equations of either the QL or the FL algorithm can be solved by any general purpose numerical techniques.

When the QL and FL algorithms are solved by Newton-like methods, like the PE algorithm, each involves solving a nonlinear system of at least C equations, and the algorithm may fail to converge, or may converge to infeasible solutions [13,16]. When all three algorithms are solved by Newton-like methods, they involve solving the same number of nonlinear equations, and hence have approximately the same space and time complexities [13,16].

When the QL and FL algorithms are solved by the successive substitution method, like the PE algorithm, either algorithm may converge very slowly in some cases, although they converge quickly for most networks [13,16]. When all three algorithms are solved by the successive substitution method, their space complexities are all $O(KC)$ because of their similar structures. Moreover, for the networks in which $N_c > 1$ for all c, the QL algorithm requires $(10KC - K - C)$ additions/subtractions and $(6KC + C)$ multiplications/divisions per iteration, while the FL algorithm requires $(10KC - K - C)$ additions/subtractions and $(7KC + C)$ multiplications/divisions per iteration, as contrasted to $(4KC - K)$ additions/subtractions and $(3KC + C)$ multiplications/divisions for the PE algorithm. For networks in which $N_c = 1$ for all c, all three algorithms require the same number of operations. Hence, the time complexity of either the QL or FL algorithm is $O(KC)$ per iteration and is identical to that of the PE algorithm when all three algorithms are solved by the successive substitution method.

4   Accuracy of the Solutions of the Algorithms

We have experimentally evaluated the accuracy of the solutions of the QL and FL algorithms relative to that of the PE algorithm. We choose to compare the QL and FL algorithms against the PE algorithm because it is the most popular and most widely used of the many alternative approximate MVA algorithms. In each of these experiments, two thousand random networks were generated and solved by each of the three approximate algorithms and by the exact MVA algorithm. The mean absolute relative errors in estimating the quantities, X_c, R_c, and $Q_{c,k}$, relative to the corresponding exact values, X_c^*, R_c^*, and $Q_{c,k}^*$, were calculated in each case according to the following formulae:

- For throughput, $\Gamma_X = \frac{1}{C} \sum_{c=1}^{C} \left| \frac{X_c - X_c^*}{X_c^*} \right|$;
- For response time, $\Gamma_R = \frac{1}{C} \sum_{c=1}^{C} \left| \frac{R_c - R_c^*}{R_c^*} \right|$;
- For average queue length, $\Gamma_Q = \frac{1}{KC} \sum_{c=1}^{C} \sum_{k=1}^{K} \frac{|Q_{c,k} - Q_{c,k}^*|}{Q_{c,k}^*}$.

Also, the maximum absolute relative error in $Q_{c,k}$ was noted:

$$\Lambda_Q = \max_{c,k} \frac{|Q_{c,k} - Q_{c,k}^*|}{Q_{c,k}^*}.$$

For each of these error measures (M), we calculated the sample mean $(\overline{M})$ and sample standard deviation (S_M) over the 2000 trials in each experiment. We also recorded the maximum value of Λ_Q $(\max(\Lambda_Q))$ over the 2000 trials in each experiment.

4.1 Experiments for Multiple Class Separable Queueing Networks

In the first set of experiments, two thousand random networks were generated and solved by each of the three approximate algorithms and the exact MVA algorithm for each number of classes from one to four. The parameters used to generate the random networks are given in Table 1. The mean absolute relative errors in throughput, response time, queue length, and the maximum absolute relative errors in queue length are shown in Table 2. Additional statistics on error measures are presented elsewhere [16]. In these the experimental results, the QL

Table 1. Parameters for generating multiple class separable queueing networks

Server discipline:	Load independent
Population size (N_c):	Class 1: Uniform(1,10)
	Class 2: Uniform(1,10)
	Class 3: Uniform(1,10)
	Class 4: Uniform(1,10)
Number of centers (K):	Uniform(2,10)
Loadings ($D_{c,k}$):	Uniform(0.1,20.0)
Think time of customers (Z_c):	Uniform(0.0,100.0)
Number of trials (samples):	2000

algorithm always yielded smaller errors than the PE algorithm for all randomly generated networks. We found that the FL algorithm yields larger errors than the PE and QL algorithms for some networks, although it yielded smaller errors

Table 2. Summary of statistical results of each algorithm for multiple class separable queueing networks whose parameters are specified in Table 1

Measure	Algorithm	1 class	2 classes	3 classes	4 classes
$\overline{\Gamma_X}$	PE	0.40%	0.73%	0.82%	0.90%
	QL	0.31%	0.67%	0.79%	0.88%
	FL	0.05%	0.47%	0.67%	0.80%
$\overline{\Gamma_R}$	PE	0.59%	0.99%	1.04%	1.09%
	QL	0.45%	0.91%	0.99%	1.06%
	FL	0.06%	0.63%	0.84%	0.96%
$\overline{\Gamma_Q}$	PE	0.69%	1.23%	1.45%	1.64%
	QL	0.55%	1.15%	1.40%	1.61%
	FL	0.11%	0.83%	1.20%	1.47%
$\max(\Lambda_Q)$	PE	15.19%	14.82%	14.63%	16.20%
	QL	13.13%	14.41%	14.49%	16.12%
	FL	10.82%	11.98%	13.64%	15.62%

than the PE and QL algorithms for most of the networks among our test cases. We also found that the error of the FL algorithm rises faster than those of the QL and PE algorithms as the number of classes increases. By applying the statistical hypothesis testing procedure [16], we can further conclude that, on the average, the accuracy of all three approximate MVA algorithms decreases as the number of classes increases, and the FL algorithm is the most accurate while the PE algorithm is the least accurate algorithm among the three algorithms for multiple class separable queueing networks with sufficiently small population. However, these conclusions are only valid for small networks with a small number of classes, and small customer populations as governed by the parameters in Table 1. Although we would like to have experimented with larger networks with more classes and larger populations, the execution time of obtaining the exact solution of such networks prevented us from doing so.

4.2 Experiments for Single Class Separable Queueing Networks

In order to gain some insight into the behavior of the three approximate MVA algorithms for larger networks than those whose parameters are specified in Table 1, the second set of experiments was performed. This involved five experiments for single class separable queueing networks. We chose single class separable queueing networks because it is feasible to obtain the exact solution of such networks. The parameters used to generate the random networks in each of these experiments are given in Table 3. The detailed experimental results for these five experiments are presented elsewhere [16].

In these experiments, we also found the QL algorithm was more accurate than the PE algorithm for all randomly generated single class separable queueing networks. Moreover, we found that both the PE and QL algorithms always yield a higher mean response time and a lower throughput relative to the exact

Table 3. Parameters for generating single class separable queueing networks

Parameter	Experiment	Value
Population size (N)	1	Uniform(2,10)
	2	Uniform(20,100)
	3,4,5	Uniform(2,100)
Number of centers (K)	1,2,3	Uniform(2,10)
	4	Uniform(50,100)
	5	Uniform(100,200)
Loadings (D_k)	1,2,3,4,5	Uniform(0.1,20.0)
Think time of customers (Z)	1,2,3,4,5	Uniform(0.0,100.0)
Server discipline	1,2,3,4,5	Load independent
Number of trials (samples)	1,2,3,4,5	2000

solution. These results are consistent with the known analytic results [5,13]. We also found that the FL algorithm tended to yield a lower mean system response time and a higher throughput relative to the exact solution. However, some networks for which the FL algorithm yields a higher mean system response time and a lower throughput have been observed. By applying the same statistical testing procedure as in the first set of experiments [16], we conclude that given a network, as the population increases, the accuracy of the FL algorithm degrades. Moreover, given the network population, when the number of centers increases, the accuracy of the FL algorithm increases and the FL algorithm yields more accurate solutions than the other two algorithms. When the network is congested, the average queue length at some centers is large, and the approximations of both the PE and the QL algorithms lead to better approximations than those of the FL algorithm. These results are also consistent with the results of the first set of experiments.

4.3   Examples

We investigated some specific examples of single class separable queueing networks to illustrate how the QL algorithm dominates the PE algorithm, and the FL algorithm is the most accurate in low congestion networks, but the least accurate in high congestion networks among the three approximate MVA algorithms. The network parameters of four such examples are given in Table 4. For these cases, the absolute value of the difference between the approximate response time and the exact response time is used to measure the accuracy of an approximate MVA algorithm. Figure 3 shows the errors for the PE, QL, and FL algorithms as a function of the population for Example 1. The corresponding graphs for the other three examples all have exactly the same form. From this we conclude that the basic form of the curves shown in Figure 3 is robust across broad classes of single class separable queueing networks.

Table 4. Network parameters of examples

Example	Parameters (The subscript c on network parameters is dropped since $C=1$.)
1	$C = 1, K = 2, D_1 = 1.0, D_2 = 2.0, Z = 0.0, N \in [1, 50]$
2	$C = 1, K = 2, D_1 = 10.0, D_2 = 20.0, Z = 10.0, N \in [1, 50]$
3	$C = 1, K = 3, D_1 = 10.0, D_2 = 20.0, D_3 = 30.0, Z = 0.0, N \in [1, 50]$
4	$C = 1, K = 3, D_1 = 10.0, D_2 = 20.0, D_3 = 30.0, Z = 50.0, N \in [1, 50]$

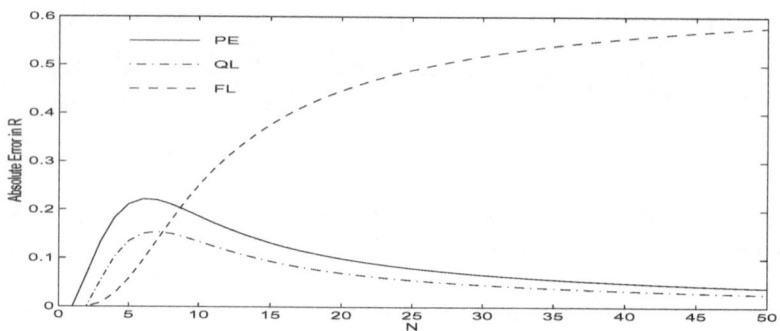

Fig. 3. Plot of the absolute error in R vs N for Example 1

5   Summary and Conclusions

Two new approximate MVA algorithms for separable queueing networks, the QL and FL algorithms, are presented. Both the QL and FL algorithms have approximately the same computational costs as the PE algorithm. Based on the experimental results, the QL algorithm is always more accurate than the PE algorithm. Moreover, as with the PE algorithm, the solutions of the QL algorithm are always pessimistic relative to those of the exact MVA algorithm for single class separable queueing networks. Specifically, both the PE and QL algorithms always yield a higher mean system response time and a lower throughput for single class separable queueing networks. These properties, which we have observed in the experiments described here, have been formally proven to hold as well [13,16]. The FL algorithm is more accurate than the QL and PE algorithms for noncongested separable queueing networks where queue lengths are small, and is less accurate than the QL and PE algorithms for congested separable queueing networks where queue lengths are large.

The FL algorithm must be used only with caution since its accuracy deteriorates as the average queue lengths increase. The QL algorithm always has higher accuracy than the PE algorithm. In particular, the QL algorithm dominates the PE algorithm in the spectrum of different approximate MVA algorithms that trade off accuracy and efficiency. The IAMVAL library which includes the QL and FL algorithms can be integrated into existing commercial and research queueing network analysis packages to replace the PE algorithm library.

References

1. Y. Bard. Some extensions to multiclass queueing network analysis. In: M. Arato, A. Butrimenko and E. Gelenbe, eds. *Performance of Computer Systems*, North-Holland, Amsterdam, Netherlands, 1979.
2. F. Baskett, K. M. Chandy, R. R. Muntz and F. G. Palacios. Open, closed, and mixed networks of queues with different classes of customers. *Journal of the ACM*, 22(2):248-260, April 1975.
3. W.-M. Chow. Approximations for large scale closed queueing networks. *Performance Evaluation*, 3(1):1-12, 1983.
4. K. M. Chandy and D. Neuse. Linearizer: A heuristic algorithm for queueing network models of computing systems. *Communications of the ACM*, 25(2):126-134, February 1982.
5. D. L. Eager and K. C. Sevcik. Analysis of an approximation algorithm for queueing networks. *Performance Evaluation*, 4(4):275-284, 1984.
6. C. T. Hsieh and S. S. Lam. PAM – A noniterative approximate solution method for closed multichain queueing networks. *ACM SIGMETRICS Performance Evaluation Review*, 16(1):261-269, May 1988.
7. S. S. Lavenberg and M. Reiser. Stationary state probabilities of arrival instants for closed queueing networks with multiple types of customers. *Journal of Applied Probability*, 17(4):1048-1061, December 1980.
8. K. R. Pattipati, M. M. Kostreva and J. L. Teele. Approximate mean value analysis algorithms for queueing networks: existence, uniqueness, and convergence results. *Journal of the ACM*, 37(3):643-673, July 1990.
9. M. Reiser and S. S. Lavenberg. Mean value analysis of closed multichain queueing networks. *Journal of the ACM*, 27(2):313-322, April 1980.
10. P. J. Schweitzer. Approximate analysis of multiclass closed networks of queues. *Proceedings of International Conference on Stochastic Control and Optimization*, 25-29, Amsterdam, Netherlands, 1979.
11. P. J. Schweitzer, G. Serazzi and M. Broglia. A queue-shift approximation technique for product-form queueing networks. Technical Report, 1996.
12. K. C. Sevcik and I. Mitrani. The distribution of queueing network states at input and output instants. *Journal of the ACM*, 28(2):358-371, April 1981.
13. K. Sevcik and H. Wang. An improved approximate mean value analysis algorithm for solving separable queueing network models. submitted for publication, 1998.
14. E. de Souza e Silva, S. S. Lavenberg and R. R. Muntz. A clustering approximation technique for queueing network models with a large number of chains. *IEEE Transactions on Computers*, C-35(5):419-430, May 1986.
15. E. de Souza e Silva and R. R. Muntz. A note on the computational cost of the linearizer algorithm for queueing networks. *IEEE Transactions on Computers*, 39(6):840-842, June 1990.
16. H. Wang. *Approximate MVA Algorithms for Solving Queueing Network Models*. M. Sc. Thesis, Tech. Rept. CSRG-360, University of Toronto, Toronto, Ontario, Canada, 1997.
17. J. Zahorjan, D. L. Eager and H. M. Sweillam. Accuracy, speed, and convergence of approximate mean value analysis. *Performance Evaluation*, 8(4):255-270, 1988.

Extending SMART2 to Predict the Behaviour of PL/SQL-based Applications

Juan Luis Anciano Martin[1], Nunzio Nicoló Savino Vázquez[2], José Antonio Corbacho[3] and Ramon Puigjaner[2]

[1] Dept. of Computer Science and Information Technology
Universidad Simón Bolívar
Aptdo. 89000. Caracas, 1080-A. Venezuela
janciano@ldc.usb.ve

[2] Dept. of Mathematics and Computer Science
Universitat de les Illes Balears
Crtra. de Valldemossa, Km. 7.5. Palma, E-07071. Spain
{dminsv9,dmirpt0}@ps.uib.es

[3] Dept. of European Projects. TransTOOLS C.A
World Trade Center Building s/n
Isla de la Cartuja. Seville, E-41092. Spain
jacorbacho@transtools.com

Abstract. Information Systems are nowadays becoming more and more complex and the use of the parallel and distributed approaches has introduced new difficulties in trying to guarantee the performance of end-user applications. In addition, the increasing volume of data to be stored, managed and processed requires to have a well-tuned database and well-designed-and-optimised database programs. SMART2 was developed as an initial solution to cop with the problem of predicting the performance of SQL-based relational programs. In this paper an extension of the SMART2 workbench for predicting the performance of PL/SQL applications is presented. The proposed tool provides end-users with a graph-oriented formalism for specifying the essential characteristics of the application he/she is conceiving and capabilities for matching software components and operational environment.

1 Introduction

When considering a database application as a Software Performance Engineering product, one feasible option to be taken into account is the one of using simulation techniques specially when analytical models cannot be easily established by simple inspection of the software structure and the operational environment. The main advantage of the performance modelling and simulation approaches is their ability to intervene into the earliest phases of the application's life cycle. Moreover, application models can be refined throughout the life cycle phases thus offering a good tool, as far as performance evaluation is concerned, for option validation during the development phase and for supporting activities such as capacity planning and load testing during the operational phase. In [2][3][9]

R. Puigjaner et al. (Eds.): Tools'98, LNCS 1469, pp. 292–305, 1998.
© Springer-Verlag Berlin Heidelberg 1998

simulation was intensively applied for establishing performance models of the activity queries in relational and active DBMSs, considering the hierarchy of low level models (disks and CPU).

As an effort to introduce the principles of the Software Performance Engineering discipline into the universe of relational database applications and event-oriented programming from the end-user point of view, in this paper a simulation-based workbench for predicting the performance of PL/SQL applications is presented. The proposed tool is based on providing end-users with a graphical notation for specifying the essential characteristics of the application he/she is conceiving and the ability to match the software components with the parameterised operational environment (RDBMS, hardware, network and operating system) on which applications are executed. The workbench was conceived as a component of HELIOS[1] [5][6], a CASE tool for predicting the behaviour of second generation client-server systems, that extends the functionality of SMART2[2].

The workbench interacts with end-users to establish the hardware and software configuration for a PL/SQL application to be analysed. From the user inputs, the workbench generates a four-layered dynamic and static performance simulation model that represents the end-user application, the PL/SQL engine, the ORACLE RDBMS, and the hardware and network components. By simulating some target application, the workbench provides results related to the communication servers, the usage of CPU, network, disks and the statistics on the execution of the user application. For this last logical component, results are provided at different levels: transaction, program and overall application.

This paper is organised as follows: Section 2 describes the overall workbench's architecture, modules and functions. The layered structure of the dynamically generated performance model is described in section 3. Section 4 presents the mechanism for specifying PL/SQL applications in the workbench. Section 5 summarises the mechanisms for workload specification in the proposed workbench. Section 5 presents an example of how an end-user application could be specified using the workbench. Finally, section 6 summarises the conclusions and further studies related to this research.

2   The SMART2-Extended Workbench

SMART2[2][13] is a performance evaluation tool for relational transactional applications. As database applications are becoming more complex and their resource comsumption is highly increasing, the goal of SMART2 is to help in the performance prediction of a database system in order to assist designers in making choices on critical issues during the whole lifetime of the project. Though

---

[1] Hierarchical Evaluation of Large Information Open Systems ESPRIT IV Project n. 22354. Research group conformed by IONA Technologies (Ireland), University of Southampton (United Kingdom), IFATEC/REDWOOD (France), TransTOOLS (Spain), Ecóle Polytechnique Fédérale de Lausanne (Switzerland) and the Universitat de les Illes Balears (Spain)

SMART2 is based on simulation techniques, it uses analytical Valued Query Execution Plans to evaluate the cost of a query or a transaction in terms of time and resource consumption. In this section, the essential features of SMART2 extended in the new workbench are described and related with the new provided PL/SQL processing facilities.

2.1   Underlying Modelling Method

Within software performance engineering[14], the proposed workbench is mainly dedicated to apply performance prediction (and possibly testing) to PL/SQL applications using simulation techniques. The main advantage of the modelling and simulation approach is its ability to intervene very early within the life cycle of an application, as early as the conception phase. Moreover, application models can be refined throughout the phases of the application life cycle, thus offering a good mean for option validation during the development phase and for supporting activities such as capacity planning and load testing during operational phase. Therefore, depending on the application life cycle phase considered, an end-user of the workbench could be either a PL/SQL application designer/developer, in conception and development phases, or a PL/SQL application manager in operational phase.

Having the previous premises, the first aim is the one of proposing a method that can be applied in every phase of the software life cycle. The method shown in figure 1, originally proposed in SMART2 and kept and extended in the workbench, is composed of four steps:

- **Component definition**: In this step, the user can define the essential characteristics of the hardware and software platforms where his/her applications run. During this step, components as processors, controllers and devices, the LAN (Ethernet), IP-routers and versions of DBMS servers are defined. The workbench includes some predefined components for servers, disk and drivers (models based on the SCSI or SCSI2 technologies), workstations, PC, terminals, ORACLE v6.0, ORACLE v7.0 and the PL/SQL engine.
- **Configuration definition**: Architecture includes hardware and system description and is termed *configuration* in the method. It is in this step when user puts together the hardware and software components to define the final operating environment where his/her PL/SQL application will be executed.
- **Application definition**: Application is the step devoted to the software specification and is based on the data and transaction models description. The data is mainly specified as the structure of the database and its corresponding estimated size. Transactions are specified through a graph-based formalism called *PL/SQL Transaction Graphs*. *Transaction Graphs* are indistinctly used for specifying user-defined transactions (PL/SLQ blocks and stored procedures) or the database dynamic behaviour (triggers and stored procedures).
- **Scenario definition**: During this step, the user can specify the entry load of the transactions and locate the data required by the application. Thus, a scenario is the merge between a configuration and an application.

- **Evaluation and Results Analysis**: When the user believes his/her scenario is fine, he/she is ready to run a simulation and get some performance results. Results are grouped in performance objects (server machines, software servers, transactions, programs, etc.). and are based on average, standard deviation, maximun and minimum values obtained from the whole simulation. However, most of them are presented with their confidence interval, to check how relevant is the execution of the simulation. This information can be displayed in different ways and analysed to determine bottlenecks and perform further capacity planning studies for the systems and operational environment.

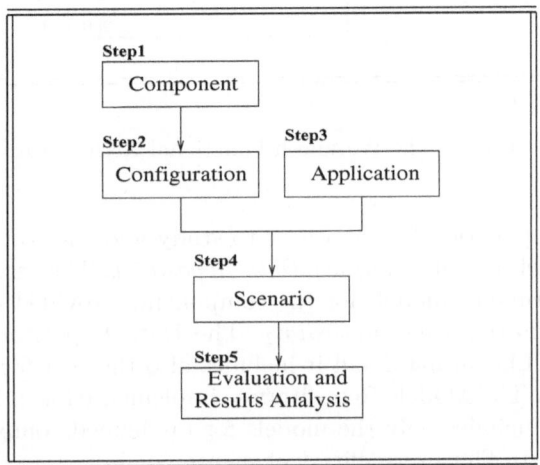

Fig. 1. The Method proposed by the workbench

2.2   Architecture

The workbench was conceived as a Java application interacting with the Oracle 7.3.2 RDBMS and with QNAP2V9, an interpreter of QNAP2[8], a modelling language with basic type extensions and simulation capabilities. Figure 2 shows the general architecture of the workbench.

The modules that compose the workbench are the following:

- **Man Machine Interface**. The interface aims at providing the user with a friendly way to enter the information required by the workbench platform and to obtain the results of the simulation. The interface items handled completely match with the step of the modelling method prevously described.
- **Repository**. The repository has two data domains derived from two different sources. The first one is related to the information the user provides

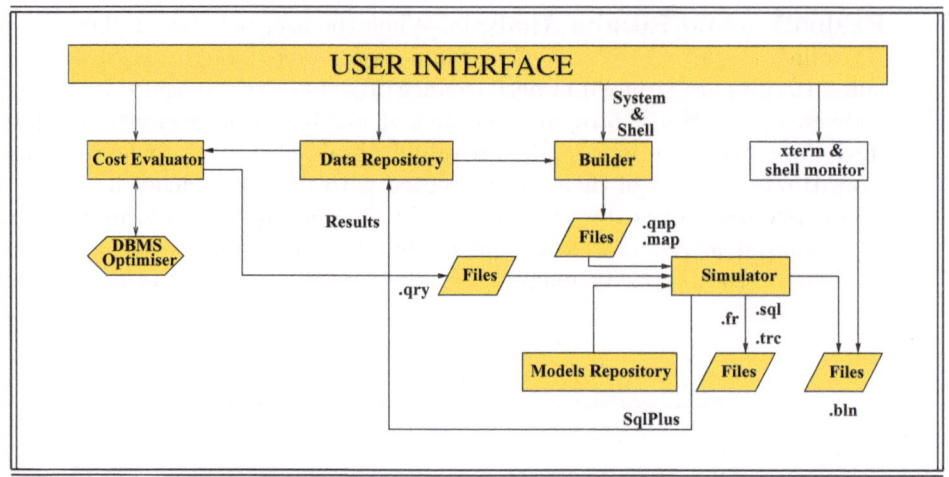

Fig. 2. The Workbech Functional Architecture

about the application he/she wants to study and the static data needed by the workbench and it is termed *Data Repository*. The second one is related to the performance models for the components provided by the workbench and it is termed *Models Repository*. The Data Repository is implemented as an ORACLE database and it includes also the cost formulas to evaluate SQL queries. The Models Repository is implemented as a library of QNAP2 macros and includes only the models for predefined components (hardware and software). The user-defined elements (mainly regarding PL/SQL applications) are not stored in the Models Repository since they are stored as data during the Application stage. The models repository was specified using HOOMA[11][12], an object-oriented method for specifying queuing network simulation performance models.

– **Builder**. The Builder is the module that generates the final simulation model for the environment (hardware, network, RDBMS and PL/SQL application) that the user wants to study. It reads the database and, given a scenario, generates the dynamic QNAP2 objects (referring to the PL/SQL application) and retrieves the needed QNAP2 macros from the models' repository. Its output is the QNAP2 program representing the system to be simulated.

– **Simulator**. The Simulator is the core of the system. This module is in charge of launching the QNAP2 interpreter to run the simulation of the model generated by the builder. When a simulation is started and completed, it generates an output file and stores the results into the data repository. The workbench provides results related to the communication servers, CPU, network and disks and the user application. For this last logical component, results are provided at different levels: transactions, modules an overall application. The user can visualise these results in different ways using the results browsing facility provided by the interface.

- **Cost Evaluator**. This module is used only when the PL/SQL application interacts with the DBMS. Up to now only performance models for the ORACLE RDBMS optimisation techniques and evaluation of query plans are available. This module is in charge of computing the cost of a query included in a SQL statement. To do that, it uses the real query execution plan and evaluates the execution time of each operation with the help of the cost formula table store in the data repository.

3 The Hierarchy of Performance Models

As the overall structure of a distributed application is conformed by the different levels of virtual machines and hardware configuring the system, the workbench is based on generating a hierarchy of performance models that interact during the simulation process. Some of the models have a static nature, i.e. the behaviour of the components is independent from the user inputs; and some others totally depend (either in behaviour or in workload characterisation) on the user inputs.

The Models Repository stores static performance models while the builder generates dynamic performance models. Nevertheless, the static models are parameterised on the configuration and scenario features that users can establish during a workbench session. Figure 3 shows the hierarchy of performance models handled in the workbench. The workbench is four-layered as follows:

- **Hardware Layer**: Include models for the basic hardware components providing processing capabilities like SMP systems, clustering systems, I/O drivers and disks.
- **Network Layer**: Include the models for the basic hardware components providing internetworking capabilities for WANs and Ethernet-based LANs.
- **RDBMS Layer**: The RDBMS Layer provides the information necessary for simulating the execution of PL/SQL and SQL statements issued by the simulated PL/SQL application and executable database objects stored managed by the DBMS. In this sense, this layer keeps the information related with the ORACLE instances included in the user-defined distributed platform. This layer includes the needed models for the components aimed at providing the access to databases. The ORACLE v 6.0, ORACLE v7.0, Valued Query Execution Plan (VQEP), Log Writer (LGWR), Database Writer (DBWR) and PL/SQL Engine performance models belong to this layer.
- **Application Layer**: The PL/SQL Application Layer provides support for simulating PL/SQL applications. As the closest-to-user layer in the hierarchy, the Application Layer must deal both with the user specification of PL/SQL applications and the framework for simulating these applications. In this layer the abstraction of workstation set and terminal set for associating PL/SQL applications with the workload that they generate is defined. This is a hybrid layer conformed by static performance models and dynamic performance models corresponding to the application being studied. The main dynamic abstraction introduced by this layer is the *PL/SQL Transac-*

tion Graph. The static performance level is composed by a set of models representing clients and communication interfaces with the RDBMS.

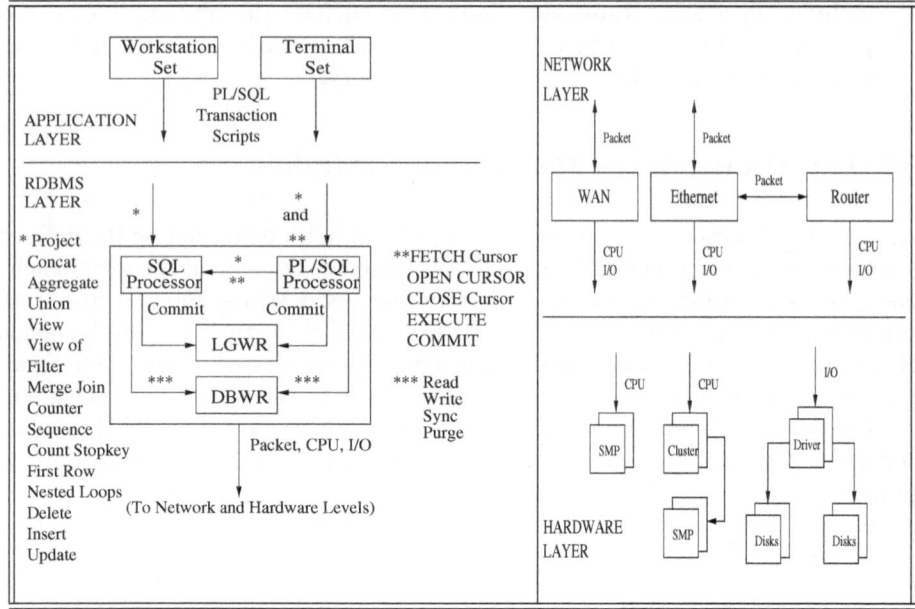

Fig. 3. Hierarchy of Performance Level in the Workbench's Models Repository

4   Modelling Paradigm of PL/SQL Applications

A PL/SQL application can be considered as a set of programs (transaction or anonymous blocks, stored procedures or nominal blocks and triggers) whose behaviour can be described by a sequence of SQL statements. Since PL/SQL is a procedural extension of SQL, services provided by the PL/SQL engine rely on services provided by the ORACLE server to process SQL statements.

Two types of operations can be abstracted from a PL/SQL program:

- **Database-independent operations**: In this category, we include all the procedural operations that a PL/SQL program can execute. Examples of these language constructs are sums, data structures accesses, variable accesses, etc. In order to simplify the domain, we have introduced another level of abstraction that goes deeper and summarises all these operations as CPU instructions.
- **Database-dependent operations**: In this category are included all the operations executed by the DBMS as a result of a SQL native Data Manipulation Language statement or a PL/SQL statement (cursors handling).

Users are provided with the following operations to model a PL/SQL application:

- **CPU Operation**: This operation summarises all the statements can be performed in a PL/SQL block that do not imply flow of control and request to the database management system, like assignments, comparison, constant arithmetic expressions, between others. The performance-affecting parameter of this operation is the number (in millions) of CPU instructions to be performed by the CPU.
- **SQL Database Operations**: Represent the request of services sent to the database management system. The following SQL DML and Control Language statements are provided:
  - **DML_OP**: Represents any of the SQL Data Manipulation Language statements to be executed in co-operation with the SQL processor of the ORACLE instance associated to the PL/SQL engine. In this category are therefore included the INSERT, DELETE, UPDATE and SELECT SQL statements. The parameter required for this type of operation is the SQL text representing the operation.
  - **COMMIT**: Commits all the changes in the database, performed since the last commit statement. There are no parameters for this type of operation.
  - **Subprogram Operations**, to specify invoacations to an application-defined sub-program. The information necessary to complete this type of operation is the name of the subprogram to be executed.
- **Database Cursor Operations**: A cursor is just a temporal structure used for maintaining query results in main memory for later processing. This structure allows the sequential processing of each one of the rows returned by a query. PL/SQL provides three basic instructions to work with cursors and provided by the workbench to users:
  - **OPEN**: Send a query to the database management system. The information for this operation is the identifier of the cursor to be opened and the SQL SELECT statement to be executed when the cursor is opened.
  - **FETCH**: Each execution of this statement returns a row from an already opened cursor. The required information for this type of statement is the identifier of the cursor to be fetched.
  - **CLOSE**: Finish the row processing in an opened cursor. The identifier of the cursor to be closed is the basic information required by this type of operation.

Here there are some examples of valid end-user operations:

- **CPU(0.2)**: Represents an operation requesting the execution of 200000 machine instructions.
- **CALL(PROC)**: Represents an invocation of a procedure called PROC. If the called procedure is a stored one, the procedure is automatically transformed in a PL/SLQ block to be executed by the PL/SQL engine.

- **OPEN(C1,"SELECT empid,sal FROM emp where sal ¡ 20000")**:
  Represents a request for opening a cursor identified by C1. This cursor will
  contain those employees that have a salary less than 20000.
- **FETCH(C1)**: Represents a request for retrieving the current pointed row
  in the cursor C1.
- **DML_OP("Update emp SET salary = salary * 1.1")**: Represents a
  SQL statement operation performing the update of the salary column in all
  the rows of the emp table.

After having conceptualised basic operations it is necessary to define the
notion of sequence of operations. In this sense, the first concept a user has to
model in a PL/SQL program is the PL/SQL program block concept. A PL/SQL
program block can be considered as a list of operations to be performed sequentially during the execution of a PL/SQL program. A PL/SQL program block
can therefore be abstractly depicted as:

- A unique identifier that identifies the program block as a reusable object.
- A sequence of operation instances, that is an operation type with values for
  its parameters. Then, each element on the sequence will be composed by:
  - The order (unique for each element on the sequence), or position from the
    beginning of the program block, where the operation has to be executed.
  - The operation instance itself.

In order to conceptualise a PL/SQL program, it is important to represent
both the execution paths (static information) and the approximate behaviour
(dynamic information). The mechanism used to represent the program behaviour
is based on probabilities. From one block B_1 the program execution can continue
in the block B_2 with probability p if and only if the $p \times 100\%$ of times the program
passes through the block B_1 continues executing the block B_2.

Following the previous reasoning, a PL/SQL functional unit (anonymous
block, procedure, or trigger) can be represented as a graph G whose nodes include PL/SQL program block identifiers. As in a PL/SQL program the same
transaction can appear in different execution paths, the transaction identifier
associated to a node is only an attribute and not the node identifier by itself.
Therefore, a node in a PL/SQL Transaction graph G is a pair (i, t), where i is a
unique identifier for the node in G and t is a PL/SQL program block identifier.
Arcs in G are weighted with probabilities, i.e. and arc is a pair (i, j, p) where i
and j are node identifiers and p is a probability.

Finally $\mathcal{F}$, the family of graphs that can represent *PL/SQL Transaction
Graphs*, has the following restrictions:

- The empty program must be represented as a transaction graph G with
  two nodes $(0,\_)$ and $(\infty,\_)$ and one arc $(0, \infty, 1)$. This means that an empty
  program has an initial and ending points and only one execution path from
  the beginning to the end of the program without execution of program blocks.
- In any transaction graph G belonging to the $\mathcal{F}$ family, for each node n that
  is the tail of at least one arc in G, the sum of weights of the arcs leaving n
  must be 1.

– The only node with no exiting arcs is the $(\infty, \_)$ one.

Finally, as a PL/SQL application is a set of PL/SQL anonymous blocks, stored procedures and triggers represented as PL/SQL Transaction Graphs, the top-level model for PL/SQL views a PL/SQL application as a set of PL/SQL Transaction Graphs.

5   The Workbench's Approach for Characterising WOrkload

The *PL/SQL Transaction Graphs* paradigm provides end-users with mechanisms for specifying the workload of a PL/SQL application at two levels:

– **Application Level**: In this high-level workload characterisation approach, the end-user can study the behaviour of the overall application in the distributed system configuration where it runs. The modelling strategy would be based on specifying the application as a set of *PL/SQL Transaction Graphs* according to the logical structure of programs. Behaviour prediction would be based on stating the number of times each application component would execute during the simulation. In this case, either a probability of launching each software component or an inter-arrival law for launching each software component can be specified.
– **Event Generation and Processing Level**: In this low-level workload characterisation approach, the user can study the impact that some program blocks can have in the overall application. The modelling strategy would be based on specifying each program block as a one-transaction *PL/SQL Transaction Graph*. The prediction of behaviour would be based on assigning the desired workload for the program block as a launching-entrance probabilistic law to the *PL/SQL Transaction Graph* representing it. The workbench would then provide results on the execution of the program block in the chosen configuration for the distributed system.

6   Modelling TPC-C as a PL/SQL Application

The TPC-C benchmark[15] is based on modelling a medium-complexity, on-line transaction processing (OLTP) system. It implements a group of read-only and update- intensive transactions that exercise the system components associated with transactional environments. The benchmark tries to represent a generic wholesale supplier workload. The overall database consists of a number of warehouses (a benchmark configuration parameter). Each *warehouse* is composed of 10 *districts* where each district has 3000 *customers*. Five different on-line and batch transactions characterise the benchmark:

– **New Order Transaction** is used to introduce a complete order through a single database transaction.

- **Payment Transaction** updates the customer's balance and reflects the payment on the district and warehouse sales statistics.
- **Order Status Transaction** asks for the status of a customer's last order.
- **Delivery Transaction** processes 10 new (not yet delivered) orders.
- **Stock Level Transaction** determines the amount of recently sold items that have a stock level below a specified threshold.

The modelling of the TPC-C application in the benchmark consists of specifying the following components:

- **Data Components**: For each one of the TPC-C tables, the cardinality (number of rows in the table), average row size and ORACLE physical design parameters (PCTFREE, PCTUSED and INITTRANS) must be specified. For each primary or secondary indexes in the TPC-C application the ORACLE physical design parameters should also be specified.
- **Processing Components**: For each one of the five TPC-C transactions, a *PL/SQL Transaction Graph* must be specified.

As an example of the TPC-C modelling, consider the following anonymous PL/SQL block corresponding to the Delivery transaction. Bracketed variables indicate external variables used to parameterise the PL/SQL anonymous block.

```
DECLARE
 DID NUMBER(2);
 ORDERID NUMBER(8);
 TOTAL NUMBER(12);
BEGIN
DID := 1;
WHILE DID <= <D_PER_W> DO
 DECLARE c_no CURSOR FOR
 & Let's term next SELECT as Op1
 SELECT no_o_id FROM NEW ORDER
 WHERE no_d_id=DID AND no_w_id=<WAREHOUSE> ORDER BY no_o_id ASC;
 OPEN c_no;
 FETCH c_no INTO ORDERID;
 & Let's term next DELETE as Op2
 DELETE FROM NEW_ORDER WHERE CURRENT OF c_no;
 CLOSE c_no;
 & Let's term next SELECT as Op3
 SELECT o_c_id iNTO CUSTOMER FROM ORDERS
 WHERE o_id=ORDERID AND o_d_id=DID AND o_w_ID=<WAREHOUSE>;
 & Let's term next UPDATE as Op4
 UPDATE ORDERS SET o_carried_id = <CARRIER>
 WHERE o_id=ORDERID AND o_d_id=DID AND o_w_id=<WAREHOUSE>;
 & Let's term next UPDATE aas Op5
 UPDATE order_line SET ol_delivery_d = $DATE
 WHERE ol_o_id=ORDERID AND ol_d_id=DID AND ol_w_id=<WAREHOUSE>;
```

```
& Let's term next SELECT as Op6
SELECT SUM(ol_amount) INTO TOTAL FROM ORDER_LINE
WHERE ol_o_id=ORDERID AND ol_d_id=DID AND ol_w_id=<WAREHOUSE>;
& Let's term next UPDATE as Op7
UPDATE CUSTOMER SET c_balance = c_balance + TOTAL
WHERE c_id=<CUSTOMER> AND c_d_id=DID  AND c_w_id=<WAREHOUSE>;
COMMIT;
DID := DID + 1;
END LOOP;
END;
```

From the PL/SQL code, the *PL/SQL Transaction Graph* can be built as:

- There are three PL/SQL program blocks in the code:
    - One corresponding to the actions performed prior to the while loop, termed as t_1 in the *PL/SQL Transaction Graph*,
    - One corresponding to the evaluation of the looping condition, termed as t_2 in the *PL/SQL Transaction Graph*, and
    - One corresponding to the sequential execution of the block inside the while loop, termed as t_3 in the *PL/SQL Transaction Graph*.
- A weighted arc joining the corresponding nodes with weight 1 represents every sequential flow of control.
- The looping execution is represented using the frequency view of probabilities. As the loops executes $< D_P ER_W >$ times, the looping expression is evaluated $< D_P ER_W > +1$ times. In this sense, the probability of exiting the loop is $\frac{1}{<D_P ER_W > +1}$ and the probability of continuing looping is 1 minus the probability of exiting the loop.

Figure 4 shows the graphical notation of the PL/SQL Transaction Graph for the TPC-C Delivery transaction and the specification of each PL/SQL Code block using the workbench-defined operations.

According to the TPC-C benchmark specification, the workload is depicted in two ways: one depending on the number of warehouses and one providing a mix of the five types of transactions.

- To specify the different configurations due to changes in the number of warehouses, an application should be defined for each value of the warehouse number parameter. The processing component of each application would be the same, i.e. the five *PL/SQL Transaction* Graphs representing the transactions. Nevertheless, although each application is based on the same data architecture (the same structure of tables and indexes) the physical information regarding table cardinalities should be different.
- To specify the execution of a warehouse configuration varying the mix of transaction the scenario definition phase of the workbench can be used under the application level of workload characterisation. As the TPC-C application is conformed by five *PL/SQL Transaction Graphs*, the mix is trivially mapped to a mix of PL/SQL Transaction Graphs executions with a probability of execution equal to the percentage of execution of each transaction in the mix proposed.

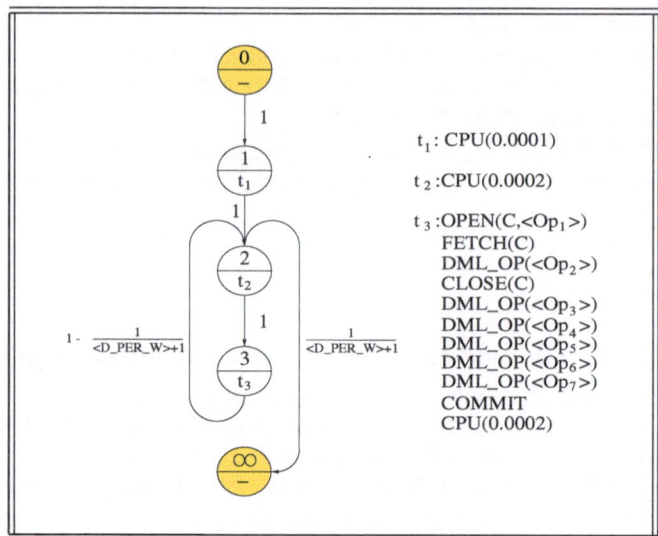

Fig. 4. PL/SQL Transaction Graph for the TPC-C Delivery transaction

7   Conclusion and further studies

In this paper, we have presented the architecture and services provided by a workbench for predicting the behaviour of database applications developed in PL/SQL. The workbench combines different techniques for specifying data, processing (synchronous and asynchronous) and workload applied to the specific domain of data manipulation programming and discrete event simulation to get performance measures for the logical components of the application. The main results obtained with the workbench are:

- An easy-to-extend implementation paradigm based on isolating the data provided by the user from the basic performance models. The use of a Models Repository implemented as a library of intermediate code with common entry point makes easy the inclusion of new models with a low programming effort.
- A two-way mechanism for characterising the workload of an end-user application first based on specifying the stochastical behaviour at the program level and then specifying the stochastical arrival laws for launching and executing the programs in the application.

Our interest now is focused on three directions:

1. Migrating the prototype to a 3GL+Java+simulation library implementation. Although the QNAP2 language is useful for prototyping simulators and validating performance models, it is not a good choice for a commercial tool since the end-user is tied to a specific simulation technology.

2. Extending the approach for predicting the behaviour of distributed PL/SQL applications. In this case, the strategy will be based on including the mechanisms for the end-user specification of a distributed database (fragments, replicas, fragments refreshment policies) and extending the DBMS models for handling the new features.

3. Extending the approach designed for PL/SQL in ORACLE environments to propose a workbench for predicting the behaviour of PL/SQL applications in other RDBMS like SYBASE and INFORMIX. In this case, the workbench's repositories would be extended with mechanisms for representing physical design features inherent to each new DBMS included.

References

1. Aiken, A., Hellerstein, J.: Static Analysis Techniques for Predicting the Behavior of Active Database Rules. *ACM Transactions on Database Systems* **20(1)** (1995) 3–41

2. Boulos, J., Boudigue, D.: An Application of SMART2: A Tools for Performance Evaluation of Relational Database Programs. *Lecture Notes in Computer Science* **977**. 1995

3. Franklin, M., Johnson, B.T., Kossmann, D.: Performance Tradeoffs for Client-Server Query Processing. In *Proc. of ACM SIGMOD International Conference on Management of Data.* Montreal, Canada. Jun. 1996. 149–160

4. Healy, K.: The Use of Event Graphs in Simulation Modeling Instruction. In *Proc. of the 1993 Winter Simulation Conference.* Los Angeles, CA. Dec. 1993

5. HELIOS Consortium: HELIOS Project Technical Annex Version 4.0. 1997

6. HELIOS Consortium: PL/SQL and Multibase Performance Models. WP2T3-d1 R2.0 Technical Report, 1997

7. Kumar, J.: Recovery Mechanisms in Databases. Prentice-Hall International. 1998

8. Potier, D., Veran, M.: QNAP2: A Portable Environment for Queuing Systems Modelling. First International Conference on Modelling Techniques and Tools for Performance Analysis. Potier (Ed.) North-Holland, 1985. 25–63.

9. Rahm, E.: Performance Evaluation of Extended Storage Architectures for Transaction Processing. In *Proc. ACM SIGMOD International Conference on Management of Data (SIGMOD '92).* San Diego, CA. Jun. 1992. 308–317.

10. SIMULOG: QNAP2 User's Manual. Jun. 1994.

11. Savino V., N. N.,Puigjaner R.: An Object-Oriented Approach for the Design of Hierarchical Queuing Network Simulation Models with QNAP2. In *Proc. Object-Oriented Simulation Conference, OOS'98.* San Diego, CA. Jan. 1998. 101–106.

12. Savino V., N. N., Puigjaner R.,Anciano M., J. L.: Including Methods and Inheritance of Hierarchical Models in HOOMA. In *Proc. Thyrtieth Summer Computer Simulation Conference, SCSC'98.* Reno, NV. Jul. 1998 (to appear).

13. IFATEC: SMART User's Guide. Release 3.0. Dec. 1996.

14. Smith, C. U.: *Performance Engineering of Software Systems.* Addison-Wesley. 1990

15. Transaction Processing Council: TPC Benchmark C Standard Specification. Revision 3.3.2. Jun. 1997. Available at http://www.tpc.org/benchmark_specifications/TPC_C/tpcc332.pdf

Performance Evaluation of Distributed Object Architectures *

Sophie Dumas[1][2] Didier Boudigue[2] Georges Gardarin[1]

[1] Laboratoire PRiSM, Université de Versailles St Quentin,
45, avenue des Etats-Unis, 78035 Versailles Cedex, France
E-mail: Georges.Gardarin@prism.uvsq.fr

[2] IFATEC, 12-14 rue du Fort de Saint-Cyr,
78067 Saint-Quentin-en-Yvelines, France
E-mail: sodumas@euriware.fr

Abstract. The development of a Distributed Information System (DIS) can lead to critical bottlenecks because of the underlying architecture, which is becoming more and more complex. Today's applications are both object-oriented and based on a new type of three-tiered client/server architecture. In this context, the capabilities of a DIS can be drastically reduced if the performances of the system are not sufficient. Recognizing these trends, industry and research are defining standards and technologies for communicating between components of a DIS and for database access mechanisms. The emerging candidates for these middleware technologies include the OMG's CORBA specification and Microsoft's proprietary solution known as DCOM. A key problem with such complex architectures is the performance issue. This paper proposes to evaluate the performance of an object-oriented DIS using a performance evaluation tool integrating analytical and simulation techniques. This tool is an extension of SMART, a performance evaluation tool for database applications, with distributed object models. These models are established using HOOMA, a hierarchical object-oriented modeling approach.
Keywords: Three-tiered Architecture, Modeling, Distributed Objects, PerformanceEvaluation, CORBA and DCOM

1 Introduction

Distributed object technology [1], [13] is proposing new component-based architectures to develop advanced information systems. New information system architectures need improved design methods and tools to guarantee the efficiency and the scalability of the applications. Defining a configuration to assure a given level of performance in a distributed object system interacting with local databases is not an easy task. The three major approaches for performance evaluation are analytical cost evaluation, simulation, and measurement of prototype

---

* This work is supported by the European HELIOS ESPRIT project (22354). The project is developed in cooperation with EPFL, IONA, TransTOOLS, UIB and UoS.

R. Puigjaner et al. (Eds.): Tools'98, LNCS 1469, pp. 306–320, 1998.

systems. Although helpful, each of these techniques is in itself insufficient to predict the performance of a given configuration and select the best arrangement of components.

Coupling them in an integrated tool seems to be a promising idea. Thus, the SMART object- oriented tool [16] has been first defined and implemented to couple a simulation tool based on queuing networks, an analytical cost model for SQL queries, and a real DBMS optimizer. The tool is object-oriented in the sense that it provides a set of objects stored in a dictionary to fill up to define hardware configurations, software components, and database tables and queries. Furthermore, the tool is extensible as new models of components (hardware or software) can be added in the dictionary.

This tool has then been extended to further take into account the distribution of components around CORBA and DCOM. To establish the queuing network models, the hierarchical object-oriented modeling approach proposed in [15] has been intensively used. This approach has then been incorporated within the SMART tool to ease the addition of new component models.

This paper gives an overview of SMART, the hybrid performance prediction tool developed in the HELIOS project and before. SMART is novel because: (i) it uses both analytical and simulation techniques, (ii) it is based on a real DBMS optimizer, (iii) it integrates an active object-oriented dictionary implemented as a database. Then, we focus on distributed object management. We propose a generic model for CORBA/ORBIX and DCOM using the aforementioned hierarchical object-oriented modeling approach. This model is generic in the sense that it can be calibrated differently for each architecture. In addition, we describe a model for the OLE-DB Application Programming Interface (API) in order to evaluate the access costs of traditional databases. Finally, we present the integration of these new models within SMART.

This paper is organized as follows: Section 2 presents our SMART performance evaluation tool. Section 3 gives an overview of the CORBA and DCOM architectures and of the OLE- DB API. Section 4 presents the approach used for the modeling and describes the resulting models. Section 5 describes the integration of these models within SMART. Finally, Section 6 concludes by summarizing the main points of this paper and introducing some future work.

2   SMART: A Hybrid Performance Evaluation Tool

This section presents the different components of our SMART simulation tool and the interactions between them. SMART is original in the sense that it integrates within a simulation engine real system components, such as the DBMS query optimizer, and analytical cost models.

2.1   Objectives

The goal of SMART is to predict the performance of a centralized database application on a given architecture, using a given DBMS. The architecture can be multiprocessor, including the shared nothing and shared memory variants. The user first describes its platform by selecting components within a library. Then, he/she picks up a given version of a DBMS among a possible set. The platform and the DBMS define the test environment. Various test environments can be evaluated, thus helping the designer to select the best environment. The application is modeled through its database requirements. More precisely, the database internal schema is defined in terms of relations and indexes. The cardinalities of relations and query relevant attributes are also specified. Typical queries and transactions are given for the evaluation, with associated frequencies. The application is then simulated on different architectures with various data placements. Performance results are given for each simulation. For a more precise definition of the input and output parameters, the reader can refer to [16].

2.2   Architecture

SMART incorporates an interactive user interface (SmartWindows) to model the environment and application, to run the simulation, and to display the results. A library of modeled objects (SmartDictionary) provides the existing environment models. A user must select the models of hardware, DBMS, and network components that are available in the SmartDictionary in order to build his complete environment via the SmartWindows interface.

As stated above, one of the originality of SMART is to include real system components within the simulation tool. A key component is the DBMS query optimizer. Today, most DBMSs integrate an optimizer capable of transforming an SQL query in a Query Execution Plan (QEP), i.e., an annotated tree of relational algebra operators. SMART uses the optimizer of the selected DBMS, which produces the QEP for each query of the application. Based on a classical analytical cost model, which can be extended to object operations [5], we have integrated within SMART an operator cost evaluator called the SmartEvaluator. The major work of the SmartEvaluator is to complete the QEP brought by the DBMS optimizer by adding several statistics concerning its analytical cost. Thus, each entry of a valued QEP is an entry of the original QEP plus the estimated CPU time consumption, the logical I/O requirements, the lock requirements, the estimated data transfer cost between client and server, the volume of data to sort, and the accessed object (tables, indexes, etc.). Each of these parameters can be set to 0.

Valued QEP are then passed to a queuing simulation engine (SmartEngine). This is the core of the system: it processes the models of the selected SMART objects (Figure 1) for the given QEPs. On activation SmartEngine checks the input data and generates a complete QNAP2 model [14] of the objects chosen in the scenario. QNAP2 is a simulation programming language based on objects and queuing networks. The language offers facilities for the definition of procedures and functions, macros, and libraries. Customers, queues, and service stations, along with their corresponding attributes, are predefined constructs of the language. The service law can be as complex as desired using customer attributes. When a simulation is completed, SmartEngine generates an output file and stores the results into the SmartDictionary. Results are available from the graphical interface or as ASCII files as well. Figure 1 summarizes the architecture of SMART. The user interacts with the SmartWindows. Key components are the SmartEvaluator, based on an analytical cost model for evaluating query plans, and the SmartEngine, based on a queuing network model. The SmartDictionary is the repository of all common objects, including libraries of models.

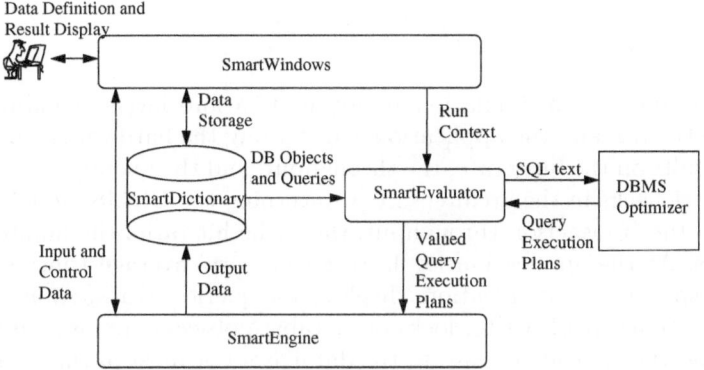

Fig. 1. SMART Architecture

2.3 Supported Models

SMART includes a library of models stored in the dictionary to design the environment model. This includes models for servers, clients, disks, networks, DBMSs, databases, and transactions. Server objects cover generic queuing models for SMP or cluster machines, and specialized models for MPP machines like the ICL GoldRush, the IBM SP2, and the nCube2. Clients are used to model a set of terminals or workstations. They are characterized by the communication traffic with the servers and the operator workloads. Various models of disks with drivers mimic the behavior of the SCSI or SCSI2 technology. The network facilities supported are the Ethernet and specific routers for WAN.

As DBMSs, SMART supports the ORACLE V6 and ORACLE V7 models. Others could be included in the near future. These models describe the process architecture of the DBMS including the multithread facilities. Furthermore they both integrate models of a sophisticated cache algorithm, a two phase locking mechanism, and a group commit protocol. The database objects are relation, index, log, and temporary area. Any of these may be spread on several disks with a uniform volume distribution. Transactions are used to define atomic units of work on the database so that the impact of locks, deadlocks, rollbacks, and commits can be modeled and taken into consideration during a simulation. Operation is the basic SMART processing entry. It can be a CPU work on a server or a client, an SQL query described in SQL by the user and translated into a VQEP for the simulation, a think-time for operator behavior modeling (keystroke, screen analysis, ...), or a block for advanced DBMS pieces of code such as triggers and procedures, stored and performed by the DBMS kernel. Finally, a transactions- script object is filled in to describe the transaction workload through probabilities of executions.

All these generic objects can be picked up from the SmartDictionary and customized for the simulation with specific parameters (database size, CPU power, network throughput, etc.).

2.4   Results

Results produced by a simulation are given at various levels including the hardware, the DBMS, and the application. Concerning the hardware components, we obtain results on the busy rate, the throughput, and the queuing state in order to locate bottlenecks in the architecture. Concerning the DBMS models, we collect results on the transaction throughput, the cache hit ratio, the number of writes and reads. At the application level, we give several average times of execution (CPU, response, communication, display) for queries, transactions, and applications. Actions (read, write, lock) on database objects are also summarized to understand the critical accesses to the database. For most of these results, standard deviation, maximum, minimum and average values are reported in order to check how relevant the execution of the simulation is.

3   Distributed Object Architectures

As stated in the introduction, the goal of our work was to extend SMART to support distributed object architectures. These architectures are designed to allow clients to transparently communicate with objects regardless of where those objects are located. To optimize application performances, and make the best possible usage of readily available hardware, a modern type of architecture, named a three-tiered architecture, distributes object accesses over a client, a processing server and a data server. Over such an architecture, object methods may be processed on a site different from the location site of the object. This section first presents the main features of CORBA and DCOM, the two distributed object architectures modeled in the HELIOS project. Then it briefly introduces OLE-DB, the API modeled for database accesses.

3.1   CORBA

In 1990, the OMG (Object Management Group) has produced an open standard called the Object Management Architecture (OMA), which has become the standard reference model for distributed object technology [11]. The central element of this architecture is the Common Object Request Broker Architecture (CORBA) [3], as shown in Figure 2. A common facility is a set of user-oriented services (structured document, email, database accesses, ...) and an object service is a set of system-oriented operations (naming, events, persistency, ...) that

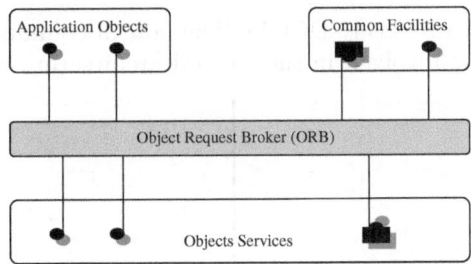

Fig. 2. CORBA Architecture

applications can use by inheritance or invocation. Products that implement this portion of the standard are referred to as Object Request Brokers (ORBs).

An ORB is a central bus to which all other components in the environment are connected, and through which they interoperate. There is a number of architectural options available to ORB designers to achieve the required functionality. In the HELIOS project, we are focusing on ORBIX [12] from IONA because it is one of the most widespread ORB in the industry. On Figure 3, a client object invokes a remote object directly, through a common facility, or through an object service. In either cases, the call results in one or several RPCs with parameter marshaling. On the server side, the Basic Object Adapter (BOA) creates and registers object instances. Object interfaces are compiled with a stub for the client side and a skeleton for the server side. The object dictionary is split between the interface repository for the client side of the ORB and the implementation repository for the server side.

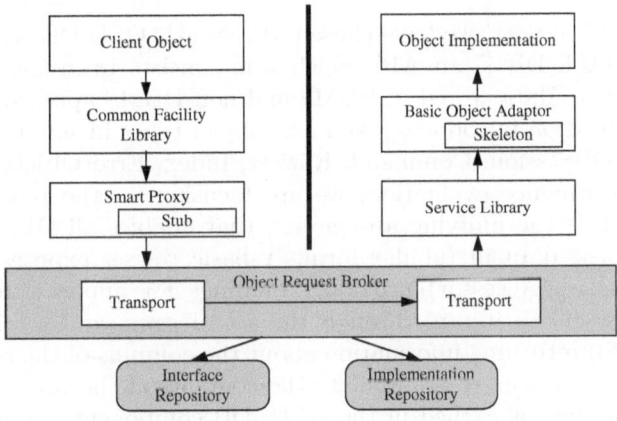

Fig. 3. ORBIX Communication Flow

3.2 DCOM

DCOM is the Microsoft counter part of CORBA. DCOM is often associated with OLE [2] to achieve Microsoft's distributed document management facility. In this paper we are most interested in distributed information systems and will restrict our focus to solely DCOM. The flow of communication between the different components involved in the DCOM architecture is shown Figure 4.

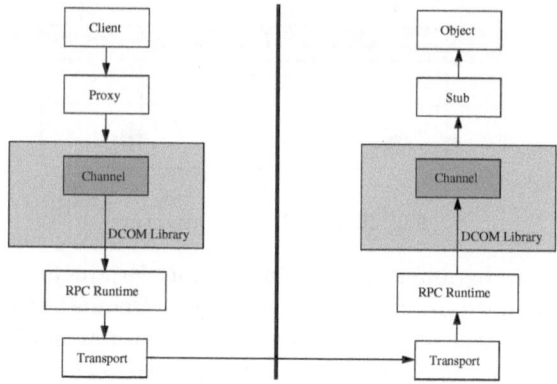

Fig. 4. DCOM Architecture

The transmission of data across the network is handled by a RPC runtime library and a channel. On the client side, the method call goes through the proxy, and then onto the channel. The channel sends the buffer containing the marshaled parameters to the RPC runtime library, which transmits it to the stub across the network. Note that the RPC runtime and the library exist on both sides of the communication [4].

3.3   Accessing a Traditional Data Server

In the HELIOS project, we have chosen Microsoft's OLE-DB API to query the data server. OLE-DB is an API which role consists in giving applications a uniform access to data stored in DBMS and non-DBMS applications [10].

The specification introduces seven new object types in supplement to OLE2: DataSource, DBSession, Command, Rowset, Index, ErrorObject, and Transaction. For performance evaluation, we are focusing on the rowset object (Figure 5), which is the unifying abstraction that enables all OLE-DB data providers to expose data in tabular form. A basic rowset exposes three interfaces: an accessor (IAccessor) providing bindings for application variables, an iterator (IRowset) to iterate through the set of rows, and a schema provider (IColumnsInfo) returning information about the columns of the rowset. Handles are used with accessors to manipulate the contents of the rows. When the row is fetched, the data is cached in the OLE- DB component. An analogy can be driven between the limited form of services provided by an OLE-DB rowset and a subset of the services offered by a BOA over an object within CORBA.

4   Models for Distributed Object Architectures

The objective of this section is to present the modeling of a distributed object architecture, which has been included in SMART to model distributed appli-

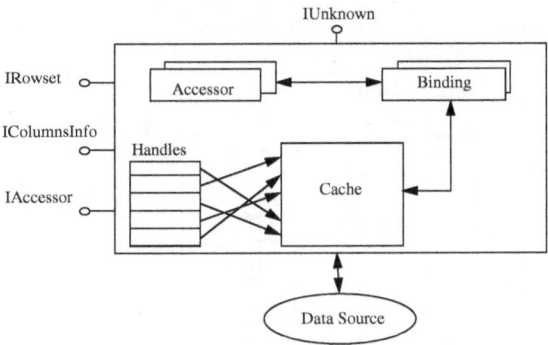

Fig. 5. Rowset Object in OLE-DB

cations. A generic cost model for CORBA/ORBIX and DCOM is defined and a specific cost model for OLE-DB is proposed. The presented models follow a conceptual simulation methodology based on queuing networks and have been mapped in QNAP2, the simulation programming language used in our performance evaluation tool.

4.1   HOOMA, a Hierarchical Object Modeling Approach

To ease the simulation of distributed object architectures (CORBA or DCOM), we use a conceptual simulation modeling method based on queuing networks. This method is known as HOOMA. HOOMA, as developed by [15], represents a system as a group of hierarchically interacting simulation models, where each one acts as an agent providing services to the others with no internal knowledge about them. A given model receives customers from higher level models in the hierarchy and sends customers to lower level models. Figure 6 presents the graphical notations used in HOOMA to specify the models representing the system to model.

A model for a system component is a set of queuing centers grouped as a black box such that component interactions are restricted to remain non cyclic. Customers are modeled as objects with attributes and are organized in a type-subtype hierarchy. A model is described in terms of customer types and classes, queuing centers, and their interactions. Depending on their relationship with other models, HOOMA distinguishes four types of objects: interface customer classes represent those clients allowed to leave a model to enter another one, internal customer classes model the transit of events strictly within a given model, interface queuing centers receive part of their clients from the outside and feed inputs to only internal queuing centers, which are used to model the behavior of the components of the real system.

4.2   Why a Generic Model for both CORBA and DCOM

Modeling the performances of a distributed object architecture may have several goals. One may want to choose among DCOM and CORBA, or to choose among

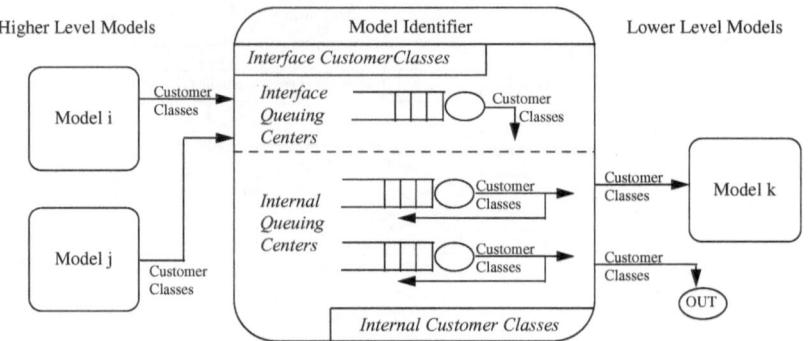

Fig. 6. Graphical Notations for HOOMA Hierarchical Models

different CORBA implementations [8]. Although there may be early stages of a project where such a choice is still open, more than often performance analysis is targeted for a given middleware and is used to predict performances, to reduce bottlenecks, and to adjust the underlying hardware support.

Our goal is to better understand the behavior of a complex Distributed Information System on a given platform, with a given architecture, and for a given application. To limit complexity, it is better to highlight the common aspects of CORBA and DCOM and to limit their differences to a few parameter values. Both architectures offer the choice between an in- process server mode, a local server mode, and a remote server mode. Servers are launched through a daemon in ORBIX and through the Server Control Manager in DCOM, but after the servers have been started this difference plays no further role. Hence, a generic model for both CORBA and DCOM is defined in the following subsection.

4.3   Generic Model

Following the conceptual model defined in HOOMA, a generic cost model for the CORBA/ORBIX and DCOM architectures has been developed in the project [9]. The main objective of this model is to evaluate the marshaling/unmarshaling cost of an object invocation, which is the major bottleneck in high-performance communication subsystems [6], [7].

Using the notations described in Section 4.1, Figure 7 gives a graphical representation of the model. The interface customer classes represent in-process requests (IN_REQ), local requests (LOC_REQ), or remote requests (REM_REQ) incoming from the user application model (U.A.). The interface queuing center (calls) is an infinite queue which main function is to become a bridge between the application, the middleware model, and the lower level models (Network, CPU). It provides services for the three interface customer classes. The internal customer classes represent either a request to be performed (INVOC) by the server or a response (RESULT) generated following a request. Internal queuing centers are single server centers representing either an in-process server queue, a local server queue, or a remote one. All the centers interact with the lower level

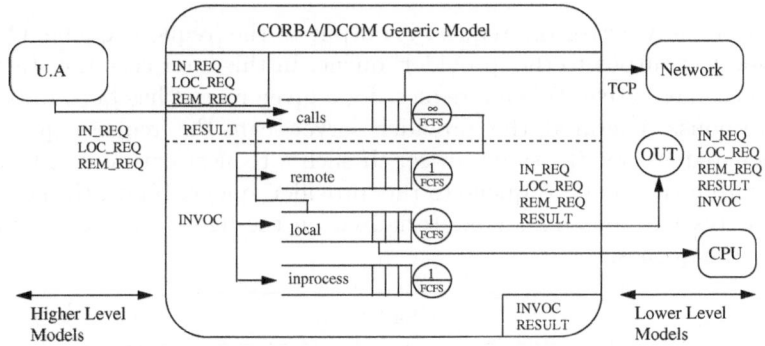

Fig. 7. Generic Model for the CORBA and DCOM architectures

models representing the network and the CPU submodels. On the figure, only a subset of the queue interactions is shown for readability.

Request customers model the invocation of a method across the distributed object architecture. A request object has attributes describing the method parameters. These attributes are used to compute the marshaling/unmarshaling costs involved in the simulation of the method call.

4.4   OLE-DB Model

Three kinds of actors are involved in the modeling of OLE-DB: the consumer which is a user application, the provider which is an instance of a rowset, and the server where the DBMS is located.

Using HOOMA notations again, Figure 8 gives an overview of the model. The interface customer classes represent requests for creating a rowset (C_CREATE), and for manipulating rows within it. Row manipulation entails insertion
(C_INSROW), update (C_UPTROW), deletion (C_DELROW), and retrieval (C_GDAT) of rows. The last request is for committing (C_COMMIT) the changes produced on the rowset. On the figure, C_xxx stands for any customer belonging to one of these classes. The interface queuing center (ole_calls) is an infinite queue which main function is to bridge the application, the OLE-DB model, and the lower level models. It services all the interface customer classes. Internal customer classes are used to keep information about all created rowsets (SET_INFO) and to send calls to the DBMS model (DB_CALL). Internal queuing centers are single server centers: 'request' is a passive queue (with no server) used to keep the pending requests for all the rowsets, 'ctrlinf' is used to keep information concerning the created rowsets, and 'provider' is used to generate the response.

To properly model OLE-DB behavior, where a provider may only serve one request at-a-time for a given rowset and can only serve requests in parallel for different rowsets, the 'provider' queue may only contain requests for different rowsets. The status attribute of a SET_INFO customer is set to active whenever a request for this rowset is in the 'provider' center, either queuing or being serviced. When the 'ole_calls' interface server inspects a new request, if the corresponding rowset is already active the request is output to the 'request' queue. Otherwise, the request is output to the 'provider' queue. In this later case the status of the rowset becomes active. When a request for a given rowset has been fully serviced and a response generated, the 'provider' server scans the 'request' queue to look for a new request for the same rowset. If such a request exists, it is transmitted directly from the 'request' queue to the 'provider' queue. If not, the status of the rowset is reset to idle. This is materialized on the figure with an arrow joining directly the queues.

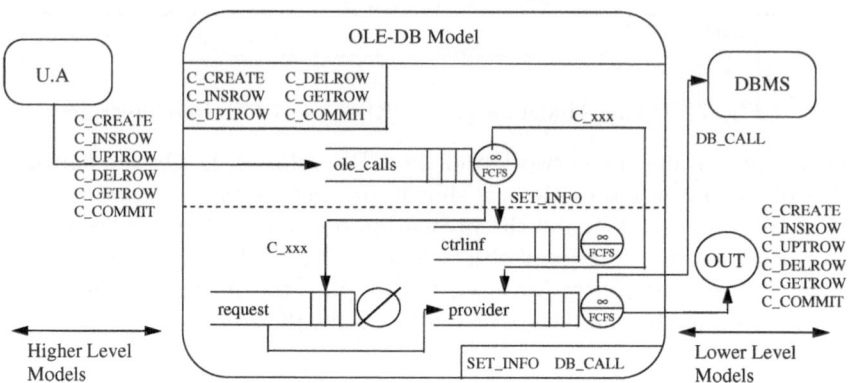

Fig. 8. Model for OLE-DB

5   Integration Within SMART

To take into account the distributed object technology in SMART, we have introduced the models described in the previous section. The user application model has been extended with operations to support binding and unbinding to remote objects. To support the distributed system aspects, models including the communication layer and the operating system buffers have been developed.

This section first presents the methodology used to integrate the various models within SMART, then proposes a view of a complete system simulation. The usage of benchmarks as a way to abstract a low level model is introduced, and finally a method to calibrate the global model for the DIS is proposed.

5.1   Integration Methodology

As SMART is centered around an object-oriented dictionary, the integration was quite easy. Mainly, new objects were defined in the dictionary to extend the user interface and enter the required parameters. At the engine level, new QNAP2 macros (for CORBA/ORBIX, DCOM, and OLE-DB models) were added in accordance with the HOOMA methodology. For further details, the user can consult [9].

For this integration, the HOOMA methodology proved to be specially helpful as the models for the added components could be designed and tested separately before their integration. It should be noted that a hybrid hierarchy may be obtained by replacing some HOOMA models in the hierarchy with other types of component models. A non HOOMA model can be either a Load Dependent Server translating the results of a benchmark into some statistical function (see Subsection 5.3) or an Analytical Model.

In addition, a model for a component can be generated instead of written by hand. This is the case for the User Application model necessary to validate the CORBA/DCOM and OLE-DB models. A transaction graph representing the flow of transactions from a given application is used as an input to a QNAP2 code generator (Figure 9). Each node of the graph is a transaction descriptor Ti, and each edge represent a possible transition weighted with a probability Pj.

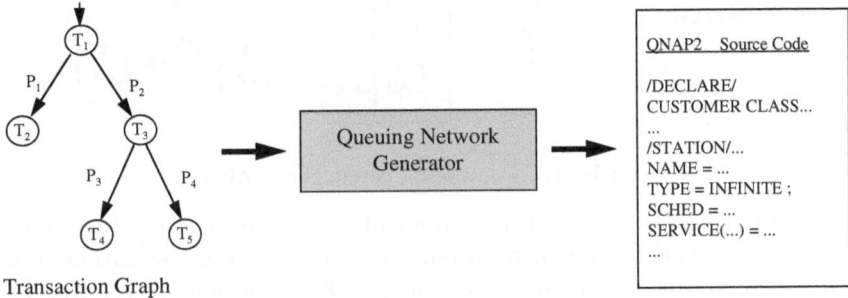

Fig. 9. Queuing Network Generator

5.2   Assembling the Parts Together

The model integration within SMART can take different forms depending on the exact DIS architecture to be evaluated. From the simplest Client/Server architecture to a modern three-tiered architecture, only the choice of the participant subsystem models and their assembling differs. A great flexibility is thus achieved in the workbench.

As an example, Figure 10 shows a possible assembling for a typical DIS target where the client is a database application, the middleware is either CORBA (ORBIX) or DCOM, and the data server is an ORACLE relational DBMS accessed through the OLE-DB API. The DBMS model as well as the models in the network and hardware layers correspond to the existing models included in the first version of the SMART workbench.

5.3   Using Benchmarks

To ease up system integration it is useful to be able to replace a subset of the model hierarchy with real measurements made for a given existing software component on a given platform (hardware + operating system). The benefit of this

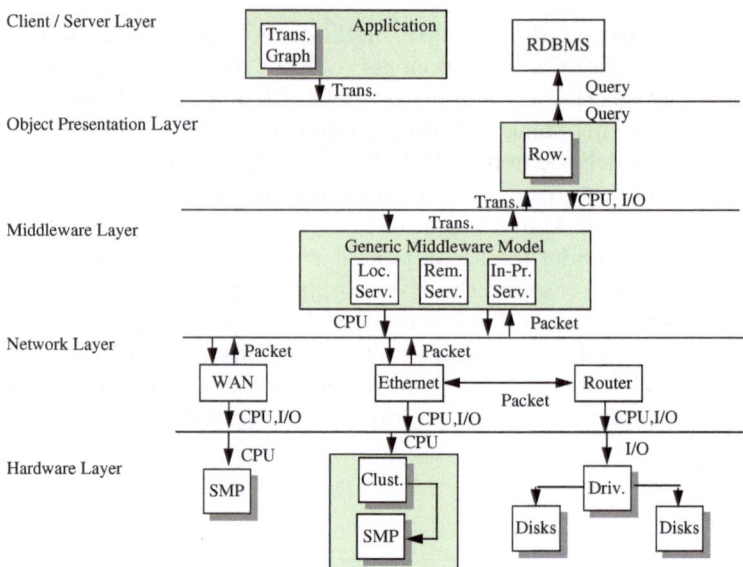

Fig. 10. Complete System Simulation

approach is threefold: (i) real measurements are more reliable than simulation results, (ii) a benchmark can be used, and (iii) the total simulation time may be drastically reduced. The use of a benchmark is especially interesting because it provides for the comparison with other results obtained with other environments. A benchmark could be installed on a simulated system, but this would entail a substantial amount of additional work to verify that the benchmark is fully supported by the model (in order to allow for comparisons), with dubious results.

A benchmark may be folded into a simulation component through the use of a Load Dependent Server (LDS), that is a special queue where the service time is computed from the benchmark results. This can be accomplish with some statistical tool such as S+.

In our case, we have developed two load dependent servers: one for the ORACLE DBMS running a benchmark designed for our needs and focusing on one object at-a-time accesses, the second for a TCP-based network running the well known TTCP benchmark. Both benchmarks were run on a Windows/NT platform. These LDS are being used to calibrate separately the particular models proposed in this paper (CORBA/DCOM and OLE-DB).

5.4   Model Calibration

QNAP2 service laws used in the model implementations are specified with an algorithmic language. This provides for the specification of service laws ranging from the definition of a rather simple multivariate function to a full analytical cost model based on customer attributes. In essence QNAP2 models are themselves hybrid models mixing queuing network and analytical techniques.

The consequence of this feature is the need to carefully calibrate the models to adjust the parameters of the embedded cost equations.

In addition, the generic model must be calibrated for each architecture before its integration within SMART. Two different sets of parameters are required. These different sets are mostly due to the two different encoding protocols, CDR (Common Data Representation) for CORBA and NDR (Network Data Representation) for DCOM. The calibration is made with a benchmark (TIMER) developed for ORBIX by Iona, that we adapted for DCOM. The benchmark is of the ping-pong type and performs a method call (two-way synchronous) in a Windows/NT environment.

6 Conclusion and Future Work

SMART is a performance evaluation tool which has been designed to assist designers in making choices on critical issues during the whole lifetime of a project. It integrates several approaches such as queuing networks, analytical cost modeling, and real system components, for finely evaluating the performance of database applications. It is able to model various environments, including parallel machines.

The work described in this paper extends SMART to support distributed object architectures, namely CORBA and DCOM. The design is based on the intensive use of HOOMA, a hierarchical object-oriented modeling approach, which proved to be a useful method to model complex systems.

Some models of benchmarking application have been developed to tune the models. Further experiences are ongoing. The ultimate goal of the project is to provide a library of reusable components with a runtime environment. The library will ease the development of fine performance models for distributed information systems. Further work is required to validate the models, and give approximations of maximum errors in performance evaluation.

Acknowledgments

The authors would like to thank Pierre de la Motte, Mustapha Hemici from Ifatec; Ramon Puigjaner, Nunzio Savino and the other members of the HELIOS team from UIB (Universitat de las Iles Baleares); Conor Doherty from Iona; Hugh Glaser, Adrian Smith from UoS (University of Southampton); Jose-Antonio Corbacho, Jorge Murcia, César Pérez-Chirinos from TransTOOLS, Spain; Yves Dennebouy, Marc Lambelin from EPFL (Ecole Polytechnique Fédérale de Lausanne). Without them HELIOS would not be such as it is now.

References

1. Bouzeghoub M., Gardarin G., Valduriez P., "Object Technology", Software Engineering series, Thomson Press, Boston, 380 p., 1997.
2. Brockschmidt K., "Inside OLE", Microsoft Press, Redmond, Washington, 1993.
3. OMG, "The Common Object Request Broker Architecture: Architecture and Specification", Revision 2.0, July 1995.
4. Microsoft Corporation and Digital Equipment Corporation, "The Component Object Model Specification", Draft Version 0.9, October 24, 1995.
5. Gardarin G., Gardarin O., "Le Client-Serveur", Eyrolles, Paris, 487 p., 1996.
6. Gokhale A., Schmidt D. C., "The Performance of the CORBA Dynamic Invocation Interface and Dynamic Skeleton Interface over High-Speed ATM Networks", GLOBECOM Conference, London, November 18-22 1996.
7. Gokhale A., Schmidt D. C., "The Performance of the CORBA Dynamic Invocation Interface and Dynamic Skeleton Interface over High-Speed ATM Networks", GLOBECOM Conference, London, November 18-22 1996.
8. Gokhale A., Schmidt D. C., Harrison T. H., Parulkar G., "A High-performance Endsystem Architecture for Real-time CORBA", IEEE Communications Magazine, Vol. 14, No 2, February 1997.
9. Dumas S., "DCOM and OLE-DB model specifications", ESPRIT Technical Report, HELIOS project (EP 22354), HELIOS/IFA/WP2T2/12.1.97, IFATEC, France, December 1997.
10. Microsoft, "OLE-DB specification" , 1996.
11. Object Management Group, "CORBA 2.0 / Interoperability, Universal Networked Objects", OMG Document Number 95.3.10, March 1994.
12. IONA Technologies, "The ORBIX Architecture", Dublin, November 1996.
13. Orfali R., Harkey D., Edwards J., "The Essential Distributed Objects Survival guide", J. Wiley & Sons, New York, 604 p., 1996.
14. SIMULOG and INRIA,"QNAP2 Reference Manual", Rocquencourt, August, 1991.
15. Savino N., Puigjaner R., "An Object-Oriented Approach for the Design of Hierarchical Queuing Network Simulation Models with QNAP2", Object-Oriented Simulation Conference, San Diego, California, January 11-15, 1998.
16. IFATEC, "SMART User's Guide", Release 3.0 Beta, December 1996.

Performance Engineering Evaluation of CORBA-based Distributed Systems with *SPE•ED*

Connie U. Smith
Performance Engineering Services
PO Box 2640
Santa Fe, NM 87504
http://www.perfeng.com/~cusmith

Lloyd G. Williams
Software Engineering Research
264 Ridgeview Lane
Boulder, CO 80302
boulderlgw@aol.com

Abstract

Systems using distributed object technology offer many advantages and their use is becoming widespread. Distributed object systems are typically developed without regard to the locations of objects in the network or the nature of the communication between them. However, this approach often leads to performance problems due to latency in accessing remote objects and excessive overhead due to inefficient communication mechanisms. Thus, it is important to provide support for early assessment of the performance characteristics of such systems. This paper presents extensions to the software performance engineering process and its associated models for assessing distributed object systems. These extensions are illustrated with a simple case study showing model solutions using the *SPE•ED* performance engineering tool.

1. Introduction

Distributed-object technology (DOT) is the result of merging object-oriented techniques with distributed systems technology. DOT is enabled and supported by "middleware" such as the OMG Object Management Architecture which provides referential transparency and high-level inter-object communication mechanisms.

Systems based on DOT offer a number of advantages to software development organizations. Developers can design and implement a distributed application without being concerned about where a remote object resides, how it is implemented, or how inter-object communication occurs. Applications can be distributed over an heterogeneous network, making it possible to run each component on the most appropriate platform. In addition, "wrappers" can be used to make commercial off-the-shelf (COTS) products and/or legacy systems appear as objects. This makes it possible to integrate COTS or legacy software into more modern systems.

Distributed object systems are typically developed without regard to the locations of objects in the network or the nature of the communication between them. However, this approach often leads to performance problems due to latency in accessing remote objects and excessive overhead due to inefficient communication mechanisms [WALD94]. The performance of these systems must then be "tuned" by fixing the locations of critical objects (e.g., making remote objects local) and replacing slow communication mechanisms with more efficient ones.

This "fix-it-later" approach leads to many development problems. Poor performance is more often the result of problems in the design rather than the implementation. Our

R. Puigjaner et al. (Eds.): Tools'98, LNCS 1469, pp. 321-335, 1998
© Springer-Verlag Berlin Heidelberg 1998

experience is that it is possible to *cost-effectively* engineer distributed-object systems that meet performance goals with Software Performance Engineering (SPE) techniques [SMIT93a], [SMIT97].

However, systems based on the OMG Object Management Architecture are relatively new and offer new challenges for performance modeling. Our previous papers extended Software Performance Engineering (SPE) methods to include specific techniques for evaluating the performance of object-oriented systems [SMIT97]. However, they did not specifically address distributed systems or issues related to the use of CORBA. This paper extends our previous work to include extensions to the SPE methods that address:

- performance engineering methods appropriate for distributed systems,
- extensions to the SPE modeling techniques to evaluate performance issues that arise when using an object request broker (ORB), and
- modeling techniques for CORBA synchronization primitives

In the following sections we: review related work, explain the SPE process extensions for distributed systems, cover the performance issues introduced when distributed systems use the OMG Object Management Architecture for inter-object communication and coordination, present the performance models for distributed systems, and illustrate the models with a case study.

2. Related Work

Gokhale and Schmidt describe a measurement-based, principle-driven methodology for improving the performance of an implementation of the Internet Inter-ORB Protocol (IIOP) [GOKH97]. Their paper presents a set of principles (first formulated by Varghese [VARG96]) and illustrates their use in improving the performance of the IIOP. Their work is aimed at improving elements of the CORBA facilities. Ours focuses on the architecture of an application that uses CORBA facilities and the effect of the inter-process communication on its performance.

Meszaros [MESZ96] presents a set of patterns for improving the performance (capacity) of reactive systems. Their work is concerned with identifying a performance problem together with a set of forces that impact possible solutions. The patterns then suggest solutions that balance these forces. Petriu and Somadder [PETR97] extend these patterns to distributed, multi-level client/server systems. Our work focuses on early evaluation of software designs via modeling. Meszaros and Petriu and Sommader propose ways of identifying solutions to performance problems but do not specify whether the problems are identified by measurement or through modeling. Since early modeling could be used to identify performance problems, their work complements ours by providing guidelines for selecting solutions.

Smith and Williams describe performance engineering of an object-oriented design for a real-time system [SMIT93a]. However, that approach applies general SPE techniques and only addresses the specific problems of object-oriented systems in an ad hoc way. It models only one type of synchronization, whereas this paper models three types. Smith and Williams also describe the application of Use Case scenarios as the bridge between design models and performance models in [SMIT97]. In contrast, this paper extends the SPE process to evaluate special performance issues in distributed systems using the earlier approach as a starting point.

Smith presents several advanced system execution model approaches for parallel and distributed processing, including remote data access, messages for inter-process communication, and Ada rendezvous [SMIT90a]. Those approaches were very general and thus complex. They focused on the features in the advanced system execution model with only a loose connection to the software execution model. It is viable to evaluate systems with those approaches, but it is better for very early life cycles stages to have a simpler approximation technique based on the software execution models to support architecture and design trade-off studies. This paper presents an approximation technique for software execution models, a simpler approach for representing the synchronization points in the execution graph and an automatic translation to the advanced system execution model.

Other authors have presented general approximation techniques for software synchronization (e.g., [THOM85]). They also adapt the system execution model to quantify the effects of passive resource contention. Rolia introduced the method of layers to address systems of cooperating processes in a distributed environment, and a modification to the system execution model solution algorithms to quantify the delays for use of software servers, and contention effects introduced by them [ROLI95]. Woodside and co-workers propose stochastic rendezvous nets to evaluate the performance of Ada Systems [WOOD95]. All these approaches focus on synchronous communication, however adaptations to the various approximation techniques could be used for an approximate analytical solution to the advanced system execution model described in section 5.2.

3. Distributed System Extensions to the SPE Process
The SPE *process* for evaluating distributed-object systems is similar to the process for other systems. However, the models require some extension to evaluate details of concurrency and synchronization. We use the software performance engineering tool, *SPE•ED,* to evaluate the performance models. Other tools are available, such as [BEIL95], [TURN92], but the model translation would differ for those tools that do not use execution graphs as their modeling paradigm. The modeling approach described in the following sections is partially determined by our tool choice.

Software Performance Engineering (SPE) is a systematic, quantitative approach to constructing software systems that meet performance objectives. In early development stages, SPE uses deliberately simple models of software processing with the goal of using the simplest possible model that identifies problems with the system architecture, design, or implementation plans. These models are easily constructed and solved to provide feedback on whether the proposed software is likely to meet performance goals. As the software development proceeds, the models are refined to more closely represent the performance of the emerging software. Because it is difficult to precisely estimate resource requirements early in development, SPE uses adaptive strategies, such as upper- and lower-bounds, and best- and worst-case analysis to manage uncertainty.

Two types of models provide information for design assessment: the *software execution model* and the *system execution model*. The software execution model represents key aspects of the software execution behavior; we use execution graphs to represent performance scenarios. The software execution model solution provides a static analysis of the mean, best-, and worst-case response times for an initial evaluation against performance objectives. The system execution model uses the software execution model solution results to study the effect of contention delays for shared computer resources.

SPE for distributed-object systems begins with the same steps used for all object-oriented systems. It begins with the Use Cases identified by developers during the requirements analysis and system design phases of the development cycle. Once the major Use Cases and their scenarios have been identified, those that are important from a performance perspective are selected for performance modeling. These scenarios, represented using Message Sequence Charts (MSCs) [ITU96], are translated to execution graphs which serve as input to *SPE•ED*. This process, originally presented in [SMIT97], is: 1. Establish performance objectives; 2. Identify important Use Cases; 3. Select key performance scenarios; 4. Translate scenarios to execution graphs; 5. Add resource requirements and processing overhead; and 6. Solve the models. If the software model solution indicates problems, analysts consider architecture or design alternatives to address the problems. If not, then analysts proceed to evaluate additional characteristics of distributed systems.

SPE for distributed-object systems adds the following model features:
* Software execution model approximate techniques for estimating the performance effect of distributed objects
* An advanced system execution model to study the effect of contention for shared objects, and other delays for inter-process coordination.

The following section describes distributed object management, then section 5 describes these additional model features.

4. Object Management Performance Issues

Distributed-object technology is enabled by middleware that allows objects in a network to interact without regard to hardware platform, implementation language, or communication protocol. The Object Management Group's (OMG) Object Management Architecture (OMA)

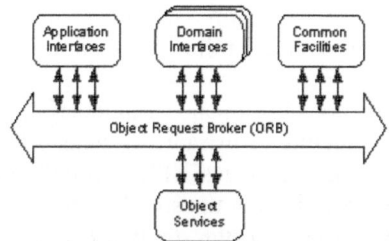

Figure 1. The OMA Reference Architecture

is a widely-used specification for a set of middleware standards that allow development of applications in a distributed, heterogeneous environment. The OMA consists of five principal components [VINO97] (Figure 1): object services, common facilities, domain interfaces, application interfaces, and the object request broker.

The core of this architecture is the Object Request Broker (ORB). The ORB is responsible for managing communication between objects without regard to: object location, implementation and state, or inter-object communication mechanisms. The OMA Common Object Request Broker Architecture (CORBA) specifies a standard architecture for ORBs. The primary performance issues that we consider are due to this component. Aspects of the ORB that impact performance can be divided into two categories: those that do not need to be explicitly modeled and those that do.

Aspects of the ORB that are vital to object interaction but do not require explicit modeling include:

- *the interface definition language*: declares the interfaces and types of operations and parameters (e.g., float, string, struct, etc.)
- *language mappings*: specifies how the interface definition language features are mapped to various programming languages
- *client stubs and server skeletons*[1]: provide mechanisms for interacting with the ORB to convert (static) request invocations from the programming language into a form for transmission to the server object and to similarly handle the response
- *dynamic invocation and dispatch*: a generic mechanism for dynamic request invocations without compile-time knowledge of object interfaces
- *protocols for inter-ORB communication*: the mechanism for ORB-to-ORB handling of request invocations

While these features affect the overall performance of a distributed system which includes an ORB, they are modeled implicitly by measuring their resource requirements and including it as "processing overhead" for each invocation of a server object.

The *Object Adapter* is the component of the ORB that actually connects objects to other objects. We also model several aspects of the object adapter by measuring their effect and including it in the processing overhead. These aspects are: registration of objects and interfaces, object reference generation, server process activation, object activation, static and dynamic invocations, communication overhead for transmitting request invocations, and processing overhead for converting requests across languages, operating systems, and hardware. We measure the overhead of each of these aspects of the Object Adapter. Performance scenarios derived from Use Cases then provide the processing details that quantify the number of times each is used.

Five aspects of the ORB that must be explicitly modeled are:

1. object location
2. process composition
3. request scheduling
4. request dispatching
5. coordination mechanisms

---

[1] In the OMA, communication is peer-to-peer, however, the terms *client* and *server* describe the roles in a particular communication when one object requests services from another.

Object location and process composition determine the processing steps assigned to each performance scenario [WILL98]. Request scheduling and request dispatching are partially determined by contention for called processes which is determined by the coordination mechanism and other processing requirements of performance scenarios. The models in section 5 quantify these aspects of the ORB. Coordination mechanisms require extensions to the Use Case and performance modeling formalisms. These are described in the following section.

5. Distributed System Models

Early in development, the SPE process for distributed systems calls for using deliberately simple models of software processing that are easily constructed and solved to provide feedback on whether the proposed software is likely to meet performance goals. Thus, our approach is to first create the software execution models as in steps 1 through 6 in section 3 without explicitly representing synchronization -- it is represented only as a delay to receive results from a server process. Section 5.1 describes these approximate models and the delay-estimation approach. Later in the development process, more realistic models, described in section 5.2, add synchronization notation to the MSCs and software execution models. They are solved with advanced system execution model techniques.[2]

For this paper, we consider the three types of coordination mechanisms between objects currently supported by the CORBA architecture [VINO97].

- *Synchronous invocation*: The sender invokes the request and blocks waiting for the response (an invoke call).
- *Deferred synchronous calls*: The sender initiates the request and continues processing. Responses are retrieved when the sender is ready (a send call, followed by a get_response call to obtain the result).
- *Asynchronous invocation*: The sender initiates the request and continues processing; there is no response a (send call to a one_way operation or with INV_NO_RESPONSE specified).

Synchronous or asynchronous invocations may be either static or dynamic; currently, deferred synchronous invocations may only be dynamic.

5.1 Approximate Models of Software Synchronization

The following sections examine the approximation strategy for each of the three types of coordination mechanisms between objects currently supported by the CORBA architecture.

5.1.1 Synchronization Types

Figure 2 shows processing flow when a client process makes two synchronous requests to a server process. The "blips" in each column represent processing activity on the corresponding processing node. The absence of a blip indicates that the corresponding processing node is not processing *this request* – shared processing nodes (the Network and Server) may process other requests at those times. Processing

---

[2] These discussions assume familiarity with execution graphs and Message Sequence Charts (MSCs). More information about these notations is in [SMIT90a] and [SMIT97].

for the first request is initiated on the Client; the synchronous request is transmitted via the Network; the Server processes the request and sends a reply; the Network processes the reply; the Client receives the reply and begins processing that will make another synchronous request. And so on.

Note that we do not explicitly represent possible ORB processing for run-time binding of the Client and Server processes. This illustration assumes that the processes are bound earlier. Analysts could model the ORB explicitly as another column in the diagrams, or implicitly by adding overhead for each ORB request.

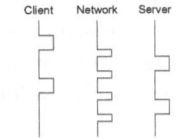

Figure 2. Synchronous Communication Flow

Figure 3 shows one possibility for the processing flow when the client sends a deferred synchronous request to the server. The client process sends the request and continues processing. The processing on the Network and Server processing nodes is the same as before. At some point in the processing the Client needs the result. The dashed line below the first Client "blip" represents

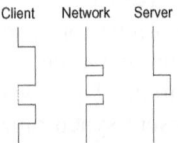

Figure 3. Deferred Synchronous Flow

the time that the Client must wait for the request completion. The second possibility, no Client wait, would omit the dashed line and show a continuous blip in the Client column.

Figure 4 shows one possibility for the flow when the client sends an asynchronous request to the server. The client process sends the request and continues processing. The processing on the Network and Server processing nodes for transmitting and processing the request is the same as before, but there is no reply.

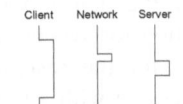

Figure 4. Asynchronous Flow

5.1.2 Approximate Software Models
These profiles are the basis for the first approximation. We create a separate performance scenario for each process in the Use Case, specify resource requirements corresponding to the "blips," and estimate the delay between "blips." The models may be iterative - the solution of each independent performance scenario quantifies its processing time. The processing time for the "dependent blips" can be used to refine the estimate of the delay between blips. In these illustrations we arbitrarily show the client and server objects on separate processors and the invocations must be transmitted through the network. If they reside on the same processor there is no delay for the network "blips."

For deferred synchronization, estimate the delay corresponding to the dashed line; if the request completes before the client processing, the delay is zero. Iterative solutions refine the delay estimates. The client process has no delay for asynchronous requests.

This model is first solved without contention to determine if this optimistic model meets performance objectives. After correcting any problems, the contention solution quantifies additional delays due to contention from other work

Each scenario may be an open or a closed model. Closed models specify the number of threads and the expected inter-arrival time of requests. Open models estimate the arrival rate of requests. Both estimates come from the processing time of the calling process, iterative solutions may be used to refine estimates.

5.2 Detailed Models of Synchronization

Detailed models of synchronization connect client requests across processing nodes more realistically reflecting the complex processing behavior. We start with the separate performance scenarios created in the approximate analysis step, and insert special notations into the MSCs at points when CORBA-based coordination is required. These lead to the insertion of special nodes into the execution graphs to represent synchronization steps. In *SPE•ED*, an advanced system execution model is automatically created from the execution graphs and solved to quantify contention effects and delays. These steps are described in the following sections.

5.2.1 MSC Extensions to Represent CORBA Coordination

The MSC notation [ITU96] does not provide graphical syntax for representing the CORBA synchronization primitives. We use elements of the UML notation [RATI97] for synchronous and asynchronous calls together with an extension of our own to show the deferred synchronous invocation. These are shown in Figure 5. The notation for synchronous invocation shows a break in the processing when the caller waits for the response. The deferred synchronous notation represents continued processing with a potential delay before receiving the reply. The arrow representing the reply will be shown at the point when it occurs, processing may continue in the called process. The notation for asynchronous invocation has a partial arrow for the call and no return arrow.

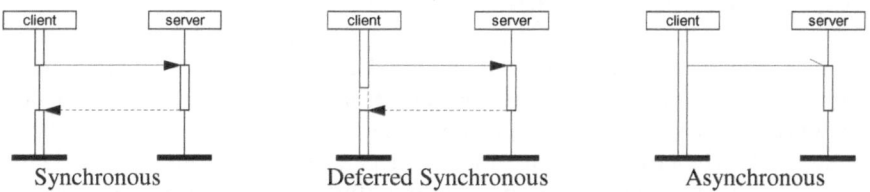

Synchronous   Deferred Synchronous   Asynchronous

Figure 5. MSC Representation of CORBA-based Synchronization

5.2.2 Software Execution Model Extensions

Figure 6 shows the new execution graph nodes that represent the three types of synchronization. The appropriate node from the left column of the figure is inserted in the execution graph for the calling scenario. The called scenario represents the synchronization point with one of the nodes from the right column depending on whether or not it sends a reply. The calling process specifies the synchronization type so the called process need not distinguish between synchronous and deferred synchronous calls. Any of the rectangular nodes may be expanded to show processing steps that occur between the dashed arrows or in connection with asynchronous calls. The expansion may contain other synchronization steps. The called process may execute additional processing steps after the reply is sent.

Next, the analyst specifies resource requirements for the processing steps and the number of threads for called processes. Each performance scenario is assigned to a processing node.

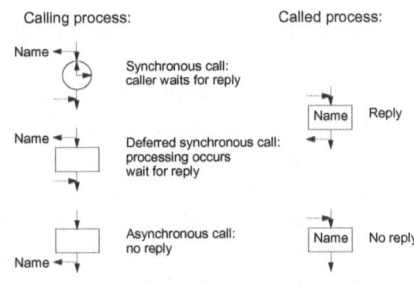

Figure 6. Execution Graph Nodes for Software Synchronization

SPE•ED uses the CSIM simulation tool to solve the advanced system model. CSIM is a simulation product that is widely used to evaluate distributed and parallel processing systems [SCHW94]. *SPE•ED* solves the software execution model to derive the computer device processing requirements, then creates the advanced system execution model and solves it with a table-driven CSIM simulation model.[3] The software execution model solution provides summary data for processing phases [SMIT90a]. This provides an efficient simulation solution at a process-phase granularity rather than a detailed process simulation.

Two CSIM synchronization mechanisms provide the process coordination required for the software synchronization: *events* and *mailboxes*. An event consists of a state variable and two queues (one for *waiting* processes and the other for *queued* processes). When the event "happens" one of the queued processes can proceed. (The waiting queue is not used in *SPE•EDs* synchronization model). An event happens when a process *sets* the event to the occurred state. A mailbox is a container for holding CSIM messages. A process can *send* a message to a mailbox or *receive* a message from a mailbox. If a process does a receive on an empty mailbox, it automatically waits until a message is sent to that mailbox. When a message arrives, the first waiting process can proceed.

A synchronous or deferred synchronous call is implemented in *SPE•EDs* advanced system execution model with a *send* to the *name* mailbox of the called process (the *name* appears in the processing node of the called process). The message is an *event* that is to be set for the "reply." An asynchronous call is also implemented with a mailbox *send*; the message is ignored because there is no reply. The calling process executes a *queue* statement for the *event*; synchronous invocations place the queue statement immediately after the send, deferred synchronous invocations place it at the designated point later in the processing. The called process issues a *receive* from its mailbox. At the reply's designated point in the processing, the called process *sets* the event it received. If there are multiple threads of the called process, the next in the receive queue processes the request. The event must be unique for the correct process to resume after the *set* statement executes.

---

[3] An approximate solution to the advanced system model is possible, but not currently in *SPE•EDs* repertoire. Several approximations in the related work section might be applicable.

In addition to the standard results reported by *SPE•ED*, the following are reported for the synchronization steps:

- mean, minimum, maximum, and variance response time for called processes
- mean and maximum number of requests and the mean time in queue (mailbox) for called processes
- throughput of called processes.

These results indicate when processing requirements should be reduced or the number of threads increased to alleviate performance problems due to synchronization. They also indicate what proportion of the total elapsed time depends on other processes. It shows the proportion of the computer resource requirements used by each scenario, and the overall device utilization.

6. Case Study

This case study is from an actual study, however, application details have been changed to preserve anonymity. The software supports an electronic virtual storefront, eStuff.[4] Software supporting eStuff has components to take customer orders, fulfill orders and ship them from the warehouse, and, for just-in-time shipments, interface with suppliers to obtain items to ship. The heart of the system is the Customer Service component that collects completed orders, initiates tasks in the other components, and tracks the status of orders in progress.

6.1 Approximate Model

The Use Case we consider is processing a new order (Figure 7). It begins with TakeCustOrder, an MSC reference to another, more detailed MSC. An ACK is sent to the customer, and the order processing begins. In this scenario we assume that a customer order consists of 50 individual items. The unit of work for the TakeCustOrder and CloseCustOrder components is the entire order; the other order-processing components handle each item in the order separately; the MSC shows this repetition with a loop symbol. The similar symbol labeled "opt" represents an optional step that may occur when eStuff must order the item from a supplier.

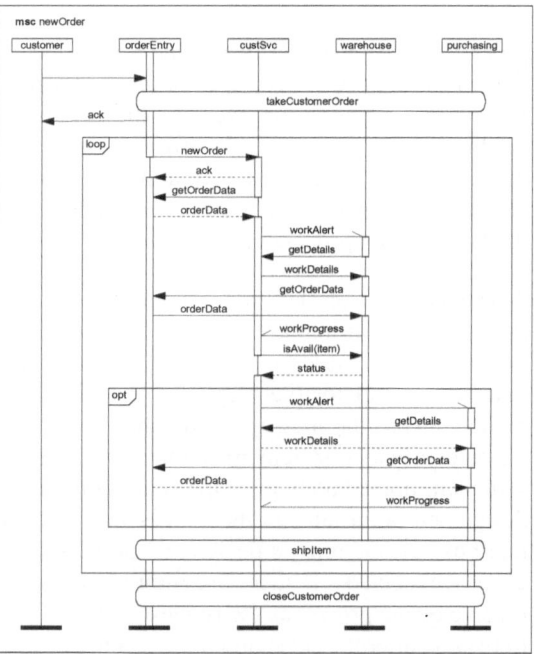

Figure 7. New order scenario

---

[4]   eStuff is a fictional web site. At the time this paper was written no such site existed.

Figure 8 shows the execution graph for the CustomerService column in the Use Case in Figure 7. Everything inside the loop is in the expanded node, ProcessItemOrder. Its details are in Figure 9. The two WorkAlert processing steps are also expanded; their details are not shown here. Each column in Figure 7 becomes a scenario. At this stage we assume that the first three scenarios each execute on its own facility, and the warehouse and purchasing scenarios share a processor. This software model depicts only the CustomerService processing node; we approximate the delay time to communicate with the other processing nodes.

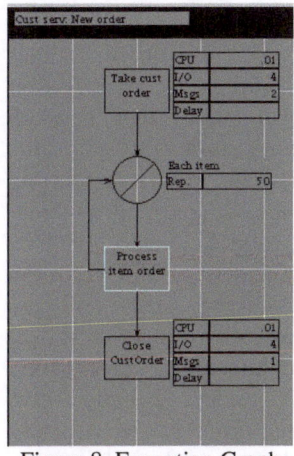

Figure 8. Execution Graph
CustomerService: New Order

The next step is to specify resource requirements for each processing step. The key resources in this model are the CPU time for database and other processing, the number of I/Os for database and logging activities, the number of messages sent among processors (and the associated overhead for the ORB), and the estimated delay in seconds for the "blips" on other processors until the message-reply is received. These values are shown in Figures 8 and 9. They are best-case estimates derived from performance measurement experiments. They may also be estimated in a performance walkthrough [SMIT90a].

Analysts specify values for the software resource requirements for processing steps. The computer resource requirements for each software resource request are specified in an overhead matrix stored in the SPE database. This matrix represents each of the hardware devices in each of the distributed processors, connects the software model resource requests to hardware device requirements, and incorporates any processing requirements due to operating system or network overhead (see [SMIT97] for a detailed description of the overhead matrix).

Figure 10 shows the best-case solution with one user and thus no contention for computer devices. The end-to-end time is 480 seconds, most of it is in ProcessItemOrder (the value shown is for all 50 items). Results for the ProcessItemOrder subgraph (not shown) indicate that each item requires approximately 9.8 seconds, most of that is in the ShipItem processing step. Other results (not shown) indicate that 7.5 seconds of the 9.8 seconds is

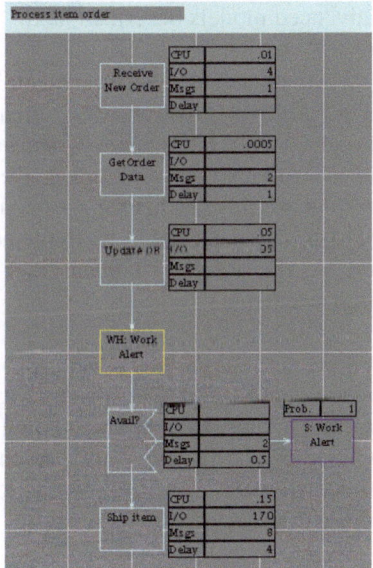

Figure 9. Execution Graph
ProcessItemOrder Expansion

due to estimated delay for processing on the other facilities. Investigation also shows that network congestion prevents the system from supporting the desired throughput. Analysts can evaluate potential solutions by modifying the software execution model to reflect architecture alternatives. We select an alternative that processes work orders as a group rather than individual items in an order. The changes to the software execution model for this alternative are relatively minor – the number of loop repetitions is reduced to 2 (one for orders ready to ship, the other for orders requiring back-ordered items), and the resource requirements for steps in the loop change slightly to reflect requirements to process a group of items. This alternative yields a response time of 16.5 seconds with the desired throughput of 0.1 jobs per second.

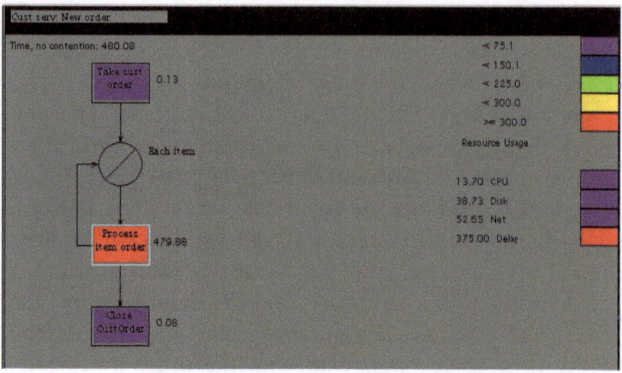

Figure 10. Best-case elapsed time.

Thus, the overhead and delays due to CORBA-based process coordination were a significant portion of the total end-to-end time to process a new order. Improvements resulted from processing batches of items rather than individual items. These simple models provide sufficient information to identify problems in the architecture before proceeding to the advanced system execution model. It is easy and important to resolve key performance problems with simple models before proceeding to the advanced models described next.

6.2 Advanced System Execution Model

This section illustrates the creation and evaluation of the detailed models of synchronization. Figure 7 shows that all the synchronization steps are either asynchronous or synchronous. Deferred synchronous calls are only useful when the results are not needed for the next processing steps. Deferred synchronous calls may also be more complex to implement. Thus, it is sensible to plan synchronous calls unless the models indicate that deferred synchronous calls result in significant improvements.

Figure 11 shows the synchronization nodes in the ProcessItemOrder step. It first receives the NewOrder message and immediately replies with the acknowledgement message thus freeing the calling process. Next it makes a synchronous call to OE:GetOrderData and waits for the reply. The availability check is now explicitly modeled with a synchronous call to WH:Avail? The processing steps here are similar to those in the approximate model.

Figure 12 shows the processing that occurs on the Warehouse facility. It receives the asynchronous request from the CS facility, makes a synchronous call to CS:GetDetails, makes a synchronous call to OE:GetOData, then (after the order is shipped) makes an asynchronous call to CS StatusUpdate.

Table 1 shows the advanced system model results. They reflect results for 10 hours simulated time with a total of 3565 CS:NewOrders during that interval. The confidence level was computed using the batch mean method; the result is 0.172 for the CS:NewOrder scenario.

It is difficult to validate models of systems that are still under development. Many changes occur before the software executes and may be measured, and the early life cycle models are best-case models that omit many processing complexities that occur in the ultimate implementation. Nevertheless, the results are sufficiently accurate to identify problems in the software plans and quantify the relative benefit of

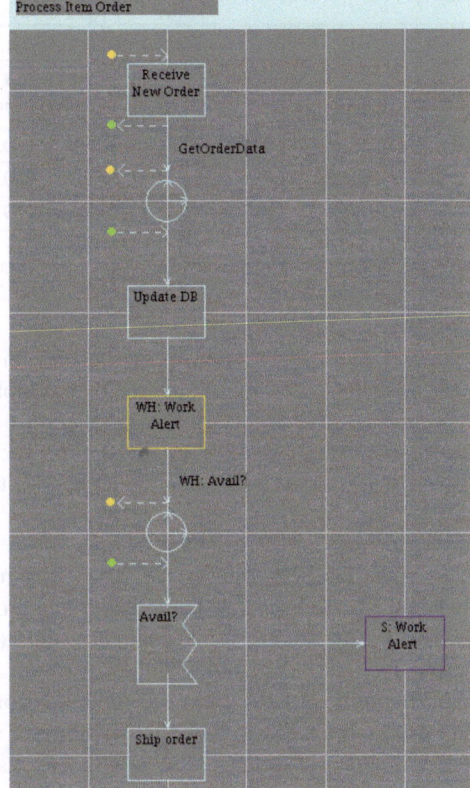

Figure 11. Synchronization in ProcessItemOrder.

improvements. In this study, the models successfully predicted potential problems in the original architecture due to network activity.

The maximum queue length and the queue time for WH:WorkAlert suggests that more concurrent threads might be desirable for scalability. The simulation results would also reflect problems due to "lock-step" execution of concurrent processes. For example, note that the mean response time for P:WorkAlert is slightly higher than for WH:WorkAlert even though they execute the same processing steps and P:WorkAlert executes less frequently (see throughput values). This is because the asynchronous calls to WH:WorkAlert and to P:WorkAlert occur very close to the same time and cause both processes to execute concurrently on the same facility. This introduces slight contention delays for the process that arrives second (P:WorkAlert). In this case study the performance effect is not serious, but it illustrates the types of performance analysis important for this life cycle stage and the models that permit the analysis.

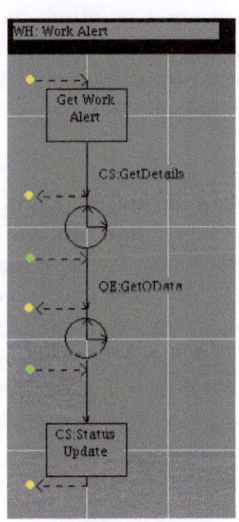

Figure 12.
WH:WorkAlert

Table 1. Advanced System Model Results

	Response Time (sec.)				TPut	Queue		
	Mean	Min	Max	Variance		Mean	Max	Time
CS:NewOrder	14.4	0.8	72.7	79.51	.1			
OE:OrderData	0.16	0	2.6	0.05	.5	0.092	5	0.19
CS:WorkDetails	0.2	0	3.7	0.05	.3	0.057	2	0.19
CS:UpdStatus	0.1	0	4.4	0.04	.3	0.004	3	0.01
WH:WorkAlert	1.3	0	9.1	1.14	.2	0.122	9	0.62
P:WorkAlert	1.4	0	9.3	1.16	.1	0.019	3	0.193

Note that most of the useful results in early life cycle stages come from the approximate software model. For example, the amount of communication and the synchronization points in the architecture and design, the assignment of methods to processes, assignment of processes to processors, an approximate number of threads per process, etc., can all be evaluated with the simpler models.

7. Summary and Conclusions

Studying the performance of software architectures for distributed-object systems, particularly those that have extensive communication and synchronization, is of growing importance. This paper presents and illustrates the SPE process and model extensions for distributed-object systems that use the OMG Object Management Architecture for inter-object communication and coordination.   Two types of models are used: approximate software models for quick and easy performance assessments in early life cycle stages, and advanced system execution models for more realistic predictions and analysis of details of interconnection performance.

Approximate software models are constructed from Use Case scenarios identified during the analysis and design phases of the development process. Then the advanced system execution models are created and solved automatically by the *SPE•ED* performance engineering tool. This simplifies the modelers task by eliminating the need for debugging complex simulation models of synchronization. It also permits an efficient hybrid solution that summarizes processing requirements by phases.

The five key aspects of the CORBA Object Adapter that determine the performance of systems and are explicitly modeled were listed in Section 4. Three of them -- process composition, process location, and synchronization type, are architecture and design decisions. Thus, it makes sense to execute these quantitative evaluations to determine the appropriate choice. Future work may explore the feasibility and usefulness of using approximate solution techniques for the advanced system execution model. This could be accomplished by implementing additional solution techniques, or by using the software meta-model to exchange model information with another tool for solution and evaluation [WILL95].

8. References

[BEIL95] H. Beilner, J. Mäter, and C. Wysocki, *The Hierarchical Evaluation Tool HIT*, 581/1995, Universität Dortmund, Fachbereich Informatik, D-44221 Dortmund, Germany, 1995, 6-9.

[RATI97] Rational Software Corporation, Unified Modeling Language: Notation Guide, Version 1.1, 1997.

[GOKH97] A. Gokhale and D.C. Schmidt, "Principles for Optimizing CORBA Internet Inter-ORB Protocol Performance," *Proceedings of the Thirty-first Hawaii International Conference on System Sciences (HICSS)*, Kohala Coast, HI, January 1997,.

[ITU96] ITU, Criteria for the Use and Applicability of Formal Description Techniques, Message Sequence Chart (MSC), 1996.

[MESZ96] G. Meszaros, *A Pattern Language for Improving the Capacity of Reactive Systems*, , Addison-Wesley, Reading, MA, 1996, 575-591.

[PETR97] D. Petriu and G. Somadder, "A Pattern Language for Improving the Capacity of Layered Client/Server Systems with Multi-Threaded Servers," *Proceedings of EuroPLoP'97*, Kloster Irsee, Germany, July 1997,.

[ROLI95] J.A. Rolia and K.C. Sevcik, "The Method of Layers," *IEEE Trans. on Software Engineering*, 21(8), 689-700, 1995.

[SCHW94] H. Schwetman, "CSIM17: A Simulation Model-Building Toolkit," *Proceedings Winter Simulation Conference*, Orlando, 1994,.

[SMIT90a] Connie U. Smith, *Performance Engineering of Software Systems*, Addison-Wesley, Reading, MA, 1990.

[SMIT93a] Connie U. Smith and Lloyd G. Williams, "Software Performance Engineering: A Case Study with Design Comparisons," *IEEE Transactions on Software Engineering*, 19(7), 720-741, 1993.

[SMIT97] Connie U. Smith and Lloyd G. Williams, *Performance Engineering of Object-Oriented Systems with SPEED*, Springer, Berlin, Germany, 1997, 135-154.

[THOM85] A. Thomasian and P. Bay, "Performance Analysis of Task Systems Using a Queueing Network Model," *Proceedings International Conference Timed Petri Nets*, Torino, Italy, 1985,234-242.

[TURN92] Michael Turner, Douglas Neuse, and Richard Goldgar, "Simulating Optimizes Move to Client/Server Applications," *Proceedings Computer Measurement Group Conference*, Reno, NV, 1992,805-814.

[VARG96] G. Varghese, *Algorithmic Techniques for Efficient Protocol Implementation*, , Stanford, CA, 1996,

[VINO97] S. Vinoski, "CORBA: Integrating Diverse Applications Within Distributed Heterogeneous Environments," *IEEE Communications*, 35(2), 46-55, 1997.

[WALD94] J. Waldo, et al., A Note on Distributed Computing, 1994.

[WILL95] Lloyd G. Williams and Connie U. Smith, "Information Requirements for Software Performance Engineering," *Proceedings 1995 International Conference on Modeling Techniques and Tools for Computer Performance Evaluation*, Heidelberg, Germany, 1995,.

[WILL98] L.G. Williams and C.U. Smith, "Performance Evaluation of Software Architectures," *Proc. First International Workshop on Software and Performance*, Santa Fe, NM, October 1998,.

[WOOD95] C.M. Woodside, et al., "The Stochastic Rendezvous Network Model for Performance of Synchronous Client-Server-like Distributed Software," *IEEE Trans. Computers*, 44(1), 20-34, 1995.

Edinet: An Execution Driven Interconnection Network Simulator for DSM Systems [*]

J. Flich, P. López, M. P. Malumbres and J. Duato

Depto. Informática de Sistemas y Computadores, Universidad Politécnica de Valencia
Camino de Vera s/n, 46071 - Valencia, SPAIN
`jflich,plopez,mperez,jduato@gap.upv.es`

Abstract. Evaluation studies on interconnection networks for distributed memory multiprocessors usually assume synthetic or trace-driven workloads. However, when the final design choices must be done a more precise evaluation study should be performed. In this paper, we describe a new execution-driven simulation tool to evaluate interconnection networks for distributed memory multiprocessors using real application workloads. As an example, we have developed a NCC-NUMA memory model and obtained some simulation results from the SPLASH-2 suite, using different network routing algorithms.

1 Introduction

Interconnection network evaluation studies usually assume that the workload generated by actual applications can be modeled by synthetic workloads. Constant message generation rate (equal for all nodes), uniform distribution of message destinations (with or without locality) and fixed traffic patterns are frequently used. However, when the designer must do the final choices, a more precise evaluation study should be performed.

Some studies have relied on trace-driven simulations [9,8]. However parallel traces generated for one architecture may never happen on another. For instance, some messages should not be generated until some other has been arrived at its destination, and this depends on the interconnection network performance, which is not being simulated when the trace file is being created.

The definitive tool to get accurate evaluation results is an execution-driven simulators [4,5]. In such simulator, an application runs on the host processor and special call-outs are inserted into the original code to instrument the required events. These events are scheduled as requests to the simulator. In our case, the events are the message send/receive primitives, and the simulator is the interconnection network simulator. In addition, a parallel application simulator is also required in order to execute the parallel code on a single processor.

In this paper, we present a new simulation tool, called EDINET, that allows executing a shared-memory application on a simulated DSM system. Our goal will be accurately to analyze the interconnection network performance using real application workloads.

---

[*] This work was supported by the Spanish CICYT under Grant TIC97–0897–C04–01.

R. Puigjaner et al. (Eds.): Tools'98, LNCS 1469, pp. 336–339, 1998.
© Springer-Verlag Berlin Heidelberg 1998

2   Edinet

The EDINET simulator is composed of two simulators. The first one is Limes [5], an execution driven simulator that allows parallel program execution and models the memory subsystem. The second one is the interconnection network simulator (NetSim) that we have already used in several evaluation studies [3,6]. The memory simulator part of Limes (MemSim) simulates the memory subsystem sending requests to NetSim in order to simulate the advance of messages.

MemSim drives the network simulator using the following commands: *InitNetSim* (starts the simulation process), *InsertRequest* (injects a new message into the network), *Simulate* (simulates from the last simulated time to the actual simulation time), *EndNetSim* (ends the simulation and collects statistics). On the other hand, NetSim issues the following commands to MemSim: *MessageArrived* (a message has just arrived at its destination node), *TimeSimulated* (the requested time has just been simulated).

The memory simulator controls the applications threads. When it needs to send a request into the network, the involved thread is stalled until all the messages due to the request has been completed.

3   Performance Evaluation

In this section we present some simulation results for a DSM system with a NCC-NUMA memory model [7]. Data distribution and process allocation are crucial in this model. In fact, some SPLASH-2 [1] applications recall that good distribution has great impact on performance. In addition, each process should be assigned to the proper processor in order to improve data locality. The best data distribution and process allocation strategies have been used in the evaluation.

The interconnection network is a 64-node wormhole switched bidirectional *k-ary 2-cube*. Three routing algorithms have been compared: deterministic, partially adaptive and fully adaptive. These routing algorithms were proposed in [3,2]. The PRAM (Perfect RAM) model is also evaluated for comparison purposes. In this model, each request served in only one cycle. Thus, we will use PRAM results as an approximation of an ideal memory subsystem and interconnection network.

Different complexity problems for OCEAN and FFT applications (SPLASH-2) are simulated. Each process is assigned to one single processor.

Performance evaluation is mainly done by means of application execution time. Taking into account that initialization phase can not be paralellized, we will not include it in the evaluation. This approach is also used in [1].

3.1   Simulation Results

Figure 1 shows the execution time for the OCEAN application. The partially adaptive routing algorithm improves performance by almost a 40 % with respect to the deterministic one. The fully adaptive routing algorithm outperforms both

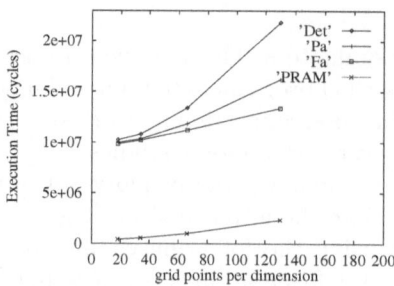

Fig. 1. OCEAN execution time.

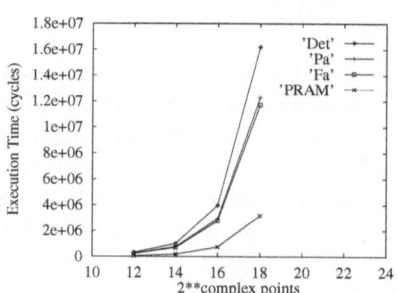

Fig. 2. FFT execution time.

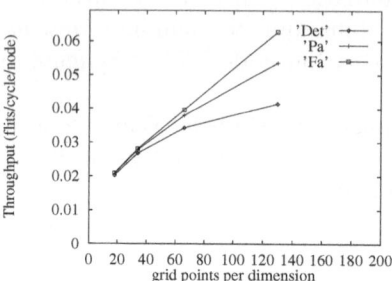

Fig. 3. Throughput for OCEAN.

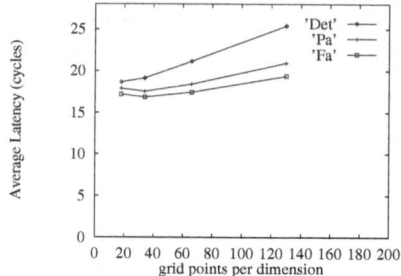

Fig. 4. Average latency for OCEAN.

the deterministic and partially adaptive one, reducing execution time by 70 % and 20 % respectively. However, the execution time achieved by the fully adaptive routing algorithm is still far from the PRAM model (by a factor of 7, approx.). Remember that the memory model considered is highly inefficient, as it does not cache remote requests.

Figure 2 shows the execution time for the FFT application. Partially adaptive reduces execution time by a 30 % over deterministic routing. Although fully adaptive routing slightly improves over partially adaptive routing, the improvement is smaller than in OCEAN. This behavior is due to the fact that the FFT application does not generate so many traffic as OCEAN does, so that the greater routing flexibility offered by fully adaptive routing is useless.

As figure 3 shows, OCEAN application generates very low network traffic rate. The maximum network throughput is reached with the fully adaptive routing algorithm at the highest complexity (0.06 flits/node/cycle). As known, the network bisection bandwidth limit is more than one order of magnitude higher. It is important to note that only a single process is assigned to each network node and a sequential consistency memory model has been assumed. Thus, global message injection is limited to 64 (the number of nodes) messages at a time. Figure 4 shows differences between the average latencies achieved by each of the routing algorithms for OCEAN application. When using adaptive routing, the improvement on the application execution time is given by the combination of lower contention and higher network bandwidth. The analysis of throughput and latency for FFT (not shown) leads to similar results.

The performance improvement of adaptive routing even with the low traffic generated by these applications and the analyzed memory model, lead us to expect important improvements of the execution time from other applications that make a more intensive use of the network. Also, more efficient memory models (CC-NUMA, COMA [7]) may demand more network traffic.

4   Conclusions

In this paper we have proposed an execution-driven network simulator that allows the evaluation of DSM's interconnection network using real application workloads. This tool can also be used to analyze the impact of memory subsystem on performance. As a consequence, both subsystems can be jointly evaluated in order to achieve the best overall performance. As an example, we have implemented the NCC-NUMA memory model and some applications have been executed using different network routing algorithms. The results show that adaptive routing improves performance over deterministic routing by a 30 %.

As for future work we plan to evaluate interconnection network performance using more realistic memory models like CC-NUMA, COMA, Simple COMA and other memory consistency models. We are also interested in evaluating irregular interconnection networks for NOWS using real applications workloads.

References

1. S. Cameron Woo et al., "The SPLASH-2 Programs: Characterization and Methodological Considerations," *Proceedings of the 22nd Annual International Symposium on Computer Architecture*, pp 24-36, June 1995.
2. W.J. Dally and C.L. Seitz, "Deadlock-free message routing in multiprocessor interconnection networks," *IEEE Transactions on Computers*, vol. C-36, no. 5, pp. 547–553, May 1987.
3. J. Duato and P. López, "Performance evaluation of adaptive routing algorithms for k-ary n-cubes," *Parallel Computer Routing and Communication*, K. Bolding and L. Snyder (ed.), Springer-Verlag, pp. 45–59, 1994.
4. S. Goldschmidt, "Simulation of Multiprocessors: Accuracy and Performance," *Ph.D. Thesis, Stanford University*, June 1993.
5. D. Magdic, "Limes: A Multiprocessor Simulation Environment," *TCCA Newsletter*, pp 68-71, March 1997.
6. M.P. Malumbres, J. Duato and J. Torrellas, "An Efficient Implementation of Tree-Based Multicast Routing for Distributed Shared-Memory Multiprocessors," in *Proc. of the eighth IEEE Symp. on Parallel and Distributed Processing*, pp. 186-189, October 1996.
7. J. Protic, I. Tartalja, V. Milutinovic, "Distributed Shared Memory: Concepts and Systems", *IEEE Parallel and Distributed Technology*, Vol.5, No 1, Summer 1996.
8. F. Silla, M. P. Malumbres, J. Duato, D. Dai and D. K. Panda, "Impact of Adaptivity on the Behavior of Networks of Workstations under Bursty Traffic", submitted to *International Conference on Parallel Processing 1998*.
9. D. Thiebaut, J.L. Wolf, H. S. Stone, "Synthetic Traces for Trace-Driven Simulation of Cache Memories", *IEEE Transactions on Computers*, vol. 41, april 1992.

Snuffle: Integrated Measurement and Analysis Tool for Internet and its Use in Wireless In-House Environment

B. Rathke[1], Th. Assimakopoulos[1], R. Morich[1], G. Schulte[1], and A. Wolisz[1,2]

[1] Telecommunication Networks Group, Dept. of Electrical Engineering,
Technical University Berlin, Germany
{rathke,thass,morich,schulte,wolisz}@ee.tu-berlin.de,
WWW home page: http://www-tkn.tu-berlin.de
[2] also with GMD-Fokus

Abstract. In this paper we describe *Snuffle*, a new measurement tool for capturing, displaying and analyzing the operation of the Internet protocol stack within end-systems. *Snuffle* is a set of modules operating in a distributed fashion and supporting an on-line analysis of network and protocol performance. This kind of tool is especially suited for wireless networks.

1 Introduction

The popular network monitoring tools (e.g. tcpdump [2], snoop [4], etherfind, Remote Network Monitoring (RMON) [5] etc.) follow the principle of observing packets traversing the network. Thus, there is only a limited possibility to infer about the internal Internet protocol variables [6]. The accuracy of this inference depends on the completeness of the trace, i.e. each lost sample falsifies the conclusions about the protocol variables and makes performance evaluations inaccurate. Therefore it is necessary to measure directly within the end-systems for precise investigation of Internet protocols and their internal state variables .

Especially in an error prone wireless environment it cannot be guaranteed, that an observer placed outside of the communicating end-systems records the same packets as transmitted or received by the observed nodes. It is known that in wireless networks operating around 1GHz or higher, small displacements of mobile systems may result in dramatically degradations of the physical link quality. In the worst case, the observed end-systems can still communicate, while the observing host has lost contact to them.

In this paper we present *Snuffle*, a tool suitable for measurements in Internet and a case study in a wireless LAN environment. *Snuffle* is currently implemented on Linux V2.0.27 and available at http://www-tkn.tu-berlin.de.

2 Design and Implementation Approach of *Snuffle*

Snuffle consists of interacting modules providing a set of measurement functionalities. The modules can be placed on different end-systems. We have defined

R. Puigjaner et al. (Eds.): Tools'98, LNCS 1469, pp. 340–344, 1998.

four types of modules: Snuffle Information Base (SIB), Tracer, Synchronizer, and Analyzer (depicted in Fig.1).

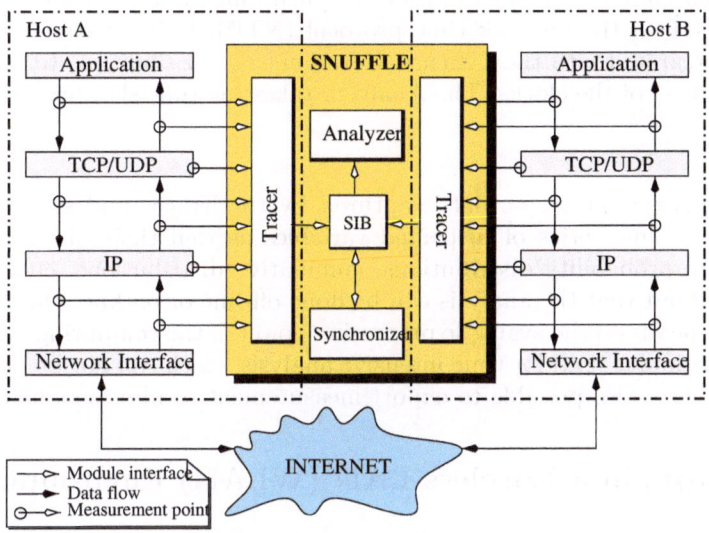

Fig. 1. *Snuffle* architecture

The Snuffle Information Base contains objects holding traced protocol data (protocol variables and header information) and derived information. A time-stamp is attached to every object defining its sampling time. We have currently implemented object classes for TCP, UDP and IP. Each object holds information about:

- Packet Header Information, e.g. TCP segment and ACK sequence numbers, window size, port numbers, IP identifier.
- Protocol Variables, e.g. TCP windows sizes (congestion window, sending and receiving windows), round trip time values, retransmission timer values.
- Derived Values, e.g. delays, cause of retransmissions, throughput.

Other modules (e.g. the Analyzer) can access objects of a SIB through an interface. This interface supports currently three functions: initialization of SIBs, reading objects from a SIB and setting filter functions.

The Tracer module is the interface between the measurement points and a SIB. The measurement points operate as samplers gathering internal protocol information and support filters for selective capturing of data. A measurement point may be placed arbitrary in the Internet protocol stack. Its implementation has to be adapted to specific Internet protocol implementations.

The Synchronizer is needed to perform accurate delay measurements between Tracers (see Fig.1), if they are located on different communication systems. To ensure correct delay measurements, clocks used by Tracers have to be synchronized. Well known approaches for clock synchronization, e.g. global positioning systems (GPS), the network time protocol (NTP), DCF or (radio) broadcasts can be integrated into the Synchronizer. Another possibility is to estimate the time skewness of the clocks. The Analyzer takes the time skewness into consideration.

The Analyzer processes data captured by the Tracer and stored in a SIB. It produces time series of inspected variables as well their distributions (e.g. conditional probability distributions, cumulative distributions, etc.). It should be pointed out that the analysis can be done off-line or on-line. On-line analysis heavily depends on the available processing power of the computing systems. The off-line method is used for time intensive analysis which can not be performed in real time. It is also possible to export measurement results to simulation tools.

3   *Snuffle* in a Wireless LAN (WLAN) Environment

We present results of measured TCP and IP throughput and TCP behavior in a WLAN environment using ARLAN[1] [1] as WLAN technology. In this scenario two hosts reside at fixed positions in a single radio cell communicating undisturbed from other hosts. Although many researches have faced the problems of TCP in WLANs by simulations (for an overview see [8]) we present results of measurements in a real environment.

Fig.2(a) shows the throughput calculated by *Snuffle* on TCP and on IP level. The measurement results show that although the IP throughput is high the TCP throughput is very low. This indicates that TCP is not suitable for this position in the radio cell. The loss rate on IP level does not exceed 10^{-6}, which is comparable to the loss rate of twisted pair cabling. Therefore losses are not responsible for the disappointing throughput of TCP. In spite of the low loss rate the number of TCP retransmissions is very high, as shown in Fig.2(b). This corresponds to Fig.2(c), showing the congestion window. Whenever a retransmission timeout occurs TCP drops its congestion window down to one segment [9]. The delay variability of packets on IP level causes retransmissions. To give an impression about the delay variability Fig.2(d) shows the delay distribution on IP level. A deeper analysis can be found in [7].

---

[1] ARLAN operates at 2.4GHz, uses Direct Sequence Spread Spectrum and CSMA/CA with immediate ACKs.

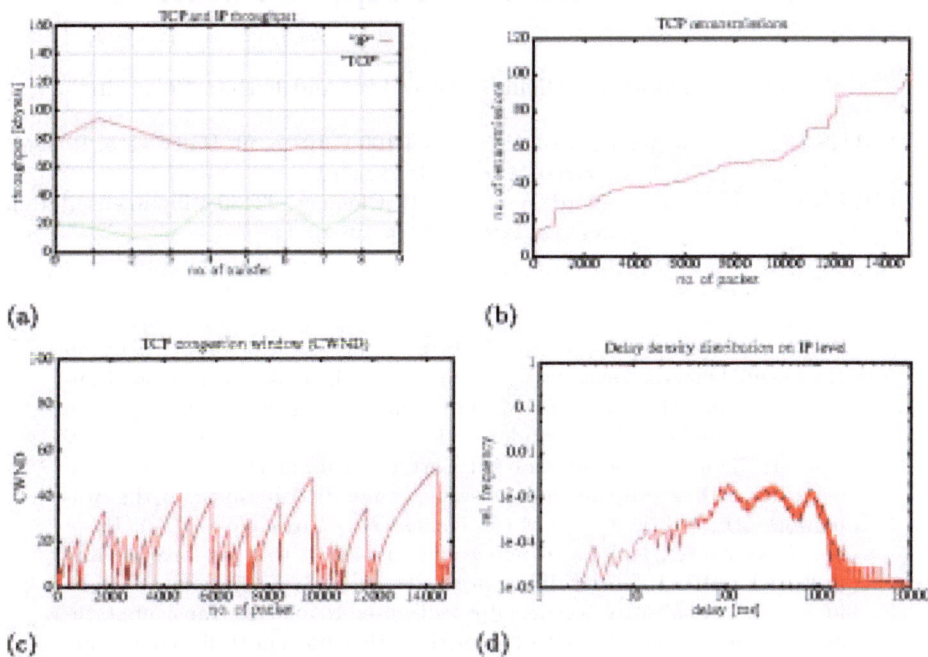

Fig. 2. Measurement results: (a) TCP and IP throughput over 10 file transfers, (b) TCP retransmissions and (c) corresponding TCP Congestion Window for the first 14000 packets. (d) Delay distribution on IP level

References

1. Arlan ISA/PCMCIA Adapter Cards, Aironet, http://www.aironet.com
2. Jacobson, V., Leres, C., McCanne,S.: Tcpdump Manual Page. Lawrence Berkeley National Laboratory, University of California, Berkeley, CA, June 1997.
3. Transmission Control Protocol. IETF, RFC 793, Sep. 1981
4. Callaghan, B., Gilligan, R.: Snoop Version 2 Packet Capture File Format. Request for Comments, RFC 1761, Internet Engineering Task Force, Feb. 1995.
5. Waldbusser, S.: Remote Network Monitoring Management Information Base Version 2. Request for Comments, RFC 2021, Internet Engineering Task Force, Jan. 1997.
6. Paxson, V.: Automated Packet Trace Analysis of TCP Implementations. Proceedings of SIGCOMM '97.
7. Rathke, B., Assimakopoulos, T.,Wolisz,A.: Internet Protocol Performance Measurements for Wireless Access using Snuffle. Technical Report, Telecommunication Networks Group, Technical University Berlin, Apr. 1998.
8. Balakrishnan, H., Padmanabhan, V., Seshan, S., Katz, R.-H.: A Comparison of Mechanisms for Improving TCP Performance over Wireless Links. IEEE/ACM Transactions on Networking, Dec. 1997.
9. Jacobson, V.: Congestion Avoidance and Control. Proceedings of SIGCOMM '88, pp. 314-329, August 1988.

A Tool to Model Network Transient States with the Use of Diffusion Approximation

Tadeusz Czachórski[1], Michał Pastuszka[1], and Ferhan Pekergin[2]

[1] IITiS PAN, Polish Academy of Sciences 44-100 Gliwice, ul. Bałtycka 5, Poland
`tadek@iitis.gliwice.pl`
[2] LIPN, Université de Paris-Nord, Avenue J. B. Clément, 93430 Villetaneuse, France
`pekergin@lipn.univ-paris13.fr`

Abstract. The paper presents a library of classes which are written in C++ and help to construct queueing network models based on diffusion approximation. The models have the form of open networks with arbitrary topology that include at the moment $G/G/1$ and $G/G/1/N$ stations. Time-dependent and autocorrelated input streams are considered as well as time-dependent service time distributions. In this framework other stations such as $G/G/c$, $G/G/1/$ *Threshold*, $G/G/1/$ *Push-out*, *leaky-bucket*, *jumping window*, *sliding window* that we have already prepared and tested their diffusion models as separate stations are to be included. The software is especially well suited to analyse transient states and to evaluate various control algorithms that prevent traffic congestion in communication networks.

1 Introduction

Diffusion approximation replaces the number of customers $N(t)$ in the queue by the value of a diffusion process $X(t)$ with properly chosen parameters and boundary conditions. The density function $f(x, t; x_0) = P[x \leq X(t) < x + dx \mid X(0) = x_0]$ is an approximation of the considered queue distribution. The complexity of this method is situated between Markov chain analysis and fluid approximation. Markovian models are able to represent any synchronization constraints, they are also well suited to express features of network traffic but their state space grows rapidly. Numerical solution of a system of e.g. 500 000 stiff and ill conditioned differential (when transient states are modelled) equations is still a challenge.

Fluid approximation is a first order approximation and it cannot give us queue distributions, hence it is useless when e.g. the loss probabilities due to buffers overflow are investigated.

We have already proposed, working together with several other authors, diffusion models for the transient analysis of some problems concerning network performances: models of leaky bucket [6], [7], jumping window [1], sliding window [9]; models of space-priority queues at a network switch: a queue with threshold [6] and with push-out algorithm [2]. We have modelled the features of traffic

R. Puigjaner et al. (Eds.): Tools'98, LNCS 1469, pp. 344–347, 1998.

along a virtual path composed of a certain number of nodes [4], jitter compensa-
tion [5] and feed-back algorithms of traffic control between nodes and sources [1].
In all these models the dynamics of flows is important. We are convinced that
the diffusion approximation is a usefool tool when applied in investigation of the
behaviour of time-dependent streams encountered in communication networks
as well as in testing various algorithms which aim to prevent the congestion in
networks or to resolve congestion problems.

We use the diffusion model with instantaneous returns [10], [11]. Owing to
this approach diffusion models are not a heavy-traffic approximation as they
were before [12]. We apply the transient solution defined in [3]. It aims to represent the pdf function of the diffusion process with elementary returns as a
composition of pdf functions of diffusion process with absorbing barriers. The
solution is obtained in terms of Laplace transforms; the originals are sought
numerically [13]. This refers to the case of constant parameters of the diffusion
equation. However, one may divide the time axis into short periods during which
the parameters are kept constant by allowing the change of values only at the
beginning of each interval. Solution at the end of an interval becomes the initial
condition for the next interval. The fact that we may shape this way the features
of input stream allows us to model various traffic patterns and to reflect the impact of control algorithms. For instance, we are able to include in the model a
correlated and time varying input stream [7].

Our resolution of diffusion equations, partly analytical and partly numerical, involves nontrivial computations and needs a careful programming to avoid
serious errors. Hence, to organize the modelling process within a common framework, we propose here a C++ library. Numerical problems that we encounter are
mostly due to the errors of the algorithm used for Laplace inversion. They are
especially visible when they are accumulated due to the procedure mentioned
above for time dependent parameters.

2   The Use of the Package

The software is composed of a set of classes representing separate modelling
problems. For example, the diffusion model of a $G/G/1/N$ station is included in
the class **GG1N**, the class **ExperimentsDevice** allows a series of experiments
for a single station, and the class **diffusionTSolver** enables the modelling of
the whole network.

A network model is represented by a C++ program written with the use
of classes; its syntax was proposed in [8]. We present below a simple example:
a network composed of a source and three stations in tandem. The source is
Poisson (squared coefficient of variation of interrarivals $C_A^2 = 1$) with intensity
$\lambda(t)$: $\lambda = 4.0$ for $t \in [11, 21)$ and $\lambda = 0.1$ otherwise. For all stations, the initial
number of customers, service intensity and squared coefficient of variation of
service time are the following: $N_i(0) = 5$, $\mu_i = 2$, $C_{Bi}^2 = 1$, $i = 1, 2, 3$.
The necessary libraries should be accessible and the function `main()` should include:

1) definition of the whole network: Network net("Network_name",1);
which gives the network name and defines the number of classes (here 1),
2) definition and naming of all classes: net.SetClassPar(CL_A, 1); ,
3) definition of stations and their inclusion into the network, e.g.

    SimpleServer source("source A", net);
    SimpleServer station1("station 1", net);

Customers leaving the network pass to the station out:

    SimpleServer out("out", net);

We should define the types of stations and give the station parameters; the
method **SetService_Source_TDiffusion** is used to set the source parameters:
class name and λ, C_A^2 for that class. **SetService_TDiffusion** sets service stations parameters: N, μ, C_B^2 for a given class; e.g. we define:

    source.SetService_Source_TDiffusion(CL_A, 0.1, 1.0);
    station2.SetService_TDiffusion(CL_A, 10, 2.0, 1.0);,   etc.

The method **SetTransition** gives the routing probabilities for a given class, e.g.

    source.SetTransition(CL_A, station1, 1.0);
    station1.SetTransition(CL_A, station2, 1.0);

4) description of the modelling session with the use of class **diffusionTSolver**.
Set the initial time, the step (time interval) and the number of resolutions before
the change of model parameters

    sol.setTime(0.0);   sol.setdT(1.0);   sol.setNbExp(1);

Set the initial number of customers for each station, e.g.:

    sol.setInitState("station 1", 5);

Start the computations for $t = 1, \ldots, 11$:

    for(i=0; i<11; i++) { sol.runExperiments(); sol.lock(); }

Change the source parameters for $t \in [11, 21)$ and increase the frequency of results:

    sol.setCountParam("source A",4.0,1.0);
    sol.lock();   sol.setdT(0.5);
    for(i=0; i<20; i++) { sol.runExperiments(); sol.lock(); }

Results (diffusion process density functions approximating queue distributions)
are written into files; each station has its own file, the records in files correspond
to time moments for which the computations are performed. These data may be
processed by a user. Fig. 1 presents mean queue lengths of stations as a function
of time. Diffusion approximation is compared with simulation.

References

1. Atmaca, T., Czachórski, T., Pekergin, F.: A Diffusion Model of the Dynamic Effects of Closed-Loop Feedback Control Mechanisms in ATM Networks. 3rd IFIP
   Workshop on Perf. Modelling and Eval. of ATM Networks, Ilkley UK (1995)
2. Czachórski, T., Fourneau, J.M., Pekergin, F.: Diffusion model of the push-out
   buffer management policy. IEEE INFOCOM '92, Florence (1992)
3. Czachórski, T.: A method to solve diffusion equation with instantaneous return
   processes acting as boundary conditions. Bulletin of Polish Academy of Sciences,
   Technical Sciences **41** no. 4 (1993)

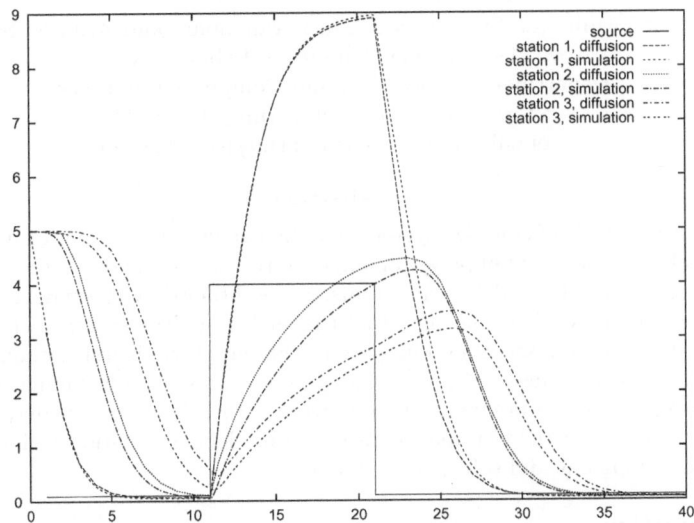

Fig. 1. Mean queue lengths of station1, station2 and station3 as a function of time — diffusion and simulation (100 000 repetitions) results; the source intensity $\lambda(t)$ is indicated.

4. Czachórski, T., Fourneau, J.M., Pekergin, F.: Diffusion Models to Study Nonstationary Traffic and Cell Loss in ATM Networks. 2nd IFIP Workshop on Performance Modelling and Evaluation of ATM Networks. Bradford (1994)

5. Czachórski, T., Fourneau, J.M., Kloul, L.: Diffusion Approximation to Study the Flow Synchronization in ATM Networks, 3rd IFIP Workshop on Performance Modelling and Evaluation of ATM Networks, Ilkley UK (1995)

6. Czachórski, T., Pekergin, F.: Diffusion models of leaky bucket and partial buffer sharing policy: a transient analysis. In: Kouvatsos, D.: (ed): ATM Networks, Performance Modelling and Analysis. Chapman and Hall, London (1997)

7. Czachórski, T., Pekergin, F.: Transient diffusion analysis of cell loses and ATM multiplexer behaviour under correlated traffic. 5th IFIP Workshop on Performance Modelling and Evaluation of ATM Networks, Ilkley UK 21-23 (1997).

8. Draga, M., Pecka, P., Rewer, A.: An object oriented language for queueing network models description. Scientific Lectures of Silesian Technical Univ., no. 30, (1996) 549-562

9. Jouaber, B., Atmaca, T., Pastuszka, M., Czachórski, T.: Modelling the Sliding Window Mechanism. ICC'98, Atlanta, Georgia, USA (1998)

10. Gelenbe, E.: On Approximate Computer Systems Models. J.ACM **22** no.2 (1975)

11. Gelenbe, E., Pujolle, G.: The Behaviour of a Single Queue in a General Queueing Network. Acta Informatica, Fasc. 7, (1976)

12. Kobayashi, H.: Application of the diffusion approximation to queueing networks, Part 2: Nonequilibrium distributions and applications to queueing modeling. J.ACM, **21** no. 3 (1974) 459-469

13. Stehfest, H.: Algorithm 368: Numeric Inversion of Laplace Transform, Comm. of ACM, **13** no. 1 (1970) 47-49

HIMAP: Architecture, Features, and Hierarchical Model Specification Techniques

Murari Sridharan, Srinivasan Ramasubramanian, and Arun K. Somani
Dependable Computing Laboratory
Department of Electrical and Computer Engineering
Iowa State University, Ames, IA 50011
email: {murari, rsrini, arun}@iastate.edu

Abstract

Accurate analysis of complex systems for their reliability and performance is a challenging task. Development of powerful and easy-to-use tools allow engineers and system designers to accurately model such systems. Several tools have been developed addressing these needs, HIMAP is one such tool that helps analyze system behavior that are used in multi-phased missions and in systems that employ scheduled maintenance. The tool accounts for the effects of phase changes, that may include configuration and behavior changes, and maintenance of components. In this paper, we describe the most important features of HIMAP and hierarchical model specification techniques that allow easy development and solution of models.

1. Introduction

As systems become more complex, it is important to ensure reliable operation in critical applications. Developing powerful and easy-to-use tools which allow engineers and system designers to specify, model and analyze such systems in an efficient and user-friendly manner is the need of the hour. In this paper we describe specification techniques for modeling hierarchically in the HIMAP modeling environment [3] and build an example to illustrate the modeling process.

HIMAP provides an ideal modeling environment as it allows the designer to specify the system as a Fault tree, a Fault tree with component repairs, a Markov chain or a Petri net. The modeler has the flexibility to choose the modeling method as appropriate to the system. HIMAP allows these high level representations to be solved directly or convert them to a markov chain and uses EHARP [1] to solve them.

In the fault tree mode, to ease the effort needed in the modeling of highly complex systems HIMAP has a feature called IN gate in the fault tree mode. This feature allows the designer to describe the system hierarchically into simpler subsystems, which can be linked through IN gates. HIMAP allows modeling repairs in the fault tree mode. The modeler can also specify repair rate as well as the number of repair persons associated with the repair of each component or a group of components. Such specification is automatically converted into a markov chain. In the Markov modeling environment HIMAP provides a standard view where the whole Markov chain generated is displayed and a single state view for viewing the transitions emanating from any state.

HIMAP also provides a very user-friendly graphical interface to specify Petri nets. To make the modeling process easier, HIMAP supports constructs like *places* and *transitions* (*timed* and *immediate*), and relationship between them in the pictorial mode. In addition, HIMAP allows the declaration of global variables, constants, and functions that include reward type, rate type, probabilistic type and enabling functions (associated with each transition). To facilitate Stochastic Reward Net (SRN) analysis, Hierarchical Stochastic Reward Nets Solver Package [6] has been developed.

The Library concept is unique to HIMAP. The library files are used to define the characteristics of components, which are used in a model. HIMAP *allows importing of*

R. Puigjaner et al. (Eds.): Tools'98, LNCS 1469, pp. 348-351, 1998

components from library files created using any of the compatible database packages and chooses the relevant fields for the component. Parameters like name, version, failure rate, repair rate are associated with each component. The modeler can create a new library or import from an existing one.

HIMAP has the capability to divide the mission into phases and develop models for each phase, use proper failure rates and solve each phase model separately [5]. HIMAP also incorporates techniques as described in [7] to accurately model Scheduled Maintenance systems.

2. Hierarchical Modeling

Modeling complex systems is very involved, both in view of the amount of work needed to model it, as well as the size of the model that needs to be solved. This makes the solution process computationally intensive. The hierarchical modeling principles can be employed in two ways. 1) A system can be decomposed into smaller models based on component types or subsystems. These models can be solved separately, and the results can be combined to produce large system solution. This approach helps solve the largeness problem. This also makes modeling of large systems simpler and the modeler has the flexibility to analyze individual subsystems independently and be able to abstract their behavior at the next higher level. HIMAP allows the modeler to choose the environment (i.e.,fault tree or Petri net) most suited to specify each individual subsystem. This assumes that the behavior of the subsystem is independent of each other [4]. 2) Even when subsystems are not independent, the model description may be identical. Moreover, the system may consist of several identical components or subsystems. This is likely to be the case when a fault tolerant or a system employing parallelism is being analyzed. In such cases, the subsystem description can be specified once, and used through instantiations, as many times as required. It is also conceivable that the pictorial view of the subsystem model is identical, but the physical association of components is different. In most cases, even most of the physical components may also be identical and only a few descriptions change. A modeling environment must allow specification of such systems as well. HIMAP specification approach allows a modeler to follow this methodology. The specification technique for hierarchical modeling in HIMAP provides a powerful modeling aid, which allows events to be shared among the instantiations of a model. We demonstrate this technique using an example.It is desired to specify a model only once. The modeler can then instantiate the unique model as many times as required. Hierarchical modeling using fault trees is implemented in HIMAP [2] by integrating specification of different subsystems into the main system through IN Gates (Fault tree mode) which serve as pipes transferring reliability characteristics of the subsystem into the main system.

To use hierarchical specification, the modeler decomposes the system behavior, creating sub-models which can be combined to solve the whole system. These sub-models may have some events that are shared. A sub-model itself can be common in different parts of the system. HIMAP facilitates specification of such commonalities and use of common sub-models. When a model is instantiated, the modeler has to specify whether it is a common sub-model which can be carried over different hierarchies. In such cases the IN gates which represent these sub-models are termed as 'Common IN gates'. HIMAP also maintains a list of all the models created during the model development process.

2.1 Example

To demonstrate our modeling technique, consider the example of modeling a Re-

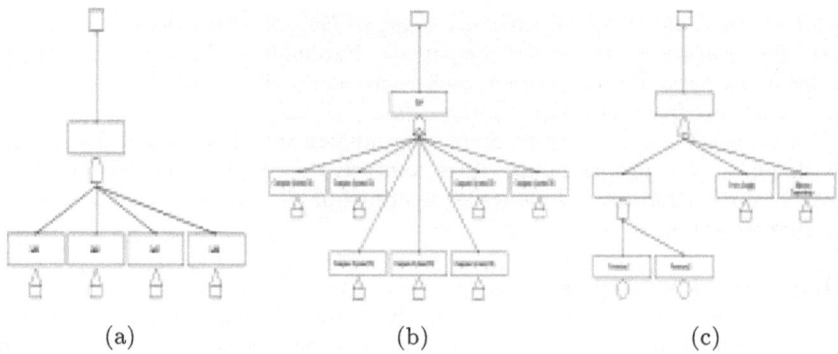

(a)   (b)   (c)

Figure 1: (a) The Research Center Model (b) The Lab Model (c) The Computer System Model

search Center. The Research Center has four Labs. The Research center would like all the labs running. Each Lab deploys Computer Systems of four types numbered 1-4. For simplicity, we assume that there are seven Computer Systems(CS) in each lab. The Lab operation requires at least 3 out-of 7 to remain fully operational. Each Computer System in turn has two processors, a Power Supply(PS) and connects to an Ethernet (EC). The Computer System will fail when both the processors fail or the PS or the EC fails. For the operation of all labs there are 2 Power supplies (PS1,PS2) and 2 Ethernet Cables (EC1, EC2) which are shared among the Computer Systems. Computer Systems of type 1,2 (CS1,CS2) use PS1 and type 3,4(CS3,CS4) use PS2. Computer Systems of type 1,3 use EC1 and type 2,4 use EC2. Lab1 consists of 3 CS of Type 1 and 4 CS of Type 2. Lab2 consists of 3 CS of type 3 and 4 CS of type 4. Lab3 consists of 3 CS of Type 1 and 4 CS of type 4. Lab4 consists of 3 CS of Type 3 and 4 CS of Type 2. Our specification technique simplifies the modeling process as the modeler needs to describe each model only once.

The Research Center (shown in Figure 1(a)) will fail even if one of the Labs fail. To describe this behavior, The Lab models are connected to an OR gate as shown in Figure 1(b). The Labs are modeled as IN gates and the modeler needs to associate the properties of each Lab type to the corresponding IN gate. The Lab will fail if 4 out-of 7 Computer Systems fail. The Computer Systems are modeled as IN gates and the modeler needs to associate the properties of the Computer System types to the corresponding IN gates. The IN gates are connected to a M-out-of-N gate. The values of M and N are specified by the modeler during the association process. The Computer System model is shown in Figure 1(c). The Computer System will fail when both the processors (Processor1,Processor2) fail or Power Supply or Ethernet fails. The failure rates of the Power Supply and Ethernet models are specified during the association process. While associating the CS model (CS1) the IN gates for power supply and Ethernet are mapped as PS1 and EC1 where PS1, EC1 are instantiated from models PS and EC. To create a model for CS Type 2, the modeler need not re-specify. The *Copy* feature in HIMAP allows the modeler to copy an already developed model. The modeler then associates the IN gates corresponding to PS and EC which are different in the instantiated model. In this case CS1 is copied and saved as CS2 and the Ethernet is associated with EC2.The PS is not associated again as PS1 remains common between CS1 and CS2. The same procedure is followed to create CS3 and CS4. Now consider creation of of model for Lab1. It is instantiated from the Lab model and there are 3 CS1 and 4 CS2 in Lab1. Each of the computer systems of type 1 is instantiated from the already developed CS1 model and the instantiations (CS11, CS12,CS13) use PS1 and EC1. Similarly each of the Computer Systems of type 2 is instantiated from CS2 and the instantiations (CS21, CS22, CS23, CS24) use PS1 and EC2. The Lab1 model is copied using the *Copy* routine and Lab2, Lab3, Lab4 models are created using the same technique as explained for the Computer model.

This model can now be solved by solving the sub-models independently and combining the results to get the final solution, or as a single fault tree. The former approach gives an optimistic view of the reliability of the system as the sub-models are treated independently. The latter approach gives an accurate solution by maintaining dependencies among the sub-models. HIMAP allows the model to be solved in both ways.

3. Conclusion

In this paper we have presented the modeling features in HIMAP and specification techniques for hierarchical modeling. Complex systems can be modeled in an easy and user-friendly manner, without having to compromise on the accuracy of the model. HIMAP allows systems to be modeled hierarchically, and facilitates individual sub-models to be analyzed separately or as one model. As implemented currently, HIMAP has the following important features: (a) Systems can be modeled as a fault tree, fault tree with repairable components, Markov chain or a Petri net. (b) Phased Mission analysis and Schedule Maintenance system modeling are incorporated to model realistic scenarios. (c) Hierarchical modeling process has been greatly simplified and designers are provided with specification techniques that reduce the amount of work needed to model complex systems.

References

1. A.K. Somani, U.R. Sandadi, A. Gupta, P.C. Leung. *EHARP: Enhanced Hybrid Automated Reliability Predictor.* Tech. Rep., DPCNL, University of Washington, Seattle, Dec 1993.

2. A. Anand and A. K. Somani. *Hierarchical Analysis of Fault Trees with Dependencies, Using Decomposition.* in the Proc. of RAMS-1998, Los Angeles, CA, pp 69-75, January 1998.

3. G. Krishnamurthi, A. Gupta, and A. K. Somani. *The HIMAP Modeling Environment.* in Proc. of PDCS-96, Sept 24-27, 1996, Dijon, France.

4. R.M. Sinnamon and J.D. Andrews. *Fault Tree Analysis and Binary Decision Diagrams.* Proc. RAMS, pp.215-220, Jan 1996.

5. A.K. Somani, J. Ritcey, and S.Au. *Computationally efficient Phased-Mission reliability analysis for systems with variable configurations.* IEEE Trans. on Reliability, Vol 41, No 4, pp. 504-511, Dec 1992.

6. T. Sakaguchi. *Development of the hierarchical Stochastic Reward Net Solver Package.* Master's Thesis, Dept. of Electrical Engineering, University of Washington, Seattle, 1997.

7. A.K. Somani, Samir Palnitkar, and Tilak Sharma. *Reliability Modeling of Systems with Latent Failures Using Markov Chains.* Proc. on Annual Reliability and Maintainability Symposium 1993.

SvPablo: A Multi-language Performance Analysis System

Luiz De Rose, Ying Zhang, and Daniel A. Reed *

Department of Computer Science
University of Illinois
Urbana, Illinois 61801 USA
{derose,zhang8,reed}@cs.uiuc.edu,
WWW home page: http://www-pablo.cs.uiuc.edu/

Abstract. SvPablo is a language independent performance analysis and visualization system that supports analysis of applications written in a variety of languages and executing on both sequential and parallel systems. In addition to capturing application data via software instrumentation, SvPablo also exploits hardware performance counters to capture the interaction of software and hardware. Both hardware and software performance data are summarized during program execution, enabling measurement of programs that execute for hours or days on hundreds of processors.

Overview

Emerging parallel systems have multilevel memory hierarchies managed by distributed cache coherence protocols or low latency message passing, all accessed by superscalar processors. To provide a language and architecture independent mechanism for performance analysis, we developed SvPablo (source view Pablo), a graphical environment for instrumenting application source code and browsing dynamic performance data.

SvPablo supports interactive instrumentation of C, Fortran 77, and Fortran 90 and automatic instrumentation of data parallel HPF programs, when compiled with the PGI HPF compiler. Interactive instrumentation provides detailed control, allowing users to specify specific instrumentation points, albeit at the possible expense of excessive perturbation and inhibition of compiler optimizations. In contrast, automatic instrumentation relies on the compiler or runtime system to insert measurement probes in compiler-synthesized code.

During execution of the instrumented code, the SvPablo library captures data and computes performance metrics on the execution dynamics of each instrumented construct on each processor. Because only statistics, rather than detailed

---

* This work was supported in part by the Defense Advanced Research Projects Agency under DARPA contracts DABT63-94-C0049 (SIO Initiative), F30602-96-C-0161, and DABT63-96-C-0027 by the National Science Foundation under grants NSF CDA 94-01124 and ASC 97-20202, and by the Department of Energy under contracts DOE B-341494, W-7405-ENG-48, and 1-B-333164.

R. Puigjaner et al. (Eds.): Tools'98, LNCS 1469, pp. 352–355, 1998.

event traces, are maintained, the SvPablo library can capture the execution behavior of codes that execute for hours or days on hundreds of processors.

Instrumentation

The SvPablo instrumentation library includes a standard interface for augmenting software performance data with hardware metrics. We have exploited this interface to capture hardware performance data on the MIPS R10000 [2]. Within SvPablo, a user can select the desired set of hardware counters via a configuation file. During program execution, the SvPablo data capture library queries the counters and records the data with extant application measurements. In addition to presenting the raw counter data, the SvPablo library also computes derived metrics for each source code line (e.g., MFLOPS and branch misprediction percentages).

Taken together, the application and hardware performance measurements provide a rich set of metrics for program analysis. Moreover, the SvPablo interface allows users to identify high-level bottlenecks (e.g., procedures), then explore increasingly levels of detail (e.g., identifying a specific cause of poor performance at a source code line executed on one of many processors).

Following execution, the SvPablo data capture library records its statistical analyses in a set of *summary files*, one for each executing process. A post-mortem utility program then merges the summary files, computing new global statistics and the resulting metrics are correlated with application source code, creating a *performance file* that is represented via the Pablo Self-Describing Data Format (SDDF) [1]. This performance file is the specification used by the SvPablo browser to display application source code and correlated performance metrics.

Analysis

Developing an interface that separates performance data presentation from language and architecture idiosyncrasies requires a flexible specification mechanism for both instrumentation points and performance metrics. Only with this separation can one readily add new metrics and support new languages, compilers, and architectures without requiring extensive modifications to the user interface.

To isolate language differences from the user interface, the performance metrics associated with each procedure and source line are organized as a hierarchy defined by a set of SDDF records. This *meta-meta-format* hierarchy contains three groups of SDDF record descriptors: *mapping, configuration* and *statistic*. Mapping records define the set of statistics associated with each instrumentable construct. In turn, configuration records indicate the statistic record names and allow SvPablo to extract the base names of all performance metrics before reading the statistics records, which define the actual performance metrics.

Finally, one of the design goals for SvPablo was creation of an intuitive, cross-architecture, language independent performance analysis interface. Realizing such a design would allow users and performance analysts to learn a single set of software navigation skills and then apply those skills to application codes written in a variety of languages and executing on a diverse set of sequential and parallel architectures.

Hence, the SvPablo implementation relies on a single interface for performance instrumentation and visualization. If the code was interactively instrumented, the user can refine the performance analysis by re-instrumenting the code while visualizing performance data from earlier executions. Regardless of the instrumentation mode, one can access and load performance data from multiple prior executions, including different numbers of processors and hardware platforms. This allows one to compare executions to understand hardware and software interactions.

Application

As an example, Figure 1 shows the SvPablo interface, together with code and performance data from an HPF program. The SvPablo interface supports a hierarchy of performance displays, ranging from color-coded routine profiles to detailed data on the behavior of a source code line on a single processor.

In the figure, the leftmost scrollbox shows the set of files comprising the HPF code, with all previously measured executions of this code shown in the scrollbox to the right. Here, the user has loaded a performance data context (i.e., a measured execution) for a 32 processors Silicon Graphics Origin 2000. After selecting a performance context, the list of procedures in the application code, together with two color coded metrics, is shown below the performance contexts scrollbox in the area labeled *Routines in Performance Data.*

The two colored columns summarize, over all processes, the mean number of calls and mean cumulative time for the routines. Clicking on a routine name loads the associated source code in the bottom pane of Figure 1, together with color-coded metrics beside each source code line. In addition, pop-up dialogs showing other statistics and detailed information about a particular routine or a particular source code line, including individual processor metrics, can be obtained by clicking the mouse on the routine name or the source code line.

Working with a group of large-scale applications, we observed that SvPablo enabled us to rapidly identify and correct performance bottlenecks. However, the key feature of SvPablo is language and architecture transparency, achieved by representing performance data via a meta-meta-format presentation of different events from different languages using the same graphical interface.

References

1. Reed, D. A., Aydt, R. A., Noe, R. J., Roth, P. C., Shields, K. A., Schwartz, B., Tavera, L. F.: Scalable Performance Analysis: The Pablo Performance Analysis Environment. In *Proceedings of the Scalable Parallel Libraries Conference* (1993), A. Skjellum, Ed., IEEE Computer Society.
2. Zagha, M., Larson, B., Turner, S., Itzkowitz, M.: Performance Analysis Using the MIPS R10000 Performance Counters. In *Proceedings of Supercomputing'96* (November 1996).

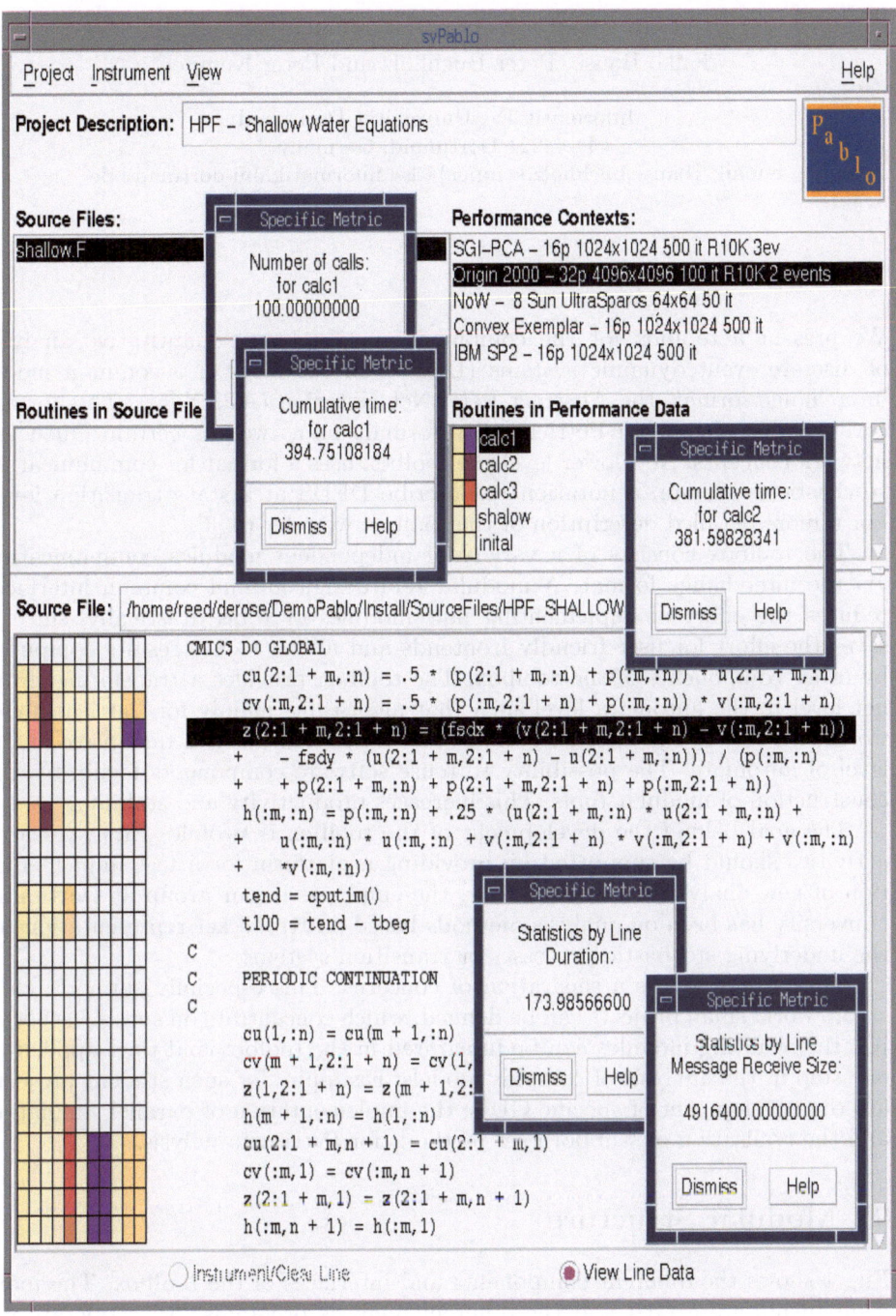

Fig. 1. Shallow Water Code (HPF Performance)

A Toolbox for Functional and Quantitative Analysis of DEDS

Falko Bause, Peter Buchholz and Peter Kemper

Informatik IV, Universität Dortmund
D-44221 Dortmund, Germany
e-mail: {bause,buchholz,kemper}@ls4.informatik.uni-dortmund.de

1 Introduction/Motivation

We present a toolbox for the combined functional and quantitative analysis of discrete event dynamic systems (DEDS) on the basis of a common model interchange format, the Abstract Petri Net Notation (APNN,[5]). This format covers a fair amount of Petri net like formalisms as well as certain Queueing network concepts. At a lower level the toolbox uses a format for communicating stochastic automata, a notation to describe DEDS at a state transition level. For a more detailed description of the toolbox we refer to [3].

The toolbox consists of a variety of independent modules communicating via the interchange format. A modular tool design around common interfaces reduces the effort of implementing new modules or tools drastically, since it saves the effort for user friendly frontends and allows to use results computed by other components of the toolbox. The toolbox provides a transformer from net level to the automata level such that algorithms mainly for Petri nets can work with the APNN interface, while state based analysis can take place at the level of automata. The possibility to reuse software components facilitates the construction of modular tools. This increases productivity and stability.

The goal behind the development of the toolbox is twofold. First, research activities should be supported by providing a platform for a fast implementation of new analysis methods. So far, the emphasis in our group at Dortmund University has been on analysis methods based on Kronecker representations of the underlying stochastic processes or transition systems.

Our second goal is a separation of concerns. This especially supports classroom work: small projects can be defined, which concentrate on specific aspects, but the resulting modules can be integrated in the toolbox and then applied as one step in the analysis of complex models. Examples for such student projects are the development of specific GUIs, the implementation of parallel simulators and the realisation of stubborn set methods for Petri net analysis.

2 Modular Structure

Fig. 1 shows the different components and interfaces of the toolbox. The main components are a GUI and the different analysis programs. All cooperate via

R. Puigjaner et al. (Eds.): Tools'98, LNCS 1469, pp. 356–359, 1998.

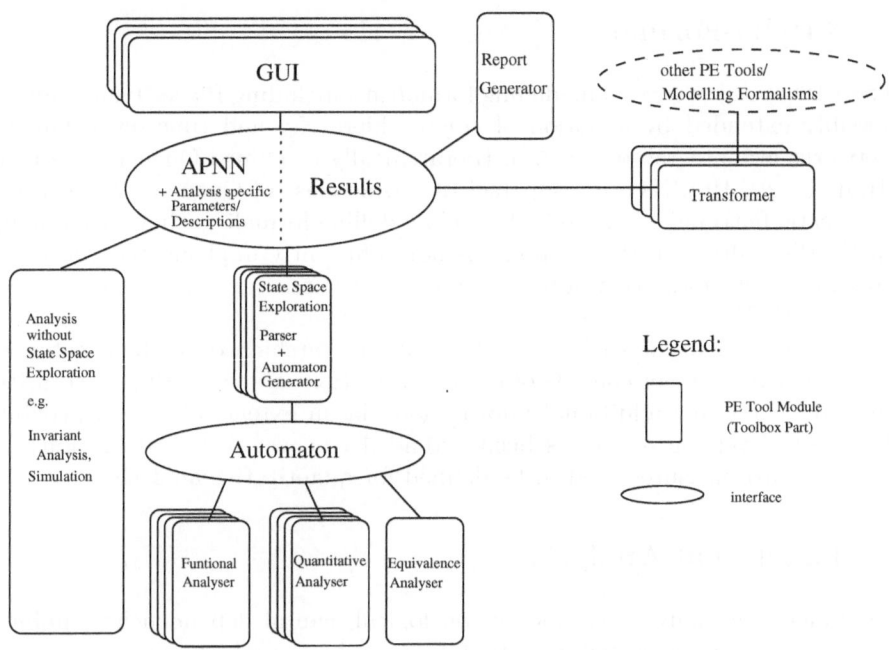

Fig. 1. Structural overview of the toolbox

APNN, a textual interface, which is complemented by the description of analysis specific parameters, e.g., the definition of quantitative measures like rewards, and by the description of the result format. This interface is the basis for the cooperation of all other tool components: the GUI which transforms the user-specified model to the APNN, and the various analysis programs which read the APNN together with further analysis specific parameters and calculate the desired results. Our toolbox provides several analysis modules for functional (qualitative) and quantitative (performance) analysis. The state based analysis tools split up into a module generating an automata description (e.g., one describing the reachability graph), and a part performing core analysis steps (e.g., calculating the steady state distribution by vector/matrix iterations). The mentioned automata description is a further interface which simplifies the incorporation of state based analysis features into our toolbox, since the modules for automata generation can be reused. The analysis programs export results in a specific output format which can be used by the GUI or report generators for result presentation.

Furthermore the toolbox also comprises transformers, which translate other formats into the APNN. E.g., software translating GreatSPN net specifications or PEP model descriptions to the APNN.

3   APNN-Format

The APNN covers several modelling formalisms including Place/Transition Nets, possibly extended by a notion of colour, hierarchy and time, even Queueing Networks are integrated as e.g. in Hierarchically combined Queueing Petri Nets (HQPNs [2]). HQPNs are a superset of a wide class of Queueing Networks and Stochastic Petri nets. Several high-level modelling formalisms have been mapped on HQPNs, although this mapping is not sufficiently implemented yet: e.g., [4] presents a transformation of SDL to Queueing Petri Nets [1], which are covered by the APNN.

The key idea of the APNN is to describe a hierarchical or modular net as a set of nets where each net consists of places, transitions and arcs. Places, transitions and arcs carry any additional information via an extendable set of attributes. The APNN version of [5] has been extended to cover reward definitions as as well. Reward measures need to be defined for quantitative analysis.

4   Functional Analysis

For functional analysis one focuses on logical, causal dependencies, timing aspects are usually neglected. Our toolbox contains a tool for invariant computation like most PN analysis tools. The resulting set of invariants is stored in a format which allows reuse of these results for other analysis tools. For state based analysis, the toolbox contains a special implementation for liveness, existence of a home space and ergodicity. For more general properties, state based functional analysis results in proving presence or absence of certain nodes or paths in the reachability graph. Our toolbox contains a model checker for CTL formulas as well [12], which profits from modular or hierarchically structured state spaces like analysis tools for quantitative analysis as described in Sect. 5.

In functional analysis equivalences are frequently employed to relief the state space explosion problem. Components of a complex model are substituted by equivalent components with a smaller state space, which often results in a significant reduction of the state space of the complete net. The available model checker supports bisimulation to reduce the state space. Equivalences are considered to some extend for quantitative analysis as well, see below.

5   Quantitative Analysis

Performance characteristics presuppose a notion of time, such that a DEDS requires appropriate timing information. In case of Markovian timing, one can perform numerical analysis based on the underlying Markov process or employ simulation. For the latter case, the toolbox provides a simulator [8], which in its current state allows the analysis of coloured and possibly hierarchically specified GSPNs.

Numerical analysis is supported by a variety of tools which employ different representations of the generator matrix. Currently available are

- a tool for conventional numerical analysis using a sparse matrix representation,
- SupGSPN, which uses a modular matrix representation based on Kronecker products [10],
- QPN-Tool [2], based on a two-level hierarchical matrix representation for certain hierarchical Queueing Petri nets,
- and an implementation of a variety of numerical solution algorithms for two-level hierarchies of automata networks, which result in a hierarchy generation either at net level or at automata level [7,9].

Structured Markov chains allow to employ performance equivalence to reduce generator matrices for their numerical analysis; methods according to [6] are implemented and can be combined with the solution tools at the automata level.

Exact numerical techniques are accomplished by approximate methods. In our toolbox, decomposition and aggregation is integrated for all models which are described in a modular or hierarchical way [8]. Thus the technique can be used for a wide class of models.

References

1. F. Bause. Queueing Petri Nets — A formalism for the combined qualitative and quantitative analysis of systems *Proc. of the 5th International Workshop on Petri Nets and Performance Models*, Toulouse (France), pp. 14–23, 1993.
2. F. Bause, P. Buchholz, P. Kemper. QPN-tool for the specification and analysis of hierarchically combined queueing Petri nets. *H. Beilner, F. Bause (eds.); Quantitative Evaluation of Computing and Communication Systems*, Springer LNCS 977, pp. 224–238.
3. F. Bause, P. Buchholz, P. Kemper. A toolbox for functional and quantitative analysis of DEDS. *Universität Dortmund, Fachbereich Informatik, Forschungsbericht Nr. 680, 1998.*
4. F. Bause, H. Kabutz, P. Kemper, P Kritzinger. SDL and Petri net performance analysis of Communicating systems. *Proc. of the 15th International Symposium on Protocol Specification, Testing and Verification*, Warsaw (Poland), June 1995.
5. F. Bause, P. Kemper, P. Kritzinger. Abstract Petri Net Notation. *Petri Net Newsletters*, No. 49, pp. 9–27, 1995.
6. P. Buchholz. Equivalence relations for stochastic automata networks. *W. J. Stewart (ed.), Computation with Markov Chains: Proc. of the 2nd Int. Workshop on the Numerical Solution of Markov Chains, Kluwer Int. Publishers (1995), 197–216.*
7. P. Buchholz. Hierarchical structuring of superposed GSPNs. *Proc. of the 7th Int. Workshop on Petri Nets and Performance Models (PNPM'97), IEEE CS-Press, 1997, 81-90.*
8. P. Buchholz. Iterative decomposition and aggregation of labeled GSPNs. *Accepted for ATPN'98.*
9. P. Buchholz, P. Kemper. On generating a hierarchy for GSPN analysis. To appear in *Performance evaluation review.*
10. P. Kemper. Numerical analysis of superposed GSPNs. *IEEE Trans. on Software Engineering*, 22(9), Sep 1996.
11. P. Kemper. Reachability analysis based on structured representations. In *Application and Theory of Petri Nets*, LNCS 1091. Springer, 1996.
12. P. Kemper and R. Lübeck. Model checking based on Kronecker algebra. *Universität Dortmund, Fachbereich Informatik, Forschungsbericht Nr. 669, 1998.*

A Reconfigurable Hardware Tool for High Speed Network Simulation

Cyril Labbé[1], Frédéric Reblewski[1], Serge Martin[2], and Jean-Marc Vincent[3]

[1] M2000, 4 rue R. Razel , 91400 Saclay, France
cyril.labbe@cnet.francetelecom.fr
[2] France Telecom/CNET/DTL/ASR , BP98, Chemin du vieux chene ,
38243 Meylan Cedex, France
serge.martin@cnet.francetelecom.fr
[3] Laboratoire LMC-IMAG , Domaine Universitaire ,
BP53X 38041 Grenoble Cedex 9, France
Jean-Marc.Vincent@imag.fr

Abstract. Estimation of rare events probabilities (such as loss rate) in high speed network remains in most cases an open problem. To address this problem, a flexible hardware testbed for simulation of ATM-based networks has been used. The goal of this article is to present this simulation technique. It is shown that this technique can be used to highlight rare events, such as realistic packet loss probability in high-speed networks.

1   Introduction

More and more High Speed Networks are intended to provide a variety of different services on a single "universal" network. Such services can have widely differing Quality of Service (QoS) requirements. At the packet (cell) level, this means differences in permissible cell loss and cell transfer delays. This measure of performance depends directly on the switch architecture and algorithms for congestion control and scheduling. That is why investigation on performance evaluation are so important.

Models used for this research are often discrete time queuing networks. This is especially true in the case of ATM (Asynchronous Transfer Mode), where slotted time is natural since all the cells have the same size. A slot is the time needed to serve a cell. Because of the small size of the ATM cell and the high link-speeds, a large number of cell events may need to be simulated to ensure satisfactory confidence intervals. A realistic packet loss probability is around 10^{-8}-10^{-9}. Such losses are rare events which are difficult to capture. Software Simulators are too limited to obtain such a probability. Although analytical techniques may be used to bound the worst-case performance, [3] these are often inadequate for modeling the switch algorithms at the needed level of detail.

The aim of this paper is to show a new approach, using emulation on a versatile architecture machine for performance evaluation of high speed networks [8, 2]. This technique is used to highlight rare events, such as realistic packet

R. Puigjaner et al. (Eds.): Tools'98, LNCS 1469, pp. 360-364, 1998

loss probability. This technique is also used to make performance evaluation on congestion control and scheduling algorithms of an ATM switch developed at the CNET.

Programmable hardware (emulation) is widely used to reproduce the functionalities of a circuit. Emulation is performed by an emulator, which can be seen as an hardware simulator. Its hardware configuration can be modified to model other circuits ; this is an "all purpose hardware emulator" based on a versatile architecture [4].

Here we will focus on the architecture, the use, and the possibilities of this tool. An ATM switch is modeled by a queuing network which is emulated by a dedicated architecture on the versatile machine. The structure of the paper is the following. The versatile architecture and software used are presented in Section 2. Section 3 presents experimental results on a eight-by-eight multistage ATM switch.

2 Hardware architecture and software environment

This section presents the hardware architecture and the software environment used to emulate queuing networks. The software is used to describe a component modeling the queuing network and the hardware simulator emulates this component.

2.1 Architecture

The hardware simulator is the M500 machine from Metasystems [4]. It acts like a giant FPGA (field programmable gate array) on which the circuit to be tested and debugged can be mapped. The emulator is based on a building bloc called PLB (Programmable Logic Bloc), static RAM and VRAM. PLBs provide register and basic logic gates, the static RAMs provide possibilities to map memories described in the netlist. The VRAMs sample all the internal nodes for logic analysis of the signal values.

All this give to the user the effective use of : 500,000 programmable logic gates (connected to each other through a programmable network), 17 Mbytes of memory (single or double port), adjustable clock frequency from 1 to 10 Mhz.

This hardware can be shaped to emulate any digital and synchronous circuit. The description of a chip is given to the Emulator by configuration files. The clock frequency, under normal conditions, is usually close to 1 Mhz. The emulator clock is under user control. All signals and register values are available on the last 7000 clock cycles, which is very useful for debugging.

This machine is from the *first generation* (1995). An up to date machine has at least 20 time more logic gates.

2.2 Software environment

The software flow leads to the files required by the emulator to reproduce the functionalities of a circuit. These functionalities are described in terms of concur-

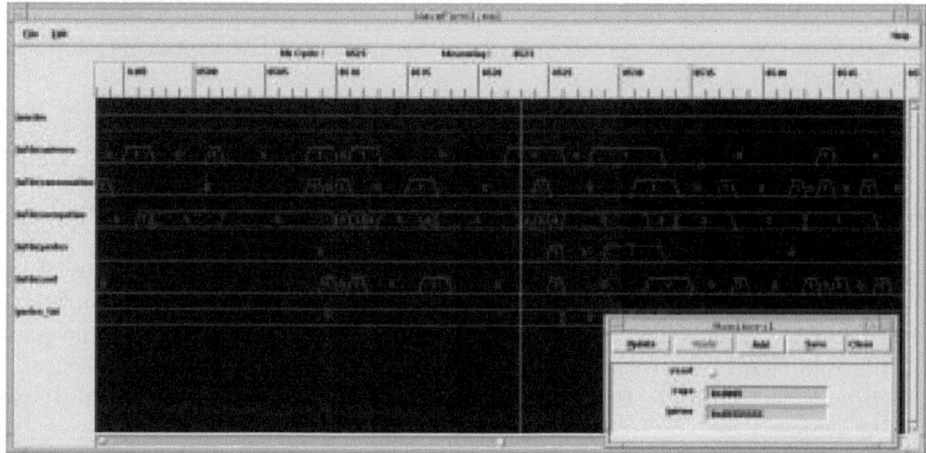

Fig. 1. The waveform window display all signals and register values on the last 7000 clock cycles.

rent processes using the VHDL language. VHDL is an efficient way of obtaining a high level description of a hardware component, which is then translated into gates by the Synopsys synthesis tools. From this representation of the components, the Metasystems compiler produces the data base required by the emulator. The software flow is detailed above :

- a VHDL (VHSIC Hardware Description Language) description of the chip is used to describe the system in terms of concurrent processes [5].
- Synopsys synthesis : this software, provided by Synopsys, translates the VHDL description into combinational logic and registers (logic gates)[5].
- The Metasystems compiler. This is the routing operation, which results in connecting the gates to each other through the programmable network of the emulator.

Those two last steps are entirely automatic.

2.3   Simulation control

Emulation is performed using the MEL tool, which loads the emulator with the configuration file, and allows run control, logic analysis, triggering features, and patterns verification. MEL can be driven by procedures written in a C-like code, which is useful for complex simulation.

All the signals or vectors (busses) can be displayed in a waveform window (cf Figure 1). Control of input signals or registers can be done through the monitor window (cf Figure 1). Any signal and register value can be displayed without recompilation.

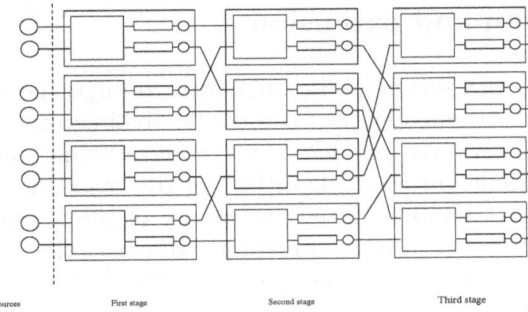

Fig. 2. A three stages eight-by-eight ATM switch modeled with discrete time queues.

3   Application to a three stages eight-by-eight switch

This section is devoted to the study of a eight-by-eight switch (figure 2). The traffic model adopted is geometric, servers of queue are deterministic, with arrival first [1]. This traffic is also call uniform traffic [9, 7]. Figure 3 shows the packet loss probability per stage. The x axis is the queue capacity K varying from 10 to 50. Each curve corresponds to a different stage. The queues of each stage have the same capacities K.

It should be noted that losses are always greater on higher stage. This is explained by the fact that the traffic following a buffer stage is more bursty than the one at the entrance. This is easily observed when doing a statistical analysis of burst length. This has been done thanks to a traffic analyzer which has been build to characterize the traffic perturbation introduce by buffers. Tagged cell can also be used to differentiate background traffic from the point to point communication.

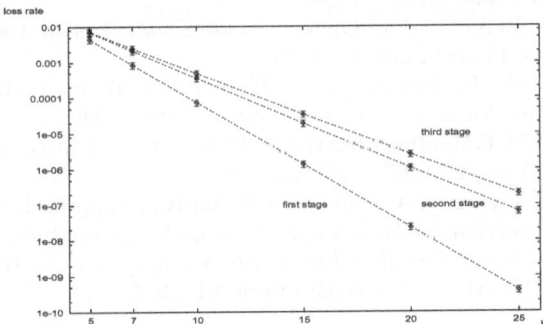

Fig. 3. Loss rate at different stages versus capacities K of queues (same capacities K at each stage), $\rho = 0.8$.

4 Conclusion and extension

In this article, a new technique for simulation of high speed network has been presented. This methodology uses a versatile architecture configured for maximum efficiency for a given problem. Analytical techniques are often inadequate for modeling the commutation algorithms at the needed level of detail. In software simulation, estimation of the probability of rare events are very difficult to obtain. The proposed tools and method overcomes the problem by a parallel approach. In one time slot, the number of treated events is in the order of the number of queues.

This new approach has been applied to the study of rare events in ATM networks. This has allowed simulation of realistic cell loss probabilities $(10^{-8}, 10^{-9})$ in a multistage ATM switch. This technology could be used to highlight other rare events with a good degree of accuracy.

This model has been extended to real service policies. In particular for studies on Fair Queuing disciplines and congestion control algorithms. More generally, this type of machine could be used to emulate numerous types of performance evaluation problems using discrete time queuing network, graphs or Petri nets.

References

1. A.Gravey and G.Hébuterne. Simultaneity in discrete-time single server queues with Bernouilli inputs. *Performance Evaluation North-Holland*, 14:123–131, 1992.
2. C.Labbé, F.Reblewski, and J-M Vincent. Performance evaluation of high speed network protocols by emulation on a versatile architecture. *RAIRO, Systèmes à événements discrets stochastiques : théorie, application et outils.*, to be published.
3. J.Pellaumail. Majoration des retards dans les réseaux ATM. *Rairo recherche opérationnelle*, 30:51–64, 1996.
4. L.Burgun, F.Reblewski, G.Fenelon, J.Barbier, and O.Lepape. Serial fault emulation. In *Proceedings of the 33rd Design Automation Conference 1996 (DAC 96)*, pages 801–806, Metasystems, France, 1996.
5. R. Airiau, J.-M. Berge, and V. Olive. *Circuit Synthesis with VHDL*. Kluwer Academic Publishers, France Telecom, 1994.
6. S. Robert and J.-Y. Le Boudec. Can self-similar traffic be modeled by markovian processes? *Lecture Notes in Computer Science*, 1044, 1996.
7. R.Y.Awdeh and H.T.Mouftah. Survey of ATM switch architectures. *Lecture Notes in Computer Science*, 27:1567–1613, 1995.
8. D. Stiliadis and A.Varma. A reconfigurable hardware approach to network simulation. *ACM Transaction on Modeling and Computer Simulation*, 7, 1997.
9. L. Truffet. *Méthodes de Calcul de Bornes Stochastiques sur des Modèles de Systèmes et de Réseaux*. PhD thesis, Université Paris VI, 1995.

JAGATH: A Methodology and its Application for Distributed Systems Performance Evaluation and Control

Sunil Santha and Udo Pooch

Department of Computer Science, Texas A&M University,
College Station, Texas 77843-3112, USA
{santha, pooch}@cs.tamu.edu

Abstract. A methodology (JAGATH) and a tool based on it for establishing the performance of a distributed system within an empirical framework are presented. A set of performance variables representing the system performance is derived in terms of a combination of a set of performance measures. These performance measures represent the actual measurements of the events in the system. These performance variables are used to display the system performance status in the form of Kiviat graphs. The causal relationship between the performance variables and the internal system control variables and the workload characteristics can be established. This can be used in a performance 'tuning' system.

1 Introduction

The methodology, JAGATH (Just Another Graphical Analysis Tool for Heterogenous systems) establishes the performance of a distributed system within an *empirical framework*. It is intended as a tool assisting in the performance management component of the distributed systems management model put forward by ISO[1]. For the tool implementation, a locally distributed system with load sharing is considered. Jobs enter the system via the nodes in the system (clients) and are processed by those and other nodes (servers) in the system.
A detailed comparison of existing monitoring tools is given in [1].

2 The System Model

Here we present a brief description of the design principle of JAGATH [2]. The general architecture is applicable to a client-server paradigm as well as systems based on distributed shared memory.

2.1 Development of the Performance Evaluation System

JAGATH can be applied to a complicated, inherently nondeterministic distributed system to establish its performance within an empirical framework. This involves the following:
 a. System Definition.
 b. Data Collection (determination of what to collect and how to collect).
 c. Data Analysis (reduction using principal component analysis).
 d. Performance Indication (displaying the results using Kiviat graphs).
 e. System Control (establishing a feedback control mechanism).

R. Puigjaner et al. (Eds.): Tools'98, LNCS 1469, pp. 365–368, 1998.

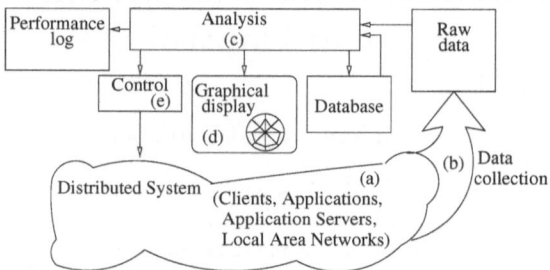

Fig. 1. Performance evaluation and control system

Figure 1 shows the basic block diagram of an application of this methodology. In it we have indicated where each of the above mentioned design phases influence the design most.

Due to limitations of space the formulas and the derivations involved with this methodology are not provided here. Refer to [2] for details.

2.2   System Definition

We would consider the distributed system to consist of several levels of abstraction [3]. One way of defining the performance of a level is by the measure of the response to the requests from the level above it. The selection of the level at which the performance evaluation is carried out depends on the performance objective [2]. Once the level for the performance evaluation is determined, the events to be measured can be selected in that level.

2.3   Data Collection and Reduction

The data is summarized in several stages. The first data reduction takes place where the observations are made. Further reductions can be done at intermediate points before being sent to the central monitoring station for final data reduction.

We use multivariate statistical methods (principal component analysis) to reduce the large number of data [4]. The underlying principle is aimed at obtaining a limited number of orthogonal variables by combining the measured variables. The lesser number orthogonal variables contain almost the same amount of performance information as the original set of variables. The reduction is possible since we combine the original variables to get the orthogonal set and unlike the original variables no two of the orthogonal variables carry the same information.

The final outcome of our reduction algorithm [5] will be the transformation matrix. This matrix will convert a vector of performance measures X containing n variables into a vector of performance variables Y containing p variables with the desired properties. (Where p is much smaller than n.) These final composite variables are used for the graphical display (Kiviat graph).

2.4   Performance Indication

In the Kiviat graphs each axis represents an almost independent phenomenon. Each axis consists of a composite performance variable. The variables can be assigned to the axes of the Kiviat graph so that the Kiviat graph for a good system

---

[1] International Standardization Organization

will have a star form. These Kiviat patterns can be interpreted and related to the structure of the system by a system analyst or a manager. Once the patterns have been identified any significant perturbation can be easily recognized [6].

2.5 System Control

It is possible to express the original performance measures as a linear combination of the final set of principal components. Hence a feedback mechanism can be introduced that causes the system to return to the range of optimum performance shown by the "good" shape of the Kiviat graph.

3 Prototype Implementation

For this case study a workstation cluster in the department of Computer Science running distributed Ada programs as the workload was used. The performance objective was to establish an empirical performance model of the system. Hence events related to requests, allocations and releasing of low level resources were identified and measured.

The prototype was executed in two distinct phases. Phase 1 programs were written in C and C++ and the real-time programs including the Kiviat display in phase 2 were written in C and Java. One objective of the design of the system of programs was to make them modular and portable to different systems.

1. System characterization phase: Performance measures were collected for a long period so that the system characteristics could be determined. The data collected was analyzed [5] to obtain the transformation matrix and other parameters which are later used to convert vectors of collected performance measures into a reduced number of performance variables in real-time. SAS^{TM} software package [7] was used for the principal component analysis and for derivations of the correlation matrix in the reduction algorithm.
2. Real-time data collection, reduction and display: Performance measures are collected periodically from the distributed system, normalized and converted into a set of performance variables using the transformation matrix. These performance variables are used in the display of a Kiviat graph (Figure 2). Parameters derived in phase one are used for the normalization of data.

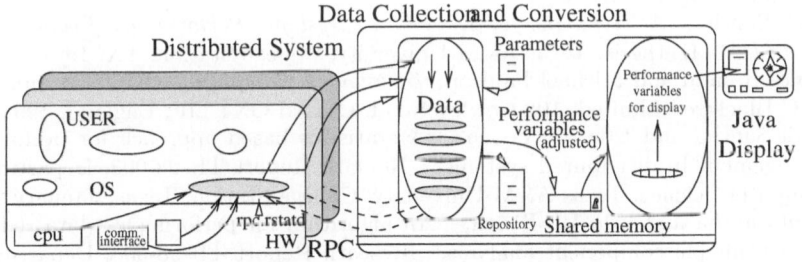

Fig. 2. Data collection, reduction and display.

The display object is implemented using $Java^{TM}$. This is designed to run as a separate process communicating with the program generating principal components using shared memory.

Kiviat Patterns The patterns in Figure 3 show various display modes of the Java application. These patterns were recorded during a case study involving 126 performance measures which were reduced to 11 performance variables.

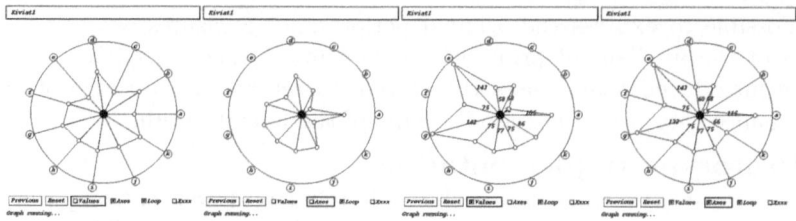

Fig. 3. Kiviat patterns

4   Conclusion

Practical use of the prototype implementation of JAGATH showed the usefulness and the validity of the methodology. The flexible implementation allowed to switch between system configurations by just exchanging the parameter files. Multiple Java applications could be invoked on different terminals with only one data collection process executing. The prototype did not implement the feedback control mechanism. The data collection and reduction program used a relatively small amount of cpu time (2.4% max.) whereas the Java Application used up to 32% (on a sun4c running SunOS 5.5). The rpc.rstatd daemon on each machine responding to the RPC calls consumed less than 0.1% of the cpu time. Usage of broadcasting or multicast messages will reduce the communication overhead. In a system possessing a synchronized clocks, a *push* technology could be used to collect data.

References

1. Sunil Santha and Udo W. Pooch, "A survey of distributed systems performance evaluation tools," in *Proceedings of the International Conference on Parallel and Distributed Processing Techniques and Applications (PDPTA'98)*, Las Vegas, Nevada, July 1998, CSREA.
2. Sunil Santha, *A Technique for Distributed Systems Performance Evaluation and Control*, Ph.D. thesis, Texas A&M University, College Station, TX, 1997.
3. James Rankin and Michael Paulson, *Distributed Computing*, chapter 3, pp. 26–29, NCC Blackwell Limited, 108 Cowley Road, Oxford OX4 1JF, England, 1993.
4. Sunil Santha and Udo W. Pooch, "A statistics based approach for performance management in distributed systems," Researh Report TR-98-003, Department of Computer Science, Texas A&M University, College Station, Texas, January 1998.
5. Sunil Santha and Udo W. Pooch, "An algorithm for performance data reduction using principle component analyais," Researh Report TR-98-008, Department of Computer Science, Texas A&M University, College Station, Texas, March 1998.
6. Pedro Sanabria, *Design and Verification of Computer Performance Measure Evaluation Analysis Techniques*, Ph.D. thesis, Texas A&M University, TX, 1977.
7. Ronald P. Cody, *Applied Statistics and the SAS Programming Language*, Prentice Hall, Upper Saddle River, NJ, 1997.

Hierarchical Stochastic Reward Net Solver Package

Tomoaki Sakaguchi and Arun K. Somani

Dependable Computing Laboratory
Department of Electrical and Computer Engineering
Iowa State University, Ames, IA 50011
email: arun@iastate.edu

Abstract. This paper describes the design and application of the Hierarchical Stochastic Reward Nets Solver Package (HSP) to compute system reliability, availability, maintainability, and other system performance metrics. This enables us to model systems with hierarchy and/or modular redundancy efficiently.

1 Introduction

System reliability, maintainability, availability and performance analyses are important and complex. Several modeling methods, such as fault trees (FTs), Markov chains (MCs), and Stochastic Petri Nets (SPNs), are used for such analyses. FTs are easy to use to develop system models, but are not suitable to describe systems with repairable components. The MC model becomes too complicated to specify by hand for any real-life system. Petri Nets (PNs) [1] provide more versatile environment than FTs and MCs.

A PN consists of a set of places $\mathcal{P}$, a set of transitions $\mathcal{T}$, and a set of arcs $\mathcal{A}$. To increase the modeling power of the PNs, temporal concept is introduced. A Generalized Stochastic Petri Net (GSPN) [2] and its enhancement Stochastic Reward Net (SRN) are temporal extensions of the basic PN. A GSPN is obtained by associating with each transition in a PN an exponentially distributed (*timed*) or a δ-function-shaped (*immediate*) firing time. A SRN is a structural extended version of a GSPN with the following added features: enabling functions and marking dependent rates or probabilities for transitions, transition priorities, and reward functions. Especially, reward functions play an important role to distinguish SRNs from GSPNs. The separated specifications of reward functions enable SRNs to model systems with less complexity at the net level in comparison to GSPNs. *Enabling functions* specify enabling conditions of transitions instead of markings. SPNs [3] are flexible, concise, and have intuitive forms. Therefore, they are more suitable to model such system. They are usually converted to continuous-time Markov chains (CTMCs) and solved.

Even though SRNs are used to specify system models, the exponential increase in the number of states of converted CTMCs cannot be avoided and may prevent the analysis from being carried out in reasonable time. Thus, the direct conversion of SRNs into CTMCs, works well only when the system model is

R. Puigjaner et al. (Eds.): Tools'98, LNCS 1469, pp. 369-373, 1998

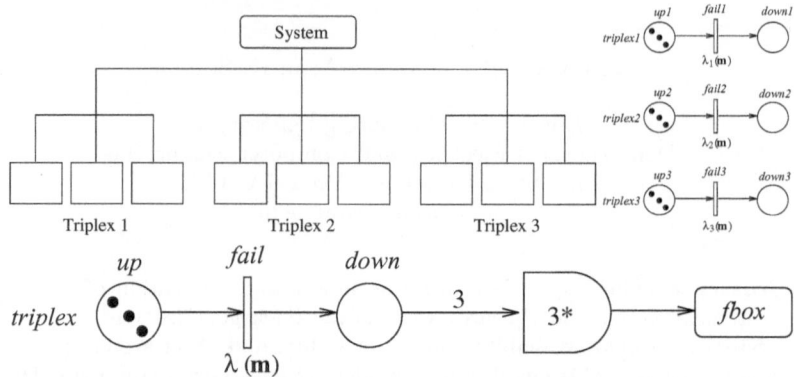

Fig. 1. A 3-triplex parallel system and its SRN and modularization.

relatively small. We extend these description and solution methods to develop the HSP [4]. As its user-interface, we adopt the enhanced version of the C-based Stochastic Petri Net language (CSPL) used in a SRN solver, the Stochastic Petri Net Package (SPNP) proposed by Ciardo et al. [3].

We pay attention to the SRN model structure and propose a new solution technique, named *modularization*, by which a SRN is divided into several subnets, each of them is solved independently, and their solutions are combined to obtain the final solution. If the system has redundancy, a subnet solution for a module can be reused as solutions for the other redundant modules. In addition, modularization makes SRNs' hierarchical analysis possible. The user-interface allows modelers to describe SRNs in the form of functions as in the C language and gives flexibility to system model specification. In order to understand the role, we will consider an example of a 3-triplex parallel system as shown in Figure 1.

2 Modularization

We develop a technique for SRN analysis, which is named *modularization*. The method allows hierarchical analysis for a given SRN that reduces the state space dramatically. The SRN model of Figure 1 may be converted into the equivalent CTMC. Since each triplex module has 4 markings (all 3 up, 2 up/1 down, 1 up/2 down, and all 3 down) and all modules are independent, the number of the marking combinations is $4^3 = 64$. Thus the SRN consists of 64 makings. This direct conversion method from SRNs into CTMCs works well when the object system is relatively small. Now, suppose a system consists of three such 3-triplex parallel systems. If the direct conversion is applied to the system, since each module has 64 states, the total number of states for this system becomes 64^3. The large state space may prevent the analysis in reasonable time.

The problems of the direct conversion method are twofold: (1) Exponential increase of state space for large system models, and (2) Inefficiency of models for systems with redundancy. Several techniques to reduce the state space have been developed. In [5, 6]. These methods make it possible to reduce the state space to solve, however, they are approximations and can be applied to only steady-state analyses. The difficulties can be overcome by *modularizing* parts of SRNs. An SRN can be partitioned into several subnets which can be solved independently [4]. Their solutions are used by including Relation functions are similar to reward functions, however, they are used to connect potions of a SRN, while reward functions are used to define rewards for specific markings.

For our example triplex1, triplex2, and triplex3, are independent of each other. This SRN is divided into 3 subnets, *triplex1*, *triplex2* and *triplex3*. Since each of them can be also treated as a SRN, it is converted into a 4-state CTMC by the ordinary solving procedure for SRNs. The whole system reliability is given by the following relation function of the 4-state CTMC solutions,

$$1 - p_{n_{\mathbf{m}}(down1)=3} \times p_{n_{\mathbf{m}}(down2)=3} \times p_{n_{\mathbf{m}}(down3)=3}, \tag{1}$$

where, $p_{n_{\mathbf{m}}(down*)=3}$ ("*" is replaced by 1,2,or 3) is the probability that place *down** has 3 tokens, which is included in the solution of the 4-state CTMC.

Fortunately, since the three subnets are identical in this example, instead of solving the three 4-state CTMCs, we just solve one of them and reuse the result as follows:

$$1 - \left(p_{n_{\mathbf{m}}(down*)=3}\right)^3. \tag{2}$$

Obviously, a solution cost for the 4-state CTMC is much lower than that for the 64-state CTMC in the direct conversion method. Modularization and relation functions allow us to analyze SRNs more efficiently than the direct conversion method and also make analyses for hierarchical systems using SRNs simpler and more efficient. The example above is ideal; however, it is obvious that the increase of state space by modularization is additive, while that by the direct conversion method is exponential.

Figure 1 also show the modularized SRN with graphical representation of the relation function (2). The right half of the figure represents the relation function (2) and the function value is expressed as *fbox*. The arc from place *down* to the AND gate means that the AND gate inputs are the 3 identical events (expressed by the label "3*" in the AND gate) that place *down* has 3 tokens (expressed by the number 3 next to the arc).

3   The Hierarchical Stochastic Reward Net Solver

HSP analyzes transient and/or steady-state behavior of of a model using the algorithms introduced in the previous sections. HSP consists of several functions which manages the analysis and execution. A modeler should provide a C++ source file, *input file*, which specifies a SRN and analysis procedures by C++ functions defined in HSP. The input file format and the predefined functions.

HSP compiles the input file, links it with HSP routines, and make an executable file corresponding to the input file; then it is executed by HSP and finally outputs analysis results.

Input files for HSP are compatible with those of SPNP; that is, they are written in *Enhanced-CSPL* or *E-CSPL*, with some extensions. Since the input file is an exact C++ file, any C++ functions can be used and any function definitions are allowed except for functions defined in HSP. A place, transition, and initialization functions are similar to CSPL with some enhancements. HSP allows users to define places in more efficiently way.

The function,

```
void module(char *module_name);
```

creates a new SRN named *module_name* during SRN specification. For example,

```
net(){
  module("net1"); place("pl1");
  module("net2"); place("pl2");
}
```

creates two SRNs named **net1** and **net2** and place **pl1** and **pl2** are defined in **net1** and **net2**, respectively. The two SRNs are analyzed separately. If there is no **module** function in the input file, the SRN is named **root** by default.

Relation functions can be defined by using any of the function available in ac_final. If a modularized SRN is complicated, FT representation of relation functions using constructs like **and**, **or**, **m_and**, **m_or**, and **fbox** is preferable.

The system shown in Figure 1 is modeled using the following description. Because *triplex1*, *triplex2* and *triplex3* have the same structures, the net structure is defined as the function **subnet()** once and each subnet is defined by calling the function from **net()** with different arguments. Since **module()** is used in **subnet()**, the three SRNs, **triplex1**, **triplex2** and **triplex3** are converted into CTMCs and solved independently. The result is obtained by the relation function defined as function **down()** in the file.

```
/** example2.cc **/
#include "user.h"
double lambda1,lambda2,lambda3;
parameters() {
  iopt(IOP_STEADY,VAL_NO);
  lambda1 = input("triplex1 rate");
  lambda2 = input("triplex2 rate");
  lambda3 = input("triplex3 rate"); }

subnet(char *name, rate_type lambda) {
  module(name);
  place("UP"); place("DOWN"); init("UP",3);
  trans("fail"); ratedep("fail",lambda, "UP");
  iarc("fail","UP"); oarc("fail","DOWN"); }

net() {
  subnet("triplex1",lambda1);
```

```
  subnet("triplex2",lambda2);
  subnet("triplex3",lambda3); }

assert() {return RES_NOERR;}
ac_init() {}
ac_reach() {}
double down() {
  double p1,p2,p3;
  p1 = pl_prob("DOWN","triplex1",3);
  p2 = pl_prob("DOWN","triplex2",3);
  p3 = pl_prob("DOWN","triplex3",3);
  return fbox(and(3,p1,p2,p3)); }

ac_final() {
    pr_transient(1000,50,down,"System Down"); }
```

4   Conclusion

We have developed techniques to specify and solve Hierarchical Stochastic Reward Nets. The HSP provides: 1) efficient methods to analyze SRNs, especially models for systems with hierarchical structure and/or with modular redundancy, and 2) convenient user-interfaces which enable us to specify models more easily and efficiently in comparison with its counterpart, SPNP; that is, they lead to less mistakes to specify SRN models.

References

1. Tadao Murata. Petri nets: Properties, analysis and applications. *IEEE Proc.*, 77(4):541–580, 1989.
2. Marco Ajmone Marsan and Gianni Conte. A class of generalized stochastic Petri nets for the performance evaluation of multiprocessor systems. *ACM Trans. on Comp. Syst.*, 2(2):93–122, 1984.
3. Gianfranco Ciardo, Alex Blakemore, Philip F. Chimento JR, Jogesh K. Muppala, and Kishor S. Trivedi. Automated generation and analysis of Markov reward models using stochastic reward nets. In Carl D. Mayer and Robert J. Plemmons, editors, *Linear Algebra, Markov Chains, and Queueing Models*, volume 48 of *The IMA volumes in Mathematics and its applications*, pages 145–191. Springer-Verlag, New York, 1993.
4. T. Sakaguchi, "Development of the Hierarchical Stochastic Reward Net Solver Package," *M.S. Thesis*, Dept. of Elect. Eng., Box 352500, University of Washington, Seattle, WA 98195, 1997.
5. H. H. Ammar, Y. F. Huang, and Ruey-Wen Liu. Hierarchical models for systems reliability, maintainability, and availability. *IEEE Trans. on Circuits and Systems*, CAS-34(6):629–638, 1987.
6. Andrea Bobbio and Kishor S. Trivedi. An aggregation technique for the transient analysis of stiff Markov chains. *IEEE Trans. on Comp.*, C-35(9):803–814, 1986.

Index